# WILBUR AND ORVILLE

*A Biography of the Wright Brothers*

## Fred Howard

DOVER PUBLICATIONS, INC.
Mineola, New York

*Bibliographical Note*

This Dover edition, first printed in 1998, is a corrected, unabridged republication of the work originally published in 1988 by Ballantine Books, Inc., New York. It contains a new preface by the author written especially for this Dover edition.

*Library of Congress Cataloging-in-Publication Data*

Howard, Fred, 1910–
    Wilbur and Orville : a biography of the Wright Brothers / Fred Howard.
        p.    cm.
    Originally published: New York : Ballantine Books, 1988.
    "Contains a new preface by the author written especially for this Dover edition"—T.p. verso.
    Includes bibliographical references and index.
    ISBN 0-486-40297-5 (pbk.)
    1. Wright, Wilbur, 1867–1912.   2. Wright, Orville, 1871–1948.
    3. Aeronautics—United States—Biography.   I. Title.
TL540.W7H69      1998
629.13'0092'2—dc21
    [b]                                                                  98–22329
                                                                              CIP

Manufactured in the United States of America
Dover Publications, Inc., 31 East 2nd Street, Mineola, N.Y. 11501

# Contents

Photographic inserts of 8 pages each will be found
following pages 116 and 276.

# Preface to the Dover Edition

It would be presumptuous to call this 1998 edition of *Wilbur and Orville* a revised edition, yet it is more than an unaltered reprint of the original. In addition to a score of corrected dates, misspellings, and inevitable typos, more than thirty textual changes have been made, very few of them detectable except to a Wright specialist with a green eyeshade, unlimited patience, and a magnifying glass. For several of these textual changes, I am indebted to a book published two years after *Wilbur and Orville—The Bishop's Boys: A Life of Wilbur and Orville Wright,* by Tom D. Crouch of the National Air and Space Museum. Crouch had reviewed *Wilbur and Orville* in a 1987 issue of *Air and Space* magazine. In the final paragraph of his review, he posed a series of questions:

> In spite of the author's best efforts, however, our most fundamental questions remain unanswered: Why did Wilbur and Orville succeed where so many others had failed? What manner of men were they, and what forces shaped them? Why does controversy continue to swirl around them?

I found that quartet of questions troubling, having assumed, naively, that they had been answered more or less adequately in *Wilbur and Orville.* Then in 1989 *The Bishop's Boys* appeared and it became clear that Crouch had intended to answer those questions himself. His third question (what "shaped" the Wrights?) is answered at great length in *The Bishop's Boys,* which is the most family-oriented of all Wright biographies, thanks to Crouch's special knowledge of the Wright family, its antecedents, and its doings. He convincingly attributes the brothers' relentless pursuit of infringers of their airplane patent to their father, Bishop Milton Wright, whose penchant for taking straying members of his denomination to court set an example for his sons.

Among the half dozen or so non-biographical books on the Wrights published during the last ten years, the most important is *Visions of a Flying Machine: The Wright Brothers and the Process of Invention,* by Peter L. Jakab. Jakab, like Crouch, is on the staff of the National Air and Space Museum. His book is a technical study of the evolution of the world's first airplane, from the Wright kite model of 1899 to the famed first Flyer of 1903. It answers in depth Crouch's first question: "Why did Wilbur and Orville succeed where so many others had failed?"

*Visions of Flight* appeared in 1990. Published that same year was *Kitty Hawk and Beyond: The Wright Brothers and the Early Years of Aviation: A Photographic History* by Ronald R. Geibert and Patrick B. Nolan, illustrated with photos from the Wright State University Archives and Special Collections. The following year saw the publication of Russell Freedman's *The Wright Brothers: How They Invented the Airplane,* a photobiography, primarily for young readers, with large clear reproductions of many of the Wright photos.

By the mid-1990s, it seemed that almost nothing new remained to be discovered or written about the Wright brothers. Even their pre-airplane careers as printers had been exhaustively examined in a 1988 issue of *Printing History* ("Wright & Wright, Printers" by Charlotte and August Brunsman). Then in 1995 the Wright story was retold from still another perspective—that of a native North Carolinian.

In *First in Flight: The Wright Brothers in North Carolina,* Stephen Kirk has ferreted out every bit of information about the brothers' half dozen excursions to the Outer Banks, the people they met there, and what happened to those people over the years. Kirk's title, like the FIRST IN FLIGHT on North Carolina license plates, is guaranteed to raise the blood pressure of Daytonians, who believe that the airplane was invented entirely in Ohio.

## ENGINEERS OR SCIENTISTS?

I have one small bone to pick with Tom Crouch and Peter Jakab. "Engineering was the key," Crouch writes in *The Bishop's Boys.* "The Wrights functioned as engineers, not as scientists." In *Visions of Flight,* Jakab is even more insistent. Distinguishing between an engineering approach and a scientific approach, he points out, enables us to comprehend Wilbur and Orville's creative processes. "The importance of understanding their strict and skillful engineering approach," he reminds readers, "cannot be overemphasized." He contrasts the brothers' "refined engineering style," their "keen engineering technique" to the working methods of other flight experimenters. Their wind tunnel experiments demonstrated their "brilliance as engineers."

Never having thought of the Wright brothers as either engineers or scientists, I find this distinction somewhat puzzling—unless it is meant to serve as a corrective to the use of "scientific" in such expressions as "their scientific approach to the problem of flight," or its use in the original Smithsonian label describing the Wright 1903 airplane. That label, reprinted in its entirety on the last two pages of *The Bishop's Boys,* includes this sentence:

> BY ORIGINAL SCIENTIFIC RESEARCH THE WRIGHT BROTHERS
> DISCOVERED THE PRINCIPLES OF HUMAN FLIGHT

The case for the use of the adjective "scientific" in this connection is made more explicit by Marvin McFarland, editor of *The Papers of Wilbur and Orville Wright.* In his Introduction, McFarland states that the publication of those two volumes "realizes the often expressed intent of Wilbur and Orville Wright to give to the world a full unvarnished account of their work, especially of their original scientific investigations as distinct from their merely technical accomplishments." Orville Wright himself made it quite clear that "scientific investigations" referred to the Wright brothers' wind tunnel experiments, when he revised the 1939 label on a reproduction of their original wind tunnel to read:

> In their scientific approach to the problem of flight they devised, in 1901, the first wind tunnel and balances giving results sufficiently accurate to be of use in designing aircraft.

The Wright brothers' most important work was done in the less semantically correct first decade of the twentieth century. It would be as pointless to call them great engineers as to number them among the century's notable scientists. Why not just admit that what Wilbur and Orville achieved defies categorization and let it go at that?

# Preface to the 1987 Edition

THE FIRST TIME I remember giving more than a passing thought to the Wright brothers was on a sunny November morning during World War II in the nose of a B-24 bomber. We were flying north along the Atlantic coast on the last leg of a radar practice mission. One radar student sat in a curtained booth behind the pilots' compartment and navigated by comparing the standard aeronautical chart with the uncertain image on the small circular radar screen. A second student rode in the bombardier's compartment and kept an accurate navigation log as a check. On the primitive radar screen of that day the Outer Banks above Cape Hatteras must have looked like nothing so much as a glittering thread of spittle, but from the nose of the noisy four-engine bomber they were sharply etched against the deep blue of the ocean and the lighter blue of Pamlico Sound. They widened out slightly above Oregon Inlet. When they reached the white dot on the map labeled Kitty Hawk, the Outer Banks blossomed into Albemarle Sound like a bulbous nose.

Kitty Hawk! The mere mention of that magic name on the interphone galvanized the crew, especially the returned veterans, who felt a kinship with that tiny collection of trees and houses down there on the sandy plain. "Reminds me of once in France," a voice said on the interphone, and trailed off into a reminiscence that had nothing to do with Kitty Hawk. In the barracks at Langley Field that night, I was inspired to compose a few banal observations of my own. "Poor Orville!" I wrote my wife. "Little did he know what a complex gadget he was giving birth to." It takes two to make a brother, however, and the most remarkable thing about that comment was the omission of Wilbur's name.

Six years passed. The Wright brothers did not cross my mind again in any significant way until 1950, when, after several postwar jobs in the Library of Congress, I found myself in the moribund Aeronautics Division, assembling aviation periodicals and annual reports of airlines for the bindery. I had heard, without giving it much thought, that the Wright brothers' papers had been deposited in the Library and that there was talk of their being edited in the Aeronautics Division to satisfy the terms of the bequest, which stipulated that the most important of the papers be published in a form that would give the brothers full credit for their scientific approach to the problem of flight—"whether or not," in the words of the executors of Orville's estate, "it appealed to general readers."

It occurred to me while vacationing on the shores of Lake Michigan that summer that it might be a good idea to dispel a little of my ignorance concerning those two bicycle mechanics who were supposed to have invented the airplane. The only book on the Wrights in the Three Oaks, Michigan, library was John R. McMahon's twenty-year-old *The Wright Brothers: Fathers of Flight.* Fortunately, I was not aware at the time how thoroughly Orville had detested that book, for I consumed it on the beach in four or five big gulps and thought it quite a story. The following year, the three-man Aeronautics Division in the Library of Congress was augmented with a two-woman typing and secretarial team, and work on the papers of the Wright brothers began in earnest under the editorship of the late Marvin W. McFarland. Arthur G. Renstrom, assistant chief of the division, handled the complex bibliographical details of the work. As the division's junior member, I was given a free hand with the Wrights' wind tunnel and propeller data and their other technical materials.

On December 17, 1953, fiftieth anniversary of the world's first airplane flights, *The Papers of Wilbur and Orville Wright* was welcomed into the world with appropriate fanfare, including a picture story in *Life* magazine. That the Library of Congress Aeronautics Division died in giving birth to those two fat volumes—enriched with more than 250 illustrations and any number of tables and footnotes in small type—was no tragedy. What was really tragic was that $25 was considered an outrageously high price for any publication in 1953, and the two volumes went the way of other unsold books and ended up on the remainder counters. A reprint edition in 1971 at almost twice the price of the original did little to increase their circulation.

It struck me as truly regrettable that the story of the invention of the airplane, told largely in the words of its creators, should have sunk from sight so quickly; and when I left the Library a few years later, I promised myself that someday, if I lived that long, I would tell the story over again in a way that would appeal to "general readers" as well as to the specialists who had been denied access to the two-volume *Papers.* There were several drawbacks to such an endeavor—five, in fact. Three biographies of the Wright brothers had already been published, and by the time I got around to redeeming my pledge, two more had appeared.

With five biographies of the Wright brothers on library shelves, there had better be a good reason for a sixth. There are two good reasons. First, what the Wright brothers did was not accomplished in a vacuum, and their story is incomplete without accounts of the efforts of other men who tried to solve the problem of flight—not only the honorable men (Chanute, Langley, Bell, et al.) but also the sometimes self-deluded experimenters, mountebanks, and outright fakers and liars whose fraudulent claims have resulted in the survival into the present decade of belief in such mythical exploits as the "lost flights" of Gustave Whitehead and that very elastic 100-foot glide made by John Montgomery of California in 1883—or was it 1884? While the author admits to a perverse pleasure in the pricking of other men's bubbles, there is no denying that the feats, real or imagined, of those early experimenters not only add a certain piquancy to the story but furnish a backdrop against which the accomplishments of the Wright brothers stand out bold and clear.

Second, most books about the Wrights give the impression that their story ends in 1909, when the brothers were at the peak of their fame and popularity, and that the rest is epilogue, except for brief accounts of their ventures into business or of Orville's twenty-eight-year feud with the Smithsonian Institution. There is little or no mention of the tragic break in their friendship with Octave Chanute, of their foray into the bloody exhibition business, or of Orville's questionable role in the aircraft production scandal of World War I, and next to nothing about the court battles over patents that caused the brothers to be vilified by many of their contemporaries as money-grubbing monopolists.

Although *Wilbur and Orville* attempts to fill in a few of these gaps, it does not pretend to be a history of early aeronautics. It contains only two references to Leonardo da Vinci (both unavoidable) and no mention whatever (except here) of Daedalus and his son Icarus of the waxen wings. It also lacks a genealogy of the Wright family. Readers who, like the present writer, do not enjoy finding themselves trapped in the branches of a family tree in the middle of Chapter One, when all they want is to get on with the story, will be happy to learn that in the following narrative the ancestry of the Wright brothers has been compressed into the first two paragraphs, which can be conveniently skipped.

## IN LIEU OF ACKNOWLEDGMENTS

For a biography to lack an "Acknowledgments" section suggests ingratitude or, worse, concealment of indebtedness. The truth in the present case is that the author is beholden to no particular person or organization. He is nevertheless deeply in debt to the many writers who have contributed in one way or another to the story of Wilbur and Orville Wright as it has been recorded over the last eight decades. Fred Kelly, author of the only authorized biography of the Wrights, is a case in point. Many years ago, when I mentioned this book as a possible project to a New York editor with whom I was corresponding, she wrote back advising caution, and asked if I was "aware of a man named Fred Kelly, who thinks that he owns all the research on the Wrights." It so happened that I knew Kelly—we were fellow commuters occasionally on the B&O local out of Washington, D.C., and I was well aware of his proprietary attitude toward the Wright brothers. Fred is probably spinning in his grave at this moment, but, like other writers whose books have been shamelessly cannibalized in the following pages, he will have to be content with the many references to his work in the notes at the back of this volume.

Kelly's was not the first book-length work on the Wrights for adults. It was preceded by John McMahon's 1930 biography, which has already been mentioned. Orville had little use for the McMahon book, because of its fictional conversations and many inaccuracies. He had no such reservations about Fred Kelly's *The Wright Brothers,* every word of which he was privileged to check before it was published in 1943. Sandwiched in between Kelly's biography and the 1951 book edited by him—*Miracle at Kitty Hawk: The Letters of Wilbur and Orville Wright*—was the third Wright biography, Elsbeth E. Freudenthal's *Flight into History: The Wright Brothers and the Air Age,* published in 1949 and characterized in Renstrom's bibliography of books by and about the Wrights as "minimizing and distorting their real contribution to the development of the aeroplane." In her acknowledgments, Freudenthal credits the Library of Congress with having been especially helpful. She seems to have been influenced by Albert Zahm, who retired as chief of the Library's Aeronautics Division in 1945, but was able to carry on his thirty-five-year campaign to discredit the Wright brothers from a study room in the Library during the years Freudenthal was researching her biography. His fingerprints are visible on many pages of *Flight into History.*

The fourth Wright biography, and the first to take advantage of the published papers, was *One Day at Kitty Hawk: The Untold Story of the*

*Wright Brothers and the Airplane,* by John Evangelist Walsh, published in 1975. At the heart of Walsh's "Untold Story" is his contention that Orville, with Fred Kelly's cooperation, engineered a coverup of Wilbur's primary role in the invention of the airplane. The book does force a rethinking of several aspects of the Wright story, but is on shaky ground in attributing solely to Wilbur many of the things that the brothers accomplished together.

The charge is sometimes leveled against Kelly's authorized biography that it scants the technical side of the story. The same charge cannot be made against the fifth Wright biography, *Kill Devil Hill: Discovering the Secret of the Wright Brothers,* by Harry Combs, with Martin Caidin. This 1979 publication lavishes such praise on the technical achievements of the brothers (their genius is "of the theoretical quality of Leonardo, Kepler, Copernicus, Einstein") that the reader is apt to be rendered awestruck by what was, after all, their commonsensical (i.e., scientific) approach to the problem of flight.

Several nonbiographical works round out the Wright story in special ways. In particular: Charles H. Gibbs-Smith's *The Rebirth of European Aviation, 1902–1908,* accurately subtitled *A Study of the Wright Brothers' Influence;* Tom Crouch's uniquely informative *A Dream of Wings: Americans and the Airplane, 1875–1905;* Ivonette Wright Miller's *Wright Reminiscences,* a rich source of family anecdotes and recollections; C. R. Roseberry's definitive *Glenn Curtiss: Pioneer of Flight,* as interesting for what it reveals of that archvillain Augustus Herring as for what it tells of Curtiss's life and work; and two books by Arthur Renstrom, my colleague in the Library of Congress so many years ago—*Wilbur & Orville Wright: A Bibliography* and *Wilbur & Orville Wright: A Chronology,* especially the latter for its invaluable Flight Log, covering the years 1900, when the Wrights made their first tentative glides, through 1918, when Orville made his last flight in a Wright aircraft.

# WILBUR AND ORVILLE

# 1

## The House on Hawthorn Street

I N 1796, Catharine Van Cleve Thompson, whose first husband had been killed by Indians, boarded a flatboat on the Great Miami River near Cincinnati, Ohio, and after a trip of ten days or so distinguished herself by becoming the first white woman to set foot in Dayton, Ohio, an act that precipitated a whole string of family firsts. Benjamin Van Cleve, her son by her first husband, became Dayton's first postmaster and the town's first schoolteacher. His marriage was the first to be recorded in the county of which Dayton is the seat and of which he was the first county clerk. He was also Dayton's first public librarian, fining library users two cents for each drop of grease found on a returned book. In the meantime, Benjamin's sister Margaret Van Cleve, who had stayed behind in Cincinnati and married an innkeeper, upheld the family's reputation for firsts by giving birth to a daughter, who, in turn, married Dan Wright and gave birth to Milton Wright, who was to become the father of Wilbur and Orville Wright.

Dan Wright had settled in Centerville, Ohio, near Dayton in 1811. He worked in a distillery until he got religion and moved to Indiana, where he took up farming and lived with his wife in the log cabin where Milton was born in 1828. By the time he was eighteen, Milton got religion like his father before him and joined the Church of the United Brethren in Christ, a nonconformist Protestant sect that had flourished in the rural districts of the Midwest since 1800. He was ordained at the age of twenty-two but taught for two years at a church school in Oregon before returning to Indiana and taking up the ministry in earnest. In 1859 he married Susan Catherine Koerner, daughter of a German-born wheelwright who had a farm in Indiana close to the Ohio line where he manufactured wagons and carriages in a woodworking shop in one of the fourteen buildings on his farm.

Milton and Susan Wright were to spend the first twenty-five years of

their marriage moving from farm to city to town through the rolling countryside of Indiana, Ohio, and Iowa. Milton's income as an itinerant clergyman was small, and he eked it out with teaching and farming. His first son,
Reuchlin, was born on a farm about fifty miles from Indianapolis in 1861.
A second son, Lorin, was born in Fayette County not far from the Koerner
homestead in 1862 and the third son, Wilbur, on a small farm near Millville
in still another Indiana county in 1867. Two years later Milton became editor
of the United Brethren weekly *Religious Telescope*. He moved his family to
Dayton, where the magazine was published, and bought the house at 7
Hawthorn Street in which Orville Wright was born in 1871. Milton and
Susan selected the names of their offspring with great care and considered
middle names unnecessary. The last child was a girl, Katharine, born in
1874. Given the family history, it was inevitable that the girl should be a
Catherine, but they spelled her name with two *a*'s, as in Catharine Van
Cleve, and with a *K*, for which there was no precedent on either side of the
family.

In 1877 Milton Wright was made a bishop and moved his family to Cedar
Rapids, Iowa. Compared to his Catholic and Anglican counterparts, Milton
was bishop in a very small pond, with a salary of less than $1,000 a year.
He preached thrift, but knew the value of a gift. The year he moved to Cedar
Rapids, he returned from one of his many trips into the hinterland with a
gift for his two youngest sons. Coming into the house with the present partly
concealed in his hands, he tossed it into the air before the boys could see
what it was. It was a toy helicopter made of cork, bamboo, and paper. Toy
helicopters in one form or another had been around for almost a century.
Usually they were powered by bow and bowstring, but the twin propellers
on this one were activated by a twisted rubber band, a type of propulsion
popularized by a young Frenchman named Alphonse Pénaud. Pénaud made
and flew several small rubber-powered, inherently stable airplanes. Lateral
stability was accomplished by bending the wingtips upward to provide a
dihedral angle. Longitudinal (fore and aft) stability was achieved by setting
the tail plane at a negative angle relative to the wings, a configuration that
serves as a model for nearly all rubber-powered toy airplanes to this day.
Pénaud's suicide in 1880 at the age of twenty-nine was to give his contribution to the flying art a faintly poetic air.

The flight of that toy helicopter in a Cedar Rapids living room was a
baptism of sorts for Wilbur and Orville Wright. Later they built some toy
helicopters for themselves and were astonished to find that the larger they
made them, the more poorly they flew. Experiments were encouraged in the
Wright household. The earliest surviving document in Orville's handwriting
includes this breathless message written on a postcard addressed to Bishop
Wright, who was in Omaha on church business at the time:

The other day I took a machine can and filled it with water then I put it on the stove I waited a little while and the water came squirting out of the top about a foot.

The postcard is dated April 1, 1881, when Orville was nine. In June that year the family moved again, this time to Richmond, Indiana, where Milton Wright took over the editorship of another church paper, the *Richmond Star.*

Richmond wasn't far from Grandfather Koerner's farm, where it was possible for the two youngest Wright boys to prowl about the outbuildings and investigate the foot-powered lathe in the carriage and wagon shop. Before long, Wilbur and Orville had built a lathe in the barn behind the house in Richmond, with a treadle wide enough to accommodate the feet of several neighborhood boys and with bearings made from marbles that revolved inside a pair of metal rings constructed from parts of harnesses found in the barn. The marbles were made of clay and disintegrated one day while a small cyclone was in progress, the boys at the treadle assuming it was the lathe rather than the wind that was shaking the barn.

It is often claimed that Wilbur and Orville inherited their mechanical aptitude from Grandfather Koerner by way of their mother, Susan Koerner Wright. Susan did have a way with tools. She once built a sled for Reuchlin and Lorin. This event has been retold and embellished with inspirational dialogue in almost every life of the Wright brothers written for young readers—with the names Wilbur and Orville slyly substituted for those of the older boys.

In Richmond, Orville came across some woodcut illustrations in the *Century Magazine* and was inspired to make a few woodcuts, using the spring of an old pocketknife as a carving tool. That Christmas, Wilbur gave him a set of engraving tools, and the resulting woodcuts were printed on their father's letterpress, an occasion that marked the beginning of a love affair with printing that was to occupy Orville for almost a decade after the family moved back to Dayton.

The move to Dayton took place in June 1884, the month Wilbur was to have graduated from high school. Although his two older brothers had attended college and his father hoped someday to send him to the divinity school at Yale, Wilbur left Richmond without receiving his diploma. During the next school year, he took courses in Greek and trigonometry in Central High School and became business manager of *The Christian Conservator,* still another church paper edited by Bishop Wright.

Orville was twelve when the family returned to Dayton. He renewed a friendship with Ed Sines, who had been his playmate during the family's earlier stay in Dayton, finding him a more satisfactory companion than

Wilbur, who was seventeen. What firmly cemented the friendship of the two younger boys was the fact that Ed Sines owned a toy printing outfit consisting of an ink pad and a set of movable rubber type. It was a short step from the printing of wood engravings to printing with type. Orville had always been an enterprising boy. In Dayton he had collected bones and sold them for trifling sums to a fertilizer factory. In Richmond, he had trafficked in metal scrap. In 1886, two years after the return to Dayton, Milton Wright talked Wilbur and Lorin into trading a jointly owned but unused homemade boat for a small printing press, which was presented to Orville, together with twenty-five pounds of type contributed by the bishop.

With Ed Sines as partner, Orville was off to a flying start in the printing business. Their most notable venture was a four-page eighth-grade school paper called *The Midget,* appropriately enough, since the printing area of the press was not much larger than a playing card. Distribution of the first and only issue of *The Midget,* however, was blocked by Bishop Wright, who disapproved of the use of one whole page to advertise the embryonic firm of Sines & Wright. Orville's next project was a larger press, which he built himself, using a gravestone as press bed. The boy printers moved their operations from the house to the Wright barn and invested two dollars in a set of display type. Soon orders for job printing began to dribble in from patronizing storekeepers.

The house in which Orville and Katharine had been born had been rented out during the family's six-year sojourn in Cedar Rapids and Richmond. It was not vacated for more than a year after they returned to Dayton, but in October 1885 they moved back into the narrow white clapboard house on Hawthorn Street that was to be their home for the next twenty-nine years. It was a two-story house with a peaked roof and green shutters on a lot less than forty feet wide. The upstairs bedrooms were small, and in the midwestern summers they were hot. The only porch was a small one at the back. The sole source of water at the time was a pump at the back door.

There were two libraries. Books on theology were kept in the bishop's cluttered study on the second floor. The downstairs library, with its fashionable sets of Irving, Hawthorne, *The Spectator,* Scott, and Gibbon, was more eclectic. It included multivolume histories of England and France, natural history books, Grimm, Andersen, Plutarch's *Lives*—a favorite of Wilbur's —and two sets of encyclopedias, whose scientific articles were staples of Orville's earliest reading.

Bishop Wright was by no means the unsmiling patriarch of tradition, although he had the beard for it and believed in the therapeutic value of an occasional spanking. The Sabbath was observed in the bishop's house, but Sunday reading and letter-writing were encouraged. Card-playing was forbidden, not as a sin but as a waste of time. Santa Claus was outlawed, but fairy tales were not, and inexpensive gifts made their appearance at the table on Christmas morning. The Wright children were familiar figures at the United Brethren Sunday school on Summit Street, but both Wilbur and Orville had read and been influenced by the writings of the agnostic Robert Ingersoll, whose works were part of the leavening of anticlerical literature in the bishop's library.

Family rapport was reflected in the choice of nicknames. The eldest son, Reuchlin, was Roosh. Lorin seems to have had no nickname, but his son Milton, born in 1892, had two, Toujours and Whackers. Orville was Bubo to his sister, and Wilbur was Ullam. Since Grandfather Koerner came from Germany, it was logical that Katharine's nickname should be Schwesterchen (German for "Little Sister") but it was usually split into Schwes (or Swes) and Sterchens, which were used interchangeably.

The well-being of the household was mirrored in the remembered story-book expressions and fossilized baby talk that crop up in the correspondence over the years and that even out of context are redolent of family life in the last quarter of the nineteenth century: "time to be abed," "afer soon," "a little waucus," "You ought to seen it! Great big sing!" "Ah! them is fine," "that chawin' gum corporation" (a reference to Orville's attempt to manufacture chewing gum from sugar and tar), "is me," and "I'll squall" (a threat of young Wilbur's). It was Wilbur who made up stories for Orville's consumption, all of which ended "and then the boiler bust." And it was Wilbur who circumvented a prohibition against teasing his sister by crooking a finger in her direction when no one else was looking, a maneuver that conveyed an insult more terrible than words and drove the young Katharine to tears.

The family was not without its quota of misfortune. Ever since the move to Richmond, Susan Wright had suffered from an ailment variously described as pleurisy and consumption. When the family settled in Dayton in 1884, her condition became worse. Two years later Wilbur was hit in the face with a bat while playing an ice-skating game called shinny and for the next four years suffered from a vaguely defined heart disorder. Homebound during those years, he seems to have done little except read and take care of his ailing mother, a situation that alarmed brother Lorin. Lorin had left home to seek his fortune in 1887. "What does Will do?" he wrote Katharine from Kansas. "He ought to do something. Is he still cook and chambermaid?" Reuchlin was married and had not lived at home for several years. With Bishop Wright sometimes away on church business, Wilbur and his mother were alone in the house during the hours when Katharine and Orville were in school, and a close relationship grew up between the two semi-invalids. Susan Wright walked downstairs each morning when she was able. Wilbur is said to have carried her upstairs each night, a touching but unlikely practice for a young man suffering from a heart disorder. Wilbur was twenty-two when his mother died on the Fourth of July 1889, and the years he might have spent in college were already behind him.

Orville turned eighteen that year. By working long hours for a Dayton printer during summer vacations, he had developed into an expert typesetter. With Wilbur's help he built a new and larger press, using the hinged bars of an abandoned buggy top to maintain pressure between paper and type. During his last year in high school, Orville took courses in Latin to meet college entrance requirements, but before the school year was over he gave up all thought of college and with Ed Sines as employee opened a print shop on a street of small stores not far from his home.

For twenty years the editing and publishing of church papers had been a part of Bishop Wright's life. Orville now decided to publish a weekly paper of his own. The first issue of *West Side News* (10¢ for six weeks, 20¢ for three months) appeared on March 1, 1889, in an edition of five hundred copies. Ed Sines's job was to gather news in the largely residential district on the west side of the Miami River, opposite the prosperous business district on the east side, and to solicit ads in the process. In addition to neighborhood news, the paper printed items of a folksy nature contributed by Wilbur or lifted bodily from *The Youth's Companion.* Before long the name Wilbur Wright appeared on the masthead as editor over that of Orville. Orville was listed as publisher.

The *West Side News* ran for a year before being converted to *The Evening Item,* a daily devoted to the interests of the West Side. The *Item* was printed for three months in a rented room on West Third Street, but it was no match for the large Dayton papers and expired in August 1890. That fall Wilbur and Orville set themselves up as Wright and Wright, Job Printers, and moved into larger quarters down the street. With Ed Sines's help, they produced such miscellaneous items as the minutes of the United Brethren Church, calling cards, advertising broadsides, and *The Tattler,* a four-page weekly for black readers written and edited by eighteen-year-old Paul Laurence Dunbar, a school friend of Orville's and the only black student in Central High School. Four lines of pre–Ogden Nash doggerel, scribbled on the wall of the printing establishment by young Dunbar, testify to his high regard for Orville's mental abilities:

> *Orville Wright is out of sight*
> *In the printing business.*
> *No other mind is half so bright*
> *As his'n is.*

*The Tattler* expired after six weeks from lack of advertising, but Dunbar continued to write poems. In 1892 he took fifty-six of his dialect verses to Orville to see if they could be printed in book form. The printshop had no binding facilities, so Orville referred Dunbar to the United Brethren publishing house in Dayton, and for $125, payable in advance, the house agreed to print five hundred copies of *Oak and Ivy,* the book that turned the four-dollar-a-week elevator operator into a literary celebrity.

By 1892 the Wright brothers' interest in printing had about run its course and they were on to something new. In his Richmond, Indiana, days, Orville had borrowed three dollars from Wilbur and bought his first bicycle. The only bicycles available then had huge front wheels, and the rider perched precariously on a saddle four to five feet above the ground. By 1890 a new type of bicycle was seen on the streets of Dayton: Both front and rear wheels were the same size. Because there was less distance to fall if the rider lost his balance, it was dubbed the "safety bicycle." Direct pedaling had been replaced by a sprocket-chain drive. Air-filled tires, ball bearings, comfortable saddles, and coaster brakes put the finishing touches to the evolutionary process, and the modified V-frame made cycling the ultimate in exercise for females, the more daring of whom donned bloomers for greater comfort in pedaling. During the early 1890s cycling became a national obsession.

Orville caught the fever first. He went in for racing after paying $160 for a safety bicycle. Wilbur waited six months, then purchased a machine at auction for half that amount. Shortly thereafter the brothers put Ed Sines in charge of their printing business and opened a shop across the street, where they became purveyors of one of the most popular forms of personal transportation ever invented. There were more than a dozen bicycle shops on the other side of the Miami River in downtown Dayton, but theirs was the only shop selling and repairing bicycles on the West Side. In 1893 they moved into a larger store on the south side of Third Street, half a block from their printing establishment. That summer they took time off to visit the Columbian Exposition in Chicago. If 1893 was a banner year for Chicago, it was a depression year for the rest of the country, but the bicycle business was hardly affected. The Wrights welcomed sales on the weekly-installment plan. They repaired and rented bicycles as well as sold them, and their business, slow at first, eventually prospered.

Now that they were successfully launched in business, Wilbur and Orville established a joint bank account on which each drew for his own use without consulting the other. There was no need to consult. Since boyhood the brothers had been partners in a relationship more binding than most marriages. Wilbur was not exaggerating when he wrote the month before he died, "My brother Orville and myself lived together, played together, worked together, and in fact thought together." Although both brothers were skeptics when it came to psychic phenomena, it was not unusual for them to begin whistling or humming the same tune at the same instant while working in the bicycle shop, as if there were a psychic bond between them —a phenomenon they themselves attributed to an association of ideas stored in a common memory.

The difference in their ages was no longer so apparent. In 1894 Wilbur was twenty-seven, Orville twenty-three. In many ways they were remarkably alike. Neither drank. Neither used tobacco, although Orville had tried it in his teens. Wilbur weighed around a hundred forty pounds and stood five feet ten. Orville was an inch or two shorter and a few pounds heavier. Their voices were similar—high-pitched and hard to tell apart if the listener was in an adjoining room.

Both had gray-blue eyes, but there was little facial resemblance. Orville had undistinguished features, more difficult to recall when he was clean-shaven than after he had grown a mustache. He had thick, curly dark brown hair. Wilbur had prominent ears, a cleft chin, and an open, firm face, stronger for the loss of his thin brown hair, which had all but disappeared by 1894. There were pronounced lines from the wings of his nostrils to the corners of his wide, expressive mouth. Wilbur was hard to rattle. Orville was more excitable, a constant talker at home or among friends. Compared to Wilbur, he was a dandy, always well groomed, even in the bicycle shop, where he wore sleeve cuffs and an apron of blue-and-white ticking to protect his clothing. He had always been the playful one, the prankster who dropped red pepper down the heat register in school and who grew up to play the guitar and go on camping trips with Katharine and her friends. Wilbur was more withdrawn. "The strongest impression one gets of Wilbur Wright is of a man who lives largely in a world of his own," wrote a former schoolmate in describing a Fourth of July picnic at which Wilbur put up the swings for the children and then stood aloof from the crowd for much of the day. At the same picnic, Katharine Wright made the laughing remark that Wilbur was the girl of the family—"not an effeminate man of course," the former schoolmate hastened to add, "(one needs only to glance at his strong face to see that), but kind and tender and 'handy' about the house."

Handy about the house both brothers certainly were. During the 1890s they added front and side porches to the house on Hawthorn Street, giving the narrow structure an air of spaciousness it had lacked before. They turned the posts themselves on a neighbor's lathe. They built a fireplace in the parlor and took a photograph of their work in which the gas-burning fire-place is the pièce de résistance among several items of middle-class elegance —mirrored mantel, floor-length lace curtains, potted palm, figured carpet, Katharine's spindly-legged writing desk, and Orville's guitar leaning rak-

ishly against the new fireplace. They developed their own glass-plate negatives and made their own prints in the darkroom in the shed behind the
house. Over the years they had developed a feeling for wood and metal, for
machinery and tools. If tools were not readily available, they made their
own.

Wilbur and Orville were among the blessed few who combine mechanical ability with intelligence in about equal amounts—if such attributes can
be said to be measurable and comparable. One man with this dual gift is
exceptional. Two such men whose lives and fortunes are closely linked can
raise this combination of qualities to a point where their combined talents
are akin to genius. But genius without an objective is genius down the drain.
Wilbur, especially, seemed to be casting about for something besides the
selling and repairing of bicycles on which to exercise his considerable talents.

Bishop Wright had hoped that Wilbur would follow in his ministerial
footsteps. When Wilbur was about twenty he had joined the United Brethren in Christ, but he left the church in protest when a split occurred in the
sect over the question of secret societies. Milton Wright was against the
existence of such societies within the church. The attitude of his opponents
on this issue so disillusioned Orville and Katharine that they too stopped
attending church when they came of age.

In September 1894, Wilbur wrote a letter to his father, who was away
from Dayton on church business. It is an uncharacteristically formal letter,
in which Wilbur seems torn between concern for his health—a concern that
had haunted the family ever since the shinny-stick accident of eight years
before—and a desire to recoup the lost college years before it is too late:

> I have been thinking for some time of the advisability of my taking
> a college course. I have thought about it more or less for a number of
> years but my health has been such that I was afraid that it might be time
> and money wasted to do so, but I have felt so much better for a year or
> so that I have thought more seriously of it and have decided to see what
> you think of it and would advise.
>
> I do not think I am specially fitted for success in any commercial
> pursuit even if I had the proper personal and business influences to assist
> me. I might make a living but I doubt whether I would ever do much
> more than this. Intellectual effort is a pleasure to me and I think I would
> be better fitted for reasonable success in some of the professions than in
> business.

"Yes, I will help you what I can in a collegiate course," Bishop Wright
replied. "I do not think a commercial life will suit you well." But Wilbur
had already changed his mind. When the bicycle trade slacked off in October

he and Orville decided to take another fling at publishing and issued a weekly advertising brochure, *Snap-Shots at Current Events,* to which Wilbur contributed timely essays on local events in a playful, labored vein under the *nom de plume* of "Weather Prophet."

*Snap-Shots* breathed its last in December 1894. Its demise was no great loss, for in 1895 the brothers moved both their bicycle and printing businesses to a third location, on Williams Street, where they began to manufacture their own bicycles. By the mid-1890s there were well over a thousand makes of bicycles registered in the United States. More than two hundred factories were turning out bicycle parts, but only fifteen joined the parts into working machines. The bulk of the business was left to small establishments like the Wright Cycle Company. For a relatively small investment it was possible to buy tubing, spokes, tires, chains, pedals, handlebars, and bearings from the factories making parts and join them together in the back room and market the product as a local one. In 1897, the left half of a remodeled building at 1127 West Third Street, owned by Charles Webbert, who ran a plumbing business a few doors to the east, offered them larger, more comfortable quarters. It was a two-story, gaslit brick building with a sizable frame structure attached that could be used for additional shop space. So they moved again, for the fourth and last time. The printing press was moved into a room on the second floor, where Ed Sines carried on as a job printer. Eventually he gave up printing altogether and joined the Wright Cycle Company as jack-of-all-trades. He handled the finishing part of the assembly work. Orville operated the enameling oven in the back of the new shop. Wilbur did the brazing with a brazier that the brothers designed themselves.

Most of the bicycles were manufactured during the slack winter months. Their costliest effort was called the Van Cleve, after their unfortunate ancestor John Van Cleve, who had been killed by Indians and whose widow had settled in Dayton in 1796. It sold for $100. The manufacture of bicycles was surely profitable, but once the business had been established it required application more than ingenuity, and it would have been odd indeed if the brothers had not kept their ears to the ground for something more challenging to turn up.

One field was wide open to men of an inventive turn of mind, and that was the revolution in transportation just around the corner. For several years railroads had been the principal means of long-distance travel on land, but the only radical change in rail transportation was the introduction of the electric interurban railway, like the one connecting Dayton with Springfield, Ohio, made possible a few years before by the generation of cheap electricity by dynamo.

The real revolution in transportation was felt in Dayton in 1896 when

Cord Ruse put together the first horseless carriage to sputter and clank along the streets of the city. Cordy, as Wilbur and Orville called him, was not truly an inventor. He was just one of the hundreds of mechanics, spawned around blacksmith shops and livery stables, who were attempting to assemble a handmade, home-built gas buggy that would work. Here was a field that was crying out for men like the Wrights to take over. But automobiles did not capture their fancies the way bicycles had, and Wilbur was so little impressed with Cordy's effort that he suggested suspending a bed sheet beneath the primitive engine mount to catch the nuts, bolts, and spare parts that were constantly vibrating loose.

Meanwhile the bicycle business flourished and life went on in the refurbished house on Hawthorn Street much as it had before. Katharine had begun to attend classes at Oberlin College near Cleveland. Lorin had married and moved to a house on South Horace Street, four blocks east of Hawthorn. Bishop Wright continued to travel on church business, sometimes as far away as the West Coast. If Wilbur and Orville were alone in the house, they took turns cooking, but in the summer, when the bishop was back and Katharine was home from college, Milton Wright and his three unmarried children were a close-knit, interdependent foursome. Only once was this tidy arrangement threatened, and that was toward the end of the summer of 1896 when Orville was stricken with typhoid fever. He was delirious part of the time, and a trained nurse was called in to spell Wilbur and Katharine in taking care of their brother in the small, hot upstairs bedroom adjoining Wilbur's. It was six weeks before the siege was lifted and Orville was able to sit up and eat a little solid food.

It had been a close call, both for Orville and for the partnership of the brothers, which was to be dissolved only by another struggle with typhoid fever sixteen years later. It would be Wilbur's turn then. What Wilbur and Orville did between those two bouts of fever is a story that has been told over and over until it has assumed the form almost of myth. In the process, the story has become encrusted with a fringe of half-truths and outright untruths, in regard not only to what the Wrights did but to what others did or, in many cases, didn't do. Fortunately, the record is clear and unequivocal as far as the Wrights are concerned, except for a few lapses here and there in those early years, where ailing memories or events recollected "to the best of one's knowledge" in long-forgotten patent suits have blurred the truth. One such circle of confusion, to borrow an expression from photography, occurred in 1896, as Orville lay delirious. Many years later he claimed that it was during this time that Wilbur read of the death of Otto Lilienthal, an event that was to influence both their lives. Wilbur himself stated explicitly that he read of Lilienthal's death in "the newspapers of that day." He naturally withheld the news until Orville recovered.

It makes a nice story: Wilbur sitting expectantly by Orville's bedside with a folded newspaper, waiting for his brother to open his eyes. But Otto Lilienthal died in Berlin on Monday, August 10, 1896. News of his death appeared in several U.S. newspapers that week and the next, but Orville did not become seriously ill until the last week in August, so either Orville's memory was playing him false or Wilbur had been entertaining himself with some very old newspapers as he sat by his brother's bedside.

Not that it matters. Orville recovered and emerged from the valley of the shadow, whole and sound. It would be more than half a century before he would be laid to rest beneath the bare wintry boughs arching over the Wright family plot in Woodland Cemetery. By that time the white clapboard house on Hawthorn Street and the red-brick bicycle shop on West Third Street would be gone—not demolished, merely transported timber by timber, brick by brick, *Arabian Nights* fashion, to Greenfield Village in Michigan by a genie named Henry Ford, not because the house and bicycle shop had any intrinsic value in themselves but because they had been intimately associated with a string of events triggered by the death of Otto Lilienthal from a broken spine.

# 2

## The Flying Men

THE WRIGHT BROTHERS were never sure where they first came across the name of Otto Lilienthal. When Orville was almost fifty, he wrote they had first read of Lilienthal and his work in a newspaper or magazine a few months before the German's death in August 1896. Later he thought it had been in 1895. Then several years after Orville himself was dead, Charles Gibbs-Smith, an inveterate searcher after truth in matters aeronautical, delivered himself of the opinion that the Wrights had first read about Otto Lilienthal in a nine-page article in the September 1894 issue of *McClure's Magazine*. The monthly *McClure's* was a staple of the U.S. cultural diet in the nineties and found its way regularly into the Wright household.

The title of the article, "The Flying Man," was apt. Its implications were irrefutable. Many men before Lilienthal claimed to have flown on a pair of homemade wings, but a single hop or jump from the roof of a barn or the top of a hill, even if the jumper survived, was hardly proof that man was capable of sustained flight. What was needed was photographic evidence. In the early 1890s halftone reproductions had begun to replace hand-engraved renderings of photographs in magazines and newspapers, and the "Flying Man" article was illustrated with ten halftones, no fewer than nine of which showed a becapped, beknickered Herr Lilienthal leaping into the air, gliding, soaring, descending, or alighting while suspended on padded armrests from a pair of wide batlike wings.

Otto Lilienthal was born in Germany in 1848. He became a mechanical engineer, and by the time he was forty was head of a factory producing small steam engines in a suburb of Berlin. Firmly convinced that the solution to the problem of human flight would be found in man's imitating the flapping flight of birds, he built a glider in 1889 and tried some glides to ascertain the best wing shape for this purpose. Over a six-year period, during which his obsession with flapping flight was happily sidetracked, he built eighteen variations of his basic hang glider, the most successful of which had a wingspread of twenty-five feet. The muslin-covered wings were curved from root to tip and constructed so that they could be folded back like the wings of a bat. A picturesque, well-rounded tail was added to the split-willow frame.

Gliding was done into the wind to take advantage of the updraft. Since the wind was not always in the desired direction on natural hill slopes, Lilienthal had an earthwork constructed on a hill near his factory, with a structure on top from whose roof he could launch himself into the wind whenever it was blowing from a westerly direction. His best gliding, however, was done in the Rhinow Hills, about forty miles from Berlin. Once afloat, he kept the glider level by shifting his legs and torso about. If the uphill wind was strong and steady, he was able to soar above one spot on the ground long enough to converse with admiring onlookers. He made over two thousand glides in all, the longest from 12 to 15 seconds in duration.

Gliding was done on Sundays, weather permitting. On Sunday, August 9, 1896, when Lilienthal was about fifty feet above the ground a sudden gust of wind thrust his wings up in front. He swung his body forward to restore the balance, but the glider sideslipped to the ground, crumpling the right wing and breaking Lilienthal's spine. He died the next day in a Berlin hospital. His last words were quoted as "Sacrifices must be made." As with most famous last words, it is doubtful that these were actually uttered, but Lilienthal had used this fatalistic expression more than once during his six years of experimenting, and the words were carved on his tombstone.

The news of Lilienthal's fatal accident renewed an interest in human flight that had lain dormant in Wilbur and Orville Wright since they first read of the German's accomplishments. The usual course they followed when a subject piqued their interest was to look it up in an encyclopedia. There were two of these in their home library, an 1875 edition of the *Britannica* and a still earlier *Chambers Encyclopedia*. Both contained articles on bird flight, but that was all. They tried the Dayton Public Library, with no better results. The only serious book on flight they found was in their own library—E. J. Marey's *Animal Mechanism: A Treatise on Terrestrial and Aerial Locomotion*. The photographs in this 1890 volume revealed the wing movement of birds in flight, but Marey was more interested in the physiological processes of flight than in the application of bird flight to human beings. When Orville recovered from his attack of typhoid fever and went back to work, any thoughts the brothers may have entertained of taking up where Lilienthal left off were put on the back burner in the new bicycle shop and allowed to simmer.

Curiously enough, it was in that same year, 1896, that the first successful aeronautical experiments were carried out in the United States, although the Wright brothers were not to learn of them until some time later. There were two sets of experiments, one conducted by a scientist, the other by an engineer. The two men were friends. Both were in their sixties.

The scientist was Samuel Pierpont Langley, secretary of the Smithsonian Institution in Washington, D.C. Since 1887 he had built and tested over thirty light model airplanes powered by twisted rubber to determine the best wing arrangement for larger models, eventually settling on a tandem design —two sets of wings, one behind the other, with propellers and power unit in between. These were no rubber-band bamboo contraptions but miniature airplanes weighing up to thirty pounds, with twin propellers driven by a light steam engine located between the two pairs of wings in tandem. Langley built seven of these and tested them by launching them from the top of a small workshop built on a scow in the Potomac River thirty-five miles downstream from Washington, D.C. None of the models flew until May 6, 1896, when a modified version of No. 5, with a wingspan of twelve feet, gave Langley his first taste of success.

So fearful of failure was the Smithsonian secretary that the only man not a member of his staff invited to witness the test was his friend Alexander Graham Bell. Langley stood on a nearby pier and watched the launching at a godlike distance from his creation. The more sanguine inventor of the telephone stationed himself and his camera in a rowboat in midstream, where he could photograph the flight if it took place. It did. The large model was catapulted out over the water. As it rose to a height of between eighty and a hundred feet, Bell snapped the only photograph made of the flight. When the steam in its boiler was exhausted, the model glided down and was so little damaged when it hit the water that it was fished out of the river and soon made ready for a second trial. The second flight, about 90 seconds in duration, was equally successful.

Langley bettered his record with another rebuilt model that November, after which he announced publicly that he was retiring from aeronautical experimentation. Two years later, during the Spanish-American War, a War Department committee invited Langley to carry his experiments to their logical conclusion by developing a man-carrying airplane for use in future military operations. Langley obliged, but since the work was done in relative secrecy, it would be several years before the world at large would learn what was going on in the two-story workshop next to James Smithson's red stone castle on Washington's Mall.

The man behind the second series of aeronautical experiments carried out in the United States in 1896 was a civil engineer by the name of Octave Chanute. Chanute was bilingual and sported a Frenchman's goatee. Born in Paris in 1832, he had been brought to New York City at the age of seven.

In 1857 he married Annie James of Peoria, Illinois, and the remainder of his long life was firmly anchored in the Midwest, where his major achievements were the design and construction of the Chicago stockyards in 1867 and the completion of the first bridge across the wide Missouri at Kansas City in 1870.

As a young man, Chanute collected whatever information he was able to find on the subject of human flight. When he was thirty-two he found his hobby was interfering with his work. Unwilling to sacrifice a profitable engineering career to such a discredited, crackpot cause, he tied red tape around his aeronautical papers and notes and resolved not to open the bundle until he could do so without detriment to his career. In 1889 he settled permanently in Chicago and established a railroad-tie works to satisfy the gluttonous appetite of the westward-expanding American railroads. He was now well enough off to untie the red tape on his bundle of aeronautical papers and begin a systematic study of man's attempt to fly. The result was a series of articles printed in *The Railroad and Engineering Journal* from October 1891 to December 1893. Published as a book in 1894, *Progress in Flying Machines,* they earned for its author the status of senior statesman of aeronautics—or aerial navigation, as it was then called—and helped to lighten a little the stigma of lunacy that had attached itself to the subject.

Octave Chanute had been chairman of the International Conference on Aerial Navigation held in the new art museum on Chicago's lakefront during the Columbian Exposition of 1893. One of the highlights of the four days of discussions about kites, balloons, and propulsion devices for nonexistent flying machines was the presentation of a paper, "The Internal Work of the Wind," by Samuel Langley. The euphonious title referred to the energy generated by momentary changes in wind direction and velocity. Langley believed that large birds utilized this energy when they soared without flapping their wings and theorized that this latent energy would someday be harnessed to provide power for human flight. It would then be possible for an airplane to circle the globe without landing, carrying only enough fuel to maintain flight in areas where it encountered extremely calm air. Many years later, Orville Wright pointed out the fallacies in Langley's theory, stating that he had seen thousands of buzzards soaring over level ground on calm sunny days, when updrafts were produced by differences between air temperatures at the surface of the earth and above it, but he had never seen a single case of a bird soaring over the same ground on a windy day when the sun was hidden by clouds. Eventually Langley himself was forced to admit that the observations on which his theory was based were not sufficiently quantitative. But "The Internal Work of the Wind," elaborately published in the Smithsonian Contributions to Knowledge series, was taken seriously in its day.

Octave Chanute also saw the sea of air as a series of swirling waves, constantly changing in direction and strength, full of tumultuous whirls and eddies like the smoke billowing upward from a chimney, but when it came to constructing a machine to navigate this uncertain sea the scientist and the engineer parted company. Langley's two successful models had been powered by small 1-horsepower steam engines. Chanute believed that power should be applied to a flying machine only after the problem of stability had been solved. That could best be done by experimenting with a hang glider like Lilienthal's, although Chanute was sure there must be a better way to maintain equilibrium than by thrashing the legs and torso about—gyrations made necessary by wind fluctuations that caused the center of pressure on a wing to move back and forth. He suspected that adjustments in the position of a wing in flight, if made automatically in response to sudden changes in the air current, would compensate for minor variations in the wind.

In 1896 Chanute took the giant step from theory to practice. He designed and constructed a man-carrying glider in which the wings were mounted on vertical axes and restrained by rubber springs, so that when struck by a wind gust they were free to swing backward at the tips and return to their normal position as the gust lessened in force. Chanute was sixty-four that summer, a brittle age for testing hang gliders, but he could afford to employ younger men to carry out the actual work of gliding. He selected three. The most reliable of these was a young carpenter and electrician named William Avery. The most eccentric was W. Paul Butusov, of Russian origin, who claimed that he had soared for miles over the treetops in Kentucky several years before in a glider of his own making. Chanute did not take Butusov's claim literally, but he found the Russian's salary requirements modest and so took him on.

The third of Chanute's assistants that summer was Augustus M. Herring, an ambitious but frustrated aeronautical enthusiast, then in his early thirties. Herring had failed to graduate as a mechanical engineering student from Stevens Institute in Hoboken in 1888. The reason, he let it be known, was that his thesis on mechanical flight was rejected by the faculty as chimerical. The truth was that the subject of his thesis, which he failed to complete, was the marine steam engine rather than flight. In 1894 Herring built and tested two Lilienthal-type gliders, to one of which he applied a movable tail controlled by a spring, in the hope that the tail vane would act like a damper in response to wind gusts. His conviction that the solution of the flight problem lay in this tail-damping contrivance (he called it his "regulator") became almost as much of an obsession with Herring as the movable-wing theory was with Octave Chanute.

In May 1895 Herring had gone to work for Samuel Langley at the

Smithsonian Institution, but resigned in a fit of temperament seven months later. Langley informed Chanute that Herring's reliability was as questionable as his discretion, in spite of which Octave Chanute employed Herring in 1896 to supervise the construction of the glider that was to embody his movable-wing concept. He also paid to have one of Herring's Lilienthal-type gliders rebuilt for testing, so that "the known," as he put it, "should be tested before passing to the unknown."

Early on the morning of June 22, 1896, Octave Chanute and his three assistants loaded the two disassembled gliders and a quantity of camping equipment onto the electric interurban that ran from Chicago around the southern end of Lake Michigan. At 8 A.M. they arrived at Miller Station, now part of Gary, Indiana, but then part of the wild dune country. Some fantastic claims have been made for what went on there during the next three or four months. Since Octave Chanute figures prominently in the later history of the airplane, and since the mendacious Augustus Herring keeps popping in and out of the Wright story with sinister regularity, it will be worthwhile to see what actually went on in the Indiana dunes as Chanute's trio of young assistants hung suspended by their armpits beneath those primitive hang gliders and thrashed their limbs about in a valiant effort to harness what Samuel Langley had so elegantly termed the internal work of the wind.

# 3

# *In the Dunes of Indiana*

THE SITE SELECTED for testing the gliders was convenient—only thirty miles from Chicago—safe, because of the gently sloping hills of yellow sand, and picturesque, because the winds had created a crescent of dunes at the foot of Lake Michigan, where each growth of tree and shrub was followed by a gradual inundation of sand and a gradual recovery, producing over the years a combination of forest, desert, and beach unique in the Midwest. Two miles from Miller Station, not far from the lakeshore, the four men pitched their tent.

The Lilienthal glider was tested first. Chanute called it cranky. On the eighth day in camp Herring made a glide of 116 feet, but the glider was so sadly out of balance that part of one wing was cut away. When Herring attempted another glide, he was hit by a wind gust. He dropped a dozen feet and landed on top of the glider, which was broken beyond repair.

"Glad to be rid of it," Chanute wrote in the diary he kept that summer. He was now free to lavish all his attention on the glider with the movable wings. It was called the multiple-wing machine, and with good reason. It consisted of six pairs of wings, mounted one pair on top of the other. The first glides made with this top-heavy apparatus were discouraging. The second time it was tried it blew over and broke. "All are afraid because of its novelty," Chanute confided to his diary.

To improve its performance, he reduced the number of wings from twelve to eight. The next day he restored the wings he had removed and tried it with two pairs of wings in front and four behind. Then the tent blew down and the glider was damaged. While it was being repaired, its wings were shifted mercilessly back and forth until it received a final configuration— five sets of wings in front, one pair to the rear, in which form it was dubbed the Katydid. On the Fourth of July, Avery and Herring made a number of jumps in it, the longest 82 feet. Satisfied with this respectable two-week start, the four men packed up and took the evening train to Chicago, planning to return later in the summer after constructing two new gliders and rebuilding the patched-up Katydid.

While the new gliders were being constructed, news of Lilienthal's fatal accident was printed in the Chicago *Tribune*. When the party returned to the dunes on August 21, Chanute had the foresight to add a fourth assistant to his original three, a Dr. James Ricketts, whom he described as a physician with a slack practice and a taste for aviation. Ricketts' services as a bonesetter were not needed, however, and with a trial glide or two by way of recompense the good doctor resigned himself to a secondary role as camp cook.

Chanute had picked a new site for this second series of experiments— a large dune five miles east of the former site with a hundred yards of sandy beach at its base. The arrival the previous June of four strangers with so much suspicious-looking equipment at sleepy Miller Station had aroused the curiosity of the natives, one of whom had sent a telegram to Chicago, with the result that two reporters and the inevitable hangers-on had turned up to witness the experiments. No reporters were anticipated at the new site. Dune Park, the nearest station on the interurban, consisted of a single house and a sandpit. The ground between the station and the beach was a series of wooded hills and swamps, so privacy was assured. To make doubly sure that reporters would not be alerted by the arrival of the party, Chanute arranged to have both cargo and crew transported from Chicago by sailboat.

Shortly after noon on August 21 the cargo was unloaded onto the beach at the foot of the sand hill. It included the rebuilt Katydid, an untried three-wing glider measuring sixteen feet across, and a still larger glider called the Albatross, designed by Chanute's Russian assistant, Paul Butusov. Constructed at Chanute's expense, the Albatross was to hang around the old man's neck for what was left of the summer like the Ancient Mariner's ill-omened bird. Before dawn the next morning a storm came up with such violence that it tore their tent on the beach to ribbons, drenched the provisions, and smashed the three-wing glider. Chanute sent to Chicago for another tent. It was a sizable one with scalloped edges like a circus tent, and its arrival by train the next day at Dune Park Station caused a small sensation. Word soon got through to the press, and reporters began to find their way to the testing ground.

For the next five weeks, Chanute's little party was plagued by storms, reporters, and absenteeism. Herring returned to Chicago to buy spare parts for the damaged glider. Paul Butusov went back for a truss for his hernia. Two days later he was called back to the city because his wife was expecting a baby. The following Sunday, Mrs. Butusov was delivered of a boy. Chanute, who had decided to spend that night at his home in Chicago, was visited by William Avery, who needed twenty dollars because his daughter was sick with typhoid fever. Neither Avery nor Butusov showed up at the camp on Monday, and when Butusov did return, he was summoned back to the city by a telegram about his baby's eyes. In spite of everything, the experiments went forward, although the only one of the three gliders tested that could be called a success was the new three-wing machine. The first time it was tried, the tips of the lower wing dragged along the ground, so the offending wing was removed and from then on Chanute called this glider his two-surface—or two-wing—machine. The Wright brothers, when they learned of its existence a few years later, nearly always referred to it as the Chanute double-decker.

Prophetic of the biplanes that were to flutter across the skies in the early years of the coming century, the double-decker was a refreshing departure from Lilienthal's bulky bat-wing design. It was smaller, its sixteen-foot wings being slightly more than four feet deep, and lighter, weighing only twenty-five pounds. The wings were rigidly trussed with wire in the criss-cross arrangement known to bridgebuilders as the Pratt truss. The tail, which consisted of two overlapping vanes like the tail of a dart, was at first firmly attached to the frame of the glider but was later fitted by Herring with a ball joint and elastic fastenings that permitted it to yield under pressure and thus serve as a gust damper like the so-called regulator on his original Lilienthal-type glider. Because of this, a controversy arose about the origin of the double-decker, and it was sometimes known as the Chanute-Herring machine. Five years later, Herring was still so sensitive on the subject that Chanute felt compelled to remind him in a steamy letter that his contribution was limited to the elastic attachments to the tail, which had proved a failure until William Avery proposed the final arrangement.

The first leaps with the machine in its two-wing form were made on August 31. Then, on September 4, Avery and Herring made about a dozen glides, of which the longest was Avery's—253 feet. On Friday, September 11, a number of good glides were made, and the five best were recorded in Chanute's diary. Although time in the air is a better criterion of superiority in a glide than distance, Avery again covered the most ground—256 feet in 10.2 seconds, compared to Herring's best—235 feet in 10.3 seconds. Lilienthal's longest glides had been 12 to 15 seconds in duration, so the glides of the double-decker were almost as good, considering that it had been tried on only four days altogether.

The Katydid was never as successful as the double-decker. To compensate for the condition of the wings, weakened from having been rebuilt so many times, Chanute surmounted them with an umbrellalike appendage called an aerocurve. Added to the clutter of wing on wing, the aerocurve made the glider so difficult to launch that it refused to lift at all until it had been overhauled and rebalanced at the new campground. Nevertheless, five successful glides were recorded for the reconstructed Katydid, ranging from 148 to 188 feet and between 7 and 7.9 seconds in duration, all made on Friday, September 11, the same day that the five long glides were made with the double-decker. In each case the longest glide had been made by William Avery. This did not sit well with Augustus Herring. Saturday afternoon, while Butusov, Avery, and Chanute were getting the Russian's big glider ready for its long-awaited launching, Herring went off by himself with the double-decker and, according to Chanute's diary, made a number of very good glides, the longest being 359 feet in 14 seconds—or within a second of the longest glide ever made by Lilienthal. No witnesses are recorded as having been present when the glides were made, but Chanute accepted Herring's figures and added the long glide to the list of the five best glides made with the double-decker the day before.

Later that afternoon Butusov's Albatross was at last ready for its first trial, but the wind became gusty. Fog began to settle over the lake, and the launching was postponed. Chanute, Avery, and Butusov returned to Chicago for the weekend, leaving Herring and Dr. Ricketts in charge of the camp. Over the weekend Herring's fit of the sulks developed into a full-scale defection. On Sunday a newspaper artist showed up to make sketches of the gliders for the Chicago *Record,* and Herring talked freely to the artist about a disagreement with Chanute. Some photographs were involved, for Herring helped himself to two glass-plate negatives belonging to Chanute and had them developed on a steam launch stranded in the vicinity. Monday morning he packed up and left. The day was wet and rainy. Chanute decided to wait for the weather to clear before leaving Chicago for the dunes. Early that afternoon, Herring knocked on his door, and there was a showdown. Herring was withdrawing his services rather than be a party to the testing of the Albatross, which he considered unsafe. Octave Chanute's record of his confrontation with Herring concludes: "O.C. let him go." When Chanute arrived at the dunes camp later that afternoon, the *Record* artist told him that Herring's action, in his opinion, had been prompted by egotism and jealousy. Avery and Dr. Ricketts agreed.

Chanute felt that Herring's defection was unfair to Butusov, but he himself was becoming uneasy about the Russian and his big glider. The gull-shaped wings of the Albatross measured forty-nine feet from tip to tip. Its weight was close to two hundred pounds unloaded, or eight times that of the trim little two-wing machine. It was not even a hang glider. The operator was expected to control the balance by moving backward and forward on an eight-foot catwalk while clinging to a pair of curtain poles fastened to the boatlike hull. It had taken two weeks to assemble the glider and another week to construct the launching ways, which resembled nothing so much as a section of roller-coaster track at the bottom of a dip.

On September 17 the Albatross was loaded with sandbags and launched by means of a towrope. As Chanute, Butusov, Avery, and Ricketts ran downhill with the rope, the glider slid down the launching track, sailed forward, then veered to one side and came down a hundred feet from the end of the launching ways. This unmanned test was followed by a nine-day wait for good weather and a wind of the right direction. Finally, at 3 P.M. on September 26, Butusov climbed aboard and the restraining rope was cut. The ungainly glider lumbered slowly down the track but stopped before it reached the end of the launching ways. It was hauled back to the top of the track. Ninety pounds of sand were substituted for the frustrated Russian, and the rope was cut again. This time the pilotless glider cleared the end of the track. After striking a nearby tree, it plowed into the sand, breaking a number of ribs and stanchions.

With relief, but with an air of having achieved at least a minimum of scientific value from this costly experiment, Chanute wrote in his diary: "This trial determines clearly that the machine will not perform soaring flight, that it will glide downward only." On this discouraging note, the camp in the dunes was broken up, and Chanute returned to Chicago with William Avery and Dr. Ricketts, leaving the unlucky Butusov to salvage what he could of his big broken bird.

The first detailed account of the gliding experiments in the Indiana dunes appeared in the *Aeronautical Annual* for 1897, the last of three yearbooks that had begun publication in 1895 under the editorship of James Means, a Boston manufacturer who, like his friend Octave Chanute, devoted a part of his fortune and a great deal of his time to the cause of aeronautics. Herring, still touchy on the subject of whose glider the double-decker really was, insisted on writing his own account of the experiments relating to it, so there were two separate articles in the *Annual* on the 1896 glides, one by Octave Chanute, the other by Augustus Herring. In his article, Herring made an audacious claim. He reported that in October 1896, a month after the Albatross fiasco, he returned to the dunes with a triplane glider, constructed by superimposing a third wing on a double-decker machine, and made glides in winds of up to 48 miles per hour. His two best glides, he wrote, were 893 and 927 feet.

Chanute had not been invited to witness these spectacular glides, nor, apparently, had anybody else. During the autumn of 1896 and the following winter, Chanute was very much in the dark as to the whereabouts and activities of his former assistant. Then, in June 1897, Herring resurfaced in Chicago, out of work. Chanute hired him to perform some tests with birdwing models and left the city on business, only to discover when he returned a few weeks later that Herring had spent the time designing a portable gold-dredging machine. "This was so palpably absurd," Chanute wrote James Means, "that I lost patience and told him we could not go on with the experiments."

Herring had had a stroke of luck in the meantime. He had found a new patron—Matthias Arnot, a young banker of Elmira, New York, whose income matched his enthusiasm for mechanics and invention. Arnot commissioned Herring to build a slightly larger copy of the double-decker. Herring paid William Avery to do the work, hired an assistant, and in September set up a camp in the Indiana dunes with Arnot to test the new glider. Reporters and photographers were welcomed and a spate of articles about the experiments appeared in the Chicago papers. Octave Chanute was present for a second week of experiments. No formal records were kept, but Chanute reported that the glides were generally 200 to 300 feet in length and 8 to 14 seconds in duration. He paid the expenses of the tests during his stay, but one week was as much as his purse could stand. By then he had spent a round $10,000 on kite and gliding experiments, and his business was beginning to suffer. He decided to retire from the field for the time being, but he was always willing to publicize a cause so dear to his heart, and on October 20, 1897, he addressed the Western Society of Engineers in Chicago on the subject of the 1896–97 experiments. Again Herring was allowed to have his say on the double-decker, and again he mentioned his record flights of October 1896 in a triplane glider, blandly adding one more detail—that his longest flight had been 48 seconds in duration, or more than triple the length of time any man, including Lilienthal, had stayed in the air until then —a glide that it would take the Wright brothers three years of practice, three gliders, and a series of wind-tunnel experiments to equal. Herring's reports of his spectacular triplane glides were received with stony disbelief. A 48-second glide, if authenticated, would have been one of the most astonishing aeronautical feats of the nineteenth century, but Chanute never mentioned such a glide in any of his writings. Even Herring may have realized he had gone too far, for neither he nor any of his supporters ever again referred to glides made in the Indiana dunes in October 1896.

Chanute had always suspected that the reason Herring left the camp in the dunes that September was that he was so elated with the success of the double-decker that he wanted to apply a motor and propeller to a flying machine of his own. Although he lacked the funds to construct such a machine, in December 1896 Herring applied for a patent on a powerplane similar to the double-decker except that a third wing was added and there was a motor between the two lower wings, a propeller in front, another behind, and a wheeled undercarriage. In January 1898 the Patent Office rejected Herring's application on the ground that his invention was based on theory and could not be proved operable, but by then Herring had Matthias Arnot in tow, and with Arnot's backing set to work to prove the Patent Office wrong. He had a biplane hang glider constructed by a boatyard in St. Joseph, Michigan, where he had moved the year before. Herring was a self-proclaimed specialist in lightweight motors, but when his machine was ready for testing in the fall of 1898, he was not able to come up with a gasoline motor to provide the 3 horsepower needed to drive his two five-foot wooden propellers. They were driven, instead, by a motor powered by a cylinder of compressed air with an operating capacity of thirty seconds.

Chanute had asked to be notified when the machine was ready for testing. On the afternoon of October 10, 1898, he received a telegram: "About ready today. If you come don't bring any strangers." Herring later claimed that sometime that same day he made the world's first powerplane flight, flying for 50 feet at an altitude of three feet above the beach at St. Joseph with his knees drawn up after a running start. St. Joseph was just across Lake Michigan from Chicago. Chanute took the night boat and arrived the next morning, but Herring was unable to get his machine off the ground and Chanute left St. Joseph with no more faith in the credibility of his erstwhile protégé than when he boarded the boat in Chicago.

The making of unwitnessed, unauthenticated flights was rapidly becoming a specialty of Augustus Herring's. On October 22 he reported that he had made a second flight of 72 feet against a wind of more than 25 miles per hour. Six days later the event was reported in the Niles, Michigan, *Mirror.* Almost a month later, an item about the flight appeared in the Chicago *Evening News,* but when Albert Zahm, secretary of the 1893 International Conference on Aerial Navigation at the Chicago Columbian Exposition, attempted to verify the story, he was unable to obtain the reporter's name or that of any witness.

Octave Chanute was not above making a few wild claims of his own. In 1900, when he retold the story of the Indiana dunes experiments in *McClure's Magazine,* he assured his readers that any quick, handy young man could master a gliding machine almost as easily as a bicycle. Wind gusts were nothing to worry about, since Herring's automatic regulator would take care of all wind gusts up to an altitude of 300 feet! Fortunately, no glider flown in the nineteenth century, Chanute's included, was ever able to attain such a height.

Nor was Chanute averse to padding the record. The longest glide ever recorded for his multiple-wing glider was 188 feet in 7.9 seconds, yet he wrote in *McClure's*: "The 'Multiple-wing' machine was provided with a seat, but, goodness; there was no time to sit down, as each glide of two to three hundred feet took but eight to twelve seconds and then it was time to alight."

In any discussion of the possibility of human flight, it was journalistically *de rigueur* in those days to include a sentence or two predicting when and how success would be achieved. Chanute's article was no exception:

> We have no reason to believe that, contrary to past experience, a practical flying-machine will be the result of the happy thought of one or of two persons. It will come rather by a process of evolution: one man accomplishing some promising results, but stopping short of success; the next carrying the investigation somewhat further, and thus on, until a machine is produced which will be as practical as the "safety" bicycle, which took some eighty years for its development from the original despised velocipede.

Chanute's prophecy was wide of the mark, but by a convenient coincidence his reference to the safety bicycle brings us back to Wilbur and Orville Wright, who all this time have been minding their bicycle business back on West Third Street in Dayton. When Chanute penned those words he had never heard of the Wrights and most likely never would have heard of them had not the brothers, early in 1899, come upon a book on ornithology that rekindled the interest in human flight which had occupied them in a desultory way ever since Orville's recovery from typhoid fever in 1896.

Wilbur and Orville mentioned this book more than once, but never by name, and its identity remains a mystery. There is a good chance, however, that it was not a book-length work at all but extracts from a book that appeared in the *Annual Report* of the Smithsonian Institution for 1892, which had been available all along in the Dayton Public Library. The extracts were a partial translation of *L'Empire de l'Air*, a panegyric on bird flight by Louis-Pierre Mouillard, published in Paris in 1881. By the spring of 1899, the Wright brothers were aware that the Smithsonian Institution had been involved in work on flight, and they may well have stumbled on the paper by Mouillard in perusing the Institution's *Annual Reports* in the public library.

In an article published the month before he died, Wilbur referred to Mouillard's book as "one of the inspiring causes in the efforts of the Wright brothers" and likened its author to a prophet crying in the wilderness, exhorting the world to repent of its unbelief in the possibility of human flight. He called *L'Empire de l'Air* one of the most remarkable pieces of aeronautical literature ever published, compared to which ordinary books on ornithology were childish. There never was a complete translation of the book into English, and Wilbur did not read French. When he quoted Mouillard in his article, he used the translation that had appeared in the Smithsonian *Annual Report* for 1892:

If there be a domineering, tyrant thought, it is the conception that the problem of flight may be solved by man. When once this idea has invaded the brain it possesses it exclusively. It is then a haunting thought, a walking nightmare, impossible to cast off.

Somewhere along the line, a typist or typesetter had transformed what the translator obviously intended to be a "waking" nightmare into a "walking" one. Mouillard had written *une espèce de cauchemar*—"a kind of (plain) nightmare." No matter. Mouillard knew whereof he spoke. He was an accurate observer of birds, but when it came to imitating bird flight he was a failure. He built six gliders in forty years, and only one made a flight of more than 100 feet. For Mouillard, who died in Cairo in 1897, the problem of flight was truly a waking nightmare.

For Wilbur and Orville, the problem of flight was never a nightmare, waking or walking, although there were times during the next few years when it seemed bent on becoming one. But in a way Mouillard was right. The idea that the problem of flight could be solved by man was a haunting thought, impossible to cast off, and it was to occupy the thoughts and energies of the brothers for the rest of their lives together.

# 4

# *The Twisted Box*

THE MOST EXPEDIENT, least expensive way to tackle the problem of human flight, as the Wright brothers saw it, was to find out first what others had done. On May 30, 1899, while other respectable citizens were celebrating Decoration Day (as Memorial Day was then called) by decking the graves of the Civil War dead with flags and flowers, Wilbur sat down at Katharine's bandy-legged desk in the parlor next to the floor-length lace curtains in the house on Hawthorn Street and addressed a letter to the secretary of the Smithsonian Institution in Washington, D.C. After a lengthy preamble expressing his faith in the feasibility of human flight, Wilbur wrote: "I am about to begin a systematic study of the subject in preparation for practical work to which I expect to devote what time I can spare from my regular business. I wish to obtain such papers as the Smithsonian Institution has published on this subject, and if possible a list of other works in print in the English language."

To make sure he would not be mistaken for a crackpot, Wilbur appended a mild disclaimer with just the right amount of high-flown humility: "I am an enthusiast, but not a crank in the sense that I have some pet theories as to the proper construction of a flying machine. I wish to avail myself of all that is already known and then if possible add my mite to help the future worker who will attain final success."

The letter was answered three days later by the assistant secretary of the Smithsonian, who sent four pamphlets free of charge, all reprints of articles already available in the Institution's *Annual Reports.* These were an account of Langley's power-model flights of 1896, Lilienthal's own description of some of his gliding experiments, a paper on soaring flight by Edward C. Huffaker, and the translated extracts from Mouillard's *L'Empire de l'Air.* The assistant secretary also sent a list of books available commercially:

Samuel Langley's *Experiments in Aerodynamics* of 1891, Octave Chanute's *Progress in Flying Machines* of 1894, and James Means's *Aeronautical Annuals* for 1895, 1896, and 1897.

The books were ordered at once. They arrived just after the bicycle business had reached its seasonal peak, giving the brothers time to devour and digest them. Wilbur and Orville were to have serious reservations about Langley's *Experiments in Aerodynamics*—a series of experiments made with a whirling arm as remarkable for the insignificance of their findings as for the elaborateness of their instrumentation—but Chanute's *Progress in Flying Machines* was a veritable Old Testament of aeronautics, to which the three *Aeronautical Annuals* were a latter-day Gospel bringing the story up to date. Almost the entire record of human flight—a mixture of myth and history —was suddenly available for study. It was a rich feast for two bicycle mechanics whose diet until then had been restricted to books on ornithology, encyclopedia articles on bird flight, and an occasional magazine piece on man's attempt to fly.

The Wrights were not interested in lighter-than-air flight. After more than a hundred years of experimenting with balloons, the most that could be hoped for along that line was attaching a motor and propeller to a rigid keel suspended beneath a lumpy gasbag, which could then be steered like a huge writhing pillow over fairgrounds if all went well or, if it didn't, would wander aimlessly with the wind like a gaseous elephant until a sharp tree branch or weather vane relieved it of its flatulence. The rigid airship would change all that, but the practical dirigible had not yet evolved.

When it came to heavier-than-air flight, Wilbur and Orville classified experimenters into two categories—those whose objective was flight by means of motor and propellers and those who attempted merely to glide. Thousands of dollars had been spent by experimenters in the first category, but the only relatively successful propeller-driven aircraft had been Langley's thirty-pound models of 1896, which, for all the Wrights knew at the time, represented a dead end. What most impressed them about the unsuccessful attempts at power flight was the wasteful procedure of mounting costly heavy machinery on a flying machine that no man would have known how to control if he had managed to get it into the air in the first place.

Hiram Maxim, the American inventor of the machine gun that bore his name, was the most lavish spender in the power category. In England, he constructed a four-ton behemoth with a wingspread of over a hundred feet. Two powerful steam engines compensated in part for the inefficiency of his two eighteen-foot propellers. "Propulsion and lifting are solved problems," Maxim told reporters in 1893. "The rest is a mere matter of time." Time ran out for Maxim on July 31, 1894, when his unbirdlike creation lumbered down an 1,800-foot track on its cast-iron wheels and struggled two feet into the air before its upward progress was arrested by a pair of wooden restraining rails, one of which broke before the power could be shut off.

In France, Clément Ader ran a close second to Maxim. He studied the flight of bats as well as birds and in the 1890s built three steam-powered batlike contraptions that ran around a circular track, propelled by feathery-looking propellers. He spent the equivalent of $100,000 in French government funds on the *Avion,* his third machine. Then, in 1897, funds were cut off by the government. Ader claimed he had flown almost 1,000 feet in the *Avion,* but when the official test results were published in 1910, his claim was shown to be false.

The sympathy of the Wrights was clearly with the second group of experimenters, the gliding men. But of these only Otto Lilienthal, Octave Chanute, and Percy Pilcher in England had produced machines capable of repeated flights. Wilbur and Orville regarded Lilienthal as a fearless experimenter and were only slightly less impressed by the Chanute experiments in the Indiana dunes. Pilcher's most notable achievement occurred in June 1897, when he had himself towed in his hang glider the Hawk, at the end of what must have been a very strong fishing line indeed, from the top of one hill in England to the top of another 750 feet away.

The thing that struck the Wright brothers most forcibly in their reading that summer was how little attention Lilienthal and other successful experimenters had paid to the problem of control. Lilienthal had maintained the equilibrium of his gliders by swinging his torso and thrashing his legs about. Chanute and Herring had tried to do so by making the wings or tail vanes of their gliders slightly movable in response to wind gusts, but to the Wrights control involved not only maintaining equilibrium but upsetting equilibrium in order to ascend and descend, or to turn and circle. To them control was the missing link in the art of flying, even though there was no flying art at the time, as Wilbur liked to point out, but only a flying problem. To be more exact, there was a whole complex of problems crying out for solution. From the vantage point of the summer of 1899, the outlook was both bleak and promising. It was bleak because all those expensive motor-powered experiments had led nowhere, and the only man then carrying on where Lilienthal had left off was Percy Pilcher, who was to die later that year when the rain-soaked tail of his glider collapsed as he was being towed into the air. At the same time the outlook was promising in that the field was wide open to anyone willing and able to preempt it.

It was a tempting challenge, and the Wright brothers lost no time in taking it up. A month after receiving the pamphlets and list of books from the Smithsonian, Wilbur and Orville were at work on a flying machine of their own. It was neither a full-sized glider nor a toylike model, but a biplane with a five-foot wingspan designed to be flown as a kite. The cloth-covered wings, which had been shellacked to make them airtight, were trussed with wire from side to side but not from front to rear, and the connecting uprights were hinged so that the upper wing could be moved forward or backward relative to the lower wing when the kite flier manipulated the two pairs of cords running from the wingtips to the sticks held in either hand. They believed that this would control the upward or downward movement of the machine, but it is doubtful that this shearing movement alone would have had the desired effect if the model's flat horizontal tail had not been attached to the wings so that when the upper wing was moved forward, the tail was automatically raised, or automatically lowered when the wing was moved to the rear.

A second type of control was built into the kite model. This was lateral control, the kind exercised by a bird to induce a turn or to correct the rocking of its wings in soaring flight. Lateral control in modern aircraft is achieved by moving the ailerons on the rear edges of the two wings in opposite directions. The fact that a bird or an aircraft alters the angles of its wings in order to turn or restore its balance seems fairly obvious today, but it was not at all obvious in 1899.

According to Wilbur, he and his brother discovered the birds' method of lateral control one day while observing a flight of pigeons. One pigeon was making an erratic sort of flight. First one wing was high, then the other. It came to them then that the pigeon had possibly adjusted the tips of its wings so as to present one wingtip at a positive angle to its line of flight and the other at a negative angle, thus turning itself into an animated windmill. When the pigeon had revolved as far as it wished, it reversed the process and began to roll the other way. "Thus the balance," Wilbur explained, "was controlled by utilizing dynamic reactions of the air instead of shifting weight."

The two brothers did not always agree on what went on in those early days. In his old age, Orville created another of those curious circles of confusion by taking a dim view of the birds' role in the development of human flight, except as an inspiration. "Although we intently watched birds fly in a hope of learning something from them," he wrote in 1941, "I cannot think of anything that was first learned in that way." He compared learning the secret of flight from birds to learning the secret of magic from a magician: "After you once know the trick and know what to look for you see things that you did not notice when you did not know exactly what to look for."

Whatever the origin of the wing-twisting idea, once the concept had been grasped, the Wrights ran up against the problem of how to apply the pigeon's method to a pair of wings made of cloth tightly stretched over a rigid wooden framework. Orville made a sketch, showing how it could be done by pivoting each wing on a metal shaft and gearing the shafts so that when one wing was tilted up the opposite wing would tilt down. Mechanically this was possible, but the weight of all that metal ruled it out, and the problem remained—how to apply this torsion principle to a light wing of wood and cloth without impairing its strength or adding appreciably to its weight.

It was Wilbur who stumbled on the solution. In those days of sixty-hour workweeks, the bicycle shop was open evenings during the summer. One night when Wilbur was minding the shop alone, he sold an inner tube for a bicycle tire. He removed the tube from the long, narrow box in which it came, and while talking to the customer, began absentmindedly to twist the ends of the open box in opposite directions. It suddenly occurred to him that if a frail pasteboard box could survive such strain, it might be possible to twist the cloth-covered wooden frame of a flying machine in the same fashion without sacrificing lateral stiffness. Ripping the ends off the box made the torsion principle more apparent. When the shop closed that night Wilbur took the box home with him and demonstrated its twisting properties to Orville. Then and there the brothers decided to utilize this principle in their five-foot kite-glider. To effect lateral control they would merely twist the right and left wings in opposite directions.

Orville told the story of the inner-tube box in some detail several years after Wilbur was dead. Recognizing a good story when he saw one, Mark Sullivan retold the story in the second volume of *Our Times,* his multi-volume history of the first quarter of the century. He called the moment when Wilbur first fiddled with the empty inner-tube box the moment when the secret of flight was discovered. He acclaimed it as a milestone in history and compared it to Newton's observation of the falling apple. When the proofs of the relevant pages of *Our Times* were submitted to Orville for checking in 1928, he considered the story a trifle tall. In a letter to one of Sullivan's assistants, he let some air out of the story, calling it an episode dramatized beyond its importance. The twisted box did not reveal a basic principle, he wrote; it merely suggested a better mechanical embodiment of a principle that he and Wilbur had already discussed several months before Wilbur picked up the empty inner-tube box.

Dramatized beyond its importance this incident may have been, but it demonstrates a significant aspect of the Wrights' story that might be called their genius for the tactile. From boyhood on, both brothers had developed a feeling for materials, for wood, cloth, metals, and wire, which was to stand them in good stead. It didn't require genius to twist an empty inner-tube box. As a matter of fact, it would be a hard thing for a person with restless fingers not to do, but to Wilbur's sensitive fingers, the bending and straining of that long, supple cardboard box conveyed a message—through who knows what chain of sensations and associations—into a product of wood, cloth, and sliding wires that would eventually enable the brothers to swoop and soar and circle almost as effortlessly as the pigeon that Wilbur pictured as turning itself into an animated windmill.

In the man-carrying Wright flying machines, this twisting of the wings, or wingwarping as it came to be called, would be accomplished by moving a series of warping wires that ran through pulleys to the wingtips. In the 1899 kite model the twisting was effected more simply. When the kite flier tilted the tops of the sticks held in his hands in opposite directions, the cords that ran from the ends of the sticks to the four wingtips would twist one pair of wings up, the other pair down.

Wilbur flew the kite model just once that summer in the low open ground on the west side of Dayton where Orville and his friend Ed Sines had flown kites as boys. The big kite responded promptly to the warping of the wings. The wing with the positive angle lifted; the wing with the negative angle dipped. The sight of a grown man flying a kite almost as wide as he was tall attracted a number of small boys. Once, when Wilbur shifted the upper wing backward by manipulating the sticks attached to the flying cords, the model turned down so sharply that a slack was created in the flying cords and the boys had to fall on their faces to avoid being hit by the diving kite.

The test of the kite model convinced Wilbur and Orville that they were on the right track. The next step would be to try out their control system on a man-carrying glider. That wouldn't be practical until the following summer, but they made a few calculations in advance. Using Lilienthal's "Table of Normal and Tangential Pressures" in the 1897 *Aeronautical Annual,* they calculated that to support a glider of the kind they had in mind would take winds of 15–16 miles per hour. Those were stronger, steadier winds than those that blew across the few open spaces left in Dayton, so on November 24 Wilbur wrote to the Weather Bureau in Washington. With Octave Chanute's experimental site in the Indiana dunes in mind, he asked for information on wind velocities in the vicinity of Chicago. The chief of the Weather Bureau himself answered Wilbur's letter, sending, in addition to the information requested, the *Monthly Weather Review* for August and September, giving the average hourly winds at all Weather Bureau stations in the United States.

Wilbur's letter to the Weather Bureau and its reply are the last documents pertinent to the Wright brothers' story before the dawn of an important new year. There would be much confusion in the public mind over whether 1900 was the last year of the old century or the first year of the new. Either way, the new year would be one long New Year's Day of stocktaking and prophesying as mankind stood poised on the threshold of the new century and peered into the shadowy abyss. What went on in the bicycle shop on West Third Street in

1900 would be of more consequence than anything that took place in the house on Hawthorn Street. Bishop Wright would continue to be absent from home from time to time, making his rounds among the scattered adherents of the Church of the United Brethren, traveling sometimes as far west as Nebraska or as far east as Pennsylvania. Lorin Wright's three older children and their baby brother would spend Sunday afternoons as usual in their grandfather's house, playing charades, singing songs, having taffy-pulls, or listening while their uncles read to them from old issues of *Chatterbox*. Wilbur was less patient than Orville. When the child on his lap showed a lack of interest, he would stretch his legs and the child would slide off onto the floor. Orville never tired of playing. When games ran out he would make candy, caramels generally, because they took longer to chew, but sometimes he made fudge, testing it from time to time with a long thermometer as it boiled down. Orville already knew how to play the guitar. In 1900 he was taking mandolin lessons. "He sits around and picks that thing," Katharine complained to her father, "until I can hardly stay in the house."

For a year and a half after graduating from Oberlin in 1898, Katharine Wright kept house for her father and brothers. Then, in January 1900, she began teaching history and Latin in Dayton at Steele High School, a monumental edifice encrusted with turrets and gables at the corner of Monument and Main. A photograph taken about that time shows her as the very model of a maiden schoolteacher in fashionable shirtwaist and high lace collar, with pince-nez secured by a slender chain to a wire hooked over one ear. A month after she started teaching, Katharine hired diminutive fourteen-year-old Carrie Kayler to come in by the day to help with the cooking and housework.

Orville was a great tease and made much of Carrie's small size, keeping track of her growth with pencil marks on the frame of the kitchen door. On the day that Carrie broke the news to the assembled family that she no longer had to stand on a chair to turn the gaslight in the kitchen up or down, Orville made her stand against the doorframe so he could check her height. It was true, he announced gravely; having shown signs of growth, she would be allowed to stay on and work for the Wrights. She stayed on for forty-eight years, graduating from white-skinned slavey to member of the family in all but name. Many of Carrie Kayler's memories of Wilbur and Orville would be kitchen-based and culinary. Orville, she remembered, excelled in the making of mundane items such as coffee and biscuits. Wilbur was the gourmet. When there was turkey to be stuffed, Wilbur did it, lining up the ingredients before him and prefacing the ceremony with much rubbing of the hands like a magician about to pull a rabbit out of a hat.

Carrie was more or less firmly established in the Wright household on Sunday, May 13, 1900, when Wilbur sat down at Katharine's writing desk in the parlor and penned the letter that would become the next document in the Wright brothers' story. It was not printed information they were after now, but advice, the kind of advice that could come only from a person more experienced than themselves, someone capable of comprehending what they were about to do and of anticipating the problems they might face. There was only one person in the United States who possessed that kind of knowledge and experience: that French-born Chicagoan, that former bridge-builder and civil engineer, that semi-retired manufacturer of railroad ties and consultant in wood-preserving, Octave Chanute.

# 5

## *A Perilous Passage*

WHEN OCTAVE CHANUTE opened the envelope with the Dayton postmark and withdrew the sheets of blue business stationery bearing the name—under a florid letterhead adorned with forget-me-nots and sun rays bursting through clouds—of an obscure bicycle company in that city, he had no way of knowing that those five pages constituted the opening salvo in an exchange of letters that would comprise as complete a contemporary record of an invention as any such record ever produced. The carefully composed opening paragraph might have given him a clue:

> For some years I have been afflicted with the belief that flight is possible to man. My disease has increased in severity and I feel that it will soon cost me an increased amount of money if not my life. I have been trying to arrange my affairs in such a way that I can devote my entire time for a few months to experiment in this field.

After assuring Chanute that they both look at the flying problem in much the same way—that it can only be solved by learning to fly first without motors and propellers—Wilbur makes so bold as to explain to the sixty-seven-year-old senior statesman of aeronautics the two causes of Otto Lilienthal's "failure": first, the German's method of practicing ("in five years' time he spent only about five hours, altogether, in actual flight . . . even Methuselah could never have become an expert stenographer with one hour per year for practice"); second, the inadequacy of Lilienthal's method and apparatus ("my observations of the flight of birds convince me that birds use more positive and energetic methods of regaining equilibrium than that of shifting the center of gravity"). Before revealing how he intends to succeed where Lilienthal failed, Wilbur makes an interesting admission:

"The problem is too great for one man alone and unaided to solve in secret." The fact that for the next six months Chanute's only clue to the existence of another Wright brother would be Orville's name in small type under that of Wilbur in the upper left-hand corner of the Wright Cycle Company letterhead makes that sentence one of the most ironic statements in the history of aviation.

"My plan then is this," Wilbur continues, and he outlines his scheme to build a tower 150 feet high with a rope passing over a pulley at the top. One end of the rope is attached to a glider at the foot of the tower, the other to a counterweight so that the glider floats free when blown away from the tower, supported partly by the wind and partly by the pull of the counter-weight. This was one of the few impractical ideas Wilbur ever committed to paper, but his intentions were praiseworthy since his object was to practice gliding by the hour rather than a few seconds at a time like Lilienthal. To rectify Lilienthal's second shortcoming—his failure to build an apparatus that can be controlled by means other than shifting the weight—he intends to construct a man-carrying glider with a means of controlling both lateral and fore-and-aft balance. The proposed glider, as he describes it, is essentially a larger version of the 1899 kite model. Not until the penultimate paragraph of his long letter does Wilbur get around to asking for a specific bit of advice: "My business requires that my experimental work be confined to the months between September and January and I would be particularly thankful for advice as to a suitable locality where I could depend on winds of about fifteen miles per hour without rain or too inclement weather."

Octave Chanute, who thought nothing of receiving letters from scientists and engineers from as far away as Australia, was sufficiently impressed by this letter from a bicycle dealer in Dayton to answer it promptly. He made no comment on Wilbur's proposed glider but pointed out that gliding down a soft sand hill was safer than practicing while suspended from a tower. He apparently considered the Indiana dunes unsuitable for experiments late in the year. He recommended instead San Diego, California, and Pine Island, Florida, because of the steady sea breezes in those localities. Perhaps even better experimental sites, he suggested, could be found on the Atlantic coast of South Carolina or Georgia.

"I shall consider your suggestions carefully in making my plans," Wilbur responded on June 1. California and Florida were too far from Dayton, however. In going through the *Monthly Weather Reviews* sent by the chief of the Weather Bureau, Wilbur noted that winds of the required strength had been reported at Kitty Hawk, North Carolina, which was even closer than the possible gliding sites on the coasts of South Carolina and Georgia suggested by Octave Chanute. Kitty Hawk was on the Outer Banks, that 200-mile strip of sand, bent like an elbow at Cape Hatteras, that acts as a buffer between the ocean and the North Carolina mainland. Transportation might be a problem. It would be no trick to get from Dayton to Norfolk, Virginia. From Norfolk the trains ran south to the rail terminal at Elizabeth City, North Carolina. But Kitty Hawk was more than thirty miles across Albemarle Sound from Elizabeth City. Since anyone arriving unannounced at such an isolated spot might have trouble finding food and shelter, Wilbur wrote the U.S. Weather Bureau station at Kitty Hawk on August 3 that he was about to conduct some kite-flying experiments and asked for information on the terrain, the winds, room and board, and transportation.

Joseph Dosher, who operated the telegraph at the Kitty Hawk Weather Bureau station, answered Wilbur's letter. He described the mile-wide beach as clear of trees and high hills for sixty miles to the south, with prevailing winds from the north and northeast during September and October. He was sorry, but it would not be possible to rent a house. "So you will have to bring tents," he wrote. "You could obtain board."

Wilbur's letter created quite a stir in the little fishing village of Kitty Hawk. It was passed from hand to hand until it either disintegrated or was lost, but not until it had received the personal attention of William J. Tate, whose wife, Addie, was village postmistress. A letter from Bill Tate soon followed Dosher's. It was a friendly, chatty letter and corrected the impression Dosher had given of the terrain as being perfectly flat. Tate told of a bare hill eighty feet high a few miles to the south with not a tree or bush anywhere to break the evenness of the wind current. The weather got a little rough by November, he warned, and ended his letter in a flourish of ampersands: "If you decide to try your machine here & come I will take pleasure in doing all I can for your convenience & success & pleasure, & I assure you you will find a hospitable people when you come among us."

When Bill Tate's letter reached Dayton toward the end of August, the man-carrying glider was already under construction. Earlier that month Wilbur had written Octave Chanute, asking him to recommend a Chicago firm that could supply spruce for the spars and to suggest a suitable varnish for the wing coverings. Chanute replied with customary promptness, recommending Cincinnati as a source of spruce closer to Dayton and enclosing a recipe for varnish, but in the end varnish was not used on the wing coverings of the 1900 glider and Wilbur unwisely decided to put off buying spruce for the spars until he got to Norfolk.

The total cost of the materials used in the glider came to fifteen dollars. In his first letter to Octave Chanute, Wilbur had stated his belief that no financial profit would accrue to the inventor of the first flying machine. Now, with work on the glider practically finished, he was having second thoughts about the matter. On September 3, during one of Bishop Wright's many out-of-town trips on church business, Wilbur wrote his father, frankly acknowledging that while he was taking up the investigation for pleasure rather than profit, there was a slight possibility of achieving fame and fortune from it. The mere thought that such a possibility even existed was enough to inject an undercurrent of excitement into the even tenor of life in the house on Hawthorn Street. On September 5, Katharine reported to her father that the household was in an uproar getting Wilbur off. It would be his first journey away from home since his visit to the Columbian Exposition in Chicago with Orville seven years before. "The trip will do him good," Katharine predicted. "I don't think he will be reckless. If they can arrange it, Orv will go down as soon as Will gets the machine ready."

Wilbur left on the six-thirty train the next evening. In addition to Katharine's trunk and suitcase, into which Katharine had thoughtfully slipped a small jar of jelly, he took with him everything needed for the gliding experiments: the bent ribs of ash, steamed to the desired curvature; the wing coverings of French sateen, which had been cut on the bias so as to brace the wings diagonally and had been sewed—on Katharine's sewing machine —so that the eighteen-foot spars could be slipped in from the side; the shaped struts, or uprights; the tools that would be needed to assemble the glider, which had been constructed so that it could be knocked down and crated; even a large tent to assemble it in.

Twenty-four hours after leaving Dayton, Wilbur got off the train at Old Point Comfort, Virginia, and took the ferry across Hampton Roads to Norfolk, where he spent Friday night in a hotel. On Saturday he went shopping for spruce. The weather was having its way over most of the United States that day. In Texas a violent hurricane was battering Galveston, whipping water from the Gulf of Mexico into the streets to depths of as much as seventeen feet, snuffing out six thousand lives, and doing damage in the tens of millions of dollars. In Norfolk, the news had not come over the wires yet, but the air was heavy and damp. The thermometer stood near 100 degrees. Respectable members of the middle class wore suits and hats in all weather in those days. Wilbur, who also wore a high starched collar, almost collapsed.

Unable to find spruce anywhere in Norfolk, he wound up Saturday afternoon in a lumberyard where, for $7.70, an obliging mill foreman by the name of Cumpston Goffigon sold him several white pine strips instead. The glider had been designed for spars of eighteen feet, but the longest Mr. Goffigon could supply were sixteen feet. Disappointed, but with the sixteen-foot pine spars added to his baggage, Wilbur boarded the train in Norfolk and Saturday evening arrived at Elizabeth City, North Carolina, where the Pasquotank River widens into Albemarle Sound after snaking its way out of the Dismal Swamp.

William Tate had sent Wilbur instructions for the next stage of his journey, the overwater trip to Kitty Hawk: "You can reach here from Elizabeth City, N.C. (35 miles from here) by boat direct from Manteo 12 miles from here by mail boat every Mond., Wed & Friday." This was much like telling a person trying to get from London to New York that he could reach New York from London by boat direct from Boston by mail boat three days a week. Joseph Dosher of the Kitty Hawk Weather Bureau station had been more coherent: "The only way to reach Kitty Hawk is from Manteo Roanoke Island N.C. in a small sail boat." But Manteo was fifty miles from Elizabeth City and Wilbur was in a hurry. To save time, he decided to visit the waterfront and hire a boat to take him direct to Kitty Hawk.

Later that week, Wilbur described the ordeal of his passage to the Outer Banks in a letter to Orville that became a family classic and suffered the same fate as Wilbur's letter to the Kitty Hawk Weather Bureau station—it was passed from hand to hand until it eventually disappeared. When Wilbur finally did get to Kitty Hawk, he jotted down a memorandum that survives as the only record of his voyage, if an incomplete one. In it, he recounted how nobody in Elizabeth City seemed to know anything about Kitty Hawk or how to get there until on Tuesday, his third day in town, he came across Israel Perry in a leaky skiff on the waterfront. Perry lived with his boy on a flat-bottomed fishing boat anchored three miles downriver. He not only knew where Kitty Hawk was, but claimed to have been born and raised there.

A bargain was struck. The heavy trunk, the long pine spars, and Wilbur's suitcase were loaded onto the skiff, and Wilbur, Perry, and Perry's boy set off down the marshy Pasquotank for Perry's schooner. Wilbur also referred to Perry's boy as a man, so he was either an adolescent on the verge of manhood or, in Wright family parlance, an "African." Black or white, man or boy, he does not figure in the Wright story until half a century later, and then only fleetingly, when a movie script about the Wrights, ground out in the Warner Brothers' Hollywood movie factory but never produced, converted the so-called boy to a big-breasted brunette with eyes only for Wilbur—an unlikely companion for Israel Perry, who appeared never to have washed, or for Wilbur, who was reasonably fussy about such matters and noticeably nervous in the presence of young unmarried women.

Fortunately the crates containing the glider had been left behind in the freight depot at Elizabeth City, for the skiff rode so low in the water that the waves lapped over its sides and all hands had to resort to bailing. Israel Perry's schooner, the *Curlicue,* was in even worse condition than the skiff. "The sails were rotten," noted Wilbur, "the rope badly worn and the rudder-post half rotted off, and the cabin so dirty and vermin-infested that I kept out of it from first to last." To make a bad situation worse, there was so little wind that it was almost dark before they passed through the wide mouth of the Pasquotank into Albemarle Sound. The remaining twenty or so miles to Kitty Hawk could have been navigated in a few hours with a fair wind, but no sooner had they headed down the sound in the direction of the Outer Banks than they were overtaken by what was probably the tail end of the hurricane that had devastated Galveston.

The rolling *Curlicue* sprang a leak and once more it was necessary to bail. Afraid of being upset if they tried to turn around, they headed into the wind, which was striking the flat bottom of the boat and driving it two feet backward for every foot it advanced. Backing up, they managed to round the light at the tip of Camden Point and take refuge in the North River, but the foresail blew loose and the boat began to roll wildly in the dark. Wilbur helped take down the foresail. Then the mainsail tore loose. When that was taken in, the stern swung around to the wind. As waves broke over the stern, they made a run over a sandbar with only the jib taking the wind. Perry refused to land and, safe but drenched, they spent what was left of Tuesday night at anchor, buffeted by the winds of the dying hurricane.

Wilbur's record of the voyage ends at this point, with the notation that "Israel had been so long a stranger to the touch of water upon his skin that it affected him very much." An echo of his lost letter has been preserved, however, in a letter that Orville wrote to Katharine from the Outer Banks a month later, referring to "those 'bars' up North River, where Israel Perry wouldn't land 'for a thousand dollars.' "

Wilbur woke up Wednesday with a sore back from sleeping on deck. He refused to eat the food that Perry provided and dined in solitary splendor on the jar of jelly that Katharine had packed in his suitcase. The boat remained at anchor until Wednesday afternoon, when the wind changed and Perry set sail for the Outer Banks. At nine that night the *Curlicue* tied up at the wharf of the sleeping village on Kitty Hawk Bay. A few houses were scattered among the trees that lined the bay, but between the houses and the lifesaving station on the beach a mile to the east there was nothing but sand. Wilbur had no intention of stumbling around in the dark in an attempt to test Bill Tate's assurance that he would "find a hospitable people when you come among us." Once again he lay down to sleep on the hard deck of Israel Perry's foul schooner, preferring the company of mosquitoes to the verminous interior of its cabin.

# 6

# The Outer Banks

ALBEMARLE SOUND WAS rich with fish, and the small village at the north end of Kitty Hawk Bay was inhabited largely by fishermen. The fishermen and their wives raised beans, corn, and turnips and kept a few pigs and cattle, but crops and farm animals were not as well adjusted to the sandy environment as the mosquitoes and wood ticks that thrived in great numbers on the Outer Banks. The name "Kitty Hawk" is said to be a corruption of "mosquito (or "skeeter") hawk," which is not a hawk at all but a dragonfly that swarms near the village at certain times of the year, presumably to feast on the insects for which it is named.

Twelve miles south of Kitty Hawk was Nags Head, a century-old summer resort of cottages built with their backs to the ocean and their front porches facing Roanoke Island across the sound. Nags Head was a favorite watering place of North Carolinians, but it was not an easy place to get to, and vacationers brought with them whatever they needed for the summer —furniture, chickens, horses, buggies, and mules. Next to the boat landing on Roanoke Sound was Nags Head's only hotel, a rambling frame structure that had burned to the ground in August 1900, a month before Wilbur made his hazardous expedition to the Outer Banks.

The fisherfolk of Kitty Hawk were insulated from the vacationers and the few year-round residents of Nags Head by a virtually uninhabited stretch of sand, unbroken except for three barren dunes four miles to the south known as Kill Devil Hills, the highest of which Bill Tate had mentioned in his letter to Wilbur, and another series of shifting sand hills four miles farther south. Below Nags Head were fifty miles of marshy meadows and beach all the way to Cape Hatteras.

Tate, born in 1860, was the descendant of a Scottish sailor who had survived shipwreck on the treacherous shoals off the North Carolina coast.

In 1874 an attempt was made to reduce the toll of lives by establishing seven lifesaving stations on the Outer Banks. One of these was located on the beach opposite Kitty Hawk and another just east of Kill Devil Hills. Each two-story station building had an enclosed lookout tower and a boathouse with a ramp for wheeling out the lifeboats on their launching cars. In 1875 a Weather Bureau station was installed alongside the Kitty Hawk lifesaving station to keep track of the hurricanes that swept the coast each fall. A telegraph line connected the weather station at Kitty Hawk to the one at Norfolk, Virginia, seventy miles up the coast. Telegrams could be sent over the government wire to the Norfolk station, from which they were relayed by phone to the local Western Union office, but Kitty Hawkers had little occasion to send telegrams, and telegraph operator Joseph Dosher seldom used the wire for this purpose.

The lifesaving stations provided seasonal employment for fishermen all up and down the coast. Members of the lifesaving crews earned fifty dollars a month when they bedded down at the stations from December to March. On stormy nights during those months, when they were not risking their lives in the surf, they patrolled the beaches with lanterns and signal flares to warn ships away from the dangerous shoals. The rest of the year they were on call, much like members of a volunteer fire department, at three dollars per call.

William Tate later became a captain in the lifesaving hierarchy. In 1900 he already wore several hats. His wife, Addie, was postmistress in name, but Bill Tate was postmaster in fact, as he had been when the Kitty Hawk post office opened in 1878. He was also a notary public and a commissioner of Currituck County, of which Kitty Hawk was the southernmost part at the time. If that tiny collection of fishermen's houses could be said to have a political boss, Bill Tate was it. His house was a quarter of a mile from the wharf on Kitty Hawk Bay—a two-story frame house with unplaned siding and a wide veranda. There was no paint on the outside walls, no plaster on the inside, no carpets on the floors, no pictures, no books, and very little furniture. Nevertheless it was one of the best houses in the village.

Kitty Hawkers led an isolated existence and no doubt would have dwelt in relative isolation for another decade or two if destiny had not come knocking at the door of the Tate house on the morning of September 13, 1900, in the person of Elijah Baum, a neighbor's boy. Elijah was not alone. He had been pressed into service as a guide by a strange gentleman, who took off his cap when Bill Tate opened the door, and introduced himself as Wilbur Wright of Dayton, Ohio, "to whom you wrote concerning this section."

It had taken Wilbur a few hours short of a solid week to find his way from 7 Hawthorn Street in Dayton to the Tate house in Kitty Hawk. His back ached and his arms were still sore from holding onto the sides of Israel Perry's boat as it rocked all night alongside the wharf on Kitty Hawk Bay. He was also hungry. When Mrs. Tate learned that he had eaten nothing but a small jar of jelly for almost forty-eight hours, she whipped him up a breakfast of ham and eggs, although eggs were not too plentiful in those parts. Until his brother Orville arrived with camping equipment, Wilbur explained, he would need room and board. Could he stay with the Tates? William and Addie Tate went into the next room to confer. When Wilbur overheard Mrs. Tate expressing fears that their spare room and plain fare would not be adequate for the well-dressed young stranger from Dayton, he went to the doorway and assured her that whatever she provided would be satisfactory. He had only one special requirement—that she boil him a gallon of water each morning and place it in a pitcher in his room. Members of the Wright family had been particular about their drinking water ever since Orville's near-fatal attack of typhoid fever in 1896.

Almost the only outsiders who came to Kitty Hawk were officials of the U.S. Lifesaving Service, whose semiannual visits were looked forward to with understandable eagerness. As soon as Wilbur had had a few days of rest, Bill Tate took him around Kitty Hawk and introduced him to the villagers and the crew at the lifesaving station. By then the weekly freight boat from Elizabeth City had delivered the crates containing the disassembled glider and Wilbur had become a figure of great curiosity.

The Monday after his arrival, he carried Mrs. Tate's sewing machine out into the yard and after cutting two feet from the French sateen wing coverings of the glider to compensate for the difference between the eighteen-foot spars he had not been able to buy in Norfolk and the sixteen-foot spars he had bought from lumberyard foreman Cumpston Goffigon, he proceeded to splice the pieces of cloth together. Twenty-eight years later the citizens of Kitty Hawk would erect a stone marker on the site where Wilbur began work on his glider, but when word got around in September 1900 that all those yards of fine sateen were to be used in a flying machine, the curiosity of the God-fearing Kitty Hawkers was tempered with suspicion. They believed in a good God, a bad Devil, and a hot Hell—the words are Bill Tate's —and more than anything else they believed that God did not intend that man should ever fly.

"I have my machine nearly finished," Wilbur wrote his father on his second Sunday in Kitty Hawk. Wilbur and Orville were no longer churchgoers, but they observed the Sabbath for their father's sake. Sunday for them was a day for putting pen to paper. The warmest, most revealing of the brothers' letters were generally written on Sunday. In his letter of Sunday, September 23, Wilbur goes to great pains to convince his father that he is in no danger. The framework of the glider can sustain five times his weight. It is trussed like a bridge. He is testing every piece. If it is upset, there is plenty of sand to cushion a fall.

Wilbur's letter is interesting for another reason. The collaboration of the Wright brothers is what makes their story so memorable, but Wilbur's letter to his father, who had been in Pennsylvania on church business while the flying-machine project had been taking shape, makes no mention of Orville. It is "my machine," "my steering arrangement," "my experiments" from first paragraph to last. Wilbur's failure to so much as intimate that Orville was involved in any way in the forthcoming experiments creates another of those troubling circles of confusion that throw their story out of focus at important junctures. The impression has always been given that they worked on the flight problem together from the beginning, but the truth probably is that Orville was never as deeply committed to the project in 1899 and early 1900 as both brothers later claimed. He seems to have drifted into the flying-machine business in the wake of big brother Wilbur, but there is no denying that he caught fire in short order.

As a matter of fact, Orville was preparing to leave for Kitty Hawk the Sunday Wilbur wrote the letter to his father. He had no trunk of his own. Wilbur had already borrowed Katharine's trunk, so Bishop Wright's things were put in what Katharine called the old trunk, and when Orville left Dayton the next day he took with him his father's trunk, loaded with camping equipment—folding canvas cots, blankets, an acetylene bicycle lamp, and a supply of coffee, tea, sugar, and other groceries that Wilbur had been unable to buy in the small store on the wharf on the bay. He also took his mandolin.

It had taken Wilbur almost seven days to get to Kitty Hawk. It took Orville four, sixteen hours of which he spent getting across Albemarle Sound in a sailboat, delayed not by winds but by a lack of them. His mind was on business part of the time. He had hired a young man named Harry Dillon to work in the bicycle shop during his absence. Katharine and Lorin were to keep an eye on things, and Cordy Ruse, contriver of Dayton's first horseless carriage, was to handle bicycle repair jobs as they turned up. "Tell Harry to sell those rolls of tire tape in the box back of what he has been selling at 5 cents a roll," Orville wrote Katharine from Elizabeth City. "They were 10-cent rolls, but we must get rid of them." Orville always insisted that he hated to write, but there were times when what he wrote could be casual, descriptive, and close to rhapsodic, as in one of his Sunday letters to Katharine depicting life in the tent that he and Wilbur erected on a sandy rise between Bill Tate's house and the ocean, six days after his arrival:

At any time we look out of the tent door we can see an eagle flapping its way over head, buzzards by the dozen—till Will is 'most sick of them —soaring over the hills and bay, hen hawks making a raid on nearby chicken yards, or a fish hawk hovering over the bay looking for a poor little fish "whom he may devour." Looking off the other way to the sea, we find the seagulls skimming the waves, and the little sea chickens hopping about, as on one foot, on the beach, picking up the small animals washed in by the surf.

But the sand! The sand is the greatest thing in Kitty Hawk, and soon will be the only thing. The site of our tent was formerly a fertile valley, cultivated by some ancient Kitty Hawker. Now only a few rotten limbs, the topmost branches of trees that then grew in this valley, protrude from the sand. The sea has washed and the wind blown millions and millions of loads of sand up in heaps along the coast, completely covering houses and forest. Mr. Tate is now tearing down the nearest house to our camp to save it from the sand.

One end of the tent was anchored to a gnarled oak that had managed to survive the smothering embraces of the sand, but two or three nights a week sudden squalls made it necessary for Wilbur and Orville to crawl out of bed and hold the tent down to keep it from being blown away. On other nights they slept nine and ten hours at a stretch to make up for lost time. They rated nights as one-blanket, two-blanket, or even three-blanket nights, although they had only two blankets apiece.

Not that they lacked creature comforts. Bill Tate made a trip to Elizabeth City and purchased dishes for them and a gasoline stove and a barrel of gasoline. Gas launches had made their appearance on Albemarle Sound, but this was the first gasoline to be used in Kitty Hawk itself. Much as the natives were fascinated by the strange ways of the two men from Dayton, they stayed away from the tent as if it had been packed with TNT. Bill Tate was an exception. An ardent fan of the Wrights, he considered installing acetylene gas lamps in his house after seeing Orville's bicycle lamp in operation and offered to buy their stove and dishes from them when they left, which he eventually did, for three dollars.

Orville did the cooking, Wilbur the dishwashing—the washing being done chiefly with sand. Tons of fish were shipped to Baltimore from the Outer Banks when the fishing season began in October, but almost no fish were to be had in Kitty Hawk unless the brothers caught their own. When they ate well, they ate bacon, canned vegetables, rice, tomatoes, eggs, corn bread, hot biscuits—made without milk—and an occasional chicken. Once they were invited to the Tates' to partake of wild goose killed out of season.

"We need no introduction in Kitty Hawk," Orville wrote in one of his long Sunday letters home. "Every place we go we are called Mr. Wright. Our fame has spread far and wide up and down the beach. Will has even rescued the name of Israel Perry, a former Kitty Hawker, from oblivion, and it is now one of the most frequently spoken names about the place. Will admits that Israel meant well."

Any fears Kitty Hawkers might have had that the Wrights were violating a divine edict by attempting to fly were allayed to some extent when they saw that the assembled flying machine was flown much more often as a kite than as a man-carrying glider. The brothers had brought their camera along, but were unable to get a picture of the glider with a man on board. In the only two photographs taken of it in the air it looks more like an overgrown kite than a proud progenitor of flying machines to come. Six-inch bow ends had been added to the wings, giving it a wingspan of seventeen feet. The wings were trussed from side to side but not from front to back, so that they could be warped for maintaining lateral balance. The warping was achieved by the movement of wires over pulleys in some fashion never clearly explained, probably by attaching the wires to a bar moved by the operator's feet, as in the glider of the following year.

Originally the 1900 glider had been designed with a tail like that of the kite model, but the Wrights foresaw possible danger or damage if the tail were to drag through the sand in landing or in gliding down steep slopes, so they shifted this large flat appendage to a position well in front of the lower wing and dispensed with a tail altogether. The rear end of this elevator, or front rudder as they called it, could be raised or lowered by hand to control fore-and-aft balance. Although the control system of the 1900 glider was the first significant improvement in glider design since Chanute's double-decker, an even more radical departure from previous practice was the belly-flop position of the operator, who lay prone on the lower wing with his feet hooked over the rear spar. The horizontal position was considered suicidal by most other experimenters, but the Wrights estimated that it reduced the head resistance of their machine by about 60 percent.

The glider was completed the first week in October and taken to the beach near the lifesaving station for testing. The winds that day were measured as 25 to 30 miles per hour at the Kitty Hawk Weather Bureau station, strong winds in which to test an untried glider, but Wilbur's failure to find eighteen-foot spars in Norfolk meant that the lifting surface had been reduced from 200 to 165 square feet, and according to Lilienthal's table in the *Aeronautical Annual,* a wind of more than 20 miles an hour would be required to fly a manned glider with that amount of supporting surface. The procedure was for one brother to lie down on the lower wing and practice using the controls while the other brother and Bill Tate flew the glider as a kite, keeping it a few feet off the ground by manipulating ropes attached to the outermost uprights. The glider's wings had been arranged in the broad V shape known as dihedral to ensure a degree of lateral stability. They soon discovered that side gusts made the V-configuration far from satisfactory, so they straightened the wings from side to side and found the glider much easier to control.

Only a total of ten minutes was spent flying the glider with a man on board. The rest of the time it was tested as an unmanned kite. On the day of its second test the wind was too light to support both the machine and a man, so they flew it once more as a kite, with ballast and without. Sometimes they used chains for ballast. Sometimes they used a boy. The boy was Tom Tate, son of Bill Tate's half-brother, Dan. Orville described Tom as a small chap who "can tell more big yarns than any kid of his size I ever saw." One of Tom Tate's brief flights was recorded in the notebook Wilbur kept that summer: "In a wind of 25 miles our machine lifted Tom (or a total weight of 50 + 70 = 120 lbs.) with a drift of sixteen pounds." What the Wrights termed "drift" has no equivalent in modern aeronautical terminology—it consisted of wing drag to which was added certain other components of drag, and bore no relation to the sidewards drift of an aircraft due to wind. These so-called drift measurements were made by attaching the cords used to fly the glider as a kite to a spring balance, such as grocers used for weighing potatoes.

The glider was tested for a third time on Wednesday, October 10. High winds had been blowing all night but by morning they had tapered off to 30 miles an hour. A few more drift measurements were made after loading the machine with chains. That afternoon, they carried the glider to a small dune nearby and erected a derrick. It was a small affair compared to the 150-foot tower that Wilbur, in his first letter to Octave Chanute, had proposed building for practicing, but it was high enough so that when the unmanned glider was suspended from the derrick, it could be made to ascend up to twenty feet by manipulating cords attached to the front rudder. After one such flight they laid the glider in the sand to make some adjustment to the ropes when a sudden gust of wind got under the wings and flung the machine several yards away, mangling the wings and front rudder so severely that the brothers thought seriously of packing up and going home.

They had not accomplished a great deal so far. They had flown the machine from two to four hours on four different occasions, but it had been flown with a man on board for only ten minutes altogether, during which they had discovered that it was not feasible to work both the front rudder and the wingwarping mechanism at the same time. They had measured the head resistance of their glider and found it to be only half that of Chanute's double-decker of 1896, although their glider was about 25 percent larger.

This was in their favor, but it was only one of several attempts they made to equate the results of their experiments with those of other experimenters, and they found the discrepancies disturbing. Even more unsettling was the discovery that the angle of incidence, which is what they called the angle between the horizon and the wings of their glider in flight, was closer to 20 degrees than the 3 degrees they had been led to expect from Lilienthal's table, an indication that their wings were not providing the anticipated lift.

They dragged the remains of the wrecked machine back to camp and after a night's rest decided to stay on and rebuild the glider rather than give up and go home. Repairs took several days. Between bouts of work on the glider, they went hunting and did some birdwatching. Then early one morning, after repairs had been completed, a 45-mile-per-hour northeaster struck the Outer Banks with such force that when dawn came the rebuilt glider, which had been anchored fifty feet from the tent, was buried beneath several wagonloads of sand. After spending half the morning shoveling it out, they took it to a nearby hill and flew it as a kite. They flew it with no load, then they loaded it with seventy-five pounds of chains and flew it that way. "We tried it with tail in front, behind, and every other way," Orville reported to the family in Dayton. "When we got through Will was so mixed up he couldn't even theorize. It has been with considerable effort that I have succeeded in keeping him in the flying business at all."

Behind Orville's lighthearted banter lay the realization that if they were ever to get any real flying experience they would have to abandon their brave plans of practicing by the hour while suspended from a tower, or lying prone on the machine in the strong winds required to fly it as a kite, and resort to gliding down a hillside as Lilienthal had done. There wasn't much time. Wilbur had been away from Dayton for six weeks, Orville for only half that time, but while the glider was rebuilding they received a telegram from Katharine saying that she had had to dismiss Harry Dillon, the young man Orville had hired to look after the bicycle shop. They decided to leave Kitty Hawk for home by October 23 at the latest.

On Thursday, October 18, they toted the glider to a small hill a mile from camp, intending to try some free glides, but the wind had fallen to a mere 10 miles an hour by the time they arrived. So as not to waste the day, they launched the unmanned glider down the hillside several times, hurling it over the brow of the hill after a four- or five-foot run. It would sail forward about thirty feet before being blown backward against the hill. Then they would splint up the breaks and try it again. That evening, Orville wrote his last letter home, sitting on an empty chicken coop next to the tent. "If the wind is strong enough and comes from the northeast," he told Katharine, "we will probably go down to Kill Devil Hills tomorrow, where we will try gliding the machine."

The largest of the three sand dunes known as Kill Devil Hills was four miles south of their camp on the stretch of beach between Kitty Hawk and Nags Head. It was somewhat crescent-shaped. Its west side, toward the sound, was littered with a few ancient stumps of trees that had been half buried by the shifting sands, but its long gentle northeast slope faced the prevailing winds and the sea and was ideal for gliding. It was an eight-mile round trip from the Wright camp to Kill Devil Hills along the narrow sand road that ran down the side of Kitty Hawk Bay, too long a jaunt to make on foot carrying a fifty-pound glider. The chances are that Bill Tate, who went along as helper, arranged for Wilbur and Orville to rent a horse and wagon by the day. The marshy shore of the bay stinks of rotting vegetation when the wind is off the sound, but a strong sea breeze was blowing on Friday, October 19—so strong a breeze that when they arrived at Kill Devil Hills they decided it was too strong for safety and went back to Kitty Hawk without having made any glides at all.

They returned the next day and made their first and only free glides of the year in winds of 12 to 14 miles per hour. They began with the wingwarping mechanism tied down so that only the front rudder was operable. One brother lay down in the center of the lower wing while the other brother and Bill Tate each grasped a wing and ran forward into the wind until the glider was supported on the air. As it gained speed, the two men ran alongside, pressing down whichever wingtip threatened to rise. The operator did his best to maintain balance by shifting his weight. He turned down the front rudder when the two men could no longer keep up with the machine and made a safe landing in the sand.

An eighteen-inch gap had been left in the covering of the lower wing through which the operator could drop his legs and assume an upright position at the last minute in order to land the glider without damaging the fabric or framework. After a few tests they found that it was perfectly feasible to let the glider settle down with the operator still in a recumbent position. Although some of the landings were made at speeds of up to 30 miles per hour, there was no damage to the lower wing, or to the operator, who found it quite comfortable except for the flying sand.

The glides made that day are rendered hazy by more than flying sand. No records were kept and all that is known of them is based on recollections recorded from one month to twenty years later. The accounts imply that both brothers took part in the experiments, but it is likely that Wilbur did all the gliding himself, as he seems to have done in 1901. The accounts do agree that about a dozen glides were made in all, with a total of two minutes in the air. The first few flights, made with the machine a safe foot or two above the side of the hill, lasted between 5 and 10 seconds. Some of the later glides were between 15 and 20 seconds in duration and 300 and 400 feet in length, very respectable times and distances compared to Lilienthal's glides and those made with the Chanute double-decker in the Indiana dunes.

What astonished the Wright brothers in these flights was that fore-and-aft equilibrium was so easy to maintain, whereas in all they had read it was considered the most difficult flight problem to be solved. Thinking that the problem of lateral equilibrium could be as easily solved, they loosened the warping wires in the last few glides, but when they attempted to operate the two systems of control simultaneously they found that lateral control was much less easy to achieve. Nevertheless, those two minutes of forward and downward motion must have been a heady experience for Wilbur and Orville, although they nowhere made a great thing of it. It was one thing to dangle by the forearms from a pair of wing-supported horizontal bars like Lilienthal. It was another thing altogether to lie motionless between a pair of seventeen-foot wings on a sea-scented updraft, using hands and brain to maintain equilibrium rather than instinctive body movements. For the first time outside of dreams, a man had been carried through the air in a prone position on a pair of wide white wings just as surely as the squeaking gulls —and had survived.

All in all, it had been a great day. When they were through, they carried the glider back up the hill and weighted it down with sand. Before they returned to Dayton three days later, they told Bill Tate he could salvage the materials in the glider if he wanted to take the trouble of toting it back to Kitty Hawk. He did. The machine was dismembered in the front yard of the Tate house and the sateen wing covering was put aside by Mrs. Tate to be made into dresses for her three- and four-year-old daughters, Irene and Pauline.

The Wright brothers had not performed any miracles at Kill Devil Hills or on the beach at Kitty Hawk. A year later, looking back at their month together on the Outer Banks in 1900, Wilbur was able to summarize what they had accomplished in a single sentence:

Although the hours and hours of practice we had hoped to obtain finally dwindled down to about two minutes, we were very much pleased with the general results of the trip, for setting out as we did, with almost revolutionary theories on many points, and an entirely untried form of machine, we considered it quite a point to be able to return without having our pet theories completely knocked in the head by the hard logic of experience, and our own brains dashed out in the bargain.

# 7

# A Two-Man Association

IN 1890, ten years before Octave Chanute prophesied in *McClure's Magazine* that the evolution of the airplane would be a long, slow process like the eighty-year evolution of the bicycle, he delivered a speech at Cornell University in which he suggested that the solution of the flying problem would be much hastened if an association were formed to devote itself to the task. It would have to be an association, he insisted, because no one man could simultaneously be

> an inventor to imagine new shapes and new motors,
> a mechanical engineer to design the arrangement of the apparatus,
> a mathematician to calculate its strength and stresses,
> a practical mechanic to construct the parts, and
> a syndicate of capitalists to furnish the needed funds.

Chanute was right. No one man was able to satisfy all those requirements. But two men were. Wilbur and Orville Wright were as capable of inventing new shapes and motors as any mechanical engineer; they had all the algebra and trigonometry necessary for calculating the strength and stresses of the necessary materials; and they were, and had been for years, practical mechanics capable of constructing the wood and metal parts of a flying machine. A syndicate of capitalists they were not, but they were the proprietors of a successful business. Its slack season allowed them time for experimenting and its profits could cover the costs if they did most of the work themselves.

In short, when Wilbur and Orville Wright returned to Dayton from Kitty Hawk in October 1900, they were already a two-man equivalent of that association of inventors, mechanical engineers, mathematicians, practical mechanics, and capitalists that Octave Chanute considered essential for the solution of the flying problem.

Chanute had had no word from Dayton since Wilbur's brief note of August 10 asking for advice on the purchase of spruce for his glider. For all Chanute knew, his Dayton correspondent had been unable to get his home-made glider off the ground or had suffered a fall and been killed like Lilienthal and Pilcher. The long silence was broken on November 16 by a letter from Wilbur that began: "In October my brother and myself spent a vacation of several weeks at Kitty Hawk, North Carolina, experimenting with a soaring machine." This projected an entirely different picture from Wilbur's previous letters—that of one man, carrying out a series of gliding experiments alone and unaided. The letter contained a description of the glider, with freehand sketches showing the curvature of the wings, the placement of the spars, and the method of trussing ("Remarkably good construction," Chanute noted in the margin), together with a report of the experiments. Compared to the numerous glides made by Augustus Herring and William Avery in the Indiana dunes in 1896 and 1897—not to mention the five hours of gliding logged by Otto Lilienthal in five years—two minutes of gliding down a sand hill on the Outer Banks in a 12-mile-an-hour wind in a balky flying machine without a tail was very small potatoes, but Chanute found the letter deeply interesting. "This is a magnificent showing," he conceded, "provided you do not plow the ground with your noses."

Sometime during the winter of 1900-1, Wilbur made an effort to enlarge his audience from one man—Octave Chanute—to the members of two European aeronautical societies, there being no such organization in the United States at the time. He drafted two articles, submitting one to the *Aeronautical Journal,* the official organ of the Aeronautical Society of Great Britain, and the other to that journal's German counterpart, *Illustrierte Aeronautische Mitteilungen.* Both articles were published in July 1901.

The *Aeronautical Journal* article, "The Angle of Incidence," was Wilbur's attempt to attach a definitive meaning to that term, which has been superseded in today's more vigorous terminology by "angle of attack." In the other article, "The Horizontal Position during Gliding Flight," Wilbur argued not only that the horizontal position reduced the head resistance of the flying machine by one-third but that landings in the prone position were less difficult and less dangerous than had been supposed. He and his brother had made repeated landings in this position in wind velocities exceeding 20 miles per hour, Wilbur wrote, without accident or damage to the machine. "Exceeding 20 miles per hour" was a substantial increase of the 12-mile wind he reported in his letter to Octave Chanute. What Wilbur had in mind may have been the landings made while the glider was being flown as a kite with a man on board on the first day of the tests. On the other hand, there was no way of knowing exactly what the wind velocity had been at Kill Devil Hills on that memorable October afternoon when the free glides were made, because the closest wind gauge was on the Kitty Hawk Weather Bureau station four miles away.

How to determine wind velocity accurately was very much on the brothers' minds in 1901. They were constructing a second glider on the basis of Lilienthal's "Table of Normal and Tangential Pressures," and accurate wind readings would be required to analyze the glider's performance. Wilbur's first letter of the year to Octave Chanute begins: "Can you give us any advice in regard to anemometers for field use?"

Chanute owned two anemometers, one English, one French. Either or both of them, he answered, were at the Wright brothers' service.

"In general we are little disposed to use anything not our own," Wilbur replied, "but as in the present case we are already planning to spend about all we feel that we ought to on our this year's experiments, it is possible that we shall later call on you for the loan of this instrument." He went on to describe the new glider and invited Chanute to witness its testing when they returned to the Outer Banks that summer. Chanute said nothing in his next letter about visiting Kitty Hawk, but he did say he would be making a trip sometime in May or June and inquired when the best time would be to visit the brothers in Dayton. Wilbur recommended a Sunday, when both he and Orville would be free from interruptions from the bicycle business. It so happened that Chanute arrived on a Wednesday, but by then the timing of his visit did not matter, for the Wrights had just made an important change in what they called their business arrangements.

The change in arrangements had been occasioned by a chance encounter on a Saturday night early in June with Charles E. Taylor, a thirty-three-year-old machinist. The bicycle shop was kept open Saturday evenings to accommodate customers who worked the usual six-day week, and Taylor had dropped in for a chat. Charlie Taylor's wife was the niece of Charles Webbert, the Wright brothers' landlord, whose name was sculptured in large letters above the second floor of the bicycle shop. Taylor had moved to Dayton from Kearney, Nebraska, in 1894 and opened a machine shop, in which he did occasional jobs for Wilbur and Orville. Recently he had sold the shop and taken a job with the Dayton Electric Company as supervisor, but he missed working with tools.

The upshot of that friendly visit was that the week before Chanute visited Dayton, Charlie Taylor went to work for the Wright Cycle Company at thirty cents an hour, or five cents more than he had been getting at the electric company. He opened the shop at seven o'clock each morning, an hour or two before Wilbur and Orville arrived, and cycled home for lunch. He brought a breath of fresh air—and cigar smoke—into the staid Wright establishment on West Third Street. Charlie was the father of two (Orville called him "Pop"; the brothers were "the boys" to Charlie). Wilbur and Orville never smoked. Taylor, a heavy smoker, once bragged that he smoked about twenty-five cigars a day. Occasionally he let go with what he described as "a heckety-hoo"; the brothers never swore, although they had sharp tempers and according to Taylor would get into shouting matches during arguments. It was Taylor's presence in the bicycle shop that made it possible for Wilbur and Orville to spend all their time with Octave Chanute during his visit to Dayton on June 26 and 27.

Chanute brought with him the portable French anemometer. Its workings required explaining, the printed instructions being in French. Aside from this, it is not known what was discussed during the two days of his stay, but arrangements must have been made for his trip to Kitty Hawk later that summer and he must certainly have been taken to the workroom behind the bicycle shop to examine the new glider, for he was planning to resume experimenting himself that year. When he stopped off in Dayton, he was on his way to Chuckey City, Tennessee, where Edward C. Huffaker, who had once worked for Samuel Langley at the Smithsonian Institution, was building a glider for Chanute on new and novel principles. The old man was still convinced that the secret of flight lay in making the wings of an aircraft responsive to wind gusts, and the wings of his new glider were being constructed so that they would vary their curvature automatically with changes in the wind. Paper tubes were to be used for framing instead of wood. The framework was to be jointed so that the machine could be folded and unfolded rapidly.

Chanute left after lunch on the second day of his visit. The lunch was served in the small dining room of the Hawthorn Street house, with Bishop Wright present and Katharine presiding. Carrie Kayler waited on table. Her recollections of that luncheon constitute the only record of the first meeting of the venerable sage of aeronautics with the Wright brothers. Katharine, an apprehensive hostess, cautioned Carrie that if the two melons for dessert were not equal in quality she was to serve Mr. Chanute a slice of the better melon only, but when Carrie cut into the melons she judged one of them too unripe to serve and cut the remaining melon into five pieces. Katharine considered a fifth of a melon an inappropriate dish for a visiting engineer who had been born in Paris, France, and after lunch vented her displeasure on fifteen-year-old Carrie—who remembered the incident vividly fifty years later, long after the melon eaters were in their graves.

Two days after leaving Dayton, Chanute wrote the Wrights a letter from Chuckey City, in which he made the Wrights an unusual proposition. He proposed that they invite Huffaker to their camp near Kitty Hawk that summer. Huffaker would help them test their new glider if they would assist

Huffaker in testing the glider he was building in Chuckey City. Chanute would pay Huffaker's expenses and for good measure would send along a second assistant, George Spratt of Coatesville, Pennsylvania, a young man with medical training who was anxious to witness some gliding experiments. The letter in which Chanute made these proposals was redolent of failure. He admitted that Huffaker lacked mechanical instinct and that Spratt was an amateur. The mechanical details and connections of the paper-tube glider were weak, but he suggested that Wilbur and Orville might "extract instruction from its failure."

If the Wrights resented Chanute's attempt to involve them in the testing of a glider with two such questionable features as variable wing curvature and paper tubing, they were too polite to show it. In his reply, Wilbur said they would be glad to have the assistance of Huffaker and Spratt but didn't feel it would be right to ask Chanute to bear the expense entailed unless he felt he was getting his money's worth. Chanute not only felt he was getting his money's worth but as if in gratitude for the brothers' compliance sent them a clinometer, an instrument for measuring angles of elevation or inclination, fitted with a leveling bubble like a sextant. The gift of the clinometer was acknowledged by Wilbur on July 6, with a very low bow: "We are of course delighted with so beautiful a little instrument and our pleasure in it is very much increased by the fact that it is to us a token of your friendly interest in us and our experiments." The next day Wilbur and Orville left the bicycle shop in charge of Charlie Taylor and boarded the train for North Carolina.

The Wright family looked on these trips of the brothers as vacations, but the first few weeks of their stay on the Outer Banks in 1901 were anything but a vacation. They were beset by rain, thirst, sickness, mosquitoes, sand fleas, and at the very start by that other scourge of the rural and urban poor —bedbugs. The brothers spent an uncomfortable first night in Bill Tate's house in a bed with a sagging spring. Orville's first Sunday letter home was embellished with a sketch of a cross section of the bed, showing Wilbur at the bottom, while Orville hangs on to the side. "The fellow in the bottom," wrote Orville, "could get along pretty comfortably, for when he was attacked by any foe (which roams at large over most of the beds in these southern places) he had the opportunity of slapping back, but the poor fellow on the side was in a pretty fix, having both hands occupied, and had to endure the attacks as best he could."

For the second time, the journey from Dayton to Kitty Hawk had been accompanied by meteorological portents of awesome proportions. The day before they reached Kitty Hawk, the anemometer on the Weather Bureau station on the beach registered winds of 93 miles per hour before the anemometer cups were torn away. Their arrival had been preceded by seven weeks of drought. It was followed by seven days of rain. The morning after their unrestful night at Bill Tate's house, they set off with their freight along the wagon road that bordered the sound. The future base of their operations was to be Kill Devil Hills, not Kitty Hawk. However, the name Kitty Hawk has attached itself to the brothers' experiments and to their various machines with such an undying grip that visitors to the place are sometimes surprised to find that the site of the Wright experiments is quite remote from the little fishing village whose name has been bandied about the world for the better part of a century in connection with what really went on at Kill Devil Hills four miles away.

They had obtained permission in advance to erect a shed to house their new glider about a thousand feet from the bottom of the largest of the three Kill Devil Hills. They called this hill Big Hill and estimated its height, which varied from year to year, as about one hundred feet. The two lesser hills were sixty and thirty feet high. They called the smaller of these Little Hill and the larger West Hill because it lay to the west, over toward the sound.

They arrived at the campsite Friday morning, July 12, in a drenching downpour. Once their tent was up, they were virtual prisoners inside it, except when they ventured out to hammer in the tent stakes that kept pulling out of the wet sand. Before the day was over they were driven by thirst to unlimber their pump and drill for water in the rain but lost the bit of their drill in the sand and were reduced to drinking the rainwater that ran down the sides of their tent into a dishpan. Orville was sick that night, probably from drinking soapy rainwater. Before leaving Dayton, the farsighted brothers had taken the precaution of rubbing the tent canvas with soap to fend off mildew.

Orville recovered the next morning and they began work on the shed that was to house the new glider. It took them a week to finish the building, which measured sixteen by twenty-five feet and was seven feet high at the eaves. The roof was covered with tar paper. The walls of loblolly pine were braced against the winds with wooden props. There were no windows but both ends of the shed were hinged so that they could be propped open and used as awnings.

In 1900 the brothers had looked with dread on the northeasters that covered their tent and everything in it with sand. In July 1901, after the seven-day storm that heralded their arrival was over, they would have welcomed a fair-sized northeaster. The week's rain had left a lush breeding ground for mosquitoes along the edges of the sound and in the puddles around their camp. Summer vacationers down the beach at Nags Head maintained that the mosquito menace reached a peak every ten or twelve years, with the insects coming off the sound like waterspouts and descending on the residents like swarming bees; 1901 seemed to be such a year. The mosquitoes arrived on July 18 in a mighty cloud, according to Orville, almost darkening the sun. That same day, Wilbur and Orville's peace of mind was threatened by an even more inauspicious arrival—that of Edward C. Huffaker of Chuckey City, Tennessee, who descended on them bearing the disassembled pieces of Octave Chanute's new glider.

# 8

## The Camp at Big Hill

WILBUR AND ORVILLE knew Edward Huffaker as the author of *On Soaring Flight,* one of the four pamphlets sent to them by the Smithsonian Institution in 1899. The pamphlet reported some rather languid experiments conducted by Huffaker one sunny day on the Mall outside the Smithsonian building in Washington, where he was employed until 1898. To prove that birds soared on currents of rising, sun-heated air, he fanned fine strands of China silk into the air, after which initial impetus they were observed to rise as high as the towers of the Smithsonian. By utilizing these rising currents human flight might become possible, Huffaker suggested, especially since "the maneuver of flying in circles is very simple and is one which could be easily reproduced." He didn't say how.

Huffaker, like Augustus Herring, was a protégé of Octave Chanute. Langley had hired him for aeronautical work at the Smithsonian on Chanute's recommendation, but his habit of reading documents with his feet on the table and his ability to squirt a stream of tobacco juice into a spittoon on the other side of the room did not escape the notice of his fastidious employer. Nevertheless, Langley praised the younger man's work in his introduction to Huffaker's paper on soaring: "I put trust in the good faith with which he reports his observations and in the conscientious care with which he has made them." If Huffaker was truly careful and conscientious on the day he fanned those strands of China silk into the air on Washington's Mall, he had undergone a sea change between then and July 18, 1901, when he appeared at the Wright camp at Kill Devil Hills.

Chanute, who was not expected for another two weeks, had instructed Huffaker to keep a daily record of gliding experiments until his arrival, but when the Wrights examined Huffaker's records after the season was over, they found them to be as inaccurate as the man was shiftless. He was given to laying stopwatches and anemometers in the sand and to using the Wrights' boxlike camera as a stool. One of his specialties was delivering lectures on character building for the benefit of the sons of Bishop Wright. Wilbur and Orville could be forgiven for looking forward with trepidation to the appearance of a second Chanute-dispatched assistant, but they were pleasantly surprised when George Spratt showed up a week after Huffaker's arrival. His medical background was ill defined (he had given up medicine for farming several years before), but his presence was a welcome counterpoise to that of Huffaker. He was a good worker, a kindred spirit who had thought hard and long about the problem of human flight, and a congenial companion with a fund of funny stories and a melancholy streak. Wilbur and Orville made a valiant but vain effort to cure him of what he called the "blues," which seems to have been nothing more or less than an inferiority complex brought on by his inability to utilize his aeronautical theories in practical ways like the Wrights.

Morale improved with Spratt's arrival, but the mosquitoes persisted. "The sand and grass and trees and everything was fairly covered with them," Orville wrote home. "They chewed us clear through our underwear and socks." He and Wilbur had brought along mosquito nets but no mesh was fine enough. The four men tried going to bed early and wrapping themselves in blankets with only their noses exposed. When that proved ineffective, they hauled stumps from the sound and built smudge fires about the camp. George Spratt soon found the heat and smoke from the fire unbearable and dragged his cot into the clear air, only to drag it back into the smoke again in desperation. The mosquitoes were worse than the smoke.

In spite of Huffaker and the mosquitoes, work proceeded on the new glider. Since the first machine had failed to lift and perform as Lilienthal's table had predicted, the lifting surface of the new machine was twice that of the old. Until then, the largest glider ever successfully flown had been Pilcher's with 165 square feet of supporting surface. Lilienthal's had 151 square feet; Chanute's double-decker, 134. With wings twenty-two feet wide and seven feet deep, the Wright 1901 glider had more than 300 square feet of lifting surface and weighed close to a hundred pounds. The front rudder —or elevator—was 18 square feet in area, about the same as the front rudder on the 1900 machine. Again there was no tail, but this year the glider was equipped with a pair of skids like sled runners to protect the front rudder in landing. There was another pair of low skids beneath the gap in the lower wing left for the operator's body. The front rudder was pivoted about one-third of the way back from its leading edge so that it could be raised or lowered by means of two arms running from the rear edge of the rudder to the hands of the operator. The wingwarping mechanism was activated by movements of the operator's feet.

The glider was assembled and ready for testing on Saturday, July 27, two days after Spratt's arrival. An auspicious wind arrived the same day, sweeping away most of the mosquitoes. To save the labor of toting the machine back up the hill after each glide, they planned to launch the glider as a kite with the operator on board. Then when sufficient altitude was gained, the kite ropes would be cut and the glider would either soar over the same spot or descend slowly to the sand. But when the wind was measured with Chanute's anemometer, it was found to lack three or four miles of the 17 miles per hour required for the kite method of launching, so they carried the machine to Big Hill, where they had made a dozen glides in 1900, and once more used manpower to launch the glider. The operator took a few steps before lying flat on the lower wing, then the two men holding up the wingtips ran forward until the operator felt himself supported by the wind and shouted, "Let go." There was no shortage of helpers in 1901. In addition to Huffaker and Spratt, Bill Tate was on hand and so was his half-brother, Dan.

Wilbur did all the gliding on that first day of tests, as he seems to have done during the entire 1901 season. The first eight attempts to launch the glider were failures, but by moving farther back on the lower wing with each trial, Wilbur finally became airborne and made the best glide of the day—315 feet in 19 seconds. There were two more good glides, in one of which he suddenly found himself rapidly losing speed at an altitude estimated by Spratt as eighteen feet (Huffaker, with customary exaggeration, made it forty feet). By manipulating the front rudder Wilbur made a flat landing without damage to the machine. The brothers found this the most encouraging feature of the day's experiments, since it showed that their glider could make a safe descent even when their wings suddenly lost their lift, a condition that had proved fatal to Lilienthal. Although they did not know it at the time, this was because they had placed the horizontal rudder—their elevator—in front rather than behind the wings, in which position it helped to parachute the machine to earth.

On the whole, the Wrights were less impressed with the performance of their machine than were the onlookers. It had failed to pick up speed in gliding downhill and Wilbur had had to apply roughly four times as much front rudder as he had used in the 1900 glides to keep the machine from either running into the ground or rising so high as to lose all headway. Suspecting that the trouble was due to the size of the rudder, they reduced its area from 18 to 10 square feet. Detecting no improvement, they flew the machine as a kite and found that it required a 23- to 25-mile-an-hour wind to support it at a gliding angle of 3 or 4 degrees, indicating that the machine had only about one-third of the lift predicted by Lilienthal's table. There was more bad news the next day when they tested the pull of the machine on the kite ropes with spring scales and discovered that the total resistance was much more than they had anticipated.

That night Wilbur carefully itemized in his diary the good points in the tests made to date: his 19-second glide, the sturdiness of the machine, its response to the wingwarping mechanism, and the fact that they had experimented safely with a machine of a size that others had considered impractical and unsafe. Against these, he set down the four discouraging aspects of the experiments so far: a significant lack in lifting power, the difficulty of maintaining fore-and-aft control with the front rudder, the increase in resistance, and the failure of the machine to pick up speed in downhill glides.

Thinking that the loss of lift might be due to the porosity of the wingcovering, they constructed two small model wings. They covered both with the plain white muslin they had used on the new glider instead of French sateen and varnished or shellacked one of the wings to make it airtight. Earlier that year, Wilbur had braved the feminine atmosphere of a Dayton dry-goods store to select a weave of the proper quality and strength. He had fingered several materials before purchasing several bolts of Pride of the West muslin —an excellent choice, for when the two small model wings were tested side by side, the cloth proved to be so tightly woven and closely textured that the brothers could detect no difference in lift between the airproofed wing and the wing covered with plain untreated muslin.

The kite tests had increased the Wrights' suspicions that the difficulty with the front rudder was due to a sudden reversal in the travel of the center of pressure. The movement of a hypothetical center of pressure on an airplane wing in relation to the aircraft's center of gravity lies at the heart of the control problem. It is not an easy concept to grasp, but when Wilbur put his thoughts on the subject on paper a few months later, he expressed it graphically:

> The balancing of a gliding or flying machine is very simple in theory. It merely consists in causing the center of pressure to coincide with the center of gravity. But in actual practice there seems to be an almost boundless incompatibility of temper which prevents their remaining peaceably together for a single instant, so that the operator, who in this case acts as peacemaker, often suffers injury to himself while attempting to bring them together.

In Lilienthal's hang glider the center of gravity lay somewhere within the operator's body and was made to coincide with the center of pressure by movements of the operator's limbs and torso. In the Wright glider, the center of gravity was fixed, since the operator was unable to move his body to any great extent; to make the two centers coincide, the position of the center of pressure was altered instead, by moving the front rudder up or down. At that time, it was assumed that in all but deeply curved wings the center of pressure moved steadily forward as the angle of the wing with the horizon—the Wrights' angle of incidence—became smaller, just as it would if the wing were a perfectly flat surface. But if the center of pressure were to reverse its direction when the wing reached a critical angle and move rapidly to the rear, as the Wrights were beginning to suspect, the operator would have to apply more and more front rudder to keep the glider from plowing into the ground. That is exactly what seemed to have been happening in many of the glides made so far.

In 1899 Edward Huffaker had detected this reversal in the travel of the center of pressure while experimenting with a small model for Octave Chanute. George Spratt had also investigated the travel of the center of pressure on various curved surfaces, and while the 1901 glider was being assembled, both men had pointed out to Wilbur and Orville that they might encounter this phenomenon once they began to glide. The brothers believed they had guarded against this eventuality by using a wing curvature of 1 in 12, the curvature on which Lilienthal had based his table of air pressures. Now they were not so sure.

The Wrights gave Huffaker and Spratt credit for suggesting that the cause of their trouble might be this reversal of the travel of the center of pressure, but it was they who designed a simple, ingenious experiment to determine if this was really the case. They simply removed the upper wing of their glider and flew it as a kite with two short ropes attached to the front of the wing. They flew it first in a wind of 18 miles per hour, so that the wing assumed an angle of 6 degrees with the horizon; there was an upward pull on the ropes, indicating that the center of pressure was in front of the wing's center of gravity. They then flew the wing in a wind of 22 miles per hour, which reduced the wing's angle to 4 degrees; the pull on the ropes was then downward, so that the wing was just skirting the ground, indicating that the center of pressure had moved to the rear behind the center of gravity and was pulling the rear edge of the wing up.

It now seemed that the reason their 1900 glider had been so much more responsive to movements of the front rudder was that the center of pressure on the wings of that machine had not reversed itself at low angles of incidence. The camber (ratio of depth of curvature to chord) of those wings had been 1:23. To make the wings of their new glider conform to those of Lilienthal's successful gliders, they had deliberately increased the camber until it was 1:12 with a man on board. Realizing that this had been a mistake, they proceeded to flatten the wings of the new glider by inserting a third spar in the lower wing; wires attached to king posts on this extra spar trussed down the ribs of both wings, giving them an effective camber of 1:19. This, they reasoned, would cause the center of pressure to move forward at almost any angle the wings might encounter in a normal glide without reversing itself and thus eliminate the difficulty with the front rudder.

While the wings were being reconstructed, they altered the front spars, which had presented a flat surface to the wind, so that they now blended smoothly with the wingcovering. This reduced the resistance of the framing from eight or nine pounds to less than six and, together with the reduced camber of their wings, tended to correct Wilbur's fourth discouraging factor —the failure of the glider to pick up speed in downhill flight.

Octave Chanute arrived for a week's stay on Sunday, August 4. The reconstructed Wright machine was flown as a kite the next day, but it was not tested as a glider until Thursday, August 8, when thirteen successful glides in winds ranging from 10 to 14 miles per hour were recorded by Chanute. Seven were 12 seconds or more in duration. The longest distance covered was 389 feet. Chanute recorded four even better glides the next day. The two best, 14.5 and 17.5 seconds in duration, were made in winds of about 25 miles per hour. The experiments were abruptly terminated at the end of the longest glide when Wilbur, skimming along about a foot above the ground, became so preoccupied with raising his low left wing that he neglected to turn the front rudder up. The skids dug into the sand, throwing him forward onto the rudder, which suffered a number of broken ribs. Wilbur suffered a bruised nose and a black eye.

It was a disappointing week for Octave Chanute. The paper-tube glider constructed for him by Huffaker was too frail and flimsy to fly and too fragile to survive a heavy rain. Wilbur took a photograph of the rain-soaked remains silhouetted against Big Kill Devil Hill. That September he sent a print to George Spratt with the proviso that he not show it about too promiscuously. "I took it as a joke on Huffaker," he confided to Spratt, "but afterward it struck me that the joke was rather on Mr. Chanute, as the whole loss was his. If you ever feel that you have not got much to show for your work and money expended, get out this picture and you will feel encouraged."

Chanute left for Chicago on Sunday, August 11, via Elizabeth City, where he placed an order for $5.39 worth of groceries to be delivered to the four men remaining in camp. A habitual gift-giver, he sent a lantern back with the groceries and added three cans of hash "to fill up the chinks." The old man was not above kibitzing from a distance. He had not been back in Chicago a week before he was urging the brothers by mail to make sure the center of gravity in their glider coincided exactly with the center of pressure. "Also," he advised, "do not fail to test the efficacy on the stability of cutting holes in the apex." His letter arrived too late to be of any practical value, but whatever the apex may have been, the Wrights had no intention of cutting holes in it.

It rained four days in a row after Chanute's departure, in spite of which the brothers got in four sessions of gliding after repairing the front rudder. They no longer had trouble maintaining fore-and-aft equilibrium, but they now encountered another problem that left them profoundly puzzled. To turn right or left, all they needed to do, they thought, was manipulate the wingwarping mechanism. The wing with the greater angle would then rise and the glider would turn smoothly about the low wing. To their surprise, in some of the dozen glides made that week, the glider turned about the high wing, a phenomenon that completely upset their theories about the dynamics involved in turning. This disheartening experience and the rainy weather so dampened their spirits that they decided to strike camp and go home before the month was over.

George Spratt left on Friday, August 16. Huffaker left two days later, taking with him one of Wilbur's blankets. "He looked rather sheepish on departure," Wilbur observed in a letter to George Spratt, "which I attributed at the time to the fact that he was still wearing the same shirt he put on the week after his arrival in camp." Wilbur and Orville left Kitty Hawk in Dan Tate's spritsail boat at daybreak on Tuesday, August 20, in a state of dejection. Their vaunted wingwarping system had proved to be as unpredictable for purposes of making a turn as Lilienthal's data were for computing the lift of their glider. Wilbur worried himself into a summer cold on the train ride home. "When we looked at the time and money which we had expended," he wrote several years later, "and considered the progress made and the distance yet to go, we considered our experiments a failure. At this time I made the prediction that man would sometime fly but that it would not be within our lifetime." In one of the few after-dinner speeches Wilbur ever made, he was even more explicit: "I confess that, in 1901, I said to my brother Orville that man would not fly for fifty years." By the time Orville got around to recounting the story of those depressing hours on the train to Fred Kelly, his biographer, he had magnified Wilbur's prediction twenty times over. "On the way home," wrote Kelly, "Wilbur declared his belief: Not within a thousand years would men ever fly!"

# 9

# *Trade Secrets*

WILBUR'S PESSIMISM ABOUT the prospects for human flight was in keeping with prevailing sentiment. The September 1901 issue of *McClure's Magazine* contained an article—"Is the Airship Coming?"—that has been quoted gleefully time and again to illustrate the shortsightedness of scientists. Its author, Simon Newcomb, was a respected astronomer and head of the Nautical Almanac Office of the Naval Observatory in Washington. Ignoring the flights of the steam-powered models made by his fellow scientist Samuel Langley in 1896, Newcomb prophesied that the first successful flying machine would be the handiwork of a watchmaker and would carry nothing heavier than an insect. Two years later he increased the payload. "It may carry two or three buttons," he predicted in *The Independent,* "but will not carry more than four."

Another celebrated prophet in the first year of the century was H. G. Wells. Wells wrote half-a-dozen articles that appeared in the *North American Review* and were later made into a book that became a best-seller. His subject was life in the year 2000. Wells foresaw the cities of the future festooned with suburbs; he foresaw the network of highways they would require; he foresaw the coming revolution in women's status; but when it came to the airplane, he was as cautious as Wilbur. A successful airplane will have soared and come home safe and sound, he prophesied, "long before the year 2000 A.D., probably before 1950."

As for Wilbur's prediction, the mood that engendered it did not outlive his cold. Over the Labor Day weekend Orville went into the shed that served as a darkroom in the Wright backyard and developed the glass-plate negatives that had been exposed at Kill Devil Hills in July and August. The resulting photographs would have caused the scales to drop from Simon

Newcomb's eyes if he could have seen them. As it was, they helped to hasten Wilbur's recovery from his depression. What did even more to revive Wilbur's flagging interest in the flying business was Octave Chanute's invitation for him to address the Western Society of Engineers at their September meeting in Chicago on the subject of gliding experiments. The lecture was to be illustrated with lantern slides, and the prospect of seeing his and Orville's handiwork projected on a screen in a partly darkened hall before an august body of midwestern engineers was tempting. Wilbur made a show of thinking it over. Katharine made a show of nagging him into it. Just two weeks after Wilbur predicted that man would not fly within his or Orville's lifetime, Katharine was writing her father, who was out of town on church business again: "We don't hear anything but flying machine and engine from morning till night. I'll be glad when school begins so I can escape."

The engine Katharine spoke of had nothing to do with flying machines. Charlie Taylor had become a fixture around the bicycle shop during the brothers' absence and on their return there was a sudden spurt of activity in the workroom behind the store, where a recently acquired drill press and band saw were being installed. The tools were to be driven by belts attached to an overhead line shaft, driven in turn by a small homemade one-cylinder motor fueled by illuminating gas. This air-cooled motor had been designed and built by the brothers in 1896 and had been used in the bicycle shop ever since.

While the workroom was being refurbished, Wilbur worked on his speech. Orville and Katharine asked him if it would be witty or scientific. "Pathetic," he replied. Chanute, as president of the Western Society of Engineers, made all the arrangements at the Chicago end. When he inquired if Wilbur had any objections to the society's making it a ladies' night, Wilbur responded: "I will already be as badly scared as it is possible for a man to be, so that the presence of ladies will make little difference to me, provided I am not expected to appear in full dress, &c." He was reassured to learn that only about sixty members and their wives would be present and that business rather than formal dress would be the order of the day.

Wilbur alighted from the train in Chicago at seven-thirty on the morning of September 18, 1901, and breakfasted alone before finding his way to Octave Chanute's house on the fashionable Near North Side. He was wearing Orville's overcoat. Compared to his younger brother, Wilbur was no fashion plate (whenever Katharine reminded him that his trousers bagged at the knees, he would heat a flatiron and press his pants himself), but he let himself be bullied into borrowing some of Orville's finery for his talk to the Western Society of Engineers. His lecturing attire that night included one of Orville's shirts and collars, Orville's cuffs, and Orville's cuff links.

Chanute had had lantern slides made of photographs of the two Wright gliders. These were flashed on a screen at the front of the hall as Wilbur read his paper. Chanute had also provided lantern slides of Lilienthal's and Pilcher's gliders and of his own multiple-wing and double-decker machines. These were projected in succession as Wilbur described the manner in which nineteenth-century experimenters had tackled the flying problem. The larger part of his talk, however, was devoted to the Wright experiments of 1900 and 1901.

The engineers in the audience were no doubt able to follow Wilbur's speech without difficulty. Their wives may have been left behind when he got into such subjects as lift and drift, angle of descent, and the horsepower required to keep an aircraft in the air, but the whole audience must have nodded in agreement when Wilbur pointed out the disastrous difference between an airplane and a vehicle that operated in the water. A steamship, for instance, would stay afloat and continue to move whether its engines were delivering a thousand horsepower or only one. But if the horsepower in a propeller-driven airplane suddenly dropped to one, the airplane would simply cease to fly. "However," Wilbur went on, "there is another way of flying which requires no artificial motor, and many workers believe that success will first come by this road. I refer to the soaring flight, by which the machine is permanently sustained in the air by the same means that are employed by soaring birds. In other words, it is possible to maintain a glider in the air by utilizing the rising current of air blowing up the side of a hill." To illustrate this point, the next slide showed what Wilbur described as "one of those very slow glides at a time when the machine was practically at a standstill."

The lantern slide had been made from the best photograph taken of the 1901 glider in flight, a memorable picture in spite of the fact that only half the glider is visible. Orville's failure to center the image on the slow glass plate was due to his aiming the camera at a point in advance of the machine, but the glider had not moved forward as expected because it was truly soaring. Incomplete as it is, the photograph contains a wealth of satisfying detail. Wilbur lies prone on the lower wing, ten feet or more above the sand hill, his hawklike profile silhouetted against the sky, the knees of his baggy trousers protruding beneath the gap in the lower wing. The sun shines through the muslin covering of the front rudder, outlining the protective skids beneath it, and shines through the wings, revealing the glider's sturdy framing. While the picture was still on the screen, Wilbur made what is the only reference in his writings or in his brother's to the part photography played in their experiments—and to the part it played in reviving their spirits when they were at their lowest ebb on their return from Kitty Hawk the month before:

In looking at this picture you will readily understand that the excitement of gliding experiments does not entirely cease with the breaking up of camp. In the photographic darkroom at home we pass moments of as thrilling interest as any in the field, when the image begins to appear on the plate and it is yet an open question whether we have a picture of a flying machine, or merely a patch of open sky.

The last lantern slide showed the unmanned 1901 glider being flown as a kite on the side of Big Kill Devil Hill. The two men holding the kite cords are under the glider rather than in front of it. "It will be seen that the machine not only pulls upward," Wilbur read from his paper, "but also pulls forward in the direction from which the wind blows, thus overcoming both gravity and the speed of the wind." In the blurred photograph, the men certainly seem to be tugging mightily at the ropes to keep the glider from taking off into the wind. "We tried the same experiment with a man on it," Wilbur continued, "but found danger that the forward pull would become so strong that the men holding the ropes would be dragged from their insecure foothold on the slope of the hill." Having provided the midwestern engineers and their wives with this mild whiff of the perils involved in aeronautical experimentation, Wilbur concluded his lecture with a brief summary and returned to Dayton.

The ripples created by his speech fanned out beyond Chicago as soon as it had been printed in the December issue of the society's journal under the modest title "Some Aeronautical Experiments." Chanute ordered three hundred reprints struck off, half of which he distributed broadside to his aeronautical, scientific, and engineering correspondents throughout the world. During the next few months the paper was reported, abstracted, or printed in full in the *Engineering Magazine,* the *Scientific American, Fielden's Magazine,* and the British *Automotor Journal.* The magazine *Flying* got maximum mileage out of the speech by publishing it as a series in four separate issues over a period of ten months. It was included in its entirety in the 1902 *Annual Report* of the Smithsonian Institution, which also published it in the same pamphlet format as the four publications sent to the Wrights in 1899 by the assistant secretary. In 1903 a translation appeared in *Wiener Luftschiffer-Zeitung,* and the Parisian *Le Pays* entertained its readers with an account of gliding experiments conducted in the United States by a "Monsieur Wilbug Bright."

"Some Aeronautical Experiments" went on to become the Book of Genesis of the twentieth-century Bible of Aeronautics and was reprinted in one form or another at least five times after the Wright brothers achieved international fame. By then it was solely of historical interest, but in the early years of the century it was eagerly studied by would-be aviators and inventors all over the world. Its plain language and straightforward exposition, not to mention its air of integrity, was a refreshing antidote to such overblown articles as Augustus Herring's "Recent Advances Toward a Solution of the Problem of the Century" in the 1897 *Aeronautical Annual* and Huffaker's pretentious paper on the minutiae of soaring.

The printed version of "Some Aeronautical Experiments" differed from the spoken speech in one important respect. Some minor changes had been made in response to Chanute's urging: "Do not be afraid of making it too technical." What these minor changes were no one will ever know, for no stenographic record was made of the speech and Wilbur's original manuscript has long since disappeared, but it is possible to identify one passage as having been inserted in the printed version at the last moment:

> After our return from Kitty Hawk we began a series of experiments to accurately determine the amount and direction of the pressure produced on curved surfaces when acted upon by winds at the various angles from zero to 90 degrees.

This refers to a series of experiments with model airfoils made sometime between September 18, when Wilbur addressed the Western Society of Engineers, and November 17, when he submitted a revised manuscript of his speech for publication in the society's journal. The experiments did not end on November 17 but continued for several more weeks. They were conducted in a homemade wind tunnel in the gaslit workroom behind the bicycle shop and were the most crucial and fruitful aeronautical experiments ever conducted in so short a time with so few materials and at so little expense. After two years of experimenting, the Wright brothers were beginning to realize that what blocked their way to a solution of the flying problem was not one great gate that would fly open when unlocked with a secret key but rather a series of small sealed doors that would have to be pried open, one after the other. The most pressing problem they faced when Wilbur returned from Chicago in September 1901 was where to begin.

While drafting his lecture, Wilbur had included some disparaging remarks about the way he and his brother had been misled by the data of other experimenters. Orville contended that it wasn't right for two Johnny-come-latelies to decry the work of others unless they could prove the others wrong. Wilbur reluctantly agreed, and the offending remarks were deleted from the speech. Since the manuscript was not due until mid-November, there was still time to test the validity of Lilienthal's table of pressures in the 1897 *Aeronautical Annual* on which they had based the design of their two gliders.

They decided first to test the angle at which a tiny model wing must be exposed to the wind to exactly balance the pressure on a small square plate facing into the wind. With typical ingenuity, they mounted the two test surfaces on the rim of a bicycle wheel laid flat, free to move as the wind struck the surfaces. Finding the natural wind unsatisfactory, they mounted the wheel horizontally on a spar in front of a bicycle and averaged out irregularities by riding the bicycle at a constant speed back and forth in a near-calm until they had determined the angle at which the lift of the model wing exactly balanced the pressure on the small flat plate. According to Lilienthal's table, the angle should have been 5 degrees. The Wright bicycle test showed it was closer to 18 degrees.

A horizontal bicycle wheel is not the most sensitive measuring instrument, so they devised a second method of testing the two surfaces against each other by attaching them to a rod free to move about a vertical axis. This balancing vane, as they called it, was set in a wooden trough made from a starch box, a common enough household item in those days, and exposed to a fan driven by the one-cylinder illuminating-gas motor that Charlie Taylor had helped them build after their return from Kitty Hawk. The imbalance between the pressure on the flat plate and the lift imparted to the curved surface was recorded by drawing lines on wallpaper scraps fastened to the bottom of the starch box. The wallpaper was left over from a recent decorating spree. "I am now absolutely certain that Lilienthal's table is very seriously in error," Wilbur wrote Chanute, "but that the error is not so great as I had previously estimated."

The brothers found this method of testing the properties of miniature wings so promising that they set to work replacing the starch-box apparatus with a bona fide wind tunnel, not the world's first but the first to yield results of value in constructing a practical airplane. Although primitive by modern standards, it was a model of compactness, efficiency, and economy compared to the whirling-arm devices with which Langley and Lilienthal had tested model surfaces in the open air. The tunnel proper was a sixteen-inch-square wooden box six feet long with a glass viewing window on top. A metal fan, operated by a belt from the overhead line shafting, was mounted on a stand apart from the tunnel to avoid vibration. The flow of air it provided was directed into the tunnel by a wooden cone and straightened by a honeycomb of sheet metal.

The instruments used for testing—the real heart of the tunnel—were as devilishly ingenious as they were phenomenally inexpensive. Their function was to determine the lifting properties and the resistance to the air of miniature wings of various shapes and curvatures and to determine the angles to the airstream at which these surfaces began to lift and the angles at which they ceased to lift. The instruments to which the surfaces were attached for testing were called balances. There were two of these—a lift balance, for measuring relative lift, and a drift balance, for measuring drag.

Since the so-called surfaces were mostly less than six inches long, the Wrights were concerned with measurements of relative efficiency rather than lift in pounds and ounces. A relative measurement requires a standard against which to measure the object being tested. In the lift balance, the standard was at first the one used in the bicycle-wheel test, a metal plate set squarely against the airstream, but the plate caused troublesome variations in the air current and was replaced with four metal strips of equivalent area, which hung like small soldered banners from a crossbar, giving the balance an even more makeshift appearance. The model surface was mounted on an arm at the angle to be tested and the amount of imbalance between it and the standard surface was indicated in degrees by a pointer that could be observed through the glass panel on top of the tunnel.

George Spratt was responsible for the basic idea behind the other balance. While fighting off mosquitoes at Kill Devil Hills, he and the brothers had discussed methods of determining the drift—that is, the drag—of model wings in a testing machine. Spratt had suggested it would be more practical to measure drift as a ratio of drift to lift than to attempt to measure it directly, and the Wrights had incorporated Spratt's concept in their drift balance.

Neither balance was a thing of beauty, being constructed partly of bicycle spokes and old hacksaw blades ground down by Charlie Taylor, but they yielded results with possible errors of less than 5 percent. The model surfaces presented no problems whatever. The materials needed and the tools to shape them were all at hand in the bicycle shop. With tin shears, hammers, files, and a soldering iron, they manufactured more than fifty small wings out of tin, galvanized iron, 20-gauge steel, solder, and wax. Thus equipped, they set out to discover the effects of a moving airstream on flat surfaces and curved, on thin surfaces and thick, on wings with pointed tips and wings with rounded ends, on wings with sharp leading edges and wings whose front edges had been thickened with layers of wax or soldered tin.

It had seemed logical to Langley that a sharp leading edge would cut the air with less resistance than a blunt rounded edge, but that turned out not to be true when the Wrights made a model of Langley's sharp-edged wing and tested it in their tunnel. They had never had a high regard for Langley's experimental work. Now their own experiments were confirming their suspicions regarding Langley's data and scientific methods. In *Experiments in Aerodynamics,* Langley described an experiment in which he attached a square flat plate to his whirling-arm apparatus and inclined it to the wind at various angles from 45 to 0 degrees. The Wrights repeated the experiment in their wind tunnel and plotted their data on graph paper, as Langley had done. Langley's curve was satisfying and smooth. Theirs had an inexplicable hump in it at 30 degrees. When they went back to Langley's book and examined the table of data on which Langley had based his graph, they discovered that the data did indeed indicate a hump at 30 degrees, but this would have destroyed the smoothness of the curve, so Langley had tagged the datum with an asterisk, keyed to the footnote "Omit."

As Wilbur and Orville's regard for Langley's work declined, their respect for Lilienthal's climbed. They made and tested a thick, almond-shaped surface with pointed ends like the model wing Lilienthal had used on his whirling-arm device. Lilienthal's data, they found, were as correct as it had been possible for him to make them with the crude methods at his disposal. The discrepancies that they had noticed were due to the fact that his table was applicable only to one particular wing shape and curvature.

They now had a general idea of the performance of wings of various shapes, curvatures, and aspect ratios—the ratio of the length of a wing (its span) to its width (or chord)—but they were beginning to sense a lack of direction in what they were doing. With the revised version of Wilbur's speech on its way to the printers on November 17, they settled down to conduct what was to be their crowning work of the year—a series of systematic tests of thirty-eight model surfaces, mostly of single wings but sometimes wings in tandem and sometimes superposed in layers of two or three. On their lift balance they made forty-three tests, in each of which the angle to the airstream of each small wing or combination of wings was varied at fourteen intervals between 0 and 45 degrees. The angle to the airstream at which lift began was determined within one-quarter of a degree. Another forty-eight series of measurements were carried out on their drift balance for twelve angles from 0 to 45 degrees.

What was recorded in each case was the angle of displacement indicated by the pointer on the scale of the balance. Calculating the relative lift and the ratio of drift to lift from the data was a time-consuming task and would come later, but they carried out the computations for the most interesting and the most promising surfaces and graphed the results, letting "the lines run where they will." None of their curves was pleasingly smooth throughout. Some were downright disturbing and resembled cones of volcanoes. They devised a "recheck vane" to verify the accuracy of their more unbelievable findings.

This systematic series of experiments took about three weeks. All that time Charlie Taylor had been carrying on more or less alone in the front of the shop, but the bicycle business was, after all, their livelihood, and they discontinued the experiments the first week in December.

The correspondence between Wilbur and Octave Chanute reached a high tide that autumn and winter. As the files in Chanute's cluttered Chicago study—so cluttered with flying machines suspended from the ceiling,

Wilbur had observed during his visit, that he could not see the ceiling—began to bulge with data and descriptions of the Wrights' wind-tunnel work and occasional charts on blueprint paper, a subtle change of roles was taking place. Octave Chanute is no longer the mentor. He is now the pupil, listening raptly as Wilbur pipes the tune and leads the old man a lively dance across the quicksands of theory. Chanute functions largely as a sounding board, but is warmly appreciative. "It is perfectly marvelous to me how quickly you get results with your testing machine," he writes Wilbur in November. Later that month: "I am amused with your apology for writing long letters, as I find them always too brief." There is much discussion back and forth regarding aeronautical nomenclature, which is in a chaotic state, causing Wilbur to complain, "I get lost now and then."

"I am delighted to hear that you 'get lost now and then'!" Chanute replies gallantly. "I do also."

Chanute not only got lost, he displayed at times a certain obtuseness. Unable to believe that so much information could be obtained with so little expenditure of time and money, he offered to help finance the Wrights' wind-tunnel work. Wilbur put him off. "Practically all of the expense of our aeronautical experiments lies in the time consumed," he explained, "and we do not wish to increase the temptation to neglect our regular business for it." When Chanute learned that the experiments had been terminated, he became insistent. "I happen to know Carnegie," he wrote. "Would you like for me to write to him?"

"I think it possible that Andrew is too hardheaded a Scotchman to become interested in such a visionary pursuit as flying," Wilbur replied, and the matter was dropped.

Determined to help, Chanute offered his services as a human calculating machine. "You will need to publish a table for each form of surface and aspect," he reminded Wilbur. "This will involve considerable figuring, and if I can help you in this respect, I shall be quite at your service." The Wrights were perfectly capable of making the calculations themselves, but it was mathematical drudgery of the type performed electronically nowadays, and they accepted the offer gratefully.

Chanute spent the first two months of 1902 in California, taking with him one of the fattest envelopes he had ever received from Dayton. Into it, Wilbur had packed not only one of his long Sunday letters but a whole theory of aerodynamics, two sets of wind-tunnel measurements—one for each of the balances—instructions for converting the angular measurements to "gliding angles" and "resultant pressures" through the use of trigonometric functions, a page of formulas for computing glides, a detailed diagram of the forces involved, and a list of terms and definitions. The last two sentences of his letter were veined with irony. "I hope you enjoy your sunning in California," he wrote. "My vacation is about over as our busy season is now at hand."

Chanute worked on the computations, off and on, through the summer of 1902. Orville began work on a new and larger wind tunnel in the fall, and Wilbur advised Chanute to hold up further work until their data could be checked in the new tunnel, but Chanute was weary of the task and completed the computations anyway. The new series of tests was never carried out. Chanute put the last of his tabulations in the mail on December 29, 1902, and set off on a trip abroad.

Publication of the wind-tunnel findings had already been discussed. In 1902 Chanute was working on a chapter he was to contribute to the English edition of Hermann Moedebeck's *Pocket-Book of Aeronautics.* The Wrights agreed that he should include some of their findings, but the hemming and hawing over just what phases of the work should be made public went on for several weeks, and in the end, mention of their experimental work was confined to the fact that they had refined and corrected certain of Lilienthal's coefficients.

Nothing more was said about publication until September 1908, when the brothers made a public pronouncement regarding their wind-tunnel work in the *Century Magazine*: "As soon as our condition is such that constant attention to business is not required, we expect to prepare for publication the results of our laboratory experiments, which alone made an early solution of the flying problem possible." By the time those words appeared in print, the Wrights had skyrocketed to fame and there was no time to prepare the detailed descriptions of the shapes, thicknesses, and curvatures of the model wings without which the figures compiled by Chanute would have been meaningless.

When Wilbur died in 1912, the tables were no nearer publication than in 1908. Orville devoted much thought to the matter in his old age, but he was adept at procrastinating and when he died in 1948 wind tunnels many times more complex than the Wrights' had wrung secrets from the air that the Wright brothers had never dreamed of. In 1953, when the most important of the papers Orville's heirs had given to the Library of Congress were published and the results of the 1901 wind-tunnel experiments were finally made public, the world was no longer panting for an opportunity to pore over those columns of superannuated figures. Yet locked in those tables back in 1902 were some of the most remarkable trade secrets of the century.

# 10
## *Well-Digging*

A WORLD'S FAIR was scheduled to open in St. Louis in 1903 to celebrate the hundredth anniversary of the Louisiana Purchase. Like the Chicago fair of 1893, it was to open a year late, but as early as January 1902 the directors of the Louisiana Purchase Exposition were formulating rules for an aeronautical competition with prizes totaling $150,000, including a grand prize of $100,000 for the best flight by an airship or flying machine. As soon as the prize money was announced, the newspapers began to blossom with accounts of flying machines being constructed in cellars, garrets, and stables by inventors who had the flight problem solved except for such insignificant details as whether to use steam, electricity, or even water power as a motive force.

The Wright brothers, armed as they were with knowledge about the aerodynamic properties of wings of various shapes, curvatures, and aspect ratios, could not afford to ignore a first prize of such magnitude. But they were only too well aware how far the problem still was from solution, and they looked upon the injection of mercenary incentives into the enterprise as something of a nuisance. Not so Octave Chanute, who was to have a share in formulating the rules for the St. Louis competition. The failure of the glider built for him by Huffaker in 1901 had only momentarily dampened his determination to resume experimenting. All that was missing was an incentive and that was provided in the spring of 1902 by Charles Lamson, a kite enthusiast who ran a jewelry store in Long Beach, California, not far from Pasadena, where Chanute was wintering with his ailing wife. Lamson had recently patented a kite based on his "oscillating wing" principle, that is, with wings free to rock fore and aft about a transverse axis. Intrigued as always by the idea of wings automatically adjusting themselves to the vagaries of the wind, Chanute wrote Wilbur from California in March 1902 that he was thinking of having Lamson build him an oscillating-wing glider, an idea that must have struck the Wrights as exceedingly chimerical. He was planning at the same time to rebuild his multiple-wing and double-decker gliders of 1896 in order to compare the performances of all three machines with the Wright glider the next time Wilbur and Orville went to Kitty Hawk. That such a venture would saddle the brothers with the job of providing living quarters for Chanute and an assistant or two in the camp at Kill Devil Hills, not to mention housing for the three gliders, did not prevent the grand old man of aeronautics from making a further request of the Wrights: Would they consent to rebuild the two 1896 gliders in Dayton at his expense?

If the brothers had any feelings that Chanute's proposal was even more of an imposition than his sending Huffaker to Kitty Hawk with the paper-tube glider in 1901, Wilbur was careful to conceal them in his reply. If Chanute was willing for them to commit the work to other hands, they would give the work their careful supervision. The plans, however, would have to be submitted well in advance.

Chanute's wife died in California in April, and the plans were never sent. After returning to Chicago, Chanute wrote Wilbur that Lamson was at work on the oscillating-wing glider and that he still intended to have his two 1896 gliders rebuilt. He wanted it understood, moreover, that all three gliders would be presented to the Wrights as gifts. "I think I will not experiment any more myself," he explained, "but I desire you to test the comparative merits of what I have done in the hope that you will get some good out of it."

There was absolutely nothing that the Wrights could have gained from the time-consuming, possibly dangerous, task of testing the antiquated double-decker and the two Chanute gliders with movable wings. Nor was the chore of supervising the rebuilding of the 1896 gliders to the brothers' liking. They were relieved of both responsibilities toward the end of May when fate intervened in the person of Augustus M. Herring, who was out of work and looking for a job.

Ever since Herring had worked as Octave Chanute's assistant in the Indiana dunes in 1896, his life had conformed to a roller-coaster pattern of ups and downs. Whenever success seemed within his grasp, an unforeseen calamity (according to Herring) would occur and he would have to start all over again. After making the two alleged hops in his powered hang glider in October 1898, he bent his energies to developing a steam engine for airplanes. A fire in his workshop in 1899 put an end to that. Next, he claimed to have developed a successful gasoline motor, but he fell ill and the work done by others during his illness, he said, was so poor that he was obliged to cancel several orders. On recovering, he sought Chanute's support in developing an airplane motor that would weigh only sixteen pounds with a half-hour's supply of fuel. Chanute's support was not forthcoming. The project would have gone by the boards in any event, for Herring suffered another bout of illness and was confined to his house until February 1901. The following month in a letter to Chanute, he made the fatuous assertion that he had in some respects accomplished much more than the ten principal aeronautical experimenters whose work was covered in an article Chanute had recently written for a supplement to the *Encyclopaedia Britannica.*

"Go on and demonstrate some important results and there will be no lack of appreciation in my writings," Chanute replied. He did not hear from Herring again until January 5, 1902, when Herring wrote blaming his long silence on business troubles, a general breakdown, and nervous prostration. What had prompted Herring to resume his correspondence with Chanute was news of the glittering prizes being offered by the promoters of the St. Louis fair. Herring was now willing to bury all differences and join Chanute in producing a flying machine that would have "a first class show" of winning the $100,000 grand prize. Chanute was not about to pour a small fortune down that hole but replied that while he was in no position to avail himself of Herring's proposal, he might have something else to suggest later on.

Sometime during the spring of 1902, while waiting to hear from Chanute, Herring had traveled to London, where he was interviewed by Hiram Maxim, the expatriate American inventor, who was also thinking of resuming aeronautical experimenting. The interview left Maxim with some doubts about Herring. "Tell me confidentially what you think of his ability and experience," he wrote his friend Octave Chanute. "Can he be easily managed or is he an impossible customer to deal with?" Chanute replied candidly that while Herring "possessed considerable ability, knowledge and mechanical instinct,—(how came you to judge him so accurately at first sight) he cannot be easily managed."

The day after Chanute penned those words, some psychic influence propelled Herring to Octave Chanute's house in Chicago, where he was soon pleading for the job of rebuilding the two 1896 gliders—"to beat Mr. Wright," as he inelegantly phrased it. Chanute was willing to give his former protégé another chance, but before taking Herring on, he asked Wilbur if he would agree to having the two 1896 machines rebuilt in St. Joseph, Michigan, by Herring rather than in Dayton under the brothers' supervision. "It will be all right with us," Wilbur replied. "To tell the truth, the building of machines for other men to risk their necks on is not a task that I particularly relish."

Before putting Herring to work, Chanute decided not to reconstruct his only successful glider—the double-decker—for the reason that Herring was still so very touchy on the subject of its origin that he would consider the rebuilt machine his own and Chanute had already promised that it would be a gift to the Wrights, together with his other two gliders. Wilbur attempted to decline the unwanted gifts in a letter that is a masterful mixture of diplomacy, evasiveness, and plain unction, but Chanute was adamant.

On July 3, 1902, Chanute traveled to Dayton to visit the Wrights, and the question of who was to test the multiple-wing and Lamson machines at Kitty Hawk came up. Herring was still hoping to hear from Maxim, so the logical choice was William Avery, the Chicago carpenter who had shared the gliding with Herring in the Indiana dunes in 1896. It was understood that whoever Chanute's assistant was, he would be required to assist the brothers in their own experiments. "On the other hand," Wilbur reminded Chanute, "it was our experience last year that my brother and myself, while alone, or nearly so, could do more work in one week than in two weeks after Mr. Huffaker's arrival." Wilbur hastened to make it clear that George Spratt, the ex-medical man from Pennsylvania, would be as welcome at their camp in 1902 as he had been in 1901 if he should be able to come. The important thing was that neither Wilbur nor Orville should be required to operate the two Chanute gliders, a point that Wilbur drove home with a wicked twist of logic, arguing that if either of the brothers flew the Chanute machines and the tests were failures, this would raise suspicions that they had not acted fairly.

Avery at first declared that he would be available only until mid-September, then that he would not be able to leave Chicago until October, or perhaps not at all. Maxim in the meantime had heeded Chanute's warning about the difficulty of managing Herring, and as time went on and no word came from England, it became obvious that Herring would be the one to accompany Chanute to Kitty Hawk. The Wrights reluctantly agreed to invite him to their camp, but not until Wilbur had committed his misgivings to paper. "In a former letter I expressed a preference for Mr. Avery," he wrote Chanute, "because several things I had heard about Mr. Herring's relations with Mr. Langley and yourself seemed to me to indicate that he might be of a somewhat jealous disposition, and possibly inclined to claim for himself rather more credit than those with whom he might be working would be willing to allow." The brothers had good reason to be wary of Herring. They were constructing a new glider to fly at Kill Devil Hills that summer based on what they had learned in their wind-tunnel experiments and had no desire to reveal the results of their research to a rival as unscrupulous as Herring was rumored to be, but they had no choice short of denying the use of their camp and experimental grounds to their good friend Octave Chanute.

Bishop Wright was away from Dayton most of the summer, but Katharine was home on vacation and kept him informed by mail, incidentally preserving for posterity a picture of her brothers at work on the wingcoverings for the new glider: "Will spins the sewing machine around by the hour while Orv squats around marking the places to sew. There is no place in the house to live but I'll be lonesome enough by this time next week and wish that I could have some of their racket around."

Wilbur and Orville had planned to leave for Kitty Hawk in July but were delayed for several weeks by "that church business," as the family called it. An official of the United Brethren in Christ had mishandled funds in a manner that smacked of embezzlement. Bishop Wright was all for removing the offending churchman from office, but a clique in favor of whitewashing the culprit threatened to deprive Milton Wright of his ministry as well as his bishopric. The young Wrights sprang to their father's defense. Wilbur spent the better part of three weeks in Huntington, Indiana, going over the church's accounts, after which he wrote a tract exposing the whitewashers. Three years later the matter would be settled in the bishop's favor, but for the time being there was nothing more the three nonchurchgoing Wrights could do to further their father's cause, and no reason for Wilbur and Orville to delay their departure any longer.

It had been a trying summer. "They really ought to get away for a while," Katharine wrote her father on August 20. "Will is thin and nervous and so is Orv. They will be all right when they get down in the sand where the salt breezes blow. . . . They think that life at Kitty Hawk cures all ills, you know."

Kitty Hawk was still not an easy place to get to, but when Wilbur and Orville emerged from the Elizabeth City, North Carolina, rail depot just before 6 P.M. on August 26, they had a stroke of luck. Tied up at the wharf on the waterfront across from the station was the schooner *Lou Willis*. Its skipper, Captain Franklin Midgett of Kitty Hawk, was planning to sail direct to Kitty Hawk before dawn the next morning and agreed to transport the Wrights. Their trunks, camping equipment, and crates of glider parts had already been stowed away for the night in the railroad baggage room and freight depot, which closed at six. The brothers raced back into the station and were just in time to retrieve their belongings and transfer them to the *Lou Willis*. This done, they picked up a barrel of gasoline at the Standard Oil Company warehouse as the workmen were leaving for the day. By another stroke of luck, Orville, whose specialty as chief cook was biscuits, located a store whose proprietor unlocked the door just long enough to sell him a portable oven, after which he picked up some cans of baking powder at one of the few grocery stores still open. At 3:45 A.M., they set sail. At four o'clock the next afternoon, after a journey slowed by almost no wind or wind of the wrong direction, the *Lou Willis* tied up at the wharf in Kitty Hawk.

Bill Tate was too busy to assist the Wrights that year, but his half brother, Dan Tate, was on hand to ferry the brothers and the heaviest part of their freight to Kill Devil Hills in his spritsail boat. Their camp building had suffered badly from the weather, sinking almost two feet at either end, so that the roof had a hump in it like a camel. With Dan Tate's help, they spent more than a week raising the sunken ends of the building and putting in foundations for a sizable addition to serve as living quarters. They were determined to camp in comfort in 1902. Battens were added to the exterior walls of the building to make them windproof and sandproof. The roof was straightened and tar-papered. They had even brought along a bicycle geared to navigate the sandy road between their camp and Kitty Hawk, cutting the time for the round trip from three hours to one. They drilled a sixteen-foot well for their old pump, which enabled them to brag that they were now supplied with the best water in all Kitty Hawk.

They called the addition to their 1901 camp building their living room, although it was actually kitchen, dining room, and bedroom combined. It was not without creature comforts—a "soft-top" dining table (oilcloth over two thicknesses of burlap), dining-room chairs upholstered with excelsior and burlap, and a pair of "patent beds" reached by a ladder and consisting of two thicknesses of heavy burlap stretched between wooden frames up among the rafters. The photograph they took of their kitchen when it had been set in order is an enduring record of their attempt to introduce an element of Daytonian decorum into a wooden shack on a windswept beach on the Outer Banks. Cups and pans hang in orderly rows beneath shelves of neatly stored cans and boxes and jars. Five eggs on an egg rack are said to have been arranged in numbered sequence. There is no contemporary evidence for this, but the Wrights were not above penciling dates on eggs if the eggs were laid by their own hens. There had been a chicken coop at the brothers' camp at Kitty Hawk in 1900; Orville's 1902 diary contains a single reference to a hen in the camp at Kill Devil Hills; many years later he would report that a hen had been running about outside the camp building in mid-December 1903—but aside from these scattered references, the fowl kept by the Wright brothers in their camps on the Outer Banks are not much more substantial than their phantom privy—if there was one. Sanitary arrangements, in those days, were not something to write home about.

On Monday, September 8, they cleaned out the workshop behind the living room, killing two mice in the process and driving away some hungry razorbacks, mongrel descendants of the hogs that Roanoke Islanders once kept along the shores of the sound. That afternoon they began assembling the new glider. Its wings were not slavish enlargements of any single airfoil but a synthesis of all the efficient characteristics of the model wings tested in their tunnel. They measured thirty-two feet from tip to tip, ten feet more than the wings of the 1901 machine, but thanks to the high aspect ratio (the span of the 1902 wings was six times the chord rather than three, as in 1901), the total wing area was increased by only fifteen square feet. The lesser curvature of the new wings, whose camber varied from 1:24 to 1:30, added to their aerodynamic efficiency, and additional lift was provided by the new horizontal front rudder, a trim ellipsoid with pointed tips, that replaced the bulky rectangular front rudder of 1901. The same Pride of the West muslin was used as wingcovering, but it was applied more smoothly, the ribs having been notched where the spars fitted into them and the joints wrapped with tire-lacing cord and varnished. On Wednesday they were far enough along to fly the upper wing as a kite. It soared with ease in a 12-mile-an-hour wind. As they suspected, the longer, narrower wing had much more lift and less drag than the cumbersome wings of their 1901 glider.

In their previous gliders, the wingwarping mechanism had been worked by movements of the operator's feet. In the 1902 glider, the wings were warped by sidewise movements of the operator's hips resting in a wooden yoke attached to the warping wires in such a fashion that if one wing was high, a movement of the hips to that side provided the required correction. In making a turn, an instinctive movement toward the center of the turning circle would bring the inside wing down. They called this wooden yoke their "cradle." Although it kept the operator from slipping sidewise down the wing in a turn, it was hard on the hipbones, which, in the case of the Wright brothers, had little natural padding. Eventually, they padded the cradle for greater comfort.

Another major innovation was the addition of a vertical tail—two fins six feet high. The tail was fixed so that it could not be moved to left or right like a ship's rudder, but the spars to which it was attached were hinged and held in position by springs so that the tail assembly would swing upward if it struck the ground on landing. What had so discouraged the Wright brothers at the end of their 1901 season had been the occasional tendency of the machine to swing about the wing with the positive angle when the wings were warped. By rights it should have swung about the wing with the negative angle—the low wing. They had concluded that this strange behavior was due to the fact that the wing with the positive angle exposed more of its underside to the airstream. The resulting drag more than counterbalanced the effect of the wingwarping and slowed the high wing down. In their new machine, they reasoned, the increased pressure on the side of the fixed vertical tail toward the inside of the bank or turn would automatically resist this unwanted turning movement.

By Friday, September 19, after ten days of hard work, the glider was ready for testing. Dan Tate helped them carry it to Little Hill, the smallest of the three Kill Devil Hills, with a gentle slope of 7 degrees. They flew it first as an unmanned kite. The flying cords in this test were almost vertical, proving that the hundred-pound glider could soar effortlessly in a wind with an upward trend of only 7 degrees. Later that day they made about twenty-five glides, with either the front rudder (their elevator) or the hip cradle tied down, to accustom themselves to the new set of controls. Not only was the hip cradle new, but they had made a change in the mechanism operating the front rudder so that the movements of the two arms required to turn the rudder up or down were the reverse of what they had been in 1901.

On Saturday they took the machine to Big Hill. Down its steeper slopes Wilbur made the first glides of the year using both controls at the same time. The reduced size and altered shape of the new front rudder gave ample fore-and-aft control, and in none of the glides did the machine swing about the high wing like the 1901 glider. In Wilbur's longest glide, the wind struck the machine from the side, lifting the left wing up. As Wilbur moved his hips to the left to bring the high wing down, he intended at the same time to turn the front rudder down, but he forgot that the movements of the rudder arms had been reversed and turned the rudder up instead of down. His own account of what happened next shows that his error brought about the first stall of a Wright glider.

Almost instantly it reared up as though bent on a mad attempt to pierce the heavens. But after a moment it seemed to perceive the folly of such an undertaking and gradually slowed up till it came almost to a stop with the front of the machine still pointing heavenward. By this time I had recovered myself and reversed the rudder to its full extent, at the same time climbing upward toward the front so as to bring my weight to bear on the part that was too high. Under this heroic treatment the machine turned downward and soon began to gather headway again.

To diminish the disturbing effect of a side wind like that which had led to Wilbur's error, the Wrights modified the trussing of their wings, making the tips four to six inches lower than the center. The wings appeared to sag slightly, but so well built was the glider that during the next few weeks they were able to land, without damaging the machine, at full speed in sandy hollows with only the tips of the wings touching the ground. Only once that year did the glider incur damage that took more than a few hours to repair.

That was on Tuesday, September 23, when Orville made his first free glides of the year.

They had made several short glides that morning on the slope of Little Hill with the hip cradle fastened down to familiarize themselves with the proper movement of the front rudder before taking the machine to the steepest slope of Big Hill to practice using both controls at once. The change in the wing trussing eliminated much of the trouble from side gusts, but they found that it was advisable to turn the front rudder down a little when warping the wings in order to speed up the machine and accelerate the warping action. On his third or fourth glide, Orville discovered that one wing was a little high and became so absorbed in moving the cradle toward the high wing that he forgot to turn the front rudder down and failed to notice that the machine had reared up at a sharp angle. Dan Tate and Wilbur shouted warnings, but their voices were carried away by the wind. When Orville finally noticed his predicament, he was thirty feet above the surface of the hill, slipping rapidly backward toward the ground. The result, as Orville reported it in his diary, "was a heap of flying machine, cloth, and sticks in a heap, with me in the center without a bruise or a scratch."

"In spite of this sad catastrophe," Orville's diary continues, "we are tonight in a hilarious mood as a result of the encouraging performance of the machine both in control and in angles of flight." Angle of flight was the angle at which a glider could glide or soar in an uphill wind of a certain strength. While it was not practical to measure accurately the angle a wing made with the horizon in flight, it was possible with the clinometer Octave Chanute had given them in 1901 to measure the slope of the hill up which the wind was blowing. Their 1901 glider, when flown as a kite, would soar only when the slope was 15 to 20 degrees, whereas their new glider had soared on the side of Little Hill, which had a slope of about 7 degrees. This was an even better angle of flight than that of the buzzards they observed soaring above Kill Devil Hills that year.

The day after Orville's accident, Bill and Dan Tate drove into camp with the crate containing Chanute's multiple-wing glider. The oscillating-wing glider made by Lamson in California was still on the way. Chanute and Herring would not arrive for another ten days. In the meantime, the Wrights were looking forward to the arrival of friendly, outgoing George Spratt, with whom they had enjoyed arguing the fine points of aeronautical theory at their camp the year before. While waiting for Spratt to arrive, they spent three days splicing broken spars and ribs and repairing the damaged glider. The day they completed the repairs it rained and the hollows in the sand for a mile around the camp were turned into ponds. Then the sun came out, the wind fell, and the mosquitoes were soon thick in the grass along the sound and about the three Kill Devil Hills. For some reason, the mosquitoes avoided the camp, but Nature rallied her forces in the form of a field mouse that prowled about the shelves of foodstuffs in the camp kitchen at night, keeping Wilbur and Orville awake in their patent beds under the roof. Orville constructed what he called a death trap for the mouse. At eleven o'clock one night he was awakened by the mouse crawling over his face. He recorded the incident in his diary the next day: "I found on getting up that the little fellow had only come to tell me to put another piece of corn bread in the trap. He had disposed of the first piece. I have sworn 'vengeance' on the little fellow for this impudence and insult."

In the end, vengeance was the Lord's, not Orville's. The little fellow was found dead under a trunk.

On Saturday, September 27, they carried the repaired glider to Little Hill, but the wind was so light they could not get started with sufficient speed to glide the full length of the hill. The following Monday they made several good glides down the side of Big Hill, but again the wind died down and they returned to camp. Tuesday morning they were about to resume practice when they saw two heavily burdened men laboring across the sand in the distance. Suspecting that the men were George Spratt and Captain Midgett, helping him with his luggage, they walked over to the camp, only to find that the visitor was their brother Lorin.

Lorin's role in the Wright story is slightly less obscure than that of Reuchlin, oldest of the four Wright brothers. Reuchlin had married in his twenties and moved to Kansas City, Missouri, where he worked as a book-keeper until 1901, when he took up farming and moved his family to a farm near the town of Tonganoxie, Kansas. Lorin had also married early, but he resisted the siren call of Kansas City and Tonganoxie and settled in Dayton, where he produced the progeny that made Wilbur and Orville's celebrated unclehood possible. His appearance at Kill Devil Hills was not unexpected, but he had left Dayton earlier than he intended and arrived the day Wilbur and Orville were expecting George Spratt. Captain Midgett brought Spratt from Elizabeth City on the *Lou Willis* the following day. Before nightfall there were two new patent beds among the rafters of the camp building.

Several new gliding records were set the week of Lorin's and Spratt's arrival—three glides of more than 500 feet and five glides between 20 and 25 seconds in duration. The fixed vertical tail had corrected the tendency of the machine to turn about the high wing when the wings were warped to restore equilibrium, but every now and then a new phenomenon was encountered that was even more difficult to explain. Instead of righting itself in response to the wingwarping control, the machine would start sliding sideways with frightening rapidity toward the low wing. Its tip would strike the ground, and the machine would swing about the grounded wingtip, driving it further into the sand. On such occasions the brothers considered themselves lucky to escape unhurt. They called this phenomenon "well-digging." Although well-digging occurred only rarely, it demonstrated that their system of control could not be considered perfect until they discovered the reason for this curious state of affairs and devised a means of correcting it. How they did this makes a quietly dramatic story, comparable to the story of Wilbur and the twisted inner-tube box that led to the successful application of their wingwarping principle. Or rather, it makes two stories—Orville's and Wilbur's.

Here is Orville's version as he told it to his biographer Fred Kelly: Thursday night, October 2, the three Wright brothers and George Spratt sat up until ten o'clock, arguing aeronautical theory—nothing unusual during Spratt's stay in the camp, except that Orville imbibed one cup of coffee too many. When the four men at last climbed into their beds under the roof of the camp building, he was unable to get to sleep and as he tossed and turned in the dark he tried to figure out the cause of well-digging. Orville was not one to count sheep aimlessly. He was able not only to explain the well-digging phenomenon to Wilbur and the others at breakfast the next morning but to propose a solution to the problem as well. He did not present his explanation right off. Afraid that Wilbur in his capacity as big brother would pretend to have already figured the problem out himself, Orville took the precaution of first winking across the breakfast table at Lorin. The wink was meant to alert Lorin to the possibility that Wilbur might try to appropriate Orville's explanation as his own—admittedly, a rather complicated message to communicate with a single sly wink. Having administered this cautionary gesture, Orville launched into his explanation of the well-digging phenomenon and his remedy for it.

If the right wing, say, were low and the operator a little slow in shifting his hips in the cradle to the left to correct the imbalance, gravity would take over before the increased angle of attack on the low wing had a chance to bite the air, and the machine would start sliding to the right like a ball rolling down an inclined plane. The increased pressure on the right side of the fixed tail would make the situation worse by causing the tail to slew around to the left, so that when the right wingtip hit the ground it would be forced into the sand with a screwing motion. Hence well-digging. The cure for well-digging, therefore, would be to make the tail movable, like a ship's rudder. If the tail in this case could have been moved to the left at the time the right wing had been given a greater angle of incidence, it would have created a torque in the opposite direction and given the low wing a chance to rise.

Contrary to Orville's expectations, Wilbur did not claim he had already solved the problem himself. He merely thought the matter over for a few seconds, then made a suggestion of his own. Since the operator of the glider had enough to do—what with manipulating the front rudder arms with both hands and the warping cradle with his hips—why not attach the wires controlling the movement of the tail to the wires controlling the wingwarping? In Orville's version of the story, it is Wilbur who points out at the breakfast table that a particular relation exists between the desired pressure on the tail and the warping of the wings and that this relation makes it possible to combine the two controls in one. In the above example, for instance, when the operator moves his hips to the left (to drop the left wing by giving it a downward warp), the rudder moves left at the same time to increase the pressure on that side (and incidentally to relieve the pressure on the other side, which could cause a fixed tail to swing about the low wing in a well-digging situation).

So much for Orville's version of the story. Wilbur's version appears in the deposition he made in a patent suit in 1912 and attributes the discovery of the cause of the well-digging phenomenon to both brothers. The solution is not arrived at in a single sleepless night but in the course of several days, during which they experimented to make sure that the fixed vertical tail was the cause of the difficulty. In the meantime, Orville—not Wilbur—notes that a relation exists between a movable rudder and the warping of the wings, which makes combining the two controls in a single activating device possible.

There are no breakfast-table revelations in Wilbur's version, but strangely enough the explanation and solution of the problem expounded by Orville at the breakfast table in Kelly's authorized biography have been lifted almost verbatim from Wilbur's 1912 deposition. This creates a second circle of confusion on top of the first by making it appear that Orville, many years after Wilbur's death, was taking sole credit for what was really a typical act of collaboration. Then, in 1953, the only contemporary record of the well-digging problem and its solution—Orville's diary entry for October 3, 1902—was finally published. It concludes: "While lying awake last night, I studied out a new vertical rudder."

Either way, Orville's coffee-induced solution to the well-digging problem (if it was his) and Wilbur's implementation of it were to have even more important consequences than those that followed Wilbur's twisting of an empty inner-tube box in the bicycle shop in 1899. What the Wrights had stumbled on in the course of their gliding experiments at Kill Devil Hills in 1902 was the discovery that the principal function of the vertical rudder in an aircraft is not to steer but to supplement and refine the action of the lateral control mechanism. This was not an insignificant discovery, for it completed and brought to a patentable stage the Wrights' three-dimensional system of airplane control, which is the basic system used today in all winged vehicles that depend on the atmosphere for their support.

# 11

## Movable Wings

AT NOON ON Saturday, October 4—the day the Wrights began work on
the new tail for their glider—Dan Tate drove down from Kitty Hawk with
a telegram from Octave Chanute. Chanute was at Elizabeth City with
Augustus Herring waiting for transportation to the Outer Banks. On Sunday
the two men managed to get as far as Manteo on Roanoke Island, where
they hired a spritsail boat to ferry them to Kill Devil Hills in the rain. There
was another heavy downpour that night, and for the second time in a week,
Wilbur and Orville sat up until 10 P.M. discussing flying and matters of
mutual interest with their fellow campers.

During their ten-day stay, Chanute and Herring were to witness the first
glides ever made with the operator controlling the machine about all three
axes. The two six-foot vertical vanes of the fixed tail had been replaced with
a single movable rudder five feet high and fourteen inches deep, now activated by movements of the hip cradle. None of the glides was spectacular
in length or duration, but with the vertical rudder operating in conjunction
with the warping of the wings, Wilbur and Orville were now able to restore
the equilibrium of their machine and to make turns right or left without fear
of the low wingtip digging into the sand. It should have been obvious to
Chanute that by manipulating the surfaces of a glider that made no claim
whatever to automatic stability, the brothers had achieved almost complete
mastery of control in the air, but the old man clung to his belief that the
secret of flight lay in making the aircraft automatically stable by allowing
the wings to wobble about one axis or another, as in the two hang gliders
he had hired Herring to fly for him.

The reconstructed multiple-wing machine was uncrated and assembled
Monday. That evening Herring made two attempts to glide in it. In the
second attempt he traveled for 20 feet before one wing hit the sand and a

wing brace was broken. Wednesday he tried again, but could not attain sufficient speed to sustain a glide on a slope as steep as 13 degrees. Friday he tried several times to fly the glider on an even steeper slope of 15 degrees in a 20-mile-per-hour wind, but without success. Saturday Wilbur and Orville made a gallant attempt to get the multiple-wing machine off the ground by flying it as a kite with Herring on board in a wind so strong that it scoured several feet off the top of Big Hill. Still the multiple-wing machine refused to fly.

Chanute blamed Herring for its failure. In mid-July he had made a trip to St. Joseph, Michigan, to see how the work was coming along. He considered the workmanship excellent, but Herring could never leave well enough alone and Chanute had made the mistake of approving Herring's proposal to lighten the glider by giving new forms to the wings and making them smaller—with the result that the wings twisted even in light winds, and all attempts to keep the glider in the air were hopeless.

The glider built by Lamson in California was brought from Elizabeth City on the *Lou Willis* in the middle of the week, but it was not uncrated and examined until Saturday, when it had become apparent that further experiments with the multiple-wing machine were a waste of time. The Lamson, or oscillating-wing, glider had three superimposed wings with pointed tips, an immovable cruciform tail, and a large rectangular front rudder like that on the Wrights' 1901 glider. But when the machine was tested at Kill Devil Hills, the rudder was not attached, and it was flown as a hang glider without any means of control except movements of the operator's limbs and torso. Its movable wings, like those of the multiple-wing machine, were restrained by springs, but unlike the wings of the other glider, which pivoted about a vertical axis, were mounted so that they could rock, or oscillate, about a transverse horizontal axis as the center of pressure moved back and forth.

The glider was taken to Little Hill on Monday, October 13, where Orville took two pictures of it in the air. In one it is being flown as a kite. The kite ropes are taut and vertical, showing that the forty-pound machine was capable of flying as a kite without a man on board. The other photograph shows Herring in flight, hanging by his armpits with his legs drawn up in a sitting position a few feet above the ground. The longest flight made in this fashion was about 50 feet. Tuesday morning the glider was taken out for a second series of tests. According to Orville's diary, Herring "soon decided to take it inside again to take its weight and ascertain its center of lift," and the tests were never made. It is not clear why, but the chances are that Herring refused to make them.

There is a curious passage in John McMahon's *The Wright Brothers* that tells how Herring fainted when he was about to ascend in a Chanute glider

at the Wright camp in 1902 and had to be revived by George Spratt. If there
is a grain of truth in this story, it probably applies to the morning of
Tuesday, October 14, when the oscillating-wing machine was about to be
tested for the second time. Herring had passed a troubled, somewhat sleepless night. To quote Orville's diary again: "We were all awakened about 2
o'clock in the morning by an announcement by Mr. Herring that the chicken
had been stolen by a fox. As he had not always proved a true prophet in
his previous predictions that it would be stolen in the night, we took little
stock in the announcement. Daylight revealed the chicken safe and sound."
A man capable of waking his sleeping campfellows in the middle of the night
to report the nontheft of a chicken by a possibly nonexistent fox was quite
capable of feigning illness the next morning—or actually fainting—to avoid
making any more glides in a rickety glider with oscillating wings, slack
trussing, and weak joints, as Chanute himself was later to admit. At any rate,
no further attempts were made to prove or disprove the efficacy of the
rocking-wing arrangement, and Chanute and Herring left for Manteo that
same afternoon on the first leg of their journey home.

Lorin had left for Dayton the day before. Spratt stayed on for another
week, the third member of a congenial trio. With less cooking and less work
to do around the camp, there was more time to wander in the woods when
the brothers were not gliding or to stroll along the beach, collecting starfish,
dried horseshoe crabs, and shells to bring back to landlocked nieces and
nephews in Dayton, together with bottles of genuine seawater and sea sand.
"Spratt is a fine fellow to be with in the woods," Orville wrote Katharine,
"for he knows every bird, or bug, or plant that you are likely to run across."
It was characteristic of Spratt that in the first letter he wrote to the Wrights
after returning to Pennsylvania, he should try to reimburse them for the
expenses of his three-week stay in their camp. Wilbur's manner of refusing
payment was equally characteristic:

> Regarding the ten dollars you enclosed, will say that we refused to accept
> any pay from either Mr. Chanute, Mr. Herring, or my brother Lorin,
> for camp expenses so we see no reason to make an exception in your case.
> Moreover we feel that your help was worth more than your board, so
> you owe us nothing anyhow. But as I do not wish that money to be the
> first thing you see when you open the letter, I will send it later. We owe
> you, not you us.

Strictly speaking, all that the Wrights owed George Spratt, aside from
his help and the pleasure of his company in those walks through the woods
and along the beach, was the concept on which the drift balance used in their
1901 wind-tunnel experiments had been based. At the time, Spratt was

perfectly willing to let two unknown bicycle mechanics utilize an idea he himself had suggested, but the melancholy Pennsylvanian was given to brooding and he was to brood to the end of his life about the significance of his suggestion and the degree of credit he received for it.

In one way, Spratt had been amply repaid during his stay at the Wright camp in 1902: He had been privy to the discovery that led to the perfection of the Wright system of control. He had witnessed more than a hundred glides by the brothers. Since he spent the night of October 20 in the village of Kitty Hawk in the house of a Dr. Cogswell before leaving for Elizabeth City, it is probable that he stayed at the camp long enough to witness the glides made that day by Wilbur and Orville—their best yet, including five of more than 500 feet, between 21 and 25 seconds in duration.

After Spratt left, they continued the experiments with Dan Tate's help, crowding an estimated 250 glides into two days' practice, increasing the record for distance to 662 1/2 feet and for duration to 26 seconds. So sure were they now of their mastery of the glider that they flew one day in a wind of 30 miles an hour without encountering any problems in control. Experimenting in strong winds, they found, made it easier for two men to launch the machine by running forward with 250 pounds of glider and operator between them, with the wind doing most of the work. Bringing the glider back up the hill with the wind at their backs was easier still. The last glides of the season were made on Friday, October 24, down the side of West Hill within sight of Roanoke Sound. A passing steamer—it may have been the *Ocracoke* making its regular Friday run from Manteo to Elizabeth City— drew in close enough to give its passengers a chance to gape at the big white glider coasting down the sandy hillside.

Things were going so well that Wilbur and Orville would have liked to stay another two weeks, but Dan Tate was to take charge of a fishing crew the last week of October and their excursion-rate railroad tickets expired the last of the month. They broke camp on Tuesday, October 28. In a stinging drizzle driven by winds of more than 30 miles an hour, they walked the four miles to Kitty Hawk. The *Lou Willis* was waiting to take them to Elizabeth City, but the wind died down and progress was so slow that Captain Midgett transferred the brothers and their belongings to a boat called *The Ray,* which reached Elizabeth City at 8:45 P.M. Their average speed for the thirty-six-mile voyage had been close to one mile per hour. Nevertheless, their spirits were high when they boarded the train in Elizabeth City. In the last six days of gliding they had made more than 375 glides, and the total for their five weeks of experimenting in 1902 was somewhere between 700 and 1,000. They intended to continue gliding practice when they returned the following year, so the 1902 machine had been left behind in the camp building. The two Chanute gliders had been stored up among the rafters, not because the Wrights intended to subject them to further tests, but because Chanute continued to insist that they were a gift to the brothers.

Incredible as it seems, Chanute still looked on the Lamson machine with its rocking wings as an alternative solution to the flying problem. A few days after leaving Kill Devil Hills he wrote Wilbur to be sure to test the oscillating-wing machine carefully with a bag of sand before trusting a man on it. A few days later he wrote Major Hermann Moedebeck, editor of the *Illustrierte Aeronautische Mitteilungen,* that the Lamson glider promised "great steadiness when the springs have been thoroughly adjusted and practice gained with it." So sure was he that Wilbur and Orville would be interested in making further tests of the glider with oscillating wings that in an article containing a description of it—which appeared in the French journal *L'Aérophile* in August 1903, before the Wrights left that year for Kitty Hawk—he wrote that although only a few tests of the glider had been made in 1902, "more are to be carried out in 1903."

When it became obvious that the brothers had no intention of testing either of the Chanute gliders, Chanute thought he would salvage what he could of his work by putting the two gliders on display, first by exhibiting them at the St. Louis fair of 1904, then at the Aero Club of America show in New York in January 1906, and finally at the 1907 aeronautical congress held in conjunction with the 300th anniversary of the founding of Jamestown, Virginia. Neither glider was ever put on display, however, for the simple reason that it would have taken six to eight weeks of the Wrights' time to get the moldering machines crated and shipped from Kitty Hawk, if mice had not finished them off in the meantime. What made such proposals particularly onerous to the brothers was Chanute's insistence that the machines were theirs—theirs to fly, theirs to elicit instruction from, theirs to maintain and preserve.

Wilbur and Orville eventually tired of this game. In April 1907, four and a half years after the gliders had been stowed away among the rafters of the camp building at Kill Devil Hills, Wilbur wrote Chanute: "Our development in the building of power flyers and the lack of a better place for storage have prevented us from giving these gliders the attention our duties as custodians really demanded, but something should now be decided as to their final disposition, or it will be too late."

It was soon too late. The following winter the roof of the camp building was ripped off in a violent storm and the two gliders, like the hundreds of marine vehicles that had foundered over the years on the shoals nearby, were consumed by the raging elements. The internal work of the wind, which Octave Chanute had so vainly sought to harness as a solution to the flying problem, had had its way with them at last.

# 12

## *Two Talks*

AFTER LEAVING Kill Devil Hills on October 14, 1902, and before returning to their homes in the Midwest, Octave Chanute and Augustus Herring stopped in Washington, D.C. Chanute wanted to pay a call on Samuel Langley. Herring would also have liked to see Langley. He knew that Langley was working in relative secrecy on a man-carrying aircraft for the War Department and hoped to trade whatever knowledge of the Wrights' methods and construction he had picked up during his stay at their camp for a job at the Smithsonian Institution. As a friend of Samuel Langley, Chanute had access to the secretary's office in the Smithsonian castle on Washington's Mall. Herring was reduced to writing a letter.

Langley was naturally interested in learning what the Wrights had been up to, but he exchanged only a few words with Chanute before being called away to keep a previous appointment. He wrote Chanute the next day, apologizing for his abrupt departure and expressing regret that he had been prevented from obtaining a more detailed description of the extraordinary results the Wright brothers were achieving. He also mentioned that he was in receipt of a letter from Herring—which he suspected was an indirect application for employment—stating that Herring would like to submit some ideas on airplane wing arrangement, form, and curvature, ideas that Langley surmised were based on observations of the new Wright glider.

Chanute was afraid that Langley was seriously thinking of rehiring Herring, and his reply to Langley's letter was a thinly veiled warning against such an action. "I have lately gotten out of conceit with Mr. Herring," he wrote, "and I fear that he is a bungler." Langley had already decided not to give his former employee another chance. His curiosity had been aroused, however, by the hints in Herring's letter and by what little Chanute had had time to tell him of the glides at Kill Devil Hills. On October 19 he sent a wire to Wilbur at Kitty Hawk: "Mr. Chanute has interested me in your experiments. Is there time to see them? Kindly write me." Wilbur's answer was that a visit would be impractical because he and his brother intended to break camp soon. The Wrights had no intention of sharing their hard-won gains with the secretary of the Smithsonian. Langley next tried to reach the Wrights through their mutual friend Octave Chanute. "I should be very glad to hear more of what the Wright brothers have done, and especially of their means of control," he wrote Chanute on December 7, 1902. He would be glad to have either brother visit Washington at his expense if they were willing to communicate their ideas on the subject. Chanute sent Langley's letter to the Wrights, calling it cheeky, and asked them to let him know how to answer it. Wilbur replied that neither he nor Orville had time to visit Washington and let it go at that.

In the same letter Wilbur mentioned that Langley had recently sent him a Smithsonian pamphlet entitled *The World's Greatest Flying Creature*. He could not resist adding, "Perhaps you have noted the mention contained therein of the Maxim and Lilienthal machines." Wilbur was being droll. The subject of the pamphlet was the extinct flying reptile known as the great pterodactyl. There was no mention of Maxim or Lilienthal in the paper, but in his introduction Langley had included three pages of illustrations, comparing the supporting area, weight, and horsepower values of his steam-driven model airplane of 1896 with similar values of the great pterodactyl, a condor, a turkey buzzard, a wild goose, and a hummingbird. The point of Wilbur's remark was that Langley seemed to consider his own flying machine the only one worthy of comparison with the wide-ranging display of winged wildlife in the illustrations. But the joke misfired: When Chanute next wrote, he complained that he had gone through his copy of the Smithsonian paper again without finding any mention of Maxim or Lilienthal.

Wilbur apologized. "I really had no intention of sending you on a wild goose chase through the pamphlet for the reference to Lilienthal's & Maxim's machines," he protested. He was sorry if his little joke had made trouble for Chanute. The misunderstanding over this harmless bit of drollery, while not significant in itself, was a harbinger of more serious misunderstandings to come. Chanute made no mention of it in his next letter, being occupied with personal matters. It had been eight months since his wife died and he was preparing to take his two daughters on a trip abroad, sailing from Boston on January 3. One of the objects of his trip was to stir up interest throughout Europe in the aeronautical contests that were to be a feature of the Louisiana Purchase Exposition at St. Louis in 1904. As the world's foremost authority on aerial navigation, he was given a warm welcome in the capitals of Italy, Austria, Germany, England, and particularly France, where the seventy-one-year-old bilingual Chicagoan was feted as "the

American inventor, who, if not extremely well known among ordinary mortals, is a veritable celebrity among 'aviators.' "

Promoting the St. Louis aerial contests may have occupied Chanute's daylight hours, but it was certainly not the subject of the talk he gave, in French, at a dinner given in his honor by the Aéro-Club de France in Paris on April 2, 1903. His subject was gliding experiments in the United States —his own and those of the Wrights. He had prepared the ground well in advance by distributing more than a hundred copies of Wilbur's 1901 Chicago lecture to his European correspondents, many of them in France, where "Some Aeronautical Experiments" had aroused envy as well as interest in the breasts of patriotic Frenchmen like Ernest Archdeacon, a wealthy French lawyer, who had taken a sporting interest in fast-moving vehicles from bicycles and motorcycles to balloons and automobiles and who had recently found heavier-than-air flight eminently worthy of his patronage.

Chanute's talk was not recorded verbatim, but it was reported in some detail by Archdeacon in the next issue of *La Locomotion*. In his talk, Chanute managed to create a false impression of his role in the Wright experiments. He was not a petty man, but there was a bee buzzing around in his bonnet that told him the Wright brothers would never have achieved what they had without his advice and guidance. The truth was just rubbery enough to bend a little here and there, and by sprinkling his talk with ambiguous statements for his listeners to interpret, Chanute made it appear that the Wrights were his collaborators or, even more incorrectly, his pupils pure and simple. "Admitting that he was no longer very young," wrote Archdeacon, "he took pains to train young, intelligent, and daring pupils, capable of carrying on his researches by multiplying his gliding experiment to infinity. Principal among them, certainly, is Mr. Wilbur Wright of Dayton, Ohio." The teacher-pupil relationship was stated even more explicitly in the report of Chanute's talk that appeared in the April issue of *L'Aérophile*. The truth, of course, was that the Wright brothers had never been particularly interested in Chanute's experiments. Their gliders represented a radical departure from his, but in both the *Locomotion* and *Aérophile* accounts of the talk, illustrations of the Wrights' 1902 glider were labeled "*L'appareil Chanute*," or "Chanute machine."

In his talk, Octave Chanute inadvertently did the Wrights an additional disservice by revealing the three-axis control system that they were later to patent. Chanute was extremely patent-minded himself. When he forwarded Langley's "cheeky" letter to Wilbur the previous December, he advised, "I think you had better patent your improvements." Wilbur assured him that the brothers were about to file a patent soon. This they did on March 23, 1903, without consulting a patent attorney, only to have their claims rejected twice in the next four months on the grounds that some of the claims were vague and difficult to understand. In July the Patent Office recommended that the brothers hire an attorney skilled in patent practice to reformulate their claims. They did not get around to consulting an attorney until early in 1904, when they were advised to patent not a flying machine but their system of controlling an aircraft of any kind about all three axes. The most important feature of this system, one that rendered it unique and absolutely essential for smooth flight, was the simultaneous warping of the wings and movement of the vertical rudder. It was this feature that was revealed in print in both Archdeacon's account of Chanute's talk and in the report in *L'Aérophile*. In the words of the anonymous *Aérophile* reporter: "The aviator controls direction in the horizontal plane by operating two cords which act by warping the right or left side of the wing and by deflecting at the same time the rear vertical rudder." In patent parlance, this constituted "prior disclosure" if the patent was filed after the date of the disclosure. The 1903 date of first filing protected the Wrights in the United States but not in all European countries.

Ironically, Chanute's disclosure of the Wrights' three-axis system of control had not the slightest effect on the development of aviation in France or any other country. Archdeacon supplemented his report in *La Locomotion* with an exhortation to French aeronauts not to permit "the greatest scientific revolution that has been since the beginning of the world to be realized abroad," but Frenchmen eager to imitate the Wrights were less interested in Chanute's description of the Wright control system than in the drawings of the three Chanute machines and the Wright 1902 glider published in the August 1903 issue of *L'Aérophile*. The drawings illustrated Octave Chanute's article "Aerial Navigation in the United States," an expanded version of his April 2 talk to the Aéro-Club. The drawing of the Wright glider was greatly simplified and gave no indication of how the machine was controlled or how the control surfaces were manipulated. In the ensuing rush to emulate the Americans and get in the air, no Frenchman made any attempt to construct a Chanute glider, but several machines *du type de Wright* made their appearance. This was not surprising, considering that Chanute had given the impression that the successful Wright glider was for all practical purposes an improved version of his double-decker of 1896.

There is always the possibility that the words Chanute spoke on the night of April 2, 1903, relegating the Wrights to the status of devoted collaborators and talented pupils had been misinterpreted, but there is no gainsaying the words he himself wrote in his article in the August *Aérophile*. After paying tribute to Lilienthal and Pilcher and describing at some length his own 1896–97 experiments, he continued: "The invitation to amateurs to repeat these experiments remained unacted upon till 1900, when Messrs. Wilbur and Orville Wright of Dayton, Ohio, took up the question." In summing up, he concluded: "It is thus seen that there has been a gradual evolution from Lilienthal onward."

By placing himself squarely between Lilienthal and the Wrights in the chain of aeronautical evolution, Chanute was creating a myth that was to bedevil the Wrights for years to come. When Wilbur went to France in 1907, he found everywhere an impression that he and Orville had made their first experiments in a Chanute glider. They had contributed a little mechanical skill while Chanute provided the science and the money; then when success had finally been achieved, the magnanimous elder statesman of aeronautics had modestly stepped aside and permitted the brothers to reap the reward.

The seeds that Chanute sowed in his *Aérophile* article and in his talk to the Aéro-Club were to grow into weeds in the garden of his friendship with Wilbur and Orville. In 1903, the relationship was cordial enough on the surface but undertones of resentment and irritation can be detected in the correspondence. Chanute was apparently willing to overlook the wild-goose chase Wilbur had led him through the pages of the Smithsonian pamphlet on the great pterodactyl the previous December, but he could not fail to notice the astringent note that found its way into some of the letters he received from Wilbur during the summer of 1903. With an engineer's reverence for tables of figures, Chanute was engrossed in analyzing the data of the glides he had recorded during his stay at Kill Devil Hills in 1902 and asked Wilbur to send him a sample computation, showing how he and Orville computed the various components of a glide. The Wrights were well beyond the stage in which the analyzing of glides was of any practical value. Nevertheless, Wilbur went to considerable trouble to compile a table listing figures for eight components of six glides made at six different speeds. Chanute had difficulty decomposing the various elements in his own data and went on at great length regarding the discrepancies he was encountering. When he asked Wilbur to send him a detailed analysis of eight of the glides made on October 8, 1902, Wilbur saw fit to draw the line. It was his and Orville's opinion, he let Chanute know, that a glide would have to be absolutely uniform in course, speed, and every other respect for such computations to be useful unless errors of 50 percent or more were acceptable. Chanute did not agree, which caused Wilbur to remark caustically, "I am really a little rusty at figuring percents of error in such a case but, at a guess, say we put it at 100,000 percent—at any rate it is more than 50 percent."

The correspondence over gliding computations went on for another month and ended amicably enough, but the letters between Dayton and Chicago that summer were concerned with a more serious matter that ended with Wilbur becoming openly exasperated and with Chanute feeling hurt and misunderstood. The bone of contention was an article on gliding in the United States that Chanute was writing for another French periodical,

*Revue Générale des Sciences.* The article was not to appear until November 30, but the dispute over how the Wright glider was to be described in it went on all through July. When Chanute sent a copy of his article to the Wrights for review, Wilbur noted that the depth of curvature of the wings of the glider had been given incorrectly and he objected to the statement that the vertical tail was operated by "twines leading to the hands of the aviator."

"Really, this is news to me!" commented Wilbur. "Would it not be well to strike out that clause?"

Chanute had already sent his article to the *Revue* for translation. Time was of the essence. "Kindly advise me as soon as possible," he wrote Wilbur. "How is the vertical tail operated? I fear that it will not do to strike out the clause altogether."

Instead of answering the question, Wilbur cited three additional errors that he and Orville had detected in the article but had not thought important enough to mention. "But the statement in regard to the 'twines' leading to the 'hands' is more serious, and we hope it will be omitted."

"I have yours of the 22d, but it does not answer the question," Chanute wrote as soon as he received Wilbur's letter. " 'How is the vertical tail operated?' "

The vertical tail, Wilbur informed Chanute the next day, was operated by wires connected to the wires that operated the wingwarping. "This statement is not for publication," he warned, "but merely to correct the misapprehension in your own mind." Until the question of patents was settled, he continued, "I only see three methods of dealing with this matter: (1) Tell the truth. (2) Tell nothing specific. (3) Tell something not true. I really cannot advise either the first or third course."

"I was puzzled by the way you put things in your former letters," a chastened Chanute replied. "You were sarcastic and I did not catch the idea that you feared that the description might forestall a patent. Now that I know it, I take pleasure in suppressing the passage altogether." If Chanute had ended his letter there, the flap over the *Revue* article would have ended as amicably as the matter of the gliding computations, but he went on: "I believe however that it would have proved quite harmless as the construction is ancient and well known."

In the context of Wilbur's last letter, "construction" could refer only to the simultaneous operation of wingwarping and rudder, the key to flight control, which had been literally wrested from the air above Big Kill Devil Hill in October 1902 by Wilbur and Orville after three years of risking their lives on imperfectly controlled gliders. That this discovery should be called ancient and well known by as knowledgeable a historian of aeronautics as Octave Chanute would be recalled with bitterness a few years later. Nevertheless, Wilbur's next letter to Chicago was conciliatory. He thanked Chanute for striking out of the *Revue* article the sentence relating to steering, then added—a little unreasonably, considering that the brothers' main concern all along had been prior disclosure of their patent claims—"You have, however, entirely mistaken the ground of our objection to it. The trouble was not that it gave away our secrets, but that it attributed to us ancient methods which we do not use."

None of these slight cracks in the cup of friendship was visible, however, when Chanute returned from Europe in May. He brought with him an anemometer for the Wrights, purchased in Paris to replace the French anemometer that the brothers had been using in their experiments since 1901 and which they had insisted on returning to Chanute in December 1902. Chanute had written Wilbur that he was planning to visit Dayton in order to deliver the anemometer, as well as "a lot of miscellaneous information which I can best deliver in person."

The visit took place on June 6, 1903. All that is known of the "miscellaneous information" comes from two letters written the following day—one from Orville to George Spratt: "Mr. Chanute thinks the dirigible balloon is fast losing favor in France, and that the French are getting worked up over gliding"; the other from a letter written by Chanute to Samuel Langley, who had evidently not given up hope of discovering what the Wright brothers were up to: "It is only yesterday that I had the opportunity of seeing the Messrs. Wright, and mentioning your hint. They say that for the present they would prefer to accept no financial aid from anyone."

During Chanute's visit the final arrangements were made for a second lecture in Chicago by Wilbur, a sequel to his lantern-slide talk of 1901, utilizing photographs of the 1902 glider. There was no reluctance on Wilbur's part this time. As a matter of fact, he had been toying with the idea of taking to the road as a professional lecturer, no mean way to make a living. Chautauquas and Lyceums were well-established cultural institutions with guaranteed audiences avid for speakers who could lecture on the unusual. Wilbur had gone so far as to write to the Redpath Lyceum Bureau, proposing that he lecture on human flight. The bureau was interested. If Wilbur would lighten his lecture with humor, the bureau responded, something might be worked out. But human flight was not a laughing matter to Wilbur, and his platform career died aborning.

His second appearance before the Western Society of Engineers in Chicago took place on June 24, 1903, and his talk was printed in the society's journal for August, illustrated with eight photographs of the 1902 glider in flight. The title, "Experiments and Observations in Soaring Flight," required clarifying, since even an audience of engineers was likely to confuse soaring with ordinary downhill gliding. The words used to differentiate these two modes of flight show that Redpath Lyceum lost a skillful speaker and popularizer when Wilbur Wright decided not to take to the road:

> When I speak of soaring, I mean not only that the weight of the machine is fully sustained, but also that the direction of the pressure upon the wings is such that the propelling and the retarding forces are exactly in balance; in other words, the resultant of all the pressures is exactly vertical, and therefore without any unbalanced horizontal component. A kite is soaring when the string stands exactly vertical, thus showing that there is no backward pull. The phenomenon is exhibited only when the kite is flown in a rising current of air. In principle soaring is exactly equivalent to gliding, the practical difference being that in one case the wind moves with an upward trend against a motionless surface, while in the other the surface moves with a downward trend against motionless air.

During the discussion period that followed the lecture, Wilbur proved himself equally capable of "talking on his feet." It so happened that the current issue of the *National Geographic Magazine* contained an article by Alexander Graham Bell on his novel cellular kites composed of masses of tetrahedral cells. Wilbur was well aware that Bell's faith in this type of construction as a solution to the flying problem was leading the inventor of the telephone into a blind alley, but his reply to a question from the audience ("Have you followed the late experiments of Professor Bell, and what do you think of them?") carries no hint of this: "It is a very bad policy to ask one flying machine man about the experiments of another, because every flying machine man thinks that his method is the only correct one. Professor Bell is working on the plan of getting a machine of very great structural strength and one which he thinks can be maintained easily. I think his principal idea is simply the method of construction—to get something strong."

A few of the questions related to power flight. One member of the audience asked for Wilbur's opinion on the flying machine of the future. Would it be propelled by flapping wings or would it be driven by a screw propeller? "As none of our experiments has been with power machines, my judgment of the relative merits of screws and wings may be of little value," Wilbur answered. "I suspect that in efficiency they are not far from equal."

Wilbur's tongue must have been in his cheek when he uttered those words, for no one in the world on that June night in 1903 could have been more knowledgeable about the relative merits of flapping wings versus propellers—unless it was his brother Orville—and Octave Chanute must have smiled, for he was the only person in the audience that night who was aware that the Wrights had almost finished constructing a flying machine that they intended to test at Kill Devil Hills before the year was out and, what was more, had designed and built a lightweight motor and a pair of the most efficient propellers in existence to fly it.

# 13

## The First Flyer

OCTAVE CHANUTE, after witnessing the Wright brothers' successful glides of October 1902, had urged them to apply a motor and propeller to their glider. Realizing that a more rigid structure would be needed to carry the weight and withstand the vibrations of a power plant, the brothers took the first step in that direction by making a structural change in their glider before leaving camp. They added stay wires between the front and rear uprights except at the end sections of the wings. The entire center section of the glider and the leading edges of both wings were thus made stationary. Only the rear outer edges of the wingtips could now be flexed, much like the movement of ailerons on a modern aircraft. They tried out this new system, which they called end control, on their last day of gliding and were pleased to discover that it worked just as satisfactorily as warping the entire wing.

When they returned to Dayton, they set to work designing an entirely new machine. They called it their "Flyer" to distinguish it from their previous machines. Squat, stumpy, and nowhere near as graceful as their 1902 glider, the first Wright Flyer was an ugly duckling of sturdy handcrafted workmanship. Its saving grace was the care that went into every detail of its construction. In their gliders they had used spoke wire for trussing. In the Flyer they used the best wire obtainable—Roebling multi-strand wire, named after the man who used it to good advantage in designing the Brooklyn Bridge. No turnbuckles were used. The fit was so tight and exact it was necessary to force the uprights into position.

The uprights themselves were newly designed. It was widely accepted at the time that struts and other aircraft members presented the least resistance to the air if they were fish-shaped in cross section, with rounded front edges and sharp rear edges, but when the Wrights tested various uprights in their wind tunnel in January 1903, they found that uprights rectangular in cross section and with rounded edges, front and rear, presented the least resistance to the air of all the shapes tested. Chanute, during his visit to Dayton in June 1903, seriously questioned the accuracy of these findings, but the brothers had learned to distrust all measurements but their own, and the Flyer's uprights were designed with corners simply rounded. The skids that had proved satisfactory for landing their gliders in sand were retained but extended several feet forward and braced to withstand the impact of landing the much heavier Flyer. Longer skids reduced the danger of rolling over and provided extra support for the front horizontal rudder, which was now a double elevator surface, spreading 58 square feet for better control of the heavy machine. The vertical rudder was also changed from a single to a double surface, with a total area of more than 20 square feet. The wingcovering was still unvarnished Pride of the West muslin, but the cloth was now stretched over both top and bottom sides of the ribs, and the ribs themselves were an improvement in strength and lightness over the solid spruce ribs of the Wright gliders. Each rib was made as light as possible by reinforcing two thin wood strips of the proper curvature with blocks of wood, wrapped into the ribs with glued paper at the place of insertion.

Lorin's son Milton was allowed to play in the bicycle shop whenever he got the chance. Forty-five years later he could still remember the sights and smells—the spruce shavings on the floor, the smell of glue in the sticky glue pot, the array of tools whose uses were largely a mystery to a ten-year-old —yet he did not believe that anything out of the ordinary was going on. He assumed that the manufacture of flying machines went on in other bicycle shops as well. There was never room enough to assemble the entire machine in the workroom behind the shop. The center section alone took up so much space that it blocked the passage leading to the back room. When a customer entered the shop, one of the men would have to go out the side door and around to the front to wait on him. The Flyer's wingspan was 40 feet 4 inches, the chord 6 feet 6 inches, giving a total wing area of more than 500 square feet. When the machine was finally put together in the camp at Kill Devil Hills, one of its distinguishing characteristics was the droop of the wings. They appeared too weak to support their weight, the tips being fully ten inches lower than the central wing section when the machine was on the ground. The droop was deliberate, however. It was meant to minimize the effect of wind gusts from the side. Not as readily noticeable was the lack of symmetry. Like the Venetian gondola, whose right half is wider than the left to counterbalance the weight of the gondolier, who stands on the left, the Flyer's right wing was four inches longer than its left to provide additional lift for the motor and its accessories, which weighed about fifty pounds more than the operator, who lay prone on the lower wing to the left of the motor.

Construction of the Flyer began in February 1903 and went on into the summer. There were no major problems in construction, but serious problems were confronted when the Wrights tried to procure a motor and design propellers for the new machine. In the fall of 1902, they had sent letters to a number of motor manufacturers, hoping to purchase a relatively vibration-less motor weighing not more than 180 pounds. Ten manufacturers bothered to reply, but they were either unable to build a motor to the brothers' specifications or too busy to undertake such an unprofitable job, so Wilbur and Orville decided to build a motor themselves with Charlie Taylor's help. Its design was largely a joint effort. One or the other of the brothers would make a rough sketch of the part they were discussing on a piece of scratch paper. Charlie would spike the paper above his bench and get to work.

The crankcase was cast by a local foundry using the strongest aluminum alloy then obtainable. Taylor machined the block in the shop. He also made the crankshaft from a slab of high-carbon tool steel, turning it down to size on the lathe in the bicycle workroom. When finished, the motor was a simplified version of a contemporary automobile motor, with four water-cooled, horizontal, in-line cylinders but without fuel pump or carburetor. Fuel was injected directly into the cylinders by gravity from a tank with a capacity of about a quart and a half, fastened to a strut near the upper wing. The slim vertical radiator was made of several lengths of metal tubing of the kind found in apartment-house speaking tubes, flattened to reduce their capacity. There were no spark plugs. The spark was created by opening and closing two contact points in each cylinder. The cylinders were primed in advance with a few drops of gas. Dry batteries provided the spark until after starting, when a throw-knife switch bought at a local hardware store was thrown to switch the current from the batteries to a low-tension magneto driven by the twenty-six-pound flywheel. The speed of the motor could be regulated by retarding or advancing the spark, but it was impractical for the operator to alter the speed in flight.

The motor took six weeks to build. With valves popping noisily, it was first tested in the workroom behind the bicycle shop on February 12, 1903. The valve cages had vents but were neither flanged nor water-cooled, and after a few minutes they became red-hot. Sickening fumes and smoky exhaust filled the workroom, but at least the motor worked.

Bishop Wright had been keeping a diary ever since he was twenty-eight, in a style that was sometimes telegraphic, sometimes florid, sometimes both at once. The entries concerning the doings of his two youngest sons include occasional passages of endearing naïveté, such as this sentence from the entry for February 13, 1903: "The boys broke their little gas motor in the afternoon." What the good bishop was referring to with such devastating offhandedness was the second test of the world's first successful airplane motor. The test ended when dripping gasoline froze the bearings and broke the engine body.

A new casting could not be delivered for another two months. During that time the valves were fitted with heavier springs so that fuel consumption was eventually cut in half and output was increased to almost 16 horsepower —an illusory amount, however, for after the first few minutes of operation the heat generated by the valves and the red-hot valve cages preheated and expanded the air to such an extent that output dropped to around 12 horsepower. This was still more than the 8 horsepower they had conservatively counted on. Rather than increase the size of the Flyer to take advantage of this windfall, they added to its weight by strengthening and bracing its framework.

They anticipated no problems at all in designing propellers. Using their tables of air pressures, they calculated the thrust necessary to sustain their Flyer in flight. The next step was to design a propeller that would provide this thrust with the power at their command. "Very generally speaking," Samuel Langley had written in *Experiments in Aerodynamics,* "there is a very considerable analogy between the best form of aerial and of marine propellers." If the sea of air seemed not unlike the sea of water to a famous scientist like Langley, then all the Wrights had to do to design aerial propellers was to apply the theory used to design marine screws, substituting air pressures for water pressures. But when they pored over everything they could find on the subject in the Dayton Public Library, they discovered that all such formulas were of an empirical nature. Marine screws were designed by varying size and pitch until a propeller was produced that could supply the required performance. What was more unsettling, ship screws operated at an efficiency of about 50 percent, whereas Wilbur and Orville calculated that propellers with an efficiency of at least 66 percent would be needed to provide the necessary thrust for their Flyer.

They had neither the time nor the money to spend in trial-and-error propeller experiments. If they were to design propellers on the basis of calculation alone, they would have to devise a workable theory of propeller action first. Nobody has described the difficulties they faced better than Orville in an article he wrote for the *Century Magazine* five years later:

> What at first seemed a simple problem became more complex the longer we studied it. With the machine moving forward, the air flying backward, the propellers turning sidewise, and nothing standing still, it seemed impossible to find a starting-point from which to trace the various simultaneous reactions. Contemplation of it was confusing. After

long arguments we often found ourselves in the ludicrous position of each having been converted to the other's side, with no more agreement than when the discussion began.

In the house on Hawthorn Street, the verbal hassles over propeller action often took place after dinner, when Katharine's teenage helper, Carrie Kayler, was doing the dishes in the kitchen. The men's voices would become louder and louder; then there would be a pause and the next time Carrie peered into the lace-curtained living room she would see Orville sitting erect on one side of the fireplace, arms folded, and Wilbur slouched in his chair on the other side, legs stretched out, hands behind his head. The argument would have lapsed into an angry silence. The discussions in the bicycle shop were more uninhibited. Five of the Wright brothers' notebooks bristle with formulas, diagrams, tables of provisional data, and random notations relating to propellers, but the closest one can come today to reconstructing their theory of propeller action is this: Whereas a marine screw moves through a relatively dense medium, somewhat like the advance of a screw into a piece of wood, the action of an aerial propeller is like that of a wing moving rapidly along a helical course in a vertical rather than a horizontal plane. It is the cumulative lift of those rotating wings that provides the thrust that propels the flying machine through the air. Thrust, therefore, must depend on several discrete but interdependent factors: the shape of the propeller blade; its pitch, or the angle at which it strikes the air; the speed at which it turns; the speed at which the machine travels forward; and the speed of the air slipping backward through the advancing, rotating blades. They began in December 1902 by analyzing the thrust of a fan twenty-eight inches in diameter driven by their small one-cylinder shop motor. By February 1903 they were working with a propeller eight feet in diameter. By March they were using their tables of lift to design propeller blades with a predicted efficiency of 66 percent.

The results of all this discussing, theorizing, and experimenting were two propellers a little over eight feet in diameter, made of three laminations of spruce, glued together, then shaped with hatchet and spokeshave. They decided to use two propellers instead of one, mounted behind the wings rather than in front to ensure that the lifting surfaces would not be moving through air stirred up by the whirling blades. Not only would two propellers act on a greater quantity of air but by running one clockwise and the other counterclockwise, any twisting effect on lateral control would be eliminated.

Transmitting power from the motor to the propellers was no problem. Sprockets and chains used to drive bicycles came ready-made. Chains strong enough to drive propellers were another matter, but the Wrights knew where to turn. The Diamond Chain Company of Indianapolis supplied them with chains of the type used in early automobile transmissions, made to their specifications. A minor problem—how to reverse the direction of one of the propellers—was solved very simply by crossing one set of chains in a figure eight and encasing the chains in metal tubes to keep them from flapping.

By June they were confident that estimates of their propellers' efficiency would prove correct within a percentage point or two. In a letter to George Spratt, Orville reached a state of near-euphoria in describing what they had gone through to achieve that goal: "We had been unable to find anything of value in any of the works to which we had access, so that we worked out a theory of our own on the subject, and soon discovered, as we usually do, that all the propellers built heretofore are *all wrong,* and then built a pair of propellers 8 1/8 ft. in diameter based on our theory, which are *all right!* (till we have a chance to test them down at Kitty Hawk and find out differently). Isn't it astonishing that all these secrets have been preserved for so many years just so that we could discover them!!"

Wilbur and Orville had been carrying on a lively correspondence with George Spratt ever since Spratt left their camp in October 1902 for his home in Coatesville, Pennsylvania. While the brothers were wrestling with propeller theory, Spratt had become ensnared in some complicated aeronautical theories of his own, from which Wilbur tried to extricate him by engaging him in the brothers' rough-and-tumble game of bouncing ideas off each other, but Spratt was not as resilient as Wilbur and Orville. "I see that you are back at your old trick of giving up before you are half beaten in an argument," Wilbur observed in one of his letters to Coatesville that April. "I felt pretty certain of my own ground but was anticipating the pleasure of a good scrap before the matter was settled. Discussion brings out new ways of looking at things and helps to round off the corners." Spratt's self-esteem suffered, however, whenever he compared his own progress with that of the Wrights, and much ink was wasted trying to cure him of his "blues." "You should by all means avoid lying awake at nights studying out problems as you did sometimes at Kitty Hawk," Wilbur wrote in the same letter. His efforts to bolster Spratt's sagging morale sometimes revealed more of Wilbur's character than it did of Spratt's:

> You make a great mistake in envying me any of my qualities. Very often what you take for some special quality of mind is merely facility arising from constant practice, and you could do as well or better with like practice. It is a characteristic of all our family to be able to see the weak points of anything, but this is not always a desirable quality as it makes us too conservative for successful business men, and limits our friendships to a very limited circle.

In May, when Spratt complained that the brothers' method of "rounding off the corners" by switching sides in the middle of an argument struck him as dishonest, Wilbur replied:

> It was not my intention to advocate dishonesty in argument nor a bad spirit in a controversy. No truth is without some mixture of error, and no error so false but that it possesses some elements of truth. If a man is in too big a hurry to give up an error he is liable to give up some truth with it, and in accepting the arguments of the other man he is sure to get some error with it. Honest argument is merely a process of mutually picking the beams and motes out of each other's eyes so both can see clearly. Men become wise just as they become rich, more by what they *save* than by what they receive. After I get hold of a truth I hate to lose it again, and I like to sift all the truth out before I give up an error.

Octave Chanute was expected to spend a week or two at Kill Devil Hills as usual. Spratt had been invited again, but Wilbur and Orville wanted no more Edward Huffakers or Augustus Herrings. One air-minded friend of Octave Chanute did try to wangle an invitation to the camp in 1903. That was Captain Ferdinand Ferber, a French artillery officer who had been experimenting with gliders since 1899 without much success. After Chanute sent him a copy of Wilbur's 1901 talk to the Western Society of Engineers, he became an enthusiastic follower of the Wrights and had a carpenter construct for him a flimsy imitation of the 1901 Wright glider, in which he made a handful of glides. Upon hearing Chanute's 1903 after-dinner talk to the Aéro-Club de France, Ferber's patriotic fervor was fanned to such a flame that he wrote a letter to Ernest Archdeacon asserting that *"the airplane must not be allowed to be perfected in America"*—the italics were added by Archdeacon when he appended Ferber's letter to his report of Chanute's talk in *La Locomotion*— and urging that wealthy sportsman-lawyer to establish prizes for gliding in order to lure Frenchmen into competition with the Wrights.

A few weeks after Chanute returned to the United States, he received a letter from Ferber, asking for an invitation to the Wright camp for the purpose of taking gliding lessons. The Wrights were naturally suspicious of Ferber's motives, but when Chanute sought advice on how to respond to this request, Wilbur remained silent, whereupon Chanute informed Ferber that there was little chance of his being invited to the Wright camp. Two days later Chanute wrote Wilbur: "Not hearing from you, I have written to Capt. Ferber that his statement that the flying machine must not be permitted to be completed in America, and that he is building a motor machine, has put a flea in your ear, and that you are thinking."

It was not much of a flea. In 1903 Ferber had been making some grandiose experiments near Nice with a propeller-driven biplane glider suspended from a whirling arm almost a hundred feet in diameter. According to his next letter to Chanute, the best speed he was able to attain with this apparatus was a little over 2 miles an hour. "Mr. Wright therefore has still time to beat me," he added. Chanute translated Ferber's letter and sent it to the Wrights, who were not the least upset by the Frenchman's efforts to not let the airplane be invented in America. "Captain Ferber need have no fears that we are offended at his patriotism," Wilbur replied. "If we had facilities for entertaining him, and nothing but gliding on the program, and four months instead of less than two in our season, he would have been very welcome."

The Wrights' stay at Kill Devil Hills that year was to be closer to three months than two. Each trip to the Outer Banks had seen a staggering increase in the amount of goods and supplies needed to see them through the season. They had planned to leave Dayton by mid-August, but the first batch of goods was not ready for shipment until September 9. In 1903 they had to transport not only a flying machine weighing, with all its accessories, close to 650 pounds, but an imposing collection of tools and equipment. Their array of instruments alone included their new French anemometer, their clinometer, binoculars for birdwatching, camera and tripod and a supply of glass-plate negatives, stopwatches, tachometers, and a coil box with batteries for starting their motor. There were rifles for sport and game, plenty of bedding for late-autumn nights, burlap for making new patent beds among the rafters, mosquito netting, reading materials, French and German grammars, even a worn carpet or two to hang against the windy walls of their drafty living room. They also took with them a motley collection of odds and ends from the bicycle shop that was to stand them in good stead —bicycle hubs, carbide cans, a supply of Arnstein's hard tire cement—and of course eating and cooking utensils and enough food to last until they could order groceries from Elizabeth City on a regular basis. Octave Chanute made a last-minute attempt to be of assistance. "I have here a little nest of dishes and cups for camping purposes," he wrote from Chicago. "If it can be of use to you, it is very much at your service."

"We thank you for your offer of the loan of your camp tableware," Wilbur wrote back on September 18, "but I think that, with the additions we are ourselves sending this year, we will have all we need." Five days later, the brothers left Dayton.

Bishop Wright saw them off at the railroad station at 8:55 in the morning. Always there hung over these farewells the realization that one or the other of the brothers might not return alive. Now two additional hazards had been added to their experiments—an explosive gasoline motor and a pair of whirling propellers. Nobody knows the words that seventy-four-year-old Milton Wright spoke to his sons that morning in the depot at Dayton, but it is said that he gave his sons a dollar to cover the cost of sending a wire as soon as their Flyer should have made a successful flight.

# 14

## A Race with the Weather

IT HAD TAKEN Wilbur and Orville four years to master the art of travel to and from the Outer Banks. In 1903 they wasted no time in Elizabeth City but caught the *Ocracoke* on its night run to Manteo on Roanoke Island, where they arrived at one-thirty in the morning, Friday, September 25. At Manteo they hired a steam launch to ferry them the rest of the way to Kill Devil Hills. For once, the trip had been without incident, although they knew a heart-stopping moment or two when they got off the train at Elizabeth City and discovered that the freight depot on the wharf across the way, through which all shipments passed on their way to Kitty Hawk, had burned down the week before. Poking about among the ruins, they spotted a large can that looked suspiciously like one of the carbide cans shipped from Dayton the week before the fire. On closer inspection the can turned out to have once been full of lard, and on arriving at Kill Devil Hills, they found that their first shipment of goods had escaped the fire and was waiting for them at the campsite, together with the lumber they had ordered for the new and larger building they planned to erect to house their Flyer. The Flyer itself was still on the way.

A February storm with 90-mile-per-hour winds had lifted their old camp building from its foundations and set it down two feet to the east. By Saturday morning it was back in place and they were setting up their kitchen and working on a French-drip coffeepot to alleviate the shortage of eggs, which were used to settle coffee grounds in those pre-percolator days. That afternoon they began work on the foundations of their new building. A few feet west of the old camp building, it was larger and roomier than its neighbor—nine feet high at the eaves, forty-four feet long, and sixteen feet wide—and braced on two sides against the wind with two-by-fours. Both ends were fitted with doors hinged at the top. A photograph taken from the top of Big Kill Devil Hill that October shows the Flyer's shed and the camp building nestling side by side on the sandy plain with no other human habitation anywhere in sight.

There was no shortage of human companionship, however. The men at the lifesaving station a quarter of a mile away on the beach would pick up the brothers' mail at the post office in Kitty Hawk and deliver it in person, glad of an excuse for dropping in at the camp for a chat. In return, the members of the lifesaving crew were presented with mounted photographs of themselves, taken the year before by the Wrights. Although Bill Tate rarely appeared at the camp, having turned over to his half-brother, Dan, the job of assisting Wilbur and Orville, there were frequent visits from other Kitty Hawkers.

To gain the greatest amount of practice in the air before trying out their Flyer, the brothers worked on the new building only on rainy and calm days and practiced gliding and soaring on days when the wind and weather permitted. On their first Monday in camp, conditions were so inviting they carried the 1902 glider to Big Hill and with Dan Tate's help made so many flights in 20- to 30-mile-per-hour winds that they lost count. The most successful soaring flight was Wilbur's in which he covered only 52 feet although he was in the air for 26 seconds. On October 8 Captain Midgett's sailboat, the *Lou Willis,* tied up at Kitty Hawk with the crates containing the Flyer. They were hauled down to Kill Devil Hills on the sand road along Kitty Hawk Bay the next morning. Before unpacking the crates, Wilbur and Orville made another attempt to glide, but a storm was coming up and they brought the glider back to camp, where they hurried to put the hinges on the north door of their new building before the storm broke. Just as they finished, the rain came pouring down.

The storm lasted four days. The new building had not yet been completely braced and the brothers lay awake most of the first night, expecting to hear it take off in the direction of Big Hill. Orville, the family expert on night alarms, climbed down from his patent bed under the roof and reported that the floor at the north end of the camp building was under water. The next morning the wind dropped from 50 to a mere 30 miles an hour. "And the evening and morning were the first day," wrote Wilbur in his next long Sunday letter home. The second day was spent bracing the new building from the inside and unpacking the Flyer, while the wind worked itself into a frenzy. At four o'clock it reached 75 miles per hour and threatened to pull the tar-paper roofing off the north end of the building. Orville, in Wilbur's overcoat, ventured outside with a ladder, a hammer, and a mouthful of nails. The wind soon blew the overcoat up over his head, so that Wilbur was obliged to hold it down while Orville nailed the tar paper back onto the roof. "The wind and rain continued through the night," Wilbur's account of the second day ends, "but we took the advice of the Oberlin coach, 'Cheer up, boys, there is no hope.'"

On the morning of the third day, their doorstep was six inches under water and the water was sloshing against the undersides of the floorboards of their living room. At noon, the wind dropped and the rain stopped temporarily. Without realizing that they were probably close to the eye of a hurricane, they took the 1902 glider out and made two glides, the second of which ended when an unexpected gust caught Orville and he came down so fast he grazed the top of Wilbur's head with one wing and broke two spars in landing. Before they could get the machine indoors, the storm recommenced in all its fury, breaking the door of the camp building when one of the props slipped away from under it. On the fourth day they stayed indoors, islanded in a sea of puddles, wet sand, and pelting rainwater. While the storm lasted, five vessels ran ashore between the Kill Devil lifesaving station and the entrance to Chesapeake Bay sixty miles to the north. Wilbur, who fancied he was something of a weather prophet, attributed the foul weather to a "cyclone" that stood off the coast and threatened the Outer Banks for four days until "it reared up so much that it finally fell over on its back and lay quiet."

The day the storm ended, the brothers began work on the upper wing of the Flyer. The rear spar was now entirely enclosed in the wingcovering, so that the underside of the wing was as smooth as the top. Both Wilbur and Orville took delight in the smoothness and perfection of the Flyer's wing as it took shape under their hands. "It is the prettiest we have ever made," Orville wrote his father, "and of much better shape." Wilbur considered it far ahead of anything they had built before.

Their plans to make the first tests of the Flyer by November 1 went badly awry. Several times during the next two months they had reason to believe that all their fine work had been in vain. On October 19 they noticed that the observed gliding angles for four long glides made that day were much larger than the calculated angles, indicating that something was radically wrong with their calculations. The calculations used to design their Flyer were based on the assumption that their anemometer habitually over-recorded. Now they weren't so sure. If the anemometer had been under-recording all along, more power would be needed to get the Flyer off the ground than their motor could provide. The next day Orville wrote a post-card to Charlie Taylor: "Flying machine market has been very unsteady the past two days. Opened yesterday morning at about 208 (100% means even chance of success) but by noon had dropped to 110. These fluctuations would have produced a panic, I think, in Wall Street, but in this quiet place it only put us to thinking and figuring." It also put them to (literally) running calibration tests on their anemometer, one brother running with the hand-held instrument beside the glider being flown by the other brother. A little additional figuring convinced them that although the anemometer recorded more nearly accurately than they had assumed, the error was not large. They were still on the safe side.

On the afternoon of Wednesday, October 21, they made nine excellent glides of between 400 and 450 feet in length, many at forty to sixty feet above the sides of Big Hill. The encouraging aspect of these glides was not the distance or the awesome altitudes but that the beginning of each glide was, for all practical purposes, soaring, the machine moving over the ground at a speed of only one or two feet per second. Wilbur's best glide of the day was an astounding 59 seconds in duration, bettered only by Orville's earlier glide of 1 minute 1.5 seconds. After observing these glides, Dan Tate volunteered the opinion that all the glider needed to keep it indefinitely in the air was a coat of feathers "to make it light."

On October 23 George Spratt arrived on his third annual visit, bringing the brothers' lonely first month in camp to an end. They obliged their visitor with a score of glides the following week, six of them over one minute in duration, the best being Orville's glide of October 26—1 minute 11.8 seconds, a world record that would stand until broken by Orville himself eight years later. Winter weather arrived with Spratt. It rained off and on during the two weeks of his stay, creating ponds in the sandy hollows about the camp, so that the countryside looked more like a marsh than the sandy dune country it normally was. The wind and rain were not as violent as during the four-day storm, but the cold was more bone-chilling and long-lasting. Carpets were hung inside the walls of the camp building to keep out the drafts. At night the three men suffered intensely from the cold in their bunk beds among the rafters until they improvised a stove from one of the empty carbide cans brought from Dayton, punching holes in its sides and adding a stovepipe, dampers, and cast-iron legs.

The afternoon they transformed the carbide can into a wood-burning stove, Wilbur told Dan Tate to collect a supply of driftwood for fuel. Dan was a hard man to handle. He complained that it was unreasonable to expect him to collect driftwood since they could buy as much wood as they wanted from Jesse Baum for three dollars a cord. Instead of going to the beach to collect firewood, Dan went home to Kitty Hawk. A few weeks earlier he had announced on arriving at the camp one morning that the price of fish had gone up. Since his usual income came from fishing, the Wrights interpreted this as a roundabout way of asking for a raise. Although weekly wages on the Outer Banks ranged from $3.50 to $5.00, the Wrights needed Dan's help at the time and agreed to pay him $7.00 for a seven-day week of ten-hour days, with lunch and an hour's traveling time thrown in for good measure. But Tate was so awkward at working about the camp that his ten-hour day

*The house at 7 Hawthorn Street, in Dayton, where Orville Wright was born.* (Library of Congress)

*Wilbur (left) and Orville on the back porch of the Hawthorn Street house, 1910.* (Smithsonian Institution, National Air and Space Museum)

*The parlor of the Hawthorn Street house at the time the Wright brothers were in the bicycle business.*
(Wright State University)

*Wilbur Wright, 1867–1912.*
(Wright State University)

*Orville Wright, 1871–1948.*
(Wright State University)

*Bishop Milton Wright,*
*1828–1917.*
(Wright State University)

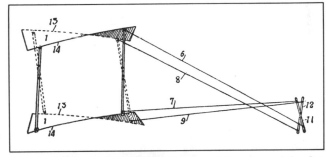

*Simplified side view of the wings of the 1899
kite-model, showing how wingwarping was
achieved by cords attached to the wingtips.*

*The camp at Kitty Hawk, 1900.* (Library of Congress)

*The first Wright glider, 1900, being flown as a kite.* (Library of Congress)

*Wilbur washing pots and pans in the sand, Kitty Hawk, 1900.* (Wright State University)

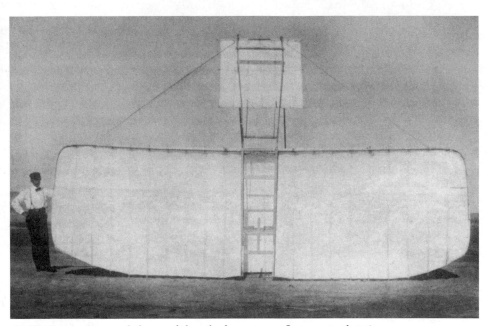

*Orville beside the upended 1901 glider, the largest ever flown up to that time.*
(Wright State University)

*Wilbur in the 1901 glider, moving so slowly he is practically soaring.*
(Wright State University)

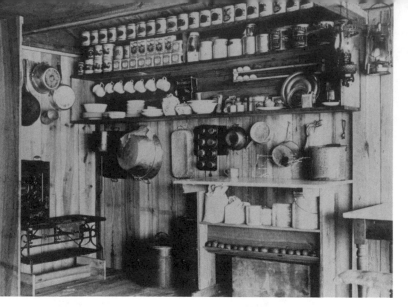

*Kitchen of the camp at Kill Devil Hills, 1902.* (Wright State University)

*Wilbur and Dan Tate launch the third Wright glider with Orville at the controls, October 1902.* (Library of Congress)

*Wilbur makes a right turn in the 1902 glider from West Hill. Big Kill Devil Hill is in the background.* (Library of Congress)

*The first Wright Flyer, outside the camp buildings at Kill Devil Hills, November 1903.* (Library of Congress)

*Start of the world's first successful airplane flight, December 17, 1903. Orville lies prone on the lower wing; Wilbur runs alongside. Estimated distance and time: 120 feet in 12 seconds.* (Library of Congress)

*The 1903 Flyer at the end of Wilbur's 59-second flight, its front rudder frame smashed in landing.* (Wright State University)

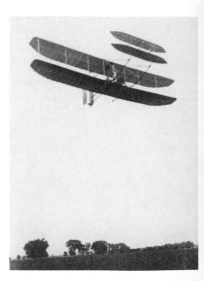

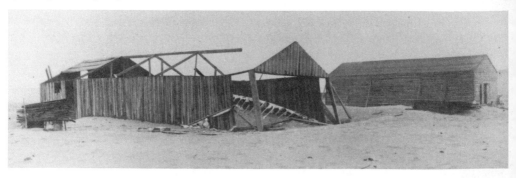

boiled down to doing the dishes and helping to carry and launch the glider on the few days each week Wilbur and Orville were able to glide. In their opinion, their helper had been spoiled. They referred to his defection as a strike. If so, it failed. Dan Tate forfeited his place in history by staying away from the camp for good.

His presence was hardly missed. Spratt pitched in while the brothers worked on the Flyer and helped construct the sixty-foot monorail to be used in its launching. By November 5 the machine was in a more or less finished state, and Wilbur and Orville ran up the motor for the first time. Suddenly they were faced with a crisis. The sprocket wheels on the propeller shafts that conducted the transmission chains from the motor had almost half a turn of play. This was of no consequence once the propellers were turning at a uniform rate, but the magneto did not produce a satisfactory spark at first and the propeller shafts vibrated ominously at every missed explosion. The shafts of steel tubing had been tested in Dayton and found capable of withstanding several times the power they would receive from the Flyer's motor, providing the power was transmitted smoothly. The motor's twenty-six-pound flywheel was too light, however, to absorb the shocks and strains of missed explosions. All at once as the motor racketed away, filling the shed with exhaust, it backfired. The crossarms that connected the propeller shafts to the airframe were jerked loose, and one of the shafts was badly twisted.

Wilbur and Orville made a quick decision. The twisted shaft would have to be repaired and both shafts strengthened, something that only Charlie Taylor back in Dayton was equipped to do. It was now two o'clock in the afternoon. It would take several days to ship the shafts back to Dayton but much time would be saved if they were to go that afternoon with Captain Jesse Ward of the Kill Devil lifesaving station, who was leaving for Manteo at 4 P.M. in his gasoline launch. The trick would be to get the shafts from Manteo on Roanoke Island to the railroad depot on the mainland for shipment to Dayton. The main purpose of Spratt's trip to Kill Devil Hills that year had been to witness a flight of the Flyer. There was no longer any chance of that, so he agreed to leave with Captain Ward at 4 P.M., taking with him the two propeller shafts and a letter of instruction for Charlie Taylor.

The day after Spratt left, Octave Chanute arrived. His visit could not have been more ill-timed. The cold, rain-laden wind that greeted him when he disembarked from Captain Ward's gasoline launch at Kill Devil Hills dampened his hopes of witnessing even a gliding flight. Wilbur and Orville did their best to exhibit their prowess in soaring, but the wind was so irregular and cold that they gave up after four or five attempts. The camp building was unpleasantly cold in spite of the carpets hung against the walls and the rags stuffed in the chinks. The warmest day of Chanute's one-week stay was Sunday, November 8, so warm that the door of their living quarters was propped open part of the time, but Sunday was the one day of the week on which the Wrights refused to work or fly.

Observing the Sabbath did not rule out conversation, and the three men sat up until eleven that night talking. Chanute had passed through Washington on his way to North Carolina and had brought with him photographs of Samuel Langley's man-carrying airplane, which had floundered into the Potomac River a few seconds after being launched from the top of Langley's workshop-houseboat on October 7. The machine had been fished out of the water to the accompaniment of derisive hoots from the press and was now being reconditioned for a second trial. Chanute was frankly surprised that the Wrights had not also been besieged by reporters. The Langley machine weighed about the same as the Flyer but was powered by a motor four times as powerful as the Wrights'. The most telling difference between the two machines for Octave Chanute, however, was the manner of their launching. The Wright launching system, which Spratt had helped construct, consisted of a sixty-foot monorail made of four fifteen-foot two-by-fours covered with a thin metal strip, held upright in the sand by wooden crosspieces. A small wooden truck moved along the rail on two metal rollers made from modified bicycle hubs. Across the truck was placed a six-foot plank, on which the skids of the Flyer rested on takeoff. A third bicycle hub, attached to a crosspiece under the horizontal front rudder, kept the machine from nosing over on the track. Chanute was greatly amused to learn that, whereas Langley had spent a large part of the thousands of dollars allotted to his project by the War Department on his elaborate catapult launching device, the total cost of the "junction railroad," which was what the Wrights called their launching system, was four dollars.

Tuesday was too cold even to work on the motor, so the three men huddled about the stove most of the day and talked about flying. In Chanute's eyes, the Wrights were aviators par excellence. It was not what they flew, it was how they flew it. He had been trying to buy the batlike, steam-powered *Avion* constructed by Clément Ader in France in the 1890s so that Wilbur and Orville could repair it and fly it for him. Although one can sympathize with the old man's desire to have his own gliders flown by competent operators, that he could seriously consider having the brothers risk their necks on the antiquated Ader machine is cause for wonder, since any picture of the machine ever published showed that it would have been capable of flight only in a Jules Verne novel. "He thinks we could do it!" Orville wrote his father and sister the following Sunday. "He doesn't seem to think our machines are so much superior as the manner in which we handle them. We are of just the reverse opinion."

Fortunately for Chanute's pocketbook, the Ader machine was not for sale. It had already been presented to a Paris museum, where it was to fill loyal Frenchmen with pride as the first power machine ever to fly—until the official report of its tests was finally published and the claim turned out to be fraudulent. In 1903 the Wrights were still willing to forgive Chanute a few blind spots. His true feelings for the brothers were better expressed by what he did after leaving Kill Devil Hills. In Manteo he purchased two pairs of gloves and had them sent back to the camp as a parting gift.

With no company to entertain and the propeller shafts not yet returned from Dayton, the Wrights were hard put to pass their time profitably. Gliding was no longer practical. The glider had been stored in back of the old camp building, where heat from the carbide-can stove had so dried out the wooden framework that it was unsafe for further gliding. It could still be used for trying out the junction railroad. The day Chanute left, two of the four sections of track were laid on the side of Big Kill Devil Hill. The glider was placed on the wooden truck and set on the starting rail. One brother lay prone on the lower wing while the other ran alongside to balance the moving machine. Satisfied that the truck would support the heavier Flyer as it moved smoothly along the rail on the bicycle hubs, they returned to camp and spent the rest of the day reading and chopping wood.

One day they hung the Flyer by its wingtips to test the strength of its framing. The framework was strong enough but the cloth wrinkled severely, so they altered the trussing to spread the strain more evenly. When they repeated the test, the machine supported a 440-pound load in the center without any sign of stress or strain.

Another day they devised an experiment to determine the power lost to friction as the transmission chains passed over the sprocket wheels. Chanute, with half a century of engineering experience behind him, had alarmed them during his visit by predicting a 20 percent loss in power from this source. They had allowed for a loss of only 5 percent. There was no laboratory at their disposal but they needed none. Suspending one of the drive chains over a sprocket wheel, they hung bags of sand on either end approximately equal in weight to the pull on the chains when driving the propellers, then slowly added weight to one side until the sprocket wheel began to move. The loss due to friction, calculated from the added weight, was just about equal to their original estimate of 5 percent.

On days when it was too cold outside for splitting wood, they stayed indoors and contrived new ways of calculating the performance of their Flyer. Orville reported the results in a letter to Charlie Taylor: "While the shafts were away we had lots of time for thinking and the more we thought, the harder our machine got to running and the less the power of the engine became, until stock got down to a very low figure." Orville employed the stock market analogy more than once to indicate the rise and fall of their hopes for the Flyer. "After figuring a while," he wrote in his diary on November 15, "stock in flying machine began dropping rapidly till it was worth very little! After supper it took a turn for the better and is now on par." And in a letter to his sister the next day: "Stock in flying machine sells one day at 175 and the next at about 17. Last night it got down to 3 but before bed time had gone up to about par, where it now stands."

At night they studied languages by lantern light. Chanute had written from Europe early in 1903 that he was sending them articles of aerodynamic interest in French and Italian. "If you are at all rusty in those languages," he admonished, "you had better brighten up." The advice was heeded, no doubt with help from Katharine, who taught modern languages as well as Latin at Steele High School. While they waited for the propeller shafts to arrive at Kill Devil Hills, Orville brushed up on his French and spent an hour a day on German, struggling valiantly to translate an article on their 1902 glider, with the vocabulary of his German grammar as the only dictionary.

Tuesday, November 17, was a warm and pleasant day. When they went to bed that night the stars were shining in an almost cloudless sky, but a north wind came up at midnight, a cold rain fell, and by morning the ponds about the camp were frozen over and the water in their washbasin was frozen solid to the bottom. It was their coldest night so far and as such required an adjustment in their classification of nights according to the number of blankets required for comfort. Wilbur explained this complicated classification system in a letter to his father and sister: "In addition to the classification of last year, to wit, 1, 2, 3, and 4 blanket nights, we now have 5 blanket nights, & 5 blankets & 2 quilts. Next comes 5 blankets, 2 quilts & fire; then 5, 2, fire, & hot-water jug. This is as far as we have got so far. Next comes the addition of sleeping without undressing, then shoes & hats, and finally overcoats. We intend to be comfortable while we are here."

Captain Midgett's *Lou Willis* was their lifeline to civilization, but it was not a very reliable one. The day the cold weather set in, they were about out of groceries. In expectation of the arrival of the *Lou Willis* with a sizable order of foodstuffs from Elizabeth City, they had a hearty meal at noon but were reduced to dining on condensed milk and crackers that night. The *Lou Willis* arrived the following day, bringing not only the groceries but the long-awaited propeller shafts, which Charlie Taylor had shipped from Dayton ten days before and which had lain most of that time in the freight depot at Elizabeth City.

The strengthened shafts were mounted on the Flyer that afternoon. Once again the motor was run up and once again flying-machine stock hit bottom. The motor ran so erratically that both sprocket wheels came loose inside of seconds, and nothing the brothers did to tighten the nuts that locked the sprocket wheels to the propeller shafts did any good. They went to bed that night badly discouraged, but got up the next morning determined to find a solution to the problem.

The solution was at hand. They had brought it with them from Dayton and had been using it to seal every letter that went back to Dayton from the Kitty Hawk post office. Orville had bought a batch of writing paper and envelopes when they got off the train in Norfolk that September. "The young lady in the store recognized me at once as of the aristocracy," he wrote Katharine when he arrived in camp, "and so palmed off these envelopes without gum. As I will have to spend the next half hour heating up some tire cement to seal it, I will have to close now." Securing the nuts on the sprocket wheels was of more importance than sealing ungummed envelopes, but in each case the agent was the same: Arnstein's hard tire cement for fastening tires to the rims of bicycle wheels. To see if Arnstein's cement would do the job, they heated the propeller shafts and sprockets, then melted some of the cement and poured it into the threads. When everything was screwed up tight and the cement had hardened, the trouble with loose sprocket wheels was over.

With the propellers back in operation they made a few tests before attempting a flight. They were aware that there was a considerable difference between the thrust of propellers in static tests and the thrust in flight. To determine the actual thrust, they placed rollers under the skids of the Flyer. Since their spring balance, the kind used by grocers, could not record the anticipated amount of thrust, they attached a rope to it, ran the rope over a pulley, attached a fifty-pound box of sand to the rope, and measured the remaining pull on their scales. Tested in this fashion, the propellers turning at 352 revolutions per minute delivered 132 pounds of thrust. According to their calculations, this was almost 40 pounds more than would be needed to get the Flyer off the ground. "Stock went up like a sky rocket," Orville wrote Charlie Taylor the next day, "and is now at the highest figure in history."

The brothers' scruples against working on the Sabbath did not extend to anemometer testing. They once more tested this instrument on Sunday, November 22, running with it over a measured course, with and against the wind, until they were quite sure of the exact extent to which the anemometer overrecorded. They had already tested their starting track and its truck using the 1902 glider. Now they loaded the truck with sand and noted that it ran smoothly over the track down a slope of a little over 1 degree. They tested the Flyer's hip cradle, which had been padded for greater comfort, to determine the pressure required to change the angle of the wingtips up to 12 degrees. The pressure was an acceptable 14 pounds. Running the propellers at 350 revolutions per minute, they tested their motor's gas consumption and calculated that the small tank held enough gasoline for 18 minutes of operation, or enough for a flight from Kill Devil Hills to the Kitty Hawk lifesaving station and back.

On Tuesday, November 24, the Flyer was ready for a flight, but as they eased it sideways out of the shed on its track, one of the bicycle-hub rollers under the track broke. It was replaced. Then the other hub broke under the strain. They took a photograph of the machine and rolled it back into the shed. Wednesday morning the broken hubs were repaired. Before removing the machine from its shed, they made a last-minute test, suspending it by the wingtips with a man on board and with the motor running. There was almost no vibration. The Flyer was at last ready for its maiden flight, but just as they were getting ready to take it out of the shed, a drizzling rain began to fall. It fell all afternoon.

Thursday was Thanksgiving Day. From the Wrights' standpoint, there was not much to be thankful for. The wind increased, the temperature dropped. Friday it snowed. While the wind howled about the frame building and the woodsmoke poured out of the stovepipe at its southeast corner, the brothers killed time by putting together an automatic flight-data recorder with which to prove or disprove the accuracy of their propeller calculations. It consisted of a Veedor revolution counter mounted on the motor and their anemometer mounted with a stopwatch on a strut next to the operator, all three instruments connected by levers and string so that they could be started when the machine moved down the track and stopped simultaneously on landing. The anemometer would record the distance through the air, the stopwatch the time of flight, and the Veedor counter the number of turns of the motor and hence of the propellers. Airspeed and power expended could be calculated from the recorded data.

Saturday was a little warmer. They ventured into the unheated Flyer shed and mounted the recording instrument on the machine. Then they ran up the motor several times with the Veedor counter attached, two to three minutes at a time. After half a dozen such runs, they noticed that something was wrong with the propeller shafts again. Shutting off the motor, they discovered a crack in one of the shafts. This distressing turn of events called for another conference and another decision.

They decided on the spot not to waste any more time on tubular shafts. It was now obvious that only solid shafts made of high-grade tool steel could withstand the shocks of premature or missed explosions from the Flyer's motor, but unless they acted fast, winter would make a flight test of the Flyer impossible. It had taken ten days for the present shafts to reach them from Dayton. There was only one way to get new shafts quickly and that was for one of the brothers to return to Dayton, have the shafts made, and bring them back with him on the train. Orville went at once to the Kill Devil lifesaving station and made arrangements to leave for Manteo. His departure on Monday, November 30, was the signal for two days of weather that would have been perfect for testing the Flyer. Wilbur filled in the time by splitting enough stumps and logs to last them as firewood for the rest of their stay.

Wednesday, December 9, nine days after leaving Kill Devil Hills, Orville boarded the train in Dayton with the new propeller shafts. He had traveled the same route to North Carolina and back no less than eight times in the last four years. There was nothing new to be seen from the window as the train rocked and swayed through the wintry Ohio countryside, but he had brought along a newspaper to while away the hours. One item in the paper caught Orville's eye and provided him with enough food for thought for the entire trip. A second and final effort to fly Samuel Langley's man-carrying airplane had been made the day before, and for the second time, pilot and plane had plunged into the Potomac.

It has been suggested many times that the Wright brothers were in a race with Samuel Langley in 1903 to see who would get off the ground first. In reality, they did not feel the least bit threatened by the airplane on which Langley was reported to have spent large sums of government money. If they were engaged in a race at the time, it was a race with the weather. They had promised their family they would be back in Dayton by Christmas.

Nevertheless, Langley's expensive failure set Orville to figuring. When he was back in camp with the propeller shafts, he added up the costs of the untested Wright Flyer, including in the total all the money spent on the two sets of shafts, on his train ticket to Dayton and return, on everything he could think of so far. The total came to less than $1,000—a startling contrast to the $73,000 that Samuel Langley had spent in his unsuccessful attempt to achieve human flight.

# 15

# *An Experiment in Aerodynamics*

IT HAD TAKEN Samuel Langley five years to design, build, and test the man-carrying airplane that he called his Aerodrome ("with scant regard for etymology," as C. H. Gibbs-Smith has noted). Although Langley's first love was astronomy, his interest in flight went back to 1886, when a paper on the soaring of birds delivered at a scientific meeting so captured his fancy that he proposed to the trustees of the Allegheny Observatory, of which he was director, that he be allowed to build a whirling table for aerodynamic research on the grounds of the observatory near Pittsburgh. Funds were provided by a Pittsburgh millionaire. Langley moved to Washington, D.C., to become secretary of the Smithsonian Institution in 1887, the year the whirling-table experiments began, and the work was carried out by assistants.

The so-called whirling table was a pair of thirty-foot arms driven by a steam engine. To the ends of these racing arms were affixed a few stuffed birds—buzzards, a frigate bird, a California condor, an albatross—but the major part of the research was a study of the reactions of flat metal surfaces held at various angles as they moved through the air at speeds up to 100 miles per hour. The findings were reported in 1891 in a handsome Smithsonian publication, *Experiments in Aerodynamics,* in which the detailed drawings of the instrumentation lavished on those experiments made the Wrights' wind-tunnel instruments, improvised from hacksaw blades and bicycle spokes, seem like relics of an engineering stone age. Elaborate instrumentation was no guarantee of accuracy, however. The experiments were conducted in the open on a hilltop 400 feet above the Ohio River, and the winds had a way of "vitiating the results"—an expression of Langley's that was picked up and used by his friend Octave Chanute in Chanute's first letter to Wilbur Wright.

Langley's studies were concerned with aerodynamics, not practical aeronautics. He was not seeking an efficient lifting surface like the Wrights in their wind-tunnel experiments a decade later, but one aspect of his work held out great hope for human flight. When he analyzed his data, Langley showed by a feat of mathematical legerdemain that the work required to maintain an inclined plane—and by inference an airplane wing—in horizontal flight diminished as the velocity increased. For years to come, this paradoxical assumption, known as Langley's Law, was to gleam like a will-o'-the-wisp on the horizon of every aeronautical experimenter who took it seriously.

While conducting the whirling-table experiments from a distance, Langley began his first real aeronautical studies in Washington, where he tested a number of small model airplanes similar to the rubber-powered models on which Alphonse Pénaud's fragile fame is based. Unproductive in themselves, these small-model tests led to the series of experiments with steam-powered models that culminated in three successful flights over the Potomac River in 1896. When Langley's account of those flights appeared in *McClure's Magazine* the following year, he intimated that he was retiring from the field, having "brought to a close the portion of the work which seemed to be specially mine—the demonstration of the practicability of mechanical flight."

At the same time that he was announcing publicly that he was handing on the torch to others, Langley was seeking help from Octave Chanute and other influential friends in soliciting government funds with which to build a large man-carrying version of his successful models. He did not have long to wait. His *McClure's* article had included a pointed reference to the value of aeronautical surveillance in time of war, a reference that did not go unnoticed by the McKinley administration during the war with Spain. In December 1898 the War Department agreed to pay Langley $50,000 to design and construct a man-carrying airplane for possible military use.

As administrator of the country's most prestigious scientific institution, Langley was in an enviable position when it came to producing such an aircraft, but in some ways the wealth of manpower and resources at his disposal was a hindrance. An accomplished draftsman himself, he required detailed drawings of all parts of his man-carrying Aerodrome, and not until the drawings were approved could the work be carried out. There was no improvisation, no casting about the shop for odds and ends, such as bicycle hubs to use as rollers, nor would it ever have been acceptable for any of the ten machinists and carpenters working on the Aerodrome to heat Arnstein's hard tire cement and pour it into the threads of a sprocket nut that refused to stay tightened.

Although Langley's work in astronomy and astrophysics had given him a well-earned reputation as a scientist, his approach to the problem of mechanical flight was far from scientific. The design and construction of the Aerodrome's wings, which were merely enlarged copies of the wings of the successful tandem models of 1896, were entrusted to an experienced Smithsonian carpenter. There were no preliminary experiments like those carried out in the Wrights' makeshift wind tunnel. Had there been, Langley would have discovered early enough that the sharp leading edges of the Aerodrome's wings produced unnecessary drag, that their curvature was not the most effective, that their aspect ratio—the wings were forty-eight feet from tip to tip but more than eleven feet from front to rear—was all wrong, and that although the wings had a total lifting area of 1,040 square feet, or more than twice that of the Wright Flyer, the tandem arrangement of one wing behind the other produced less lift than a biplane arrangement would have done.

Before beginning work on the Aerodrome, Langley employed as his assistant twenty-two-year-old Charles M. Manly, who came directly to the Smithsonian on graduating from engineering school in June 1898. Manly had a way with motors. Langley had satisfied himself in advance that the New York firm of Stephen M. Balzer could provide a lightweight motor powerful enough to propel the airplane he was about to build, but after spending thousands of dollars in a vain attempt to construct the motor Langley wanted, the Balzer firm was on the verge of bankruptcy. In 1900, Manly took over. He redesigned Balzer's five-cylinder rotary motor and converted it to a water-cooled fixed radial, developing up to 52 horsepower. Considered a marvel in its day, it was to survive two duckings in the Potomac and, like the ill-starred Aerodrome, become a revered museum piece without having any effect whatever on the subsequent development of aviation.

While Manly was perfecting the motor, work on the aircraft went ahead in South Shed, the two-story workshop behind the main Smithsonian building on Washington's Mall. The Aerodrome's framework was of tubular steel, drawn as thin as possible for lightness. The two seven-foot propellers, mounted between the wings on either side of the motor, were made of cloth tightly stretched between wooden arms anchored in metal hubs and secured with guy wires. Langley encountered the same trouble with twisted and buckling propeller shafts that the Wrights were to face in 1903; but this was corrected, and the Aerodrome was all but complete by the end of 1902.

In the meantime, the small, dilapidated houseboat-workshop used to launch the thirty-pound models had been replaced by a new floating workshop large enough to house the full-sized Aerodrome and to sleep a staff of eight workmen and a military guard. It was surmounted by an eighty-five-foot launching track, a turntable, and a powerful spring-loaded catapult. No provision was made for kite or gliding tests of the Aerodrome before its first catapult launching, but Langley, a firm believer in models, had a quarter-size model built in order to study its flying characteristics. Powered by a small gasoline motor, the model made two flights in 1901 and was then laid aside until June 1903, when both the man-carrying Aerodrome and its quarter-size model were placed in the houseboat and towed down the Potomac from Washington and anchored at a wide bend in the river opposite Widewater, Virginia.

Langley had tried to develop the Aerodrome in secrecy, even though news of the project had been leaked to the press a month before the formal agreement with the War Department had been concluded. He gave orders that the grass be allowed to grow long about South Shed to give the impression that the building was unoccupied, but such tactics did not fool newspapermen whose appetite for the sensational had been whetted by the Spanish-American War. It was not surprising, therefore, that a party of reporters should set up camp in July 1903 on the pestiferous banks of the Potomac within sight of the Aerodrome's launching platform, and begin a vigil that was to last for three malarial months. The newsmen's diet of sandwiches during most of that time did little to alleviate their anger at being refused any information at all about what was going on inside the houseboat. They referred to it in their articles as "the ark," and it soon became something of a tourist attraction, gawked at by passengers on the Washington & Richmond Railroad, whose cars passed along the Virginia shore, and by the passengers on the night boat to Norfolk, which trained its searchlight on Langley's ark each night about dark as the steamer passed Widewater.

On August 8, the reporters were rewarded with a flight. It was not the man-carrying Aerodrome that was ejected from the top of the houseboat, however, but the quarter-size model. Manly later compared the flight to that of a huge white moth, a more apt analogy than he may have intended, for the model made a fluttering sort of flight, speeding up and slowing down, rising and falling, covering about 1,000 feet before hitting the water. The 9:30 A.M. launching caught the newsmen by surprise. They reached the scene in their flotilla of rowboats just in time to see a sailcloth thrown over the aircraft as it was being hauled from the river. The next day's Washington *Star* raised such a clamor about the "absurd secrecy" that Manly broke his long silence. The experiment had been entirely successful, he said. The required data had been obtained.

While the experiment proved absolutely nothing about the ability of the large Aerodrome to sustain forward flight, an important lesson might have been drawn from the erratic flight of the model. After the flight it was discovered that the reason for the variations in speed and altitude was that a zealous workman had filled the fuel tank to overflowing, so that gasoline ran into the air intake pipe on the motor. What this demonstrated was the folly of entrusting even such a simple task to an unsupervised workman. Langley himself had not been present. He had taken the train to Widewater the day before, but conditions had not been right for a flight, so he had returned to Washington, leaving up to Manly the decision whether or not to test the model the following day.

Although Samuel Langley had a reputation for refusing to delegate authority, it had been his custom from the whirling-table days to design a program of experimentation and to leave its implementation to others. Little by little he seems to have relinquished conduct of the complex Aerodrome project to young Charles Manly. After the test of August 8, Manly, in a supreme act of delegation on Langley's part, was given authority to make a trial flight in the man-carrying Aerodrome at the earliest opportunity, while the secretary of the Smithsonian went about his business in Washington, thirty-five miles upriver.

Manly's knowledge of every feature of the Aerodrome and its motor, as well as his light weight—125 pounds—made him the ideal candidate for Aerodrome pilot. The pilot would be expected to steer the big machine while standing in the pilot's car, the cloth-surrounded space between the two front wing sections. Like all early experimenters except the Wrights, Langley considered control secondary to automatic stability, and the two steering wheels in the pilot's car had been installed almost as an emergency measure, one to move the tail up or down, the other to control the movement of a vertical cloth rudder positioned between the two pairs of wings. Several years later the Smithsonian Institution issued a lavishly illustrated *Langley Memoir* in which the gear trains and linkages of the Aerodrome's control system were reverently described. Typical of the exquisite care that went into the detailed drawings that preceded their construction is the following thighbone-connected-to-the-shinbone passage illustrating the means by which the tail was connected to one of the wheels in the pilot's car:

Referring to the general plans in Plates 53 and 54, and to the details in Fig. 1 of Plate 56, the main stem of the Pénaud tail is seen to be connected by a pin to the horn (17), which is brazed to the clamping thimble, braced to the rear end of the midrod, the horn (17) being larger than the stem of the tail and set at an angle to the vertical tube (16), the pin connection permitting the tail to swing up and down.

And so on for five more sentences of equivalent length. As for lateral control, there was none, nor had much thought been given to landing the Aerodrome. It was expected to make a flight of a few miles, after which it would simply splash down in the Potomac and the pilot would be picked up by rowboat or tug.

Manly would have preferred a ground-level launching to being catapulted into space from sixty feet above the river, but the launching apparatus had worked for the quarter-size model, and Langley could see no reason why it would not work for the full-sized machine. A more probable reason for this decision was that a large part of the War Department's $50,000 had gone into the fifteen-ton launching apparatus and not to have made use of this costly facility would have been an admission of its basic inutility. As a matter of fact, the War Department money had all been spent long ago. To pay the Aerodrome staff, Langley had had to draw $10,000 from two Smithsonian funds and an additional $13,000 from the Hodgkins Fund, a $250,000 bequest made to the Institution by Englishman Thomas George Hodgkins.

With the money rapidly running out, a favorable day for a test flight did not occur until September 3, but with everything in readiness the Aerodrome's battery produced too weak a spark to start the motor, and the dry cells reserved for such an emergency were found to have deteriorated from the river damp. It was just as well no flight was made. On closer inspection, the glue in the wings was found to have softened. During the next five weeks, while the weather itself deteriorated, the wings were taken apart, reglued, and bound with tape.

On Wednesday, October 7, the weather finally cleared. The telephoto lenses of the cameras on the Virginia shore were focused on the Aerodrome poised on the steel superstructure of the houseboat. Reporters clambered into rowboats and headed for the middle of the river. Two tugboats chugged downstream and anchored in the anticipated line of flight, ready to fish the Aerodrome and its pilot from the water. A little before noon, Manly appeared on the roof of the houseboat in his flying togs—cork-lined life jacket, white duck pants, cap, and automobile goggles. Sewn into his left trouser leg was an aneroid barometer for indicating altitude.

When the engine was started, a skyrocket was fired to alert the photographers on the shore. The tugboats hooted. A second rocket was fired as the catapult was released. With a loud, grinding noise, the Aerodrome shot down the track, the last twenty feet of rail dropping downward at an angle to give it added speed. After leaving the track, the machine continued to travel forward and downward until, in the words of one of the reporters in the rowboats, "it simply slid into the water like a handful of mortar."

Manly grabbed the guy wires above his head as he went under. Pulling himself free, he swam away from the sinking Aerodrome as fast as his cork life jacket would allow. When he looked back and saw that the machine had settled on the shallow river bottom, he paddled back and sat down on the wreckage and waited to be rescued. The first person to reach him in a rowboat was a reporter seeking an interview. Tight-lipped, Manly refused to talk, but as other reporters clustered around and threatened to print their own versions of what had happened, he grudgingly granted a brief interview in which he said the disaster had been caused by improper balancing of the machine.

Langley later issued an official statement from his office in Washington, where he had spent the day, blaming the accident on a guy post that had become caught in the section of the launching track that dropped away as the Aerodrome left the houseboat. The newspapers were less concerned with the cause of the accident than with the fact that Langley's failure vindicated the press's skepticism regarding the possibility of human flight. The Washington *Post* gleefully reported that the Aerodrome was as incapable of flight as a dancing-pavilion floor. The *New York Times* editorialized that a man-carrying airplane would eventually be evolved if mathematicians and mechanics worked steadily for the next one million to ten million years. Overnight the Aerodrome became the butt of popular jokes, on the vaudeville stage as well as in the press.

Langley was not about to give up. The top-heavy houseboat was towed back to Washington and tied up at the foot of Eighth Street, where it could be stared at by any passerby. New wings were fitted to the Aerodrome. The small lug at the end of the plane's forward guy post that was supposed to have caused the accident by catching on the launching track was removed. By mid-November the engine had been thoroughly cleaned and tested, and the reconditioned machine was ready for another trial. Secrecy was no longer possible, so a more convenient site was selected—the point where the Anacostia River flows into the Potomac, about two miles due south of the Smithsonian building.

Tuesday, December 8, began as an ideal day for a flight. An almost perfect calm prevailed over the Potomac. Word that something was afoot spread throughout the capital and by noon the waterfront at Eighth Street was crowded with curious onlookers. River traffic on the icy river was light in December, and it was late afternoon before a tugboat could be found to tow the houseboat to the new test site. Its progress was plainly visible to watchers with binoculars and spyglasses from the highest tower of the Smithsonian castle. What they saw was not especially reassuring. The river's surface was dotted with floating ice. A shifting wind had come up, and the wings of the Aerodrome on the launching track, sixty feet above the water, were being buffeted by gusts of up to 18 miles an hour, first from one side, then from the other. The decision to make a flight under such unfavorable conditions had been left up to Manly. Langley's exact whereabouts on that gloomy afternoon are uncertain. The *New York Times* reported that he was on the tug. Other accounts placed him on the houseboat. Manly decided to go ahead. Not wanting to be hampered by excess clothing when he came down in the water, he was attired only in long underwear, stockings, light shoes, and a cork-lined life jacket. Dr. Francis Nash, a military surgeon, stood by on the houseboat in case his services were needed.

It was almost dark when the restraining cable was released and the Aerodrome darted forward into the gloom. Once again there was a crashing, rending sound as it left the starting track. Instead of following a slanting path into the water, it quivered upward until it was in a nose-up position, where it was sustained for a fraction of a second by the whirling propellers. Then with the wind threatening to drive it backward onto the houseboat, it slipped tail first into the icy Potomac.

For the second time in his life, Manly found himself in the water beneath the twisted Aerodrome. His life jacket was caught in the metal fittings of the upended pilot's car and his head was pressing against its floor. Tearing himself loose from the life jacket, he dove and rose to the surface, only to bump his head against the underside of a cake of ice. He made another dive and surfaced just as one of the workmen on the houseboat plunged into the freezing water to come to his aid. Both men were hauled to safety as Langley watched. Inside the houseboat, Dr. Nash cut the frozen underwear from Manly's body, wrapped his shivering patient in blankets, and administered half a tumblerful of whiskey, a course of treatment that caused the well-bred Manly to deliver (in the words of a member of the Smithsonian staff who was present) "the most voluble series of blasphemies that I have ever heard in my life."

Outside, in the cold and the dark, Langley was treated to still another unhappy sight. In their eagerness to salvage the damaged Aerodrome before it sank, the crews of the tugboat and the houseboat fastened a line to the tail and yanked it forward so vigorously the framework snapped in two. As the pieces of the Aerodrome were lashed to the stern of the houseboat like a harpooned whale, Langley's sixteen-year experiment in aerodynamics came to an ignominious end.

A halfhearted attempt was made to blame the failure on the launching mechanism again, but it is generally conceded today that inherent structural weakness was the cause. The only photograph taken at the time tends to bear this out. The light was too faint for the fast-shuttered official cameras, but an alert newspaper photographer managed to snap a picture from a nearby rowboat. Blurred, grainy, and underexposed, the photograph catches the twisted frame and tail and crumpled rear wings of the Aerodrome in the act of disintegrating, at the moment the big machine begins its downward plunge into the Potomac.

The devastating and prolonged uproar in the newspapers over the Aerodrome's second failure was the press's revenge for Langley's penchant for secrecy. It struck a responsive chord in a public only too willing to poke fun at professors and scientists in general and at the Smithsonian's "stuffers of birds and rabbits" in particular. Despite the howls of derision from all quarters, including Congress, Langley wanted to carry on his experiments, but the War Department's report on the tests put an end to his hopes, and he died in 1906, presumably of a broken heart. The last three years of his life were not particularly happy ones, but if a broken heart caused his death, it was occasioned less by the failure of his Aerodrome than by a scandal that broke in 1905, involving the embezzlement of $70,000 of Smithsonian funds by one of his most trusted associates. A brief biography written the year of his death by his good friend Cyrus Adler concludes with this ringing tribute to Langley's contribution to the future of aviation:

> Whatever form this may take or whatever modification may be made as to the result of experiment, the laws of aerodynamics will be the laws which Mr. Langley discovered, and the aeroplane or other form of machine heavier than air will be based upon the models which he made and which actually flew.

But Langley's Law, the only law of aerodynamics for which the secretary of the Smithsonian was famous, has long since been discredited, and his tandem-wing models of 1896 had no progeny.

The only significant contributions made by Samuel Pierpont Langley to the future of aviation, then, were the flights of his two thirty-pound models of 1896. This was the part of Langley's work that Wilbur Wright was referring to in a letter he wrote to the new secretary of the Smithsonian in 1910, in which he pointed out that although the first practical demonstration of the possibility of mechanical flight had been claimed by others, Langley's demonstration had a convincing character that none of the others possessed. "It had a great influence in determining my brother and myself to take up work in this science," Wilbur wrote, "and without doubt it similarly influenced others."

# 16

## *The First Four Flights*

THE NEW PROPELLER shafts were installed on the Flyer Saturday
morning, December 12, the day after Orville returned to Kill Devil Hills.
The machine was rolled out of the shed and placed on the starting track that
afternoon, but the wind was too light to risk taking off from the level ground
with only sixty feet of track. The wind freshened the next day, but as usual
on Sunday, they neither worked on the machine nor attempted to fly.

The wind on Monday, December 14, was again not strong enough for
taking off from the level. The Wright brothers were determined to make a
flight, however, and decided to move the starting rail and the machine to
Big Hill for a downhill start. At half past one, they ran up a prearranged
signal on a pole at one end of the Flyer's shed, where it would be visible to
the men at the Kill Devil lifesaving station. Not wanting to make a flight
without witnesses, they had extended a blanket invitation in advance to
everyone within a radius of six miles of their camp, including all the inhabi-
tants of Kitty Hawk, the few year-round residents of Nags Head, and the
fishermen in isolated cottages in between. The impracticality of alerting so
scattered a population by flying a signal from one of their camp buildings
had not escaped them, but they knew they could at least count on the
presence and help of the surfmen and anyone who happened to be in the Kill
Devil lifesaving station at the time.

Shortly after putting out the signal, they were joined by five men from
the station, two small boys, and a dog. The men helped move the heavy Flyer
the quarter of a mile to Big Hill, balancing it by hand while rolling it
along the rail, moving each fifteen-foot section of the track from the rear to
the front as they went along. The entire sixty feet of track was then laid on
the hillside on a gentle slope of about 9 degrees, and the Flyer was placed
in position at the high end of the track. Before starting the motor, a photo-

graph was taken of the machine, with four of the men, the two boys, and the dog lined up alongside. When the propellers were turned over, their noisy paddling and the clatter of the transmission chains made such a terrifying addition to the motor's racket that the dog and the two small boys took to their heels.

Wilbur and Orville tossed a coin for first whack. Wilbur won. He lay down on the lower wing with his hips in the padded wingwarping cradle, while Orville made a last-minute adjustment to the motor. When everything was ready, Wilbur tried to release the rope fastening the machine to the rail, but the thrust of the propellers was so great he could not get it loose and two of the men had to forcibly push the Flyer backward a few inches until the rope slipped free. Orville ran beside the machine, balancing it with one hand. In the other hand he held a stopwatch, which he started as the Flyer lifted from the rail.

Wilbur turned the big front rudder up sharply, not realizing how sensitive it would be in flight. The Flyer surged quickly upward until it was almost fifteen feet above the hillside, losing headway as it climbed. To regain speed, Wilbur turned the rudder down too far. The Flyer sank to the ground in a nose-up position. In the excitement, he forgot to shut off the motor. The left wing hit the side of the hill, and the machine slewed around, digging the skids deep into the sand, breaking one of them, and splintering a strut, a brace, and a spar in the front rudder. It was all over in 3 1/2 seconds. Although the Flyer had traveled over 100 feet, the Wright brothers did not consider this a true flight. All the same, they were elated. The test had proved four important things about the untried Flyer. Its strength in flight was satisfactory, the motor was reliable, the power sufficient, and the launching system both safe and practical. There was now no question of final success.

Anxious for the good word to reach home as quickly as possible, Wilbur sent a telegram to his father the next day from the Kitty Hawk Weather Bureau station: "Misjudgment at start reduced flight one hundred twelve power and control ample rudder only injured success assured keep quiet." The secretive ring of that "keep quiet" was deceptive. On the very day that Wilbur was making his unsuccessful attempt to fly, Bishop Wright back in Dayton had been preparing a typewritten description of the Wright Flyer and a brief biographical sketch of his two youngest sons for release to the press—but not until a satisfactory flight had been made.

Wilbur and Orville worked all day Tuesday on repairs and completed the work at noon on Wednesday. The wind was at last strong enough for a start from level, so they laid the track in the sand near the Flyer's shed and took out the machine. By the time it was set up on the track, the wind had dropped. They decided to wait until it rose again before alerting the men at the lifesaving station on the beach.

A stranger came along while they waited. He stopped plodding through the sand long enough to look at the Flyer on the starting rail and ask what it was. A flying machine, said the brothers. Did they intend to fly it? the stranger wanted to know. They replied that they did, as soon as they had a suitable wind. The stranger looked at the machine for a while longer, then said he reckoned it would fly—if it had a suitable wind! Ten years later, when Orville retold the events of that week in the magazine *Flying,* he speculated that what the stranger had in mind when he repeated their words "a suitable wind" was the 75-mile-an-hour gale of early October. There is no mention of an unidentified stranger in Orville's 1903 diary. The entry for December 16 ends uneventfully. "After waiting several hours to see whether it would breeze up again we took the machine in."

During the early morning hours of Thursday, December 17, the wind rose. By dawn the puddles and ponds left in the hollows around the camp by the recent rains were encrusted with ice. After breakfast, Wilbur and Orville went outside and measured the wind with their hand-held anemometer. It was not quite gale strength, a cold, gusty north wind of from 22 to 27 miles per hour. They went back indoors to wait for the wind to slacken, but at no time that morning did it drop below 20 miles per hour. With their minds set on being home by Christmas, they decided to go ahead. At 10 A.M. they hung out the signal for the men in the lifesaving station.

While waiting for the station men to show up, they laid the starting rail in the sand in a slight hollow that had been a shallow puddle a few days before. The wind had whipped it dry, leaving a hard-packed, practically level surface, ideal for supporting the crossties under the track. From time to time they went inside the camp building to warm their hands at the carbide-can stove. Before they finished laying the starting rail, three men from the lifesaving station showed up—John Daniels, described by Orville as a giant in stature and strength; Will Dough, who had been present at Wilbur's abortive flight on Monday; and Adam Etheridge. A fourth surfman, Bob Westcott, had been left in charge of the station back on the beach. He went up in the tower of the station house and trained a spyglass on the Wright camp.

The lifesaving stations on the Outer Banks were sociable, hospitable places in those days. It was not unusual for men and boys to walk the beach with the men on patrol or to drop into the station house for a visit and stay for supper. Two such hangers-on followed the three surfmen to the Wright camp that morning—W. D. Brinkley, a lumber buyer from Manteo, who was investigating the possibility of salvaging lumber from one of the recent wrecks off the coast, and Johnny Moore, a teenager from Nags Head. Wilbur and Orville had laid the starting rail close to the camp buildings to lighten the work of moving the 600-pound Flyer from its shed to the launching site. The men helped them set the machine on the track. Then the motor was started and given a chance to warm up.

It was Orville's whack now. He lay down with his hips in the padded cradle and the toes of his shoes hooked over the small supporting rack on the trailing edge of the wing. He did not don automobile goggles like Charles Manly before his first precipitous plunge into the Potomac on Langley's Aerodrome, nor did he have an aneroid barometer sewed into his trouser leg for indicating altitude. Both he and Wilbur that morning wore their usual business suits, starched collars, neckties, and caps.

At 10:35 Orville slipped the rope restraining the Flyer. It started slowly down the track, Wilbur holding the right wingtip to balance it on the rail. On Monday, Orville had been unable to keep up with Wilbur's headlong dash down the slope of Big Hill. On Thursday, Wilbur had no trouble keeping up with Orville as the Flyer rolled down the track against a wind of more than 20 miles an hour. The Flyer's speed through the air when it reached the end of the track was close to 30 miles per hour, but its speed over the ground was only about 7 miles per hour, making it possible to record the start of the flight on one of the slow photographic plates of 1903, even though the sky was overcast. Orville had set the camera on its tripod before the flight, focusing the center of the ground glass on a point just short of the end of the track. Before taking his place on the Flyer he had inserted a plate holder in the back of the camera, withdrawn the black slide, and entrusted the rubber bulb that activated the shutter to the large hand of John Daniels, after instructing the surfman to squeeze the bulb as the Flyer neared the end of the track.

Daniels did exactly that. As the clattering machine lifted into the air and the wooden truck under its skids dropped away in the sand, the camera shutter clicked open and for a fraction of a second light poured through the lens, impressing its pattern of bright and dark on a five-by-seven-inch glass plate. Then the shutter snapped shut, trapping inside the black bellows of the camera one of the great moments of this century. It would be several days before the first print made from the fragile glass-plate negative would emerge from its bath of developer in the red-lit darkroom behind the house on Hawthorn Street in Dayton. When it did, it would reveal a photograph of accidental excellence, but Orville was too busy that December morning to worry whether Daniels had snapped the shutter at the right moment or not. Like Wilbur on December 14, he was finding that the big two-surfaced front rudder, turned sharply upward at the moment of takeoff, was difficult to manipulate. It was balanced so near the center that the slightest movement of the control lever started it moving upward or downward of its own accord, with the result that the Flyer would rise until it was about ten feet in the air and then, when the direction of the rudder was reversed, dart suddenly for the ground. One of these downward darts ended the first flight about 100 feet from the end of the starting track, or about 120 feet from the point where it had risen from the rail. The impact cracked one of the skids and set the stopwatch on the flight-recording instrument back to zero. Wilbur in the excitement of the moment forgot to stop the stopwatch in his hand, so the time of the flight had to be estimated. They made it 12 seconds.

The true import of those few seconds in the air, as compared to all other flights made by man before 10:35 A.M., December 17, 1903, has nowhere been expressed as accurately and concisely as in Orville's 1913 *Flying* article, where he described the flight as

the first in the history of the world in which a machine carrying a man had raised itself by its own power into the air in full flight, had sailed forward without reduction of speed, and had finally landed at a point as high as that from which it started.

The witnesses of the flight helped Wilbur and Orville carry the machine back to the starting track, where repairs were made to the cracked skid. Then all six men and Johnny Moore went inside the camp building to warm up. Not much is known about the boy Johnny Moore (his age is given as sixteen in one place, eighteen in another) aside from the fact that he was a year-round resident of Nags Head who caught crabs for a living. A story survives about the Moore family cow, which refused to come home to be milked when its calf died, whereupon Johnny and his mother, who told fortunes for twenty-five cents a head, skinned the calf, stuffed the skin with straw, and propped a false calf against a fence to lure its mother home. That's all that is known of Johnny Moore until December 17, 1903, when his lifeline crosses that of the chicken that has been haunting the Wright story since 1900, when Orville wrote a letter to his sister from Kitty Hawk while sitting on an empty chicken coop. In 1903, only a year after Augustus Herring woke his sleeping campmates at Kill Devil Hills at 2 A.M. to announce that the chicken had been stolen by a fox, the imperishable chicken makes another appearance.

Laying hens were scarce on the Outer Banks. As the men warmed their hands around the stove in the Wrights' living quarters, Johnny spotted a box of eggs under the kitchen table. He had never seen so many eggs in one place before and asked one of the men from the lifesaving station where the Wrights got them. The station man feigned surprise. Hadn't Johnny seen the small hen running about outside? It laid eight to ten eggs a day. Johnny went outside to inspect the high-yield hen. A few minutes later he came back in and reported, "It's only a common-looking chicken." Common-looking or not, what was a small hen doing running around outside the Wright camp building in a 20- to 27-mile-an-hour wind on December 17, 1903? The unanswered question lends a dreamlike resonance to that otherwise well-documented morning, as if the little creature is running about the camp building still, in an eternal December wind—just as that mysterious stranger of the day before will be forever trudging through the sand at the foot of Big Kill Devil Hill, brooding about the "suitable wind" whose hurricane force would make it possible for the Wright Flyer to fly.

The small hen, if she hadn't already been blown away, retreated to the far side of the camp building when the Flyer's noisy motor was started again at 11:20, and Wilbur took off on the second flight of the day. He too had trouble with the large front rudder, and his flight, like Orville's, was an undulating one. Although the two flights were about the same in duration, the second flight covered an estimated 175 feet. The increase in distance was attributed to a slackening in the speed of the wind.

Half an hour later, Orville made the third flight. They had decided to make all flights as close to the ground as possible. While safer, this made it difficult to maneuver in gusty winds. Both brothers were gratified, however, to find that the response of the warping mechanism was so much more prompt and effective in fast powered flight than in slow glides. Orville was prepared now for the peculiar behavior of the sensitive front rudder and made more careful adjustments, so his flight was steadier and longer than Wilbur's—a little over 200 feet in 15 seconds. It ended when a side gust lifted the Flyer from twelve to fifteen feet in the air, after which the wind, in Orville's words, "sidled the machine off to the side in a lively manner." Wilbur took a picture of the machine from the rear just before it landed, with the right wing almost touching the ground. It is not a photograph to go down in history, but it was the only one taken of the 1903 Flyer in the air beyond the end of the starting rail.

At noon Wilbur made the fourth and longest flight of the day. By the time he had covered 300 feet he was more familiar with the feel of the front rudder. His progress was less undulating, and the Flyer ambled along on a more or less even keel, its motor popping confidently, the large propellers biting the cold wind, the transmission chains clanking in their metal-tube guides. There is no telling how much farther Wilbur might have flown across the sandy plain if he had not turned up the front rudder to clear a small hummock about 800 feet from the starting point and, when he turned the rudder down again, turned it down too far, so that the Flyer plowed into the sand. Its speed over the ground against the strong wind had never been more than 10 miles an hour, so Wilbur was not thrown from the machine, but the front rudder frame was badly smashed.

The times and distances of the first three flights had only been estimated. The fourth flight was carefully measured—852 feet in 59 seconds. Two photographs were taken of the Flyer after it landed. One, taken from the camp, showed the starting rail so that the relatively small size of the Flyer would serve as pictorial proof of its distance from the end of the track. The other, taken at the landing site, showed the damage to the front rudder. When the picture taking was over, the station men helped the Wrights carry the machine back to the camp and set it down outside the shed. As they stood a few feet away, talking over the last, long flight, a powerful gust of wind got under the wings of the Flyer and flipped it over.

The men rushed to hold it down. Wilbur grabbed the uprights in front, but the wind threatened to carry his slight frame away with the machine and he let the wooden struts slip through his fingers. Orville and John Daniels grabbed the rear uprights. Orville had to let go, but Daniels retained his grip and was carried along inside the Flyer, entangled in the rigging wires. As Orville described it later, the large surfman was shaken about like a rattle in a box until the Flyer finally came to a stop and he rolled out on the sand, scared but sound. The others considered it a miracle that he had escaped with only a few painful bruises and scratches.

The damage to the Flyer was more serious. Almost all the ribs of both wings were broken beyond the rear spars. One spar and a number of uprights were splintered. The legs of the engine frame had all snapped off, and the chain guides were badly bent. There would be no more flights in the 1903 Flyer. After their helpers returned to the lifesaving station, Wilbur and Orville had lunch. Then they washed the dishes and set off on the windy four-mile walk to Kitty Hawk to send the wire countermanding Wilbur's cryptic injunction to his father in Tuesday's telegram ("success assured keep quiet").

Joseph Dosher was still manning the telegraph key at the Weather Bureau station on the beach. He tapped out Orville's telegram to Bishop Wright on the afternoon of December 17 while in another corner of the room the brothers examined the wind velocities for the day on the bureau's wind-recording instrument.

That their Flyer had gotten off the ground was no longer news in Kitty Hawk. Captain S. J. Payne of the Kitty Hawk lifesaving station just down the beach must have been informed by phone of the impending flights by Bob Westcott at the Kill Devil station, for he claimed to have seen at least one of the flights through a spyglass. The plain between Kitty Hawk and Kill Devil Hills was as bare of vegetation as a desert, so the captain's line of sight would have been unobstructed, but even with the most powerful glass, it is doubtful that he could have made out much of what was going on at the Wright camp from his three-story perch above the beach—four miles away.

Whether Joseph Dosher, Captain Payne, or anyone else in Kitty Hawk realized the sensational nature of the events of that day is something else again, but somebody at the Norfolk end of the Weather Bureau wire evidently did. Before James Gray, the Norfolk operator, had a chance to relay Orville's message to Western Union for transmittal to Dayton, he was back on the wire with a question for Dosher in Kitty Hawk. Would it be all right to give the news to a reporter friend?

Wilbur and Orville's answer was an unequivocal no. Orville had already spelled out a plan of action for the release of the news in a letter to his father and sister four weeks before: "If we should succeed in making a flight, and telegraph, we will expect Lorin as our press agent (!) to notify the papers and the Associated Press." Orville's exclamation point was significant. The Wright brothers were not shunning publicity, they were actually courting it—but on their own terms and in their own good time.

# 17

## Fiction and Fact

I T   W A S   A L M O S T  dark when  Carrie Kayler went into the kitchen of the house on Hawthorn Street to prepare the evening meal for Bishop Wright and Katharine. She had just lit the gas jet in the kitchen when the doorbell rang. It was a Western Union messenger with a telegram for the bishop. Carrie signed for it and after taking it upstairs to Milton Wright's study went on about her business in the kitchen.

In a little while Bishop Wright came downstairs with the telegram in his hand, looking pleased. "Well, they made a flight," he told Carrie. When Katharine walked in the door a few minutes later, he gave her the telegram to read:

> Success four flights thursday morning all against twenty one mile wind started from Level with engine power alone average speed through air thirty one miles longest 57 seconds inform Press home # # # # Christmas.
>
> Orevelle Wright   525P

The message had suffered in transmission. Capital letters appeared where they should not, a word had been crossed out, "Orville" had been misspelled, and Wilbur's long flight had shrunk from 59 to 57 seconds, but there was no mistaking the words "inform Press." Katharine Wright, prim schoolteacher with the pince-nez, knew what was expected of her. Telling Carrie not to serve the meal until she returned, she walked the four blocks to Lorin's house and gave the telegram to her brother, who was eating his dinner. Either on the way home or shortly thereafter, she sent a wire to Octave Chanute announcing the successful flights. Only then did she sit down to dinner with her father. The two of them were in high spirits that night. It was Carrie's impression that the euphoria was created less by news of the four flights than by the certainty that Wilbur and Orville would be home for Christmas.

Lorin Wright didn't let his duties as press agent interfere with his dinner. He finished eating before making the rounds of the Dayton newspaper offices with the telegram and copies of the typewritten statement prepared by Bishop Wright three days before. At the Dayton *Journal* office he killed two birds with one stone by telling his story to Frank Tunison, who represented the Associated Press in Dayton. But Frank Tunison was unimpressed. Like most editors, he had been convinced of the impracticality of heavier-than-air flight by the failure of Langley's Aerodrome. If the Wrights' longest flight had been 57 minutes instead of 57 seconds as in the telegram, he told Lorin, it might be worth a mention. As all newspaper readers knew, the Brazilian daredevil Alberto Santos-Dumont had been making much longer flights up and down the boulevards of Paris in his semi-rigid airship all last summer. A flight of less than a minute in North Carolina could not possibly be of interest to readers of the *Journal* or its city editor—or the Associated Press.

Two Dayton papers did print news of the flights the next day. The *Daily News* relegated the story to an inside page under the heading DAYTON BOYS EMULATE GREAT SANTOS-DUMONT. The *Evening Herald,* likewise unable to distinguish between a gasbag and an airplane, carried a page-one headline: DAYTON BOYS FLY AIRSHIP. The Cincinnati, Ohio, *Enquirer* also printed the news on its front page under what Bishop Wright denounced as "flaming headlines."

The stories in the Dayton *Evening Herald* and the Cincinnati *Enquirer* were not fruits of Lorin's press agentry. Both stories were datelined Norfolk, Virginia, where Orville's telegram to his father had been taken off the Weather Bureau wire by James Gray for transfer to Western Union. There are two versions of what happened after Gray tapped a message back to Dosher at Kitty Hawk, asking permission to give the news to a reporter friend, and the Wrights turned him down.

In the version current during Orville's lifetime, Gray's reporter friend was Harry P. Moore of the Norfolk newspaper *Virginian-Pilot.* Gray may not have shown Moore the telegram but he must have revealed its contents, for Moore tried to pin down the facts by long-distance telephoning, probably to the lifesaving station at Kill Devil Hills. Moore or someone did get information from a source other than the telegram, since the headlines on page one of the December 18 *Virginian-Pilot* included four facts not in Orville's wire: the vehicle was a heavier-than-air apparatus, not an airship; it was built on the box-kite principle (that is, it was a biplane); it had two propellers; and the brothers had spent years of hard work before achieving success.

The second version of how the news was leaked in Norfolk did not find its way into print until three years after Orville's death. In that version, Gary's reporter friend was Ed Dean, who regularly covered the Weather Bureau for the *Virginian-Pilot.* Dean and the paper's city editor put the story together on the night of December 17, and it was not until their words were about to be set in type that Harry Moore appeared and asked the city editor if he knew about the flight. Moore was not even a reporter at the time. He worked in the paper's business office and it was never clear just how he managed to hear of the flights. Whichever version is true, Dean or Moore, or maybe both, worked with the city editor to beef up the few known facts into a gaudy page-one news item with no fewer than five headlines. The first headline ran all across the top of page one of Friday's *Virginian-Pilot:*

FLYING MACHINE SOARS 3 MILES IN TEETH OF HIGH WIND OVER
SAND HILLS AND WAVES AT KITTY HAWK ON CAROLINA COAST

This was followed by four smaller headlines:

NO BALLOON
ATTACHED
TO AID IT

Two Years of Hard, Secret
Work by Two Ohio Brothers
Crowned with Success

ACCOMPLISHED WHAT
LANGLEY FAILED

With Man as Passenger Huge
Machine Flew Like Bird
Under Perfect Control

"The problem of aerial navigation without the use of a balloon has been solved" was the first sentence under the last headline. The chief inventor was "Wilber" Wright. "Wilber" was well groomed, raven-haired, and swarthy. He had piercing deep blue eyes and an extremely long sharp nose. His brother Orville was sandy-haired. He had sparkling black eyes and a magnificent physique. The flying machine was likened to a big box that rose to a height of sixty feet, thanks to the action of an "underwheel." Both brothers were elated with the flight. Both were quoted. " 'It is a success,' declared

Orville Wright to the crowd on the beach after the first mile had been covered." When "Wilber" landed at the end of his three-mile flight, he let himself go. " 'Eureka,' he cried, as did the alchemist of old."

The *Virginian-Pilot* story was offered to twenty-one other papers by wire. Only five bought it, and only one, the Cincinnati *Enquirer* with the flaming headlines, put it on the front page. Once the ice was broken, the Associated Press relented and distributed the story to its subscribers, adding a few inventions of its own, such as a fan-shaped rudder protruding from the navigator's car, six-bladed propellers, and a hillside launching device.

The house on Hawthorn Street was soon besieged by the press. On December 22, reporters called all day long, asking for pictures of the brothers and their flying machine. Other inquiries arrived by mail. "My sons Wilbur and Orville are expected under the parental roof—always their home —within a few days, when they will read your letter of the 19th inst.," was the bishop's reply to one such request. Until then, he wished to clear up a few misrepresentations. "All reported as to what Orville or Wilbur said is not unlikely, but probably mythical." (So much for Wilbur's "Eureka!") He also labeled as mythical the "push upward" and added a touchingly accurate postscript on the relationship of his two youngest sons:

> P.S. Wilbur is 36, Orville 32, and they are as inseparable as twins. For several years they have read up on aeronautics as a physician would read his books, and they have studied, discussed, and experimented together. Natural workmen, they have invented, constructed, and operated their gliders, and finally their "Wright Flyer," jointly, all at their own personal expense. About equal credit is due each.

Press inquiries were not restricted to Dayton. On the morning of December 19, as Wilbur and Orville were breaking up camp and crating the dismembered Flyer for shipment back to Dayton, they received two telegrams. The *Woman's Home Companion* asked for photographs. The New York *World* wanted to know the brothers' price for exclusive rights to their story. Later in the day John Daniels, recovered from his bruising experience inside the wind-toppled Flyer, came over from the lifesaving station with another batch of telegrams. The insistent New York *World* now asked that the brothers wire a 600-word account to them at once; the *Scientific American* wanted pictures; the *Century Magazine* wanted their exclusive story, with photographs. One of the telegrams was from Octave Chanute: "Pleased at your success. When ready to make public please advise me." The telegram that interested them most was the inquiry from the popular monthly, the *Century Magazine,* but all that the Wrights cared about at the moment was getting home by Christmas. Even Octave Chanute was made to wait for a reply—but not as long as the four and a half years the *Century Magazine* would have to wait for the exclusive story the brothers eventually promised it.

On December 23, Orville got off the train at Huntington, West Virginia, long enough to send a final telegram to 7 Hawthorn Street: "Have survived perilous trip reported in papers. Home tonight." They were met at the train in Dayton by Katharine, their father, brother Lorin, and a handful of reporters. The reporters were handled with dispatch according to Bishop Wright, that minor Pepys, who recorded the encounter in his diary thus: "They had some interviewers in the way but suppressed them."

Carrie had prepared a feast for the family's first meal together in three months. There was more of everything in the kitchen, with the unfortunate exception of fresh milk. Milk had been in short supply on the Outer Banks and Orville's thirst for this delicacy was such that Carrie, after refilling his glass several times, found it necessary to add a little water as a "stretcher." The deception was detected by Orville, who accused Carrie of dairying the milk—a phrase that was promptly added to the lexicon of Wright family expressions.

The traditional Christmas dinner took place at Lorin's house. Those austere Christmases that Lorin's generation remembered—with a single orange and an inexpensive present at each place on the breakfast table Christmas morning—belonged to the past. Orville's Christmas present to Katharine that year was a set of silver forks and pearl-handled table knives. Remembrances of some sort were received from that inveterate gift-giver Octave Chanute and were duly acknowledged by Wilbur three days after Christmas.

Since Katharine's telegram of December 17, Chanute had been left in the dark, wondering just how many of the fantastic details about the Wright flights he read in the papers were true. Christmas came and went without any word from Dayton. On December 27, sounding more puzzled than piqued, he wrote a short note to Wilbur, with this plaintive opening paragraph: "I have had no letter from you since I left your camp, but your sister kindly wired me the results of your test of Dec. 17. Did you write?" He was leaving for St. Louis that night to address the winter meeting of the American Association for the Advancement of Science on the subject of aerial navigation. "It is fitting that you should be the first to give the Association the first scientific account of your performance. Will you do so?"

Wilbur's immediate response was a telegram: "We are giving no pictures nor descriptions of machine or methods at present." This somewhat peremptory message was followed by a letter written the same day. The letter included a full and satisfying account of the four flights of December 17, but no explanation of why their old friend had been left cooling his heels for so long. Nor did Wilbur explain why they had refused to prepare a statement for Chanute to deliver to such a distinguished organization as the American Association for the Advancement of Science. They had their reasons of course. Chanute's talk to the Aéro-Club de France in Paris earlier that year, in which he had revealed details of their control system and intimated that the brothers were pupils of his, made Wilbur and Orville think twice before permitting the elderly Chicagoan to speak for them again. Several times during the past year, Chanute had placed serious strains on his friendship with the Wrights by his inability to comprehend or appreciate what they were trying to accomplish. Consciously or unconsciously, they must have resented the last sentence of the letter he had written Katharine, thanking her for her telegram announcing the four flights ("I earnestly hope that they will do better"). That remark could well have been in the back of Wilbur's mind when he wrote in his letter to Chanute describing the events of December 17: "Those who understand the real significance of the conditions under which we worked will be surprised rather at the length than the shortness of the flights made with an unfamiliar machine after less than one minute's practice."

Chanute's address to the scientists meeting in St. Louis on December 30 included only the briefest mention of the flights by the Wright brothers. "How they accomplished this," he added, "must be reserved for them to explain." Explain they did, six days later, in a carefully worded statement to the Associated Press, deploring the *Virginian-Pilot*'s fictitious story and presenting their own 500-word factual report of the four flights of December 17. Then this:

> As winter was already well set in, we should have postponed our trials to a more favorable season, but for the fact that we were determined, before returning home, to know whether the machine possessed sufficient capacity of control to make flight safe in boisterous winds, as well as in calm air. When these points had been definitely established, we at once packed our goods and returned home, knowing that the age of the flying machine had come at last.

They encountered the usual difficulties in getting their story to the public. All but one paper omitted the paragraph decrying the numerous falsified accounts already published. One paper converted Wilbur's 852-foot flight to a flight made 852 feet up in the air. And more than one editor, mindful of the Langley fiasco, made sneering references to Wilbur and Orville's conclusion that the age of the flying machine had come at last. That much-abused expression had been used so often before, by Alexander Graham Bell and Octave Chanute among others, that the world at large remained unconvinced.

When the boxes containing the dismantled Flyer finally arrived in Dayton, they were stored in a shed behind the bicycle shop, where they would remain for many years, all but forgotten. Their contents had little or no value, historic or otherwise, in 1903. Charlie Taylor remembered, when he was eighty, that Wilbur and Orville's first words to him when they were back in the bicycle shop had to do with building a new motor to replace the one damaged after the Flyer's last flight. "They were always thinking of the next thing to do," said Charlie. "They didn't waste much time worrying about the past."

# 18

## *The Year of the Fair*

WHEN THE Wright brothers returned to Dayton in December 1903, they faced the toughest decision they would ever have to make. Wilbur described their situation in a letter written some time later: "We found ourselves standing at a fork in the road. On the one hand we could continue playing with the problem of flying so long as youth and leisure would permit but carefully avoiding those features which would require continuous effort and expenditure of considerable sums of money. On the other hand we believed that if we would take the risk of devoting our entire time and financial resources we could conquer the difficulties in the path to success before increasing years impaired our physical activity."

In the end, the Wrights had no choice. On December 17, 1903, the gates of their uneventful middle-class existence had banged shut behind them. There was no turning back.

The decision was made a little easier by the fact that, although the edge was off the bicycle business, they were financially secure, at least for a time. In January 1904 they had $4,900 tucked away in two savings and loan associations in Dayton. Most of the money had come from the sale of a 320-acre farm near Casey, Iowa. The farm had been owned by Bishop Wright until 1902, when he sold it at the request of Reuchlin and divided the money equally among his four sons. Rather than abandon the business altogether, they decided to ease themselves out of it gradually. Bicycles already in production would be completed and sold. Any repair jobs that came in would be handled by Charlie Taylor when he was not working on the new Flyer under construction in the workroom behind the bicycle shop. For practice, they would need a flying field suitably isolated but not too far from home. They found just such a site eight miles northeast of Dayton at Simms Station, a stop on the interurban trolley line that ran to Springfield,

Ohio. Paralleling the trolley tracks was a wagon road known as the Dayton–Springfield Pike. At Simms Station it crossed the road running southeast to Yellow Springs, a small college town below Springfield. Within the protective elbow of the crossroads was Huffman Prairie, part of a dairy farm owned by Torrence Huffman, president of the Fourth National Bank of Dayton. Huffman agreed to let the Wrights use the land rent-free on condition that they shoo any grazing cows and horses out of the way before making any flights.

Huffman Prairie was irregular in shape, a quarter of a mile wide, almost half a mile long, and so covered with grassy hummocks that Wilbur once likened it to a prairie-dog town. They would have to watch out for trees, but there were only half a dozen of these, all close to the barbed-wire fence with the exception of a single honey locust, which could easily be avoided if they flew an oval course within the confines of the field. The one disadvantage was that everything that went on at the site was visible to traffic on the two roads that bordered the field and to passengers in the Dayton–Springfield interurban cars. In time, Amos Stauffer, whose cornfield bounded the pasture on the east and south, and David Beard, who tenant-farmed the land across the Springfield Pike, could be counted on to become accustomed to the sight of the white-winged Flyer. The same could not be said of the passengers in the passing trolleys, but prying eyes could be eluded by timing flights between the passages of the cars.

Another possible disadvantage of the new setting—which bothered Wilbur and Orville not at all—was that at Huffman Prairie in 1904 the Wright story loses its allure for those who have fallen under the spell of what has come to be called the Kitty Hawk mystique. There would be no seabirds wheeling and squealing over the prairie, no sound of surf, just the jingle of farmers' teams passing up and down the road to Springfield or Yellow Springs and the interurban cars, with their wrought-iron baggage racks and chattering chandeliers, hissing to a stop at Simms Station. No miracles would take place in banker Huffman's pasture. The long, slow process of perfecting an imperfect flying machine would be as tedious at times as the sowing of corn by farmer Stauffer in the adjoining field, but the harvest, when it came, would be more bountiful than those four brief flights over the sandy plain between Kitty Hawk and Big Kill Devil Hill.

Work on the flying machine went on all winter back in the bicycle shop in spite of interruptions, diversions, and distractions. A satisfactory patent would have to be filed if the Wrights were to receive a return on the money they were about to invest in their invention. In 1903 they had been rebuffed by the Patent Office when they bypassed the legal profession and filed their own patent. Now they sought professional advice. Wilbur made two trips to Springfield in January 1904 to consult with patent attorney Harry A.

Toulmin. To avoid the possibility of having to make a demonstration of their Flyer to satisfy the patent examiners, who were known to be skeptical when it came to power flight but accepted glider flights as a reality, Toulmin persuaded the brothers that their patent should cover their three-axis system of control rather than a flying machine per se. All during the spring of 1904 the patent claims were labored over, but rephrasing and revisions were required and the patent was not finally accepted and published until May 22, 1906, three years and two months after the Wright brothers had initiated the do-it-yourself process in 1903.

One minor distraction that winter raised Wilbur's blood pressure to the point where he found it necessary to compose a series of angry letters. That was the publication of an article, "The Experiences of a Flying Man," in the February 4 issue of *The Independent,* the weekly magazine that only four months before had published the paper by Professor Simon Newcomb presenting scientific proof that a practical flying machine was an impossibility. "The Experiences of a Flying Man" was a clever pastiche, concocted from Wilbur's two addresses to the Western Society of Engineers and the brothers' press release of January 6, 1904, supplemented by a few fantastic details from newspaper reports of the flights of December 1903. What incensed Wilbur almost more than the article's inaccuracies was the use of his name as its author.

The day after the article appeared, a vitriolic letter from Wilbur was on its way to the editor of *The Independent.* Three weeks later a paragraph buried in the magazine's editorial columns explained to readers that two recent articles accepted for publication, of which the "Flying Man" article was one, had been submitted by a literary agent and later disclaimed by the gentlemen whose names were attached to them. The magazine very much regretted the error. Not at all satisfied by this meek apology, Wilbur sharpened his pen for an attack on the perpetrator of the forgery, one D. A. Willey of Baltimore, who made a specialty of writing articles over the names of well-known persons. "Please do not think that because your colossal impudence was the means of getting you into trouble it will also be the means of getting you out again," Wilbur's letter began. It concluded: "*The Independent* will probably publish a further statement regarding the matter. If not I will." The further statement demanded by Wilbur was published as a footnote to the editor's column in the March 10 *Independent,* but in the smallest type this side of legibility.

One curious aspect of the whole affair was that the article was not mentioned in any of the letters exchanged between Wilbur and Octave Chanute for almost two months, although Wilbur knew the photograph of the Wright glider on the first page of the article to be one taken by Chanute during his stay at the Wright camp in 1902. Chanute, unknown to Wilbur, had supplied Willey with the photograph and copies of Wilbur's two lectures under the impression they were to be used in an article published over Willey's own name. When Wilbur finally did refer to the forgery in a letter to Chanute on March 29, Chanute was as indignant at the deception as Wilbur. "I suggest that you consult a lawyer and advise me of what can be done," he advised, but Wilbur doubted that Willey was solvent enough to justify the costs of a damage suit, and he let the matter drop.

Another gnatlike distraction, not quite as unsettling to Wilbur and Orville as it was to Octave Chanute, was a letter the brothers received that winter congratulating them on the success of their Flyer but warning them that their experiments would probably result in interference suits. The writer had apparently beaten the Wrights to the Patent Office and patented a machine similar to theirs. He had recently had a cash offer to sell all rights to interference suits but had refused out of consideration for the brothers. To avoid litigation and eliminate competition, he suggested that they form a joint company to market the Wright Flyer—"the basis being a 2/3 interest for you two and a 1/3 interest for me."

The writer of this astonishing letter was none other than Augustus Herring, who had been lurking in the wings ever since October 1902, when he had stopped in Washington on his way home from the Wright camp at Kill Devil Hills in a vain attempt to exchange his knowledge of the brothers' progress for a job at the Smithsonian. Orville sent a copy of Herring's proposal to George Spratt, calling it a "very generous offer." Wilbur sent a copy to Octave Chanute with the comment:

This time he surprised us. Before he left camp in 1902 we foresaw and predicted the object of his visit to Washington, we also felt certain that he was making a frenzied attempt to mount a motor on a copy of our 1902 glider and thus anticipate us, even before you told us of it last fall. But that he would have the effrontery to write us such a letter, after his other schemes of rascality had failed, was really a little more than we expected. We shall make no answer at all.

Chanute was genuinely alarmed at the threat of an interference suit. In January 1903, Herring had written Chanute that he had an idea for a flying machine that could easily win the $100,000 first prize at the St. Louis fair in 1904. It would be capable of staying in the air for ten hours—forty, if a larger model were built for ocean crossings. Later that year, after Herring had moved from St. Joseph, Michigan, to Freeport, Long Island, he wrote Chanute another letter, in which he mentioned casually that he had got a number of flights with a small gas motor. His habit of dropping vague hints in his letters left recipients wondering whether there might not be a grain of truth in what he claimed. Chanute offered his services to the Wrights in case of a patent suit.

"You seem to regard the Herring letter with more seriousness than we do," Wilbur replied. "We do not anticipate any trouble in the Patent Office from him, and do not think he has any intention of interfering there." No such suit evolved of course, for the reason that Herring had no patents. His flying-machine patent application, rejected in the United States, had been accepted in England and patented there in 1898 at Chanute's expense, but neither man considered it worth the annual renewal fee and it had been allowed to lapse. In February 1904, Herring wrote Chanute for information about the aeronautical competition at St. Louis. It was the last letter to pass between the two men. Chanute did not deign to reply.

To the Wright brothers, the coming aerial contest at the St. Louis exposition was both a distraction and a goad. In 1902 they considered competing for prizes a nuisance. In 1904, with the successful flights of their first Flyer behind them, it was impossible to pretend disinterest. When the fair opened that spring it threatened to surpass the Chicago Columbian Exposition of 1893 in popularity and attendance—a perfect showcase in which to display the Wright Flyer to the world.

The principal drawing card of the contest was expected to be the Parisian airship builder and operator Alberto Santos-Dumont. Although the competition was open to flying machines as well as airships, Santos' new airship was considered the most likely winner of the $100,000 grand prize. Santos had become the darling of Paris in 1901 after winning the 100,000-franc Deutsch prize for his daring seven-mile flight from St.-Cloud to the Eiffel Tower and return. Excitable, vain, always nattily attired from his wide-brimmed panama hats to the elevator shoes that compensated for his small stature and slight build, the Brazilian-born Santos was at the same time passionately air-minded. A large part of his inherited coffee fortune had gone to maintaining his standing as the world's foremost aeronaut. Two years before the St. Louis fair opened, he had used his influence with the committee planning the aeronautical competition to have the grand-prize contest changed from a grueling St. Louis-to-Chicago airship race, which nobody could have won, to three flights over a ten-mile circuit of the fairgrounds.

In February 1904, Wilbur and Orville went to St. Louis to inspect the grounds over which the flights would be made. An aeronautical amphitheater of fourteen acres was under construction. Hemmed in by buildings and trees, it had been designed for airships rather than flying machines. Contestants would be required to take off within this restricted area and land within fifty yards of the starting point. Whereas there would be $50,000 in subsidiary prizes for airships, gliders, balloons, kites, and even toy airplanes, flying machines would have to compete for the grand prize or nothing.

"A flight of even one mile by such a machine would be an event of great importance in aeronautical history," Wilbur pointed out to the rules committee, "yet your rules would give it no recognition even to the extent of a brass medal." The committee was unmoved, but it made one rule change that favored the Wrights. The requirement that contestants land within fifty yards of the starting point was changed so that flying machines would be allowed to land on a fifty-yard landing strip outside the fence of the amphitheater. After returning to Dayton, the Wrights notified the rules committee that they wanted to test their new machine before officially entering the contest.

In April they began work on a shed in which to assemble the new Flyer at Huffman Prairie. Like the 1903 building at Kill Devil Hills, it had braced walls and a large door at each end that could be propped up like an awning. Bad weather slowed its completion. There was a further delay when that old "church business," which had delayed the brothers' departure for Kitty Hawk in 1902, came once more to a head and there was another attempt to depose Bishop Wright. Wilbur spent a week writing letters in defense of his father and made a three-day trip to United Brethren headquarters in Huntington, Indiana. The dispute was to drag on for another year, but by the middle of May Wilbur was back in Dayton and the new Flyer was finally assembled in the shed on Huffman Prairie.

The 1904 machine was more sturdily constructed than the original Flyer and eighty pounds heavier. To supply power for the additional weight, the new engine had a slightly larger bore and developed up to 16 horsepower. Knowing that it would be impossible to keep the existence of the big white Flyer a secret, Wilbur and Orville concluded that the best way to avoid unwanted publicity would be to make a clean breast of what they were up to. Accordingly, they sent a letter to each of the daily papers in Dayton and Cincinnati, announcing that they would begin flying at Huffman Prairie on Monday, May 23. They made only two requests of the press: that reports not be sensational and that no photographs be taken.

About forty persons were on hand Monday morning at Huffman Prairie —a dozen reporters, the Wrights' father, their brother Lorin, Lorin's family, and a sizable group of friends. It rained all morning. The Flyer was not taken out of its shed until the wind, which had been blowing at 25 miles an hour during the rain, had died away to almost nothing. It was next to impossible to accelerate the Flyer to flying speed with only a little more than a hundred feet of track and no headwind, but the reporters had begun to grumble, so the Flyer was placed on the starting rail and the motor was run up to give the newspapermen some idea of how the machine operated. The Wrights decided to try a short hop. The motor was missing, and the Flyer slid off the end of the track without ever leaving the ground. The trouble with the motor was traced to the improper flow of air over the intake pipe. This was corrected Tuesday. Wednesday the Flyer was readied for a flight, but once again bad weather intervened. Thursday only a few reporters showed up. Lorin and his family stayed home. Bishop Wright went to Huffman Prairie on the trolley.

It rained off and on all morning. After lunch there was a break in the weather and the Flyer was taken out of the shed. At 2 P.M., Orville lay down on the lower wing with his hips in the warping cradle. The propellers were turned over and the motor was started. One of the spark points had become detached, so that only three cylinders were firing, but a storm was coming up again and there was no time to tinker. Orville tripped the release line. Wilbur ran beside the Flyer, balancing it until it left the track. The machine rose about six feet, then dropped to the ground so suddenly that several spars were broken. The brothers had to work fast to remove the front rudder so the damaged machine could be moved into its shed before rain poured down on the prairie. The distance flown over the ground had not been measured. Bishop Wright called it 25 feet in his diary; the reporters made it 30; Orville later gave the distance as 60 feet. To the Wrights it had not been a flight at all, but the few reporters present had been waiting four days for a story and they made the most of it.

It so happened that on the very day Orville was making the first, failed flight of 1904, Chanute was writing a letter to Wilbur in which he remarked, "I am glad to see that the newspapers have not yet found you out." The next morning he was no doubt surprised to see a short item with a Dayton dateline in the Chicago *Tribune* under the headline

TEST OF FLYING MACHINE IS
DECLARED A SUCCESS

The *New York Times,* however, printed the story on its first page under the heading

FALL WRECKS AIRSHIP

and blamed the aborted flight on a "derangement" of the Flyer's motor. As the brothers had requested, none of the reports was sensational, and Wilbur was able to write Chanute a few days later: "The fact that we are experimenting at Dayton is now public, but so far we have not been disturbed by visitors. The newspapers are friendly and not disposed to arouse prying curiosity in the community."

It is generally taken for granted that the Wrights did their best to make a flight in the presence of reporters on May 26, 1904, but it has also been suggested that their failure to fly was an ingenious deception to forestall future attention by the press. The most convincing evidence to support this theory is a passage from a letter Wilbur wrote a few years later in connection with a plan to demonstrate the Wright Flyer in a foreign country (the demonstration never took place): "No doubt an attempt will be made to spy upon us while we are making the trial flight . . . but we have already thought out a plan which we are certain will baffle such efforts as neatly as we fooled the newspapers during the two seasons we were experimenting at Simms." But Wilbur might just as well have meant that they fooled the newspapers by making flights at a time when the press refused to believe they were capable of flying and so ignored them. Deliberate or not, the failure of the Wrights to fly in the presence of reporters during the week of May 23, 1904, worked like a charm. It would be sixteen months before another reporter set foot on Huffman Prairie.

Two weeks after Orville's accident of May 26, the repaired Flyer was launched with Wilbur at the controls. Sixty feet from the end of the starting track, he made a mistake in manipulating the front rudder and nosed into the ground. Another two weeks were spent making repairs. "We certainly have been 'Jonahed' this year," Wilbur wrote Chanute on June 14, "partly by bad weather, and partly by being compelled to use pine spars in our wings, which causes breakages difficult to repair quickly." Eventually spruce became available, and on June 21 they made three landings without any breakage whatever. They were confident now that with a little more practice they would be ready to compete for the grand prize at the St. Louis fair. "In a light wind," Wilbur predicted to Octave Chanute, "we ought to be able to cover the course in eighteen or twenty minutes easily." This was optimistic, to say the least, considering that their longest flight at Huffman Prairie so far had measured only 225 feet, and the competition called for three flights over a ten-mile course.

On June 17, Santos-Dumont arrived in New York with his airship and its accessories packed in three two-ton crates. After a welcome befitting an international celebrity, he traveled to Washington at the invitation of President Theodore Roosevelt. From the White House he was whisked to the Naval Academy at Annapolis for a secret discussion with Admiral Dewey and other military leaders on the potential uses of airships in war. By the time he reached St. Louis, Santos was in a position to wring a few concessions from the rules committee, the most important being that the ten-mile, L-shaped course was changed to a six-mile round trip between two markers. Because Santos-Dumont's new airship, his seventh, was the most advanced in the world, it was widely believed to be the only aerial vehicle capable of winning the grand prize. The Wright brothers were under no such illusion. Like all other airships at the time, except for the dirigibles with rigid internal frames being developed in Germany, Santos' No. 7 was a dirigible-balloon —a flexible, sausage-shaped, hydrogen-filled envelope pointed at both ends. Beneath it was suspended a rigid keel supporting a catwalk on which motor, propeller, and operator were stationed out in the open. A tremendous amount of power was required to overcome the enormous drag of the flabby gasbag. Knowing how difficult it was to maneuver an airship in any wind at all, the Wrights thought of Santos' No. 7 as the tortoise in the coming contest. Their 1904 Flyer was, of course, the hare. "It is true that the tortoise beat the hare in a great historic race," Wilbur wrote Chanute on June 21, "but if the hare can open its eyes a little sooner next time or keep from breaking its legs or neck, it might turn the tables on the tortoise next time in a rather surprising way." Four days later, while flying close to the surface of Huffman Prairie in a 15-mile-per-hour wind, the Flyer began to undulate and struck the ground while going at full speed, damaging a spar and the struts that supported the front rudder. There was another heartbreaking interval of repairs that the hare could ill afford if it were to beat the tortoise.

The tortoise was having troubles of its own. The crates containing Santos' airship were opened in St. Louis on June 27 in the presence of U.S. customs officers, and the cover was left off the crate containing the gasbag. Twice that night, the exposition guard left the crate unattended to get coffee. At 7 A.M. the next day, one of Santos' mechanics discovered that four long slashes had been made through three layers of the folded silk, rupturing the fabric in a dozen places. The vandal was never caught or identified, but bitter accusations and counter-accusations were exchanged by Santos and the embarrassed fair officials. When an exposition guard hinted publicly that Santos or one of his French mechanics had sabotaged the airship because he was afraid of losing the competition, the volatile little Brazilian left St. Louis in a rage and withdrew from the contest.

Since the September 30 deadline for entering the competition was still three months off, the Wrights decided not to part with the $250 entrance fee until they could be more certain of winning. The last accident to the Flyer had been caused by their inability to control its undulations. Suspecting that the center of gravity was too far forward, they moved the engine and the operator's position farther to the rear. The results were so unsatisfactory that they spent most of July restructuring the machine. It continued to undulate unless they kept the front rudder turned down slightly. This created additional drag that could only be overcome by the application of more power, but there was no power to spare. They solved the problem, paradoxically, by adding seventy pounds of iron bars as ballast to the framework under the front rudder. The drag created by the bars, they calculated, was less than the drag the motor had to overcome when they flew with a turned-down front rudder.

Things went a little better during August. Of the twenty-four flights made that month, seven were 30 seconds or more in duration. On August 22, Wilbur and Orville each made flights of about a quarter of a mile, as far as they could travel safely in a straight line without starting to circle. Only five landings resulted in injury to the Flyer, and all the damage was minor until the twenty-fourth flight of the month on August 24. Orville had been in the air for only seven seconds when a gust of wind caused the Flyer to dive toward the ground. Instead of pulling back on the control handle in his right hand, he pushed forward instinctively with all his might, turning the front rudder down to its maximum and driving the Flyer into the ground at such a steep angle that it came to rest on the splintered rudder frame with its tail in the air. Orville was thrown forward onto the ground with the front spar of the upper wing across his back.

This was Orville's first serious scrape with death since the glider accident of September 23, 1902, from which he had escaped without a bruise or a scratch. He was even luckier on August 24, 1904, for his back might have been broken if the impact of the crash had not created a two-foot gap in the center of the spar that fell on top of him. Although he escaped this time with nothing worse than bruises and a scratched hand, he admitted to being sore all over. The brothers were farsighted enough to realize that without a lot more practice any attempt to fly the difficult course at St. Louis would result in an even worse disaster. With Orville's accident, the $100,000 grand prize went glimmering.

The air over the fairgrounds was proving as resistant to conquest as the air above Huffman Prairie. The Louisiana Purchase Exposition was a world's fair, but the only national aeronautical exhibits were of a low order. The German contribution was a demonstration of the making of maps from stereoscopic photographs taken from balloons. England contributed a plant for the production of hydrogen for balloons and airships. France sent an airship, but it won no prizes and was ripped on a nail as it was being moved into its hangar, the escaping hydrogen instantly asphyxiating a colony of sparrows nesting under the eaves. The most popular American aeronautical attraction was a shoddy concession in which two paying passengers at a time were sent aloft in a basket beneath a captive balloon tethered to a 1,000-foot cable and hauled back to earth by an asthmatic electrical winch. The balloon's fabric was in such poor shape that on one occasion the gasbag burst at an altitude of 500 feet, but enough gas remained in a remnant of the bag to parachute the passengers safely to earth.

Octave Chanute did his best to dignify the U.S. contribution by entering his celebrated double-decker in the gliding competition. To demonstrate the resurrected machine he employed the Chicago carpenter William Avery, who had built and flown the original double-decker in 1896. To launch the glider from the level aeronautical concourse he devised a launching apparatus in which the operator stood on a small dolly or flatcar, holding the glider. One end of a towrope was attached to the glider, the other to a large revolving drum 400 feet away. As the towrope was wound on the drum, the glider was pulled forward rapidly, ascending like a kite. When the operator felt he was safely airborne, he released the towrope and began his glide.

Like most Chanute gliding experiments, the St. Louis demonstrations were subject to a series of minor mishaps. To Chanute's dismay, Avery wasted valuable time trying unsuccessfully to procure a gasoline motor to operate the launching drum. When he arrived in St. Louis on Labor Day, the fair officials were practicing rigid economies and were reluctant to furnish him with the facilities he needed. It was not until October 7 that he made his first flights, with an electric motor operating the launching drum. In his best glide he ascended thirty-five feet before releasing the towrope and covered 175 feet. After that he made almost daily demonstrations until October 25, when he came to grief in an incident reminiscent of the 1896 Albatross fiasco at the Indiana dunes. The towrope had been used in a kite-flying contest without Avery's knowledge and had been frayed in several places by rubbing over the roofs of buildings. In spite of Chanute's instruction that he was to examine the rope before every flight, Avery failed to do so, and as he was being towed into the air in his official try for one of the two glider prizes, the towrope parted, and he sprained his ankle so badly in alighting that he had to withdraw from the glider competition.

"He is getting over it," a frustrated Octave Chanute wrote Wilbur, "but greatly regrets not winning the prize, which he says would have been as easy as picking money off the street."

The deadline for the $100,000 grand-prize competition had been extended to October 31, but as contenders failed to appear or met with accidents, aeronautical interest at the St. Louis fair centered on a fifty-three-foot airship, the *California Arrow,* the creation of an American, Thomas Baldwin, then in his mid-forties. Less than half the length of Santos-Dumont's No. 7 and powered by a secondhand motorcycle motor, the *California Arrow* had no chance of winning the coveted grand prize and little chance of gaining enough speed to win any prize at all with the 210-pound Baldwin as its pilot. That handicap was overcome when Baldwin hired a slim young balloonist named Roy Knabenshue to do the piloting. Knabenshue's daring and his light weight made him an ideal airship pilot. On October 25, with no previous experience in piloting an airship, he went up in the *California Arrow* and flew a figure S above the admiring fair crowds. While he was over the Transportation Building, his motor died and he drifted out of Missouri and across the Mississippi before coming down in Illinois, fifteen miles away. As the deadline for the grand-prize competition drew near, the desperate contest officials began to offer compensatory prizes for more feasible aerial feats. One of these—$500 for a flight of one mile from the aeronautical concourse and return—was won by the *California Arrow* on October 31. Contrary to William Avery's belief, however, there was no money to be picked up off the street at the fair. The St. Louis exposition was in the red. All available funds were impounded, including aeronautical prizes, and Baldwin and Knabenshue had to be satisfied with fame for the time being, rather than fortune. There was thus a bright side to the Wright brothers' failure to enter the competition, for even if they had done so—and had won —they would have risked their necks in vain.

# 19

## The Finished Flyer

WHAT PREVENTED Wilbur and Orville from obtaining the necessary practice in the summer of 1904 was their inability to launch their Flyer in light winds and calms. Sixty feet of track had been sufficient for taking off into a wind of more than 20 miles an hour at Kill Devil Hills. At Huffman Prairie the winds were seldom that strong. Whenever the wind changed direction they would have to start over, realigning the track so they could take off into the wind. A staggering amount of work was involved. It finally became clear that they would never get the practice they needed unless they devised a means of getting their Flyer into the air regardless of calms or changes in wind direction.

The Wright brothers solved the launching problem in the cheapest and simplest way possible by using the most available form of energy at their disposal—gravity. In September 1904 they erected a portable starting derrick, a pyramidal structure of four poles, with a line running over a pulley at the top. One end of the line was attached to 600 pounds of metal weights suspended under the derrick (their weight would be doubled before the year was out). The line ran under fifty feet of starting track, over a pulley at the front of the track, and back over the top of the track to the Flyer, to which the other end of the line was attached. The line holding the weights under the derrick was geared with ropes and pulleys so that when the metal weights were hoisted to the top of the derrick and released, they exerted a pull of more than 300 pounds on the Flyer. Added to the thrust of the propellers, this was enough to accelerate the machine to flying speed by the time it reached the end of the track. Before each flight, the Flyer was held in place by a wire anchored to a stake driven into the ground, and the weights were hauled to the top of the derrick. After the propellers were set in motion, the operator tripped the catch that released the holding wire, the weights began their drop, and the machine accelerated along the track. The brother not on the Flyer ran alongside, steadying it by one wingtip until it lifted from the track under the combined pull of the towline and the thrust of its propellers.

Wilbur made the first ten starts with this device. Seven resulted in true flights. On September 15 he made his first turn in the air and came down after accomplishing half a circle. On the morning of September 20 he attempted his first circle but flew instead an S-shaped course and landed with his wingtips grazing the barbed-wire fence separating Huffman Prairie from farmer Stauffer's cornfield. That afternoon he tried again, and without straying beyond the boundaries of the field flew his first complete circle. His distance over the ground was 4,080 feet; his time in the air, 1 minute 36 seconds. To measure distance, they simply rolled a wheel from the starting track over the course flown to the landing point and multiplied the number of turns of the wheel by its circumference, which happened to be eight feet.

Wilbur's circumnavigation of Huffman Prairie was witnessed by Amos T. Root, whose report of that event has long been acclaimed as the first eyewitness account of an airplane in controlled flight. Root was a Medina, Ohio, merchant of beekeeping supplies. He was also the publisher of an obscure little trade magazine, *Gleanings in Bee Culture.* His account of the Wright brothers' first circle was printed in the January 1, 1905, issue of that magazine under the epigraph "What Hath God Wrought?" Its tone is that of a talk delivered to a class of fidgeting boys by a Sunday-school teacher, which Root was: "Dear friends," it begins, "I have a wonderful story to tell you—a story that, in some respects, outrivals the Arabian Nights fables—a story, too, with a moral that I think many of the younger ones need, and perhaps some of the older ones too if they will heed it."

Root's only discernible moral is aimed at the bee trade: If inventors of new types of beehives would do as much research as the Wrights brothers have done before applying for a patent, they would save themselves time and money. He goes on to describe the experiments made by the Wrights at Kitty Hawk and at Huffman Prairie. His account is enlivened by sparkles of naïveté. Wilbur is the Flyer's "intrepid manager." Its shed is "the little house where it is kept nights." The usually phlegmatic Charlie Taylor, who spent part of his time that year at Huffman Prairie timing flights with a stopwatch when he was not working on airframe repairs, shakes "from head to foot as if he had a fit of the ague" as the Flyer shoots down the track. Here is Root's eyewitness account of the first circling flight ever made by a heavier-than-air machine:

> The machine is held until ready to start by a sort of trap to be sprung when all is ready; then with a tremendous flapping and snapping of the

four-cylinder engine, the huge machine springs aloft. When it first turned that circle, and came near the starting-point, I was right in front of it; and I said then, and I believe still, it was one of the grandest sights, if not the grandest sight, of my life. Imagine a locomotive that has left its track, and is climbing up in the air right toward you—a locomotive without any wheels, we will say, but with white wings instead . . . coming right toward you with the tremendous flap of its propellers, and you will have something like what I saw. The younger brother bade me move to one side for fear that it might come down suddenly; but I tell you friends, the sensation that one feels in such a crisis is something hard to describe.

Amos Root's presence at Huffman Prairie on September 20, 1904, may not have been a coincidence. His trip of almost two hundred miles from Medina to Dayton by automobile, no mean feat in those days, may have been made at the invitation of the Wrights so that a printed account of their Flyer in flight would be available as proof of their ability to fly—not in a widely read newspaper or magazine but in a publication with such a restricted circulation that the publicity would not attract curiosity seekers or the press. Although Root sent a copy of his article to the *Scientific American* and gave the editor permission to use it in any way he saw fit, that popular weekly paid no attention to the story at all.

Octave Chanute had been invited to witness the experiments earlier in the year, but he had been too tied up with business to make the trip. On October 5 Wilbur wrote that word of what was going on at Huffman Prairie was spreading through the neighborhood, and it might be necessary to discontinue experiments. If Chanute wanted to witness a flight it would be well to come within the next few weeks. Chanute arrived in Dayton on October 15. Orville had made his first circling flight the day before. He tried to repeat the performance in Chanute's presence, but on his first turn he was unable to straighten out and after only 30 seconds in the air was forced to land at such a high speed that the machine slewed around, breaking both skids and both propellers and damaging the engine. Chanute left Dayton without having seen a satisfactory flight.

The Wrights were being Jonahed again. On October 26 they broke both skids and one propeller. On November 1 the stake to which the restraining wire was anchored pulled from the ground and the Flyer, without an operator on board, started down the track as the weights dropped. Orville managed to reduce the damage to a few broken struts by flinging himself across the lower wing. The next day he broke the tail in starting. On November 3 Wilbur flew his second complete circle but broke both propellers and a spar in landing.

The spell of bad luck was broken on Wednesday, November 9. There had been an election the day before in which Republican Theodore Roosevelt had won a landslide victory for the presidency. The next day Wilbur, Orville, and Bishop Wright, loyal Republicans all, took the interurban trolley to Huffman Prairie, where Wilbur celebrated with what came to be known as his victory flight. He circled the field four times in five minutes, landing only when the Flyer's engine showed signs of overheating. On the first of December, Orville duplicated Wilbur's feat, and on December 9 flying was discontinued. The brothers were ready for a rest and the 1904 Flyer was ready for the scrap heap—except for its motor and transmission system, which were salvaged. Many years later, when Orville was asked what had become of the rest of the machine, he was not quite sure but thought the wings had been burned when they began assembling a new machine in 1905. Cremation would have been fitting. The 1904 machine had served its purpose. It was a learning tool, not a museum piece worthy of preservation like the first Flyer of 1903—or the swanlike machine of 1905, which was to rise phoenixlike from its ashes.

Before completing work on the new machine, the Wright brothers felt that, with two five-minute circling flights behind them, they were in a position to open negotiations for the sale of their invention. The time had come to look for some return on their investment of ingenuity and daring. The maximum reward for their efforts, they concluded, would be obtained not by selling Flyers to individuals but by offering machines to one government or another for use in time of war. What they had in mind was the scouting abilities of the airplane rather than its destructive potential. They shared a belief held by many in the first years of the century that the airplane would end war altogether by enabling rival armies to observe every move made by their opponents, thus making it impossible for either side to gain an advantage, a theory that seems as preposterous today as current theories of deterrence may seem a century from now.

On the evening of January 3, 1905, Wilbur paid a call on his congressman, Robert M. Nevin, who had not yet returned to Washington after spending the holidays in Dayton. Nevin suggested that the procedure to follow in making a sale to the U.S. War Department would be for the Wrights to address a proposal directly to him. He would deliver the proposal to the Secretary of War in person and set up a meeting between the brothers and the appropriate War Department officials. On January 18 a letter from the Wrights was on its way to Congressman Nevin, stating in businesslike terms that they had produced a flying machine in which they had made two flights of five minutes each at speeds of 35 miles per hour. They were prepared to supply the government with similar machines for a contracted price, together with all the scientific information on flight accumulated during their five years of experimenting.

When the letter arrived in Washington, Nevin was ill and unable to make his promised visit to the Secretary of War. The letter was forwarded routinely to the War Department, where it was routed to the Board of Ordnance and Fortification, the same agency that had provided Samuel Langley with $50,000 for the development of a man-carrying airplane, only to see the money sucked into the Potomac behind Langley's collapsing Aerodrome to loud catcalls from the press. Since then, the Board had received so many requests for assistance in developing flying machines that a stock reply had been composed for use in responding to letters from would-be inventors and cranks. The letter of the president of the Board to Congressman Nevin, dated January 24, 1905, consisted of a formal acknowledgment of Nevin's letter "of the 21st instant," followed by the stock reply and a second paragraph freshly composed:

> I have the honor to inform you that, as many requests have been made for financial assistance in the development of designs for flying-machines, the Board has found it necessary to decline to make allotments for the experimental development of devices for mechanical flight, and has determined that, before suggestions with that object in view will be considered, the device must have been brought to the stage of practical operation without expense to the United States.
>
> It appears from the letter of Messrs. Wilbur and Orville Wright that their machine has not yet been brought to the stage of practical operation, but as soon as it shall have been perfected, this Board would be pleased to receive further representations from them in regard to it.

The Wrights, of course, had made no appeal for financial assistance, and a flying machine that had been making five-minute flights at 35 miles an hour was hardly as far from a stage of practical operation as the Board's letter implied. Obviously there had been a misunderstanding. Nevertheless, scorn and ridicule have been heaped upon this poor letter ever since it was forwarded to the Wrights by their congressman. To this day their supporters, with a single exception, wax indignant at the mere mention of its existence. The exception is John Evangelist Walsh, who broke the mold in 1975 by putting himself in the shoes of the members of the Board of Ordnance and Fortification when they received the Wrights' proposal. "Imagine the U.S. Secretary of Defense, in 1975," Walsh wrote in *One Day at Kitty Hawk,* "receiving out of nowhere a letter in which the writer announces he has constructed a rocket in which he has already visited Mars and returned safely to earth, and is willing to make the rocket available to the government on contract. But even that would not adequately express the army board's depth of puzzlement, for in 1975 rockets are facts of life, while in 1905 flying machines for all but the Wrights were still in the realm of Jules Verne."

Misunderstanding or not, Wilbur and Orville construed the Board's reply as a flat turndown that left them free to pursue a sale to some other government. As a matter of fact, eight days before making the proposal to the U.S. War Department through their congressman, they had sent a letter to England, announcing that they were prepared to sell an airplane to the British War Office. Taking into account the week or more it took a letter to reach London from Dayton, it would be correct to say that they approached the two governments simultaneously.

The British had been showing an interest in the brothers' experiments since December 24, 1902, when Patrick Y. Alexander, a well-to-do member of the Aeronautical Society of Great Britain, had appeared at the house on Hawthorn Street with a letter of introduction from Octave Chanute. Alexander had spent a large part of his fortune on furthering aeronautics in England and was eager to meet the two Americans who had made the only notable advances in gliding since the experiments of Percy Pilcher, the Englishman killed in a gliding accident in 1899. The Wrights were as favorably impressed with Alexander as he was with them. Although he was unable to take advantage of the invitation, he was the only person aside from Octave Chanute and George Spratt invited to their camp at Kill Devil Hills in 1903.

On October 23, 1904, the Wrights played host to still another member of the British Aeronautical Society, Lieutenant Colonel John B. Capper, whose visit was preceded by a letter of introduction from Alexander. As an aeronautical expert attached to the British Balloon Factory, later the Royal Aircraft Establishment, Colonel Capper was on an official visit to obtain what information he could on the state of aeronautics in the United States. After visiting Octave Chanute in Chicago, he traveled to St. Louis, where he witnessed William Avery's flights in Chanute's double-decker glider at the 1904 fair. He also observed the American concession in which paying passengers were taken aloft in a balloon. The balloon, he reported to his superior at the British Balloon Factory, was made of the rottenest fabric imaginable. "It is no use, however, I have already learnt, pointing out anything to an ordinary American," he wrote; "they are all so damned certain they know everything and so absolutely ignorant of the theory of aeronautics that they only resent it."

Capper's low opinion of American aeronautics underwent a radical change when he stopped in Dayton with his wife, Edith, on their return trip east. He had been looking forward to seeing the Wrights make a flight, but Wilbur and Orville explained that a demonstration would attract too much attention from the press—a polite way of preventing the Englishman from getting too close to their Flyer. Instead, they showed him photographs of their recent flights. Neither brother had flown more than a single circuit of Huffman Prairie at the time of Capper's visit, and none of the pictures taken so far showed the machine more than a few feet off the ground, but the colonel saw that the Wrights had made greater strides than any of their predecessors and urged them to submit a proposal in writing for the sale of a flying machine to his government.

On January 10, 1905, the Wrights wrote Colonel Capper that they were ready to make such a proposal. Capper turned their letter over to the British War Office, and on February 11 the Director of Fortifications and Works wrote the Wrights asking for their proposal. On March 1, the Wrights complied. They offered to furnish a machine capable of carrying two men and flying for fifty miles without refueling. No payment would be required until a series of trial flights had been made. If none of the flights was at least ten miles, the contract would be void. The price: 500 British pounds for each mile covered in the longest trial flight. This meant that if the trial flight covered ten miles, the cost to the British would be 5,000 pounds, the equivalent of 25,000 American dollars. If the trial flight covered fifty miles, the price would be a whopping 50,000 pounds, or $125,000.

Having no such sums at his disposal, the Director of Fortifications and Works referred the proposal to the Royal Engineer Committee. The committee responded on May 13, 1905, that the capabilities of the proposed machine were too uncertain to render an agreement advisable. However, the British military attaché in Washington would be ordered to visit Dayton to witness a trial flight. If his report was favorable, negotiations would be resumed. Although the Wrights had no intention of making a trial flight until a contract had been signed, they looked forward to the arrival of the military attaché, hoping that photographic evidence of their Flyer's capabilities would prove as convincing to him as to Colonel Capper.

Meanwhile, a new Flyer had been under construction in the workroom behind the bicycle shop. In turning before alighting, the 1904 machine had tended to sideslip and to remain in a tilted position while landing. To see if this tendency could be overcome by varying the proportion of rudder to wingwarping, the vertical rudder and wingwarping controls were disconnected in the 1905 machine, and a separate handle was used to control the movement of the vertical rudder. If the vertical rudder were controlled independently, the Wrights figured, stability about the vertical axis would have to be increased. To supply the needed increase and to prevent the front rudder from slipping sidewards in a turn, they inserted two vertical semicircular vanes between the upper and lower elevator surfaces. They called these appendages blinkers because of their resemblance to the blinkers attached to horses' bridles to eliminate distracting side vision.

The 1904 motor was installed in the new machine. Its performance had improved with age because of the smoothing of pistons and cylinders by wear. In April 1905 it averaged 18 horsepower in shop tests. By the end of the year it would deliver more than 20. At the same time, the Wrights were working on another, more powerful motor. They would tinker with the new motor for the next year or two until it was capable of producing about 25 horsepower continuously, or more than twice the power of its 1903 proto-type.

While work went on in the bicycle shop, Wilbur and Orville made a halfhearted search for a more secluded flying field. By timing their flights between passages of the interurban trolleys, they had managed to escape observation in 1904 until November 9, when Wilbur made his long flight in celebration of Theodore Roosevelt's election victory. While Wilbur was still in the air, an unscheduled car bearing two officials of the interurban railway line came down the track alongside Huffman Prairie and braked to a stop. The two men got out to watch. After Wilbur landed, they crossed the pike and introduced themselves. Their amazement at what they had seen was exceeded only by their reticence, for there was not a word in the papers the next day that the general manager and chief engineer of the Dayton, Spring-field & Urbana Interurban Railway had witnessed the first five-minute flight in history, but to Wilbur and Orville the message was clear. If flights longer than five minutes were to be made at Huffman Prairie, sooner or later they would be observed by passengers on the passing trolleys, and reporters would come flocking.

They asked Octave Chanute for advice. After ruling out the Indiana dunes where Chanute had done his own experimenting, they asked him if he knew of any suitable prairie land in Illinois, something neither too accessible nor inaccessible. Chanute suggested that it might be worth their while to examine the Kankakee marshes about fifty miles from Chicago. "I think they are being drained," he added uncertainly—after which the Wrights gave up the search and resigned themselves to coping with the disadvantages of Huffman Prairie.

In May, just as the new Flyer was ready to be assembled, that old "church business" came once more to a head. A tract written by Wilbur was published in defense of his father's position in the three-year-old controversy over the mishandling of church funds. Wilbur spent a week at a United Brethren conference in Michigan, where the tract was distributed with telling effect. Thanks to the efforts of his literary, nonchurchgoing son, Milton Wright was able to retire on May 20, 1905, with his bishopric intact.

When Wilbur returned from Michigan, the new machine was assembled in the shed at Huffman Prairie. There was still no word from the British military attaché, and the brothers' determination not to make any flights before a contract had been signed began to weaken. On June 23, Orville made a trial flight to check the new control system, but he had trouble manipulating three control mechanisms at once and was unable to straighten the wings in landing. Four cracked ribs in the lower left wing was the result. Wilbur had the same difficulty the next day, breaking the spar and bow end of the same wing in landing. Suspecting that the so-called blinkers contributed to the difficulty, they removed these vertical surfaces. Although one or two blinkers were used in most later Wright machines, they do not appear in any photographs of the 1905 machine taken after June 23.

As the summer wore on and the British military attaché failed to appear, the few tests they intended to make of the new machine evolved into a season of full-fledged flying, and the delays and disappointments they had experienced in 1904 began to repeat themselves in earnest. While making a test of the repaired Flyer on July 14, Orville encountered the old trouble with the front rudder. After a twelve-second undulating flight, the Flyer darted to the ground and rolled over. Orville was thrown violently out through the broken upper wing. This time he escaped without a scratch.

Flying practice was interrupted by even more bouts of foul weather than in 1904. When conditions did permit flying, an astonishing amount of sheer physical drudgery was involved. The Flyer had to be removed, sideways, from the shed so that the tail and front rudder could be bolted on. Sixty feet of track had to be laid and up to 1,200 pounds of metal weights hoisted to the top of the starting derrick. After each flight, 700 pounds of airplane and motor had to be lifted on wheeled supports and hauled back to the starting rail over the bumpy, often soggy surface of the prairie, an exhausting task that greatly reduced the number of flights it was possible to make in a single day.

The Wrights gave up all pretense of running a bicycle business that summer. Charlie Taylor spent his whole working day either at Huffman Prairie or in the bicycle shop manufacturing spare parts to replace ribs, spars, uprights, bow ends, and propellers as fast as they were smashed or splintered. In recalling those busy days, Taylor has preserved for posterity an illuminating glimpse of Wilbur's reactions to the opposite sex as the three men rode the interurban trolley back and forth between Dayton and Simms Station: "If an older woman sat down beside him, before you knew it they would be talking and if she got off at our stop he'd carry her packages and you'd think he had known her all his life. But if a young woman sat next to him he would begin to fidget and pretty soon he would get up and go stand on the platform until it was time to leave the car." From his perspective as the only cigar-smoking, married man of the three, Taylor would have the last word on the Wright brothers and sex: "I think both the boys were mentally flying all the time and simply didn't think about girls."

The first two weeks in August it rained almost every day. Huffman Prairie was under water and the Flyer's shed could be reached only by jumping from hummock to hummock. During the rainy spell, a new front rudder was constructed. The twin elevator surfaces were increased in area from 50 to 84 square feet and positioned twelve full feet in front of the wings. In flights made toward the end of August, their new front rudder had the effect of dampening the undulations that had caused Orville's accident of July 14. Manipulating the separate vertical-rudder handle was not easy, however, and Wilbur was twice forced to land to avoid hitting a fence. Thinking that steering would be made easier if the vertical rudder was also enlarged, they increased its area from 20 to 35 square feet and began at last to reap the rewards of three months of unrequited labor. On September 7 Wilbur flew four circuits of the field, twice running into a flock of birds, one of which was killed and fell on top of the upper wing, where it stayed without falling off until Wilbur banked the Flyer in a sharp turn. The next day Orville flew the first figure eight flown by either of the brothers.

The third week in September it rained again. The Wrights took advantage of the lull in flying to put the finishing touches on the 1905 machine. The wings of their first two Flyers had had a noticeable droop to counteract the effect of side gusts. Such gusts were neither so frequent nor so strong near Dayton as on the Outer Banks. While waiting for the rain to stop, they rewired the wings, trussing them so that they were perfectly straight from tip to tip except for a slight dihedral at the center. They also designed and constructed a new set of propellers.

The propellers used in 1904 and 1905 were wider and thinner than those used on the first Flyer. The Wrights suspected that the reason these propellers were not yielding the thrust that their calculations indicated they should was that the blades were being twisted from their normal shape in flight. To test this assumption, they mounted the equivalent of a small elevator behind each propeller blade. They called these small elevator surfaces "little jokers." When set at an angle so as to reduce the pitch of the propeller and balance the pressure that they suspected was distorting the blades, the little jokers did indeed indicate that the loss of thrust was caused by the bending of the thin propeller blades in flight. The blades of the propellers constructed that September, the so-called bent-end propellers, were given a backward sweep to prevent their bending under pressure.

Aside from two changes made a few weeks later (the vertical rudder was moved three feet further to the rear and twenty-eight pounds of iron bars were lashed to the front rudder to bring the center of gravity forward another few inches) the 1905 Flyer was in its final form by the end of September and ready for a series of rigorous endurance tests. The front horizontal rudder, supported by a pair of long, gracefully curving skids, was now twice as far in front of the wings as at the beginning of the season. It is this increased distance from the wings of both front and rear rudders, not to mention the lack of the clutter created in later Wright machines by the addition of seats and levers, that makes the Flyer of 1905 the most aesthetically pleasing of all Wright airplanes.

Any early Wright airplane takes a little getting used to. To modern eyes, the front rudder at first glance appears to be the tail. The propellers seem to be pulling the wings forward rather than pushing them from behind. Once this error in perception is acknowledged, the 1905 Flyer no longer seems to be flying backward in the old photographs. It soars forward with a swanlike grace that the stumpy first Flyer and its 1904 successor sadly lack—a paradoxical combination of fragility and strength, lightness and weight, simplicity and complexity—the practical airplane that men had been striving for years to create but that only the Wright brothers, by 1905, had come even close to perfecting.

# 20

# *A Bold Performance in California*

IN HIS LETTERS to Wilbur, it was Octave Chanute's custom to enclose newspaper clippings that would keep the Wright brothers informed of the work of other aeronautical experimenters. "I enclose an account of a bold performance in California," he wrote Wilbur on April 4, 1905. "I will write to Montgomery for particulars."

Chanute had known John Joseph Montgomery ever since the Chicago World's Fair of 1893. Montgomery, who was thirty-five that summer, had already earned a reputation in California as an unsuccessful inventor whose specialty was electricity but whose obsession was the flying problem. The Montgomery clan had become worried about the long hours John was spending in his makeshift laboratory in the barn on the family ranch near San Diego and had packed him off to the Columbian Exposition in Chicago, where he was attracted to the four-day International Conference on Aerial Navigation like a moth to a flame. Octave Chanute, as chairman of the conference, was in a position to furnish Montgomery a platform for expounding his eccentric theories of flight. The outcome was a paper printed in the conference proceedings, describing some of Montgomery's own mild experiments in air and water flow. Chanute's *Progress in Flying Machines,* published the following year, revealed that Montgomery had also conducted experiments with gliders, and it is with the account of those experiments in Chanute's book that the story of John Montgomery gets off the ground.

At some unspecified time in the past, Montgomery had constructed a forty-pound glider with a twenty-foot wingspread and a movable horizontal tail, in which he had made a glide of about 100 feet after giving a jump into the air without previous running. The glide was made against a wind of 8 to 12 miles an hour. As he carried the glider back up the hill it began to twist in the wind. One wing caught on some shrubbery and "quick as a flash" the

130-pound young man was tossed eight to ten feet in the air. Montgomery was not hurt, but the machine was smashed past mending. He later built two more gliders of different design. Both were incapable of flight.

Since no discrepancies in his report of his gliding experiments were pointed out by Montgomery in his subsequent correspondence with Chanute, it must be assumed that the account in *Progress in Flying Machines* was as accurate and complete as the two men between them were able to make it at that late date. (Chanute did not seem to be bothered by the two obvious absurdities in the account: the impossibility of making a 100-foot glide by simply jumping into the air without a running start, and the fact that it would take a wind of more than hurricane force to hurl a 130-pound man eight to ten feet into the air.) Nevertheless, Montgomery's single glide was to become the most flexible glide in history, shifting about in time and expanding from "about 100 ft." in the 1894 account in Chanute's book to a definitive 603 feet in 1962.

After returning to California, Montgomery sought Chanute's help in putting his chimerical aerodynamic theories into publishable form. Chanute soon became exasperated and accused his correspondent of confounding pressure with energy and statics with dynamics, pointing out that Montgomery had assigned a motive power to gravity in the air that gravity had never exhibited on land or sea. Displeased with one of Chanute's critical comments, Montgomery broke off the correspondence in November 1895. In 1897 he accepted a part-time teaching job in the San Francisco Bay area at Santa Clara College, then a school for boys and young men run by the Jesuits. He was listed in the school catalogue as professor of geometry, but his meager salary of thirty-five dollars a month plus room and board forced him to confine his fitful aeronautical experiments to the testing of model gliders until 1903, when an offer of financial support was made by airship designer and pilot Captain Thomas Scott Baldwin.

The Captain designation applied to airship operators at the turn of the century was no more authentic than the Professor preceding the names of professional balloonists and parachute jumpers. In Baldwin's case, Professor would have been just as appropriate. A circus-trained tightrope walker, he also performed as an aerial artist on a balloon-borne trapeze and in 1887 made a spectacular jump in a parachute of his own design from a balloon 1,000 feet above Golden Gate Park, San Francisco. Parachute jumping soon became popular at state and county fairs. When Baldwin became too heavy for jumping, he began experimenting with a series of cigar-shaped airships, culminating in his *California Arrow* of 1903. That November he wrote John Montgomery, with whom he had been corresponding since January, that he was having trouble with propellers and would be glad to try out any ideas the Santa Clara professor might have for a more efficient propeller. The following month he visited Montgomery at Santa Clara. Baldwin had more than propellers in mind. Predicting that more money could be made in exhibition jumping from balloons if a glider was substituted for a parachute, he offered to finance the construction of a man-carrying glider along the lines of Montgomery's latest tandem-wing model. On April 28, 1904, Montgomery signed an agreement with Baldwin to produce a glider to be dropped from an ascending balloon for exhibition purposes and a few weeks later was writing his brother Richard that he and Baldwin were working away like beavers. If the man-carrying glider performed as well as the model, they expected to clear over $100,000 the first year.

The phantom riches vanished over the horizon as suddenly as they had appeared. By the time the glider was completed, Baldwin had solved his airship problem by purchasing a more powerful motor secondhand from Glenn Curtiss, motorcycle racer and manufacturer of Hammondsport, New York. On August 3, 1904, with a new oak-frame-and-fabric propeller whirling away in front of his two-cylinder Curtiss motor, he piloted the *California Arrow* over San Francisco Bay in the first closed circuit made by an aircraft of any kind in the United States. Then he packed up his airship and headed for the St. Louis fair. Baldwin's success at St. Louis marked the end of his friendship with Montgomery, who accused him of having stolen the idea for his new propeller. Furthermore, Montgomery claimed, Baldwin had received from him the equivalent of an education in aeronautics during his visits to Santa Clara, and therefore he, not Baldwin, was the real inventor of the *California Arrow.* This was not the last time that Montgomery was to feel he had been betrayed by men who appropriated his aeronautical secrets and used them for their own advantage.

The glider constructed at Santa Clara during Baldwin's stay now belonged to Montgomery. It was unlike any other glider ever constructed. The two twenty-four-foot sinuous wings, covered with oiled muslin, were attached one behind the other to an ashwood frame and supported by wires connected to two guy posts. This tandem-wing configuration had been abandoned by nearly all other experimenters after the failure of Langley's Aerodrome, but Montgomery insisted that the two wings of his glider were in reality the front and rear components of a single wing and in some mysterious fashion gathered power from the air. The disproportionately large tail consisted of two semicircular vanes close behind the rear wing. It could be moved up and down by a lever manipulated by the operator, who sat on a saddle between the wings with his feet in a pair of stirrups. The trailing edges of the rear wing could be pulled down on one side or the other by wires connected to the stirrups. Photographs show the glider to have been an apparatus halfway between a parachuting device and a glider with rigid wings. Montgomery himself spoke of the wings as being inflated in flight. The Santa Clara College monthly magazine, *The Redwood,* once referred to the Montgomery glider with naïve accuracy as a dirigible-parachute.

The glider was tested in the summer of 1904 by being dropped with and without weights from a cable stretched between two poles, after which Montgomery made a number of flights down a steep hillside with the assistance of three cowboy friends. His next move was to salvage what he could of Baldwin's idea for exhibition flights. A friend, John Leonard, put him in touch with Fred Swanton, who operated the Santa Cruz Beach Cottage and Tent City concession at the north end of Monterey Bay where the area's first casino had recently opened. Customers were lured to Swanton's concession on holidays by parachute jumps performed by Daniel Maloney, a twenty-six-year-old aerial artist known professionally as Professor Lascelles, and by Frank Hamilton, who owned the two balloons that carried the parachutists aloft. Montgomery convinced Swanton that even larger crowds would be attracted to his beachside concession if the aerial artist were to descend in a glider rather than dangling from a parachute. Swanton witnessed a few flights of a large unmanned Montgomery model in December, and on March 16, 1905, went to the Leonard ranch near Santa Cruz to see young Daniel Maloney make his first daring descent from a balloon in Montgomery's man-carrying glider.

About twenty men were on hand to manage the restraining ropes while Frank Hamilton's hot-air balloon was inflated. After two aborted ascensions, Maloney succeeded in cutting the lift rope when he was about 800 feet above the ground. The glider plummeted several hundred feet before it straightened out and spiraled rapidly to earth, just missing the ranch house and landing in an apple tree. Maloney made a second drop the next day from an altitude he said was 1,100 feet. Montgomery gave the altitude as 2,000 feet, although all such figures must be taken with a grain of salt, since they were estimates only. A third flight, to which the press was invited, was made on March 20 from an altitude that Montgomery estimated as 3,000 feet. "The problem of aerial navigation is solved," Maloney told a San Francisco reporter on alighting.

News of the flights spread throughout the country. The newspaper account of a bold performance in California that Octave Chanute enclosed in his letter to Wilbur Wright of April 4, 1905, was one such report. On the same day that Chanute sent Wilbur the clipping, he wrote Montgomery for the first time since 1895. Montgomery was only too glad to renew the correspondence and to unburden himself on the subject of Thomas Baldwin: "Captain Baldwin entered into a contract with me to put my ideas in practical form, apparently for an honest purpose, but in reality to obtain some of my knowledge relating to aero-dynamics and to rob me of the results." Chanute sent Montgomery's letter to the Wrights to read with the comment: "I regret that he has gotten into a wrangle with Baldwin and I fancy that in this and in the development of his aeroplane he is like the young bear who had all his troubles still to come."

To John Montgomery the future had never seemed so free of troubles. Fred Swanton and his beachside concession were forgotten as demands for public exhibitions poured in from as far away as San Diego. Frank Hamilton, owner of the two indispensable balloons, took over as manager. Before any commercial performances were given, however, there was to be a free exhibition flight at the Santa Clara campus to celebrate the college's annual President's Day on Saturday, April 29, and to honor the school's newly famous professor and his wonderful glider. "The Fathers say it is the greatest invention of the age," Montgomery wrote his mother, "and are going to make the first exhibition a grand affair."

By midmorning Saturday more than a thousand spectators had gathered for the event, including reporters and photographers from twenty-five newspapers. The red and white college colors were everywhere. Even the white wings and tail of Montgomery's glider, which had been blessed that morning by a Jesuit father and christened the *Santa Clara,* were tipped with red. At 11 a.m. Hamilton's big balloon began to bulge and writhe as hot air was piped into it from a fire in a nearby pit. When it had assumed a proper pear shape, the students holding the restraining ropes brought it over the glider. The lift rope was attached, and Daniel Maloney in circus tights and spangled trunks straddled the Santa Clara's carpet-covered saddle. The spectators broke into cheers as the balloon was released and the glider sprang suddenly skyward. When Maloney was between 2,000 and 4,000 feet above the ground—the estimates varied as usual—he cut the lift rope. The gasbag bounded upward, then tumbled to earth as the hot air gushed out of it, leaving a smoky condensation trail behind.

Record-keeping was not one of Montgomery's strong points. Neither he nor any of his helpers used a stopwatch to determine the time it took Maloney to reach the ground. Most printed accounts gave the time as between 15 and 20 minutes, although one newspaper report seen by the Wright brothers gave the time of ascent and descent combined as 7 minutes. There was only a slight lack of consensus, however, about what happened next. Montgomery's own breathless account of the descent in his next letter to Octave Chanute was no more ecstatic than the newspaper reports: "The crowd was spellbound and swayed between feelings of intense fear and delight according as they beheld the downward darting, swift whirling, with the machine tilted sidewards more than 45°, only to pass gracefully again to its gliding movement." When the glider was about 1,000 feet above the ground it struck a current of rising air and seemed to remain motionless for a few seconds, after which it circled rapidly to the ground and landed in a grain field half a mile from the college campus.

Montgomery looked on Maloney's spectacular flight as vindication of all those abstruse theories of his that Octave Chanute had criticized as unscientific. In May 1905, he proudly sent Chanute two copies of a thirty-page pamphlet entitled *The Aeroplane,* designed for sale at public exhibitions of his glider. Actually a reprint of a special supplement to the May issue of the Santa Clara College *Redwood,* the pamphlet included reports of Maloney's flights at the Leonard ranch and his April 29 triumph, as well as a brief biography of Montgomery. The most impressive part of the pamphlet was a thirteen-page section, "The Aeroplane: A Scientific Study," by John J. Montgomery, Ph.D. (Montgomery had been given an honorary doctorate by Santa Clara College in 1901). The study made available for the first time in print Montgomery's theories of fluid movement that explained the secret of flight, theories based on "unrecognized mechanical principles." On May 30, Chanute sent one of his two copies of the *Aeroplane* pamphlet to Dayton, where Wilbur and Orville were preparing their 1905 Flyer for its first trials.

"Do you consider the part signed by Mr. Montgomery a bona fide article," Wilbur wrote back, "or is it a deliberate bit of charlatanism?"

"Much of it is bosh," replied Chanute, "but it is entirely bona fide."

Before receiving the *Aeroplane* pamphlet, the Wright brothers considered Maloney's flights the most wonderful exhibition of daring since the world's first parachute jump in 1797. After reading the pamphlet, they considered the flights foolhardy. The photograph of the *Santa Clara* in the pamphlet showed it to be aerodynamically unstable and potentially dangerous. Chanute had tried to obtain data from Montgomery with which to calculate the glider's performance, but all he received were measurements of size and weight. To ascertain the necessary data, he advised Montgomery to borrow an anemometer and other instruments from the local Weather Bureau office if the instruments weren't available at Santa Clara, but Montgomery was too busy constructing a second glider and arranging for commercial exhibitions to worry about such matters.

The first exhibition of a Montgomery glider before a paying audience was made on May 21, 1905, at the racetrack on the fairgrounds at San Jose, a few miles from the Santa Clara College campus. Montgomery's brother Richard designed a cloth advertising banner for the occasion ("Most daring feat ever accomplished by man"), illustrated with a crude sketch of the *Santa Clara* being flown by Maloney in circus togs, while Hamilton's collapsing balloon belches dark bursts of hot air in the background. One of these magenta-tinted banners was on display for many years in the Smithsonian Institution, and it has been reproduced many times in aeronautical histories and in advertisements for the aerospace industry, creating the impression that Maloney repeated his amazing flight of April 29 many times throughout the state of California.

He did not repeat it at the San Jose racetrack on May 21, 1905. The trouble at the racetrack began with Frank Hamilton, whose wife was manning the ticket booth. A professional parachute jumper himself, Hamilton wanted to fly the *Santa Clara* and garner some of the publicity that Maloney had been receiving. Montgomery refused, whereupon Hamilton demanded $500 in advance for the use of his two balloons. While the crowd waited restlessly, a compromise was reached in which a desperate Montgomery agreed to turn over all the gate receipts to Hamilton. The unpleasantness was intensified when hangers-on pried open a gate at the rear of the racetrack, and hundreds of freeloaders poured in. The balloon was finally inflated and the ascent began. When the glider was less than 200 feet above a grove of eucalyptus trees, the lift rope snapped. Maloney glided safely to earth, missing the trees but landing in a mass of booing spectators.

The *Santa Clara* had been damaged in landing. Montgomery's second, untried glider was taken from its place beneath the trees next to the racetrack and readied for a flight. The ascent was only too successful. The balloon, with the glider still attached to it, was soon out of sight of the spectators at the racetrack. The unfortunate Maloney drifted with the wind for almost an hour before the hot air in the balloon cooled and he was able to land near Gilroy, thirty miles from San Jose. Montgomery explained what had happened in a letter to Octave Chanute. A balloon rope had become entangled with the glider, making it impossible for Maloney to cut loose with safety. To the newspapers, Montgomery told a different story. His second glider had been sabotaged as it rested unguarded under the trees during the confusion that followed the opening of the gate at the rear of the racetrack. So many bolts had been loosened, so many wires twisted and rods bent that for Maloney to have cut his lifeline to the balloon would have meant certain death.

Montgomery's next move was to initiate two legal actions against the saboteur, whom he identified publicly as Captain Thomas Baldwin. Baldwin, who had been in Oregon on the day of the racetrack fiasco, filed a countersuit for libel. All three suits were eventually dropped, but the events of May 21 had undermined Montgomery's confidence. He abandoned plans for commercial exhibitions for the time being and returned to the Santa Clara campus for the next demonstration of his glider. The occasion was the annual encampment at the college of the League of the Cross Cadets, a militant temperance organization of young men who dressed in military tunics and wide-brimmed campaign hats. Maloney was a former member of the cadets. With the booing of the rowdy crowd at the San Jose racetrack still ringing in his ears, he was determined to equal or better his flight of April 29.

The morning of July 18 was bright and windless, a perfect morning for an ascent. When everything was in readiness, Maloney shouted, "Let go," and the temperance cadets released the restraining ropes. The ropes slid through the rings on the side of the rapidly rising balloon with the usual snapping and lashing. When Maloney was an estimated 3,000 feet in the air, he released the glider. All accounts agree that the *Santa Clara* made an uneventful initial glide, but accounts of what happened after those first few seconds vary in particulars. Montgomery himself claimed only that the rear wings began to flutter and flap, after which the glider turned over on its back and dived toward a tannery adjoining the college vineyard. A low groan went up from the temperance cadets. They removed their hats. Father Richard Bell of Santa Clara took off his biretta and administered a final blessing as the glider landed upside down in the middle of the tannery yard. Maloney was carried on a litter to the college infirmary, where he died half an hour later.

The cause of the accident would remain a matter of conjecture. In one newspaper account, Montgomery was reported to have said as he reached the dying Maloney, "My God, it's awful! How could it have happened? The rope must have caught and crumpled the wing." He later wrote that one of the restraining ropes had fallen on the glider as it was withdrawn from the balloon during the launching and had wrapped itself around the right rear wing, bending it downward and breaking the post to which it was guyed, but in that case the *Santa Clara* would not have glided so smoothly during the first few seconds after its release.

When news of the fatal flight reached Dayton, Wilbur wrote Octave Chanute:

> The tragic death of poor Maloney seemed the more terrible to me because I knew it was coming and had tried in vain to think of some way to save him. I knew a direct warning would tend to precipitate rather than prevent a catastrophe. The Montgomery pamphlet showed an entire misapprehension of the real facts regarding the distribution of pressures and the travel of the center of pressure with increasing speed, and it seemed to me something awful that poor Maloney should cut loose high in the air and lightly cause the machine to dart and describe circles without knowing that there were critical points beyond which it would be absolutely impossible for him to right the machine.

In September, Chanute wrote Wilbur that Montgomery had had offers of money from promoters to exhibit his machine around the country and was building another glider. "If Prof. Montgomery resumes experiments," Wilbur warned, "he ought by all means to make a few flights himself to make sure that the machine acts in all respects as his theories lead him to expect." But Montgomery would never admit that the failure of the *Santa Clara* could have been caused by structural weakness or flaws in its design. By November 1905 he had constructed two new gliders and engaged David Wilkie to fly them. Wilkie, an electrician and motion-picture projectionist, was one of the three so-called cowboys who had helped Montgomery make the first tests of the *Santa Clara* in the summer of 1904. Once again a cable was strung between high poles in the hills and a new glider was hoisted up with Wilkie astride. After seventeen drops from the cable, Wilkie was considered trained.

The second and last exhibition of a Montgomery glider before a paying audience took place at the Idora Park racetrack, Oakland, California, on February 22, 1906. Wilkie did not cut loose from the balloon until he reached 1,200 feet according to the Oakland *Tribune*—2,000 feet according to Montgomery, who described the start of the flight as beautiful, a point the newspapers the next day seemed to have missed. The *Tribune* reported that the glider fell in terrifying circles. Wilkie in panic had taken his feet from the stirrups that controlled the movement of the trailing edges of the wings, so that the rear wings were free to oscillate, a condition perilously close to the fluttering that preceded Maloney's fatal fall. When the glider was a few hundred feet from the ground, Wilkie regained control and landed in a grassy area a quarter of a mile from the racetrack, his face skinned, his nose bleeding freely. The intrepid young electrician attempted a second flight a few days later, but when the balloon was nearly inflated a gust of wind nuzzled a weak spot near the top and the big bag split from top to bottom.

The great San Francisco earthquake of 1906 occurred before another demonstration could be made, and the depression that followed the quake put an end to Montgomery's experiments. On May 27 he wrote a long, complaining letter to Octave Chanute, citing the reverses and mishaps he had suffered at the hands of the "fools and knaves" with whom he had been obliged to associate. Disillusioned for the second time in his life with the California inventor, Chanute forwarded the letter to Wilbur with the comment that Montgomery had little idea of the trouble he would have, "first to secure stability, and then to apply a motor and propeller, if he ever gets as far as that." Montgomery never did get that far, and his tandem-wing gliders would have been all but forgotten today had not their inventor, a few years later, become the subject of a promotion campaign that had the effect of elevating John Joseph Montgomery to a pedestal where he is still revered by many as the misunderstood aeronautical pioneer who "opened for all mankind the great highway of the sky" but who lived to see the credit go to Wilbur and Orville Wright.

# 21

## *The Thorn Tree*

THE RAINS THAT turned Huffman Prairie into a quagmire were over by Monday, September 25. The Wright brothers spent every day that week at the flying field. Wilbur was unable to get a start Monday, but he redeemed himself Tuesday by flying for 18 minutes, completing sixteen rounds of the field before his gas supply was exhausted and he was forced to land. The longest flight the next day was a disappointing 3 minutes, because of engine trouble. The trouble was traced to a chunk of rubber lodged in the gas pump. It was removed and a screen was inserted in the supply pipe on Thursday, after which Orville made one of the most significant flights ever made by either of the brothers since it provided the solution to the last major problem of controlling their Flyer in the air.

The problem, which had occurred intermittently during 1904, was the occasional failure of the machine, while turning or circling, to respond promptly when the hip cradle was moved toward the high wing to restore lateral balance. In the 1905 machine, they had purposely disconnected the rudder and warping controls to see if varying the proportion of rudder to warping would correct the problem. The trouble continued. On September 12 Wilbur stalled the machine when turning a short circle. A few days later, Orville was unable to level the wings and stop circling. The same thing happened on Thursday, September 28. When Orville had been in the air for a little over 8 minutes, he passed over the Flyer's shed at the eastern edge of Huffman Prairie and headed toward the honey locust tree that stood alone in the prairie about 1,500 feet from the shed and served as a turning point at the western end of the Flyer's oval course. Orville was flying about fifty feet above the ground. The tree was forty feet in height.

The honey locust is not a tree to tangle with. Its twigs and trunk are covered with hardwood spines up to four inches long and with clusters of three-pronged, needle-sharp thorns, for which reason it is sometimes called the thorn tree. As Orville banked to the left to make his eighth sweep about the west end of the field, he noticed that he was headed straight for the thorny branches of the honey locust and shifted his hips to the right in the padded warping cradle in order to raise the left wing. The low wing refused to respond and the Flyer continued to slip toward the menacing spines on the branches of the tree. Assuming instinctively that the only way to avoid being impaled on the sharp spikes was by landing the machine before it slid into the tree, Orville turned the front rudder down to its extreme position. To his surprise, the left wing immediately began to rise. At the same time, for no apparent reason, the machine turned to the right, away from the tree —but not before a long, sharp thorn had been driven into a wooden upright with such force that a branch was torn from the tree. With the danger now past, Orville turned the front rudder up to its opposite extreme so that, instead of landing, the Flyer scraped its skids over the surface of the prairie, then rose and swept on a foot or two above the weeds, grass, and clover and landed safely in front of its shed, the thorn-tree branch still firmly nailed to one of the uprights.

Wilbur and Orville went over what had happened until they were able to ferret out the cause of the Flyer's failure to respond to movements of the hip cradle. The failure was due, they decided, to the machine's having to carry an extra load in flying the short tight circles required to stay within the boundaries of the field. In addition to its own weight, the Flyer had to sustain the load resulting from centrifugal force. With the engine already operating at full power, the machine was unable to maintain sufficient speed to sustain itself in the air, and the low wing, moving at a slower speed than the high outside wing, was in a stalled condition and refused to respond to the warping. The remedy, then, was to turn the front rudder down momentarily and let gravity supply the extra power needed. That the machine had swerved sharply away from the tree was explained by the fact that when the Flyer was in a steeply banked position, the horizontal front rudder performed more like a vertical rudder than an elevator.

By providing the solution to their last major control problem, Orville's thorn-tree flight made as significant a contribution to the brothers' success as Wilbur's idle twisting of an empty inner-tube box back in 1899. "When we had discovered the real nature of the trouble," Wilbur wrote in summarizing the experiments of 1905, "and knew that it could always be remedied by tilting the machine forward a little, so that its flying speed would be restored, we felt that we were ready to place flying machines on the market."

Confident that he now had complete control of the machine, Orville flew fourteen rounds of the field on Friday before exhausting the gasoline supply. On Saturday he circled the prairie several times again, coming down after

17 minutes. As usual, a few drops of oil had been applied to the transmission bearings before the Flyer was launched. This lubrication was adequate for short flights, but on Saturday the rear bearing overheated, forcing Orville to land before the gas ran out. A three-gallon fuel tank was fitted to the machine the following week, and on Tuesday, October 3, Orville flew 15 miles around and around the field, but again the rear bearing overheated and he landed after 25 minutes. An oil cup was added to the troublesome bearing and on Wednesday he flew for 33 minutes. Overheating of the front transmission bearing brought the flight to an end. This must have been the flight that Orville had in mind when he told Fred Kelly many years later, "I used to think the back of my neck would break if I endured one more turn around the field." On Thursday, October 5, Orville's neck was given a rest and Wilbur took over. Oil cups had been fitted to both transmission bearings. Wilbur took off but landed after less than a minute to avoid hitting a fence. The Flyer was brought back to the starting rail and launched on the longest flight of 1905—24 1/5 miles in 38 minutes, at an average speed of 38 miles per hour. It would have been longer if the brothers had not neglected to replace the gasoline consumed in the aborted first flight of the day.

At first, only Bishop Wright, Lorin and his family, banker Huffman, and a few close friends had been invited to witness the flights at Huffman Prairie. As the flights grew longer, Wilbur and Orville saw to it that a few influential civic leaders and local merchants and businessmen were on hand, men who could be trusted not to talk to reporters but whose word as witnesses would come in handy later on. Aside from the presence of these invited guests, the flights had been made in almost perfect secrecy until Tuesday, October 3, when two interurban trolleys passed the prairie during the 25 minutes Orville was in the air. The still longer flight he made the next day was witnessed by ten relatives and friends.

That night a long-distance telephone call was received in the house on Hawthorn Street: A Mr. Fay of the Cincinnati *Commercial Tribune* wanted to know about the flights at Huffman Prairie. Until then the brothers had not been bothered by reporters, aside from three newspapermen who had descended on the prairie one Saturday in September when it had been impossible to fly because the rains had turned the pasture into a swamp. Mr. Fay was evidently given short shrift, but his call signaled an end to the relative privacy in which their experiments had been conducted. At least fifteen spectators appeared at Huffman Prairie the next day to witness Wilbur's record-breaking flight of October 5. Wilbur identified three of them by name, then wrote in his diary "about a dozen others present."

Among the dozen others was Luther Beard, managing editor of the Dayton *Journal.* Beard sometimes rode the same trolley as the Wrights and made inquiries about their progress from time to time by phone, but nothing about the flights had appeared in the *Journal,* probably because short airship flights were no longer news and Beard, like most newspaper editors, did not know the difference between an airship and a flying machine. A flight of more than twenty minutes by a flying machine was news, however, and a rival Dayton paper, the *Daily News,* scooped the *Journal* the very day that Luther Beard was watching Wilbur's 24-mile flight. The city editor of the *Daily News* had recently been badgered by interurban trolley passengers who had seen the Wright Flyer in the air and wanted to know why his paper wasn't printing the news.

The inquiries were effective. On the afternoon of October 5, the Dayton *Daily News* informed its readers that the Wright brothers had been making sensational flights every day at Huffman Prairie. One flight was described during which "according to reliable witnesses the machine soared gracefully for some 25 minutes, responding to all demands of the rudder," an obvious reference to Orville's 15-mile, 25-minute flight of Tuesday, which had been witnessed by a local hardware merchant, a post office employee, a traveling salesman from nearby Germantown, and Dayton druggist William Fouts. The story was picked up the next day by the Cincinnati *Post,* but with the help of a few influential friends the Wrights succeeded in keeping the news from going out over the wires, an achievement that gave rise abroad to a report that they had suppressed the news by buying up the entire edition of a Dayton newspaper.

The day after the *Daily News* story appeared, so many men and women armed with cameras lined the fences at Huffman Prairie that flights were discontinued until the excitement died down. The Wrights did not take to the air again until October 16, when Wilbur came down with engine trouble after a single circuit of the field. His aim was to better the record with a flight of more than one hour before winter made flying impossible. For a flight that long to be accepted as credible by a skeptical world would require the testimony of a witness with a greater understanding of what was involved than any of the Daytonians who had been present at Huffman Prairie—a witness, say, with the reputation of Octave Chanute. Chanute had seen only one power flight by the Wrights. That had been on October 15, 1904, when Orville had smashed the skids and propellers of the 1904 machine in landing after a flight of only 24 seconds. Now, a year later, they were more sure of their machine and their skill in handling it. As soon as their balky motor was back in condition, they notified Chanute of their intention to set the record above one hour. On Monday, October 30, he received a wire from Dayton. "Trial Tuesday. Can you come?" Chanute left Chicago that night. On the back of one of Wilbur's recent letters, he made a brief notation that tells what happened: "Went to Dayton to see last flight of season at the beginning of November. Prevented by great storm."

The storm put an end to the Wright brothers' hopes to better Wilbur's 24-mile, 38-minute flight of October 5. The Flyer was dismantled and stored. The shed on the prairie was turned over to Torrence Huffman, who had other uses for the lumber and tore it down. When the interurban cars stopped at Simms Station thereafter and the passengers looked out the windows at the field across the Dayton–Springfield Pike, all they saw were banker Huffman's cows and horses, grazing once more undisturbed among the grassy hummocks of the prairie.

# 22

## *One Million Francs*

E V E R   S I N C E   T H E  first, distorted reports of the flights of December
1903 reached Europe, the French had been frantically trying to catch up with
the Wrights. The two most persistent experimenters were Ferdinand Ferber,
the French artillery captain who had tried to wangle an invitation to the
Wright camp in 1903, and Ernest Archdeacon, the wealthy lawyer who had
written the report of Octave Chanute's 1903 talk to the French Aéro-Club that
was printed in *La Locomotion*. Archdeacon had appended to his report an
extract from a letter by Ferber exhorting patriotic Frenchmen not to allow
the airplane to be invented in America. In March 1904, Ferber made a number
of glides in the sand hills on the Channel coast below Calais in a glider modeled on the Wrights' 1901 machine. His best glide was only 9 meters in length.
At the same site, a biplane glider with a fixed vertical tail constructed at
Archdeacon's expense was tested by young Gabriel Voisin, later to become a
famous aircraft designer and manufacturer. Archdeacon blamed the poor
performance of his glider on Chanute's failure to provide him with enough
information. In his 1903 talk to the Aéro-Club de France, Chanute had mentioned the Wrights' system of lateral control by warping the wings and simultaneously moving the vertical rudder, but of the half dozen gliders *du type de
Wright* constructed in France in 1904, only two had any means of lateral
control. These were both built by Robert Esnault-Pelterie. In each, a pair of
movable flat surfaces called *élevons* were positioned in front of the wings like
primitive ailerons. Neither of these gliders flew.

Typical of the French approach to the flying problem was the belief that
large cash prizes would tempt experimenters to come up with solutions. In
March 1904, Henri Deutsch de la Meurthe, an oil-rich benefactor of ballooning and aviation, established a prize of 25,000 francs for the first airplane
flight of one kilometer in a closed circuit. In November, Ernest Archdeacon

put up a like amount, so that the Grand Prix Deutsch-Archdeacon, as it came to be called, amounted to 50,000 francs, or $10,000. In March 1905, Archdeacon wrote the Wright brothers a challenging letter, offering to come to Dayton to see them compete for the prize. The Wrights were not about to reveal their solution of the flight problem to possible imitators for a paltry $10,000 and replied evasively that they might try for the prize when other arrangements permitted. A few weeks later they received a letter from Captain Ferber, who wanted to purchase a Wright Flyer. At the time, they were still awaiting a visit from the British military attaché in Washington. Assuming that Ferber was acting on behalf of the French government, they put his letter aside for the time being.

There had been no falling off in the number of letters exchanged by Wilbur and Octave Chanute in 1905, but it was not until May, when Chanute asked the brothers outright how near they were to producing a practical flying machine for use in war, that Wilbur mentioned the unsuccessful effort they had made that January to interest the U.S. War Department in a Flyer, and when he did mention the matter, he referred to it in a curiously round-about way, without revealing that their offer to sell a Flyer to the British War Office had been made at the same time. "The American Government has apparently decided to permit foreign governments to take the lead in utilizing our invention for war purposes," Wilbur wrote in answer to Chanute's query. "We greatly regret this attitude of our own country but seeing no way to remedy it, we have made a formal proposition to the British Government and expect to have a conference with one of its representatives, at Dayton, very soon."

Astonished that the United States would allow a foreign government to take the lead in utilizing the brothers' invention, Chanute offered to put a flea in the ear of the U.S. War Department. The offer was ignored, but in Wilbur's next letter he related the whole sad story—Congressman Nevin's failure to present their proposal directly to the Secretary of War and the government's reply, which they had interpreted as a flat turndown. "We still do," he added contentiously, as if French-born Octave Chanute had put the native-born Wrights on the defensive. "We would be ashamed of ourselves if we had offered our machines to a foreign government without giving our own country a chance at it, but our consciences are clear." Just how clear can be adduced from the final paragraph of Wilbur's letter:

It is no pleasant thought to us that any foreign country should take from America any share of the glory of having conquered the flying problem, but we feel that we have done our full share toward making this an American invention, and if it is sent abroad for further development the responsibility does not rest upon us. We have taken pains to see that

"Opportunity" gave a good clear knock on the War Department door. It has for years been our business practice to sell to those who wished to buy, instead of trying to force goods upon people who did not want them. If the American Government has decided to spend no more money on flying machines till their practical use has been demonstrated in actual service abroad, we are sorry, but we cannot reasonably object. They are the judges.

When summer came and went without any word from the British military attaché who had been ordered to visit Dayton, the brothers decided to renew their proposal to the U.S. War Department. On October 9, 1905, they addressed a letter directly to the Secretary of War, pointing out that their previous proposal had received scant consideration from the Board of Ordnance and Fortification. Once more, with bureaucratic inevitability, their letter was forwarded by the Secretary of War to the Board of Ordnance and Fortification, and once more the first thing they saw when they opened the Board's reply was the stock paragraph used in responding to cranks and indigent inventors. The second paragraph, however, was entirely new. Before a contract could be considered, the president of the Board advised them, they would have to furnish a description and drawings of their machine, together with its approximate cost and date of delivery.

The Wright brothers replied on October 19, making it clear that the Flyer had been developed at their own expense and they had no thought of asking for financial assistance from the government. Before they could frame a proposal that would meet the Board's requirements, they would have to know what those requirements were. The government's response was that "the Board does not care to formulate any requirements for the performance of a flying machine or take any further action until a machine is produced which by actual operation is shown to be able to produce horizontal flight and to carry an operator." To be fair, the Wrights' proposal had not stated that they had actually produced a flying machine capable of flying for twenty-five miles at more than 30 miles an hour, only that they were ready to furnish such a machine on contract. Nevertheless, Wilbur and Orville looked upon the Board's second turndown as not only flat but final. Octave Chanute made another offer to intercede by presenting the brothers' case directly to Theodore Roosevelt, but the Wrights were not interested in Chanute's putting a flea in anybody's ear, least of all that of the President of the United States.

Chanute had also volunteered his help in the English negotiations, and Wilbur had promised to let him know when the British military attaché visited Dayton, but the attaché failed to appear. "We are not anticipating an immediate visit from the Britishers, as we have not heard from them for several months," Wilbur wrote Chanute on October 19, "and do not expect anything until we write or stir them up in some indirect way." They stirred the British up in the most direct way that same day by addressing a letter to the War Office in London. The letter amended their previous proposal by guaranteeing a trial flight of at least fifty miles rather than ten. This effectively increased the minimum price of a Flyer to the British from $25,000 to $125,000.

The British War Office in the meantime had initiated an inquiry to find out what had become of the report of the military attaché's visit to Dayton. The inquiry revealed that the attaché, Colonel Hubert Foster, who was accredited to Mexico as well as the United States, had been in Mexico in May 1905 when he was ordered to make the visit and had not returned to Washington until October. On November 18 he was prodded into asking the Wrights when he could come to Dayton to witness a flight. He was welcome to come at any time, was their reply, but only to satisfy himself of their claims through conferences with witnesses of their flights. No demonstration flights would be made until a contract had been signed. Colonel Foster was planning to retire in December and was not about to set off on a wild-goose chase into the Ohio wilderness. He informed the Wrights bluntly that his instructions were to witness a flight, not to interview witnesses. "There is thus a deadlock" were his final words on the subject. He returned to England, and the following February the British War Office notified the Wrights officially that the terms of their proposal were unacceptable. This constituted another turndown, but not as flat a one as they had received from their own government, for the reason that the news of their long flights of September and October 1905 had by then been accepted by the British as authentic.

Wilbur and Orville had kept the press in ignorance of their experiments at Huffman Prairie to avoid the ludicrous distortions of fact that had colored the first reports of their flights at Kill Devil Hills in 1903. When it became obvious that they would not be able to improve on Wilbur's 38-minute record of October 5, they sent accounts of what they had accomplished in 1905 to the three individuals who could be counted on to spread the news in the three European countries most likely to purchase a Wright Flyer. The announcements were sent in the form of letters, all on the same day, November 17, 1905—one to Georges Besançon, editor of the French monthly *L'Aérophile;* one to Carl Dienstbach, New York representative of the German journal *Illustrierte Aeronautische Mitteilungen*; and one to Patrick Alexander, the wealthy member of the Aeronautical Society of Great Britain who had triggered the English negotiations by sending Colonel John Capper of the British Balloon Factory to call on the brothers in 1904.

Alexander read the Wrights' letter to the Aeronautical Society at the society's December 15 meeting in London. Its contents were accepted as truthful, but they had no effect whatever on the negotiations with the British War Office, which had reached a deadlock before the letter was made public.

The November 17 letter to Carl Dienstbach was printed in February 1906 in *Illustrierte Aeronautische Mitteilungen,* with observations by the editor that amounted to a personal attack on the Wright brothers. The reason for the attack was the publication in the French journal *L'Aérophile* of two letters written by the Wrights to Captain Ferdinand Ferber, in one of which a reference to Kaiser Wilhelm had been translated into French in such a way that it could be construed as an insult to the German Emperor. The Wrights had put aside Captain Ferber's letter about purchasing a Flyer until October 9, when they wrote that they were now prepared to offer a flying machine on contract, the cost to depend on the length of a trial flight. Ferber wrote back, asking the Wrights to set a definite price, but warning them that because of the progress he himself had been making, the French government was not willing to pay as high a price for a Flyer then as when he had first written in May. In fact, Ferber was out of favor with his superiors at the moment because of some inconclusive experiments he had been making that year with a small propeller-driven glider launched from a cable. Wilbur and Orville did not know this, but they were not taken in by the claims of the progress being made by the mercurial French artillery captain. It is difficult to distinguish flattery from sarcasm in their reply. "No one in the world can appreciate your accomplishment as much as we can," they responded. France was indeed lucky to have Ferber, but since other governments would not want to be overtaken, the value of the Wright machine to other countries would increase accordingly. "With Russia and Austria in a troubled state and the German Emperor in a truculent mood," the letter continued, "a general conflagration could break out at any moment." Since France was so far ahead of these other countries—thanks to Ferber—the Wrights were willing to reduce the price of a machine and instructions in its use to one million francs, then the equivalent of $200,000 (the letter did not state what the price was being reduced from).

Neither of the letters to Ferber had been meant for publication, and the brothers considered their appearance in the December 1905 *Aérophile* outrageous, not only for the omission of all embarrassing references to Ferber's own insignificant experiments but for the liberties taken in translation. "The German Emperor in a truculent mood" came out *l'Empereur allemand cherchant noise,* which Chanute translated back into English for Wilbur as "seeking a fuss." The editor of *Illustrierte Aeronautische Mitteilungen* not only questioned the credibility of the Wrights' November 17 letter but let his readers know that its authors had referred to the Kaiser as a disturber of the peace of Europe.

Whereas the Wright brothers' claims were as widely disbelieved in Germany as they were believed in England, their November 17 letter to Georges Besançon created a traumatic schism in aeronautical circles in France. The letter had been intended for publication in Besançon's monthly *L'Aérophile,* but because the December issue was late that year and would not appear until January 1906, Besançon arranged to have the letter translated and published in advance in the November 30 issue of *L'Auto,* a daily for sports fans published in Paris.

The initial French reaction has been described as one of near-stupefaction. Frenchmen had always found it hard to believe that the Wrights had made four flights of less than a minute in 1903. Now they were expected to believe that they had been making flights of more than half an hour in 1905. In the Parisian periodical *Les Sports,* Ernest Archdeacon, patriotic patron of French aviation, repeated publicly the challenge he had made in his letter to the brothers in March: If they could really fly that well, why did they not come to France and snap up the Deutsch-Archdeacon prize of 50,000 francs for a single closed-circuit flight of only one kilometer? If they did not, the glory would go to others, for their invention would be quickly copied. Wilbur forwarded a copy of the clipping from *Les Sports* to Octave Chanute, noting that he and Orville had had a good laugh at Archdeacon's suggestion that their invention could be so easily copied. Chanute was in his cluttered upstairs study in Chicago when he opened the envelope containing the clipping. "As I read it," he wrote Wilbur, "I burst into such laughter that one of my daughters was alarmed and ran up to find out what was the matter. I could only gasp: 'It is—because—Archdeacon—is such—an ass!' "

The tremors created in France by the publication of the letter to Besançon were felt as far away as Mansfield, Ohio, 120 miles from Dayton. Mansfield was the hometown of Frank S. Lahm, a wealthy American businessman, head of a firm, located in Paris. Then in his late fifties, Lahm was recognized as the dean of balloon pilots of the Aéro-Club de France. As the most prominent American member of that organization, he determined to find out for himself if his fellow Ohioans had actually accomplished what they claimed. The day after Wilbur and Orville's letter appeared in *L'Auto,* he sent a cable to his nephew Henry Weaver, Jr., in Mansfield, Ohio: "Verify what Wright brothers claim. Necessary go Dayton today. Prompt answer cable."

Henry Weaver, Jr., was the son of Lahm's brother-in-law, who manufactured the overhead cash carriers used in department and dry-goods stores in those days. Henry Sr. was a busy man, so Lahm had addressed the cable to Henry Jr., knowing that he would be more free to make the trip to Dayton than his father. The cable made no sense to young Weaver, who had never heard of the Wright brothers. Thinking it had been meant for his father, who was in Chicago on business, he transmitted the dozen words of cabalese by telegram to his father's hotel. The telegram was delivered to Henry Sr. in the middle of the night. He had no more idea who the Wright brothers were than Henry Jr., but the word "claim" in the cable sounded a note of urgency in his businessman's brain. Before going back to bed, he sent a telegram, addressed simply to "Wright Brothers, Dayton, Ohio," requesting an explanation.

The telegram was received at the Wright Cycle Company on West Third Street on Saturday morning, December 2. Wilbur and Orville could make neither head nor tail of it and sent a wire to Weaver requesting an explanation from him. Utterly confused, Weaver sent a second wire to the Wright brothers, asking if they knew F. S. Lahm of Paris. The brothers didn't know Lahm, but they had read of his ballooning exploits in France and assumed he was a Frenchman. "Yes," they wired back, "Lahm the French aeronaut." The word "aeronaut" jogged Weaver's memory. He had once read something about two brothers named Wright who had experimented with gliders in North Carolina. Concluding that his aeronautical brother-in-law was about to abandon ballooning for gliding and had ordered a glider from the Wright brothers—who were no doubt asking too high a price—Weaver was overcome by a still greater sense of urgency and sent the brothers a third telegram, announcing that he was leaving Chicago and would be at the Algonquin Hotel in Dayton the next morning.

Weaver arrived at the Algonquin at 7 a.m., Sunday, December 3. No firm by the name of Wright Brothers was listed in any of the hotel's directories, so he went to the telegraph office, where he learned that his three telegrams had been delivered to a bicycle company on West Third Street. Knowing that it would be futile to visit a place of business on Sunday morning, he returned to the hotel, where he found Orville waiting for him in the lobby, looking more like Edgar Allan Poe, Weaver thought, than a flying-machine inventor. The comedy of errors reached a climax when Weaver introduced himself as the brother-in-law of the man in Paris who had ordered a glider from the Wrights. But everything came sharply to a focus when Weaver gave Orville Lahm's message to read. "Verify what Wright brothers claim" made sense to Orville. This was what he and Wilbur had been waiting for—the opportunity to prove to a disinterested party that they had done what they claimed they had done, but without having to make a demonstration flight.

The rest of the morning was one long love feast between Orville and the manufacturer from Mansfield, Ohio. It began with a trip on the interurban trolley to Simms Station. After being shown over Huffman Prairie, Weaver was introduced to farmer David Beard across the pike, who assured him there was absolutely no doubt that the flights had taken place. Even more convincing was an interview with Amos Stauffer, who farmed the fields adjoining Huffman's pasture. "Well, the boys are at it again," Stauffer remembered remarking to the helper with whom he had been cutting corn on October 5, the day Wilbur made his 38-minute flight. "I just kept on shocking corn until I got down to the fence," he told Weaver, "and the durned thing was still going round. I thought it would never stop."

When Weaver and Orville returned to Dayton, they dropped in on William Fouts, the druggist whose loose tongue had been responsible for the story in the *Daily News* which had brought such a flood of sightseers to Huffman Prairie that the brothers had been forced to discontinue their experiments. Weaver was also taken to the home of Charles Billman, secretary of the West Side Savings and Loan Association, who provided Weaver with further corroboration of the flights. Later that day he visited the house on Hawthorn Street and met Katharine, Bishop Wright, and Wilbur. He found Wilbur even quieter and less demonstrative than Orville. When he was back home in Mansfield, Weaver wrote his brother-in-law a detailed account of his trip to Dayton. Because his visit had taken place on a Sunday, he had been able to interview only a few of the many witnesses of the Wright flights, but he was absolutely convinced of the reliability and integrity of the brothers. "Neither is married," he threw in for good measure. "As Mr. Wright expressed it, they had not the means to support 'a wife and a flying machine too.' "

Frank Lahm's brother-in-law was not the only man who traveled to Dayton that year to find out if the Wright brothers were lying. On December 12, Wilbur and Orville were interviewed by Robert Coquelle, reporter for *L'Auto,* the Parisian daily that first printed the letter to Besançon. Coquelle cabled his editor from Dayton: "The Wright brothers refuse to show their machine, but I have interviewed the witnesses, and it is impossible to doubt the success of their experiments."

Coquelle's highly colored, romanticized account of his visit was published in *L'Auto* in four daily installments under the title "Conquête de l'Air par Deux Marchands de Cycles." The Wrights estimated that 95 percent of everything Coquelle claimed to have seen and heard in Dayton was purely fanciful. The 5 percent residue of truth did little to alter the attitude of the anti-Wright faction in the French Aéro-Club. The first installment of Coquelle's story was published December 23. It was the chief topic of discussion at the meeting of the Aviation Committee of the Aéro-Club that night. The members of the committee—which as its name implied were more interested in flying machines than in airships and ballooning—were soon aligned in two groups of unequal size, those few, like Besançon, Lahm, and Captain Ferber, who believed the Wrights, and those who, like Ernest Archdeacon, could not believe that the Wright Flyer had been developed to the point where it could stay in the air for more than half an hour. When it became apparent that there was no reconciling the two factions, Besançon suggested that the discussion be postponed until the next meeting, by which time Coquelle's three remaining articles would have been published and Lahm would have had a chance to translate Weaver's letter into French so that it could be read aloud to the members.

When the committee met again, late in the afternoon of December 29, twenty members were present, including Frank Lahm, Captain Ferber, Georges Besançon, and Robert Coquelle. The excitable Ernest Archdeacon chaired the meeting. After Lahm had read Weaver's letter and Coquelle had given a brief account of his trip to Dayton, the discussion began, quietly at first, then more vociferously, with several members gesticulating and speaking at once, while Archdeacon banged on the table with a metal ruler and called for order.

Lahm was challenged on two points. Since it was known that the Wrights were not wealthy, who had financed all those expensive experiments? Lahm's answer that the brothers had done all the work themselves was greeted with skepticism. He had no answer at all for the second question: Since American reporters were known to be among the most aggressive and enterprising in the world, why had there been nothing about the Wright flights in the U.S. newspapers? Archdeacon continued his attack on the Wrights' credibility at the regular monthly dinner meeting of the Aéro-Club de France that night. Momentarily relenting, he said that if what the brothers claimed was really true, it was one of the greatest achievements in the history of the world, and he proceeded to draft a cable to Theodore Roosevelt, informing the President of the United States that it was his duty to see that his government gave the Wrights a sum equal to one million francs. When Frank Lahm pointed out that the President was not in a position to give away money, Archdeacon shot back, "Didn't they give money to Langley?" The meeting broke up several hours later, with the majority of the members present strong in the belief that the Wright brothers had perpetrated a brazen *bluff américain.*

All this time the negotiations that the Wrights had initiated with the devious but energetic Captain Ferber had been progressing independently, without regard to the opinions of Archdeacon and other doubting members of the French Aéro-Club. When Ferber first informed his superiors that the Wrights had offered to sell a flying machine to the French government for one million francs, he was treated like a visionary for believing that such a machine existed, but his chief had second thoughts about the matter and suggested that a commission be appointed to visit Dayton and confer with the Wrights.

On November 15, Ferber wrote asking the brothers if they thought the visit of such a commission advisable. Yes, they replied, they thought it highly advisable, the sooner the better. The formation of a commission would take time, however. In the interim, Ferber went to work behind the scenes. The next move in this international game was a cable from Ferber to the Wrights, dated December 13: "Friend with full powers for starting terms of contract will sail next Saturday." The mystery of just who Ferber's friend might be was intensified by the receipt of a cable five days later from Frank Lahm: "Am working for you. Avoid publicity."

Wilbur and Orville were of the opinion that Ferber's friend would represent a syndicate of sportsmen. Chanute, when apprised of the impending visit, suspected that the emissary would be an agent of the French War Department, dispatched as a civilian to save the department embarrassment in case the Wright brothers were found to be bluffing. When the Wrights received a letter from Ferber on December 27, identifying his friend as a Monsieur Fordyce, representing a syndicate that intended to purchase a Flyer and turn it over to the French government, the brothers' growing distrust of Ferber made them change their minds. It now seemed evident that Fordyce really did represent the French government.

Fordyce arrived on December 28. Like everyone else who traveled to Dayton and met the brothers face to face, he was impressed by their frankness and sincerity and by the presence in the house on Hawthorn Street of their clergyman father, never a drawback when it came to convincing visitors from abroad of the integrity of his two youngest sons. At seventy-seven, Bishop Wright was still the indefatigable diarist he had been since 1857, when he began this conscientious method of record-keeping at the age of twenty-eight. Two laconic entries extracted from his diary for 1905 attest to the rapidity with which the deal with Fordyce was consummated:

*Thursday, December 28.* A Frenchman by the name of Arnold Fordyce came to investigate and drive a trade for a flying machine. They agreed on terms.

*Saturday, December 30.* In the afternoon, Wilbur and Orville sign up the contract with Mr. Arnold Fordyce, of Paris, to furnish a flyer &c., for one million francs.

# 23

## Fame, But Not Wealth

NEWS OF WHAT THE Wright brothers had accomplished in 1905 drifted back over the Atlantic from France. American newspaper and magazine writers were skeptical. If such sensational flights were being made in a populated part of the United States, the *Scientific American* asked its readers on January 13, 1906, "is it possible to believe that the enterprising American reporter, who, it is well known, comes down the chimney when the door is locked in his face—even if he has to scale a fifteen-story skyscraper to do so—would not have ascertained all about them and published them broadcast long ago?" Claiming that it had a right to exact further information before placing reliance on French reports, the magazine asked the Wrights to either deny or confirm the claims made in the letter to Besançon published in the January *Aérophile*. The request was made to order for Wilbur's sharp pen. "As you profess to have obtained the data of what you term 'alleged experiments' direct from a published letter signed by ourselves," he replied, "and do not discredit the authenticity of the letter but only the truthfulness of the statements, we are at a loss to understand why you should desire further statements from such a source."

The Wrights' claims were not questioned by the Aero Club of America, an organization founded in New York in the fall of 1905 by members of the Automobile Club of America. When Alexander Graham Bell, the Aero Club's most famous member, was asked by reporters wherein the Wright Flyer differed from other machines, he replied succinctly: "It flies." Although most of the other members were millionaire sportsmen, Wilbur and Orville were invited to join the club, and did so in January 1906. In February, Albert F. Zahm, a prominent if not especially affluent member, wrote the Wrights a letter, asking them to prepare a formal statement of their flights for publication. Zahm had helped Octave Chanute organize the International Conference on Aerial Navigation in Chicago in 1893 and in 1902 had offered to exchange information on wind-tunnel experiments with the Wrights. Wilbur sent him a chart of wind pressures on a square plane. Zahm did not reciprocate, although he had been conducting experiments in a forty-foot wind tunnel at Catholic University in Washington, D.C., where he headed the Department of Physics and Mathematics.

There was a sycophantic streak in Professor Zahm. His letter on behalf of the Aero Club was so effusively congratulatory that Wilbur in his reply was moved to comment on "the kindness that breathes from every line." As to a statement for publication, the brothers would be only too happy to comply. On March 2, they addressed a letter to the secretary of the Aero Club, similar to those sent to Besançon and Alexander for dissemination abroad. The letter was released to the press as an official Aero Club Circular and in this form reached the desk of the editor of the *Scientific American*. The wily editor knew better than to ask the Wrights for confirmation a second time. Instead, he mailed a questionnaire to the seventeen witnesses of flights whose names were appended to the Aero Club Circular. Witnesses were asked to give the date of each flight they had seen, together with the estimated altitude and speed of the aircraft. Eleven of the seventeen witnesses replied. Answers to the questions varied widely—the Flyer's speed was given as anywhere from 7 to 30 miles an hour—but they all confirmed that on the days specified the Wrights had made flights of the duration they claimed.

On April 7, 1906, the *Scientific American* recanted and printed the complete text of the Wrights' letter to the Aero Club of America. This added to the brothers' fame, but fame was one thing, fortune another, and two days before the scientific weekly reversed its position on the Wrights, their deal to sell a Flyer to the French for one million francs fell through.

When the Frenchman Arnold Fordyce arrived in Dayton during Christmas week 1905, Wilbur and Orville were sure that he represented the French Ministry of War, but as Captain Ferber had written, he really did represent a syndicate of businessmen who wanted to purchase a Flyer and present it to the French Army. Ferber had persuaded Henri Letellier, whose father was proprietor of the Parisian newspaper *Le Journal*, to head the syndicate. Purchasing an airplane for one million francs as a gift to the French nation was not as altruistic as it seemed. The members of the syndicate would garner awards and decorations from the government in return, and *Le Journal* would score a scoop over its rival Parisian dailies by being the first to cover the trial flights. Arnold Fordyce, Letellier's secretary, had been dispatched to Dayton to obtain the Wright brothers' signature to a contract guaranteeing world rights to their invention. He was not to quibble over price, merely to make sure that the syndicate did not become the victim of a hoax.

The contract signed by Fordyce and the Wright brothers on December 30, 1905, did not guarantee an outright sale of a Flyer for one million francs. It was an option to buy if certain terms were met, the terms being that the Wrights must make a trial flight of fifty kilometers before August 1, 1906, and instruct others in the operation of the machine. They must also deliver formulas and information that would enable the French to manufacture flying machines of other sizes and speeds. Exclusive world rights to the invention would be limited to three months, after which the Wrights would be free to sell to other governments. If an agreement on terms was not reached by April 5, 1906, the option would lapse. The French would get no Flyer, and the Wrights would be paid 25,000 francs by way of compensation.

When Fordyce returned to Paris, Letellier presented the contract to the Minister of War and was assured that he and his associates would receive the proper credit for their patriotism. The Flyer's price was considered ridiculously high, but at the time France and Germany had locked horns in a struggle over which nation should establish a protectorate over Morocco, the sole remaining piece of the African jigsaw puzzle that had not yet been firmly put in place by one of the imperialist European powers. By making loans to the Sultan, the French were in the best position to do this, but they were being challenged by the Germans, who had appeared on the scene in the guise of champions of Moroccan independence. If an armed conflict should ensue, the use of scouting planes in that sparsely settled corner of Africa might just tip the scales in favor of the French. The Ministry of War was therefore willing to provide the 25,000 francs to be held in escrow and forfeited to the Wright brothers in case a final agreement had not been signed by April 5. A commission of three military men and two civilians was appointed by the ministry to travel to Dayton to negotiate terms.

Arnold Fordyce was one of the two civilians on the commission. He believed implicitly in the ability of the Wrights to fulfill the terms of any contract they signed. As a counterweight to Fordyce, Commandant Henri Bonel, Chief of Engineers of the French General Staff, was appointed to head the commission. Bonel had witnessed the unsuccessful tests of Clément Ader's *Avion* in 1897 and was a confirmed skeptic when it came to flying machines. The two men reached New York on March 18 and were joined in Dayton a few days later by Captains Jules Fournier and Henri Régnier of the French embassy in Washington and attorney Walter Berry, American legal adviser to the embassy.

The existence of the commission was a well-kept secret. Fordyce had stayed at the Algonquin Hotel during his previous visit. The five-man commission lodged instead at the less palatial Beckel House. To avoid detection, the military members dressed like businessmen. The meetings in the room above the bicycle shop went unnoticed until a telegraph office employee alerted a local reporter to the large number of coded messages being cabled to Paris by the Frenchmen at the Beckel House. The reporter accosted Fordyce and Bonel in the hotel lobby one night as they returned from the theater. Fordyce, a former actor, saved the day by explaining with appropriate aplomb that the commission was in Dayton to study the city's "water pipes." Hydraulics was of no interest to the reporter's paper, and the commission was able to conduct its business thereafter without interference from the press.

In time, Commandant Bonel became an even more zealous disciple of the Wrights than Fordyce. He recommended that the deal be closed before the option expired, but by the end of March the Moroccan question had become moot. Its settlement had been left to a multinational conference at Algeciras in Spain. Germany's hypocritical concern for Moroccan independence badly misfired, and when it became clear that the question would be settled in France's favor, a clique at the War Ministry openly opposed Bonel's recommendation. A rash of cables from Paris demanded an increase in the requirements for the Flyer's speed and altitude and an unreasonable increase in the exclusivity period—the time that must elapse before the Wrights would be free to sell their invention to other governments. The original three-month period was increased to fifteen months. The Wrights balked. The ministry reduced its demands to twelve months. The Wrights agreed to five, then six.

Four days before the option agreement expired, Wilbur sent a telegram to French-speaking Octave Chanute, seeking his help in the negotiations. Chanute arrived in Dayton on Monday, April 2, took part in the final meeting above the bicycle shop, and returned to Chicago that night. Tuesday was a day of waiting, as cables were exchanged with the War Ministry. At three o'clock on the afternoon of April 5, the brothers were shown the ministry's last cable, insisting that they agree to a twelve-month exclusivity period and a 300-meter altitude requirement. The Wrights refused, and the commission was recalled. The day after the option expired, Wilbur and Orville made a last-ditch offer in writing to Bonel, agreeing to all the War Ministry's demands and accepting the twelve-month exclusivity period on condition that the United States government be excepted. The offer was considered, then rejected, and the 25,000-franc forfeit, the equivalent of $5,000, was paid to the Wrights in October 1906. Oddly enough, although it was the first money they had made since giving up their bicycle business, it was earned, not by selling, but by not selling a flying machine.

A month after the French option expired, the Wrights prodded the War Office in London into reopening the British negotiations. They now offered to sell a single Flyer and instructions in its use for $100,000. For an additional $100,000 they would sell data and formulas for the designing of machines of other sizes and speeds. They suggested that the British military attaché in Washington come to Dayton to discuss the new proposal. Lieutenant Colonel Edward Gleichen, who had succeeded Colonel Foster, the former attaché, visited Dayton on August 8, 1906. Like the two preceding British emissaries, Gleichen was completely captivated by the Hawthorn Street household. To supplement his official report of the visit, he wrote a lengthy monograph in which he described Wilbur and Orville as "intelligent looking, not 'cranks,' apparently honest—their venerable father being a bishop of some hazy denomination—and with little or none of the usual braggadocio of the Yankee inventor." They were modest, even shy, Gleichen reported, characteristics that contrasted sharply with their determination not to take a penny less than the prices quoted in their latest offer.

In 1904 the Wright brothers had made an equally favorable impression on Colonel Capper, when he made the trip to Dayton at the time of the St. Louis fair. In May 1906, Capper was appointed superintendent of the British Balloon Factory at Farnborough and in that capacity was to be consulted on all aeronautical matters. He advised the War Office not to purchase a Wright Flyer. Not only was the price too high but in his opinion current British experiments would, within a reasonable time, produce a flying machine much like that of the Wrights.

Actually, the British were lagging far behind the French. The best they had accomplished at the time the War Office received the brothers' new proposal had been tests of a huge kite-glider, designed and flown by Samuel Franklin Cody, an eccentric American expatriate who had toured England in the 1890s in a Wild West show and decided to stay. Cody traded on a facial resemblance to Buffalo Bill Cody, to whom he was not related, and dressed accordingly. With Colonel Capper's help, he would construct and make a brief flight in the first English propeller-driven aircraft, but that would not be until 1908, and the flight would end in a crash.

What Capper was pinning his hopes on in 1906 was a tailless glider with swept-back wings being developed by a British lieutenant, John W. Dunne. By producing inherent stability, this tailless configuration would supposedly enable student pilots to learn to fly at once without undergoing the long training period that the English believed would be required for piloting a Wright Flyer, but Colonel Capper was clutching at a straw when he hinted to the War Office that the Dunne machine would rival the Wright Flyer. The first tests of the glider would not be made until 1907, in secret in Scotland, with Capper himself doing the gliding, and its only successful flight would end after eight seconds when the glider smashed into a wall. The colonel, who had donned a fencer's mask for his maiden flight, escaped with a cut ear. The addition of a motor to the machine the following year would be no more successful. In 1906, however, Capper's high hopes for a British solution to the flight problem were behind the decision of the British War Office not to purchase the world's only practical flying machine and the secrets that led to its creation. Wilbur and Orville were notified of the decision in December 1906, unaware that it was based on the advice of their good friend Lieutenant Colonel John Capper.

Not long after the French commission left Dayton, the moribund negotiations with the U.S. War Department showed signs of reviving, thanks to the efforts of two members of the Cabot family of Boston. Brothers Samuel and Godfrey Cabot had followed the experiments of the Wright brothers since 1903 and each had made offers, through Octave Chanute, to finance the experiments. The offers had been politely refused. In April 1906, Godfrey Cabot learned that Wilbur and Orville had offered to sell an airplane to the U.S. War Department and had been turned down. Shocked, he dashed off a letter to his relative Senator Henry Cabot Lodge, protesting the treatment the Wrights had received from their own government. Senator Lodge sent the letter to Secretary of War William Howard Taft. Taft forwarded it to the Board of Ordnance and Fortification, the agency responsible for the ill treatment of which the letter complained. The matter might have ended there, in the bureaucratic morass, if Godfrey Cabot had not traveled to Washington and paid a personal call on General William Frazier, president of the Board, after which Cabot assured the Wrights that any proposal they made in the future would be given careful consideration by the Board.

"We are ready to negotiate whenever the Board is ready," they wrote, thanking Cabot, "but as the former correspondence closed with a strong intimation that the Board did not wish to be bothered by our offers, we naturally have no intention of taking the initiative again."

Samuel Cabot was not involved in his brother's endeavor to revive the expiring U.S. negotiations, but Octave Chanute had been in Boston that summer and had left with him extracts of the correspondence between the Wrights and the Board, which had been forwarded by Wilbur. Upon looking through this material, Samuel Cabot's enthusiasm for the Wright brothers became tempered by the fear that they were asking too high a price for their invention and that meanwhile someone else might succeed in producing a practical airplane. "It seems to me there are probably several methods that might succeed without infringing their patents," he wrote Chanute, "and that probably their most valued asset was their first having done the trick, which they are losing by delay." Chanute was inclined to agree and forwarded Cabot's letter to the Wrights. Its receipt triggered a debate between Wilbur and Chanute that was to go on, by mail, all during the autumn of 1906.

"Our friends do not seem to exactly understand our position in the matter of supposed delay," Wilbur pointed out. He and his brother were merely refusing to let their hand be forced. "If it were indeed true that others would be flying within a year or two, there would be reason in selling at any price but we are convinced that no one will be able to develop a practical flyer within five years." When he and Orville saw men laboring year after year on aspects of the problem that they had overcome in a few weeks, they realized that the time required might be even longer—many times five years.

Chanute might have dropped the subject there, but for one sentence buried in the body of Wilbur's letter: "Even you, Mr. Chanute, have little idea how difficult the flying problem really is." Mr. Chanute rose to the challenge. "I cheerfully acknowledge that I have little idea how difficult the flying problem really is and that its solution is beyond my powers," he admitted when next he wrote, "but are you not too cocksure that yours is the only secret worth knowing and that others may not hit upon a solution in less than 'many times five years'?"

Wilbur's next letter was conciliatory: "The world does not contain greater men than Maxim, Bell, Edison, Langley, Lilienthal, & Chanute. We are not so foolish as to base our belief (that an independent solution of the flying problem is not imminent) upon any supposed superiority to these men and to all those who will hereafter take up the problem." He still insisted, however, that a quick solution to the problem was not possible.

"I do not understand what you have in mind in saying that 'The nature of the flying problem seems to us to absolutely forbid a quick solution,'" was Chanute's rejoinder. "For if it involves discovering a secret, it is possible that others may stumble upon it."

"It is the complexity of the flying problem that makes it so difficult," Wilbur explained. "It is not to be solved by stumbling upon a secret, but by the patient accumulation of information upon a hundred different points."

"I did not believe that there was a secret," Chanute replied, "but your previous letter squinted that way, and I wanted to bring you out."

At the heart of the debate that went on between Wilbur and Octave Chanute all that autumn was not the existence of a secret but the length of time it would take someone else to produce a practical flying machine. The Wrights could not conceive of the problem being solved in any way other than the orderly scientific way in which they themselves had solved it over a six-year period. Chanute could be disconcertingly naïve at times, but he had his ear to the ground and was more aware than the Wrights of the frenzied attempts being made to overtake them. "I still differ with you as to the possibility of your being caught up with if you rest upon your oars," he warned Wilbur. "It is practice, practice, practice which tells and the other fellows are getting it." Chanute knew whereof he spoke. No fewer than six propeller-driven flying machines were constructed and tested in Europe in 1906. Two built by Gabriel Voisin for Louis Blériot failed to leave the ground, but one of the two monoplanes tested by Trajan Vuia, a Hungarian living in Paris, made a hop of 80 feet. In Denmark, J. C. R. Ellehammer made a 140-foot merry-go-round flight while tethered to a center pole. The one aircraft to make a flight of any consequence, however, was a cumbersome biplane designed by Alberto Santos-Dumont with the help of Gabriel Voisin.

Santos had built six new airships since withdrawing from the aerial competition at the St. Louis fair in 1904. In his book *Dans l'Air,* published the same year, he predicted it would take man half a century to achieve mastery of the air without the aid of balloons. In 1906 the resilient little Parisian-Brazilian performed an abrupt about-face. In his workshop in a suburb of Paris he began construction of a biplane that looked less like a flying machine than a collection of cloth-covered open-ended boxes insecurely assembled on a wheeled undercarriage. It had a wingspan of thirty-three feet, six "side curtains" between the wings, and no tail. A pine framework covered with white cloth, jutting forward from the wings, was tipped with a large box-kite cell that could be manipulated for steering. The operator stood erect in a balloonist's basket in front of a 25-horsepower motor whose crankshaft was connected directly to an eight-foot propeller behind the wings.

This ungainly aircraft was given its first tentative test while suspended from Santos's sixty-foot airship No. 14, for which reason it was known ever after as the *14-bis.* Its first free flight was made in Paris in the Bois de Boulogne in August 1906, but there was not enough power for a hop of more than a few meters. Its propeller, which had been smashed in landing, was replaced and a more powerful, 50-horsepower motor was installed. On September 13, trailing clouds of smoke, the *14-bis* traveled through the air for about 7 meters before sinking onto its undercarriage, which collapsed, shattering the propeller again. While Gabriel Voisin repaired the damaged biplane, Santos took part in the first international Gordon Bennett Balloon Race, starting from Paris on September 30. Ever the innovator, he carried no ballast in his balloon. He equipped it instead with a 6-horsepower motor and two propellers, one to force the gasbag upward, the other to force it earthward. During the flight his sleeve became entangled in the complicated machinery and he came down a hundred miles from Paris with a painfully bruised arm.

With this latest disaster behind him, Santos returned to the *14-bis* and made an official try for the Coupe Archdeacon, a silver trophy donated by Ernest Archdeacon for a flight of twenty-five meters, or about eighty feet. On October 23, after several trial runs, in one of which a landing wheel came loose and in another a propeller blade flew off, the *14-bis* flew an estimated 60 to 70 meters over the grass of the Bois de Boulogne. The undercarriage collapsed during the landing as usual, and the propeller was shattered for the third time. No one thought to measure the exact distance, but it was well over the twenty-five meters required to win the Coupe Archdeacon. In the hysteria of the moment, the French reporters confused the Coupe Archdeacon with the Grand Prix d'Aviation Deutsch-Archdeacon for a one-kilometer flight over a closed circuit. The debate between Wilbur and Octave Chanute over the time it would take for someone to equal the Wrights' record was still going on when word reached Chicago that Santos had made a flight of one kilometer. "I fancy that he is now very nearly where you were in 1904," Chanute crowed to Wilbur on November 1.

The news was grist for the Wrights' mill. "This report gives such an excellent opportunity for exercising our powers as prophets that I cannot resist making a forecast before the details arrive," Wilbur wrote Chanute the next day. He predicted that the so-called flight would turn out to have been a jump of less than a hundred meters. "When someone goes over three hundred feet and lands safely in a wind of seven or eight miles it will then be important for us to do something," he added. A week later, a clipping from a French newspaper containing an accurate account of Santos' flight reached Chanute, and he was forced to eat humble pie. "Santos is not now as far along as you were in 1903," he conceded. Wilbur had easily won the first round of the debate.

There was one more prize the *14-bis* was capable of winning—the 1,500-franc Aéro-Club de France award for a flight of a hundred meters—and on November 12, before hundreds of spectators in the Bois de Boulogne, Santos made five attempts to win it. He had equipped the *14-bis* with a pair of octagonal horizontal surfaces between the wings to correct the loss of lateral balance that had ended the short flight of October 23. The longest flight he was able to make on the morning and afternoon of November 12 was 80 meters, but just as the sun was about to set, the *14-bis* made a long run over the ground and lifted itself into the air. Cameras clicked. Ernest Archdeacon in the back seat of the official Aéro-Club automobile was able to keep abreast of the shaking, vibrating aircraft as the crowds ran alongside. When the *14-bis* lurched and began to falter, Santos shut off the motor and the large boxlike machine landed on its two wire-spoked wheels, which once more collapsed. Women screamed and cried. Some fainted. Archdeacon stood up in the back of the Aéro-Club car and bellowed congratulations. Santos was plucked from his wicker basket and carried in triumph about the park. There was no doubt about the distance this time. It was measured and found to be 220 meters, or more than twice the length of the 300-foot flight that Wilbur had said would cause the Wright brothers concern.

It was Wilbur's turn to eat humble pie. He called Santos' flight "the first real indication of progress that has been displayed in France in five years." But if anyone would struggle into the air in less than the five years that Wilbur had predicted it would take, it would not be Santos in the *14-bis*. That gauche biplane made only one fifty-meter hop after winning the Aéro-Club prize. Nevertheless, its flight of November 12 was the longest ever made in Europe. At the time it was made, the Wright brothers had not been in the air for thirteen months and about all they had to show for the year they had spent in vain attempts to market flying machines was a flurry of unwanted publicity. Speculation about the brothers and their mysterious Flyer tended to increase the longer they did not fly. "There is much in the papers about the Wright brothers," their father wrote in his diary on the last day of November. "They have fame, but not wealth, yet."

What prompted Bishop Wright to append that qualifying "yet" to his diary entry for November 30 was a visit the brothers received the same day from Ulysses D. Eddy, a New York businessman who had read something about the Wrights in a newspaper and had come to Dayton to satisfy his curiosity. Eddy was a former associate of Flint and Company, New York, a firm that specialized in promoting and selling such lethal items as submarines, cruisers, and torpedo boats under the leadership of Charles R. Flint, known to muckrakers as the Father of Trusts, a title in which he took a perverse pride. Eddy suspected that a flying machine that could be used for scouting in time of war would be a suitable subject for exploitation by his friend Flint. Like so many visitors to 7 Hawthorn Street, Eddy fell under the spell of this unpretentious middle-American household, but he was not too spellbound to talk business. "It seems the favorable conditions we have been awaiting for six months have now arrived," Wilbur wrote Octave Chanute the next day. He called Eddy's proposition the best from a financial standpoint they had had. "There is nothing definite yet," he admitted, "but we are to meet the people interested in New York next week."

Wilbur and Orville had already planned a trip to New York to attend the second show of the Aero Club of America. The club's first show had been held earlier that year in the 69th Regiment Armory in New York from January 13 to 20. The Wrights had wanted to restrict their contribution to photographs of their gliding experiments, but at the last minute they were asked to send their 1903 motor for display. The metal from the damaged crankcase of that motor had long since been recast, so they sent instead the motor's crankshaft with the flywheel attached. It arrived too late for the show's opening, but was exhibited during the last few days in makeshift fashion on a box covered with wrapping paper, a few feet from what appears to be, in a surviving photograph, a spittoon. The Smithsonian contributed one of Langley's steam-driven models, and Augustus Herring exhibited the two wooden propellers that had driven his compressed-air-powered flying machine of 1898 in what he still maintained was the world's first power flight. Herring was one of the earliest members of the Aero Club of America. His home on Freeport, Long Island, was within commuting distance of the club's New York headquarters, where he hobnobbed with the wealthy sportsmen who comprised a part of the membership. He was treated with respect because of his former association with Langley and Chanute.

The second Aero Club show, held in New York from December 1 to 8, 1906, was a grander affair than the first. The Wrights were to be represented by their completely new, 30-horsepower motor, so designed that it could be mounted vertically on the lower wings of their Flyer, rather than horizontally as in the past. When Wilbur and Orville boarded the train for New York on the evening of December 5, they were accompanied by the Englishman Patrick Alexander, who had spent the day with them in Dayton. It was Alexander's second visit that year. He had showed up in April a few weeks after the French commission left and had startled the Wrights by inquiring casually if the commission was still in town. Since the existence of the commission was a closely guarded secret, the brothers suspected that Alexander's visit had been made on behalf of British intelligence. Assuming that the purpose of his December visit was to draw them out, they made a point of being close-lipped and unresponsive. The three men were to remain friends, but friendship did not prevent Wilbur from referring to Alexander when he met him again in Europe in 1908 as "certainly the strangest man I have ever known."

Octave Chanute met the brothers in New York, and they attended the aero show at the Grand Central Palace in the company of Augustus Post, secretary of the Aero Club of America. On December 6, Ulysses Eddy took Wilbur and Orville to the offices of Flint and Company and introduced them to Frank R. Cordley. Cordley, one of the more conservative members of the firm, was not as given to enthusiasms as Charles Flint, but he was as favorably impressed with the brothers in that affluent office setting as Eddy had been in the modest parlor on Hawthorn Street. Charles Flint was in Europe, but as soon as he returned, the Wrights were told, a formal agreement would be drawn up under the terms of which Flint and Company would act as their business agent. The proposed arrangement seemed the perfect conclusion to a year of fruitless negotiations. When Wilbur and Orville left New York the next day, they could not be blamed for looking forward—a little prematurely, it turned out—to the time when the onerous task of seeking a purchaser for their Flyer would be taken out of their hands entirely.

Before returning to Dayton, they made a side trip to Coatesville, Pennsylvania, to visit George Spratt. Wilbur had written their old friend that they were making a trip to New York and might stop off at Coatesville on the way home—"if you are still alive and willing to spend a day spinning yarns for us as in the old days at Kitty Hawk." The three men had not met since Spratt left the camp at Kill Devil Hills in November 1903, but they had continued to correspond. Pessimistic by nature, Spratt wrote a letter to the brothers a few weeks after leaving camp that elicited this stern advice from Wilbur: "I am sorry to find you back at your old habit of introspection, leading to a fit of the blues. Quit it! It does you no good and it does do harm. I have sometimes thought that this is the result of your living and working too much alone." In 1905 Spratt wrote the Wrights that he had made an important aeronautical discovery, but they could not make head or tail of it.

The hours the three men spent in talk during that weekend in Coatesville in 1906 were no doubt devoted more to discussions of aeronautical theory than to recollections of life in the camp on the Outer Banks. As the years passed and fortune as well as fame came to the Wrights, the gap between the achieving brothers and the melancholy Pennsylvanian continued to widen. In 1909 Spratt sent them a disturbing letter, accusing them of depriving him of credit for the design of the drift balance used in their 1901 wind-tunnel experiments. "We have not wished to deprive you of the credit for the idea," Wilbur replied, "and when we give to the world that part of our work, we shall certainly give you proper credit. . . . But while we considered the idea good," he went on, "I must confess that I am surprised and a trifle hurt when you say that the advice and suggestions we gave you in return 'cannot be considered in any degree a fair compensation.' I suppose when two men swap stories each thinks his own story better than the other's, and it is about the same when men swap ideas."

In the years that followed, the introspective Spratt was to remember with resentment rather than pleasure those nights at Kill Devil Hills when the wind howled about the drafty camp building and the three men swapped ideas while sitting on the floor to avoid breathing the smoke that poured from their carbide-can stove. In 1922, Orville made one of those vain attempts he was forever making to compile a history of the Kitty Hawk years and wrote Spratt asking for copies of the letters he and Wilbur had written to Coatesville describing their wind-tunnel and propeller experiments. Spratt refused to surrender the letters. Once more he rehearsed his old grievance about the drift balance and accused the brothers of having been secretive and obstructive and lacking in vision and generosity. After Orville's death, the draft of a letter to another Pennsylvanian was found among his papers, in which Orville commented on Spratt's bitter accusations. "Not wishing to add to the sorrow of an already unhappy life," he wrote, "I have refrained from making any reply to them."

# 24

## Bell's Boys

IN 1906 THE threat to the Wrights' supremacy in the air came from Europe. In 1907 the threat came from closer to home in the person of five men calling themselves the Aerial Experiment Association. The association was headed by Alexander Graham Bell. Its most dynamic member was Glenn Hammond Curtiss of Hammondsport, New York. In 1906, Curtiss's interest in aeronautics was limited to supplying motors for Tom Baldwin's airships, one of which was afloat under the skylight of the 69th Regiment Armory at the first Aero Club show in January. In April, Baldwin's airship plant was destroyed in the San Francisco earthquake, and he moved his airship operation to Hammondsport, where he could work more closely with the Curtiss Manufacturing Company. Later that year both Curtiss and Baldwin became acquainted with the Wright brothers through circumstances that were made to seem exotic by an entry in Bishop Wright's diary for September 6, 1906 ("Saw Baldwin's airship float out west. Wilbur went after it—got home at 10:30 at night"), which summons up the spectacle of a long-legged Wilbur racing across the Ohio countryside in the dark in pursuit of a runaway airship. The circumstances surrounding the meeting of the four men were a little more mundane.

Baldwin had contracted to make flights at a fair in Dayton starting Labor Day, September 3, and Curtiss had come along to make repairs on the airship motor. Sometime during the first or second day of the fair when the winds were too strong for a flight, the four men met and Wilbur and Orville were allowed to examine Baldwin's tethered airship at close hand. They reciprocated by inviting Baldwin and Curtiss to the bicycle shop, where a lively discussion took place on the subject of propellers, airships, flying machines, and motors. The wind did not become light enough for Baldwin to venture into the air until Thursday. His airship was not capable of more than 8 miles an hour and was blown out of the fairgrounds. Wilbur helped Curtiss haul it back. The same thing happened Friday, with Orville lending a hand as well as Wilbur and Curtiss.

After leaving Dayton, Baldwin wrote the brothers a letter thanking them for their help. His only regret was that they had not had time to extend their discussion on the subject of propellers. Curtiss also wrote them a letter in which he had this to say about the airship's propellers: "It may interest you to know that we cut out some of the inner surface of the blades on the big propellers, so as to reduce the resistance and allow it to speed up, and it showed a remarkable improvement." If indeed this improvement was due to a suggestion made by the Wrights—and Curtiss's letter does not indicate that it was—it is the only item of information gleaned by Curtiss during fair week in Dayton that can be shown to have been put to practical use. Nevertheless, Wilbur and Orville would attach a sinister significance to those discussions in the bicycle shop, claiming that Curtiss's rapid progress in the air two years later was due, at least in part, to information that they unwittingly imparted to him at the time.

One of the topics known to have been discussed was the motor that Alexander Graham Bell had ordered from Curtiss for use in aeronautical experiments at the inventor's Canadian estate. Bell's official residence was in Washington, D.C., but in 1893 he built a cedar-shingled mansion on a promontory jutting into one of the ocean inlets on Cape Breton Island, Nova Scotia, and gave it the Gaelic name of Beinn Bhreagh. Beinn Bhreagh—he pronounced it Ben Vree-ah—had eleven fireplaces, two conical towers, and more than the normal number of gables, dormers, balconies, and freestone chimneys. The grounds were ideal for aerial experimentation. "Alec is simply gone over flying machines," Mrs. Bell wrote her mother the year after the big house was completed. Bell had been present at the first successful flight of Langley's steam-driven model in 1896, and in 1907 was one of the first American notables to concede publicly that the Wright brothers had solved the flight problem. He would not concede, however, that theirs was the only solution. Kites, he believed, would lead to an alternative solution. In 1899 he built a box kite more than fourteen feet long from tip to tail, but the wind on the kite field at Beinn Bhreagh was not strong enough to get it off the ground.

Shortly thereafter, Bell was smitten with a radical idea: He would construct his future kites out of tetrahedral cells. A tetrahedron is a three-sided pyramid whose base and sides are composed of four equilateral triangles. By covering two of the four sides of each tetrahedral cell with cloth and amassing the cells so that the air was free to move through them from front to rear, he was able to construct light, remarkably strong kites. Since each cell was braced in three dimensions by its framework of wood or aluminum

tubing, wire bracing was not required. Speed would suffer from the enormous drag created by the large number of cells used in this type of construction, but the inventor of the telephone was not interested in speed. He
considered the Wright Flyer dangerous because of the high speeds needed
for taking off and maintaining lift in flight. It was his hope that the extreme
dihedral of the hundreds of small V-shaped wings in a tetrahedral, propeller-
driven kite would provide the automatic stability that would make slow
speeds of 10 to 15 miles an hour feasible. In the ideal flight of a propeller-
driven, man-carrying kite, as Bell envisioned it, the kite would be towed over
ground or water until it was airborne, then the operator would drop the
towline and the kite would proceed under its own power. To land, the
operator would simply turn off the motor and the big kite would sail to a
slow, safe landing, or, if the wind was strong enough (this was his most
fantastic hope of all), the operator would drop a line to a man on the ground
who would tether the kite, and the operator would climb down a rope ladder
as the kite continued to soar.

After trying a variety of configurations, Bell settled on a wedge-shaped
honeycomb of ten-inch cells for his man-carrying kite. The cells were turned
out by the hundreds in the big kite house at Beinn Bhreagh, where two sides
of each cell were covered with red silk by girls and women from the neighboring town of Baddeck. The silk was red for a good reason. Much of the
litigation required to protect Bell's telephone patent could have been
avoided if he had kept written and pictorial records at the time. He insisted
that every stage of his kite experiments be adequately documented and
photographed, and because red registered as darker than it really was on the
color-blind film of that day, the big red kites stood out sharply against the
blue sky, which photographed white.

The *Frost King,* Bell's first kite large enough to support a man, contained
1,300 silk-covered cells. In December 1905, while flying at a considerable
height in a 10-mile-per-hour wind, it was photographed lifting a 165-pound
man a few feet off the ground as he clung to a rope suspended from the kite.
A few weeks later, Bell exhibited some of his tetrahedral kites at the first
Aero Club show in New York. In the adjoining Automobile Club of America show Glenn Curtiss was exhibiting the light motors manufactured in his
motorcycle plant. Bell was convinced that the young engine expert from
Hammondsport was just the man to supply him with a motor for his first
propeller-driven man-carrying kite. Later that year, he placed an order
for the motor that Curtiss discussed with the Wrights during fair week in
Dayton.

The motor was still not finished when Bell stopped at Hammondsport
on his way up to Nova Scotia in the spring of 1907. The ostensible purpose
of his visit was to hurry up work on the motor, but he also wanted to see

if Curtiss would be willing to assist in the kite experiments at Beinn Bhreagh. Curtiss could hardly be expected to give up a lucrative business and a career as a motorcycle racer to devote himself to aeronautics in a remote area of Canada. But Bell made him a tempting offer: If Curtiss would deliver the motor in person and provide instruction in its use, he would be paid twenty-five dollars a day plus expenses. Curtiss accepted, and early in July arrived at Beinn Bhreagh with a four-cylinder, 20-horsepower motor.

Alexander Graham Bell was sixty that year and could well afford to recruit younger men to do his experimenting for him. Two young recruits, both recent graduates of the University of Toronto, were at Beinn Bhreagh when Curtiss arrived—John A. D. McCurdy, who preferred to be known as Douglas, the second of his middle names, and Frederick W. ("Casey") Baldwin (no relation to Thomas Baldwin, the airship man). A third young assistant, who had heard of Bell's forthcoming experiments and volunteered his help, was Lieutenant Thomas E. Selfridge, a 1903 graduate of West Point. Selfridge was officially detailed to Baddeck, Nova Scotia, by the U.S. Army after Bell addressed a request to his friend President Theodore Roosevelt to have Selfridge assigned to Beinn Bhreagh because of his interest in the military applications of aeronautics.

Curtiss left Canada at the end of July to take part in the motorcycle races at Providence, Rhode Island, where an accident in a hill-climbing event left him so badly banged up that he abandoned his career as a motorcycle racer. After a spell in the hospital he returned to Beinn Bhreagh. There, on October 1, 1907, the four young men and Alexander Graham Bell established the Aerial Experiment Association—AEA for short—with the avowed purpose of "getting into the air." Each member of the association had a title. Bell was chairman; Casey Baldwin, chief engineer; Douglas McCurdy, treasurer and assistant engineer; Selfridge, secretary; Curtiss, director of experiments. Mabel Bell, the inventor's wife, was not officially a member, but she had funded the organization for a one-year period with $20,000 of her own money and was recognized by the younger members as "the little mother of us all." One of her functions was serving tea in front of the logs blazing in the stone fireplace of the paneled living room at Beinn Bhreagh, while her gray-bearded husband argued aeronautics with the younger members between patriarchal puffs on his pipe.

The meetings held in these comfortable surroundings were curiously formal. Motions were made, seconded, and voted on; minutes were conscientiously recorded. Chairman Bell was addicted to copious note-taking, fearful that the potential value of the most insignificant suggestion might be lost unless it was immediately transcribed. In spite of this careful habit, the aging inventor was inclined to be impulsive and impatient, and his ideas of how the AEA was to get into the air were often at variance with those of the younger members. The mechanical background and resources of twenty-nine-year-old Glenn Curtiss, who had never been to college, set him off from McCurdy, Baldwin, and Selfridge, all in their mid-twenties, all university graduates, and all from well-to-do families. But in one respect Bell's Boys, as they were sometimes called, were united: While they tolerated Bell's preoccupation with tetrahedral kites, they were eager, to a man, to get into the air by almost any other means. When the AEA was established, Bell had reluctantly agreed that each member would be given a chance to build and experiment with a flying machine of his own design but not, he made it clear, until the large, man-carrying kite under construction in its hangar on the waterfront at Beinn Bhreagh had first been tested in flight.

The big kite was called the *Cygnet,* French for "little swan." It was fifty-two feet wide, ten feet high, and more than two hundred pounds in weight without motor, propeller, or operator. With its formidable array of 3,393 tetrahedral cells, partially covered with red silk and enclosed in a wedge-shaped framework of aluminum tubing, it looked like anything but a swanlet. There was a crawlway in the center with room for the operator to lie prone and room behind him for the motor and propeller. A pointed triangular bow projected about six feet forward from the crawlway.

On December 3, fitted with pontoons but without motor, propeller, and operator, the *Cygnet* performed well as a kite while being towed over the water between Beinn Bhreagh and the town of Baddeck. Three days later it was tried again as a kite, but with a man on board. After being christened by Mabel Bell with a cup of water, the unswanlike behemoth was moved on its launching raft to a waiting excursion steamer. Two towlines were attached from the steamer, one to the raft on which the kite was poised, the other to the *Cygnet* itself. Lieutenant Selfridge lay prone in the crawlway, dressed in oilskins and bundled in rugs to protect him from the winter wind. As the steamer began its tow, the big red kite lifted from the raft and rose gradually until it reached an altitude of between 150 and 200 feet. It maintained that altitude for a full seven minutes. Then the wind slackened and it began to descend. From his nest of oilskins and rugs, Selfridge was able to see only straight in front of him because of the *Cygnet*'s pointed prow. He was not aware that the kite was losing altitude until just before the pontoons hit the water and it was too late to release the towline. Baldwin and McCurdy on the excursion steamer were prepared to cut the towline in case of emergency, but at the crucial moment the plume of smoke from the steamer's stack completely concealed the *Cygnet,* and the big kite was dragged to pieces through the water at the end of the taut towline. Selfridge wriggled out of the mass of twisted aluminum tubing and tattered silk and was picked up by a motorboat and taken aboard the excursion steamer, where he was plied with stimulants.

At a meeting of AEA members in front of the big stone fireplace that night, Bell bowed to a majority decision that the next aircraft to be constructed by the association would be a biplane rather than a kite. It was further moved, seconded, and voted that AEA activities should be moved temporarily to Hammondsport, so that the new apparatus could be constructed in the motorcycle plant under Curtiss's supervision.

A few weeks after the *Cygnet*'s demise, Glenn Curtiss wrote the Wright brothers a letter from Hammondsport on Aerial Experiment Association stationery, in which he offered to supply them, gratis, with one of the new 50-horsepower motors turned out by his firm. He mentioned in passing that he had lately "been getting rather deeply mixed in Aeronautics," a fact that the Wright brothers had already gathered from the letterhead, on which Curtiss was listed as AEA director of experiments. Wilbur thanked Curtiss for the offer but assured him that the new Wright motor would satisfy all their needs. "We remember your visit to Dayton with pleasure," his reply concluded. "The experience we had together in helping Captain Baldwin back to the fairgrounds was one not soon to be forgotten."

The tone of Wilbur's letter might have been less friendly if the Wright brothers had known at the time that Bell's Boys were about to produce a series of flying machines, one of which would fly considerably farther than the 220 meters covered by Santos-Dumont in the *14-bis,* and that it would take the Aerial Experiment Association closer to five months to accomplish such a feat than the five years Wilbur had predicted it would take back in the autumn of 1906.

# 25

## *The Brothers Abroad*

NEGOTIATING A CONTRACT with Flint and Company was not a mere matter of signing on a dotted line. Less than a week after the Wright brothers returned to Dayton on December 12, 1906, Orville was back in New York, summoned by a telegram from Charles Flint. Flint offered the Wrights half-a-million dollars for all rights to the Flyer and its manufacture outside the United States. Both brothers made another trip to New York in January, during which the half-million-dollar deal was scrapped, and an arrangement was worked out whereby the Flint firm would handle the foreign business and the Wrights would have control of the terms and places of selling. The company would pay all expenses and collect 20 percent commission on all business up to $500,000 and 40 percent thereafter. The German and Austrian business would be handled through the Mauser gun people. The French were lukewarm for the moment; how to deal with them would be decided later. Charles Flint would handle the British business himself, which he proceeded to do through an exchange of coded cables with a Lady Jane Taylor in Scotland, a heavyhanded approach that was abandoned when a British postal official raised questions about the meaning of certain code words in the cables and an outraged Lady Jane complained that her situation was very much like sitting on a thistle. Flint also wanted to handle the Russian market himself. He offered the Wrights $50,000 to make a private flight in the presence of the Czar before signing a contract, but Wilbur and Orville flatly refused to make any demonstration flights before a contract had been signed.

Only once did they consider making an exception to this policy, and then only because such a flight would have shocked the U.S. War Department out of its complacency. The occasion was the 1907 Jamestown Exposition celebrating the 300th anniversary of the founding of the first permanent

English settlement in America on an island in the James River in Virginia. The exposition was to open April 26 with a parade of battleships in Hampton Roads at the mouth of the river below Jamestown. Since the flotilla was to be reviewed by President Theodore Roosevelt and high-ranking officers of the Army and Navy, what if—and the Wrights' idea remains to this day one of the most tantalizing what-if's of history—what if they were to assemble one of their new machines in the old camp at Kill Devil Hills, fly seventy-five miles north to Hampton Roads, circle the battleships, and vanish southward, leaving the President and his party with mouths agape, aware that the air had been conquered but not quite sure by whom. When the truth came out, embarrassed War Department personnel would have trouble explaining to the President of the United States that the world's first practical flying machine had been offered to them three times, and that three times they had let it slip through their fingers.

Before undertaking the 150-mile round trip, they ran some experiments on the Miami River in Dayton to make sure that a Flyer equipped with pontoons and hydrofoils would be able to take off and land on the shallow waters of Currituck Sound. A motor and propellers were mounted on a platform supported by a pair of cylindrical pontoons. When accelerated to 20 miles an hour, the front edges of two steel hydrofoils between the pontoons lifted almost clear of the water, but when the water ceased to flow over their tops, they promptly lost their lift. The Dayton *Herald* the next day entertained its readers with a photograph depicting the antics of this "modern water bird." That night a dam above that section of the Miami River broke, whereupon the brothers read the handwriting on the wall and canceled the project. It was just as well. The problem of taking off from water would not be solved for another four years, and it would be solved not by the Wright brothers but by their hated adversary, Glenn Curtiss.

A few days after the hydrofoil tests were discontinued, Wilbur became involved in a fourth attempt to sell a Flyer to the U.S. government. While in New York, he was introduced by Cortlandt Field Bishop, president of the Aero Club of America, to Bishop's brother-in-law Herbert Parsons, U.S. congressman from New York. Parsons immediately interested himself in the Wrights' cause. He sent President Theodore Roosevelt a clipping about the brothers from the *Scientific American.* The President forwarded the clipping to Secretary of War William Howard Taft, recommending that action be taken. Taft once more passed the buck to the Board of Ordnance and Fortification, adding his endorsement to that of the President. The outcome was a cautiously worded letter to the Wright brothers, stating that the Board would be glad to hear from them on the subject of their Flyer if they desired to take any action in the matter.

Presidential pressure had at last forced the Board to open the door, if only just a crack. It happened that at just that time Wilbur disappeared from the scene as abruptly as if he had been dropped through a trapdoor, and it was up to Orville to initiate a new round of negotiations. The Board asked for a formal proposal. Orville complied, quoting a price of $100,000 for one machine and instructions in its operation. The Board next wanted to know if the price included exclusive use of the machine by the United States. Orville replied on June 15 that a recent contract precluded them from offering such a right. This was followed by a long silence on the part of the Board, during which the door seemed to have been quietly closed again. At least it had not been slammed.

The contract Orville referred to—the brothers' agreement with Flint and Company—had been the cause of Wilbur's precipitous withdrawal from the negotiations. The firm's agent in Paris had come under the influence of the anti-Wright faction. Charles Flint, thinking that the best way to convince his skeptical agents in Europe that the Wrights had a salable product to offer would be for them to meet one of the brothers face to face, booked passage for Wilbur on the steamship *Campania,* leaving New York on May 18. Arriving in London a week later, Wilbur was met at Euston Station by Hart O. Berg, Flint and Company's representative in England, France, and Russia.

Hart Berg was one of those American industrial missionaries who flourished in Europe before World War I. His mission was the promotion of products of Yankee inventive genius—machine guns, submarines, and automatic pistols, leavened occasionally with a less lethal item such as the electric automobile. His headquarters were in Paris, where he had been subjected to the opinions of Ernest Archdeacon and other Frenchmen who scoffed at the idea that the Wrights could have made long flights without being noticed by the press. Berg had never seen a picture of either of the brothers. "Still," he wrote the New York office of Flint and Company the next day, describing his meeting with Wilbur in the railroad station in London, "he was the first man I spoke to, and either I am Sherlock Holmes, or Wright has that peculiar glint of genius in his eye which left no doubt in my mind who he was."

The cosmopolitan Berg was won over by Wilbur's self-assurance but taken aback by the meagerness of his luggage, which consisted of a single suitcase "about the size of a music roll." Wilbur had left Dayton in a hurry, assuming he would be gone only a week or two. The first thing Berg did was to take Wilbur to a tailor shop and have him measured for a dinner jacket and dress suit. They spent the rest of the afternoon talking business. Berg contended that it would not be feasible to deal directly with the governments of England and France. Wilbur agreed that there was not much chance of a sale in England but was against forming a company in France to sell Flyers to the government. He favored approaching the government directly. Berg was not quite sure how to take Wilbur or how to interpret what more than one reporter would refer to in the coming months as Wilbur's sphinxlike smile. "About 5 o'clock in the afternoon," Berg wrote in his letter to the New York office, "I think, you will distinctly note that I said 'I think,' I brought about some sort of action in his mind, and think he was on the point, you will note that I say that 'I think he was on the point,' of veering around from the government to company methods."

Berg had already discussed the formation of such a company with Henri Deutsch de la Meurthe, the French capitalist known as the oil king of Europe. He wanted Wilbur to meet Deutsch in Paris before making any overtures to the French government. "I think he agreed," his letter went on, "you will note that I distinctly say 'I think he agreed,' to go to Paris with me Monday."

"I am much pleased with Wright's personality," Berg's report concluded. "He inspires great confidence and I am sure that he will be a capital Exhibit A."

Over the weekend Wilbur and Berg were joined by Frank Cordley, the Flint partner whom Wilbur had met in New York the previous December. All three traveled to Paris on Monday, where Wilbur was introduced to Henri Deutsch de la Meurthe. Deutsch was all for forming a company as Berg suggested, but thought it would be prudent to first sound out the new Minister of War, who was not familiar with the recommendations of the French commission that had been sent to Dayton in March 1906. Because of his connections, Deutsch was able to deal personally with the minister. After examining the commission's findings, the minister told Deutsch it would be feasible for the government to consider purchasing a flying machine from the proposed company, providing the machine could reach an altitude of 300 meters. That altitude requirement was one of the rocks on which the negotiations of 1906 had foundered. Wilbur no longer thought it a matter of great importance, so with Deutsch's enthusiastic approval, the Flint attorney in Paris proceeded to draw up articles of incorporation for an international company. Deutsch agreed to purchase the only large block of shares offered for sale in France.

While this was going on, Commandant Bonel, who had headed the French commission in 1906, ran into Arnold Fordyce, who had also served on the commission. Bonel let Fordyce know that the commission's recommendations were at last bearing fruit, assuming that Fordyce would share his mood of jubilation. Instead, Fordyce "in an almost rambunctious mood" (Wilbur's phrase) relayed the news to his employer, Henri Letellier, son of the proprietor of *Le Journal.* Letellier went at once to the Minister of War and protested angrily that he had spent good money to obtain an option from the Wright brothers in December 1905 and did not want to see the glory of its fulfillment go to Deutsch. The War Minister, General Georges Picquart—a key figure in the Dreyfus case—had been improperly accused of forgery and imprisoned for a time. Although he had been pardoned and promoted on his release, he had no desire to find himself at the center of another political cyclone, and informed Deutsch that any business the government did with the Wrights would have to be done through Letellier and *Le Journal.* Deutsch, thinking he had been used by Wilbur and Berg only to attract additional financing, indignantly withdrew from the proposed company. Not until July 8, when Wilbur came face to face with the oil king at the balloon races at St.-Cloud, was he able to explain that neither he nor Berg had any contractual ties with Letellier.

Nevertheless, in their efforts to deal directly with the French government, Wilbur and Berg became hopelessly locked in a Laocoön-like struggle with the Letellier crowd (the "disreputable Letellier crowd," Wilbur called them): Henri Letellier, Letellier's father (owner of *Le Journal*), Arnold Fordyce, and French Senator Charles Humbert. Fordyce was evidently not tarred with the same brush as the others, for he would remain a friend of the Wright brothers. The most venal of the other three was Senator Humbert. In time, he would become vice-president of the Senate's committee on army affairs, in which capacity he acquired the habit of compiling dossiers on important personages several decades before the practice was adopted by J. Edgar Hoover in the United States. During World War I, he would buy a controlling interest in *Le Journal* with funds secretly supplied by the Germans through an intermediary who was subsequently convicted of treason and sentenced to death. Humbert himself was arrested, although the charges against him were dropped when wartime fevers had cooled.

In 1907 Senator Humbert was secretary of the Chamber of Deputies' budget committee, the bottleneck through which any appropriation for the purchase of a Wright Flyer would have to be funneled. On June 24 the proposal for the sale of a Flyer was presented to the senator by Arnold Fordyce, who reported the next day that the price must be adjusted upward, from 1,000,000 francs to 1,250,000. The extra quarter-million francs was the price of Humbert's services for expediting the deal. Appalled at this unabashed bribe-seeking, Berg issued an ultimatum. If action was not taken on the proposal as it stood, he and Wilbur would leave at once for Berlin to negotiate a sale to Germany. A somewhat chastened Humbert told Berg to return in two days for his decision. Three days later Wilbur and Berg were informed that the proposal had been accepted "in principle," and they settled down to await further word from the War Ministry. With a trip to Germany still a possibility, Wilbur did some shopping and visited a tailor in the rue d'Antin. Unable to return to London to pick up the finery ordered there, he was fitted for another dress suit and a long frock coat. "Please have Orville send me an American Express money order for $150," he wrote his father. "I cannot hob-nob with the Emperor when I get to Berlin without some clothes." The prospect of Wilbur in a swallowtail coat titillated Orville, who wrote his brother, "I would give three cents to see you in your dress suit and plug hat!"

Communications between Wilbur in Paris and Orville in Dayton were not always that cordial. To avoid the delay of two to three weeks involved in asking and answering questions by mail, inquiries requiring an immediate reply were sent and answered by cable. Details were left to letters. The inevitable confusion began on June 13, when Wilbur asked Orville for his consent to increase the altitude requirement in the French proposal to 300 meters, or approximately 1,000 feet. Orville had the U.S. negotiations in mind when he cabled his ambiguous answer: "Thousand in America, hundred ft. in France." To Wilbur this appeared to be an indirect refusal by Orville to do any business in France at all. Five days later the altitude matter became critical and Wilbur cabled Dayton: "It is question whether refuse 1,000 ft. in Europe," to which Orville responded: "Will fulfill terms with exception of height within the time. May require an addition for 300 meters." Wilbur interpreted this to mean that Orville would need additional time to make changes in the Flyers then under construction. He found this exasperating because Orville hadn't indicated how much additional time would be necessary.

The day before Senator Humbert was to let Berg know definitely whether the million-franc deal would go through, Wilbur received the most baffling cable yet from Orville: "Not approve offer to French war dept. Have not yet received any information from Flint & Co. Do nothing without I consent. Keep me informed." Wilbur was completely in the dark as to what Orville was objecting to or what Flint and Company had to do with it, but it turned out not to matter. At noon the next day word came through Fordyce that the French cabinet had refused action on the Wright proposal, and Wilbur cabled his brother: "Every trade is off. Send specifications of what is limit German Government. When can you come?" (It had been agreed that Orville and Charlie Taylor would join Wilbur in Europe as soon as a flying machine and one of the new motors had been shipped.) "Can come when you think it necessary," was Orville's cabled reply.

By July 3, the on-again, off-again French negotiations had come full circle, and Senator Humbert promised to arrange a meeting with the Minister of War. Before the meeting could take place, the ministry suggested several drastic changes in the proposal, the most important of which was extending the exclusivity period to a full year. On July 9, Wilbur, Berg, and Fordyce were ushered into the ministry office and granted an audience with

Major A. L. Targe rather than the War Minister. To everyone's surprise, the major did not insist on some of the more unreasonable changes that had been suggested. Encouraged by this turn of events, Wilbur cabled Orville: "You and Charlie come here as soon as possible. Expect to close."

Ten days were spent rewording the proposal, but when the three men returned to the War Ministry on July 19, they were confronted not by the amiable Major Targe but by a General Roques, who demanded that the exclusivity period be extended to a full three years. Wilbur and Berg insisted that the proposal be accepted as it stood or not at all. Four days later they were asked to put their proposal in the form of a contract. Wilbur and Berg then drafted a contract specifying a six-month exclusivity period and turned it over to Fordyce at the office of *Le Journal,* where Fordyce and Commandant Bonel saw fit to revise sections of the draft. Thoroughly disgusted, Wilbur refused to take any further action in the matter until Orville arrived.

Orville left Dayton on July 18. Two days before his departure, the bewildering game of cabled questions and answers reached a climax with his disconcerting cable to Wilbur: "Cannot get an answer to letter or telegram to Flints. All ready. Delay caused by them. Can we dispose of them?" Wilbur had no idea why his brother was urging that they disassociate themselves from Flint and Company. He was enlightened by a letter that reached Paris a few days after the cable but had been written several days before the cable was sent. In it, Orville ticked off his complaints against Flint's New York office. "I am so completely disgusted with them that I would like to sever our connection with them. We employed them in order that we wouldn't have to be bothered with business all the time. But they have been *so* tricky that it keeps us busy watching them." In the same letter, Orville blew off steam in regard to the way Wilbur responded to his cabled questions. "I have practically no information of what is going on. When you cable, you never explain anything so that I can answer with any certainty that we are talking about the same thing."

Wilbur's need to blow off steam was even greater than Orville's. When he learned that Flint and Company's so-called trickiness consisted largely of the failure of the New York office to answer Orville's letters, he wrote his father: "Flints were quite right in keeping silent. If they had attempted to communicate or negotiate directly with Orville, there would have been a fuss here immediately." That was merely the postscript to the blistering letter Wilbur wrote on July 20, in which he unloaded his pent-up frustrations onto the rest of the family, knowing that Orville was on his way and out of reach for the time being. In the bishop's last letter Wilbur noted "a tendency to complain that I have not written fully, and that my telegrams are not explicit." This was incomprehensible. "Do you suppose I was so foolish as to mix letters and cables?" Three paragraphs later, Wilbur is still hammering away. "How could I base cables on letters which portrayed a situation entirely different from that existing two weeks later? I foresee things of this kind so easily that I make the mistake sometimes of assuming that Orville also understands." It was a long letter. In the sixth paragraph, Wilbur is on the verge of forgiving Orville but cannot quite bring himself to do it. "Well, I will stop complaining. I suppose he has been so worried that he has not been really himself. But it would have been better if he had attended energetically to his own department and avoided interference with mine."

Writing that letter no doubt exorcised a few of the frustrations Wilbur was experiencing in his dealings with the French, but he also had a need to disabuse "you people in Dayton" of the notion that he was, as Berg had expressed it, any man's Exhibit A. That he was determined not to be used in such a fashion is clear from a passage in a letter he wrote to Katharine three days before he penned the vitriolic letter to his father:

> When I first came over, Berg & Cordley thought that they were business men and I was merely a sort of exhibit. But their eyes have gradually opened, and now they realize that I see into situations deeper than they do, that my judgment is more often sound, and that I intend to run them rather than have them run me.

The nine weeks Wilbur spent in Paris before being joined by Orville were not devoted entirely to business. He did his duty as an American sightseer without succumbing entirely to the charms of the French capital. Because he did not understand French, he was able to preserve his middle-American values in the midst of the meaningless babble all about him and to report on what he saw with an unjaundiced eye. "In Paris the parks are the play grounds of the people," he wrote his father. "In day time they are filled with children wearing little black silesia aprons or rather coats coming about to their knees, to keep their clothes clean. It is very amusing, but shows French thrift." French domestic architecture did not appeal to him. Unlike the porches and front yards of Dayton, the open spaces in French houses were in the center of the dwellings where only the owners could enjoy them. To Wilbur, this was "not the American way."

He haunted the picture galleries in the Louvre when he had nothing else to do. The French academicians survive today in the bright shadow of the Impressionists, but in 1907 Wilbur considered their work the finest in the Louvre. "While I do not pretend to be much of a judge, I am inclined to think that in five hundred years it will be recognized as some of the greatest work ever done," he wrote his sister. He thought the *Mona Lisa* was not much better than the black-and-white prints he had seen of it back in Dayton and was sorry Katharine could not be in Paris, prancing through the Louvre with red Baedeker in hand like other schoolteachers he had seen. When he visited Notre Dame, he complained that the nave was not much wider than a storeroom and that the high windows made the interior very dark. "It was rather disappointing as most sights are to me," he reported. "My imagination pictures things more vividly than my eyes."

During Wilbur's first two months in Paris he met most of the men seriously concerned with aviation in France—Ernest Archdeacon and Georges Besançon, among others, and of course the Wrights' fickle champion, Captain Ferdinand Ferber. The brothers' opinion of Captain Ferber had never been very high, and the Frenchman's duplicity became only too obvious in a letter he wrote to the editor of *L'Aérophile* published in the June issue. After describing his meeting with Wilbur in glowing terms, he went on to argue that the million francs the Wrights were asking for a flying machine (Ferber made it a million and a half) may have been a fair price in 1905, but that their Flyer was worth only 50,000 francs in 1907—a rather precipitous depreciation, considering that the experimenting being done by the French that year was not remotely comparable to what the Wrights had done in 1904 and 1905.

Wilbur was invited as a matter of course to witness the French Aéro-Club's balloon contests at the club's aero park at St.-Cloud. He was also invited to go ballooning with Alan Hawley of the Aero Club of America in Hawley's new balloon, *La Mouche.* At four-thirty in the afternoon of July 17, it soared aloft at St.-Cloud with four men in the basket—Wilbur, Hawley, and two Frenchmen—and drifted in a wind of 25 miles per hour at an altitude of from 1,000 to 2,000 feet. Wilbur made use of the experience in two ways. First, he was able to investigate the winds at the altitude above the French countryside that he or Orville would be required to fly if their contract was approved by the War Ministry. Second, he utilized his experience in writing "Flying as a Sport—Its Possibilities" for the *Scientific American.* That article involved a mild bit of deception in that it included a graphic description of what the world looked like from a flying machine, although until then all Wilbur had seen from the air when he looked down had been the sandy plain below Big Kill Devil Hill or the few familiar trees at Huffman Prairie and the interurban stop at the crossroads—hardly sights to induce sportsmen to exchange the safety of solid ground for the uncertainties of the eddying upper air. The world from the air, as Wilbur pictured it in the *Scientific American,* was a much more interesting place:

> Once above the treetops, the narrow roads no longer arbitrarily fix the course. The earth is spread out before the eye with a richness of color and beauty of pattern never imagined by those who have gazed at the

landscape edgewise only. The rich brown of freshly turned earth, the lighter shades of dry ground, the still lighter browns and yellows of ripening crops, the almost innumerable shades of green produced by grasses and forests, together present a sight whose beauty has been confined to balloonists in the past.

The brief article contrasted the ease with which a sportsman in a flying machine returns home to the discomfort experienced by a balloonist. "In ballooning," Wilbur wrote, "a few glorious hours in the air are usually followed by a tiresome walk to some village, an uncomfortable night at a poor hotel, and a return home by slow local trains," an accurate description of the unexciting sequel to the three-and-a-half-hour flight of Hawley's *La Mouche.* After packing the balloon and paying the farmer for the rent of the wheatfield in which they landed, the four men had supper at a little village nearby, then transported the deflated balloon and themselves by cart to Orléans, where they spent the night before returning to Paris the next day.

Balloons were not the only objects bobbing about the skies of France that summer. On the morning of July 8, Wilbur dressed hurriedly and went up on the roof of the Hotel Meurice. He was just in time to see the sharp-nosed French airship *La Patrie,* with its crew of four in an open goldola shaped like a lifeboat, pass over the Arc de Triomphe and turn directly over the hotel before heading back to its base at Fort d'Issy. Allowing for a wind speed of about 8 miles per hour at roof level, Wilbur estimated *La Patrie*'s speed to be 15 or 16 miles per hour, indicating that the airship would have difficulty maneuvering in winds of 10 miles per hour or more. He was able to check the speed more accurately during the Bastille Day ceremonies at Longchamps, when *La Patrie* sailed majestically over the parade ground in an almost absolute calm. Clocking the time it took the airship to travel its own length over the ground, he found its speed to be 8.7 meters per second, or about 20 miles per hour, which proved that newspaper reports had greatly exaggerated the airship's speed.

These observations were not made merely to satisfy Wilbur's curiosity. The prospect of selling Wright Flyers to the airship-conscious Germans was not very good. Ever since the successful trial flight in October 1906 of the third of Count Ferdinand von Zeppelin's dirigibles—called zeppelins after their designer and builder—the country had been afflicted with zeppelin fever. An even larger dirigible, the count's fourth, was under construction in 1907. It would be more than twice as long as *La Patrie,* and its hydrogen capacity four times as great. The director of the Mauser gun works, Isidore Loewe, through whom Flint and Company intended to deal with the German government, was of the opinion that the officials having the final say in the purchase of a Wright Flyer would be terrified of losing their standing with the Kaiser if they recommended such a purchase and the Flyer turned out to be inferior to the new zeppelin for scouting purposes. This state of affairs might improve, Loewe suggested, if Wilbur were to prepare a paper for presentation to the appropriate German officials portraying the superiority of flying machines to airships.

The result was "Comparison of Airships with Flyers," written the day after Wilbur returned to Paris from his balloon trip to Orléans. In it, he estimated the cost of an airship the size of *La Patrie* to be ten times that of a flying machine. He cited other disadvantages of semi-rigid airships and dirigibles—their vulnerability to gales, the huge sheds needed to house the monsters, and the army of attendants and the wagon train of gas generators and auxiliary equipment that must follow airships wherever they go. "Attention is also called to the fact that the flying machine is in its infancy," he pointed out, "while the airship has reached its limit and must soon be a thing of the past."

Although it was true that the airplane was in its infancy then, three decades would pass before the *Hindenburg* disaster would place its fiery imprimatur on Wilbur's otherwise prescient paper. But the fate of *La Patrie* proved his point. While the French airship was being repaired near Verdun that November, a strong wind came up. More than a hundred soldiers trying to hold it down with ropes were dragged along the ground until ordered to let go. With no one on board, *La Patrie* sailed away like an aerial *Flying Dutchman*. It crossed the Channel, was sighted over Wales, and after touching down briefly in Ireland was blown out to sea and never seen again.

Orville arrived in Paris on Sunday, July 28, and the brothers set to work revising anew the much-revised contract. Fordyce made additional changes when he translated it into French. On the last day of July it was given to Senator Humbert, who presented it to the Minister of War just as vacations were getting underway. Since nothing could be done until Major Targe returned from vacation, Wilbur and Berg boarded a train for Berlin to try their luck there. Orville, left behind in Paris, was introduced to the cat-and-mouse game that Wilbur had been playing since May with Letellier's men and the War Ministry. On August 6, after Major Targe returned, Orville learned that Senator Humbert had tried to convince the major over lunch that the Wrights were frauds. He did not succeed, and Fordyce assured Orville that the contract would be put through without delay. Instead, it was submitted to a technical committee for evaluation. There was another week of waiting, during which Orville dined occasionally with Frank Cordley, made the obligatory visits to the Louvre, and behaved so as not to bring discredit to the household of a United Brethren bishop. "We have been real good over here," he informed his father. "We have been in a lot of churches, and haven't got drunk yet!" Drinking was not a subject for levity with Bishop Wright. "I did not anticipate that either of you would become intemperate or debauched," he wrote, "but I want you to show the foreigners that you are teetotalers, and in every way maintain that high character that is most proper to have, and which in the eyes of the best in America is the most approved."

The less abstemious Charlie Taylor arrived in Paris on August 11. He was there to help assemble the Flyer that had been shipped from Dayton in July and was stored temporarily in the customhouse at Le Havre. Reporters were trailing the Wrights. There was no telling what stories might appear in the papers if it was discovered that their mechanic was in France, so Charlie was put up around the corner from Orville's hotel in a small hostelry in the rue d'Alger, where he registered in relative anonymity as C. E. Taylor of Lincoln, Nebraska. Orville spent what time he could with Taylor. They went for walks in the Tuileries gardens and ascended the Arc de Triomphe together, but Charlie was a fish out of water in Paris. There was nothing for him to do, and he soon became homesick.

Wilbur, meanwhile, was in Berlin with Hart Berg, sounding out the Germans. There was still some hard feeling against the Wrights because of the mistranslation in *L'Aérophile* of their letter to Ferber two years before, but Wilbur's paper comparing airships with flying machines had been read with great interest by Captain Richard von Kehler, an influential member of the German airship establishment. "Captain von Kehler is becoming very much excited," Wilbur wrote Orville from Berlin. "In fact I think we will soon have the whole pot boiling."

Alas, the prospect of doing business with the Germans in the immediate future proved as illusory as settling quickly with the French. On August 17 Wilbur returned to Paris, where a final French proposal was drawn up. When Fordyce made what Wilbur described as "all sorts of ridiculous objections to the form of it, saying it was not good French, &c., &c.," the brothers concluded that the French were acting in bad faith. They notified the War Minister that they were withdrawing all offers, and Wilbur returned to Berlin to see if anything further could be done there. Frank Cordley was also in Berlin. On September 24 he received instructions from Flint and Company to proceed to England to confer with a mysterious Mr. Stewart. Wilbur wired Orville to be ready to leave Paris for London on short notice if the Stewart business proved to be serious. It did, and Orville set off on one of the wildest goose chases the Wrights were to make in Europe in 1907.

Mr. Stewart turned out to be the current owner of the Barnum and Bailey and Buffalo Bill Shows, but he had not sought out the brothers. It was the other way around. Wilbur had made the first move back in March by writing the Barnum and Bailey business headquarters in Bridgeport, Connecticut, that he and his brother had developed a practical flying machine and would be interested in communicating with someone able to handle the exhibition part of the business when the time came. The time had come. From a circus owner's point of view in 1907, a flying machine that could fly was as exploitable as an elephant with wings. When Orville arrived in London, he found a letter from Wilbur containing several suggestions for the exploitation of their invention by Barnum and Bailey. The most practical of these was for making flights at fairs and pleasure resorts. The least practical suggestion, which must have sent poor Daniel Maloney spinning in his grave, was for dropping a manned Wright glider from a balloon if a suitable landing ground could be found within a mile of the show grounds. What Mr. Stewart had in mind, however, was for the Wrights to train a celebrated French automobile racer to make exhibition flights in an open-air amphitheater at an exposition to be held in London in 1908. Orville didn't think much of the idea, and it was dropped when he received a cable from Wilbur urging him to come to Berlin at once to help prepare a proposal for a sale to the Germans.

In Berlin the brothers were able for the first time to deal directly with the officials concerned, but the same old fear of being hoaxed precluded the signing of a contract. Nevertheless, Wilbur and Orville achieved in three weeks in Germany what they had been unable to achieve in three months in France—a gentleman's agreement that a contract would be given serious consideration if they returned in the spring. Before leaving Berlin, Wilbur wrote a letter to Katharine in which he described a cartoon that had appeared in a German newspaper satirizing the brothers' efforts to peddle flying machines in Europe:

> The Gebrüder Wright are represented as bargaining over the sale of a "cat in a bag." Orville is at one end bargaining with France while I am working Russia at the other end. France has a wheelbarrow full of money and is down on its knees begging us to accept it. The pile is marked 3,900,000 francs. Orville with a pipe in his mouth leans indifferently against the bag containing the wonderful machine, and with a bare glance at the 3,900,000 frs. holds up four fingers to indicate that 4,000,000 frs. is our bottom price. At the other end I am almost equally indifferent, though Russia is represented as pulling its last rouble out of its pocketbook.
>
> As soon as France scrapes up another 100,000 frs. we will sell out and come home.

But France did not scrape up any francs at all, and the dealings with Russia were only slightly less fanciful than the pipe the cartoonist put in Orville's mouth. On November 14, Wilbur and the homesick Charlie Taylor sailed for the United States. Orville stayed in Paris for another three weeks, preparing drawings of the Wright engine so that duplicate engines could be manufactured there for possible use in Europe when, and if, the brothers returned in the spring.

# 26

## *A Letter of Information*

IN 1907 THE United States could no longer afford to assign aeronautics to the pigeonhole in which it had been allowed to languish since Langley's Aerodrome splashed into the Potomac in 1903. Ever since the Union Army sent its first balloon aloft during the Civil War, anything having to do with aeronautics had been assigned to the Signal Corps, so it was in this branch of the service that an Aeronautical Division was at last established on August 1, 1907. Lieutenant Thomas Selfridge was assigned to the new division on August 3 before being sent to Nova Scotia to participate in the experiments being carried out there by Alexander Graham Bell's Aerial Experiment Association. Lieutenant Frank P. Lahm, another young West Point graduate, was assigned to the division a few days later.

Twenty-nine-year-old Frank P. Lahm was the son of Frank S. Lahm, the American expatriate who had created a virtual schism in the Aéro-Club de France in December 1905 by dispatching his brother-in-law to Dayton to investigate the Wright brothers' flights. In 1906 the elder Lahm made a trip to Dayton himself to meet Wilbur and Orville, and after returning to France addressed a letter to the Paris *Herald* vouching personally for the claims of the brothers. The Lahms, father and son, were ardent balloonists. The elder Lahm was to have represented the Aero Club of America in the first international James Gordon Bennett Balloon Race starting from Paris in September 1906, but he had to return to the United States for his daughter's wedding, and his place was taken by his son, then doing a tour of duty at the French cavalry school at Saumur. Young Lahm landed in Yorkshire after a 400-mile trip and won the race for the American Aero Club. In the summer of 1907, he was still in France, recuperating from a relapse of an earlier case of typhoid fever. On August 1 he was convalescing in the garden of a former private school at St.-Germain when his father walked into the garden with two luncheon guests, Wilbur and Orville Wright.

The meeting with Lieutenant Lahm marked a turning point in the Wrights' relations with the U.S. War Department. Shortly after the meeting, Lieutenant Lahm wrote a letter to the Chief Signal Officer, Brigadier General James Allen, second-highest-ranking member of the four-man Board of Ordnance and Fortification, urging that the brothers' latest proposal for the sale of a Flyer receive favorable action from the Board. It would be unfortunate, he said, if the United States should not be the first to take advantage of the unquestioned military value of the Wright Flyer.

Lahm's letter had the desired effect. The Board's long-delayed response to the brothers' proposal of June 15, 1907, reached Orville in Paris in October, while Wilbur was in Germany. The proposal had been considered, but $100,000 was more than the Board had at its disposal. Nothing could be done without a special appropriation from Congress, and that would take time. After discussing the matter with Lieutenant Lahm, Orville wrote the Board on October 30 that he and Wilbur would make every concession to provide a basis of agreement. Fair treatment meant more to them than a high price. If the Board was interested, one of them would return to America for a conference at once. Two weeks later, without waiting for a reply, Wilbur was on his way back to the United States, having decided that a fair price on which to base negotiations for the sale of a Flyer would be $25,000, or a quarter of what they had previously asked.

Wilbur stopped off in Washington on the way home and met with three members of the Board. The Board had only $10,000 to apply toward the purchase of a Flyer, he learned. It would take until March to obtain the rest of the money from Congress. Wilbur arrived in Dayton somewhat disillusioned, but when he returned to Washington on December 5 to attend a formal meeting of the Board, his frankness of manner and self-confidence worked their usual magic, and the Board assured him that the entire $25,000 would be forthcoming by drawing on an emergency fund left over from the Spanish-American War. An outright purchase was not possible, however. Bids would have to be solicited first. On December 23, 1907, an "Advertisement and Specification for a Heavier-Than-Air Flying Machine" was issued by the Signal Corps, seeking bids for an aircraft capable of carrying two men at a speed of 40 miles an hour and of staying in the air for at least one hour and landing without serious damage. There were a number of other requirements—such as that it must be possible to take the machine apart, transport it on an Army wagon, and reassemble it without difficulty—all tailored closely to what the Wrights had to offer.

The purpose of the call for bids had been to forestall criticism and sound out public sentiment, but criticism was not forestalled and public sentiment was far from reassuring. "There is not a known flying-machine in the world which could fulfill these specifications," proclaimed the *American Magazine of Aeronautics*. James Means, erstwhile editor of the *Aeronautical Annuals* of 1895–97, thought that if the Signal Corps really wanted a flying machine, the conditions would have been made easier. "I believe that Minerva came forth fully fledged, from the head of Jupiter," he wrote Octave Chanute, "but I hardly think that the perfect flying machine will appear in such sudden fashion."

To discourage irresponsible or impecunious bidders, each respondent was required to deposit with the Signal Corps a certified check amounting to 10 percent of his bid, to be forfeited in case of failure. Since the specifications were impossible of fulfillment by anybody but the Wrights, only one bid was expected, but by the February 1, 1908, deadline forty-one had been received, ranging from $850 to a cool $1 million. Nineteen were discarded as too preposterous for consideration, including one from a federal prisoner who promised to deliver an airplane in exchange for his release, another that was merely a crude sketch on wrapping paper, and another from an inventor who offered flying machines for $45 or $65 per pound, depending on the model preferred. Of the remaining twenty-two bids, only three were accompanied by certified checks. The lowest was from a J. F. Scott of Chicago, who had only $100 on hand with which to satisfy the requirement for a check, so his bid was limited to $1,000. He soon asked the Army to cancel his bid, which the Army was only too happy to do since it was now in an embarrassing position. The Wrights had been underbid. Another bidder had offered to produce a flying machine for only $20,000. Since the rival bidder had a formidable reputation in aeronautical circles, the Board could not afford to ignore his bid and would have to scrape up funds for two machines instead of one if both should prove successful.

The low bidder was the irrepressible Augustus M. Herring, who has no peer in the annals of aeronautics as an inventor of unseen aircraft and maker of unobserved flights. Wilbur and Orville were of the opinion that Herring had taken it for granted that the Army contract would go to the low bidder and that he would then make arrangements with the Wrights to carry out the contract for him on a commission basis. Herring traveled to Dayton and made the brothers just such a proposition, but he was naturally rebuffed, and when the Army agreed to accept both bids, he was obliged to go through the motions of constructing an airplane that would meet the Signal Corps's requirements.

In 1907 Herring had opened a machine shop on upper Broadway in New York, where he claimed to be engaged in some kind of aeronautical work. His overblown reputation was due in large part to his warm personal friend Carl Dienstbach, a New York City musician who served as U.S. correspon-

dent for the German journal *Illustrierte Aeronautische Mitteilungen*. Dienstbach's promotional efforts on behalf of his friend were admirably demonstrated in an article, "Herring's Work," in the May 1908 *American Aeronaut,*
in which he stated unblushingly that Herring's work was "at least equal, and
it may be, paramount to that of the Wrights themselves." He promised that
the government would witness the result of Herring's studies when the
airplane being constructed for the Army was unveiled. He parlayed the
upcoming Army tests into a competition in which Herring would meet
the Wright brothers, those "equally famous adepts," in "the most remarkable rivalry America has ever witnessed."

Wilbur and Orville were too familiar with Herring's past, and too busy,
to worry about competition from such a source. The successful outcome of
their negotiations with the United States was followed in March by the
signing of a contract with the French. In 1907 they had preferred dealing
directly with the War Ministry in Paris, but when a private syndicate for
the manufacture and sale of Wright Flyers in France was finally put together
by Hart Berg in March 1908, the Wrights were quite willing to sign a
contract with the syndicate, especially since Deutsch de la Meurthe, whose
involvement in the previous negotiations had so offended the Letellier group,
was considered a prospective stockholder. None of the Letellier men were
in the new syndicate, which was headed by Lazare Weiller, an enterprising
French businessman with a finger in many pies, including the lucrative Paris
taxicab business. La Compagnie Générale de Navigation Aérienne, the
French Wright company, was capitalized at 700,000 francs, or $140,000. The
Wrights would receive the lion's share of the stock, royalties on all machines
constructed, and a substantial sum in cash on the completion of demonstration flights in France.

In one way, the ten-month delay in concluding a contract with the
French was all to the good. The Wright Flyer would now be making its
debut on both sides of the Atlantic at almost the same time, and the effect
would be doubly astounding. On the other hand, the delay made it possible
that the Wrights might be overtaken either in Europe or in the United States
before they had made a single demonstration flight. Santos-Dumont's
21-second flight of November 1906 in the *14-bis* had inspired a trio of French
experimenters to take up where Santos left off. Léon Delagrange, a Parisian
artist and sculptor, was one of the three. He had purchased a biplane from
the factory set up by Charles and Gabriel Voisin. Like most early Voisin
machines, Delagrange's had an elevator in front, as in the Wright Flyer, a
boxlike tail that served as vertical rudder, and no mechanism whatever for
lateral control, although the so-called side curtains, inserted between the
wings of some Voisin machines, contributed to lateral stability, as did the
slight dihedral of the wings, making flying difficult in all but the lightest of

winds. Delagrange managed to better Santos' record with a 40-second flight on November 5, 1907, at Issy-les-Moulineaux, the drill grounds near Paris that the War Ministry made available to the French Aéro-Club as a flying field. Only slightly more successful than Delagrange was Louis Blériot, a prosperous manufacturer of automobile headlamps, who crashed a monoplane of his own design in April 1907 and almost ended his career that summer by trying to fly an apparatus with wings in tandem like Langley's Aerodrome. In September he smashed the rebuilt tandem machine after a flight of 600 feet. He then built a monoplane with a remarkably modern configuration in which he made two half-kilometer flights in November and December before destroying this machine also. Octave Chanute would one day write of Blériot that he had "built and broken more machines than any other aviator in the world."

The most successful of this trio of French aviators in 1907 was Henri Farman, a former bicycle and automobile racer. The son of an English journalist living in Paris, Farman was British by birth but had spent all his life in France and knew only a few words of English. Like Léon Delagrange, he flew a Voisin biplane, which he continually altered and modified in an effort to win the Deutsch-Archdeacon prize for the first closed-circuit flight of one kilometer. His best performance in 1907 was a 74-second flight at Issy on November 9, in which he covered slightly more than one kilometer but failed to complete the circle that would have won him the prize. Wilbur and Orville witnessed some of Farman's flights at Issy in 1907. They did not consider his attempts to force his clumsy biplane into the air much of a challenge. "I note from several remarks in your recent letters that you evidently view the present situation in aviation circles with very different eyes from what we do," Wilbur wrote Chanute on the first day of 1908, after Chanute had made a halfhearted attempt to reopen the debate over how long it would be before others overtook the Wrights. "I must confess that I still hold to my prediction that an independent solution of the flying problem would require at least five years."

In 1908, the five-year gap threatened to close more rapidly than Wilbur was willing to admit. On January 13, the Grand Prix d'Aviation Deutsch-Archdeacon was won with great éclat by Henri Farman at Issy. In flying the first complete circle in Europe, he had to make wide skidding turns to compensate for sideslip and to avoid stalling. That spring, Léon Delagrange and Farman engaged in a friendly game of leapfrog, each attempting to outdo the other. At Issy on March 21, Farman flew 2 kilometers in 3 1/2 minutes. On April 11, Delagrange flew 4 kilometers in 6 1/2 minutes. The following month, Delagrange shipped his Voisin to Rome and broke his own record on May 30, flying for 15 1/2 minutes before a vast crowd that included the King and Queen of Italy. In Milan on June 23, Delagrange stayed aloft for 16 1/2 minutes, only to be outflown on July 6, when Farman flew for 20 kilometers at Issy in 20 minutes 20 seconds. Shortly thereafter Farman was lured to the United States with an offer of $25,000 to display his flying skill in a four-city tour beginning in Brooklyn at Brighton Beach racetrack. On August 1, 10,000 paying customers showed up, but Farman refused to fly in the 15-mile-per-hour wind. The next day a crowd of only 1,000 waited three hours to see a 40-second flight during which the Frenchman was never more than fifteen feet off the ground. The backers of the tour were soon deeply in debt. The tour was canceled, and Farman returned to France with his Voisin.

In sharp contrast to the American failure of Farman's boxlike Voisin was the success, earlier that summer, of the biplane that won the *Scientific American* trophy for the first public flight of one kilometer in the United States. The winning biplane had been constructed by Alexander Graham Bell's Aerial Experiment Association. In December 1907, the association had moved its headquarters from Nova Scotia in Canada to Hammondsport, New York, where Glenn Curtiss's motorcycle works made it possible for the four young AEA members, whose interest in tetrahedral kites Bell had found disappointingly low, to get into the air by the flying-machine route. In January 1908, Glenn Curtiss, Lieutenant Tom Selfridge, and the two Canadian AEA members, Douglas McCurdy and Casey Baldwin, set to work to show the world that they could achieve in a little over six months what had taken the Wright brothers five years to accomplish.

To accustom themselves to the feel of the air they made half a hundred glides down the snowy flanks of a hillside near Hammondsport in a seventy-five-pound hang glider made of bamboo and cotton sheeting. These AEA gliding experiments would soon have been forgotten if Lieutenant Tom Selfridge, as secretary of the Aerial Experiment Association, had not addressed a letter to the Wright brothers on January 15, beginning: "I am taking the liberty of writing you and asking your advice on certain points connected with gliding experiments, or rather glider construction, which we started here last Monday." Because the Wright brothers would later claim that whatever success the AEA eventually achieved was due to the information they supplied in response to this request, both Selfridge's letter and the brothers' reply warrant careful perusal.

Lieutenant Selfridge asked specifically for three items of information: the results the Wright brothers had obtained on the travel of the center of pressure on curved and flat surfaces; a good method for constructing ribs that would retain their curvature in flight; and a good means of fastening the cloth and spars to the ribs.

The Wrights replied on January 18 that much of the information requested had already been published and would be found in Wilbur's 1901 and 1903 addresses to the Western Society of Engineers, in Chanute's article in the November 1903 *Revue Générale des Sciences,* and in the Wright patent of May 22, 1906. The tone of the brothers' letter was cordial and polite. Its central paragraph was a detailed answer to Selfridge's inquiry regarding the travel of the center of pressure—information that had been available, in Wilbur's first Chicago address, ever since 1901, except for two facts: that reversal of travel begins when the angle of attack is from 12 to 18 degrees and that in gliding flight the travel occurs between the center of the wing and a point one-third back from the front edge. In response to Selfridge's request concerning glider ribs, the Wrights replied: "The ribs of our gliders were made of second growth ash, steamed and bent to shape." As to Selfridge's third request—for a good means of fastening cloth and spars to the ribs—there was no response at all.

It is impossible to say precisely what use, if any, the Aerial Experiment Association made of the information supplied by the Wright brothers. In the case of the AEA glider, it was none at all, for the glider had been built and was being used for practice when Selfridge wrote his letter. The four publications mentioned by the Wrights had been available for some time to anyone interested enough to ferret them out. As a matter of fact, the AEA members had already made a study of the Wright patent and had come to the conclusion that wingwarping placed an undue strain on the wings. What use the AEA made of the Wrights' explanation of the travel of the center of pressure is anybody's guess; such niceties as experiments to acquire this information firsthand or to determine the best camber and aspect ratio for wings were noticeably lacking in the AEA's pragmatic approach. As to rib construction, the method described by the Wrights, which they themselves had abandoned in 1902, could have been of little or no use, for the ribs of the AEA machines were constructed not of ash, steamed and bent to shape, but of four laminations of ash and spruce glued together.

In all likelihood, the Aerial Experiment Association would have gone about its task exactly as it did if the Wrights had not answered Selfridge's letter. The first flying machine produced by the association bore little resemblance to the Wright Flyer, except that the elevator was in front and the vertical rudder behind. Because Lieutenant Selfridge had risked his life and undergone a ducking in testing Alexander Graham Bell's big man-carrying kite, he was the first of the four young AEA members to design a flying machine. This was a biplane with a wingspan of forty-three feet, driven by a single pusher propeller powered by a Curtiss air-cooled motor of 25 horsepower. It was called the *Red Wing* because its wings were covered with the same kind of red silk used in Bell's big tetrahedral kites. There was no lateral control, but the wings, tapered to their pointed tips, were bowed toward each other in the hope that the droop of the upper wing and positive dihedral of the lower would provide a measure of inherent stability.

Lieutenant Selfridge had been called to Washington on Army business, so the honor of piloting the first AEA machine fell to Casey Baldwin. Equipped with sled runners, the *Red Wing* rose from the frozen surface of Lake Keuka on March 12 and flew for 319 feet. A second trial was made on March 17, but the wingcovering was so soaked with rain that the machine flew only about 120 feet before spinning in on its left wingtip. Selfridge returned from Washington to find his bright red brainchild a sodden wreck.

The next AEA machine, designed by Casey Baldwin, was the *White Wing,* so named because the supply of red silk had been exhausted and its wings were covered with plain white muslin. It was much like the *Red Wing* but had a tricycle landing gear instead of sled runners and movable wingtips for lateral control. The hinged wingtips were operated like ailerons by ropes attached to a wooden yoke on the shoulders of the operator, who instinctively moved his body toward the high wing to restore balance. Each of the four AEA members was given a chance to fly the *White Wing* at a trotting track near Hammondsport. Between May 18 and May 23, when the machine turned turtle and was wrecked, five flights were made. The longest lasted 19 seconds, during which Glenn Curtiss covered more than 1,000 feet, his wheels touching the ground once or twice between takeoff and landing.

The next AEA machine, a strengthened and improved version of the *White Wing,* was christened the *June Bug* by Alexander Graham Bell because it reminded him for some strange reason of that insect. It had been designed by Glenn Curtiss and it was in the *June Bug* that Curtiss first gained fame as an aviator by winning the *Scientific American* trophy, a silver artifact, between whose onyx base and the American eagle at its apex were a globe of the earth, a miniature of Langley's tandem-wing Aerodrome, and a motley assortment of winged horses and riders. It was to be awarded each year for three years beginning in 1908—the first year for a straightway flight of one kilometer or more. Knowing that the Wrights had flown many times that distance in 1905, the editor of the *Scientific American* did his best to lure the brothers into the competition. One of the stipulations, however, was that the airplane must use wheels, rather than a track, in taking off. With two contracts in the offing, the Wrights did not think it worthwhile to alter their machine's method of starting for the dubious honor of walking away with the magazine's flamboyant trophy.

A twenty-two-man delegation of the Aero Club of America was among the crowd of spectators and reporters assembled on July 4 at the trotting track near Hammondsport to witness Curtiss's try for the trophy. Bad weather held up the proceedings until 6 P.M., when Curtiss took off and came down several hundred feet short of one kilometer. The *June Bug* was pushed back to the starting point, and Curtiss took off once more. This time he made it to the finish line and beyond, covering 5,090 feet, or a little over a kilometer and a half, in 1 minute 42 1/2 seconds. Between July 10 and the end of August, the *June Bug* made eight flights of a minute or more, the longest being a flight of 2 miles in 3 minutes made by Douglas McCurdy on August 29, during which he flew the AEA's first figure eight. Two days later, Curtiss flew the first circle.

In June 1908 the *Scientific American* printed an account of the flights of the *White Wing,* to which the following sentence was added: "The builders will duplicate this machine for anyone desiring one for $5,000, delivery to be made within 60 days." When Orville read those words, he wrote Wilbur, who was then in Europe preparing for flights in fulfillment of their French contract: "Curtiss et al are using our patents, I understand, and are now offering machines for sale at $5,000 each, according to the *Scientific American.* They have got some cheek!"

The report turned out to be false, but when news reached France that Glenn Curtiss had won the *Scientific American* trophy on July 4 in a machine equipped with movable wingtips, Wilbur also became alarmed and advised Orville to inform Curtiss that their patent covered broadly any adjustment of the wings, including movable wingtips, used in combination with the vertical rudder. He urged Orville to inquire at the same time if Curtiss would like to take a license to operate under the Wright patent for exhibition purposes. On July 20 Orville wrote Curtiss, pointing out that the fact that they had referred Selfridge to their patent in their letter of January 18 did not mean that they had given the AEA permission to use the methods covered by that patent.

Curtiss replied that the matter of the patents had been referred to AEA secretary Selfridge and that, contrary to newspaper reports, he did not expect to do anything in the way of exhibitions. The newspaper reports had not been entirely wrong, however. The *June Bug*'s success had brought a $10,000 offer for Curtiss to make exhibition flights in St. Louis, but Bell put his foot down. He had spent years in the courts defending his telephone patents, and although he did not personally believe that movable wingtips infringed the Wrights' wingwarping claim or that it was necessary to use the vertical rudder in conjunction with movable wingtips, he foresaw that the AEA would be flying into a storm cloud of litigation if its members went in for exhibition flights or manufactured flying machines for sale.

Nevertheless, the Wright brothers were more certain than ever that the Aerial Experiment Association had profited from the information contained in their letter to Selfridge. How else could the association have progressed from gliding experiments to a flight of a kilometer and a half in six months?

Grover Loening, the aeronautical engineer who knew Wilbur and worked closely with Orville in the first American Wright Company, wrote many years later that both brothers were adamant in claiming that they had released priceless data on wing surfaces in their letter to Selfridge of January 18, 1908. But the only data on wing surfaces in that letter concerned the travel of the center of pressure, and no one has ever shown that the Aerial Experiment Association put that information to use in any practical way.

Infringement of the Wright patent was another matter altogether. That was a matter for the courts to decide. The time was not yet ripe for that, but when it was, it would be Glenn Curtiss, rather than the Aerial Experiment Association, who would draw the first flash of fire from the Wright brothers in their flame-breathing defense of their 1906 patent.

# 27

## *Return to Kitty Hawk*

THE NEW WRIGHT FLYERS were designed to carry two men in a sitting position, pilot on the left, passenger on the right. A lever controlling the front rudder (the elevator) was at the pilot's left; the wingwarping and vertical rudder controls were combined in a single lever between the seats. While the sitting position would be more comfortable for the operator, the new controls would require a good deal of practice before their operation became automatic. With this in mind, the Wright brothers equipped their 1905 Flyer with seats, control levers, and one of their new, more powerful motors, and prepared to get into the air for the first time since 1905. The days when they could experiment in relative privacy at Huffman Prairie were gone forever. The stretch of beach below Kitty Hawk was still the most suitable practice site and, for reporters, the least accessible. On April 4, 1908, they shipped their modified Flyer to Elizabeth City, North Carolina. Two days later Wilbur left Dayton to ready their old campsite at Kill Devil Hills for its reception.

The trip to the Outer Banks was attended by the usual mishaps. Wilbur had arranged for transportation from Elizabeth City to Kitty Hawk in Captain Franklin Midgett's sailboat, the *Lou Willis,* but the *Lou Willis* did not appear until Wilbur's second day in town. When it did show up, it was manned by the captain's son, Little Spencer Midgett. The Mighty Midgetts, as the family has sometimes been called, had lived on the Outer Banks since the eighteenth century. Many men of the family were in the Lifesaving Service. They were a stocky, broad-shouldered breed, so the chances are that Little Spencer was not as tiny as his cognomen implied. His father arrived later in the day, piloting a gasoline launch with the pompous name of *B. M. Van Dusen.* It was too late to make the return trip to Kitty Hawk, so Wilbur spent another night in his hotel. It could not have been a very restful one. There were three fires in town that night.

The next day he purchased a fifty-two-gallon barrel of gasoline and enough lumber and hardware for a new building, after learning from Captain John Daniels of the Lifesaving Service, whom he met in the depot at Elizabeth City, that the old camp buildings at Kill Devil Hills were in ruins. That evening the *B. M. Van Dusen* chugged into Kitty Hawk, and the *Lou Willis* followed with as much of the lumber as it could carry. The next morning Little Spencer Midgett hitched up the family wagon and drove Wilbur to Kill Devil Hills in a windy drizzle, while Truxton Midgett and his uncle Ezekiel sailed the *Lou Willis* down the bay to the old fish landing, as close as they could get to the former campground, and unloaded the lumber.

John Daniels had not exaggerated. The building that had housed the 1903 Flyer had been buffeted to pieces by the wind. The side walls of the 1902 camp building were standing, but the floor of the old living quarters was under a foot of sand. Earlier that year some boys had come by and ripped the burlap from the bunks in the loft and the wingcovering from the 1902 glider. The friendly lifesaving crew invited Wilbur to move into the Kill Devil station until a new building could be erected. When he moved in with the surfmen, Wilbur was in a depressed mood. Almost a week had gone by since he left Dayton, and much valuable time had been wasted. "I will expect you to arrive with relief Saturday," he wrote Orville on April 11. "I am not sure I can hold out much longer than that."

Wilbur's second week away from home was filled with a whole new set of frustrations and aborted endeavors. He had hired two "semi-carpenters" in Kitty Hawk to help with the foundations of the new building. After the foundation posts were put in Monday, he discovered that only half the necessary lumber and hardware was on hand to finish the job. Little Spencer had sailed the *Lou Willis* back to Elizabeth City to pick up the rest of the lumber, but his sails were blown off and he didn't tie up at the wharf in Kitty Hawk until Wednesday afternoon, too late to sail the lumber down to Kill Devil Hills. That same morning, Wilbur had looked out from the lifesaving station and seen a man wandering about the demolished camp buildings in the rain. Thinking it was one of the semi-carpenters, he walked over and found that the man was Charles Furnas, a Dayton mechanic, who had been bitten by the flying bug and hoped someday to learn to fly. Either Furnas had gone to Kill Devil Hills on his own or Orville had decided that Charlie Taylor was needed in Dayton and had sent Furnas on ahead to help. In either case, there was nothing at first for Furnas to do and no place for him to stay except at the lifesaving station, which was already overcrowded. A worried Wilbur wired Orville to postpone his departure for five days. It was just as well. Before the week was over, Orville came down with a chill.

Wilbur was having a health problem of his own. Accommodations at the lifesaving station were not up to Hawthorn Street standards, and he was suffering from diarrhea. On Thursday a driving rain and winds of up to 40 miles an hour kept the men indoors. Friday, the *Lou Willis* had still not appeared with the lumber, so Wilbur sent Furnas up to Kitty Hawk to see what had happened. It turned out that Thursday's high winds had driven the waters of Kitty Hawk Bay away from the wharf, leaving the *Lou Willis* stranded high and dry. The energetic Furnas rounded up all available Midgetts and had them transfer the lumber to a flatboat and had it towed to the old fish landing. When the lumber was carted to the campsite, it was discovered that the siding for the new building and the sheeting for the roof were still in Elizabeth City. It was about this time that the drum of gasoline began to smell. When Wilbur siphoned the gas into an empty metal drum that had been on the site since 1903, he found that half of the fifty-two gallons had leaked away, thanks to the Mighty Midgetts, who had thrown the barrel off Little Spencer's wagon with such force when it was unloaded at the camp the week before that it had sprung a leak.

Still suffering from diarrhea, Wilbur set off on foot for Kitty Hawk Saturday morning to persuade Captain Midgett to take the *B. M. Van Dusen* to Elizabeth City and pick up the remaining lumber. "It is a little hard having to pay for a special trip at a fancy price when he made three trips without bringing anything," Wilbur grumbled to his diary. There was more Midgett trouble on Monday. Little Spencer went home with a headache without giving Wilbur a chance to hire a replacement, but by nightfall the rafters of the new building were up. Tuesday, the floor was laid and the side walls erected. Wednesday, the roof was sheeted. Thursday, the big hangar doors were hung. Friday, Wilbur fixed up the kitchen. Saturday morning, two Kitty Hawkers drove into camp with two carloads of flying-machine freight and the news that Orville was at the old fish landing with the 1905 Flyer, which had been stored in the depot at Elizabeth City. Orville also brought the stove and groceries Wilbur had ordered earlier in the week. Saturday night, after sitting down to a meal better suited to Ohio palates and bowels than the fare at the lifesaving station, the three Daytonians went to bed, each in his own fashion—Wilbur in a patent bed up among the rafters, Orville on boards thrown across the ceiling joists, Furnas on the floor.

They spent the next week assembling the Flyer. The brothers hoped to make a few short flights to familiarize themselves with the new controls before news of what they were doing leaked out. On Friday, May 1, before the machine was completely assembled, the Norfolk *Virginian-Pilot* published a sensational story of their having made a ten-mile flight over the ocean. The New York *Herald* decided to investigate, but before sending a reporter to that outrageously inaccessible bit of seacoast, the paper enlisted the services of D. Bruce Salley, a free-lance reporter from Norfolk whose beat included the Outer Banks as far south as Cape Hatteras.

On Monday, May 4, Salley checked into the Tranquil House in Manteo on Roanoke Island. Manteo was eight miles from Kill Devil Hills as the crow flies, about as close to the Wright camp as an enterprising reporter could get without forgoing such refinements of civilization as hot meals and telegraphic communication with the outside world. Tuesday morning Salley had himself ferried to the Outer Banks in a wheezy gasoline launch operated by Captain Midgett—not the skipper of the *B. M. Van Dusen* but another Captain Midgett, who happened to be the nephew of Walter Midgett of the Kill Devil lifesaving crew. No doubt it was through the Midgett grapevine that the Wrights' presence on the Outer Banks had become known. After wading ashore, Salley and the captain tramped through the sand hills and reached the Wright camp about noon. While Wilbur's diary does not record what they were told, Salley evidently got the impression that the brothers were not yet ready to fly and did not return to Kill Devil Hills the next day, when the first flight of 1908 was made.

Like all Wright flights on the Outer Banks, Wednesday's flight was launched without benefit of derrick and falling weights. Wilbur used almost 100 feet of the 115-foot starting rail before struggling into the air against a 15-mile wind. He was so occupied with manipulating the combined warping and vertical rudder handle in his right hand that he neglected the horizontal front rudder control in his left and landed after twenty-two seconds without shutting off the motor. Two wheel-trucks were placed under the wings, and with the help of two men from the lifesaving station, the Flyer was wheeled back to the camp building. Each turn of a wheel multiplied by its circumference gave the distance flown over the ground, in this instance 1,008 feet.

Reporter Salley learned of the flight by telephone from one of the men at the lifesaving station. His secondhand report of a 1,000-foot flight was sent out over the Weather Bureau wire that night by Alpheus Drinkwater, who manned the bureau's station at Manteo, and was printed on page one of the New York *Herald* the next day. The *New York Times* also carried the story, together with a few embellishments picked up along the way, such as that a flight to Hampton Roads (seventy-five miles from Kill Devil Hills) would be made the following day in the presence of representatives of the United States and foreign governments. But it rained on Thursday, and no flights were made at all.

Conditions were ideal for flying on Friday. Wilbur, Orville, and Charles Furnas hurried through breakfast and had the Flyer on the starting rail by

7 A.M. Because it was difficult to determine just how much movement of the hand levers produced the desired amount of control, only one of the nine starts made that morning lasted as long as twelve seconds. The first real flight of the day was made after lunch by Orville—954 feet in 31 seconds. Salley, concealed in the underbrush half a mile or more away, watched the proceedings through field glasses. He was so overcome by his first sight of a flying machine in the air that he left his hiding place and ran over to the camp. Again Wilbur's diary is silent on what the reporter was told or what he was allowed to see, but it was not until after Salley was gone that Wilbur made the most successful flight of the day—2,230 feet in 59.5 seconds

Alpheus Drinkwater tapped out Salley's eyewitness account of Friday's flights that evening on the Weather Bureau wire. Bishop Wright noted in his diary the next day that the report appeared in two Dayton dailies and three Cincinnati papers, one of which stated that the Wrights had traveled eight miles out over the ocean at an altitude of 3,000 feet. The New York *Herald*'s more sober account, written by star reporter Byron R. Newton, was printed on an inside page as if the information on which it was based, attributed to "D. Bruce Salley, a spectator," was somehow suspect. James Gordon Bennett's air-minded *Herald* had no intention of being scooped, however, and before the day was over Byron Newton was on his way to Manteo. He arrived Monday, May 11. William Hoster of the New York *American* signed into the Tranquil House the same day. The two reporters were joined Tuesday by Arthur Ruhl of *Collier's Weekly,* James Hare, a pioneer news photographer, also from *Collier's,* and P. H. McGowan, U.S. correspondent of the London *Daily Mail.*

Several times that week, after the little band of journalists waded ashore from a hired launch, lanky, loose-jointed Salley guided them through the woods of live oak, holly, and loblolly pine along the marshy shores of the Outer Banks to a place of concealment from which they could observe the Wright camp through field glasses. William Hoster would one day write that they were required to trek ten miles through underbrush, part of it on hands and knees. Arthur Ruhl, in his contemporary account in *Collier's,* reduced the distance to four or five miles, although thanks to heat, ticks, sand fleas, chiggers, and mosquitoes, it seemed more like thirty-five. Fifteen years later, Byron Newton would recount the agonies endured by the reporters as they hacked their way to their hiding place through patches of dense jungle infested with wild cattle, hogs, turkeys, moccasins, rattlers, and blacksnakes—flora and fauna that evoked smiles from native Kitty Hawkers— but the amazement of the newsmen at seeing an airplane in the air for the first time was genuine enough.

The Wright brothers knew they were under surveillance. Like good double agents, the Kill Devil lifesaving crew, while keeping the newsmen informed of what was going on at the Wright camp, kept Wilbur and Orville informed of the movements of the reporters, whose heads could be seen bobbing up and down from time to time behind the sand hills in the distance. So long as the newsmen did not interfere with practice, the brothers were more amused than angered at these antics.

Wilbur and Orville flew three days that week. On Monday, May 11, the wind was too light for a start from the level, so they laid the launching rail on the side of Big Hill. Orville made a 71-second flight after a gravity-assisted takeoff, then Wilbur made a circling flight of 2 1/2 minutes. At eleven o'clock, Orville ended the third flight by failing to turn quickly enough and landed sideways a considerable distance from the camp. They dragged the Flyer back to its shed and spent the rest of the day overhauling the machine. They were interrupted that afternoon by Alpheus Drinkwater of the Manteo Weather Bureau station and a Mr. Grant, who claimed to be the Norfolk attaché of the bureau. The men said they were making repairs on the telegraph line along the beach, but the motivation for their visit seems to have been curiosity, for they left the area when it became clear that flying was over for the day.

The newsmen's vigil on Tuesday was in vain. Furnas and the brothers were so exhausted from hauling the 800-pound machine through the soft sand to Big Hill and back the day before that no flights were attempted.

On Wednesday there were more uninvited visitors. Wilbur's flight of less than one minute that morning was witnessed by a young man who identified himself as J. C. Burkhart of Ithaca, New York. They suspected Burkhart was a reporter disguised as a native, but learned later he was actually a Cornell University student who had come all that way "to investigate the scientific part." When they returned to camp after the second flight of the morning, they found another visitor—Arthur Ruhl of *Collier's*. Ruhl had interviewed the brothers in 1907 before they left for Europe. The Wrights liked Ruhl and invited him to stay for lunch, but the journalist declined. He was unaware that they knew other reporters were hiding in the underbrush along the sound and was afraid of compromising his fellow reporters. A dozen more visitors appeared after lunch—a man, a woman, and ten children, natives of Collington Island at the south end of Kitty Hawk Bay. The man and his wife had trudged through the sand lugging the smaller children in the hope of seeing a flight. The Wright brothers would have been glad to oblige, but the wind had risen to more than 20 miles an hour and they didn't want to fly in such winds until they were more familiar with the new controls.

At 6 P.M., after the wind had dropped to 15 miles an hour, Wilbur made a circling flight and returned to the starting point in 2 minutes 40 seconds. Then Orville made a larger circle in 3 minutes 20 seconds. By also landing at the starting point, he circumvented the onerous task of hauling the machine back through the deep sand.

Confident that they were now familiar enough with the new controls to try a two-man flight, they rose early on Thursday. At 8 A.M. Wilbur took off into a southwest wind with Charles Furnas in the seat beside him, but the wind drove the Flyer so close to West Hill that he brought the Flyer down sooner than he intended. The world's first passenger flight had lasted exactly 22.6 seconds. With Furnas still in the passenger seat, Orville made the next flight. He passed safely south of West Hill, turned north, and flew around the dune they called Little Hill. The Flyer was halfway around West Hill for the second time when a hot engine bearing forced it down. The world's second passenger flight had lasted a little over 4 minutes.

After lunch they moved the track into the wind, which had been gradually shifting to the west, and Wilbur made the last and longest flight of the day by himself. He flew north of West Hill, rounded Little Hill, and continued north along the sound for half a mile before circling back and passing over the starting point about five minutes after taking off. He flew on, passing south of West Hill this time, so that the reporters had a clear view of the Flyer from their place of concealment, then continued north once more until he was out of sight of the reporters, although they could still hear the steady beat of the Flyer's engine and propellers.

The Flyer's sound was as familiar to the newsmen by then as its appearance. Both Newton and Ruhl compared it to the sound made by a grain reaper in a distant field at harvest time. Harry Harper, a British journalist who saw—and heard—Wilbur fly in France later that year, pointed out that the distinctive sound made by the Wright machines in flight was in sharp contrast to the roar made by the French machines with their more powerful motors. Like most airplane power plants at the time, Wright engines had no mufflers. They were relatively quiet nonetheless. "One did not hear much of them," Harper wrote. "What one did hear quite clearly was an odd sort of chattering, clattering sound from the crossed chains which drove the two long-bladed air-screws. And there was also a penetrating whistling sound from the air-screws themselves. The net result was a mingled whistling, chattering hum which, once heard, could never be forgotten."

After Wilbur had been in the air for 7 1/2 minutes, it was the abrupt cessation of that whistling, chattering hum that puzzled the reporters in their hot, sandy hideout on the afternoon of May 14. Not sure what the sudden silence portended, they trained their glasses on the Wright camp and saw two men race away from the camp building. The men were soon out of sight behind West Hill. When they did not return and there were no further signs of life about the camp, the reporters assumed there would be no more flights that day and headed back to Manteo to file their dispatches.

When they arrived at the Weather Bureau office, they learned from Alpheus Drinkwater, who had been in touch with the Kill Devil lifesaving station by phone, that Wilbur's long flight had ended in a crash. The disaster provided a colorful ending to the week's dispatches, and the lack of details left plenty of room for improvisation. The accident was front-page news throughout most of the country the next day. It was widely assumed that the Wright brothers had lost their only flying machine. More than one newspaper described Wilbur, although uninjured, as almost crazed with grief and disappointment.

What had happened was that Wilbur had pushed the elevator handle forward when he meant to pull it back, and the Flyer with the wind behind it had plowed into the ground at 50 miles an hour. Orville, watching through field glasses at the camp building almost a mile away, could see nothing at first but a splash of sand. He and Furnas set off on a run. The brothers had agreed that in the event of a crash the one on the Flyer should climb out immediately if he was unhurt, but Wilbur had been thrown violently against the smashed upper wing and was too dazed to move. He remained inside the wreckage for several seconds before staggering out. There was a cut across his nose and bruises on one hand and forearm and both shoulders, but he was otherwise unhurt. The three men spent the rest of the afternoon hauling the undamaged lower wing and engine back to the camp in the hot sun. The heat was so unbearable they waited until sundown to bring the rudders back to the campsite and went to bed completely fagged out.

Friday morning, when they were carting the rest of the Flyer back to the camp, they noticed two men in the distance taking photographs of the remains of the 1902 glider, which had been propped against the ruins of the old camp building. One of the men was McGowan of the London *Daily Mail*; the other was a Washington, D.C., journalist who had arrived too late to witness a flight. As the brothers drew near the camp—Wilbur hitched to the cart in what he described as a dog harness and Orville protected from the sun by what he called his Merry Widow bonnet—the reporters wanted to take a picture but put their cameras aside when the brothers made it clear they preferred not to be presented to the world as beasts of burden or clowns in funny hats.

Later that day an urgent telegram came from Flint and Company saying that one of the brothers must leave for France within a week. Wilbur decided to go without returning to Dayton. Before leaving the Outer Banks, he sent Katharine a wire instructing her to send on his trunk. The trunk was waiting for him at his hotel in New York, together with his hatbox, an indispensable piece of luggage for gentlemen travelers in 1908. "I do wish though," he wrote his sister from New York, "that you had raised the lid of my hatbox, which was unlocked, and put some of my hats in it before sending it on."

It was still undecided which brother would conduct the trials of the Army Flyer to be held that summer at Fort Myer, Virginia, across the Potomac River from Washington, D.C. "If you think best," Wilbur wrote Orville the day before he sailed, "prepare to follow me to France within a few weeks and get some practice there before we undertake to go to Fort Myer."

Wilbur's optimistic estimate of the time it would take to fulfill the French contract was as far off the mark as his estimate of the time it would take to negotiate a contract with the French in 1907. He had anticipated a stay of a few weeks then, but his visit had lasted six months. When he sailed for Le Havre on May 21, 1908, his belief that he and Orville could complete the tests in France in time to return for the trials of the Army Flyer was just as wild a dream. The brothers soon came to the conclusion that the only course to follow would be for Orville to make the demonstration flights at Fort Myer by himself, while Wilbur handled the trials in France alone.

# 28

## *Wilbur Has the Jimjams*

THE WRIGHT BROTHERS were not averse to publicity that did not distort facts or resort to sensationalism. Orville considered Arthur Ruhl's "History at Kill Devil Hill" in the May 30 *Collier's* the finest thing he had ever read about their experiments. Ruhl's story of the May 1908 flights was prefaced by an account of his 1907 visit to the Wrights' "dingy little bicycle shop," in which Orville was depicted as winning and studious-looking and Wilbur as having the "high bald head, long nose and deeply lined face of one who would apparently say something rather dry and droll if he said anything at all." Although Orville did the talking for both brothers, Ruhl noted that it was "about as difficult to get anything out of them as out of a couple of furtive wood animals."

Byron Newton established an enduring friendship with the Wrights by sending them clippings of his dispatches to the New York *Herald* about the flights. He later won their respect by severing his connection with the *Herald* in protest against the sensational way in which that paper—as Orville put it in a letter to Wilbur—tried to "palm off old stuff as revealing our secrets." On Thursday, May 28, the *Herald*'s New York delivery wagons had been plastered with signs announcing that the Wright brothers' secrets would be revealed in the paper the next day. The so-called secrets, which covered half of page one and all of page two of the New York and Paris editions of the *Herald*, consisted mostly of information and diagrams from the Wright French patent of 1904, embellished with an imaginatively retouched photo of the Wright Flyer, one propeller before the wings, the other behind.

Publication of these less than sensational revelations was timed to coincide with Wilbur's arrival on May 29 in Paris, where his first order of business was to revive the flagging spirits of the men who had signed the

French contract. As he described the situation to Orville, "I found our affairs here about like Peter Cartwright reported religion to be on one of his circuits—'looking upward'—in other words flat on its back." The day after Wilbur's arrival, Léon Delagrange flew for 8 miles at Rome and Henri Farman made the first two-man flight in Europe at Issy with Ernest Archdeacon as passenger. Lazare Weiller, the taxicab king, was about to drop out of the French Wright company. Hart Berg was for letting him go. Not so Wilbur. A few days later he was able to write his brother: "Our position is improving rapidly as it always does when one of us is here to meet people and infuse a little confidence in them."

On his second day in Paris, Wilbur visited the factory of Bariquand and Marre, the firm commissioned to build duplicate Wright motors. Before leaving France in 1907, Orville had provided the necessary drawings and had had the original Wright motor shipped from the customs shed at Le Havre to Paris, but the French mechanics had not been able to get the original motor to run. Wilbur showed them how and was assured that two new motors would be ready for testing within a week. When he returned to the factory at the end of ten days, the duplicate motors were still not ready and the mechanics' attempts to run the original had damaged it in various ways. "I fear they will have the old American motor ruined before I can get it out of their hands," Wilbur complained to his diary on June 9. "They are such idiots! and fool with things that should be left alone. I get very angry every time I go down there."

Wilbur's next order of business was to find a field where he could make demonstration flights in fulfillment of the French contract. He and Berg made several forays into the countryside, but found no satisfactory sites among the carefully cultivated fields close to Paris. The most suitable site was a hundred miles away—the artillery testing ground, two to three miles long, at Camp d'Auvours near Le Mans—but it was being used at the time by the French Army, so they settled for Les Hunaudières, a racecourse ringed with poplars in the piney wasteland south of Le Mans. The racetrack was half a mile long and a quarter of a mile wide. The ground inside the track was full of ruts but smooth enough for landing on skids. The chief advantage of Les Hunaudières was its nearness to Le Mans, then a city of 75,000, where a room in an automobile factory was made available to Wilbur for assembling the Flyer that had been stored in crates in the customs shed at Le Havre ever since the summer of 1907. The factory belonged to Léon Bollée, president of the Aéro-Club de la Sarthe, the *département* in which Le Mans was located. Bollée was a roly-poly, bearded little man of 240 pounds who knew as little English as Wilbur knew French, but he was the proud owner and pilot of a spherical balloon that went by the name of *Au*

*Petit Bonheur,* and a mutual interest in aeronautics made the two men fast friends.

On June 16, Wilbur moved into a hotel in Le Mans where no one spoke English but where he was as comfortable as he had ever been while away from home. The hotel dining room was the scene of his first encounter with alphabet soup. "I was a little astonished and disturbed the other evening when I sat down to dinner," he wrote Katharine, "to find my soup, which was a sort of noodle soup, turning into all sorts of curious forms and even letters of the alphabet. I began to think I had the 'jimjams.' "

Wilbur really had the jimjams in the big room at the Bollée factory when he opened the crates shipped from Le Havre and got his first look at the machine he was expected to fly. In a scathing letter to Orville, he itemized what he found: broken ribs, wingcoverings torn and smeared with silver paint from the skids, smashed radiators, a broken seat, magneto coils torn up, possibly a bent propeller shaft. He had always suspected that Orville was careless and impetuous when not under the direct supervision of his older brother. Forgetting that only ten days before he had written Orville that he believed the French had opened the crates in 1907 and examined their contents, he now blamed Orville for everything:

> I opened the boxes yesterday and have been puzzled ever since to know how you could have wasted two whole days packing them. I am sure that with a scoop shovel I could have put things in within two or three minutes and made fully as good a job of it. I never saw such evidence of idiocy in my life. Did you tell Charley not to separate anything lest it should get lonesome?

Orville responded by blaming the damage on the customs officers. In his old age he would chuckle over Wilbur's letter when he showed it to friends, but it could not have inspired many chuckles when it arrived in Dayton toward the end of June 1908. Work on the U.S. Army Flyer was already behind schedule, and Orville and Charlie Taylor had their hands full constructing parts for five more machines to be shipped to Wilbur in France. The publicity created by the May flights at Kill Devil Hills made it difficult for Orville to get any work done. People kept dropping into the bicycle shop, wanting to talk. Metal manufacturers, scenting profits in a future aeronautical industry, were plying him with suggestions for the use of their products. Inventors by the dozen were offering their inventions at what they considered rock-bottom prices. There was a tenfold increase in the mail pouring into the office above the shop. Most of the letters could be ignored, some could be answered with Katharine's help, but inquiries from scientific and aeronautical journals asking for authorized accounts of the May flights required Orville's personal attention, as did the recently reopened negotiations with the British.

In April, before leaving to join Wilbur at Kill Devil Hills, Orville had written the War Office in London that he and Wilbur would like to revive the discussions that had come to a standstill in December 1906 when the War Office had turned down their second offer to sell the British a Flyer. Unknown to Orville, the Wrights' English friend Lieutenant Colonel John Capper was still being consulted on all matters pertaining to the negotiations. The British were still pinning their hopes on Samuel Cody's big biplane then under construction at Farnborough. Not wanting to cut off the possibility of doing business with the Wrights altogether, Capper suggested that the War Office reply of June 10 (signed not by Capper but by an underling named J. M. Bull) should include a list of specifications that would have to be met by any machine purchased by the British government. Several of the specifications struck Orville as unreasonable. The machine, for instance, would have to be capable of climbing to 5,000 feet with a full load and durable enough to remain in the open for one month without deteriorating. On July 27, Orville wrote again, asking the War Office to clarify some of the more ambiguous specifications. Capper's reply of August 12 (again over the signature of J. M. Bull) included an entirely new specification that brought the third round of negotiations effectively to a close, namely, that the machine must be started without the aid of a launching rail and falling weights. Half-a-dozen exclamation points were used by an indignant Bishop Wright in relaying to Wilbur in France the contents of J. M. Bull's second letter to Orville: "They ask only that an applicant should jump over the moon! through a hoop!! six times!!!"

As if Orville's plate was not already full that summer, Wilbur saddled his brother with a task that he himself, as the writer of the family, was better qualified to perform. Before sailing for Europe, he had dropped into the *Century Magazine* office in New York and informed the editors that the Wright brothers were now ready to furnish that popular periodical with the exclusive account of their flying experiments that had been promised the editor not long after the first flights of December 1903. What Wilbur had in mind was not merely an article to satisfy public curiosity about the Wright brothers but one that would signal a warning to infringers of their patent. On the morning of his visit to the *Century* office, the New York papers had carried stories of two short flights made the day before by Lieutenant Selfridge at Hammondsport in the Aerial Experiment Association's second biplane, the *White Wing.* The movable wingtips of the *White Wing,* Wilbur believed, infringed the brothers' wingwarping claim. It was therefore important, he admonished Orville, "to get the main features originated by us identified in the public mind with our machine before they are described in connection with some other machine. A statement of our original features ought to be published and not left covered up in the patent office. I strongly advise that you get a stenographer and dictate an article and have Kate assist in getting it in shape if you are too busy."

Writing a magazine article on top of everything else he had to do was a tall order for Orville, who hated putting pen to paper anyway, but when the *Century* editors offered $500 for an illustrated account, he set to work and completed a 5,000-word article in less than three weeks, a feat that might not have been possible if Wilbur had been looking over his shoulder. Wilbur assumed that Orville would of course put off the onerous task of writing until the last minute and on June 28, six days after the manuscript had been sent to New York, he wrote a letter from Le Mans, spelling out several subjects that he wanted Orville to touch upon in the article, especially Chanute's 1903 talk to the Aéro-Club de France and the subsequent scramble of French experimenters to build and fly machines *du type de Wright.* He was still at it a week later: "I hope you bring out in your *Century* article the fundamental difference between our methods & those of Chanute, and call attention to the fact that we have obtained very broad patents on the general combinations as well as the particular constructions employed." But when "The Wright Brothers' Aeroplane" appeared in the September *Century*—attributed to both brothers, incidentally, although Orville's name was given first—it contained nary a whisper of the subjects Wilbur had wanted Orville to include, except for a single offhand reference to the fact that "movable rudders working in conjunction with the twisting of the wings" were a feature of the basic Wright patent.

Orville's article began with Bishop Wright's gift of a toy helicopter to his two youngest sons in 1878 and concluded with the May 1908 flights at Kill Devil Hills. It was illustrated with nine photographs—one of the 1902 glider in flight, seven of the Huffman Prairie flights of 1904 and 1905, and another of Orville's 12-second flight of December 17, 1903, the first publication of this now famous photograph. Orville purposely provided the magazine with poor-quality prints of all the photographs so that details of the machine would be too indistinct for imitators to copy, but as the first authentic popular account of the invention of the airplane, his article has been mined ever since for information about the Wright brothers. It contained a masterful description of the mental gymnastics that accompanied their search for an efficient propeller, and its long penultimate paragraph portraying what it was like to take off, fly, and land in a fast-moving aircraft provided a number of vicarious thrills for readers who had as little hope in

1908 of ever making an airplane flight as the modern reader has of making a flight to the moon.

Orville seems to have had some doubts about the value of his work. When the $500 check arrived, he wrote the magazine that he would "be glad to make such adjustment as is satisfactory to you," if events before the publication of the article made it worth less than the money he had been paid for it. It is doubtful that Wilbur, toiling away in Léon Bollée's automobile factory while Orville worked on his article, would have countenanced such a show of humility. A mechanic named Bertrand had been assigned to help Wilbur, but damp weather had shrunk the Flyer's torn wingcovering, and Bertrand was not much help. "I was the only one strong enough in the fingers to pull the wires together tight, so I had all the sewing to do myself," Wilbur grumbled in a letter to Orville. "It took a day and a half. My hands were about raw when I was not half done." Bertrand supposedly understood a little English, but a little was worse than none, and Wilbur's own command of the language threatened to desert him when he wrote in another letter to Orville: "It is almost impossible to explain what I want in words to men who only one fourth understand English."

The work done on the old American motor by Bariquand and Marre turned out to be so bad that Wilbur spent most of two days "fixing at things" before it could be mounted on the Flyer. On July 4—no holiday in France —he ran up the motor in a test. He was standing directly in front of the motor with his shirtsleeves rolled up, reading the tachometer, when one end of the hose connecting the radiator to the motor body came loose, sending a spurt of boiling-hot water onto his left side above the heart and spraying his left forearm up to the elbow. Fortunately, Léon Bollée was in the room, watching the test. He caught Wilbur as he staggered backward, let him down gently to the floor, then ran to his office and returned with picric acid, which he applied to the burns.

The press, always on the alert for stories about Wilbur, made the most of the incident. According to one account, he was rendered temporarily unconscious by the excruciating pain. According to another, he insisted on walking the mile back to his hotel from the factory. To allay the family's traditional fears about his health, he wrote a humorous letter home, describing the ministrations of the "hoss doctor" who came to the hotel later that day to dress the burns with oil-soaked cotton. After the doctor left, the oil dripped down Wilbur's arm to his fingertips and half filled his shoes. "I thereupon removed all the stuffing, like the fat man in A. Ward's show," he wrote, "and dressed the burns myself with more sense."

The burns were no joking matter. They left a blister as big as Wilbur's hand on his left side and another a foot long on his forearm. For several days he could not bend his left arm. There was nothing the matter with his right arm, however, and he relieved his pent-up feelings by directing a scalding stream of invective at Orville with his pen:

> I would really save time by getting into bed and staying there till entirely well, as nothing is done down at the shop except irritate my arm and nerves. If you had permitted me to have any anticipation of the state in which you had shipped things over here, it would have saved three weeks' time probably. I would have made preparations to build a machine instead of trying to get along with no assistance and no tools. If you have any conscience it ought to be pretty sore.

When Wilbur began assembling the Flyer, he estimated it would take three weeks to complete the job. It took almost seven. On Tuesday, August 4, the front framing was bolted back and the finished machine was placed on a two-wheeled, rubber-tired carriage and towed behind one of Léon Bollée's automobiles to Les Hunaudières under cover of darkness. The shed constructed for it at the racetrack was similar to those built for the machines at the camp on the Outer Banks except that it had a dirt floor. Since Wilbur intended to live in the shed and sleep beside the Flyer, an outdoor privy had been erected a discreet distance away—a refinement nowhere in evidence in any photograph ever taken of the camp at Kill Devil Hills. The shed was equipped with a stove and utensils so that Wilbur could eat breakfast and lunch without leaving the racecourse. René Pellier, a leading citizen of Le Mans and one of the largest manufacturers of tinned goods in France, saw to it that Wilbur was well supplied with the finest canned sardines, anchovies, and asparagus available. Just off the road to Le Mans was a small restaurant where good meals could be had, and close by was a farmhouse where Wilbur could get water and buy milk. A small boy who lived in the farmhouse was reputed to speak English as well as French—at least, when Wilbur inquired, *"Parlez-vous anglais?"* the boy replied politely, *"Oui, monsieur."*

On Wednesday, August 5, Wilbur was ready to fly, but there was a storm. He was not displeased when the rain continued on Thursday, for his arm had not yet completely healed. The weather began to clear on Friday. On Saturday the good weather held. "As the day was the finest for a first trial we have had for several weeks," Wilbur wrote Orville, "I thought it would be a good thing to do a little something."

If we go back four or five years—making allowances for developments in technology since the early years of the century—and compare what Wilbur and Orville did on the morning of December 17, 1903, when they made the world's first airplane flights, to what the Russians did on October

4, 1957, when they sent the world's first satellite hurtling into orbit about the earth, then the "little something" that Wilbur did on August 8, 1908, can best be compared to the first American landing on the moon on July 20, 1969, for the world was ushered into the air age that Saturday at the little country racetrack near Le Mans just as surely as it was ushered into the age of space sixty-one years later by Neil Armstrong's first feathery footsteps on the surface of the moon.

# 29

## *"Nous sommes battus"*

BY MIDMORNING SATURDAY the small grandstand at the racetrack near Le Mans was only partly full. Everyone lounging on the bleacherlike steps of the unpretentious grandstand was hatted, the men in panamas with turned-down brims or straw boaters, the women in the veil-covered, top-heavy hats of the period. It was not a large crowd, but it included a number of journalists from Paris, who had been waiting since Wednesday to see Wilbur fly, and several members of the Aéro-Club de France, led as usual by Ernest Archdeacon. Four of the Aéro-Club members present had experimented with flying machines: the brothers Ernest and Paul Zens, who had made a few hops the previous Tuesday in a biplane of their own design before it hit a haystack and capsized; René Gasnier, who only the day before had been experimenting with a Voisin-type biplane; and Louis Blériot, who had flown for 8 1/2 minutes at Issy-les-Moulineaux on July 6 in his eighth aircraft, a monoplane that he would manage to wreck before the month was out, as he did most of the aircraft with which he had experimented so far.

The more farsighted of the spectators had brought lunches with them. At noon the Flyer was still in its shed and there was nothing of interest to be seen inside the racetrack enclosure except Wilbur's launching derrick and track. To Aéro-Club members who had watched French aviators take off and land on rubber-tired wheels, the eighty feet of wooden starting rail, the four-legged pylon, twenty feet high, and the 1,500 pounds of cast-iron disks waiting to be hoisted to its apex with block and tackle, did little to dissipate a feeling that the Wright brothers and their Flyer might be after all *un bluff gigantesque.* All alike, however, were waiting to see if Wilbur could fly as well or stay in the air as long (if at all) as the great French aviator Henri Farman. Farman's career was in temporary eclipse—he was still in New York trying to collect the money promised him for his canceled American tour—but he had won the Armengaud Prize of 10,000 francs on July 6 for the first flight of over fifteen minutes ever made in France.

At two o'clock there was a flurry of excitement when the doors of the shed next to the grandstand were propped open and the big white Flyer was moved crabwise out of its hangar. The tail assembly was bolted into place and the machine was hauled to the launching rail. Wilbur, dressed in a gray business suit and wearing his usual high starched collar, fussed with the Flyer for the better part of the afternoon, while Ernest Archdeacon pointed out to his friends those features of the huge Wright biplane that would prevent it from performing as well as the French machines.

Wilbur would not be hurried. Not until six-thirty, when there was a virtual calm, were the propellers turned over and the engine started. Setting his cap on his head with the peak to the rear to keep it from blowing off, he took his place in the seat to the left on the lower wing. The heavy metal weights beneath the pyramidal starting derrick were released, and the Flyer began to move along the track, slowly at first. As its speed accelerated, Hart Berg's chauffeur, a man known to posterity only as Fleury, ran alongside, steadying the machine by one wingtip.

Four seconds after the weights began their descent, the Flyer leaped into the air. To Wilbur it was a routine launching. To the watching Aéro-Club members, accustomed to the long, lumbering takeoffs of the French machines, it was a revelation. A cheer went up from the grandstand, but cheers changed to cries of alarm and feminine screams as Wilbur headed toward the poplars at the end of the racetrack. In French biplanes, turning and circling were delicate maneuvers requiring plenty of room. Aéro-Club members who had seen Farman and Delagrange fly at Issy were convinced that the Flyer would slide sidewards into the trees. It did no such thing. Wilbur banked it sharply in a turn, then straightened out and swept down the other side of the racetrack oval at an altitude of about thirty-five feet and made his second turn with ease.

None of the spectators had ever seen a banked turn before, nor had any of them seen anything to compare with the way Wilbur had made his first circuit of the course without leaving the cramped confines of the clearing in which the racetrack was located. Many Frenchmen seriously believed that if the Wright brothers had really flown, it was only because they were accomplished acrobats who had been trained by Octave Chanute to balance their machines in flight. The Flyer's speed of between 35 and 40 miles an hour was not so great, however, but that Wilbur could be clearly seen, sitting erect, almost immobile, applying no more pressure to the levers held in either hand than he would apply to the handlebars of a bicycle. In actual fact, controlling the unstable Flyer was not quite that easy. By his own admission, Wilbur made no fewer than ten mistakes during the flight, but he was able to correct them so rapidly that the spectators were not aware he had made any mistakes at all. When he reached the trees at the end of the field, he turned again and after completing his second circuit came down at a sharp angle. The Flyer slid smoothly over the ground on its skids and came to a stop fifty feet from the starting rail. The flight had lasted exactly 1 minute 45 seconds.

The little crowd of men and women at the racetrack near Le Mans that day was of a different order of magnitude from the horde of cheering Frenchmen at Le Bourget who would greet Charles Lindbergh at the end of his 33 1/2-hour flight to Paris two decades later. But the emotions generated by Wilbur's flight of less than two minutes were no less electric and just as powerfully charged with wonder, amazement, and admiration. The spectators exploded out of the grandstand. They surged onto the field and surrounded the Flyer. Wilbur, having been disbelieved for so long by so many, was not yet prepared to be believed in so vigorously. His usually impassive features were said by one journalist to have paled with emotion. Another reported that his face was flushed with pleasure. Hart O. Berg, whose faith in Wilbur dated from the day in May 1907 when he saw Wilbur for the first time as he stepped off the train in London, was reported in the New York *Herald* to have kissed Wilbur on both cheeks, French fashion, but it transpired later that a reporter had made the story up as a joke on the imperturbable Berg.

Strangely enough, the frantic efforts of Farman and Delagrange to overtake the Wrights had redounded to the benefit of the brothers. It had taken only two circuits of a provincial racecourse to convince the members of the French Aéro-Club that the wobbling flights of their countrymen were the flutterings of fledglings compared to the controlled and birdlike circling of Wilbur's Flyer. The few pilots present were left gasping with admiration. Paul Zens, who had waited since morning to see Wilbur's short evening flight, told a reporter, "I would have waited ten times as long to have seen what I have seen today. Mr. Wright has us all in his hands."

"The whole conception of the machine—its execution and its practical worth—is wonderful," René Gasnier exclaimed. "We are as children compared to the Wrights."

Louis Blériot, after Farman and Delagrange the most experienced French pilot, was equally ecstatic. "I consider that for us in France, and everywhere," he said, "a new era in mechanical flight has commenced. I am not sufficiently calm after the event to thoroughly express my opinion."

The reaction of the press was summed up in Sunday's *Le Figaro,* which called Wilbur's flight not a success but a triumph, a decisive victory that amounted to "a revolution in the scientific world." Overnight the expression "birdman" came into being. When the French aviation journalist François

Peyrey wrote—and published in the short space of a month—the first small book devoted entirely to the brothers, it was inevitable that its title should be *Les Premiers Hommes-oiseaux: Wilbur et Orville Wright.*

Only a few hundred men and women had seen Wilbur fly on Saturday. On Monday, a crowd of 2,000 overflowed the grandstand at Les Hunaudières and spread out along the edges of the racetrack. Wilbur made two flights. The first lasted only 42 seconds.. After completing three-fourths of a circle, he found himself heading for some poplars at the edge of the course. Too low to go over the trees, he decided to land and made a sharp turn. The diameters of the turns he usually made at Les Hunaudières were between 300 and 500 feet. When measured later, the diameter of the turn made on this occasion was less than 100 feet. The maneuver created a sensation.

Between flights, Wilbur created a small sensation of another kind. Hart Berg had been circulating among the crowd, requesting that no photographs be taken of the machine except from a distance, but as the Flyer was being wheeled past the grandstand, Wilbur observed a French Army captain taking pictures. He leaped the fence and confronted the Frenchman, demanding that the plates in his camera be handed over or destroyed. When the captain refused, Wilbur folded his arms and waited, the focus of all eyes, until the plates were handed over.

The second flight that day was not unlike Saturday's two circuits of the field except that it included a figure eight. Flying figure eights was no novelty to Wilbur. To the wide-eyed French it was a dazzling accomplishment. Among the members of the French Aéro-Club on hand Monday was Léon Delagrange, who had come from Paris to see just how his two flights of more than a quarter of an hour at Rome and Milan earlier that year could have been so peremptorily overshadowed by Wilbur's flight Saturday of less than two minutes. "It is marvelous, I assure you, marvelous," was his comment on the incomparable ease with which Wilbur was able to fly figure eights. Although Delagrange would later qualify some of the remarks he made in the heat of the moment, his attitude at the time was best expressed by three words spoken to a reporter from *Le Matin* the next morning before he returned to Paris: *"Nous sommes battus* [We are beaten]."

On Tuesday, a crowd estimated at 3,000 waited hours to see a flight that did not take place until just before sunset. When the shed doors were thrown open, there was an audible buzz among the spectators. Men ran here and there for a better vantage point from which to view the Flyer as it emerged from its hangar. The younger men climbed trees about the perimeter of the racetrack. The flight lasted almost 4 minutes and consisted of three circuits of the field, during which Wilbur reached an altitude of about seventy feet, or twice that of previous flights. The crowd cheered wildly as each circuit was completed.

On Wednesday, Wilbur felt sure enough of himself to make a 7-minute flight in a light wind. Two brief flights that evening were cut short when the winds became dangerously gusty. That Wilbur had made flights in winds of any strength at all was considered another sensation.

On Thursday, he made his longest flight at Les Hunaudières—seven circuits of the field in a little over 8 minutes. His purpose in making such a flight was not to display his flying skill or see how long he could stay in the air; he was merely trying to familiarize himself with the new machine and to learn to manipulate the control levers smoothly before making the trial flights required by the French contract. He was afraid the constant cheering would be so distracting as to cause him to make mistakes. In the second flight of the morning he climbed to almost a hundred feet, but in completing his second circuit of the track, he made a tight turn, consuming power so rapidly that he had to turn the front horizontal rudder down to increase his speed. To do this he moved the lever in his left hand forward. At the same time, he intended to move the right-hand lever to the rear to relieve the pressure on the inside of the vertical rudder, but his right hand, in slavish imitation of his left, moved forward instead of backward. Losing power fast, Wilbur found himself too close to the ground to climb and was forced to land before he could straighten his wings. There was a sound of snapping and splintering wood as the left wing smashed into the ground and the left skid collapsed. Wilbur stepped out unscathed, but several spars and all but one or two ribs in the left wing had been shattered. Oddly enough, the accident added to Wilbur's reputation rather than detracted from it. The French airship designer Henry Kapferer, who was among Thursday's spectators, pronounced the accident as fine a demonstration of the practicability of flying as any of the flights Wilbur had made so far. Edouard Surcouf, another airship designer, was quoted in the New York *Herald* the next day as saying, "Mr. Wright is as superb in his accidents as in his flights."

The need to repair the Flyer gave Wilbur a rest from flying and time to assess the change in his and Orville's fortunes. The letter he wrote to Orville the day after the accident, describing the reaction to his flights at Les Hunaudières, was positively exultant:

> The newspapers and the French aviators nearly went wild with excitement. Blériot & Delagrange were so excited they could scarcely speak, and Kapferer could only gasp and could not talk at all. You would have almost died of laughter if you could have seen them. The French newspapers, *Matin, Journal, Figaro, L'Auto, Petit Journal, Petit Parisien,* &c., &c., gave reports fully as favorable as the *Herald.* You never saw anything like the complete reversal of position that took place after two or three little flights of less than two minutes each.

There were a few holdouts against the chorus of praise. Patriotic, unbending Ernest Archdeacon insisted that the French machines were superior to the Wright Flyer because they had wheels and could start without the help of falling weights and rails. Louis Blériot qualified his initial comments on the superiority of the Wrights, and expressed doubts that Wilbur's Flyer would be capable of making the two fifty-kilometer flights required by the French contract.

There was no doubt in Wilbur's mind about his machine's ability to make fifty-kilometer flights, but the small size of the field at Les Hunaudières would make it necessary to turn two to three times every minute he was in the air and the irregular ellipses resulting would make accurate measurement of the distances covered difficult. These obstacles were unexpectedly overcome when the French Army had a sudden change of heart and announced that the artillery range at Camp d'Auvours, which Wilbur had preferred as a practice ground from the start, would be available as a flying field after all. On Wednesday, August 19, the repaired Flyer was placed on its rubber-tired carriage and towed behind Léon Bollée's automobile to the new and larger shed built for it at Camp d'Auvours, seven miles east of Le Mans.

On the same day in Dayton, Ohio, Orville boarded the train for Washington, D.C., to prepare for the trials of the U.S. Army Flyer. Once again, as at Kill Devil Hills on December 17, 1903, each brother would have his turn. It was Orville's turn now to garner some of the honors and plaudits that were being showered so prodigally on Wilbur on the other side of the Atlantic.

# 30

# *Fort Myer*

T H E  U. S.  A R M Y ' S venture into aeronautics was not confined to the purchase of flying machines. At an air carnival in St. Louis, the Chief Signal Officer, General James Allen, had been favorably impressed by the performance of Thomas Baldwin's airship, the same airship that Wilbur and Orville had helped Baldwin recover when it blew away from the fairgrounds in Dayton in September 1906. The outcome was a contract with Baldwin for Signal Corps Dirigible No. 1, signed in February 1908, a few days after the Wright brothers signed a contract with the Signal Corps for a flying machine.

Baldwin's Army dirigible was constructed in Hammondsport, New York. Although Aerial Experiment Association secretary Tom Selfridge designed the propeller and Glenn Curtiss the motor, the airship had no connection with the AEA work on flying machines being carried out in Curtiss's factory in Hammondsport at the same time. A miniature affair compared to the airships then flying in Europe, it was not a dirigible with rigid steel framing inside the envelope like the German zeppelins but was similar to one of Santos-Dumont's dirigible-balloons—a silvery gray gasbag about ninety feet long, pointed at both ends, below which was suspended a skeletonlike keel of spruce. In the Army tests, Tom Baldwin stood in the open at the rear of the keel and manipulated the cruciform rudder, and Glenn Curtiss stood on a platform at the front end of the keel and operated the engine and a large biplane elevator positioned between the engine and the propeller. Both elevator and rudder were manipulated by means of tiller ropes, making the airship difficult to control if there was any kind of wind tugging at the ropes.

Signal Corps Dirigible No. 1 was delivered to Fort Myer in July 1908 and passed its speed test on August 14, maintaining an average speed of 19.61

miles per hour, and its endurance test on August 15, with a flight of 2 hours 10 minutes. A stipulation of both the Baldwin and the Wright contracts was the training of at least two Army officers in the operaton of each aircraft. Three lieutenants from the Signal Corps Aeronautical Division were taught to fly Baldwin's airship: Frank P. Lahm, whom Wilbur and Orville had met in Europe in 1907; Benjamin D. Foulois, who in time was to become as fast a friend of the brothers as Lieutenant Lahm; and Thomas Selfridge, who had been recalled from his work with the Aerial Experiment Association at Hammondsport. The three lieutenants were also members of an Aeronautical Board headed by Signal Corps Majors George O. Squier and Charles S. Wallace, set up to supervise the airship and flying-machine tests and to ensure that the specifications of both contracts were met.

The dirigible had passed its tests, and the training flights were underway when Orville arrived at Fort Myer on August 20. The parade ground, where the Army Flyer's tests were to take place, was an irregular tract west of Arlington National Cemetery, 1,000 feet in length, 700 feet wide at the south end, and about 100 feet wider at the north. It was ideal for dress parades and polo matches but was as small an area for flying practice as the Wrights had ever used. While it was smaller than Wilbur's flying field at Les Hunaudières, the accommodations for assembling and housing the Flyer were far superior, and Orville had all the help he needed in preparing and launching the machine. The fourteen Army men who had assisted in the tests of Baldwin's airship were to perform a similar service for Orville's Flyer. The corrugated-iron shed across the road from the parade ground known as the balloon building had been used as a hangar for the Signal Corps dirigible. It was cleared out after the airship tests were completed so that Orville could assemble the Flyer there with the assistance of the two Charlies—Charlie Furnas, who had been of such help at Kill Devil Hills in May, and Charlie Taylor, who seems to have become just a little jealous of the other Charlie. (Orville had written Wilbur in June: "Chas. Taylor is crazy to get into the experimenting again.")

In Washington, Orville stayed first at the St. James Hotel, then at the Cosmos Club on Lafayette Square a block from the White House. The move was made at the instigation of Albert Zahm, the air-minded professor of mathematics and physics from Catholic University in Washington and a leading light in the Aero Club of America. He would die in 1954 harboring a pathological grudge against the Wrights, but in 1908 he was on the best of terms with both brothers. His attempt earlier that summer to arrange a meeting by mail between Wilbur and a beautiful heiress had elicited the following response from Wilbur: "When Orville gets down to Washington I fear my chances will be gone, so far as the young lady is concerned. But I will console myself with the thought that 'my loss is his eternal gain,' as they say at funerals." Although Orville did indeed meet "some very hand-some young ladies" in Washington, he admitted to his sister he would have trouble remembering their names if he ever met them again.

Interest in the upcoming trials of the Army Flyer was whetted by the appearance of Orville's article in the September *Century Magazine,* but there were few signs of the contest between the Wrights and Augustus Herring to provide the Army with a flying machine, which Herring's ardent pro-moter Carl Dienstbach had predicted would be "the most remarkable ri-valry America has ever witnessed." About the only indication that the Signal Corps sweepstakes was still on was an article in the September *American Review of Reviews,* in which the fine hand of Dienstbach could be detected, stating that Herring's "work has been more or less shrouded in mystery, but it is still of such a character as to make him the 'dark horse' in the present race for aerial supremacy." There was much curiosity regard-ing the flying machine that was to rival the Wright Flyer, especially after Herring let it be known that he was thinking of flying it to Washington, rather than shipping it by rail, as Orville had been reduced to doing. Report-ers who approached the inventor in his shop on Broadway were told that the machine was automatically stable, that the gust of wind that disturbed the balance of the machine could be used to right it. Glenn Curtiss suspected that this was achieved by some kind of gyroscopic action, but nobody knew for sure. The only person who seems to have caught a glimpse of Herring's machine before it was delivered was Byron Newton of the New York *Her-ald,* who wrote Orville that it was "a little thing with a pocket edition of a motor." It was to have been delivered to the Signal Corps on August 13, two weeks before the Wright Flyer, but when Herring reported that he had hurt a finger in a test of his motor, which had been shaken to pieces in the test, the Signal Corps extended his delivery date to September 13. On Sep-tember 11 Herring announced to the press that the Army machine was now finished and ready. However, some points remained to be perfected. The Signal Corps generously extended his delivery date another thirty days to October 13.

Orville's Flyer was delivered to the balloon shed at Fort Myer on August 20, eight days before its delivery deadline, and assembled in five days. The motor was installed on the lower wing on August 25 and tested on the twenty-seventh. It was essential that the motor run at its greatest efficiency. If the Flyer made 40 miles per hour in its speed test, the Wrights would receive the contracted price of $25,000. For each mile per hour above 40 they would receive an additional $2,500, and for each mile per hour the speed fell below 40, $2,500 would be subtracted from the contracted price. The first day the motor was tested, it stopped twice after having run for only ten seconds. The next day, the axle bearings became hot. The day after that, it began to skip. The skipping was traced to poor gasoline. After sight-feed oilers had been put on all outside bearings, the motor ran with the required reliability.

On Tuesday, September 1, the operations necessary to fulfill the Army contract began, starting with the portability test. The tail and front rudder of the Flyer were unbolted and tucked between the wings. The machine was then hauled up an incline onto an Army combat wagon and towed from the balloon house to the tent on the parade ground that would be its home until work on the shed being erected for it could be finished. Wednesday was a day of jinxes. As the Flyer was taken out of the tent and placed on the starting rail it slipped off the track and lurched to the ground. "No damage," reported the log kept by the Signal Corps, but while a helpful lieutenant was "untwisting ropes at derrick, rope at the front end of track broke, letting 400 lbs. of iron down on the chin of 1st Lieut. Creecy, U.S.M.C." Richard Creecy of the U.S. Marines was a friend of Tom Selfridge, and although the Signal Corps log does not say so, his chin seems to have suffered as little damage as the Flyer.

On Thursday, September 3, word went around Washington that Orville might finally fly. A sizable crowd assembled at the parade ground that afternoon—government officials, members of foreign embassies, anyone, in fact, curious enough to board a streetcar and cross the Potomac to see what all the fuss was about. The President's twenty-year-old son, Theodore Roosevelt, Jr., was there, and reported to his father that the crowd numbered less than one thousand. More sober estimates put the number at under five hundred.

Shortly after four-thirty the Flyer was taken from the tent and placed on the launching rail. The motor refused to start, but after a second try it sputtered to life and the weights under the derrick thumped to the ground. With a popping of valves and clattering of propeller chains the Flyer left the starting rail, brushing the tops of the weeds on the parade ground with its skids before beginning its sharp rise. A collective gasp of astonishment was supplanted by a hearty burst of handclapping. When Orville reached the south end of the field he turned east toward Arlington Cemetery at an altitude of about thirty-five feet and followed the cemetery wall back toward the north end of the field. As he banked and passed over the road where most of the spectators were congregated, a few of them ducked. Most roared their approval. The Flyer was on its second circuit of the field when Orville made the inevitable error with the new control handles and found himself heading for the tent at the south end of the field below the level of the tent top. He came down just in time, landing in a swirl of dust, damaging both skids and the front rudder braces. As he stepped from the Flyer, he was startled to note that there were tears in the eyes of three or four of the reporters who came running up to interview him.

The sensation created among onlookers and reporters by this flight of 1 minute 11 seconds was not reflected in the stories printed in the newspapers the next day. It was not considered front-page news, even in Washington. That city's *Evening Star* carried the story on page three under a querulous headline:

FLY? WHY, OF COURSE

Orville Wright Electrifies Army
Officers with Feat

STAYS UP OVER A MINUTE

The difference between the newspaper reaction to Orville's first flight at Fort Myer and that accorded Wilbur's first flight in France was understandable. The flights made by Delagrange, Blériot, and Farman in Europe had been witnessed by many of the reporters at Les Hunaudières, and the superiority of Wilbur's brief performance was immediately apparent. Only a few of those present at Fort Myer on September 3 had ever seen an airplane in the air, and newspaper editors had no way of knowing that Orville's circuit and a half of the parade ground was in any way different from the straightway flights made by Curtiss's *June Bug* at Hammondsport in July or by Farman's Voisin at Brighton Beach. The story of Orville's flight on page 5 of the New York *World* was almost as much concerned with the possibility of the crowd being hit by what it called the "vessel" as with the flight itself.

A larger crowd showed up at Fort Myer on Friday. It was not disappointed. Orville flew for 4 minutes 15 seconds. On Saturday, Charles Flint came down from New York to see a flight, but high winds and rain ruled out flying. Orville's dislike of New York businessmen had begun when Wilbur was in Europe in 1907 and letters and telegrams from Orville in Dayton to Flint and Company in New York had gone unanswered. His feelings toward Charles Flint had not softened in the meantime. "As usual he has started a lot of embarrassing reports," Orville wrote his father after Flint had returned to New York without seeing a flight. He did not say what the reports were.

Two men whose presence at Fort Myer Orville resented more than Flint's were Aerial Experiment Association members Glenn Curtiss and Lieutenant Tom Selfridge. Curtiss had talked with Orville and had examined the Army Flyer at first hand. He described what he had found in a letter to AEA chairman Alexander Graham Bell. The wings of the Wright machine, he wrote, had a curvature like the segment of a circle (which was not true). He thought the Wright propellers odd, and since they were three times as wide at the tip as at the hub, he suspected they presented great resistance (actually they were the most efficient aerial propellers so far designed). "No attempt is made anywhere on the machine to reduce resistance," he reported. This seems like a peculiar comment for Curtiss to have made unless one realizes that the struts and other vertical members of the AEA machines were fish-shaped in cross-section, that is, rounded in front but tapered to a sharp edge at the rear. The AEA experimenters had taken Albert Zahm's word for it that the fish shape produced the least resistance in flight, whereas the Wright's wind-tunnel experiments had demonstrated that air resistance was at a minimum when all four corners of the struts were rounded. Curtiss, whose experience until 1908 had been largely in the design and manufacture of lightweight motors, did not think very highly of the Flyer's motor, which he found "rather crude and not exceptionally light." Orville had a correspondingly low opinion of the Curtiss motor on Baldwin's airship. "They have not been able to make the motor on the dirigible run more than a minute or two without missing about half its explosions," he reported in a Sunday letter to Wilbur. "Ours runs without a miss. Selfridge has been trying to find out how we do it!"

Lieutenants Selfridge and Foulois were scheduled to make exhibition flights in the Signal Corps dirigible at the state fair in St. Joseph, Missouri, later in September. Foulois had been sent on ahead to make the necessary preparations. Curtiss followed to make sure that the motor would be in shape for the flights, but Selfridge was left behind to sit in judgment on the Wright Flyer as a member of the Aeronautical Board. Orville found this hard to swallow. He was convinced that the information he and Wilbur had provided in the letter to Selfridge of January 18, 1908, had been responsible for the success of the AEA *June Bug.* "I like Foulois very well," he wrote Wilbur, "but I will be glad to have Selfridge out of the way. I don't trust him an inch. He is intensely interested in the subject, and plans to meet me often at dinners, etc. where he can try to pump me. He has a good education, and a clear mind. I understand that he does a good deal of knocking behind my back. All the others I think are very friendly."

Orville's letter to Wilbur was written Sunday, September 6. As usual, he did no flying on the Sabbath. The French aviator Léon Delagrange had no qualms about flying on Sunday. On September 6 he made the longest flight ever made in Europe by staying in the air for seven seconds short of half an hour at Issy near Paris. It made the front page of more than one U.S. newspaper on Monday. The crowds that came to Fort Myer on Monday afternoon to see Orville beat Delagrange's record had to be satisfied with a flight of 55 seconds. He flew twice on Tuesday. In the first flight he made thirteen circuits of the field and landed after 11 minutes to put on goggles. The second flight was called off after 7 1/2 minutes on account of darkness.

Tuesday's flights were mere warm-ups for Orville's performance the next day. Augustus Post, secretary of the Aero Club of America, was staying at the Cosmos Club that week. When he knocked on Orville's door early Wednesday morning, Orville was dressed and ready to go. It was too early to breakfast at the club, so the two men had rolls and coffee in a little restaurant near the White House and arrived at Fort Myer a short time later. By 8 A.M. the Flyer was out of the large shed on the parade ground in which it was now housed and on the starting track. Only a score of persons witnessed the takeoff half an hour later, mostly soldiers cleaning fieldpieces or grooming horses outside the gun shed and stable across the road from the parade ground. No reporters were present. To keep track of Orville's progress, Augustus Post made a mark on the back of an envelope every time the Flyer circled the parade ground. When he made the fifty-seventh mark on his envelope, Orville landed, having set a world endurance record of 57 1/2 minutes.

Official Washington had settled down to its daily routine when word of what had happened at Fort Myer spread through the corridors of government buildings across the river. When it became known that there might be another flight that afternoon, desktops were slammed down. Offices were shut up. Government officials, reporters, embassy personnel, and the merely curious poured across the river by the thousands. At 5:19, in the presence of a huge throng that included the Secretaries of War, Navy, Commerce, and Labor, Orville once more took to the air. He made only fifty-five circuits of the field this time, but he flew wider circles and his time was 62 minutes 55 seconds. The crowd, satisfied that it had seen the world's first flight of more than one hour, melted away, heading for home and dinner, unaware that there was more to come. The light was fading and the moon was rising, partially obscured by mists, when Lieutenant Lahm climbed into the Flyer beside Orville and was treated to a 6-minute flight, which broke the world record for two-man flight set by Orville himself at Kill Devil Hills on May 14.

For the next three days, Orville set a new world record with almost every flight. Thursday, September 10, he flew in a 10-mile-an-hour wind. Charlie Taylor climbed onto the slanting roof of the Flyer's shed with a pot of white paint. When fifty minutes had passed, he painted a big 50 on the roof for Orville to see. Then a large 55. When Orville had been in the air for one hour, Charlie raised both hands. Motorists tooted horns. Everyone cheered wildly. Orville came down after completing one more circuit of the field. He had been in the air for 1 hour 6 minutes and set a world altitude record by flying at 200 feet. Friday, Octave Chanute arrived at Fort Myer in time to see

Orville break Thursday's record with a flight of 1 hour 11 minutes, during which he performed two figure-eights. Saturday, 5,000 men, women, and children pressed about the edges of the parade ground and watched Orville break his endurance record for the fourth day in a row. The flight lasted fourteen minutes over the hour and set a new altitude record of 310 feet. Before the day was over, he broke the record for two-man flight by flying for 9 minutes with Major Squier of the Aeronautical Board as passenger.

In four days, Orville had set nine world records. Reporters felt justified in picturing the brothers as locked in a transatlantic contest in which the impetuous younger brother was outstripping the older, more cautious Wilbur. And, while there was never any real competition between the two, it was certainly obvious to anyone following their exploits that Wilbur's progress in France was disappointingly slow compared to the steady progress being made by Orville at Fort Myer. Wilbur's first two flights at Camp d'Auvours on August 21 added up to only four minutes. There were times during the next ten days when the Flyer could have been placed on the track while Wilbur waited for a break in the weather, but rather than disappoint the throngs that showed up whether he flew or not, he preferred to keep the Flyer in the shed until he could be absolutely sure of the day's weather. The Flyer's shed at Camp d'Auvours was larger than that at Les Hunaudières. Wilbur's living quarters were separated from the Flyer by a partition of wooden packing cases. His bed, a heavy piece of canvas nailed to strips of wood, could be hauled up and stored under the roof during the day. There was a small gasoline stove on which he made breakfast. Nearby was a small inn where Madame Pollet served plain, well-cooked meals in her cheerful sanded kitchen.

Wilbur did not make a flight of any consequence at the new field until September 3, when he stayed in the air for 10 minutes 40 seconds. Two days later he at last hit his stride with a flight twelve seconds short of 20 minutes. Then on Thursday, September 10, spurred by the news of Orville's 57-minute flight of the day before, Wilbur flew before a crowd of 3,000 for almost 22 minutes, reaching an altitude of 120 feet, a record for Europe, although Orville was to reach 200 feet a few hours later on the other side of the Atlantic. In a Sunday letter to Orville, written the day after Orville had set his ninth world record in a row, Wilbur admitted defeat in the mock contest: "The newspapers for several days have been full of the stories of your dandy flights, and whereas a week ago I was a marvel of skill now they do not hesitate to tell me that I am nothing but a 'dud' and that you are the only genuine skyscraper. Such is fame! Your flights have naturally created an immense sensation in Europe and I suppose that America is nearly wild."

His pleasure at Orville's success notwithstanding, Wilbur still considered that thirty-seven-year-old Orville functioned best when he was under the supervision of his big brother, even with four thousand miles of ocean between them. Before leaving New York for France in May, he had written Katharine: "If at any time Orville is not well, or dissatisfied with the situation at Washington, especially the grounds, I wish you would tell me. He may not tell me such things always." No sooner had Orville reached Washington than a stream of instructions and advice began to flow from Le Mans to Fort Myer, replete with underlinings for the benefit of Younger Brother, who had showed himself incompetent to the point of idiocy when he packed the Flyer that Wilbur had had to put together in France. "In your flights at Washington I think you should be careful to begin practice in calms and *keep well above the ground.* . . . Be awfully careful in beginning practice and go slowly. . . . I can only say be exceedingly cautious. . . . Be careful of your electrical connections. . . . Be exceedingly cautious as to wind conditions and thorough in your preparations." Wilbur's performance as a mail-order Polonius reached its climax in a letter in which he had nightmarish visions of his pale and shaking younger brother, worn out from socializing, falling asleep at the controls of the Army Flyer:

> I advise you most earnestly to stick to calms till after you are sure of yourself. Don't go out even for all the officers of the government unless you would go equally if they were absent. *Do not let yourself be forced into doing anything before you are ready.* Be very cautious and proceed slowly in attempting flights in the middle of the day when wind gusts are frequent. Let it be understood that you wish to practice rather than give demonstrations and that you intend to do it in your own way. Do not let people talk to you all day and all night. It will wear you out, before you are ready for real business. Courtesy has limits. If necessary appoint some hour in the day time and refuse absolutely to receive visitors even for a minute at other times.

Then, as if Wilbur thought there was some small possibility of one of Professor Zahm's seductive heiresses finding her way into the all-male Cosmos Club after dark, he added: "Do not receive *any one* after 8 P.M. at night."

In spite of the inevitable lionizing and the invitations to lunch and dinner, most of which he saw fit to ignore, Orville remained in good physical shape and suffered nothing worse than a bloodshot left eye from a leaking goggle during his 66-minute flight of September 10. After flying every day that week, the weather gave him a three-day respite. Easterly winds blanketed the parade ground with dust on Monday, September 14. Orville spent the day overhauling the engine. Tuesday, high north winds made flying impractical. The winds continued Wednesday, but there were signs of clearing. "The next flight of the aeroplane probably will be with a passenger in addition to the operator," the Washington *Star* informed its readers Wednesday evening. "Lieut. Selfridge is slated as the lucky man."

Orville had misgivings about the projected flight, knowing that Selfridge, as secretary of the Aerial Experiment Association and as one of the pilots of the AEA *White Wing* and the prize-winning *June Bug,* would be making mental notes of any features of the Wright Flyer that might profitably be adapted to future AEA machines. There was nothing in the Army contract requiring that each member of the Signal Corps Aeronautical Board should be given a ride, but Orville had given his good friend Lieutenant Lahm the first passenger flight and had broken the two-man record when he flew Major Squier on Saturday. Furthermore, it was likely that the two men he must train to operate the Flyer would be selected from among the three youngest members of the board—Lahm, Foulois, and Selfridge. Lieutenant Foulois had been sent to Missouri to fly the Signal Corps dirigible before he could be given a flight, and since Selfridge had been ordered to follow Foulois to Missouri at the end of the week, he was the obvious choice as Orville's next passenger.

Wilbur, meanwhile, had been doing his best to catch up with Orville. On Wednesday, September 16, he covered 30 miles at Camp d'Auvours in 39 minutes, breaking the European endurance record of 29 minutes 53 seconds set by Delagrange September 6. On Thursday morning, September 17, Delagrange broke his own record, flying a few seconds over half an hour, but failed to better Wednesday's record set by Wilbur.

Walther Nernst, the German scientist who would win the Nobel Prize for chemistry a dozen years later, saw Delagrange fly Thursday morning at Issy, after which he boarded a train in Paris and arrived at Le Mans in time to see Wilbur fly for 33 minutes in a golden sunset at Camp d'Auvours— at about the same time that Orville and the two Charlies at Fort Myer, where it was still early afternoon, were preparing the Army Flyer for Selfridge's passenger flight. Walther Nernst, with what he had seen that morning still fresh in his mind, was in an ideal position to compare Wilbur's performance with that of Delagrange. "He nearly went crazy with enthusiasm over my flight," Wilbur wrote Katharine. "'It was so different,' he said."

Early next morning, a huge crowd collected at Camp d'Auvours to see Wilbur make an official try for the Coupe Michelin, the 20,000-franc prize for the longest flight made in France before the end of the year. He had just about completed preparations at the starting rail when he was called to the Flyer's shed by Hart Berg. A cablegram had arrived—a *papier bleu,* one of those cryptic messages on blue paper that had a reputation for striking terror to the hearts of Frenchmen who received telegrams so seldom that blue paper had come to be associated with bad news. The news in this instance was rendered all the more horrible by a lack of details. Orville's Flyer had crashed on the parade ground at Fort Myer on Thursday. Lieutenant Selfridge had been killed. Orville had been injured—how badly, it was still too early to tell.

There are two conflicting descriptions of Wilbur's reaction to the news. One was written a quarter-century after the event by Lieutenant Colonel Edward Gleichen, the English military attaché who had met the Wrights in Dayton in 1906 and traveled to Camp d'Auvours to make arrangements for a flight with Wilbur. According to Gleichen's account, when he arrived he was told by Hart Berg that Wilbur had just received a cable containing bad news. Gleichen found Wilbur sitting in his tent with his head in his hands, unable to speak, tears streaming down his face, shoulders trembling convulsively. When Wilbur stretched out his hand in greeting to the Englishman, it was shaking "like an aspen." This account, however, is highly questionable. Wilbur was to take up many passengers during the four months he spent at Auvours, but there is no record that Gleichen was ever one of them. When Wilbur received the news of Orville's accident, he was in the shed with the Flyer, not in a tent; and, having been so often depicted by reporters as sphinxlike, it is doubtful that he would have let himself be observed weeping.

More believable is the account published the year after the accident by the French journalist François Peyrey. Peyrey was with a party of sportsmen who had come to Camp d'Auvours to see Wilbur try for the Coupe Michelin. Peyrey wrote that for a long time after the cable came, Wilbur stayed in the shed without saying a word to anybody, pacing feverishly around the Flyer, absentmindedly twisting a piece of wire in his hands. Finally he announced that he would go to Le Mans, where any subsequent messages would reach him more quickly. He set off alone, bent over the handlebars of his bicycle, along the country lanes under the pines and horse chestnuts, where any tears he had to shed could be shed in private.

A second cable reached Le Mans later that day: Orville's condition was as good as could be expected. He would recover. Katharine had left Dayton for Washington and would soon be at his bedside.

# 31

# A Tragedy and a Comic Interlude

AT FORT MYER across the Potomac River from Washington, D.C., the afternoon of Thursday, September 17, 1908, was sunny and cool. The high winds that had kept Orville from flying Wednesday had died down to a manageable 4 miles an hour. By 4 P.M., 2,000 people or more had gathered to see him fly with Lieutenant Selfridge as passenger. A few minutes after 5, the young lieutenant took his seat in the Flyer beside Orville after doffing his military jacket and campaign hat and handing them to a friend. Charlie Taylor and Charlie Furnas turned over the propellers, and the motor began its rhythmic popping. As the weights beneath the starting derrick were released, Selfridge waved to his friend, probably Richard Creecy (the Marine lieutenant on whose sturdy chin 400 pounds of metal from the same starting derrick had been inadvertently dropped the day before Orville made his first flight at Fort Myer). Lieutenant Creecy was described in one of the newspaper reports of the day's events as Selfridge's closest friend.

At 175 pounds, Selfridge was Orville's heaviest passenger so far. Instead of skimming the tops of the weeds and grasses after leaving the starting rail, the Flyer slid along the ground on its skids for almost a hundred feet before rising rapidly to the usual lusty cheers from the crowd. Making short turns and keeping well within the oval formed by the Army buildings to the west and the wall of Arlington Cemetery to the east, Orville flew three circuits of the parade ground at an altitude of a little over a hundred feet. Things were working so smoothly he decided to enlarge his oval course by making wider turns. As he made his first wide turn over the Flyer's shed at the south end of the field, he heard or felt—he was never sure which—a slight tapping behind him. Although he found nothing wrong when he glanced hurriedly over his shoulder, he concluded that the safe thing to do would be to shut off the motor and glide to a landing. But before he could do so, he heard two loud thumps, and the Flyer began to lurch and shake. At the same moment, several spectators saw an object fly from the machine and arc through the air before falling to the ground. Thinking that one of the propeller transmission chains had snapped off, Orville shut off the motor. The next moment, the Flyer veered to the right and headed for the trees in the cemetery. When Orville tried to bring the machine back on course by moving the warping and rudder lever, nothing happened. Overtaken by a dreamlike feeling of utter helplessness, he continued to work the lever in his right hand. Suddenly the right wing rose until the Flyer was facing directly north up the field. Orville immediately rocked the warping lever to the right to level the wings. The machine responded by going into an almost perpendicular dive.

All this time Lieutenant Selfridge had not said a word, although he had turned to look at Orville once or twice to see if he could read in Orville's face the meaning of those two ominous thumps. As the machine started for the ground, Selfridge uttered an almost inaudible "Oh! Oh!" The first fifty feet of the plunge took less than a second, but to Orville the fall seemed to last for half a minute. He kept releasing the front rudder lever a little each time before giving it another pull, although he could see that the rudder was bent to its limit and the cloth was bulging up between the ribs. When the Flyer was about twenty-five feet from the ground, it seemed to Orville that the machine had begun to right itself, but it was too late. The wings had already begun to crumple from the strain.

The Flyer hit the parade ground with terrific force, not far from the gate in the cemetery wall. The skids collapsed, the wings turned up, the motor tore loose and struck the ground with a thud like a small earthquake. For a second or two the Flyer and its occupants were entirely concealed in a boiling cloud of dust. A tense silence pervaded the parade ground. Nobody moved. Then everybody seemed to move at once and there was a wild dash onto the field. Three mounted cavalrymen galloped ahead, followed by half a dozen reporters and more soldiers on foot and on horseback. As the crowd closed in, a cavalry officer could be heard shouting, "If they won't stand back, ride them down." Adding to the confusion were the cries and questions of the men and women who had remained at the edges of the parade ground and the honking of horns by drivers wanting to offer their automobiles as ambulances. Gradually the clouds of dust stirred up by the crush of men and horses settled, and the extent of the damage became visible. The Flyer's wings were twisted out of shape, its skids smashed to kindling. The left propeller was intact but both ends of the right propeller were broken off. One of the broken pieces dangled by a shred of its fabric covering. Orville and Selfridge were pinned beneath the upper wing, their faces buried in the dust.

Orville was lifted out first and laid on the grass, moaning softly. It took several men to lift the debris from Selfridge's unconscious body. His khaki uniform, ripped and torn by the impact, was matted with dust and with blood from a six-inch gash on his head. Charlie Taylor helped Lieutenant Creecy remove Selfridge from the wreckage, then he stooped over Orville and undid Orville's necktie and opened his shirt. Two physicians among the spectators forced their way through the cordon of mounted soldiers. A Dr. Watters of New York did what he could for Orville. Three Army surgeons, who had been watching the flight from an open car, drove up and attended to Selfridge. A few minutes later a horse-drawn ambulance arrived from the post hospital, but it was thought best to move both men by stretcher. When the hospital orderlies lifted Orville onto the stretcher, Charlie Taylor was thrust aside. As Orville was borne away, his face bloody from a cut over his left eye, Charlie leaned against an upended wing of the wrecked Flyer, buried his face in his arms, and sobbed. A newspaperman tried to comfort him, but he was past comforting until Dr. Watters assured him that the chances for Orville's recovery were good. Then he pulled himself together and took charge of carting the wrecked Flyer back to its shed.

A sizable group of Army officers, newsmen, and notables congregated on the porch of the Fort Myer hospital that evening, waiting for word from the doctors. The Signal Corps's Major Squier paced up and down, muttering from time to time, "It's frightful! It's frightful!" The French military attaché was there. So was Octave Chanute, who had stayed on in Washington to see another flight by Orville. He told reporters that the accident had been caused by a defective propeller, although all anyone knew for sure was that the object seen to fly from the machine before the crash had been a broken propeller blade. Also on hand was Charles Flint, who had made a second trip to Washington to see Orville fly, only to see him crash.

It was dark when the Army surgeons released a statement to the reporters on the porch. Orville had sustained a fracture of the left thigh, several broken ribs, and severe scalp wounds. He was much shocked but was reacting well. Lieutenant Selfridge had suffered a fracture at the base of the skull and was being operated on in an attempt to save his life. At 8:10 P.M., five minutes after the operation was completed, Selfridge died without regaining consciousness. Lieutenant Creecy broke down completely when he heard the news.

Bishop Wright was in Greens Fork, a small town near Richmond, Indiana, on the day of the tragedy. It was thought best not to tell him of the accident until the next day, whereupon he made the following unemotional entry in his diary: "Orville injured. Orville's disaster at 5; Selfridge's death." When the news reached Dayton, Katharine took a leave of absence from her teaching job at Steele High School and boarded the train for

Washington. She was met at Union Station Friday afternoon by Lieutenant Lahm and driven to Fort Myer, where she was taken to Orville's bedside by Charles Flint.

Katharine was allowed to stay with her brother for only twenty minutes. Orville had had a bad day. He did not learn that Selfridge had died until that morning after his leg had been reset and the minor bruises he had suffered all over his body had begun to pain him severely. The two Charlies had brought to his bedside a piece of the broken propeller and some other broken parts for him to examine, and he was already trying to determine, in his feverish condition, the cause of the accident. It would be several weeks, however, before he would be able to examine the wrecked Flyer and reconstruct the sequence of events that preceded and followed the breaking of the propeller.

Eight days before the accident occurred, an eighteen-inch split had been discovered in one of the Flyer's eight-and-a-half-foot propellers. The split blade was repaired by nailing down the loose piece and gluing cloth over the split. In the meantime, Orville sent to Dayton, where brother Lorin was in charge of things during his absence, for a new pair of propellers. The propellers arrived Wednesday, September 16, and were fitted on the machine the same day. They were nine feet in length but had the same twelve-inch maximum blade width as the old eight-and-a-half-foot propellers. Tests made in the shop at Dayton had shown that these "big screws," as the brothers called them, were able to withstand twice the stress they would receive in flight. Nevertheless, a longitudinal crack developed in one blade of the right propeller just seconds before the fatal crash, causing it to flatten and lose power. The unequal pressures on the two blades set up a vibration, which created the tapping that Orville heard—or merely felt. The vibration loosened a stay wire fastened to the tube in which the propeller axle turned, permitting the axle to swing slightly, bringing the undamaged blade of the propeller in contact with the upper stay wire leading to the vertical rudder in the tail. The wire tore loose, wrapped itself around the propeller blade, and with a loud thumping sound broke it off. The broken blade was the object that was seen to fly from the machine, but it was the vertical rudder, loosened by the loss of the stay wire, that caused the Flyer to swerve first right, toward the cemetery, then left, so that it was heading north up the field. Since Orville was then in an ideal position for gliding to a landing, he moved the wingwarping lever to the right to straighten his wings and also moved it forward to move the vertical rudder to the right. But the rudder, without its upper stay wire, was so severely tilted out of the vertical that it functioned as an elevator, sending the Flyer into its fatal dive.

Wilbur, with customary clarity, had the final say on the accident: "The splitting of the propeller was the occasion of the accident; the uncontrollabil-

*Many Frenchmen believed the Wright brothers were* bluffeurs *until Wilbur made a few short flights at this racetrack near Le Mans in August 1908.* (Wright State University)

*The Wright airplane being moved into the hangar at the racetrack after Wilbur's accident of August 13, 1908.* (Smithsonian Institution, NASM)

*Orville circling the Fort Myer parade ground, September 9, 1908,
the day on which he broke three world records.*
(Smithsonian Institution, NASM)

*Fort Myer, September
17, 1908. End of the
flight in which
Lieutenant Tom
Selfridge was killed and
Orville severely injured.*
(Smithsonian Institution,
NASM)

*Orville is borne on a
stretcher from the scene of
the crash.*
(Wright State University)

*Mrs. Hart Berg and Wilbur just before her flight as his first woman passenger, at Camp d'Auvours, France, October 7, 1908. The cord around the bottom of her skirt inspired the hobble skirt fad.* (Smithsonian Institution, NASM)

*Wilbur, by the French cartoonist Mich.*

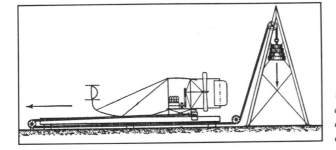

*Until 1910, most Wright aircraft were launched from a starting rail by weights dropped from a derrick.*

*A sunset flight by Wilbur at Camp d'Auvours, September 1908.* (Wright State University)

*Wilbur on the field near Pau, France, where he flew in February and March 1909.* (Smithsonian Institution, NASM)

*Orville watches as Wilbur checks the wind before a flight at Pau.* (Wright State University)

*Wilbur steadies the 1909 Army Flyer by one wingtip as Orville takes off.* (Wright State University)

*Huge crowds swarmed across the Potomac from Washington to witness the tests of the Wright Army Flyer at Fort Myer in July 1909.* (Smithsonian Institution, NASM)

*Germans flock to Tempelhof Field near Berlin to see Orville fly, September 1909.* (Wright State University)

*Governors Island, September 1909: Wilbur supervises removal of the wheel trucks used to move the Flyer.* (Wright State University)

*October 4, 1909. Wilbur's 20-mile flight up the Hudson, from Governors Island to Grant's Tomb and back, gives hundreds of thousands of New Yorkers their first sight of an airplane in the air.* (Smithsonian Institution, NASM)

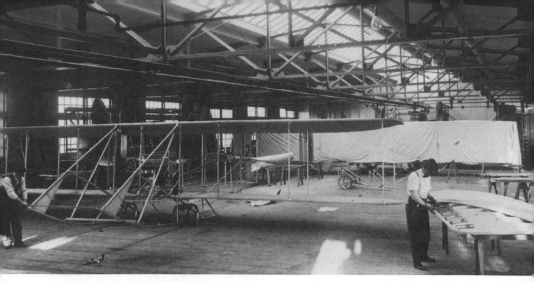

*Assembly department of the Wright Company factory, Dayton, 1911.*
(Wright State University)

*In the exhibition business—the Wright brothers at the International Aviation Tournament, Belmont Park, Long Island, October 1910.*
(Wright State University)

*The 70-mile-an-hour Wright "Baby Grand" racer at Belmont Park. It was wrecked before it could compete for the coveted speed trophy.*
(Wright State University)

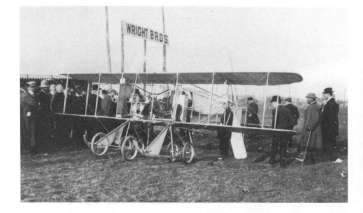

*Orville clinging to the upset glider.*
(Smithsonian Institution, NASM)

*Orville soaring in his 1911 glider.*
(Library of Congress)

*Hawthorn Hill in Oakwood, Orville's home
from 1914 to 1948.*
(Wright State University)

*On the lawn at Hawthorn Hill, 1915. John McMahon is one of the two men on Orville's right; on Orville's left: Bishop Wright, Katharine, Earl Findley, and nephew Horace. (Library of Congress)*

*Orville at his summer retreat on Lambert Island in Georgian Bay. (Wright State University)*

*Scipio, Orville's St. Bernard, on the porch at Hawthorn Hill. (Library of Congress)*

*The reconstructed Hawthorn Street house and the West Third Street bicycle shop, side by side in Greenfield Village, Dearborn, Michigan. (Smithsonian Institution, NASM)*

ity of the tail was the cause." He did not reach that conclusion until eight months later, after he had returned from Europe and had had a chance to discuss the matter with Orville. At the time of the accident, he was four thousand miles away in France and could only guess at the cause of the disaster. He was quite sure at first that it was due to what today would be called human, or pilot, error. In a letter he wrote to Katharine the Sunday after the accident he blamed himself as much as he blamed Orville:

> I cannot help thinking over and over again, "If I had been there, it would not have happened." The worry over leaving Orville alone to undertake those trials was one of the chief things in almost breaking me down a few weeks ago and as soon as I heard reassuring news from America I was well again. A half dozen times I was on the point of telling Berg that I was going to America in spite of everything. It was not right to leave Orville to undertake such a task alone.

When it eventually became clear that a split propeller blade, rather than Orville's socializing, had led to Selfridge's death, Wilbur found other means of shouldering the blame. "In so far as the responsibility falls upon anyone," he wrote Octave Chanute, "I suppose it falls upon me as I did the testing of the screws." The tests, which had been run in the spring of 1908 before Wilbur left for Kitty Hawk, had been made by applying pressure in the form of a block laid on the concave side of the blades of the new nine-foot propellers. The block had prevented the blades from flattening and splitting as one blade did on September 17. After the accident, the Wright propellers were redesigned and made heavier at the point of weakness. The blades were further strengthened with canvas all the way down their concave sides, and the tubes supporting the propeller axles on all new Flyers were braced so that no amount of vibration could ever again make it possible for the propeller blades to reach the wires bracing the vertical rudder in the tail.

Katharine remained in Washington for the entire six weeks of Orville's stay in the hospital at Fort Myer, fending off visitors and coping with the flood of good wishes and get-well messages that threatened to inundate the sickroom. Octave Chanute was his usual helpful self. He helped Katharine frame a letter to the Signal Corps requesting an extension of time for the trials of the Flyer. A nine-month extension was granted, giving the brothers to the end of June 1909 to fulfill the terms of their contract. After returning to Chicago at the end of September, Chanute gave Wilbur a firsthand report of his brother's progress. Orville's broken thigh had knitted so that his left leg would be no more than one-eighth of an inch shorter than his right. His temperature had almost hit 102 degrees at times and he was still weak from the liquid diet, but the patient was quite out of danger. He had recovered his pluck and "the old genial smile had come back." Katharine had been devotion itself. She had stayed at the hospital every night and gone without so much sleep that he had had to remonstrate with her about it.

Before leaving Washington, Chanute became involved indirectly in an incident that concerned the Aerial Experiment Association. During the first week of his convalescence, Orville was permitted few visitors aside from Octave Chanute, Lieutenant Lahm, and Major Squier. On Wednesday morning, September 23, three AEA members dropped in at the Fort Myer hospital to pay their respects to Orville—Alexander Graham Bell, Douglas McCurdy, and Casey Baldwin—but were forbidden by Orville's doctor to see the patient. Instead, they "left cards" and set out on foot for Arlington National Cemetery to view Selfridge's casket, which had been placed in the receiving vault, waiting the arrival of Selfridge's father and brothers from the West Coast. The funeral was to take place on Friday, and all three men had been designated honorary pallbearers. They cut across the parade ground on their way to the gate in the cemetery wall. When they came to the Flyer's shed, they spoke to the guard in charge, a Sergeant Downey, who let them enter the building, where the wrecked Army Flyer had been crated for return to the Wright bicycle shop in Dayton. The case containing the bloodstained wings had not yet been nailed shut, and as the three men peered into it, Alexander Graham Bell pulled a measuring tape from his pocket and made at least one measurement, after which the three men went on their way.

Word reached Orville and Katharine that the three AEA members had been allowed to examine the wreckage of the Flyer. Suspecting the worst, they asked Octave Chanute to find out what he could about the incident. After interviewing Sergeant Downey, Chanute informed Katharine that according to Downey, a dispute had arisen among the three men about the width of the wing, and Bell had said, "Well, I have a tape in my pocket and we will measure it." Two days after the measuring incident, Tom Selfridge was buried with appropriate military honors in Arlington National Cemetery. His martyrdom as the first person to die in the crash of a propeller-driven flying machine did little to allay the suspicions of Orville and Katharine and other members of the Wright family that the examination of the wrecked Army Flyer by the three AEA members had been motivated by more than idle curiosity.

Another incident that occurred at Fort Myer during Orville's stay in the Army hospital provided a modicum of comic relief. That was the delivery, twice postponed, of Augustus Herring's Army airplane. After the accident in which Selfridge lost his life, a rumor began to circulate that Herring would renege on his Army contract, using as an excuse that he was about to close negotiations for the sale of his aeronautical patents to a foreign syndicate or some foreign government. When challenged by reporters, Herring dismissed the rumor. "I shall keep my contract with the government," he said, smiling. "If I were offered five millions for my machine tomorrow it would make no difference about the government contract."

Herring once intimated to a *New York Times* reporter that his flying machine was radically different from Orville's. That it certainly was different was revealed when its so-called technical delivery took place on October 12, the day before the deadline of Herring's second extension. There is some controversy about how it was delivered. Most accounts state that it was delivered in a single suitcase, but a photograph in *Harper's Weekly* of Herring and an assistant on their way to Fort Myer clearly shows the assistant carrying two suitcases. Herring himself claimed that the suitcases contained parts of one of the airplane's two 22-horsepower motors and that the airplane was delivered in a wardrobe trunk—or "innovation trunk," as a member of the Signal Corps Aeronautical Board mysteriously referred to it. In any event, Herring seems to have fulfilled the contract requirement that the flying machine be transportable in an Army wagon by transporting it to the balloon shed at Fort Myer from nearby Alexandria, Virginia, in a taxicab.

The next day Herring returned to the balloon shed and in the presence of the Aeronautical Board assembled what he identified as the center section of a biplane. It could be controlled in flight, he said, by twisting the struts next to the pilot's seat. The Aeronautical Board, perhaps in desperation, perhaps because it seemed like the only logical thing to do, gave the inventor a third monthly extension—to November 13—so that he could complete the machine before making any flights in it. Until then, Herring had welcomed the attentions of the press. When asked for details about his machine as he left Fort Myer, he became strangely reserved and antagonized reporters by refusing to let them see what was inside the two suitcases. "I don't like publicity," he told them, which was in itself news.

The technical delivery of the Herring flying machine was the subject of some outright guffaws in big-city newspapers. "The Herring airship is packed in a suit case," commented the New York *Herald.* "This is the safe way to use it." The popular illustrated journal *Harper's Weekly* took Herring more seriously. Three pages of its October 24, 1908, issue were devoted to his life and work. The overall title, "The Problem of Flight Solved," was followed by two subtitles, the second of which read: "The Aeronautical Board of the United States Army assembled at Fort Myer is reported to be convinced that this invention has positively and finally solved the question of flight by man." William Inglis, the gullible journalist who interviewed Herring, had no doubts about his subject's integrity. "His gaze meets yours with the utmost frankness," Inglis wrote, "and yet it is impossible to escape the belief that the intelligence back of those eyes is busy with something else even while the man gives candid answers to every question."

Some of Herring's candid answers revealed that his age was thirty-five (actually he was forty-three), that his father was a millionaire, that he had sold thousands of motors to motorcycle manufacturers, and that his flying machine, which was only one-fourth as large and heavy as the Wright Flyer, was composed of sections so that its wingspan could be varied from fifteen feet to thirty-three, depending on the load to be carried. The Herring machine could carry from six to twelve men, whereas the Wright machine could carry only two. No catapult was needed to launch it. A run of five to ten feet would suffice in a wind. Although his new flying machine was as safe and easy to use as a motorcar, he told the man from *Harper's,* "there is always the liability that some little thing like a bolt or screw might work loose." The Aeronautical Board had therefore granted him permission to conduct preliminary flights away from Fort Myer, over grounds where he would not be "diverted by turns."

The first and only trial of Herring's Army airplane was purported to have taken place in the early morning near Hempstead, Long Island, on October 28, 1908. It was raining, Herring said, and he assembled his aircraft in such a hurry that he left out some important parts altogether. He flew for only 300 feet before rain on the battery wires caused a crash. There were no injuries. The chances are there was no flight either and no witnesses, although Herring testified in court several years later that one other person had witnessed the flight—a person he was able to identify only as "a neighbor's boy—or somebody else." With Herring's $2,000 deposit still in hand, the Aeronautical Board, having granted the Wright brothers a nine-month extension of their contract because of Orville's accident, could not in all fairness deny Herring a similar extension because of his. A fourth and final extension was granted, to June 1, 1909.

Orville was released from the Fort Myer hospital on October 31 and boarded the train for Dayton that night with Katharine as traveling companion. "He is brought out from the depot on a wheeled chair," Bishop Wright wrote in his diary the next day. "His mind is as good as ever and his body promises to be in due time." The family doctor, however, took a dim view of the Army's antiquated method of treating fractures by traction and put the injured leg in a cast. Twice during the next two weeks, Charlie Taylor shoved Orville in his wheelchair from the house on Hawthorn Street, which had been turned into a virtual florist shop by well-wishers, to the shop on Third Street, where the wrecked Fort Myer machine had been uncrated for his inspection. By mid-November, Orville was hobbling about the house on crutches and with Katharine's help answering some of the five hundred letters that had piled up during his convalescence. By the end of the year he had exchanged the crutches for a pair of canes. His leg was out of the cast, and he appeared to be on the road to complete recovery.

The Fort Myer accident was Orville's fifth scrape with death. The first had been at Kill Devil Hills on September 23, 1902, in the third Wright glider, when he wound up in "a heap of flying machine, cloth, and sticks in a heap, with me in the center without a bruise or a scratch"; the second on August 24, 1904, when the second Flyer crashed and a spar that broke just above Orville's back protected him from injury; the third on July 14, 1905, when he was thrown violently through the top wing of the upended Flyer onto the soggy surface of Huffman Prairie, miraculously unscathed; the fourth on September 28, 1905, when he landed safely after the wing of the Flyer had scraped a branch of the thorn tree in the middle of the prairie with such force that thorns were driven into one of the wooden uprights. On September 17, 1908, Orville was not quite so lucky. In addition to the injuries identified by the Army doctors, X rays made a dozen years later revealed three hipbone fractures and a dislocated hip—unsuspected injuries that were to cause him occasional severe pain to the end of his long life.

# 32

## Camp d'Auvours

ON SEPTEMBER 21, 1908, four days after the tragedy at Fort Myer, as if to show the world that Orville's accident did not mean an end to the breaking of world records by the Wright brothers, Wilbur flew for 1 hour 31 minutes at Camp d'Auvours near Le Mans before a cheering throng of 10,000. As he climbed out of the Flyer, almost frozen, he is reported to have said, "This will cheer Orville up a bit," words that were picked up by French journalists and emerged from Wilbur's mouth, in the Parisian papers, as *"Orville sera content, là-bas, à l'hôpital!"* Wilbur no longer avoided the gentlemen of the press. He put them to work. They considered it a privilege to be allowed to haul the Flyer out of its shed and to fetch and carry tools for the great Wilbur. France had clasped this son of Dayton to its bosom as it had no other American since Benjamin Franklin.

Wilbur's apparent indifference to his fame was a constant source of wonderment to press and public. He lived and slept in the shed with his Flyer, his only companion an ugly, low-slung mongrel whose name, by a predictable coincidence, was Flyer. When adopted, Flyer was half starved and had a figure like an hourglass. Within a month he looked like a beer keg. One Sunday, when Wilbur had locked the door to keep the curious at bay while he wrote a letter to his sister, someone moved Flyer's box outside the shed to a position under one of the high windows and climbed up on the box to gaze at Wilbur inside the shed, while half a dozen others waited in line for a turn. "Flyer," Wilbur wrote Katharine, "like a well-trained dog sat in his box and watched them through the whole proceeding without creating the least disturbance." On one occasion, soldiers were called on to handle the unruly crowds who tried to force their way into the shed. One woman eluded the soldiers and bored a peephole through the back of the shed with a gimlet, an incident that caused Wilbur to complain in his next letter home that he couldn't even take a bath without a hundred or two people peeking in at him. "I sometimes get so angry at the continual annoyance of having the crowd about that I feel like quitting the whole thing and going home," he wrote his father, "but when I think of the sacrifices some of them have made in the hope of seeing a flight I cannot help feeling sorry for them when I do not go out." He cited the case of a seventy-year-old man who made a sixty-mile round trip by bicycle every day for nearly a week in the hope of seeing a flight. "The distance overcome and perservance to see the flights is pathetic," replied Bishop Wright. "What compassion Jesus showed toward the multitude drawn out by curiosity!"

The scriptural parallel was apt. Almost every evening a multitude of two to three thousand men, women, and children, rich and poor, found their way to Camp d'Auvours. They came as often just to see Wilbur as to see him perform the miracle of flying. In time he became resigned and was even amused by the adultation lavished upon him by all levels of society. Princes and millionaires, he wrote Orville, were thick as fleas. He was just as popular with workingmen as with royalty. While assembling the Flyer in Léon Bollée's automobile factory in Le Mans, he had worked the same hours as Bollée's workmen and had gone to lunch with them in his overalls when the noon whistle blew. After the Flyer was moved out of the factory and Wilbur began to fly, the workmen took up a collection to buy him a testimonial of their regard. They called him "Veelbur Reet," an affectionate double entendre that sounded like *vieille burette,* French for "old oilcan." Most Frenchmen found it easier to use Wilbur's first name than his last. When the song "Il Vole" ("He Flies") became popular in Paris and flying-machine fever hit the French capital, the young Spanish painter Pablo Picasso nicknamed his artist friend Georges Braque "Vilbour," although "Veelbare" was the more common pronunciation.

Wilbur's flights at Camp d'Auvours had brought a wave of prosperity to Le Mans, a city that until then had been famous, if at all, as the place where Léon Bollée manufactured automobiles. The crowds arriving daily by train from Paris were put up in the best hotels and transported to the flying field by a fleet of taxicabs known collectively as the Le Mans–Auvours Aeroplane Bus Service. Shops in town were full of "Vreecht caps," copies of a nondescript green workman's cap that Orville had bought in Paris in 1907 and that Wilbur had brought back to France with him to wear while working on the Flyer, only to find that it had suddenly become a fashionable item of headgear. There was also a lucrative business in souvenir postcards caricaturing Wilbur's birdlike features—his hawklike nose, pronounced cheekbones, and protruding Adam's apple. When Orville was making his record-breaking flights at Fort Myer, he received a postcard caricature of an extraordinarily thin Wilbur, face upthrust under a Vreecht cap, flying his airplane as a kite at the end of a long string. Across the front of the card, Wilbur had scrawled: "I'll tie a string to you next time to keep you from going too high or too far. It's too much trouble to break your records." It was one of these postcards sent to Octave Chanute by Wilbur that caused Chanute to comment in his next letter: "Dear me! How thin you have grown. Your sister said that you were emaciated and nervous but I had no idea it was to this extent."

In Le Mans, Wilbur was barraged with bouquets and presented with more baskets of fruit than he could eat in a year. He was wined and dined (though very little of the wine trickled down his throat) half-a-dozen times, beginning with a luncheon on August 16. A week later, he was presented by the Universal Peace Society with a medal for himself and another for Orville. Because of its scouting potential, the airplane was looked upon in those days —somewhat prematurely, it turned out—as a keeper of the peace rather than an angel of destruction. The reception given by the Aéro-Club de la Sarthe to celebrate Wilbur's record 1 1/2-hour flight of September 21 was memorable largely because of sixteen words out of some hundred spoken by Wilbur on that occasion which have been quoted and misquoted so often as an example of his wit, wisdom, and aversion to the after-dinner speaking that they are worth quoting again: "I know of only one bird, the parrot, that talks, and it can't fly very high."

It was a mark of distinction to have been taken up in the Wright Flyer. Of the 120 flights Wilbur made at Camp d'Auvours, more than half were made with passengers. All but two of the twenty-six flights made during the first week of October were made with a man or a woman in the seat beside him. His first passenger that week was Léon Bollée. That the Wright Flyer, with a motor delivering only 30 to 40 horsepower, had gotten off the ground with 240-pound Bollée in the passenger seat created greater astonishment than anything Wilbur had done at Camp d'Auvours up to that time. Tuesday, October 6, Arnold Fordyce was given a ride that lasted for 1 hour 4 minutes and covered 70 kilometers. Hart Berg was given his first ride Wednesday. Mrs. Berg was next. Before she took off, Mr. Berg fastened a cord about her skirt between her ankles and her knees out of deference to Edwardian ideas of propriety. As he helped her from the Flyer after a 2-minute flight, she took a few hobbling steps before the cord was removed. Among the spectators that day was an alert dress designer from Paris who foresaw a possible fad in Mrs. Berg's hobbling gait. A few weeks later the hobble skirt took the world of fashion by storm. Four of Wilbur's seven passengers Thursday were members of the Aeronautical Society of Great Britain. His passengers Friday were all French and included Henri Deutsch de la Meurthe, who had purchased 100,000 shares of stock in the French Wright Company when Wilbur moved to Camp d'Auvours.

Wilbur's sole passenger Saturday was Paul Painlevé, the French mathematician who would serve his country twice as Premier before becoming Minister of Aviation in 1930. A pouring rain dashed Painlevé's hopes of an early flight. That evening, when he was finally seated in the Flyer beside Wilbur, he waved so enthusiastically to the crowd as Wilbur was about to take off that he tripped the cord that stopped the Flyer's motor, and the entire starting procedure had to be repeated. The flight not only set a record for two-man flight of 80 kilometers in 1 hour 10 minutes but, together with the flight with Fordyce on Tuesday, fulfilled the requirements of the French contract for two passenger flights of at least fifty kilometers. The remaining requirement of Wilbur's contract was the training of three Frenchmen in the operation of the Flyer. Training was begun at the end of October but was postponed early in December because of the weather. Flights could be made on only seven days in November. Wilbur finally found time to write his first letter to Octave Chanute since July 10. He blamed his long silence on the large number of letters he had been receiving, three-fourths of which had to go unanswered. "For three months I have had scarcely a moment to myself except when I take my bicycle and ride off into the woods for a little rest," he wrote, and added a little wistfully, "How I long for Kitty Hawk!"

He longed for Hawthorn Street as well. He had given up all hope of returning home for the holidays and wanted the family to join him in Europe. Bishop Wright would be eighty that November and was not up to making the trip, but it was agreed that Katharine would once more leave her teaching job at Steele High in Dayton and accompany Orville to Europe as soon as he was able to travel. That would not be until after the first of the year, however. In the meantime Wilbur continued to live in the shed with his flying machine and the dog Flyer, heating his living quarters with a small stove after the cold weather set in. The blue-misted mornings and early twilights at Camp d'Auvours agreed with him. He began to put on weight. The first week in November he made a trip to Paris to harvest some of the official honors that had been accumulating. On November 5 he was guest of honor at a luncheon given by an elite assemblage of authors, editors, artists, and scientists that included Henri Bergson, Paul Painlevé, and Auguste Rodin. A reception was given for him that afternoon by the French Senate, followed by an Aéro-Club de France banquet, at which he accepted a pair of gold medals awarded to Orville and himself by the Aéro-Club and another pair from the Académie des Sports. A few days later the Aeronautical Society of Great Britain voted to award the society's gold medal to both brothers for their distinguished services to aeronautical science. Some of the gold medals, Wilbur confided to Katharine, were "about the size of a small can."

Ever since his first short flights at Les Hunaudières, the adulation showered on Wilbur by his French and British admirers had made him a little uneasy. "The dangerous feature," he wrote Katharine, "is that they will be too enthusiastic and that a reaction will set in." The most notable reaction to his success, however, was a positive one. French aviators were busily modifying their machines, adding various means of lateral control in an effort to catch up with the Wrights. On October 30, after installing large ailerons on the rear edges of the wings of his Voisin biplane, Henri Farman made the first cross-country flight in history, flying 27 kilometers from the flying field at Camp de Châlons to Reims in 20 minutes. Blériot had equipped his monoplane with movable wingtips before Wilbur ever flew in France, but the results had been discouraging, and it was not until he incorporated the Wrights' wingwarping system into his newest monoplane that he would achieve any great success. Within a year, the wide skidding turns of the French machines would be a thing of the past.

There were only a few signs of the negative reactions that Wilbur had expected. Griffith Brewer, the first Englishman to be taken up in the Flyer, remarked on the "quiet sarcasm" with which Wilbur greeted the advice of engineers and scientists who tried to show him how his flying machine could be improved. Frederick Lanchester, whose pioneering study *Aerodynamics* had been published in London the year before, softened his criticism with backhanded compliments when he wrote: "The Wright machine is astonishing in its simplicity—not to say apparent crudity of detail—it is almost a matter of surprise that it holds together. The Voisin machine has at least some pretensions to be considered an engineer job." He admitted, however, that Wilbur's Flyer "appears not to come to pieces but continues to fly day after day without showing any signs of weakness."

A more insidious reaction to Wilbur's success was the claim put forth by a few chauvinistic Frenchmen that their countryman Clément Ader had flown about 1,000 feet in 1897, six years before the first Wright flights of 1903. Ader was a civil and electrical engineer who had established the first telephone system in Paris in 1880. In 1890, after studying bats and their flight, he constructed and experimented with a flying machine with folding wings like those of a bat. In 1894 he received a subsidy of half a million francs from the French government to build a flying machine for the Ministry of War. Like his two previous machines, Ader's third aircraft, the *Avion,* was a batlike monoplane. It had two propellers, each powered by a 40-horsepower steam engine. Their blades were made of semi-flexible bamboo, shaped to resemble the feathers of a bird. In October 1897 the machine was tested in secrecy at the military field of Satory near Versailles before a commission appointed by the Minister of War. The test was so unsatisfactory that the government withdrew its support.

The *Avion* was reconstructed and placed on display in the Galerie des Machines at the Paris Exposition of 1900, after which a home was found for it in the Musée des Arts et Métiers, and there it might have remained as a reminder of the stone age of aeronautics if Ernest Archdeacon had not claimed—at a time when it was not generally believed that the Wright brothers had really flown—that Santos-Dumont's 1906 flights in the *14-bis* were the first powerplane flights made in Europe, if not in the world. Clément Ader indignantly refuted that claim, but the Wright brothers knew that Ader was lying when he said he had flown in 1897. Their friend Commandant Henri Bonel had been present at the test of the *Avion*. When he visited Dayton in March 1906 as head of the French commission investigating the Wright brothers' flights, he told Wilbur and Orville that the *Avion* had never flown but had been blown over and smashed while running around its circular track at Satory.

On September 5, 1908, less than a month after Wilbur made his first flight in France, *Le Matin* published a letter from the xenophobic Gabriel Voisin and his brother Charles in which the Voisins not only restated Ader's claim to have flown in 1897 but added that "it was in France that Chanute, great precursor of the Wrights, came to absorb the data about [Ader's] admirable machine from which the aviators of Dayton had learned to fly." The report of the *Avion*'s secret test would not be published for another two years, so in 1908 there was no way of disproving Ader's claim. Gradually the story of the 1897 flight of the *Avion* gained credence among patriotic Frenchmen. In December 1908, when the most elaborate aeronautical exposition ever held opened in the Grand Palais in Paris, the *Avion* was taken from the Musée des Arts et Métiers and elevated to a place of honor on a high platform between the two great stairways of the Grand Palais.

The campaign to discredit the Wrights was largely the work of a chauvinistic clique in the Aéro-Club de France. In the fall of 1908 they kept Wilbur from competing for the club's 2,500-franc, twenty-five-meter altitude prize by stipulating that the winning machine must take off under its own power without the aid of falling weights. The Aéro-Club de la Sarthe in Le Mans, of which Wilbur was an honored member, countered this affront from its Parisian colleagues by offering 1,000 francs for the first machine to reach an altitude of thirty meters. Wilbur won the prize easily on November 13 by flying at more than twice the required altitude. A few days later he delighted his fellow club members in Le Mans by showing that he could qualify for the Aéro-Club de France prize by increasing the length of the Flyer's starting rail and taking off without the aid of falling weights. In case the use of the starting rail should disqualify him, Wilbur scraped his skids along the ground before beginning to climb. He deliberately cleared the four captive balloons anchored at twenty-five meters by a few feet only, as a mild rebuke to the Aéro-Club members who had thought to eliminate the Wright Flyer from the competition.

The Wright brothers looked on the winning of prizes as something of a bother unless the prize was a sizable one. In October the London *Daily Mail* offered a prize of $5,000 (£1,000) for the first flight across the English Channel. Wilbur was sorely tempted when he was privately offered an extra $5,000 if he would compete—and win. "If I felt sure of decent weather," he wrote Orville, "I would go for it." The first letter Orville wrote Wilbur after being released from the Fort Myer hospital put an end to that. "I do not like the idea of your attempting a channel flight when I am not present," he replied. "I haven't much faith in your motor running. You seem to have more trouble with the engine than I do."

The only prize Wilbur had his heart set on winning before he left Camp d'Auvours was the Coupe Michelin, the 20,000 francs offered by André Michelin, a wealthy member of the Aéro-Club de France, for the longest flight of the year. The cup itself would go to the aero club whose member won the monetary award. With Christmas approaching, there were times when Wilbur thought of withdrawing from the competition and returning to Dayton. His 1 1/2-hour flight of September 21 was still the longest flight of the year, but Henri Farman had made two flights of more than 40 minutes each, even before installing ailerons on his Voisin at the end of October, and Wilbur was afraid that if he went home for the holidays he might be overtaken in the race for the cup. Early in the morning of December 18, he telephoned the Aéro-Club in Le Mans that he was ready to make his official try for the Coupe Michelin. The judges hurried to Camp d'Auvours. Shortly after 10 A.M., the Flyer sailed over the starting post on the first lap of the course, a wedge-shaped isosceles triangle, measuring one kilometer on each long side, 200 meters at the base. The three corners of the triangle were marked by flags. During the first dozen circuits, a strong wind blew snow across the field, but Wilbur signaled his assurance to the judges and continued to fly. After 1 hour 55 minutes, he was forced down by a clogged oil line, having covered almost 100 kilometers.

Later that afternoon, when he was thoroughly warm again, Wilbur notified the judges he would try for the Aéro-Club de la Sarthe's 1,000-franc Prix de la Hauteur. A single captive balloon was sent up 100 meters as an altitude marker. At 4 P.M., as the sun was beginning to set, the Flyer was launched into a strong wind. Wilbur flew three circuits of the field at an altitude of about twenty feet, then abruptly began to climb. The sound of his motor became indistinct, and his silhouette merged with that of the Flyer. As he flew over the marker balloon, with several meters to spare, its western side was aglow with the rays of the setting sun. He had reached an altitude of about 350 feet, as high as any man had ever been in a flying machine.

Determined to set a two-hour record for endurance before the year was over, Wilbur formally notified the secretary of the Aéro-Club in Le Mans that he would make another try for the Coupe Michelin on the last day of 1908. On December 30, as a sort of warm-up, he flew for 1 hour 53 minutes in subfreezing weather, a feat that seemed to require more stamina than his slight frame possessed. The temperature on the ground at Camp d'Auvours that day was 18 degrees Fahrenheit.

Thursday, December 31, was slightly warmer. The ground was covered with a light mantle of snow. Again Wilbur was brought down short of his goal when a broken fuel line ended his flight after 42 minutes. The broken line was repaired, and at 2 P.M. he once more began the monotonous circuiting of the triangular course. At 4 P.M. he reached his goal but kept on. Fighting a freezing drizzle of sleet and rain, he landed just as the sun was setting. He had been in the air exactly 2 hours 20 minutes 23.2 seconds. His official distance over the course was 124 kilometers, but the actual distance was closer to 150 kilometers because of the turns, or about 90 miles.

One of the bundled-up spectators that day was French Minister of Public Works Louis Barthou. Barthou had been up in airships and balloons but never in an airplane—until Wilbur, in the last flight of the year, gave him a four-minute ride in the deepening twilight. Sometime during the flight or just after it, the minister let Wilbur know that the government had decided to bestow the Legion of Honor on both Wright brothers. The award signaled the end of an eventful year for aeronautics—a year that began with Henri Farman's winning of the Deutsch-Archdeacon prize for a 1 1/2-minute, one-kilometer circuit of Issy-les-Moulineaux on January 13 and ended with the awarding of the Michelin prize to Wilbur for his seemingly endless circling above snow-covered Camp d'Auvours for 2 hours 20 minutes on December 31.

On the second day of the new year, Wilbur made four brief flights for the sole purpose of giving four of his friends in Le Mans the right to say that they had flown with the great "Veelbare." From Le Mans he traveled to Paris, where he was joined early in the morning of January 12 by Orville and Katharine. Katharine's twenty-four-year-old helper and housekeeper, Carrie, had recently been married in Dayton to Charles Grumbach, and the two Grumbachs had moved into the house on Hawthorn Street to take care of Bishop Wright while Orville and Katharine were in Europe. The day after Orville and Katharine's arrival, Wilbur set out for Pau in the south of France to complete the training of the three French pilots. Orville and Katharine dallied in Paris to give Katharine a chance to see the city and do some shopping. Then on January 16, 1909, only four months after the accident at Fort Myer, Orville demonstrated his affinity for close scrapes with death. Thirty miles from Pau, the express train in one of whose sleepers he and Katharine were riding collided with a slow local train. Two were killed, many were injured, but the worst that happened to Orville was a five-hour delay and the temporary loss of his watch and pocketbook. They were believed to have been stolen, but were later found beneath a dislodged mattress.

# 33

# *The Homecoming*

P A U, A T T H E F O O T of the Pyrenees in southwestern France, was a popular winter resort in the Edwardian era, thanks to the presence of the king of England during the season. Lately the king had developed a preference for Biarritz, and business had fallen off. To provide a new attraction for sensation-loving Edwardians, the city fathers had established a committee to lure Wilbur and his Flyer south to Pau. For a flying field the committee offered him a level unfenced area almost a mile square at Pont-Long on the gorse-covered plateau between the mountains and the maritime plain. The field was eight miles from town but only twenty minutes away by automobile. *Champs d'Aviation* signs were erected along the road to Pont-Long to ensure that none of the thousands expected to flock to Pau to see Wilbur fly would go astray.

Pont-Long was an even more ideal flying field than Camp d'Auvours. The virtual absence of trees made it possible to fly circuits of three to four miles without straying too far from the Flyer's shed—a large reddish-brown building incorporating a workshop for assembling and repairing the machine. Its sliding doors were wide enough so that for the first time the Flyer could be trundled in and out of its hangar with both tail frame and front rudder attached. Wilbur slept at the flying field as usual, but his living quarters in the commodious new shed were luxurious by comparison with those at Camp d'Auvours. His meals were provided by a French chef, selected by the mayor, and he was supplied with a special telephone line to Pau, where Orville and Katharine were ensconced without charge in a sumptuous suite in the Hotel Gassion.

Of the sixty flights Wilbur made at Pont-Long in February and March 1909, forty were made with his three student pilots, Paul Tissandier, Captain Paul Lucas-Girardville, and Count Charles de Lambert. After a few flights as passenger, the student learned to manipulate the horizontal front rudder —the elevator—in straight-line flight. He was then allowed to operate the warping and rudder control stick between the two seats, while Wilbur rode with his hands on his knees, ready to take over if the student made a mistake. On March 19, the day before Wilbur made his final flight at Pont-Long, Tissandier and de Lambert each made solo flights of more than twenty minutes, refuting the canard spread by the anti-Wright clique in France that the acrobatic ability required to manage the Wright Flyer made it next to impossible to train others in its use. The idea that the Wright brothers were well-trained aerial artists died hard. One day the Curzons, a family of vaudeville acrobats, visited Pont-Long and asked to be introduced to Wilbur on the grounds that they were in the same line of work.

In a way they were. Pau was a thriving show-business capital that winter. The city played host to a steady procession of notables who came from all over Europe to see Wilbur and his Flyer—prime ministers, generals, dukes, duchesses, counts, countesses, lords, ladies, press moguls, even a brace of kings. The visit of King Alfonso of Spain on February 20 was preceded by a careful search of the Hotel Gassion by the Spanish secret service for any traces of anarchists or antimonarchists. The king was eager for a flight, but his queen and cabinet forbade it, and he had to be satisfied with having his picture taken, sitting in the Flyer on the ground, while Wilbur explained the functions of the control handles. Portly sixty-eight-year-old King Edward of England arrived by automobile from Biarritz on March 17. He not only had no desire to fly but was observed to be engaged in conversation with a member of his suite while the Flyer was being launched. But very few of the high and mighty of Europe who came to Pont-Long were that uninterested. Many considered themselves lucky to have been photographed while tugging on the rope that hoisted the 1,400 pounds of weights to the top of the starting derrick—an operation performed quite efficiently by block and tackle or by automobile when no photographers were present.

Fashionable Europeans who made the trip to Pau found Wilbur, Orville, and Katharine as exotic and extraordinary as the Wright Flyer. Of the three, Wilbur was the most impressive physically. Reporters vied with each other in defining what it was that made him instantly recognizable as the world's premier aviator, and most agreed that it was his hawklike features. It was certainly not his clothes. Unlike the French aviators with their eye-catching scarves and fancy flying togs, Wilbur wore either a business suit and necktie when he flew or, in cold weather, a black leather motorcyclist's jacket. His trousers were described by a British journalist as "plainly strangers to the press." According to the same journalist, Orville's small, regular features and his eyes set close together failed to generate the electricity that Wilbur's features inspired in a crowd, nor did Orville possess Wilbur's dynamic manner of moving and walking—small wonder, considering Orville had recently given up crutches for a cane. When photographed in dark overcoat and derby, leaning against his cane, Orville looked every bit as debonair as if he were in the retinue of some royal family come to see Wilbur fly, but at thirty-seven he was no longer as attractive to women as when he had strummed his guitar at Katharine's parties for her schoolgirl friends. Wilbur at forty-one, on the other hand, had retained the gaunt hungry look, as if starved for affection, that women found irresistible. It was not altogether unbelievable, therefore, when it was reported shortly after Wilbur left Le Mans that he was named corespondent in a divorce suit filed by a lieutenant in the French Army. The story was traced to an enterprising reporter who foresaw that the news would attract more attention if Wilbur's name was substituted for that of the real corespondent in the suit—a French mechanic who had worked for Wilbur at Le Mans. The news service apologized, the reporter was fired, and the titillating possibility that either of the Wright brothers had ever engaged in a sexual peccadillo was blasted in the bud.

Almost overnight, Katharine became a celebrity in her own right. She was known to be a teacher of classical languages. Aside from that, her background was as shadowy and mysterious to the European press as her face in the photographs taken of her at Pont-Long, in which her features are almost always concealed under an enormous hat. There was no shortage of stories about her. It was stated seriously that her knowledge of mathematics was behind her brothers' success, and that her life's savings had kept the family from starving while the Flyer was being perfected. Her experience as a trained nurse, it was said, had hastened Orville's recovery after the accident at Fort Myer. Her name was almost always misspelled, as in the following tribute by the French aviation journalist François Peyrey: *"Mlle Katherine Wright, professeur de grec, est une femme absolument supérieure."* The fact that Wilbur and Orville were bachelors and Katharine a spinster, Peyrey postulated, was the bond that united the three youngest Wrights. When he asked Wilbur about his older brothers, Wilbur gestured vaguely. "The others?" he said. "They're married."

While he was still at Le Mans, Wilbur had accepted an offer of $10,000 from the Aeronautical Society of Rome for a Flyer and the training of an operator in its use. After he made his last flight at Pont-Long on March 20, the Flyer that had served Wilbur so well in France became the property of Lazare Weiller and was offered by Weiller to the Musée des Arts et Métiers in Paris. A new Flyer, which had been partially constructed in the big hangar at Pont-Long of parts shipped from Dayton, was sent on to Rome to be reassembled there. Wilbur and Hart Berg arrived in the Italian capital on Thursday, April 1, and on Saturday were presented to King Victor Emmanuel by the American ambassador. (In a Sunday letter to Orville, who was then in Paris with Katharine, Wilbur observed that when "His Gracious &c." sat down, his feet failed to reach the floor by about a foot.) The new Flyer was assembled in an unused automobile shop. "It makes a splendid place to set up the machine," he noted in the same letter. "It is located outside the north gate of the city, on the Flaminian Way along which Caesar passed on his way to the conquest of Gaul, &c., &c., &c."

Orville and Katharine arrived in Rome a week later and were put up in the Hotel Britannia, which boasted central heating, although there was little evidence of it in April. They were entertained by the mayor of Rome and required to traipse through cold marble palaces behind costumed servants. On April 24 they were introduced to His Gracious &c. at the field outside Rome where the little king had come to see Wilbur fly. The flying field was named Centocelle, after a nearby fort. A temporary shed had been erected there for the Flyer, but Wilbur no longer slept beside his machine; he lived, instead, in a cottage belonging to the countess whose villa adjoined Centocelle and who provided his breakfasts and saw that his quarters were supplied with fresh flowers daily. He was welcome to dine at the villa, but preferred to eat with the Italian officers at the fort. In the four weeks he was at Centocelle he consumed, by his own reckoning, forty-seven miles of macaroni.

Since the Wright brothers' contract with the U.S. Signal Corps had been extended only until June 28, 1909, their stay in Italy was limited. Wilbur flew almost every day from April 15 to 27 with the exception of Sundays and was up and down as many as thirteen times in a single day. He had some misgivings about his student pilot, Lieutenant Mario Calderara of the Italian Navy, whom he characterized as a cigarette fiend. He was not at all surprised to hear a few weeks after leaving Italy that the lieutenant had suffered a fainting spell while demonstrating the Italian machine and had injured his leg in landing.

Wilbur added a few more firsts to his record at Centocelle. He took off several times on a downslope without benefit of falling weights—and five times without use of either falling weights or starting rail, by merely taking off into the wind over the grassy ground on the Flyer's skids. On April 24 his passenger was a news cameraman who took the first successful motion pictures ever taken from an airplane. On his last day at Centocelle he gave rides to four complete strangers—another first. They were winners of a lottery organized by the Italian Aero Club.

The three Wrights left Rome for Paris at the end of April. On May 1 they went to Le Mans and were guests of honor at a farewell banquet. They left loaded down with a gold plaque bearing the city's coat of arms, a gold medal awarded by its citizens, and a bronze statuette, commissioned by the Aéro-Club de la Sarthe, in which the spirit of aviation spreads her capacious wings over Wilbur and Orville, who are staring intently at a large flying eagle anchored to the base of the statue. Armed with these spoils, the trio made their way to London. They left England two gold medals the richer, and arrived in New York on May 11 after seven days at sea, during which Wilbur discovered he had gained a dozen pounds since leaving the United States and Orville discarded his cane after finding he could walk about the deck as comfortably without a cane as with one. The highlight of their one-day stopover in New York was a luncheon given by the Aero Club of America. The alphabetical list of the eighty persons present began with John Jacob Astor and ended with Wilbur Wright.

In September 1908, when Orville was making his first long public flights in the Army Flyer, he learned that the Dayton *Herald* was planning an elaborate homecoming reception and wrote Wilbur, who hated such affairs, that he would "endeavor to suppress the 'spontaneous' uprising of our fellow citizens." The accident at Fort Myer put an end to the *Herald*'s plans, but in May 1909 the homecoming celebration could no longer be suppressed. When the train bearing Wilbur, Orville, and Katharine steamed into Dayton, any hopes the three might have had for a quiet family reunion went up in smoke. Eleven carriages were drawn up before the depot and the streets about the station were black with people. Bishop Wright and his favorite granddaughter, Leontine, were in one of the carriages, Lorin and the rest of his family in another. To the tooting of factory whistles and the booming of cannon in a thirty-gun salute, Wilbur and Orville were ushered into a carriage pulled by four white horses and driven from the depot in triumph. Thousands of welcomers were congregated in the Wrights' neighborhood on the West Side across the river. A marching band took over at the bridge and escorted the procession to the strains of "Home, Sweet Home." Chinese lanterns were strung between the elms and poplars on Hawthorn Street. The modest Wright homestead was decked with flags, banners, and toy balloons. There were welcoming speeches, a reception, and at night fireworks.

Wilbur and Orville would have been grateful if celebrating had ended with the fireworks on May 13. They were at work on a new Army Flyer that would fly faster than any machine they had designed so far, but the official homecoming festivities were still several weeks in the future and they were seldom left alone for any length of time. One distraction that could not be avoided was a trip to Washington, D.C., the second week in June to receive the Aero Club of America gold medals from the hands of the President of the United States. The presentation in the East Room of the White House was attended by President Taft's cabinet, high-ranking military and government officials, and representatives of all the embassies and legations in the capital. Afterwards there was a luncheon at the Cosmos Club, at which the brothers told General James Allen of the Signal Corps that although the new

Army Flyer would be delivered by June 28, it would be patently impossible to complete its trials by that date, whereupon General Allen gracefully extended their deadline to July 28, giving them another month in which to fulfill the terms of their Army contract.

The Flyer was delivered in eight boxes to Fort Myer. Charlie Taylor was sent ahead to begin the unpacking while Wilbur and Orville were still crating the final parts for shipment back in Dayton. They worked off and on during the first day of the official two-day homecoming celebration declared by the city of Dayton. On Thursday and Friday, June 17 and 18, schools were closed, and all nonessential business was suspended.

The festivities began at 9 A.M. Thursday with blasts from every factory whistle and the ringing of bells in every church in Dayton. The brothers, already hard at work in the bicycle shop, stepped outside in their shirtsleeves to listen. Cannon were booming on the riverfront and bands could be heard playing in the distance. After ten minutes the racket subsided and they went back to work. At 10 A.M. a carriage drew up in front of the bicycle shop to take them to the opening ceremonies. Two old friends were in the carriage —Ed Sines, Orville's partner in their old printing business, and Edgar Ellis, assistant auditor of the city. As the procession crossed the Third Street bridge and proceeded up Main Street behind a brass band, Wilbur and Orville shrank back among the cushions of the closed carriage and watched with amusement as Sines and Ellis shook the hands extended to them through the partially opened windows by people who imagined they were shaking the hands of the famous brothers.

The opening ceremonies took place in Van Cleve Park, where there was a pageant under the trees on the bank of the Miami River. Once again, as in 1796, Jonathan Dayton, in colonial costume and wig, stepped from a boat in the river onto the soil of the city that would one day bear his name. He was accompanied by heralds and colonial soldiers in costume. Two speeches from the pageant were preserved for posterity by the daily press:

> JONATHAN DAYTON. Methinks I see two great objects like gigantic birds coming from the eastward as if riding on the winds of the morning! What manner of birds can these be?
> ANOTHER MEMBER OF THE CAST. They are no other than two of Dayton's illustrious sons coming home from foreign triumphs with the greatest invention of the age.

At the point in the program designated "Responses by the Wrights," Wilbur rose to his feet. "Thank you, gentlemen," he said, speaking for both brothers, and sat down. Shortly thereafter, he and Orville were back at work in the bicycle shop after hanging canvas in the windows to shield them from the gaze of the crowds on the sidewalk. That afternoon there was a fire department parade and drill on Main Street, at which the brothers were presented with something they did not badly need—a key to the city of Dayton. At four o'clock they returned to the bicycle shop and worked until six. At 8 P.M. there was a handshaking reception at the YMCA and at 9 P.M. fireworks on the riverfront, climaxed by a pyrotechnic display featuring blazing portraits of Wilbur and Orville entwined in a smoking American flag.

The high point of the two-day celebration was the medal-presentation ceremony at the racetrack on the fairgrounds Friday morning. Reuchlin Wright had brought his wife and children from Tonganoxie, Kansas, for the event, so that all fifteen members of the Wright family were seated on the speaker's platform—Bishop Wright in clerical attire, Reuchlin and Lorin with their wives, Katharine, the bishop's three grandsons and four hair-ribboned granddaughters, and Uncles Wilbur and Orville in silk toppers and long frock coats. On the bleachers behind the platform were almost a thousand Dayton schoolchildren dressed in red, white, and blue so as to form an American flag. After the invocation by Bishop Wright, the schoolchildren rendered a medley of patriotic songs. General James Allen presented Wilbur and Orville with Congressional Medals of Honor. The governor of Ohio presented them with medals on behalf of the state, and the mayor of Dayton, not to be outdone, presented diamond-studded medals on behalf of the city. That afternoon there was a parade downtown, depicting the development of transportation. It featured an Indian runner, a sedan chair, and floats bearing an oxcart, a covered wagon, an automobile, a captive balloon, and a float-maker's impression of a Wright Flyer. There was another parade that night, observed by members of the Wright family from a festooned court of honor at the corner of First and Main streets. Its principal attraction was an automobile aglow with electric lights, driven by a family friend.

What Wilbur and Orville thought of all this can be inferred from two sentences in a letter of Wilbur's to Octave Chanute: "The Dayton presentation has been made the excuse for an elaborate carnival and advertisement of the city under the guise of being an honor to us. As it was done in spite of our known wishes, we are not as appreciative as we might be."

One unscheduled event of the month-long welcome-home orgy was the delivery free of charge of a player piano to the house on Hawthorn Street. The paper roll that came with the instrument was a player-piano version of Robert Schumann's "Träumerei." Although the Wright brothers realized the family had been made the victim of a shoddy advertising scheme, they could not resist pumping the pedals that operated the player mechanism, with the result that Schumann's mournful melody was to haunt them for the rest of the summer. On June 19, the day after honors had been heaped upon them in such unwanted abundance, they left for Washington, D.C., and for the next few weeks they could be heard humming and whistling the wordless "Träumerei" as they worked on the new Army Flyer in the big wooden shed erected for it on the parade ground at Fort Myer.

# 34

## *Cross-Country*

ORVILLE WAS TO DO all the flying at Fort Myer. Wilbur was there to see that the Army machine was properly assembled and maintained and also to ensure that when Orville resumed flying for the first time in almost a year he would not be distracted by a busy social life. They were to see a lot of Albert Zahm that summer. Zahm had left Catholic University in January to become secretary of the Aero Club of Washington, but the former professor was not able to inveigle the Wright brothers into staying at the Cosmos Club on Lafayette Square, where Orville had lived in 1908. They took rooms instead at the Raleigh Hotel on Pennsylvania Avenue, a good half mile from the Cosmos Club and its distractions, keeping to themselves as much as possible and refusing to be interviewed.

The temperature was in the nineties every day during the week the Flyer was being assembled. Charlie Furnas was not at Fort Myer that year, but Charlie Taylor was there to help and so were Lieutenants Frank Lahm and Benjamin Foulois. Lieutenant Foulois pronounced his name "Fuh-LOY." By 1931, when he had become Major General Foulois, chief of the U.S. Army Air Corps, the newspapers had learned to spell his name correctly, but in 1909, whenever his name was mentioned in connection with the flights that summer, it usually came out "Foulers," and once in a headline over an Associated Press dispatch he was identified as Lieutenant "Foulouis." However his name was spelled or pronounced, Foulois was interested in flying machines and made himself a pest with his questions. Wilbur, who looked with suspicion on all questions regarding the Flyer, would either say nothing at all or nod assent to Orville's belated reply and reluctantly add a few words of his own. Foulois was delighted when Wilbur's aloofness melted away in the hot, humid Washington weather and he was allowed to don overalls and work on the Flyer beside the brothers and Charlie.

The skids were higher in the new Army machine than in the 1908 Flyer, and the wing area had been decreased in order to increase speed. A change had also been made in the lever between the pilot seat and the passenger seat that controlled both the wingwarping and the movement of the vertical rudder. In previous machines, the lever had been a single piece of wood that could be moved backward or forward to warp the wings and at the same time tilted to right or left to move the vertical rudder. The new control stick designed by Orville was called the split-handle lever. The entire lever could be moved forward or backward to effect wingwarping, but only the top of the lever, the so-called split handle, could be moved sideways, left or right, to supply the desired amount of rudder in a turn. In practice, the lever was moved forward or backward a short distance until the Flyer began to bank, then the split handle at the top was manipulated in conjunction with the fore-and-aft movement to produce a smooth turn. The amount of vertical rudder to be applied was indicated by a piece of cotton twine eight to twelve inches long, weighted at the bottom and suspended from the horizontal crossbar between the skids. A movement of the string to the left or right showed the pilot that the machine was either slipping toward the inside of the turning circle or skidding outward, conditions that could be promptly corrected by the appropriate movement of the vertical rudder. This primitive bank and turn indicator served a secondary purpose. When the weighted string inclined too much toward the pilot, it indicated the possibility of a stall.

In spite of the heat and humidity, the Flyer was assembled within a week and ready for launching by Monday, June 28. The Signal Corps, hoping to prod the federal legislature into increasing appropriations for military aeronautics, had invited Congress to witness the maiden flight of the new Army machine. Both houses had adjourned for the afternoon and gone to Fort Myer. Senators and representatives were not allowed near the Flyer, however, and had to content themselves with posing for news photographers in the hot sun about the edges of the parade ground while the Wright brothers fussed with their machine in the distance. Restive congressmen began to complain they might as well have gone to the ball game. A light rain came up and went, leaving a 16-mile-an-hour wind in its wake. Wilbur and Orville, feeling it would be unsafe to try the new machine in such a wind, canceled plans for a flight. The Signal Corps officers wanted to placate the disgruntled congressmen by introducing them to the brothers and showing them the Flyer, but Wilbur objected and threatened to push the machine back in the shed and lock the door as he had done in France when crowds became too much of a nuisance. It was absurd, he said, for Congress to adjourn to see a flight that might not take place. The outcome was a page-one headline the next day:

WRIGHTS FAIL TO FLY

SNUB CONGRESSMEN

BROTHERS NO DIPLOMATS

Shortly before 6 P.M. on Tuesday, the Flyer was finally launched but lost speed rapidly after leaving the starting rail. The right wing struck the ground and the machine spun to a stop. The ripped fabric was sewed and Orville took off forty minutes later only to land after eight seconds. Wilbur thought the machine was improperly balanced, so eighteen pounds of iron bars were attached to the horizontal front rudder. At the next launching, the Flyer skidded almost two hundred feet across the parade ground without lifting at all. Orville thought the trouble lay in the spark lever on the motor, which had slipped back after each takeoff from lack of friction. That was corrected. He took off for a fourth time at almost eight o'clock and came down after making a single circuit of the field. Several more feet were added to the starting rail on Wednesday, after which Orville flew the length of the parade ground, made too sharp a turn, and broke a skid in landing. Thursday evening he made three flights. The longest was nine minutes, not exactly front-page news in 1909. After three aborted takeoffs and two minor accidents in three days, the question on everyone's mind was "Will Orville's next mishap be a fatal one, like his accident of September 17, 1908?"

The question was answered Friday evening, July 2. Orville had been in the air less than eight minutes when the motor stopped and he glided to what would have been a routine landing if a small dead thorn tree at the south end of the parade ground had not caught the right wing and ripped through the fabric, breaking several ribs. The machine dropped heavily to earth and both skids collapsed. Orville was badly shaken but able to walk away. While the Flyer was being hauled back to its shed, the thorn tree was picked clean by souvenir hunters, and the police had to string a rope to hold back the crowds who wanted to peer at the wrecked Flyer. Wilbur had had his fill of such crowds in France, and when he spotted a man on the other side of the rope taking a picture of the damaged machine, he picked up the closest object at hand, which happened to be a piece of the Flyer's broken frame, and hurled it at the photographer. In an incident much like the one that occurred after his second flight in France, he leaped the rope and grappled with the man for the camera. The photographer, taken by surprise, stammered that he was from the War Department. Wilbur apologized but insisted that no more pictures be taken of the wrecked machine.

The broken skids could be replaced with spare parts at Fort Myer, but the wingcovering was beyond mending. Orville returned to Dayton over the Fourth of July weekend and spent the following Monday and Tuesday making a new cloth covering for the lower wing. By Friday, July 9, the machine was ready to fly, but high winds prevented flying for the rest of the week. It began to look as if Schumann's elegiac "Träumerei" was casting a baneful spell over the trials of the new Flyer. On Monday, Orville landed after a few minutes because his motor was running unevenly. The same thing happened twice on Tuesday. A skid runner was broken in the second landing. On Wednesday, the repaired skid collapsed as the Flyer was being taken out of its shed. On Thursday, another section was added to the starting rail. Seventy more pounds were added to the falling weights, and a pit was dug beneath the starting derrick so that the weights would have an additional foot to drop. Friday morning was ideal for flying, but they waited as usual for the evening calm and were rewarded with a violent windstorm that blew down the tent that had been erected at the north end of the parade ground for the President and his cabinet, who had been invited to watch the flying.

Finally, just before 7 P.M. on Saturday, the spell of bad luck was broken when Orville stayed in the air for almost seventeen minutes and thrilled spectators by leaving the confines of the parade ground and soaring over the nearby cavalry stables and the Fort Myer powerhouse with its tall chimney. On Monday, July 19, he circled the field twenty-five times in his first flight, twenty-eight times in his second. On Tuesday, he broke the U.S. endurance record by flying for 1 hour 20 minutes 45 seconds, during which he performed three figure eights and reached an altitude of 300 feet. On Saturday, while circling the field twenty-one times, he showed that the Army machine was capable of flying tight circles with diameters as small as 200 feet.

All this while the public was being drawn to the parade ground as if by a powerful magnet. Washington society and the capital's working population came in droves across the Potomac, by trolley car, carriage, automobile, or on foot, to spend the long summer evenings at Fort Myer. Some brought drinks and sandwiches and picnicked while waiting for Orville to make a flight. The ex-President's daughter Alice Roosevelt Longworth served tea to friends from her electric automobile. The current President's young son Charlie Taft was reported to have violated nearly every rule set down by the Wrights for the taking of photographs. President Taft himself arrived in the presidential automobile on Monday evening, July 26, and was permitted to inspect the Flyer on its launching rail in the company of Vice-President James Sherman. Orville was sure enough of his control of the new Flyer by then to make a two-and-a-half-minute flight for the President and his party in a 15-mile-an-hour wind, something he would not have dared to do three weeks before.

The first of the two flights required by the Signal Corps contract—a two-man flight of at least one hour—took place on Tuesday, July 27. Black clouds gathered over Washington that afternoon. A wind of 25 miles per hour whipped across the parade ground. A crowd estimated at 10,000 was sent scurrying for shelter by a sudden squall, but the rain was over as suddenly as it began. The sky cleared, the wind died down, and the Flyer was taken out of the shed and placed on its launching rail. At 6:30, Lieutenant Lahm climbed into the passenger's seat beside Orville, aware that he might be following Lieutenant Selfridge into the aviator's Valhalla. At 6:34 P.M., President Taft alighted from his automobile in front of the presidential tent and took his place beside the members of his cabinet and other invited guests. At 6:35, Orville took off.

An hour later, the contract requirement had been fulfilled and Orville was still circling. When he was within a few seconds of surpassing Wilbur's world record for a two-man flight of 1 hour 10 minutes made at Camp d'Auvours on October 10, 1908, the crowd about the edge of the field began to yell hysterically. Automobiles honked their horns in unison. Wilbur did a gleeful little dance in the middle of the parade ground. An Associated Press reporter described this as the first sign of emotion Wilbur had shown publicly since coming to Fort Myer (the reporter had evidently not been present when Wilbur had grappled with the War Department photographer). Orville made one more circuit of the field, his seventy-ninth, and landed in a cloud of dust close to the spot where Lieutenant Selfridge had been killed ten months before. He had bettered Wilbur's record for two-man flight by almost three minutes and had helped to eliminate fears that the tragic accident of September 17, 1908, might be repeated.

The other flight specified in the Signal Corps contract was the ten-mile, two-man, cross-country speed test on which the price the Wrights received for the Flyer depended. For a flight of 40 miles per hour, they would receive $25,000. For each mile per hour above 40, they would receive an additional $2,500, and for each mile per hour the speed fell below 40, $2,500 would be subtracted. This would be the first cross-country flight in the United States, though not the first in the world—that honor had gone to Henri Farman for his 20-minute flight to Reims from Camp de Châlons on October 30, 1908. On July 23, 1909, Farman had flown 50 miles from the field near Chalons to Suippes in 1 hour 5 1/2 minutes. These flights had been made over flat terrain, however, with few obstructions to emergency landings, and neither had been made with a passenger.

After going over the grounds about Fort Myer in several directions, Orville had decided that the best course for the speed test would be a round-trip flight to Alexandria, five miles south of the parade ground. Because the weight of the two men on the Flyer might well make a difference in speed of a mile an hour or more, he selected as his passenger five-foot-one-inch, 126-pound Lieutenant Foulois. Because Foulois had experience in map reading, he was to serve as navigator as well as official observer for the

Aeronautical Board. The turning point of the flight was Shuter's Hill (sometimes spelled Shooter's) just outside Alexandria. The hill was the site of the future George Washington Masonic Memorial, the cornerstone of which had recently been laid. A telegraph instrument would be placed on the cornerstone and a telegraph line would be strung between the hill and Fort Myer for the purpose of sending a signal back to the starting point at the exact moment the Flyer crossed the Alexandria end of the course and another signal when it started back after having made its turn about the hill. A sausage-shaped captive balloon would float above the turning point. Another balloon would serve as a marker midway in the course, and an automobile would stand by to render aid in case the Flyer was forced to land before the end of the flight. Such precautions may seem excessive for a round-trip flight of no more than ten miles, but the terrain between Fort Myer and Alexandria, now laced with highways and cluttered with housing, was extremely rough in those days. There were three deep ravines to be crossed, one large forest-covered ridge, and very few cultivated lowlands suitable for landing in an emergency.

On Wednesday, July 28, the day on which the Army contract expired, 14,000 spectators were on hand to witness the Army Flyer's speed test. The direction of the wind did not matter, since the round trip would be made both with and against the wind and speeds would average out, but the wind was so strong that both captive balloons that were to serve as aerial buoys were blown away. The Wrights were given an additional three days to complete the test—until midnight July 31. On Thursday the marker balloons were back in place, but when preparations at Fort Myer were completed, word came over the field telephone from Shuter's Hill that a heavy squall was in progress there, and the test was canceled again.

The weather on Friday, July 30, was even less promising. Wind and rain temporarily disrupted the telegraph circuit on which accurate calculation of the Flyer's speed depended. Although the weather cleared, the public was convinced there would be no flight, and Friday's crowd at Fort Myer was only half the size of Wednesday's. When it became known in the District of Columbia that Orville would fly after all, those unable to cross the river in time for the flight congregated about news bulletin boards in downtown Washington with the eagerness of voters awaiting the returns of a presidential election.

At Fort Myer the atmosphere was like that of the last game of a world series. President Taft arrived and was cheered as he rode by in an open limousine, waving his hat. At six o'clock the Flyer was wheeled out and placed on its track. For the next half-hour, Wilbur and Orville were the focus of all eyes and hundreds of cameras. Katharine objected to her brothers having their pictures taken in shirtsleeves, but the most arresting photograph of the brothers taken that day shows Wilbur in shirtsleeves, the staff of a large signal flag cocked jauntily over his right shoulder, straw hat on the back of his head. He is having a last-minute conference with Orville, whose shirtsleeves are respectably concealed by the jacket of his suit, and natty little Foulois, whose Army attire includes leather puttees and the hot, high-collared tunic worn by the military in all weathers in that benighted age.

Shortly after that picture was taken, the three men approached the Flyer. The motor was started. Orville got in, and Foulois climbed through the wires bracing the front rudder and sat down in the passenger seat. There was a box compass strapped to his left thigh, an aneroid barometer to his right. A map was jammed into his belt and two stopwatches hung about his neck, the first to record the time of the flight to Alexandria, the other the time of its return. At 6:46 the falling weights yanked the Flyer down the starting rail. It skimmed over the weeds and grass for a hundred feet or so, then soared abruptly upward. Wilbur raced to the starting line in the center of the field, a stopwatch in one hand, the staff of the big signal flag in the other. When the Flyer reached an altitude of fifty feet, Orville made two circuits of the parade ground, then passed over the starting line. Wilbur hurled the signal flag to the ground and started his stopwatch. Lieutenant Foulois on the Flyer and the members of the Aeronautical Board on the ground started their stopwatches at approximately the same time. The official time would be an average of all the times thus recorded. Wilbur returned to the starting rail and watched the Flyer through field glasses until it disappeared over the trees in the direction of Alexandria.

Lieutenant Foulois pointed out to Orville the course to follow until the sausage-shaped balloon marking the halfway point bobbed into view. As they clattered along, 125 feet above the ground, the Potomac River glinted through the treetops a mile to their left. The air was bumpy and at times the Flyer sank almost to treetop level. The plan was to keep to the right of the balloon at Shuter's Hill so as to make a left turn about the hill, but the southwesterly wind kept blowing the Flyer left of course. When Orville veered right to keep the balloon on his left as planned, the crowd that had gathered on the east side of the hill to welcome the Flyer surged to the west side. Straw hats were hurled into the air and umbrellas and handkerchiefs were waved as Orville made his turn. A sudden downdraft brought the Flyer perilously close to a small group of trees, but the hill was rounded safely. Lieutenant Foulois flicked his second stopwatch as they straightened out and headed north, traveling with the wind. Orville climbed and flew along at 400 feet until another sudden downdraft caught the Flyer as they passed over the valley made by the small stream called Four Mile Run. The calm way in which Orville worked the controls to regain altitude made a lasting impression on young Foulois.

Wilbur had estimated the moment the Flyer could be expected to re-appear over the treetops to the south. His estimate was too optimistic, and when the machine failed to appear, he knew an anxious second or two. Then it was sighted to cries of "There it comes" from the crowd. The Flyer dipped out of sight once again between two ridges not far from the parade ground, after which, in the words of a watching reporter, it "crawled up the hill of air" to an audible sigh of relief from the 7,000 spectators. Orville nosed down to pick up speed and passed over the finish line at 7:08 to a wild outburst of screaming and shouting, and honking of automobile horns. He circled over Arlington Cemetery, then cut the motor and glided in for a landing. The noisy throng was momentarily still as the Flyer skidded to a stop, all but concealed in the cloud of dust thrown up by its runners. Then pandemonium resumed, and Wilbur rushed up to the Flyer. It was the first time Lieutenant Foulois had ever seen him smile.

The telegram Bishop Wright received in Dayton shortly after the speed test was over gave the time of the flight as 14 minutes 42 seconds. With Lorin's help, he set to work calculating the speed. It was not a simple matter, since the true speed would be an average of the two speeds of the Flyer—against the wind to Alexandria and with the wind to Fort Myer—and several seconds would have to be deducted for the turn about Shuter's Hill. Lorin estimated the average speed at 43 miles per hour. Bishop Wright came up with a generous 44 miles, which would have netted Wilbur and Orville a bonus of $10,000 over the 40-mile-per-hour price of $25,000. The next day they learned that the official average speed was 42.58 miles per hour. Since the Signal Corps specification said nothing about prorating that last fractional mile, 42 miles per hour was made the basis of payment, and the price the U.S. War Department paid for its first flying machine was $30,000.

Orville returned to Dayton the day after the speed test. Wilbur stayed in Washington a few more days to arrange for the training of the two Army pilots later in the year. Lieutenant Lahm, meanwhile, began a search for a more suitable training field than the dusty parade ground at Fort Myer, where the cheers of the crowd and the clatter of the Army's $30,000 flying machine were soon replaced by the barking of drill instructors and the thundering of cavalry horses' hooves.

# 35

## *Herring and Curtiss*

THE WRIGHT BROTHERS' supremacy in the air was not challenged until Louis Blériot, the feisty little French manufacturer of automobile headlamps whose fearless approach to flying had resulted in more accidents than successes, secured for himself a place in the pantheon of aviation immortals by making the first airplane flight across the English Channel in 1909. On July 13, while he was making a cross-country flight in his eleventh aircraft, a monoplane with wings that could be warped like those of a Wright Flyer, Blériot's left leg had been burned when his motor flashed back. For several days he was forced to hobble about on crutches. On July 19, another French aviator, Hubert Latham, made a bid for the London *Daily Mail*'s £1,000 prize for the first flight across the English Channel, but came down in the water with motor trouble. Rescued by a French destroyer, he returned to Calais to await the delivery of a new Antoinette monoplane from the Levavasseur factory. Blériot, still on crutches but hoping to beat Latham to the prize, set up camp on a farm a few miles from Calais. For the next few days the two men scanned the skies for a break in the weather.

Early in the morning of July 26, Blériot noticed that the wind had dropped and had himself driven in the dark to his monoplane while Latham was still asleep. Casting aside his crutches, he flew off across the choppy Channel in the rising sun. He held a course for Dover, but there was a southwest wind behind him and the first land he sighted was not the white cliffs he expected to see but the beach at Deal, several miles up the coast. Turning west, he flew on over the water until he could see the large flag being waved at the appointed landing place on the cliffs. Thirty-seven minutes after leaving Calais, he bumped heavily to earth on collapsing landing gear in a meadow close to Dover Castle, winning the *Daily Mail* £1,000 prize and, in the process, demonstrating to the world that Great Britain was no longer an island and would be subject to invasion in the future just like any other European country.

In 1909 the Wright brothers also had to share the spotlight with Glenn Curtiss, the American director of experiments for Alexander Graham Bell's Aerial Experiment Association. The AEA's first year had ended in September 1908, the month in which AEA secretary Tom Selfridge was killed in the crash of Orville's Army Flyer at Fort Myer. The day after Selfridge's funeral, the four remaining AEA members—Bell, Curtiss, and the two Canadians, Casey Baldwin and Douglas McCurdy—met in Bell's home in Washington, D.C., and voted to extend the life of the association for another six months. Mrs. Bell donated $10,000 of her own money to keep the organization alive until March 31, 1909. After the meeting, Curtiss and McCurdy went to Hammondsport to work on the fourth AEA flying machine, an improved version of the *June Bug* called the *Silver Dart* because of the silvery finish of its wingcovering. Accompanied by Casey Baldwin, the Bells went to their Canadian home in Nova Scotia, where Bell's new tetrahedral kite, *Cygnet II,* was nearing completion. One and a half times as large as the *Cygnet* of 1907, the new kite was composed of more than 5,000 tetrahedral cells covered with red silk. It was fifty feet in width. With its propeller and its motor, which was being built in Hammondsport for use on both the *Silver Dart* and the *Cygnet II,* it weighed more than 900 pounds.

Alexander Graham Bell hoped that most of the six-month reprieve granted the AEA would be devoted to proving that his propeller-driven tetrahedral kite was as practical a solution to the flying problem as the Wright Flyer. He became impatient when Curtiss and McCurdy spent the last three months of 1908 in Hammondsport fussing over the *Silver Dart* while the *Cygnet II* languished in the kite house at Beinn Bhreagh for lack of a motor to fly it. On January 12 he wired Curtiss to come to Nova Scotia at once. Before the AEA expired in March, he wanted to establish a company to exploit what the association had accomplished so far. All AEA machines, inventions, and patents would be transferred to a commercial enterprise called the American Aerodrome Company. It would be located at Hammondsport, New York. Glenn Curtiss would be manager and the AEA members would be the principal stockholders.

Curtiss did not arrive at Beinn Bhreagh until January 29. To Bell's dismay, he showed little enthusiasm for the proposed company and professed to be unable to make up his mind about it. There was reason for his indecision. At the same time that Bell was doing his best to interest Curtiss in his American Aerodrome Company, Curtiss was being wooed by telegram from New York with a tempting counterproposal—partnership in a company that just might earn for himself and his partner a possible one million dollars each.

The tempter and would-be partner was none other than Augustus M. Herring, who reappears in the guise of aeronautical entrepreneur. Since 1905, Herring had been rubbing elbows with the millionaire founders of the Aero Club of America. He was no stranger to the Aerial Experiment Association. In March 1908, he had turned up on the train carrying Lieutenant Selfridge to Hammondsport and had stayed in that city long enough to make a few suggestions regarding the construction of the association's second flying machine, the *White Wing,* with movable wingtips. On July 4, when the AEA's *June Bug* won the *Scientific American* trophy, Herring was a member of the twenty-two-man Aero Club delegation. In the fall of 1908, when the *Silver Dart* was under construction, he turned up again at Hammondsport and was invited into Curtiss's home for lengthy discussions on aircraft construction and aviation in general. The time to make money in airplanes was now, he told Curtiss, before the Wright brothers took to the courts with their patent and tried to monopolize the business. Herring hinted that he himself had patents that antedated the Wrights'.

Eighteen years of litigation over telephone patents had made Alexander Graham Bell extremely sensitive to the patent process, and some of his respect for patents had rubbed off on Curtiss, who was greatly impressed by Herring's references to his many patents and patent applications, particularly those covering devices for automatically stabilizing airplanes in flight. When Curtiss left Hammondsport for Nova Scotia at the end of January 1909, the idea had been firmly planted in his mind that perhaps the best way to break into the airplane business would be for himself and Herring to pool resources and form a joint manufacturing company. Curtiss would contribute his motorcycle manufacturing facility, and Herring would contribute all of his patents, patent applications, and devices for achieving automatic stability. What Glenn Curtiss did not know was that after the Wrights made their first flights in 1903 Herring had made the brothers a somewhat similar business proposition by offering to forgo a patent suit in exchange for a one-third share in profits from the Wrights' invention. Wilbur and Orville had recognized Herring from the start as a braggart and a liar and had ignored this preposterous proposition. Glenn Curtiss was not that astute. Either he was momentarily blinded by Herring's hints of a glittering array of patents or he was not as shrewd a businessman as his thriving motorcycle business seemed to indicate.

Eager as he was to learn more about Herring's attractive proposition, Curtiss, as director of experiments, could not very well withdraw from the Aerial Experiment Association and leave Nova Scotia just as the *Cygnet II* was being readied for its first tests. He was still trying to make up his mind whether to stay with Bell or go with Herring when the monster kite was tried out on the frozen lake at Beinn Bhreagh on February 22. With most of the citizens of nearby Baddeck in attendance, *Cygnet II* slid over the ice on its sled runners for about a hundred feet before the engine died. A second attempt at a takeoff ended with a broken gas line. On the third try, the kite gathered speed but before it showed any signs of lifting, its ten-foot propeller flew off and splintered to pieces on the ice.

The motor was removed from the kite and installed on the *Silver Dart,* and Douglas McCurdy made the first airplane flight in Canada, soaring for half a mile over the frozen surface of the lake. On February 24 he made a flight of four and a half miles, but the right wing struck the ice in landing and a wheel collapsed. The *Silver Dart*'s motor and propeller were transferred to the *Cygnet,* and three more attempts were made to get the big kite into the air. *Cygnet II* refused to leave the ice. The next day Glenn Curtiss left Nova Scotia for New York.

In the meantime, Herring had lured two members of the Aero Club of America into his net—Thomas Scott Baldwin of airship fame and Aero Club president Cortlandt Field Bishop. Baldwin was easily ensnared. Something of a snake-oil salesman himself, he was promoting his balloon and airship business in a current magazine article by recommending ballooning as a surefire cure for rheumatism, mental depression, and diseases of the lungs. Herring had no difficulty in persuading Baldwin to head balloon and airship production in the proposed company. Curtiss would supply the manufacturing plant. Cortlandt Field Bishop would supply the cash.

Bishop was one of the charter members of the Aero Club of America. The club's splendid New York City headquarters were located, rent-free, in one of the buildings he owned. As the grandson of the founder of the Chemical National Bank of New York and the bank's largest stockholder, Bishop had the reputation of a hardheaded businessman. In reality, he was nothing of the sort. An ardent print collector and bibliophile, he spent half of each year abroad, mostly in France, where he had taken up ballooning. He had inherited his wealth and was inclined to frown on titans of finance who had dirtied their hands in the climb to the top. Shy and studious, he was an easy target for the wily Herring. With Baldwin securely in his net, Herring went to work on Bishop. Having intimated to Curtiss by telegram that financial backing for the proposed company was already assured, Herring now hinted to Bishop that Curtiss had agreed to join him as partner. All that stood in the way of incorporation was a little ready cash.

With Bishop undecided and Curtiss still in Nova Scotia, Herring played his trump card. For several years, Carl Dienstbach had been championing Herring in German and American aviation journals. In the early months of 1909, Herring, with Dienstbach's help, circulated a rumor that he had received offers of up to $100,000 from syndicates in France, Germany, and Belgium to construct airplanes in those countries. The rumors had the desired effect. Cortlandt Bishop, fearful that Herring's unique talents might be lured abroad by one of those mysterious European syndicates, agreed to invest in the proposed company.

Thomas Baldwin was so fired with enthusiasm for Herring's project that when Glenn Curtiss returned from Nova Scotia, Baldwin greeted him in the railroad station in New York with the news that Bishop was about to invest $21,000 in the company. Other millionaire members of the Aero Club were expected to follow suit. There was now no question in Curtiss's mind as to which deal was the better, Bell's or Herring's. In less than a week, details were worked out and on March 3 a press conference was held in the meeting rooms of the Aero Club to announce the formation of the first American company to build and sell airplanes. With becoming modesty, Herring gave Bishop credit for the idea, admitting at the same time that he had received flattering offers from abroad for his airplane rights. "If Congress will offer no incentive to inventors to remain in their own country," Cortlandt Bishop told reporters, "the next best thing is to keep them here by private enterprise."

On March 19, 1909, the Herring-Curtiss Company was incorporated in the state of New York with a paper value of $360,000. The president of the company was an old friend of Curtiss, Monroe M. Wheeler, county court judge of the county in which Hammondsport was located. Curtiss was vice-president and general manager, Herring vice-president and director. Each vice-president would receive an annual salary of $5,000. Baldwin and Bishop were on the board of directors. Curtiss turned over to the company all his property, including his factory and real estate holdings and his share in patents applied for by the AEA. Herring agreed to assign to the company the various aeronautical devices invented by him, as well as the patents and patent applications by which the Wright patent could be circumvented. For his $21,000 investment in the Herring-Curtiss Company, Cortlandt Bishop was rewarded with an adulatory article by Carl Dienstbach in the aeronautical magazine *Fly*. The headline THE MAN OF THE HOUR appeared over a photographic portrait of the Aero Club president, who was praised by Dienstbach for performing a service of inestimable value to the cause of aeronautics in America by combining the variegated talents of Curtiss, Baldwin, and Herring in a single company. "It was not an easy task by any means to amalgamate the different activities, personalities, and developments of these three great men into one combination," wrote Dienstbach, "but Mr. Bishop was equal to the emergency, and by securing the cooperation of several of America's leading financiers, an organization was effected which purchased all of these three great Americans' aeronautical interests and cemented them into one great working whole."

Dienstbach's reference to the cooperation of America's leading financiers proved to be an exaggeration. The stampede of Aero Club millionaires wanting to take advantage of the promised profits of the new company failed to materialize. The only other investors were Bishop's brother David, a bon vivant who owned a château in France and seldom visited the United States (he invested $16,000 in the company and committed suicide two years later); International Harvester heir James Deering, who contributed $1,000; and Herring himself, who invested $5,658 of his own money.

When Alexander Graham Bell read newspaper accounts of the March 3 press conference in the Aero Club headquarters, he wired Curtiss: "Please write fully concerning your arrangement with Herring and how it affects your relations with the A.E.A." Curtiss replied that there was no reason why Bell's American Aerodrome Company should not also be established— "unless the members of the Association would care to come into the Herring combination. This would please Mr. Herring, I am sure, and I don't know but that it would be just as well for the Association." But the association members were not interested. It so happened that Bell had left some of his effects at Hammondsport during his last visit. His daughter Mrs. Marian Bell Fairchild had gone to Hammondsport to pick them up at a time when Herring was there. Curtiss introduced her to Herring, who made flattering remarks about her father's tetrahedral kites. Curtiss assured her that Herring was an authority on all kinds of aircraft, "but all the others without exception (the ones I talked to)," Mrs. Fairchild wrote her father, "were uncertain as to whether he is a genius or a fool."

Either way, Glenn Curtiss, in Bell's opinion, was traveling in fast company. Ten days before the Aerial Experiment Association was due to expire, Bell wired Curtiss that there would be a final meeting of the AEA on March 31 and warned his director of experiments that if he failed to show up he would regret it all his life. Curtiss ignored the warning. He was not present on the evening of March 31, 1909, when the three remaining AEA members gathered about the fireplace at Beinn Bhreagh for the last time. The usual formalities were observed to the end. Casey Baldwin "reluctantly moved" that the organization be dissolved on the stroke of midnight. The move was "regretfully seconded" by Douglas McCurdy. There was even a posthumous issue of the *AEA Bulletin* in which chairman Bell wrote: "The A.E.A. is now a thing of the past. It has made its mark upon the history of aviation and *its work will live.*"

There would always be some question about the form in which the work of the AEA would live—certainly not in the form of tetrahedral kites. At no time after Curtiss left Beinn Bhreagh on February 25 did the *Cygnet II* threaten to lift from the ice. The *Silver Dart,* which had been built in the hope it would capture the 1909 *Scientific American* trophy with a flight of twenty-five kilometers, managed only eight miles in its best flight, and Bell withdrew the application for the trophy. It was shipped that summer to the Canadian Army's cavalry field at Petawawa, Ontario, where it crashed on August 4 with both McCurdy and Baldwin on board. The men escaped injury, but their attempt to interest the Canadian government in AEA flying machines was a failure.

Bell's faith in his beloved tetrahedral kites never faltered. In 1912 he built a much smaller *Cygnet III,* consisting of a mere 360 tetrahedral cells, and Douglas McCurdy made a gallant attempt to get the kite into the air with a 70-horsepower motor. After checking the tracks left in the snow by its sled runners, he reported that the *Cygnet III* had traveled through the air for just one foot. What remained of Bell's inventive genius was expended on his hydrodromes—cigar-shaped hydrofoil boats driven by aerial propellers. The largest, 60 feet long, powered by two 350-horsepower engines, was demonstrated before representatives of the U.S. and British navies in 1920, but was declared too fragile for naval action at sea. "This is an old man's toy," a U.S. admiral wrote in his report, "a boat that will not fly." Years later, the huge hydrodromes and the fading red cellular kites that had survived were ensconced in a beautifully landscaped museum at Baddeck, Nova Scotia—a touching memorial to the unfulfilled dreams of the aging inventor of the telephone.

# 36

## *The Races at Reims*

FOR GLENN CURTISS, the greatest advantage in dissociating himself from the unproductive AEA experiments was that he was at last free to build airplanes without the design constraints imposed by other AEA members. He had never approved of the tapered wings of the four AEA machines or the way they bowed together at the tips. "This taper stuff," he once remarked, "is just a lot of expensive construction for nothing." The first airplane designed completely by Curtiss had been ordered by the Aeronautic Society of New York, a splinter group of Aero Club members who had grown impatient with the club's preoccupation with balloons and airships. In January 1909, Glenn Curtiss contracted to build an aircraft for the society for $5,000, but the agreement was kept secret until Curtiss had left the AEA. In March it was announced that the Aeronautic Society's airplane would be the first aeronautical product of the Herring-Curtiss Company.

Because of the yellow-ocher coating on its wings and the orange shellac on its wooden struts and bamboo outriggers, the society's machine was called the *Golden Flier,* although it was sometimes referred to as the *Gold Bug*, as if it were a successor to the AEA *June Bug,* which it was not. Its wings were short and straight and uniform in chord throughout, in sharp contrast to those of the AEA machines. The wingspan of the *Silver Dart* had been more than forty-nine feet; that of the *Golden Flier,* less than twenty-nine feet. As in almost all biplanes of those early days of flying, the elevator was in front of the wings and the propellers behind, but for lateral control, instead of the AEA movable wingtips or the flexible outer sections of the wings of the Wright machines, the *Golden Flier* was equipped with ailerons located between the wings. Its wings were rigid and could not be flexed.

One of the anticipated benefits of the Herring-Curtiss combination was that Herring's secret devices for achieving automatic stability would beget a revolutionary strain of aircraft in which the pilot would be relieved of the arduous task of keeping the airplane in straight and level flight. Curtiss had suspected that Herring's secret devices involved gyroscopic action, but the only evidence of a Herring device on the *Golden Flier* was a triangular fixed fin about two feet high, positioned between and a little above the biplane elevator surfaces of the front rudder, like the "blinkers" used on most Wright Flyers since 1905. This vertical vane may have produced a degree of stability about the vertical axis, but it also reduced maneuverability and was not used on any other aircraft turned out by the Herring-Curtiss factory.

Curtiss first demonstrated the *Golden Flier* at a former racetrack at Morris Park in the Bronx. The Aeronautic Society had leased the track from the Automobile Club of America for a flying field. It had been used solely to exhibit a curious collection of unflyable airplanes on the ground until June 16, when Curtiss made three short straightway flights in the *Golden Flier.* On June 26, in the presence of 5,000 paying spectators, Curtiss made the first circling flight ever witnessed by New Yorkers. It created a sensation, but Curtiss was less interested in crowd-pleasing than in practice. Having won the *Scientific American* trophy in 1908 for his flight of one kilometer, he was eager to win it in 1909 for the first public flight of twenty-five kilometers or more in the United States. The rules for the competition had been changed to allow machines launched from a starting rail to compete, but the Wright brothers had no interest in adding the trophy to the awards they had already accumulated.

To practice for the trophy, Curtiss rented a spacious field near the Mineola fairgrounds in western Long Island in the area known as Hempstead Plains and on July 17, after several days of practice, circled for 52 minutes in the *Golden Flier,* winning the *Scientific American* trophy with a flight of 40 kilometers. After training another pilot to fly the machine, he turned it over to the Aeronautic Society and returned to Hammondsport, where he was building a faster version of the *Golden Flier* in which to represent the Aero Club of America in the world's first international air races, to be held at Reims, France, in August.

A few weeks after the Herring-Curtiss Company was incorporated, Herring told reporters he was thinking of entering the races at Reims himself. No aeronautical authority, however, had ever seen Herring make a flight in a propeller-driven aircraft, and it was not surprising that he subsequently withdrew and left to his partner Glenn Curtiss the privilege of representing America in the races, giving as his excuse that there was still too much work to be done on the machine he was building to replace the Signal Corps machine that had been wrecked—he said—after making a flight of 300 feet on Long Island in October 1908. At that time his Army contract had been extended to June 1, 1909. Three days before the new machine was to be delivered, he notified the Signal Corps that two of his foreign patents would be forfeit if he exhibited his machine publicly prior to June 16, and he was given another thirty-day extension—to July 1. On the last day of June, General James Allen of the Signal Corps penned a peremptory letter to Herring, warning him that if he did not deliver his machine the next day, his $2,000 deposit would be forfeit. Herring responded in the only way possible, by asking the Signal Corps to declare his contract void and his deposit forfeit for reasons of nondelivery.

By then it was apparent to anyone capable of putting two and two together that the airplane Herring had once said he would fly to Washington from New York rather than ship it by rail had existed largely in his head. No one was more aware of this than Glenn Curtiss. Herring had managed to make himself unpopular with the workmen in the Hammondsport factory, where his role seems to have been like the one he played at the Smithsonian in 1895—that of fault-finder and maker of suggestions. Some of his suggestions were tried out and found to be of no value, like the triangular fin on the *Golden Flier*'s front rudder. Others were simply ignored. He had originally agreed to contribute the jigs and patterns from his New York shop to the new company. These were never delivered, perhaps fortunately, for they would have been of no use in the manufacture of anything produced in the Hammondsport plant. (It would be revealed in court many years later that the only detectable income derived from Herring's shop came from the manufacture of toy airplanes.) His patents and the secret devices that were to have revolutionized aviation remained as much of a secret to the board of directors of the Herring-Curtiss Company as they did to the public at large. When Curtiss embarked for France on August 5 with his Reims Racer, he was thoroughly disillusioned with the charlatan into whose hands, in a weak moment, he had surrendered the business he had spent so many years in building up.

The *Grande Semaine d'Aviation de la Champagne*—the world's first international air races, to which the French champagne industry had contributed 200,000 francs in prizes—was held at Reims in the heart of the champagne country from Sunday, August 22, to Sunday, August 29, 1909. The site was a racecourse three miles from Reims, expanded into a fenced-in field two miles long and three-quarters of a mile wide. Red-and-white pylons at the four corners marked an oval flying course of ten kilometers. The four grandstands accommodated 50,000 spectators. Food vendors were in constant circulation, and for those who could afford it there was an open-air buffet where champagne could be consumed to the accompaniment of gypsy fiddlers. The setting was a sharp contrast to the small provincial racetrack with its single dilapidated grandstand near Le Mans to which Frenchmen had flocked in such numbers to see Wilbur Wright fly only a year before.

Then there had been one pilot and one airplane. Now there were thirty-eight machines and as many pilots, although only twenty-two managed to get into the air. On opening day, the thousands jamming the grandstands were treated to the sight of seven airplanes in the air at once. The men and women in the buffet were so overcome by the spectacle that they stood on tables and chairs and shouted and screamed for joy.

Nominally it was an international meet, but the aviators were all French with the exception of Glenn Curtiss and the Englishman George Cockburn. Cockburn collected no prizes but distinguished himself by winning an unscheduled race with a passing railroad train. Several French-built Wright airplanes were flown in the meet, two by pilots Wilbur had trained at Pau —Count de Lambert and Paul Tissandier. De Lambert took one of the minor prizes, Tissandier took two. Another Wright machine was flown by Eugène Lefebvre, who won the smallest prize of all for placing fourth in the thirty-kilometer speed race but won the plaudits of the crowd for his steep banks and sharp turns. One Parisian paper speculated that the reason the Wright machines took so few prizes was that Wilbur was not there to fly them. When Wilbur, back in Dayton, was asked about the poor showing of the Wright airplanes at Reims, he replied that he had not expected his machines to break any records—they were built for endurance, not for racing. It was not a Wright Flyer that won the 50,000-franc Grand Prix for endurance, however, but a Voisin-type biplane manufactured and flown by Henri Farman. Farman had had a falling out with the Voisin brothers and had set up shop with his own brother Maurice. In the first airplane turned out by the Farman factory, he set a world's endurance record of 3 hours 5 minutes, landing in a glare of searchlights long after twilight on Friday, August 27.

The week-long meet reached its climax on Saturday, August 28, with the race for the Gordon Bennett trophy. The trophy and a cash award of 25,000 francs had been donated by James Gordon Bennett, owner of the New York and Paris *Heralds,* for the fastest two laps of the ten-kilometer course. Only half the value of the Grand Prix, the Bennett trophy was nevertheless the most coveted prize of the meet. Curtiss's trim little Reims Racer with its water-cooled 50-horsepower V-8 motor had been built expressly to compete in the speed races. Only one machine at a time was in the air during a race. Curtiss was first off, on Saturday morning. By diving at each corner of the course and making his turns at full power, he completed the twenty-kilometer course in 15 minutes 50.6 seconds at an average speed of 47.10 miles per hour. Next off was the Englishman Cockburn. He gave up after one lap. Then Lefebvre took over. It took him almost 21 minutes to maneuver his French-built Wright about the course. After lunch, Hubert Latham bettered Lefebvre's time by three minutes but failed to overtake Curtiss.

French hopes for the trophy now centered on Louis Blériot and his twelfth aircraft, a more highly powered monoplane than the one in which he had flown the Channel. Excitement among the French spectators in the grandstand was intense while Blériot was in the air. He landed to a great burst of applause. His countrymen had no doubt that he had won. Blériot joyfully acknowledged the applause while the judges were completing their computations. A few minutes later the Stars and Stripes was hoisted to the top of the flagpole and the band blared out "The Star-Spangled Banner." Blériot had lost the race to Curtiss by 5.6 seconds.

Although no new records were set on the last Sunday of the race, the crowd was estimated at 200,000, four times as many spectators as could be accommodated in the grandstands. Another 100,000 witnessed the final flights from the hills outside the fenced-in airfield. So many gallons of champagne had been consumed in toasting the aviators that it was rumored the champagne industry had more than doubled its investment in the races. In the remaining months of 1909, several other meets were held throughout Europe, including one in September at Brescia, Italy, at which Glenn Curtiss garnered more honors and won more cash prizes before returning to the United States.

One of the most remarkable features of the eight days of intensive flying at Reims was that there had not been a single serious injury, although there had been a number of accidents. French pilots crashed into haystacks with alarming frequency. Lefebvre in his French Wright skimmed the ground so closely at one time that spectators and press photographers had been obliged to flatten out on the ground. Blériot had two of his customary close calls. On the fifth day of the races, he made too low a turn and to avoid hitting a group of mounted soldiers in the middle of the racetrack, altered his course and ran into a fence instead. On the final day of the races, while trying to better his speed record of Saturday, he stalled on a curve, hit the ground, and tumbled out of his monoplane just as the gas tank exploded. With his usual luck, he escaped with nothing worse than slight burns on his hands.

All week, however, the Grim Reaper had been lurking behind the grandstands, cartoon fashion, sharpening his scythe. On September 7, only nine days after the bands stopped playing at Reims, Eugène Lefebvre was killed at Juvisy near Paris when the French Wright machine he was testing dove into the ground from a height of twenty feet. Captain Ferdinand Ferber, erstwhile friend of the Wright brothers, had competed at Reims but won no prizes. On September 23 he was taxiing at a fast clip after landing at a field near Boulogne when his Voisin biplane hit a ditch and overturned. Ferber was crushed beneath the engine.

The Grim Reaper who had bided his time behind the grandstands at Reims would reap a richer harvest in 1910.

# 37

# *The Last Public Flights*

GERMANY HAD NOT been represented in the air races at Reims. The country's preoccupation with dirigibles had all but precluded experimenting with flying machines. When Count Zeppelin's fourth dirigible had crashed and exploded during a sudden squall on August 5, 1908, enough money had been donated by the German people within twenty-four hours to pay for the construction of a still larger zeppelin. Three days later, Wilbur amazed all Europe with his first flight in France, and a few German army officers began to wonder if flying machines might not prove more practical for use in war than dirigibles. One of these officers, Captain Alfred Hildebrandt, had gone to Pau early in 1909 and on behalf of the Berlin newspaper *Lokal-Anzeiger* offered the Wrights a substantial fee if they would make demonstration flights in Germany to which the public could be invited as guests of the paper. The brothers accepted. When they were in Rome that April, they renewed their friendship with another German officer, Captain Richard von Kehler, whom they had met in Berlin during their first trip to Europe. Von Kehler proposed the formation of a company to manufacture Wright Flyers in Germany. The outcome was the Flugmaschine Wright Gesellschaft, established May 13, 1909, under an arrangement whereby the Wrights received 200,000 marks in cash, a block of stock in the company, and 10 percent royalty on all machines marketed in Germany, Luxembourg, Turkey, Sweden, Norway, and Denmark.

Since Wilbur had done all the flying in France, it was decided that Orville should make the demonstration flights in Germany for the *Lokal-Anzeiger*. He left Dayton on August 8, 1909, accompanied by Katharine, on leave for the third and last time from her job at Steele High School (she never did return to teaching). On August 19 they arrived in Berlin, where Hart Berg had reserved for them the Hotel Esplanade's finest suite—a sitting room with brocaded walls, two bedrooms, two baths, and a balcony over-flowing with flowers and greenery.

While they were in Berlin, the German emperor, Kaiser Wilhelm, di-verted attention from the air races at Reims by ordering Count Zeppelin to fly his newest dirigible to the German capital from its floating hangar on Lake Constance on the Swiss border, 400 miles away. The dirigible came down with a broken propeller less than 100 miles from Berlin on Saturday, August 28, but the damage was repaired and a little after noon on Sunday, the last day of the Reims meet, the big silver ship sailed majestically over the city to the ringing of every church bell in the capital. A crowd of 100,000 was waiting to welcome the new zeppelin at the Tegel parade ground on the outskirts of the city. Orville and Katharine were on the platform with the royal family as the great ship settled earthward and dipped its nose in a salute to the emperor. The climax of the ceremony occurred when Count Zeppelin descended from the control car and after paying his respects to the emperor was introduced by that august personage to the American aeronaut Orville Wright.

The following week Orville showed Berliners what an airplane could do that a zeppelin could not. On Tuesday, he flew for 52 minutes before a gathering of military officials at the Tempelhof parade ground, ending the flight only when his fuel was exhausted. On Saturday, the public demonstra-tions sponsored by the *Lokal-Anzeiger* began. After a nineteen-minute flight Orville alighted to a welcome that rivaled that of Wilbur at the end of his first flight at Les Hunaudières. Thousands of hands stretched out to touch this conqueror of the skies, as if merely touching his sleeve meant sharing in the glory of the conquest.

During the week of September 6–11, crowds as large as 200,000 came to Tempelhof to see Orville fly. The next week he took three days off and traveled to Frankfurt for a ride in Count Zeppelin's new dirigible. In the company of Captain Hildebrandt and three members of the royal family, he sailed the fifty-odd miles from Frankfurt to Mannheim, where the press of the crowd at the landing field was so great that he became separated from Hildebrandt, who was acting as his interpreter. Unable to remember the name of the hotel at which the luncheon was being given for the zeppelin party, he wandered about Mannheim completely lost until he was eventually recognized and carried off by a member of the reception committee who had been driving about the streets in a frantic search for the luncheon's missing guest of honor. On Friday, September 17, he made a 55-minute flight at Tempelhof that was witnessed by the empress, two princes, one princess, and Mr. and Mrs. Charles Flint, who were touring Europe by automobile. The crush around Orville and his sister and the two Flints was so great that

Orville was compelled to separate himself from the others to save them from the merciless pressing of the crowd.

On Saturday, September 18, Orville broke his own record for two-man flight by flying with a passenger for 1 hour 35 minutes. That afternoon he tried to break the world endurance record set by Henri Farman at Reims, but he was thwarted by a broken water pump and forced to land after 1 hour 45 minutes. That was the longest flight Orville was ever to make. From Tempelhof he went to the Bornstedt drill ground at Potsdam, twenty miles south of Berlin, to train a pilot for the German Wright company. The student pilot was Captain Paul Engelhard, a retired German naval officer. His training began on September 29 and ended with three solo flights on October 13. Orville's contract with the *Lokal-Anzeiger* for public flights had been fulfilled at Tempelhof, but the flights he made at Potsdam were far from private and at times became a form of entertainment for the royal family and their guests. Crown Prince Friedrich Wilhelm, then in his twenties, was fervently interested in flying. On October 2 he donned an overcoat to avoid being spattered with oil from the engine and was given a fifteen-minute flight. He kept urging Orville to go higher, but Orville preferred not to run the risk of reprisals from his passenger's warlike father and rose no higher than a hundred feet. Nevertheless, the prince was so pleased that when he alighted he presented Orville with the stickpin he was wearing. The stickpin was surmounted by a *W* set in diamonds. The *W* was surrounded by a crown set in rubies and stood for Wilhelm, by which name the prince was expected to succeed his father, the Kaiser, but he assumed, tacitly, that it could stand just as well for Wright.

That same day, Orville set an unofficial world altitude record by reaching 500 meters, or about 1,600 feet, during a twenty-minute flight. The previous record had been set by Hubert Latham, who reached 155 meters at Reims. Orville's record was an estimate only, but the Flyer was high enough to have been observed from a steamer on a lake three miles from the flying field at Potsdam. The excursionists on the steamer thought they were watching a box kite and were amazed at the ease with which it was being manipulated from the ground.

While Orville was making his first public flights in Europe at Berlin and Potsdam, Wilbur had been making his first public flights in the United States at New York City. The occasion was the Hudson-Fulton Celebration commemorating the 300th anniversary of Henry Hudson's ascent of the Hudson River in his ship the *Half Moon* and the 102nd anniversary of Robert Fulton's trip up the same river in the *Clermont,* the first commercially successful steamship built in the United States. Reproductions of the *Half Moon* and the *Clermont* were riding at anchor in the river when the celebration began on September 25, 1909. New York Harbor was clogged with watercraft of all kinds from small sailboats to battleships from as far away as France, Italy, Germany, Great Britain, the Netherlands, Mexico, and Argentina. To dramatize the radical changes in locomotion that had taken place in the two hundred years from Hudson's day to Fulton's and in the hundred years from Fulton's time to the present, the Hudson-Fulton Commission had established an Aeronautics Committee. The committee offered Wilbur $15,000 for a flight either ten miles long or one hour in duration, plus whatever other flights he might see fit to make during the first two weeks of the celebration. The Aeronautical Committee also offered Glenn Curtiss a contract. He was to be paid $5,000 for a twenty-mile flight over the Hudson from Governors Island in Upper New York Bay to Grant's Tomb on Riverside Drive and return or, if that was not feasible, for at least two round-trip flights across the Hudson between Grant's Tomb and the New Jersey shore.

Two hangars, one for Wilbur, one for Curtiss, were erected on the sand flats at Governors Island, which had recently been enlarged as a drill ground for the U.S. First Army. There was ferry service from Manhattan, but the fact that passes were required to get off the ferry at the island meant that Wilbur and Charlie Taylor could work without interruption after they had uncrated their Flyer on September 20. One enterprising admirer of the Wright brothers did manage to get into the hangar while the Flyer was being assembled, however. This was Grover Loening, Columbia University's first student of aeronautics, whose mother had been able to obtain a pass for her son and a letter of introduction to Wilbur from August Belmont, the New York financier. Once past the guard at the ferry dock, Loening found his way to the Flyer's shed and handed Belmont's letter to his hero in person. Wilbur merely glanced at the letter and went on working, leaving Loening standing meekly at one side of the hangar. When the young man made no move to leave, Wilbur threw him a rag and told him to clean up the oil under the engine. The rag sopped up as much oil as it could hold, after which Loening used his handkerchief. Years later, he looked back on this incident as the first step in his climb to success as an aeronautical engineer.

The ship bringing Curtiss and his Reims Racer back from Europe docked in New York on September 21. The next morning, accompanied by reporters, Curtiss took the ferry to Governors Island and on the way to his own hangar stopped to say hello to Wilbur. Grover Loening, who haunted Governors Island most of the time Wilbur was there, was aware that there was some kind of breach between Wilbur and Curtiss, but in the presence of reporters that morning all was cordiality. Wilbur returned Curtiss's greeting but excused himself from shaking hands on the grounds that his own hands were dirty and greasy. After a five-minute exchange of pleasantries, mostly about the races at Reims, Curtiss left. In the meantime, Guglielmo

Marconi, the inventor of the wireless, had come in at the back of the hangar and insisted on shaking Wilbur's hand, greasy or not.

Among the craft crowded into New York Harbor were about forty warships. It was arranged that whenever Wilbur or Curtiss was about to make a flight, a wireless message would be sent from Marconi's transmitter on Governors Island to the warships with receiving sets. Those ships would run up flags as a signal to the other ships that a flight was about to commence. At the same time, the Signal Corps would fly flags on Governors Island that would be visible to observers in three Manhattan skyscrapers. Flags would then be flown from the skyscrapers to alert New Yorkers to the imminence of a flight.

The day after his meeting with Wilbur, Glenn Curtiss left New York for Hammondsport, where he was accorded a reception that rivaled the Wrights' two-day homecoming festivities in Dayton. Since his contract with the Hudson-Fulton Commission ran for the first week of the celebration only, the Aeronautical Committee was not at all pleased that Curtiss did not return from Hammondsport until Tuesday, September 28, the day on which the little *Half Moon* and the tiny *Clermont* and their retinue of tugboats and small craft sailed up the Hudson to Yonkers, the first stop on their slow trip upriver to Albany and Troy.

Curtiss spent Tuesday night on Governors Island and was up at 6 A.M. on Wednesday, long before Wilbur, who was staying at the Park Hotel in Manhattan, had gotten off the ferry. The newspapers were playing up the aerial features of the celebration as a contest between two world-famous aviators, but it was a contest in which Glenn Curtiss was at a disadvantage. While he was in France and Italy winning laurels for the Herring-Curtiss Company, Augustus Herring had accepted $5,000 from Wanamaker's New York and Philadelphia department stores to put the Reims Racer on exhibit as soon as it was returned from Europe, and Curtiss was reduced to flying from Governors Island with an untried machine powered by a 24-horse-power motor. The soft sandy surface of the Army drill ground made taking off with a wheeled undercarriage difficult, and the flight Curtiss made on Wednesday at 7 A.M., witnessed only by an Army officer and a friend, was a short one. It was the only flight he made that day.

Two hours later Wilbur took off with the aid of a starting rail only (no weight-dropping derrick was used on Governors Island) and made a seven-minute circuit of the island. A red canoe with a waterproofed canvas covering was slung between the skids of the Flyer to serve as a flotation device in case he came down in the water. Satisfied that the canoe did not adversely affect the handling characteristics of the Flyer, Wilbur announced shortly before 10 A.M. that he would make his first public flight. Marconi's wireless signal was sent to the ships in the harbor. The Signal Corps flags were run up. The Brooklyn shore was soon lined with thousands of spectators. Thousands more crowded into Battery Park at the bottom of Manhattan.

Before taking off, Wilbur said merely that he would make another short flight over the ships in the harbor, but when the white-and-silver Flyer with the red canoe between its skids, instead of continuing north over the shipping, turned left and headed for the Statue of Liberty on Bedloe's Island, there was no longer any doubt as to his objective. The Flyer climbed gradually; then as ferryboat whistles and deeper blasts from the larger ships rent the air, Wilbur circled the Statue of Liberty at waist level and headed back to Governors Island. It so happened that the *Lusitania* was steaming down the harbor at that moment, bound for Europe, its decks lined with hundreds of passengers hysterically waving handkerchiefs, scarves, and hats. A thundering blast from the liner's foghorn greeted the Flyer as Wilbur flew past. He landed a few seconds later to the cheers of the soldiers on Governors Island.

Wilbur's third flight of the day, at 5:30 that afternoon, was cut short after twelve minutes by high winds, the same winds that turned the only other aeronautical event of the day into a fiasco. The New York *World* had offered a prize of $10,000 for the first flight up the Hudson from New York to Albany. Only an airship could be expected to accomplish such a feat in 1909. Thomas Baldwin hoped to win the prize with his new dirigible-balloon, which was faster than the one he sold to the Signal Corps in 1908. His only competitor was George Tomlinson, to whom Baldwin had sold an airship similar to his own. They took off shortly before noon from the park below Grant's Tomb and headed upriver at about 20 miles an hour, but the winds above the water were bothersome. Baldwin came down in the river with a jammed steering gear when he had gone less than four miles and was towed ashore by sailors in cutters from U.S. warships anchored in the vicinity. Tomlinson came down with oil and gas leaks on a farm near White Plains.

Hundreds of New Yorkers lined Riverside Drive on Thursday and Friday, hoping to have ringside seats when Curtiss made his flight to Grant's Tomb. They waited in vain. The winds continued strong over the weekend. Curtiss's contract expired Saturday, but he spent Sunday on Governors Island, waiting for the wind to die down. Just before dusk he made an attempt to redeem himself with a flight but returned after leaving the end of the island and encountering turbulence over the water. On Monday, his machine was dismantled and shipped to St. Louis, where Herring, acting as his agent, had arranged for him to make flights at the city's centenary celebration, beginning October 6.

It was up to Wilbur to pull the Hudson-Fulton Celebration out of its four-day slump. The wind was an acceptable 10 miles an hour on Monday morning. When he got off the ferry at Governors Island, Wilbur announced that he would make the flight that Curtiss had contracted to make—the twenty-mile round trip up the Hudson to Grant's Tomb and back. The wireless signal was sent. The Signal Corps flags were flown. Within a few minutes of the announcement, New Yorkers were scurrying in droves to the riverfront. On Governors Island, three hundred soldiers, sailors, reporters, and photographers looked on from behind ropes as the Flyer was rolled out and placed on the starting rail. At 9:53 Wilbur took off, a life jacket lashed to the lower wing at his feet, two American flags fluttering from the front rudder. As the Flyer soared up the harbor toward the river mouth, sailors came tumbling up from the bowels of the warships in the harbor and danced like dolls on the decks. Bells clanged and whistles shrieked on passing tugs and ferries, foghorns blared from the larger vessels, every craft on the water contributing to the din as Wilbur entered the air above the river. The hot gases rising from the shipping made the Flyer difficult to control, but it was clearly visible against the gray urban overcast as the crowds continued to pour from the alleys and side streets to catch a fleeting glimpse of the wide white wings and the red canoe between the silver skids.

The British cruiser *Argyle* was anchored in the river just north of Grant's Tomb. At 10:13 A.M. Wilbur made a graceful 180-degree turn about the cruiser and headed downriver with the wind behind him. It had taken 20 1/2 minutes to fly the ten miles to Grant's Tomb against the wind. With the wind at his back, he made the return trip in 13 minutes, landing 33 minutes 33 seconds after taking off. The flight had been witnessed by an estimated one million New Yorkers, almost none of whom had ever seen an airplane in the air before. It was considered an even more daring feat than Blériot's crossing of the English Channel because of the updrafts created by the vessels congregated in the harbor and the river and the unpredictable sidedrafts sweeping out from the narrow streets between the tall buildings of Manhattan.

The trip up the Hudson was planned as a curtain raiser to an even more sensational event that afternoon—a flight up and down the East River ending with a side trip to the Jersey shore—but a few minutes after four, while Charlie Taylor and Wilbur were turning over the propellers, a cylinder head broke through the motor casing with a muffled bang, ripping a two-foot gash in the upper wing and shooting twenty feet into the air. It fell within a few feet of Wilbur. The accident ended flying at the Hudson-Fulton Celebration. His Hudson River flight, Wilbur told a reporter, was the last public flight either he or Orville would make. Hereafter they would devote all their efforts to the commercial exploitation of their machines and only fly to test the value of changes made in construction. This was stretching things a little, since Orville's flights at Potsdam were still being reported in the papers, but although those flights were made before the Kaiser and his family, the German military, and a few notables, they were not, strictly speaking, open to the public.

With Orville still in Europe, it was up to Wilbur to train two officers in the operation of the U.S. Army Flyer. He went directly from New York to College Park, Maryland, eight miles from Washington by rail, where a field near the state agricultural college had been selected as a more suitable site for training Army pilots than Fort Myer. Lieutenant Benjamin Foulois had taken it for granted that he and Lieutenant Frank Lahm would be the two student pilots. To his dismay, Foulois was assigned to represent the United States at a congress of aeronautics held in France from September 8 to October 17, and Lieutenant Frederick Humphreys of the Corps of Engineers was sent to College Park in his place. Lieutenant Foulois had his heart set on learning to fly, however. He left the aeronautical congress before it was over and arrived in College Park in time to be given three lessons by Wilbur.

Training ended on November 2. All the flights were conducted without accident until, a few days after Wilbur left College Park, Lieutenant Lahm grazed a wing in landing. After being repaired, the Flyer was shipped to Fort Sam Houston in Texas. Lieutenant Humphreys's flying career was cut short when the Chief of Engineers objected to one of his men "fooling around with the Signal Corps' 'flying circus' " and ordered Humphreys back to the Corps of Engineers. Lieutenant Lahm was also ordered back to the branch of the service from which he had come—the cavalry—after it had been reported that he had "taken a woman into the air." In true bureaucratic fashion Lieutenant Foulois, who had never soloed, was sent to Fort Sam Houston to fly the Army's $30,000 airplane.

Foulois completed his pilot training by correspondence with the Wright brothers. Only $150 was allotted by the Army for the Flyer's upkeep, and he was required to dip into his own pocket to keep the machine in the air. In 1911, when the Signal Corps was given enough money to purchase two new Wright airplanes, the outmoded 1909 machine was restored and placed on display in the Smithsonian Institution in Washington, D.C., where, after almost nine decades, the oil-stained old Army Flyer is still one of the national museum's most prized possessions.

# 38

## The Patent Wars Begin

IN 1908, when the Wright brothers were making their first flights in public and it was no longer possible to deny that the age of the flying machine had dawned at last, elation over the long-delayed dawning was tempered in aeronautical circles by the fear that the future development of aviation would be seriously impeded if Wilbur and Orville should seek to wring a profit from their basic patent by taking infringers to court. A few farsighted members of the Aero Club of America sought to forestall possible litigation by urging the club's wealthier members to subscribe to a $100,000 fund with which to purchase U.S. rights to the brothers' patent. "If the subscription were really *spontaneous* and of sufficient size to justify it," Wilbur wrote Orville from Le Mans in September 1908, "I would be willing to make our American patents free." But the movement was far from spontaneous. At the end of six months all that had been collected was $11,000, including $500 contributed by Octave Chanute, who was well off but no millionaire, and it became obvious that the Wrights would have to resort to litigation if the control system covered by their patent were to yield them a profit.

Aero Club of America president Cortlandt Field Bishop met Wilbur, Orville, and Katharine in France in April 1909, when they were on their way home after Wilbur's flights in Rome. As the largest investor in the recently formed Herring-Curtiss Company, Bishop was disturbed to learn from the Wrights that they were contemplating a suit against Glenn Curtiss and the Herring-Curtiss Company. When the new company was formed in March it had been announced that its first product would be the $5,000 *Golden Flier* ordered by the Aeronautic Society of New York. The Wright brothers convinced Bishop that the machine's midwing ailerons violated the wing-warping claim of their basic patent. Furthermore, they said, whatever success Curtiss may have had in designing and flying airplanes was due to information obtained directly from the brothers. They further alarmed the Aero Club president by telling him of Augustus Herring's visit to their camp in 1902, during which he had familiarized himself with the Wright control system before it was patented. This meeting with the Wright brothers made Bishop very uneasy. "They told me certain things which, if true, put matters in a very bad light, both on moral and legal grounds," he wrote Herring-Curtiss Company president Monroe Wheeler, "and if the facts are as they state them I shall regret having anything to do with the aeroplane part of the business."

When they returned from Europe, Wilbur and Orville were busy preparing the Army Flyer for its trials at Fort Myer. It was not until the trials were over that a bill of complaint was filed on behalf of the Wright brothers, seeking to enjoin Curtiss and the Herring-Curtiss Company from selling or using flying machines for exhibition purposes. Curtiss was in France at Reims on August 18, 1909, when the papers were served on the Herring-Curtiss Company in Hammondsport. Such a flurry of publicity attended the announcement of the suit that company president Monroe Wheeler issued a statement, assuring the press that many of the alleged infringements cited in the Wrights' bill of complaint would be found to have been covered by patents taken out by Augustus Herring before the Wright brothers' basic patent had been granted in 1906. "While the plaintiffs in the case are without doubt acting in good faith in their allegations," his statement continued, "the records of the patent office, which will be produced by the defense, will easily and satisfactorily adjust what at first was regarded by the public as a stupendous litigation."

News of the action against Curtiss reached Europe a few days before the Reims races began on August 22 and created a greater furor there than in the United States. Between 1904 and 1909 the Wrights' patent attorney, Harry Toulmin, had seen to it that their basic patent was duplicated in every European country with a potential for aeronautical development, not only in France, Italy, and England, where flights were becoming more frequent, but also in Austria, Hungary, Belgium, Germany, Russia, and Spain. To the aviators and airplane manufacturers gathered at Reims the suit appeared to be less an attack on Glenn Curtiss than the opening gun in a struggle to establish an international monopoly on the manufacture and operation of all aircraft using the Wright brothers' patented system of control. Among the Americans at Reims for the races, feelings against the Wrights ran high for their having chosen this particular moment to sue Glenn Curtiss, who was the sole representative of the United States at a meet the brothers had not seen fit to enter themselves. This feeling was intensified when Curtiss won the coveted Gordon Bennett trophy. The trophy, incidentally, was topped by a large reproduction of a Wright Flyer.

The Wrights had convinced Cortlandt Bishop that the Herring-Curtiss Company wouldn't have the ghost of a chance in court, but after talking it over with Curtiss at Reims, he changed his mind and confidently told reporters that the midwing ailerons on the *Golden Flier* and the Reims Racer did not after all constitute an infringement of the wingwarping claim of the Wright patent. But Bishop's confidence in another matter was severely shaken. The Reims races provided him with the first opportunity he had had since coming abroad in April to compare notes with Curtiss. The two men made an ominous discovery. Each had assumed that the other had investigated Herring's patents and purported inventions and could vouch for their validity. Unbelievable as it seems, no one involved in the formation of the Herring-Curtiss Company—not even Monroe Wheeler, to whom the actual incorporation of the company had been entrusted because of his reputation as an experienced lawyer and county judge—had thought to approach the Patent Office to confirm the existence of Herring's patents, and in the five months since the company's incorporation the only device for maintaining automatic stability produced by Herring had been the ineffective triangular fin on the front horizontal rudder of the Aeronautic Society's *Golden Flier.*

As president of the Aero Club of America, Cortlandt Field Bishop was determined to remain neutral in the coming conflict between Curtiss and the Wrights. After he and his wife had returned from abroad, they met Wilbur in New York. Wilbur had just finished training the Army pilots at College Park, and all three—Bishop, his wife, and Wilbur—were on hand to greet Orville and Katharine when the ship bearing them home from Europe docked in New York on November 4.

Three days later there was a family reunion in Dayton, where Lorin Wright had been keeping the books for his two younger brothers. Financially, Wilbur and Orville were in good shape. In September, Orville had sent Lorin a draft for $40,000 from Germany, representing their first profits from the business there. Earlier in the year a contract had been signed with Short Brothers in England to construct Wright Flyers, and a similar arrangement was expected to be concluded in Italy. As yet, no company to manufacture Wright airplanes existed in the United States, but a move in that direction had been taken during the Hudson-Fulton Celebration when twenty-four-year-old Clinton R. Peterkin called on Wilbur at his Manhattan hotel. Peterkin's first job at the age of fifteen had been with J. P. Morgan and Company as office boy, the approved first step on the ladder to fame and riches in the days when the heroes of the stories of Horatio Alger, Jr., were accepted as role models by the upwardly mobile. Peterkin proposed to

Wilbur that he be allowed to round up backing for an American Wright Company. Wilbur condescendingly gave the young man permission to go ahead, but stipulated that only backers with established financial reputations would be considered.

Peterkin began at the top. He not only interested J. P. Morgan himself in the venture but received Morgan's word that Judge Elbert Gary of the U.S. Steel Corporation would be glad to purchase stock. With these two men lined up, Peterkin had no trouble enlisting additional backers by telephone. The Wright Company, with offices on Fifth Avenue in New York and manufacturing plant in Dayton, was incorporated on November 22, 1909, with a capital stock of $1 million and a paid-in value of $200,000. The Wright brothers were to receive $100,000 in cash, one-third of the stock, and 10 percent royalty on each machine sold. Some of the most prominent capitalists of the day were among the stockholders, men whose fame or notoriety, or both, has not yet entirely faded: Cornelius Vanderbilt, August Belmont, Robert Collier, Howard Gould. Missing from the list of stockholders were the names of Morgan and Gary. Morgan had discreetly withdrawn when he learned that the other stockholders feared they would be overshadowed if that mighty mogul of twentieth-century finance sat on the board of directors.

The presidency of the company went to Wilbur. Orville was a vice-president. Space in a Dayton factory was rented until the company could construct a more modern factory of its own. Although both brothers were to supervise the Dayton plant, they hoped that factory manager Frank Russell, a cousin of one of the stockholders, would take charge of details so that they could devote most of their time to experimental work. This turned out to be as vain a hope as their expectation two years before that Flint and Company would relieve them of the task of selling their Flyer abroad. Another mixed blessing was that the costs of all infringement suits instituted in the United States would be borne by the company. While the Wrights could now afford to pursue any and all infringers without direct cost to themselves, they soon discovered that they would have to devote more and more of their time to the pursuit.

The simultaneous use of vertical rudder and wingwarping to maintain equilibrium was as yet only a subsidiary issue in the patent dispute. In 1909 the principal issue at stake was: Did ailerons constitute an infringement of the Wrights' wingwarping claim? Thomas Hill, an attorney who had made a special study of aeronautical patents, answered the question in the journal *Aeronautics* that October, by stating that there was nothing in the Wright patent to show that the brothers had at any time meant their control system to apply to supplementary surfaces, such as Curtiss's midwing ailerons, when used in conjunction with rigid wings rather than with wings with flexible outer sections as on the Wright Flyer. The use of ailerons for lateral control, Hill wrote, was "indisputably a public right."

But the issue was one to be settled in court, not in the pages of a journal, and *Wright Company* v. *Herring-Curtiss Company and Glenn H. Curtiss*— or *Wright* v. *Curtiss,* as it was more commonly called—was tried in the U.S. Circuit Court in Buffalo, New York, on December 14 and 15, 1909. The Wrights were represented by patent attorney Harry Toulmin, who could not have imagined when Wilbur called upon him that January day in 1904 in Springfield, Ohio, that half a dozen years later he would be representing the brothers in the nation's first, precedent-setting aeronautical case. The Curtiss faction was represented by Emerson Newell, who on the first day of the trial tried to minimize Wilbur and Orville's abilities as inventors by intimating to Judge John R. Hazel that their fame was based on their skill as "airplane chauffeurs."

Judge Hazel had been awarded a federal judgeship in 1900 for his part in William McKinley's presidential campaign of that year. The appointment had been condemned as overtly political, but politics had nothing to do with the suit against Curtiss nine years later. The judge in *Wright* v. *Curtiss* would be adjudicating a technical issue on the basis of testimony from witnesses on both sides who professed to be experts in a field in which the court could be expected to have little or no previous knowledge. Although there were no clear-cut precedents to assist Judge Hazel in making up his mind, one of the first cases to come before him in 1900 had concerned the controversial Selden automobile patent. In 1879, George Selden had applied for a patent on a so-called road engine and through clever utilization of the patenting process had kept his application pending until 1895, when the first crude automobiles had begun to appear. Without ever having constructed a motorcar himself, Selden traded his patent rights for royalties to a company that undertook to sue automobile manufacturers who infringed his patent. In one such suit in 1900, Judge Hazel upheld the validity of the patent, and royalties began to pour into the coffers of the Selden interests. Henry Ford refused to pay tribute to Selden and was sued. In September 1909, three months before *Wright* v. *Curtiss* came to trial, Hazel's original decision was upheld in the U.S. District Court of Southern New York. Although Ford appealed, and although there was little similarity between the Selden and Wright patents, it would have been strange if Judge Hazel, before coming to grips with *Wright* v. *Curtiss,* had not reviewed his decision in the Selden case. That decision had been based on a broad and liberal interpretation of the Selden patent of 1895. It should not have come as too much of a surprise, therefore, that he applied the same broad, liberal interpretation to the Wright brothers' aeronautical patent of 1906.

In his opinion, handed down January 3, 1910, Hazel declared that ailerons were the equivalent of wingwarping. Dissimilarities in structure had no bearing on the case, since both mechanisms achieved an identical result. Accordingly, he granted the plaintiffs a temporary injunction preventing the Herring-Curtiss Company and Glenn Curtiss from manufacturing aircraft or making exhibition flights for profit. The victory was a short one. Curtiss appealed and was allowed to continue flying after posting a $10,000 bond. On June 14, less than six months later, the bond was returned and Judge Hazel's injunction was vacated by the U.S. Circuit Court of Appeals on the grounds that infringement had not been clearly enough established to justify the granting of an injunction.

*Wright* v. *Curtiss* was far from over. As the litigation dragged on, the reservoir of good feeling about the Wright brothers engendered by national pride in their flights of 1908 and 1909 began slowly to drain away. The public, or that part of it concerned with aeronautics, became divided into two camps. To the anti-Wright faction, it was unthinkable that Wilbur and Orville should be allowed to collect royalties from aviators and manufacturers until their patent expired in 1923 just because they had been the first men in the world to maintain equilibrium in the air by warping the wings of their Flyer. It did not help the brothers' cause that Henry Ford's challenge of the Selden automobile patent was successful. In January 1911, Judge Hazel's ruling in the Selden case was reversed by the U.S. Circuit Court of Appeals, freeing automobile manufacturers from the necessity of paying royalties to the unproductive Selden. The court went so far as to state that public interest would have been better served if the patent had never been granted. While there was little in common between the Selden case and *Wright* v. *Curtiss* (Selden had not really invented the automobile, whereas the Wrights had spent four years and risked their lives inventing the airplane), there was a feeling abroad that in both instances the motivation had been greed. In the eyes of Curtiss's supporters, Wilbur and Orville had lost their standing as inventors by becoming businessmen in a Wall Street–financed company that was using the Wright patent as a noose to strangle the development of aviation and monopolize the industry.

The Wrights were never without loyal supporters. In 1912 Orville wrote a brief introduction to the book *Practical Aeronautics* by Charles B. Hayward, praising the author's chapter on the patent litigation as the best and clearest presentation of the subject to date. Hayward likened the invention of the airplane to the invention of the telephone. "A situation analogous to that now presented in the field of aviation would have arisen," he wrote, "had the public claimed the right to help itself to Bell's telephone thirty years ago." He considered the Wright patent every bit as basic as Bell's, and since the Wrights had given permission for employment of their patented system without charge in experimental work and were only attempting to stop the manufacturing of aircraft for sale and exhibition purposes without payment of royalty, upholding their patent rights did not constitute a restrictive monopoly. It had always been possible to fly without using the Wrights' three-axis system of control, Hayward pointed out. Henri Farman hadn't used their system when he won the Deutsch-Archdeacon prize in January 1908 by flying a one-kilometer circle in a biplane without any means of lateral control. Nor had the Wrights themselves used such a system successfully until 1902, when their gliding experiments had progressed to the point where they discovered that an airplane's rudder, unlike a ship's, is a balancing rather than a steering device, and that its use in conjunction with wingwarping provided the long-sought solution to the problem of flight.

What motivated the Wright brothers in their infringement suits was not greed but the knowledge that others were making thousands of dollars by using the system of airplane control that they had spent years perfecting. They presented their side of the controversy in an article, "Are the Wrights Justified?," which appeared in *Aeronautics* in April 1910:

> When a couple of flying machine inventors fish, metaphorically speaking, in waters where hundreds had previously fished for thousands of years in vain, and after risking their lives hundreds of times, and spending years of time and thousands of dollars, finally succeed in making a catch, there are people who think it a pity that the courts should give orders that the rights of the inventors shall be respected and that those who wish to enjoy the feast shall contribute something to pay the fishers.

Adjudicating the Wright basic patent, however, turned out to be a good deal more complicated than equating wingwarping with the use of ailerons. Judge Hazel's decision of January 3, 1910, had opened a Pandora's box of questions. What Wilbur and Orville had discovered in 1902 and patented in 1906 was the basic principle of flight—the only efficient way to control an airplane in the air—and it would remain the only efficient method of operating a winged vehicle off the surface of the earth until rockets were perfected and man could venture into airless space without benefit of ailerons, rudders, and elevators.

But is such a universal system, amounting almost to a basic physical principle, patentable? The U.S. Patent Office examiners certainly thought so. Other men sincerely disagreed. A speculative approach to the problem is sometimes suggested: If the Wrights had invented the wheel, would they have been entitled to patent their invention? Or, to rephrase the question so that it parallels more closely what they actually patented: If the Wrights had invented the wheel but had patented instead the axle, without which the wheel could not be set in useful motion over the ground, would they have been entitled to collect royalties from every man who used the wheel to his profit during the duration of their patent?

Therein lies the dilemma that was to occupy lawyers, judges, the Wright brothers, Glenn Curtiss, and many others until the United States' entry into World War I made compromise a matter of national necessity. There never would be any legally satisfying answer to the question, but the battle in the courts would go on for seven long years, gathering size and momentum like a large snowball rolled down a snowy hillside, leaving exposed in its wake a dark and depressing collection of twigs, dead leaves, pebbles, and other detritus—or, in the case of *Wright* v. *Curtiss*, a sordid trail of hatred, invective, and lies that muddy the pages of aeronautical history to this day.

# 39

## End of a Friendship

ONCE THE SUITS against infringers of the Wright patent were underway, Wilbur and Orville were fair game for vilifiers and detractors. One of the more subtle attacks on their claim to be the airplane's inventors was based on the belief that the first flying machine had been the joint product of Samuel Pierpont Langley's scientific work and the Wright brothers' mechanical ingenuity, a misconception that originated in 1910.

On February 10 of that year, the Smithsonian Institution awarded Wilbur and Orville the first Langley Medal for achievement in aerodynamic investigation and its application to aviation. The medal presentation was held in the Regents room of the Smithsonian building. It began with a speech by Regent Alexander Graham Bell that was one long effusion of unqualified praise for the aeronautical research of Langley, who had given "to physicists, perhaps for the first time, firm ground on which to stand as to the long disputed question of air resistance and reactions." Quoting Octave Chanute, Bell cited the eight important research results set forth in Langley's *Experiments in Aerodynamics* of 1891, the eighth and crowning achievement being the "paradoxical result obtained by Langley that it takes less power to support a plane at high speed than at low." This was the so-called Langley's Law, which had been thoroughly discredited in practice.

Bell's speech was followed by the formal presentation address by Senator Henry Cabot Lodge. Lodge spoke more briefly than Bell, but he also attributed to Langley "the establishment of the scientific principles of aerial flight." Nothing, the senator added, could have given Langley more pleasure than to recognize the men (Wilbur and Orville Wright) "who had successfully demonstrated the soundness of his principles by their application to actual flight."

Wilbur's acceptance speech was even shorter. He too referred to Langley, but only to say that since the Smithsonian had taken a special interest in aerodynamic research because of the experiments of its former secretary, he hoped that in future the Institution would encourage the labors of others engaged in such research.

From the account of the presentation ceremony in the Smithsonian Institution's *Annual Report* for 1910, a reader could be forgiven for assuming that the occasion had been held to honor Langley more than the Wright brothers. Bell's remarks on Langley were summarized, as were the remarks of Senator Lodge. As to Wilbur's acceptance speech, the *Annual Report* merely stated that Wilbur had "called attention to the valuable scientific researches by Professor Langley." Then:

> As an indication of their early confidence in the successful solution of the problem of aerial navigation, the Wright brothers said:
> The knowledge that the head of the most prominent scientific institution of America believed in the possibility of human flight was one of the influences that led us to undertake the preliminary investigation that preceded our active work. He recommended to us the books which enabled us to form sane ideas at the outset. It was a helping hand at a critical time and we shall always be grateful.

If any reader of the Smithsonian *Annual Report* for 1910 had stumbled on the complete text of Wilbur's speech in the *Report*'s "Proceedings" section, he would have been surprised to discover that neither of the brothers had uttered those words on February 10, 1910. Wilbur had written them in 1906 in a letter to Octave Chanute. Chanute had quoted Wilbur's words in a speech he gave later that year at a memorial meeting in honor of the late Smithsonian secretary, and Chanute's tribute, together with the quotation from Wilbur's letter, had subsequently been printed in a Smithsonian pamphlet. In his 1910 medal-presentation speech, Alexander Graham Bell had quoted Wilbur's remarks to show that the Wright brothers, too, had "laid their tribute" at Langley's feet, and someone had seen fit to reprint Wilbur's words on page 23 of the *Annual Report* as if they had been the conclusion of his speech in acceptance of the Langley Medal. The net effect was to leave the reader with the impression that the Wrights' success had less to do with their own experiments and research than with Langley's "helping hand." While the words had been intended in 1906 as a sincere tribute to Langley, their publication in 1910 created two false impressions. The first can be attributed to a lapse in Wilbur's memory: It had been Richard Rathbun, assistant secretary of the Smithsonian, not Langley, who had recommended the books that enabled the Wright brothers "to form sane ideas at the outset." In the second place, although Langley's *Experiments in Aerodynamics* had been one of the books recommended by Rathbun and had been studied carefully by the Wrights, readers of Wilbur's words in 1910 had no way of knowing that the brothers had no faith whatever in Langley's research. They found Langley's profuse data, most of which concerned air pressures on flat plates rather than curved airfoils, both misleading and inaccurate.

A far more serious liability for Wilbur and Orville than the myth of their indebtedness to Langley was the charge that they had never adequately acknowledged their debt to Octave Chanute. This had been a touchy subject ever since January 1904, when the Wright brothers had sent a press release to the Associated Press describing the first four flights of December 17, 1903. Chanute had taken exception to the statement in the release that "all the experiments have been conducted at our own expense without assistance from any individual or institution" and had written Wilbur: "Please write me just what you had in your mind concerning myself when you framed that sentence in that way."

Wilbur's diplomatic response was that the statement had been made to scotch "a somewhat general impression that our Kitty Hawk experiments had not been carried on at our own expense, &c. We thought it might save embarrassment to correct this promptly."

Chanute accepted Wilbur's explanation without comment, but in his talk to the Aéro-Club de France in April 1903 he had already intimated that the Wrights were his collaborators and pupils, and the impression persisted that they had profited from his tutelage more than they were willing to admit. In *Navigating the Air,* the book published by the Aero Club of America in 1907, Charles Manly had contributed a chapter in which he deplored that so little mention had ever been made "of the fact that the success of the Wrights has been built on the very valuable work of Mr. Chanute . . . who, I understand, not only furnished the Wright brothers with the design for their first gliding machine, but also placed at their disposition his own machines with which they made their initial gliding experiments."

In the fall of 1908, after Wilbur had stunned his critics into silence with his brilliant flights at Le Mans, Paul Renard, a Frenchman who had had a hand in constructing Ernest Archdeacon's glider of 1904, wrote Octave Chanute, objecting that so little credit had been given to the older man for what the Wrights had accomplished. Professing that he never missed an opportunity to point out that the Wright brothers had been Chanute's pupils, Renard asked Chanute to identify for him just what aspects of the Wright Flyer he, Chanute, was responsible for and what they had added themselves.

Chanute replied modestly enough that he was not able to say exactly how useful he had been to Wilbur and Orville through his counsels and

publications, yet when he itemized for Renard the seven principal improvements that the Wrights, in his opinion, had added to the machines of their
predecessors, he gave them sole credit for three of these—propellers, transmission system, reliable motors—and subtly qualified the other four: placing
the elevator in front (Maxim, Chanute reminded Renard, had done this in
1894); the prone position (Chanute had indicated in his writing that this
would reduce resistance); wingwarping (Mouillard had patented this at
Chanute's insistence); and improvements due to the 1901 wind-tunnel experiments (Chanute himself had calculated the results for the brothers). Nothing
in Chanute's letter rebutted the idea that the Wrights had been his pupils,
and his statement that he had been present at part of the experiments of
1901–5 left the impression that the experiments had been conducted with his
help and advice. Actually, Chanute had witnessed only one power flight in
1904—Orville's 24-second flight of October 15, which had ended in a crash
—and not a single flight in 1905.

Chanute went on to indicate to Renard the extent of his intimacy with
the Wrights: "In eight years we have exchanged perhaps 200 letters on
questions which arose and on the progress achieved [actually the number
of letters was closer to 500 than 200]; these letters, along with two lectures
given by Wilbur Wright at my invitation before the Western Society of
Engineers in Chicago in September 1902 and June 1903, may one day serve
to tell the story of the conquest of the air."

When Chanute had opened Wilbur's first letter back in May 1900—the
letter beginning "For some years I have been afflicted with the belief that
flight is possible to man"—he could not have foreseen that the trust and
regard permeating the correspondence thus initiated would deteriorate into
bitterness and distrust by the end of the decade. Things had not quite
reached that stage in 1908 when Chanute wrote to Renard, but by then the
once-swollen stream of letters to and from the Wrights had thinned to a
trickle. The brief note Chanute received in November from Wilbur, then in
Le Mans, was the first to reach him in four months, and it would be another
six months before he received further word from the brothers—three paragraphs announcing that they were back in Dayton and at work on the new
Army Flyer. Chanute's reply was even shorter. He was being slowed down
by advancing age, he admitted, but expressed gratification at the sensible and
modest way in which Wilbur and Orville were accepting the honors being
heaped upon them. "It encourages the hope that you will still speak to me
when you become millionaires," he added. Chanute seemed convinced that
Wilbur and Orville were endeavoring to disassociate themselves from the
one man to whom they had turned for advice and encouragement back in
1900, and his conception of the brothers' debt to him for his help in those
early years had begun to magnify itself out of all resemblance to the truth.

In August 1909, when the Wright brothers sued Glenn Curtiss for infringement, Chanute lost no time in aligning himself with the defendants. "I think the Wrights have made a blunder by bringing suit at this time," he wrote the editor of *Aeronautics*. "Not only will this antagonize very many persons but it may disclose some prior patents which will invalidate their more important claims." Glenn Curtiss was making exhibition flights at a racetrack near Chicago that October, and spent two evenings with Octave Chanute discussing the pending suit. Curtiss left town firm in the belief that the Wrights had few prospects of winning.

Chanute's opinion about the suit was eagerly solicited by the press. In an interview published in the Chicago *Daily News,* he stated that while Wilbur and Orville were entitled to be rewarded for the things they had actually performed, their wingwarping claim was not absolutely original. "On the contrary," he said, "many inventors have worked on it, from the time of Leonardo da Vinci." He also discussed in this interview his relationship with Wilbur and Orville. "When the Wrights wanted to start, they wrote to me that they had read my book on gliding and asked if I would permit them to use the plans of my biplane," he said, forgetting after a lapse of almost ten years that the Wrights had asked him no such thing. Then, at a later point in the interview, again on the subject of Wilbur and Orville: "I turned over all my data which included a copy of the Mouillard patent and information given to me by Dr. Langley and his young engineers Manly, Herring and Huffaker, and made them free of it." The old man could not possibly have forgotten, however, how little the Wrights valued Langley's work, nor could he have forgotten that they warped their wings long before they saw Mouillard's patent—or what a burden to them the mere presence of Huffaker and Herring had been in their camp at Kill Devil Hills.

Chances are that the Wrights did not see the Chicago *Daily News* interview, but they did see a clipping from the New York *World* of December 12, 1909, that contained another reference to the Wright brothers' debt to Octave Chanute: "Their persistent failure to acknowledge their monumental indebtedness to the man who gave them priceless assistance has been one of the most puzzling mysteries in their careers." This article so incensed Wilbur that he dashed off a letter to its author, Arnold Kruckman. He and Orville, Wilbur wrote, had repeatedly acknowledged their indebtedness to Chanute for the biplane idea, but because most of the information regarding their work had leaked out through Chanute, it had been assumed that they had worked under his direction and with his financial assistance. Any attempt they might have made to correct such inaccuracies would give the impression they were trying to detract from Chanute's fame. "Rather than subject ourselves to criticism on that score we have preferred to remain silent, but now you find fault with our silence. We, rather than Mr. Chanute, have been the sufferers from this silence so far, and we see no immediate danger that he will not receive the credit to which he is justly entitled for his services to the cause of human flight."

The New York *World* had always taken an interest in aeronautical news, especially when it verged on the sensational. Chanute was naturally consulted on the matter of Judge Hazel's January 3, 1910, decision in *Wright* v. *Curtiss,* and his opinion was flaunted in a four-tiered headline in the *World* on January 17:

### DR. CHANUTE DENIES
### WRIGHT FLYING CLAIM

## Declares Brothers Were Not First
## by Many Years to Discover
## Balance Principle

### HAS TOLD THEM THEY ARE
### WASTING TIME IN SUITS

## "Father of Aeronautics" Says
## the Strongest Point Attacked
## Is Protected by Patents

Chanute was quoted as saying that the principle underlying wingwarping had been known for more than half a century before the Wrights incorporated it in their machine, and that even their strongest claim—the use of the vertical rudder in conjunction with wingwarping—was covered by a patent issued in 1901.

This was too much for Wilbur. On January 20, he sent a short, sharp letter to Chanute and enclosed the offensive clipping. The New York *World,* he protested, had published several articles in the past few months in which Chanute was represented as saying that when the Wrights began experimenting, wingwarping was already well known. Since there was no reference to the use of warping wings for lateral control in Chanute's 1894 book, *Progress in Flying Machines,* Chanute must be referring to publications in French of which the Wrights were not aware. "Do the French documents from which you derive your information contain it," Wilbur inquired, "and if so can you give information as to where such documents can be obtained?"

Chanute returned the clipping to Wilbur, asserting that it was the first item from the New York *World* referring to himself that he had seen. "This interview, which was entirely unsought by me, is about as accurate as such things usually are," he explained. "Instead of discussing it I prefer to take up the main principles at issue."

First, he had never told the Wrights that they had originated wingwarping. It was the mechanism by which they warped their wings that was original, and he cited three examples of "warping." Two were examples of torsion of the wings from *Progress in Flying Machines,* the third was a reference to twisting the rear of the wings, as described in the Mouillard patent of 1897. None of these were the equivalent of the Wrights' method of warping the outer sections of a right and left wing at opposing angles (one wing at a positive angle, the other at a negative) for the purpose of restoring equilibrium or making a turn. "If the courts will decide that the purpose and results were entirely different and that you were the first to conceive the twisting of the wings, so much the better for you," he continued, becoming as hot under the collar in his fifth paragraph as Wilbur had become in his first, and ending the paragraph with a pointed play on words: "I am afraid, my friend, that your usually sound judgment has been warped by the desire for great wealth."

The second principle at issue was this: If Wilbur had a grievance against Chanute, Chanute had one as well against Wilbur. It concerned a speech that Wilbur had made at a dinner given in Chanute's honor earlier in the month:

In your speech at the Boston dinner, January 12th, you began by saying that I "turned up" at your shop in Dayton in 1901 and that you then invited me to your camp. This conveyed the impression that I thrust myself upon you at the time and it omitted to state that you were the first to write to me, in 1900, asking for information which was gladly furnished, that many letters passed between us, and that both in 1900 and 1901 you had written me to invite me to visit you, before I "turned up" in 1901.

"I hope that, in future," the letter concluded, "you will not give out the impression that I was the first to seek your acquaintance or pay me left-handed compliments, such as saying that 'sometimes an experienced person's advice was of great value to younger men.'

"P.S. The statement that warping in connection with the turning of the rudder was patented in 1901 was not from me. The reporter must have gotten this elsewhere."

Wilbur waited four or five days before replying. Then, on January 29, he lashed out acidly in the longest letter he had written to Octave Chanute since 1902.

Your letter of January 23rd is received. Until confirmed by you, the interview in the New York *World* of January 17 seemed incredible. We have never had the slightest ground for suspecting that when you repeatedly spoke to us in 1901 of the originality of our methods you referred only to our methods of driving tacks, fastening wires, etc., and not to the novelty of our general systems. Neither in 1901, nor in the five years following, did you in any way intimate to us that our general system of lateral control had long been a part of the art, and, strangely enough, neither your books, addresses or articles, nor the writings of Lilienthal, Langley, Maxim, Hargrave, etc., made any mention whatever of the existence of such a system. Therefore it came to us with somewhat of a shock when you calmly announced that this system was already a feature of the art well known, and that you meant only the mechanical details when you referred to its novelty. If the idea was really old in the art, it is somewhat remarkable that a system so important that individual ownership of it is considered to threaten strangulation of the art was not considered worth mentioning then, nor embodied in any machine built prior to ours.

As to the examples of wingwarping that Chanute had cited in his letter: "I do not find in any of them any mention whatever of controlling lateral balance by adjustments of wings to respectively different angles of incidence on the right and left sides." The Mouillard patent, Wilbur maintained, did not mention control of lateral balance, let alone disclose a system for attaining it. "Unless something as yet unknown to anybody is brought to light to prove the invention technically known to everybody prior to 1900, our warped judgment will probably continue to be confirmed by the other judges as it was by Judge Hazel at Buffalo.

"As to inordinate desire for wealth, you are the only person acquainted with us who has ever made such an accusation." He and Orville believed that the physical and financial risks they had taken justified their right to enough surplus income to permit them to devote their future time to scientific experimenting instead of business. "You apparently concede to us no right to compensation for the solution of a problem ages old except such as is granted to persons who had no part in producing the invention. That is to say, we may compete with mountebanks for a chance to earn money in the mountebank business, but are entitled to nothing whatever for past work as inventors."

As to grievances, he and Orville had a grievance extending back to the early years of their association with Chanute. On one occasion they had complained that an impression was being spread broadcast that they were merely pupils and dependents of Chanute. Chanute had indignantly denied that he was responsible for that impression—yet "when I went to France I found everywhere an impression that we had taken up aeronautical studies at your special instigation; that we obtained our first experience on one of your machines; that we were pupils of yours and put into material form a knowledge furnished by you."

As to the matter of the debt owed by the Wrights to Chanute: "One of the *World* articles said that you had felt hurt because we had been silent regarding our indebtedness to you. I confess that I have found it most difficult to formulate a precise statement of what you contributed to our success." What was needed, Wilbur said, was a precise statement of the truth. "If such a statement could be prepared it would relieve a situation very painful both to you and to us.

"I have written with great frankness," the letter continued, "because I feel that such frankness is really more healthful to friendship than the secretly nursed bitterness which has been allowed to grow for so long a time." Neither he nor Orville wished to quarrel with a man toward whom they ought to preserve a feeling of gratitude. "P.S. I enclose a sample of the class of misrepresentations connected with your name. It just came in today."

The enclosure was a clipping from the Los Angeles *Express* and concerned Charles Lamson, who had built the oscillating-wing glider for Chanute that had been tested at the Wrights' camp on the Outer Banks in 1902. According to the *Express,* Lamson had been the first to patent what he called the airship feature in dispute in the Wright suit against Curtiss—in other words, wingwarping—and his patent would probably render the Wrights' claim ineffectual. Actually, Lamson had not patented wingwarping but rather the rocking-wing principle embodied in his 1902 glider. What the Wrights found particularly galling in the *Express* article was Lamson's assertion that he had built a glider for them, through the agency of Octave Chanute, and shipped it to them at Kitty Hawk in 1901, whereas the glider had been built for Chanute, not the Wright brothers; it had been shipped to Kitty Hawk in 1902, not 1901, and had been tested by Augustus Herring, not the Wrights. (That was not the last they would hear of Lamson. A few months later he brought suit against the brothers for infringement of his patent, a fruitless, time-consuming legal action that would not be settled in the Wrights' favor until 1912.)

A few days after receiving Wilbur's letter, Chanute wrote his friend George Spratt that he had gotten a "violent letter" from Wilbur, "in which he disputes my opinion, brings up various grievances, and quite loses his temper. I will answer him in a few days, but the prospects are that we will have a row." Chanute did not answer Wilbur's letter in a few days. He did not answer it at all. It was Wilbur who broke the silence after three months. "I have no answer to my last letter," he wrote Chanute on April 28, "and fear that the frankness with which delicate subjects were treated may have blinded you to the real spirit and purpose of the letter. I had noted in the past few years a cooling of the intimate friendship which so long existed between us, but it was your letter of recent date and newspaper clippings to which I referred, that brought to my mind the fact that a real soreness existed on your side as well on ours, which if not eradicated would make our friendship a mere travesty of what it once was." Wilbur's object had been not to give offense but to remove it, and as suggested in his previous letter, he urged that they draw up a joint statement that would do justice to both parties in the controversy and injustice to neither.

Chanute was preparing to sail for Europe and did not reply for several days. "I am in bad health and threatened with nervous exhaustion," he wrote on May 14. "Your letter of April 28th was gratifying, for I own that I felt very much hurt by your letter of January 29th, which I thought both unduly angry and unfair as well as unjust." He stubbornly insisted that he had never given the impression either in writing or in speaking that the Wright brothers were his pupils. He had never made *any claims,* he wrote, underlining the last two words, to have been of help to the brothers. Nor would he budge an inch when it came to giving Wilbur and Orville credit for having originated wingwarping—"but I have always said that you are entitled to immense credit for devising apparatus by which it has been reduced to successful practice. I hope, upon my return from Europe, that we will be able to resume our former relations."

While he was in Europe that summer, Chanute contracted pneumonia. He rallied to the point where he could withstand the ocean voyage home and in October returned to Chicago, where he died on November 23, 1910, at the age of seventy-eight. The joint statement proposed by Wilbur had never been prepared, and the myths about Chanute's contributions to the Wright brothers' success were free to proliferate, while the truth lay buried in the more than five hundred letters that had been exchanged by Wilbur and Chanute between May 1900 and May 1910.

Chanute was buried in Peoria, Illinois, beside his wife. A few weeks after the funeral, Wilbur wrote Chanute's son Charles regarding the disposition of the Wright-Chanute letters: "Inasmuch as this correspondence will probably have historic value in years to come, it ought to be guarded with great care against any possibility of destruction by fire or otherwise. I had intended before your father's death to suggest to him that several careful copies should be made in order to ensure their preservation." Charles Chanute replied that while Octave Chanute was ill in Paris he had had copies made of his own letters to the brothers. The eventual disposition of the correspondence would be up to the estate.

It was not until 1953, when the entire correspondence was published, that it was possible to pry loose the many misconceptions that had fastened themselves like barnacles to the history of the Wright-Chanute relationship. Wilbur and Orville had never denied that they were indebted to Octave Chanute, but it was for something less tangible than the biplane principle, and that was the encouragement he gave them. Encouragement can be a two-way street, however. Octave Chanute spent the last twenty years of his life seeking the solution to the flying problem and urging others to seek it with him, and when he died in 1910 he was in debt to Wilbur and Orville Wright—more deeply in debt than he was willing to acknowledge—for their having vindicated his faith in the possibility of a solution.

# 40

## Exit Herring

THERE WERE TIMES, in the years before World War I when the aviation industry was struggling to be born, when it seemed as if the infant industry was being strangled by its umbilical cord—the Wright patent. A dozen infringement suits were brought by the Wright Company in the United States and a score or more by the Wright companies in France and Germany before the cord was cut. The suits in the United States were not limited to those against American pilots and manufacturers. In September 1909, Wilbur wrote Orville, who was then in Berlin: "I intend to bring suit against importers of Blériot and Farman machines and I think the patent matter should be pushed in Europe also. The license proposition can be discussed to better advantage after we have shown our teeth a little." Most suits did not survive this showing of teeth. The threat of an injunction usually served to convince defendants that the brothers were serious about not permitting infringers to fly or manufacture aircraft without having first made the appropriate licensing arrangements.

Two lawsuits against foreign pilots flying foreign machines for profit in the United States did reach the trial stage. The first began with a bill of complaint filed against French aviator Louis Paulhan. Paulhan's specialty was endurance and cross-country flying. After winning 10,000 francs by placing third in the endurance race for the Grand Prix at Reims, he signed a contract for a series of flights to be made in the United States, starting at an air meet in Los Angeles early in 1910. As he came down the gangplank in New York on January 4, Paulhan was served with papers informing him that the two Blériot monoplanes and two Farman biplanes he had brought with him infringed the Wright patent. This action elicited a strong response abroad, especially from French aviators who had been invited to compete at the international air races to be held in New York in October and had no desire to place themselves within the jurisdiction of the U.S. courts.

Paulhan's case did not come to trial until January 30, so he was free to make his scheduled appearance at Los Angeles. The meet was held at a hastily constructed airfield in Dominguez Hills, January 10 to 20. Paulhan, described in handbills as "The World's Greatest Aviator," set a world altitude record of 4,165 feet and brought the total of his prize money to $19,000 by making a 45-mile cross-country flight to Santa Anita racetrack and return. On February 17, Judge Learned Hand of New York issued a preliminary injunction requiring Paulhan to post a $25,000 bond before making any more flights in the United States. U.S. marshals caught up with him six days later at Oklahoma City, whereupon he canceled his U.S. tour except for a few final flights at the Jamaica racetrack on Long Island, where he deliberately refused to accept any money to appear and where he complained he was being molested by Wilbur and his lawyers. The injunction against Paulhan, like that against Curtiss, was vacated on appeal in June 1910, but by that time Paulhan had returned to France.

The British aviator Claude Grahame-White was the subject of the other suit against a foreign pilot to reach the trial stage. He was alleged to have made a round $100,000 flying in the United States. In December 1911, the Wright Company sued Grahame-White for $50,000. On January 24, 1912, the suit was decided in favor of the complainants. Although the company was awarded a mere $1,700, the action was probably worth the expense in that it discouraged other foreign aviators from flying in the United States without payment of royalties to the Wrights.

The expenditure of time, effort, and money in the suits against Paulhan and Grahame-White was as nothing compared to that involved in *Wright v. Curtiss*. The Wright Company could afford the cost. The Herring-Curtiss Company could not. The legal expenses were staggering for those days. What kept Curtiss's company from going under during the winter of 1909–10 was the exhibition business. The Reims Racer had at last been released from bondage as a department-store exhibit, and Curtiss and two of the fliers he had trained flew off with almost as much prize money at the Los Angeles meet in January as Paulhan. Nevertheless, Curtiss had a hard time meeting the costs of the Wright suit, once he had begun the painful process of extricating himself and his Hammondsport plant from the octopuslike grip of Augustus Herring.

The conflict between Herring and the Herring-Curtiss Company had broken out into the open after Curtiss returned from Europe in September 1909. A meeting of the board of directors was called in October, at which Herring was ordered to turn over his patents, patent applications, and all the other items he had agreed to assign to the company in exchange for the voting majority of the stock. When he failed to comply with the board's request, Herring and his lawyer were summoned to a special meeting in December, at which the board voted to file an injunction requiring Herring to turn the promised materials over to the company. While documents were being drawn up to that effect, Herring excused himself and left the room. A few minutes later, his lawyer also left the room. When neither man reappeared, a search was made for the missing men by automobile about the streets of Hammondsport, at which point the story begins to resemble the scenario for a two-reel silent-motion-picture comedy.

Herring's lawyer had returned to his hotel in Hammondsport, where he made a phone call to an accomplice in the nearby town of Bath. Following the lawyer's instructions, the accomplice went into the street, hailed a passing automobile, and got the driver to agree to drive to Hammondsport, where he was to pick up the lawyer at his hotel and receive further instructions. By a cinematic coincidence, the amenable driver turned out to be Rumsey Wheeler, son of Herring-Curtiss president Monroe Wheeler, who was at that moment eager to get his hands on Augustus Herring in order to serve him the injunction that had been prepared at the meeting. In Hammondsport, Rumsey picked up the lawyer, who instructed him to drive to a secluded spot along the shore of Lake Keuka, where a friend was waiting. He was then to take the two men to Bath, where they could catch the next train for New York. All went well until they arrived at the appointed spot and young Wheeler saw the shadowy figure of Augustus Herring emerge from the bushes at the side of the lake. He became so alarmed that he sped off, leaving Herring and his lawyer to find their way on foot to the closest dwelling. The owner of the house believed their story of an automobile breakdown and put them up for the night. The next morning he drove the two men to the nearest town, from which they made their escape by train to New York.

Herring went into hiding for three weeks to avoid being served the papers requiring him to turn over his patents and patent applications to the Herring-Curtiss Company. There were no patents—there never had been any, with the exception of the patent applied for jointly by Herring and Chanute in England, which had been allowed to lapse in 1901 or 1902. By the time Herring came out of hiding, Judge Hazel's decision in *Wright* v. *Curtiss* had brought business at the Hammondsport factory to a virtual standstill. Bills piled up. Creditors complained. On April 10 the company filed a petition of involuntary bankruptcy. Herring's reaction was to file suit against the board of directors and Glenn Curtiss on behalf of the stockholders. Cortlandt Bishop, who had fallen out with Curtiss over Curtiss's ventures into exhibition flying, joined Herring in the suit, but reneged when

Herring asked him to invest an additional $16,000 in an attempt to prove that the petition of bankruptcy was part of a conspiracy to ease him out of the firm. The conspiracy charges were found to be groundless and in December 1910 a bankruptcy decree was issued.

Curtiss was free to form a new company if he could raise the necessary capital. When the Hammondsport plant was auctioned off by the trustee in bankruptcy in March 1911, he was able to buy it back for $25,100. In December the Curtiss Motor Company (later Aeroplane Company) was incorporated and Curtiss was back in business, making good his pledge that all Herring-Curtiss creditors and stockholders would be reimbursed—all, that is, except the two Bishop brothers, who had sided with Herring, and Herring himself, whose bundle of shares in the former company were now worth no more than the paper they were printed on.

Before his expulsion from the Herring-Curtiss Company, the devious Herring had become secretly involved with a company owned by W. Starling Burgess of Marblehead, Massachusetts. Burgess built yachts but wanted to get into the aviation business, and signed a contract with Herring. The first of the so-called Herring-Burgess biplanes (they were neither designed nor constructed by Herring) was equipped with a 25-horsepower Herring-Curtiss Company motor. Herring's contribution was limited to the control system, in which the vertical rudder was controlled by movements of the pilot's thumbs, a four-bladed propeller, and six of Herring's devices for automatic stability—triangular vertical vanes three feet high, fixed to the upper wing, similar to the single vane built into the elevator of Curtiss's *Golden Flier* and later abandoned. Since there were no ailerons or movable wingtips, the aircraft did not infringe the Wright patent. It landed with such force after its first and only five-second trial that Herring went right through the seat. A second Herring-Burgess aircraft boasted eight triangular vanes on the upper wing. It made half a dozen short, straightway flights before being wrecked in April 1910, after which Burgess saw fit to buy up Herring's contract.

In the legal maneuverings to unseat Herring and establish a new company, Glenn Curtiss and his lawyers had overlooked one essential—they had neglected to see that the bankrupt Herring-Curtiss Company was formally dissolved, and the more than 2,000 shares of stock in the defunct company owned by Augustus Herring ticked away quietly like a time bomb. In 1918, when Curtiss's new company was doing a booming business in war orders, the Herring-Curtiss Company rose from the dead. Herring, as its largest stockholder, filed suit against Glenn Curtiss and his associates for $5 million, charging that the 1910 bankruptcy of the company had not been involuntary but rather the culmination of a plan to conduct the business so that insolvency would ensue. Three years later there was an eighteen-week trial, during which Herring made his usual wild claims, topped by his assertion that the patent applications he had contributed to the company had been worth half a million dollars. In 1923 a verdict was rendered in favor of Curtiss. Herring appealed.

The following year it was revealed in a lengthy biographical sketch printed in an obscure southern journal that Herring had suffered a stroke which left him at least partially paralyzed. "When Will Merit Count in Aviation? The Life Story of Augustus M. Herring, Inventor of the Aeroplane" appeared in the October 1924 issue of *The Libertarian,* published in Greenville, South Carolina. The article has been drawn on ever since as a source of information on Herring's life and work. Its author, James Vernon Martin, who seems to have replaced Carl Dienstbach as Herring's publicist, was something of a minor-league Herring himself. He had worked for Herring in 1909 and claimed to have invented interconnecting ailerons, retractable landing gear, and the tractor airplane among other things, although in *The Libertarian* he was more modestly identified as "Present holder of the world's record for aeroplane efficiency and a former pupil of Mr. Herring."

Martin depicts Herring as a modern Galileo, dying in poverty and humiliation, the victim of an ill-defined aircraft conspiracy. The Herring-Curtiss Company fiasco in Martin's version is a story of unrewarded genius, in which Curtiss makes millions from the company that Herring started and into which he put all his money and his valuable patent applications. The unfortunate man has not made one penny from his inventions, yet there is very little in modern airplane design, Martin tells his readers, that is not covered by patent applications filed by Herring before 1910. It was Herring who invented the curved airfoil, and it was Herring, we are told in a section headed "Herring Encouraged Wrights and Others," who communicated to Wilbur and Orville, through Octave Chanute, the advantages of using curved airplane wings instead of flat.

Herring died of another stroke in July 1926. Most of the information in his obituary in the *New York Times* was supplied by James Martin, including the statement that the Wright brothers were given access to Herring's research discoveries after they had made a flight of a few seconds in 1903. The most characteristic touch of all—as if Herring were writing his own obituary from beyond the grave—was the revelation that he first became interested in aeronautics as a boy when he was presented with a toy helicopter by his father, an event cribbed brazenly from Orville's famous article "The Wright Brothers' Aeroplane," in the September 1908 *Century Magazine.*

The state of New York formally dissolved the Herring-Curtiss Company the year Herring died, but the suit against Curtiss was carried on by Herring's son and daughter. In 1928, the New York Supreme Court reversed the

1923 decision, which had favored Curtiss, who was now found guilty of having acted selfishly rather than in the interest of the only Herring-Curtiss stockholders who had contributed capital to the enterprise. A former Supreme Court judge was appointed to adjudicate a settlement, but Glenn Curtiss was determined to carry on the fight. In the summer of 1930 he spent five days testifying in the case. After a weekend at home he suffered an attack of appendicitis on his way back to Rochester for further questioning and died several days later of a pulmonary embolism.

Curtiss's widow had no stomach for carrying on the struggle. To divest herself of this legal incubus she settled out of court. The exact amount of the settlement was never revealed, but Glenn Curtiss, Jr., thought it was on the order of half a million, no inconsiderable fortune in those early years of the Great Depression. The only solace the ghost of Glenn Curtiss could have taken from this extraordinary windfall for Herring's heirs was that Herring himself had not lived to enjoy it.

# 41

# *The Exhibition Business*

THE BUSINESS OF manufacturing and selling Wright airplanes in Europe was proving to be unprofitable. Orville and Wilbur had reserved the British rights when they revised their contract with Flint and Company in 1907. They had licensed Short Brothers to build half a dozen Flyers in England, but there was as yet no Wright company in that country. In France and Germany, where such companies were well established, business had gone from bad to worse. In November 1910, Orville sailed for Europe to find out what had gone wrong.

The original French Wright company had gone out of business after turning all its unfinished machines and orders over to Astra, an airship company in such bad repute with French officialdom that the government was unwilling to do business with it. The German factory was in bad shape for different reasons. German Flyers had been loaded with so many would-be improvements by zealous workmen they could barely get off the ground. There had been two training fatalities. Royalties had not been paid on some of the machines sold. "I have about made up my mind to let the European business go," Orville wrote Wilbur from Berlin. "I don't propose to be bothered with it all my life and I see no prospect of its ever amounting to anything unless we send a representative here to stay to watch our interests."

The American Wright Company, on the other hand, was prospering. Two months after the company was founded in November 1909, ground was broken for a manufacturing plant in Dayton. While the building was going up, space was rented in an unused factory, where an average of two flying machines were turned out each month. When the new factory opened in November 1910, production was doubled. The company ended its first year of operation with a profit of more than $100,000, the largest part of which came from the sale and licensing of machines for exhibition flying. In April

1910, the Aero Club of America had signed an agreement with the Wrights whereby it would lend its name and prestige to air meets only after arrangements had been made for payment of royalties to the Wright Company. Although it was impossible to control wildcat flying, most exhibitions were sponsored by local affiliates of the national Aero Club, and the only way promoters of such meets could protect participants from possible infringement suits was by signing a contract with the Wrights in advance. The usual fee was 20 percent of the prize money when aviators flew for cash prizes only, or 10 percent of the gate receipts when these constituted the entire income of the meet.

There was grumbling that the Wrights were arrogating to themselves complete control of aviation in America by means of the Aero Club agreement. The brothers were not deaf to the grumbling. They were determined not to make any more public flights themselves, but when they saw thousands of dollars pouring into the pockets of fliers who were not inventors like themselves and who would never have been able to profit as they did without utilizing the control system covered by the Wright patent, they could see no reason why the Wright Company, so far ahead of its competitors in other respects, should not enter the exhibition business and train pilots to fly aircraft built by the company.

They began by employing Roy Knabenshue to oversee and manage that part of the business. Knabenshue was the young aeronaut who had piloted Thomas Baldwin's *California Arrow* at the St. Louis fair in 1904. His six years' experience in promoting airship exhibitions at state fairs made him the ideal man to organize and manage a Wright exhibition team, leaving Wilbur free to concentrate on the work involved in the infringement suits and Orville free to carry out a pilot-training program.

The brothers' old practice field at Huffman Prairie eight miles from downtown Dayton had been leased by the Wright Company. In March 1910, while it was being prepared as a training camp for exhibition pilots, a temporary flying school was established at Montgomery, Alabama, on the site of the present Maxwell Air Force Base. Orville's first pupil was twenty-one-year-old Walter Brookins of Dayton, whom the Wrights had known since he was a boy of four. Others who began their training at the same time were Spencer Crane, also of Dayton, who soon dropped out; Arthur Welsh of Washington, D.C.; J. W. Davis of Colorado Springs, who for some reason never learned to fly, but stayed on with the exhibition team as a handyman; and Arch Hoxsey, a twenty-six-year-old auto mechanic from Pasadena, California. Knabenshue had hired Hoxsey to tune up the motor of the dirigible he flew at the Los Angeles meet and, sensing Hoxsey's potential as an exhibition pilot, had hired him for the Wright team.

A hangar had been erected at Huffman Prairie in the meantime and the refurbished airfield had been renamed Simms Station, after the nearest interurban trolley stop. Orville returned from Alabama early in May, and Brookins came up from Montgomery at the end of the month to help him train a new crop of pilots. The field was only partly cleared of hummocks. Students were required to level off the remaining hummocks during their spare time and to chase banker Huffman's cows out of the way before each flight. There were five new candidates for the exhibition team: Frank Coffyn, Phil Parmalee, J. Clifford Turpin, Duval La Chapelle—a French-speaking American who had worked as a mechanic for Wilbur in France, and who was discovered to be suffering from cataracts after he almost demolished the hangar at the end of his first, and last, solo flight—and Ralph Johnstone of Kansas City, Missouri. Johnstone was the most promising pilot of the lot. He had been a trick bicyclist since the age of fifteen, his specialty being flips in midair after riding his cycle up a springboard.

Wilbur had all but given up flying, but Orville made close to 250 flights at Simms Station in 1910. During the last three weeks of May alone he managed 99 takeoffs and landings, many with passengers. Brother Lorin was given his first ride on May 21 and so, at long last, was Charlie Taylor. Wilbur made his first flight in more than six months the same day. It was the last flight he would ever make in the United States as pilot, although four days later he flew as Orville's passenger. The brothers had always made it a rule that the two of them should never be in the air together, thus ensuring that if there was ever a fatal accident, one of them would be left to carry on their work. Their six and a half minutes in the air together on May 25, 1910, amounted to a tacit admission that the most important part of their work was done. On the twelfth flight of the day, Orville took his father up for the first time. They flew round and round the renovated airfield for seven minutes. "Higher, Orville," the eighty-one-year-old bishop kept urging, "higher!" Orville's most noteworthy flight of the year was made on September 22, a day designated Aviation Day by the Greater Dayton Association in an attempt to pump life into a languishing industrial exhibit being held in the city. Bishop Wright recorded the event in his diary with customary succinctness:

> At 5:00 Orville comes on his flyer, about 2,000 feet high, turns at Williams Street, goes near our home, flies along Third Street to the limits of the city, and rising to about 4,000 feet, goes up Mad River to their grounds. Came nine miles in ten minutes, returned slower. Many thousands saw him.

The Wright exhibition team made its debut in an air show at the Indianapolis Speedway, June 13–18, 1910. On June 17, Brookins bettered the altitude record set the first day of the meet, by rising to almost 6,000 feet. As he began his descent, his motor stopped suddenly and he glided down so rapidly that he failed to reach the speedway and vanished from sight before the eyes of the terrified crowd in the grandstand, which included his parents and sister, who had accompanied Wilbur and Orville from Dayton. Wilbur left the speedway on a run, breaking through clumps of bushes and vaulting fences until he reached an open field a quarter of a mile from the racetrack, where he found young Brookins calmly smoking a cigarette beside his undamaged Flyer. At Montreal two weeks later, Ralph Johnstone set a new Canadian endurance record. At Atlantic City in early July, there was a ten-day exhibition of flying during which Brookins and Glenn Curtiss vied with each other for the plaudits of the crowds on the boardwalk. Brookins won a $5,000 Aero Club prize by setting a new altitude record and Curtiss was awarded a like amount for flying fifty miles over the ocean in ten five-mile laps along the beach.

At the Asbury Park, New Jersey, meet on August 10, Wright machines equipped with wheels made their first public appearance. The skids were retained. A pair of small wheels were simply attached to each skid. The meet began with an accident. In landing, Brookins had to swerve suddenly to avoid a crowd of about fifty photographers who had flocked onto the field for pictures. A gust of wind caught the machine and sent it spinning over backwards. Eight bystanders were slightly injured, and Brookins was plucked from the wreck stunned, with a broken nose, a broken ankle, and several broken teeth. With Brookins temporarily on the sidelines, Ralph Johnstone, who was rapidly gaining a reputation as a fearless flier, and Arch Hoxsey, who made his first public flight at Asbury Park, became the darlings of the meet. The Star Dust Twins, as they came to be called, were even more responsible for the success of the Wright exhibition business than Walter Brookins.

Most of the flights made by Johnstone and Hoxsey at Asbury Park were made in the machine shipped from Dayton to Asbury Park to replace the Flyer wrecked the first day of the meet. This was a Model B, the first radical departure in design of a Wright machine since 1903. The horizontal front rudder had contributed greatly to the maneuverability of the Wright gliders and the first slow Flyers, but the faster an airplane flew, the more difficult it was to fly a level, nonundulating course with the elevator in front. To dampen unwanted undulations, the Wrights applied a fixed horizontal surface to the tail of a Flyer, then went a step further and made this surface movable so that it worked as an auxiliary elevator in conjunction with the horizontal front rudder. The next step was to eliminate the front rudder altogether. This made it possible to shorten the skids and equip them with fixed triangular "blinkers" for additional stability. The redesigned machine was known at first as the Headless Wright, since it lacked the front framing of the swanlike creature that had sailed so serenely over Huffman Prairie in 1905. Headless Wright soon gave way to the less colorful designation Model B, although there had never been a Model A.

Brookins recovered from his accident in time to compete at the flying meet at Squantum Meadows near Boston, September 3–13. British aviator Claude Grahame-White carried off the lion's share of the prize money, but Wright Model Bs won all the endurance and distance contests. That same week, Arch Hoxsey had his first accident while flying at the Wisconsin State Fair in Milwaukee. He swerved suddenly from his course at a low altitude and, according to newspaper reports, plunged into the crowd on the cement platform before the grandstand. Five women and three men were said to have been injured. Ralph Johnstone had his first accident at Kinloch Park near St. Louis the second week in October, at an air show remembered chiefly because Arch Hoxsey gave portly ex-President Theodore Roosevelt a three-minute ride in a Model B. The day before that much-photographed event, Johnstone lost control of his machine in turning and made such an abrupt landing that his motor broke loose. Fortunately it fell on the airplane's radiator rather than on the pilot.

As the Wright team became more adept at stunting, the possibility of a fatal accident occurring during an exhibition haunted the Wright brothers. Brookins was famous for short turns and for flying circles close to the ground with his wings at angles of up to 80 degrees. Johnstone's repertory of hair-raising tricks included pirouettes and steep dives climaxed with a series of so-called Dutch rolls. Hoxsey's specialties were grapevines and the Dive of Death. The Dive of Death consisted of a circling glide followed by a steep dive and a last-minute pullout guaranteed to draw screams from sensation-hungry crowds. Three days after Hoxsey's accident at Milwaukee, Wilbur sent him a stern letter regarding the flights he and Johnstone were scheduled to make at Detroit later in September:

> I am very much in earnest when I say that I want no stunts and spectacular frills put on the flights there. If each of you can make a plain flight of ten to fifteen minutes each day keeping always within the inner fence wall away from the grandstand and never more than three hundred feet high it will be just what we want. Under no circumstances make more than one flight each day apiece. Anything beyond plain flying will be chalked up as a fault and not as a credit.

Plain ten- to fifteen-minute flights were not what the public was paying its money to see, and the Wright exhibition pilots were no more capable of resisting the exhortations of the noisy crowds than the ambitious young fliers trained by Glenn Curtiss. Exhibition flying was at bottom a bloody business. The first aviator to die in 1910 was Léon Delagrange, who had flown at Reims without making any flights of note. On January 4, 1910, he was flying before a huge crowd at Bordeaux when he made too sharp a turn and the wings of his Blériot monoplane collapsed. There followed a three-month respite from fatal accidents, ending April 2 with the drowning of French exhibition pilot Hubert Leblon after his Blériot crashed into the Bay of Biscay off San Sebastián in Spain. By the time the Wright exhibition team entered the arena in June, the pace had picked up. Between May 13 and July 3, five pilots died in Europe in aircraft accidents. On July 12, Charles Stewart Rolls, founder of the Rolls-Royce Motor Company, died during the first British air meet when the tail of his French-built Wright snapped off before a grandstand filled with horrified spectators at Bournemouth. Four more pilots died before summer was over. On September 23, the Peruvian Georges Chávez made a spectacular flight over the Simplon Pass in the Alps, but was upset by a gust when he landed. Both legs were broken below the knee and his left thigh fractured. He died four days later.

The carnage went on into the autumn—by the end of October there had been eight more fatal crashes. But the deaths had all occurred in Europe, and when the International Aviation Tournament opened at the Belmont Park racetrack near Garden City, Long Island, on October 22, 1910, there had as yet been no pilot fatalities in the United States.

France and England sent teams to Belmont Park. The United States was represented by the Curtiss and Wright teams and by a number of independent American aviators. The $5,000 race for the Gordon Bennett trophy was the red-letter event of the meet as it had been at Reims the year before. Several aircraft seen at Belmont Park for the first time had been designed with the Bennett trophy race in mind. Curtiss's candidate was a cross between a monoplane and biplane—a thirty-foot wing surmounted by a much smaller airfoil. It was powered by a 65-horsepower motor but was withdrawn from the race after Curtiss came to the conclusion that it was too far outclassed by Claude Grahame-White's powerful Blériot with its fourteen-cylinder Gnome rotary engine. Alexander Ogilvie of England entered the race with a Wright Roadster, a single-seat scaled-down version of the Model B. Ogilvie had met Wilbur in France in 1908. In September 1910 he traveled to Dayton and was given lessons in flying the Wright Roadster by Orville himself.

The Wright brothers' entry in the trophy race, to be flown by Walter Brookins, was an even smaller version of the Model B called the Baby Grand. Because the Roadster was sometimes referred to as the Baby Wright, the two machines were often confused, but there were significant differences. The Baby Grand's wingspan was twenty-one feet, giving it a total lifting surface of only 140 square feet, compared to the 180 square feet of the Roadster with its twenty-six-and-a-half-foot wingspan. Whereas the Roadster was powered by a standard Wright four-cylinder, 35-horsepower motor, the Baby Grand boasted the only eight-cylinder motor produced by the Wrights. It was capable of 50–60 horsepower. The motor was placed where the passenger sat in the two-seater Wright machines. There was so little room on the small wing that the pilot operated the elevator lever with his left arm wrapped about an upright.

Wilbur, Orville, Katharine, and Alexander Ogilvie arrived at Belmont Park on Monday, October 24, the third day of the meet, the day on which the American J. Armstrong Drexel set a new U.S. altitude record of 7,015 feet. On Tuesday, Ralph Johnstone bettered Drexel's record by 200 feet and came down chilled to the bone after encountering snow above the clouds. Twice that day, Orville, nattily attired in leather flying togs, made trial runs in the Baby Grand and was clocked at almost 70 miles per hour. On Wednesday, Brookins flew the Baby Grand in the daily distance race. He easily outdistanced his seven competitors but dropped out after twelve laps, and the race went to Hubert Latham of the French team. The Baby Grand was built for speed, not endurance. With Brookins at the controls, it was conceded to be the favorite to win Saturday's race for the Bennett trophy.

On Thursday, a howling wind filled the racetrack enclosure with autumn leaves. Hoxsey and Johnstone tried for the day's altitude record but ran into such a strong west wind at 1,000 feet that they were blown backwards with their engines wide open until they were out of sight of the astonished spectators. Hoxsey came down twenty-five miles away. Johnstone was unable to land until he reached Middle Island, fifty-five miles east of Belmont Park. Wilbur described the two flights for reporters as "just one straight forward progress, backwards."

Before making his official try for the Gordon Bennett trophy on Saturday, Brookins made a trial flight in the Baby Grand. Its eight-cylinder motor was actually two four-cylinder Wright motors assembled in a V-position on a single crankshaft. As Brookins was making a turn, one bank of cylinders ceased firing. With the wind at his back, Brookins was unable to climb. The racer hurtled to the ground with such speed that the wheels collapsed, the skids dug into the ground, and the Baby Grand came to rest upside down. Painfully injured in the groin, Brookins staggered from the wreckage in a state of shock and was hurried to the hospital by ambulance. The race was won later that day by Claude Grahame-White, averaging 61 miles an hour in his 100-horsepower Blériot. John Moisant of Chicago came in second, flying a less powerful Blériot. Ogilvie in his 35-horsepower Wright Roadster placed third.

Sunday's $10,000 prize for a flight from Belmont Park to the Statue of Liberty in New York Harbor and return was won by John Moisant. Wilbur and Orville would not let their pilots fly on the Sabbath, so the Wright team did not compete, but on Monday, October 31, the last day of the meet, Ralph Johnstone set a world altitude record of 7,714 feet, flying a Wright Roadster for the first time. This brought the Wrights' share of prize money to $15,000, to which should be added the $20,000 paid to the Wright Company for the license that precluded threats of infringement suits against other contestants.

Two days after the Belmont Park meet closed, an air show opened at Baltimore. On November 7, Arch Hoxsey assembled a Wright Model B at a railroad station outside Baltimore and flew it to Halethorpe Field, where he made three crowd-pleasing flights before a heavy rain ended flying for the day. From Baltimore, Hoxsey traveled to Denver, where an air show opened November 16 at Overland Park. Despite the wintry cold, three crack Wright pilots were all in the air at once on opening day—Johnstone circling at 1,500 feet, Brookins darting to and fro at 1,000 feet, and Hoxsey flying figure-eights somewhere in between. On the second day, Brookins and Johnstone flew back and forth in front of the grandstand, leaping imaginary hurdles, while Hoxsey climbed in wider and wider circles. When he was at 2,500 feet he made a dash for the foothills west of Denver and came down so chilled he could hardly walk.

Johnstone was first off in the day's second round of flights. He had told a reporter he would attempt no daring stunts at Overland Park, because the thin air at Denver's high altitude made stunting too risky. The warm reception given Hoxsey for his flight over the foothills earlier that day may have made Johnstone change his mind. After reaching 800 feet, he began one of the spiral glides for which he was famous. The band in the grandstand blared away. All eyes were on Johnstone as he began his descent. Everything went well until he was in his second circle, when his machine went into an almost perpendicular dive. To the horror of Brookins and other watchers on the ground, Johnstone could be seen making heroic efforts to right the machine as it hit the earth with a sickening thud opposite the grandstand. The band continued to play. The spectators poured out on the field despite the efforts of the police to hold them back.

Johnstone had died instantly. His back, neck, and both legs were broken. The bones of his thighs were forced clear through his leather flying clothes. That did not deter the men and women who clawed through the wreckage for souvenirs, tore scraps of fabric from the twisted wings, and snatched the gloves from the dead aviator's hands. Hoxsey landed as soon as he could, and when order had been restored, he and Brookins helped to lift Johnstone's broken body into an automobile. They drove out of the enclosure to the accompaniment of "A Grizzly Bear," which the band had never ceased playing.

Ralph Johnstone was the first professional flier to be killed in the United States. John Moisant, who had made such a good showing at Belmont Park, was the second. He had organized the first American air circus and taken it south for the winter. While he was flying a few miles from New Orleans on the last day of the year, his Blériot monoplane went into a nosedive from which it never recovered, and he was killed. That same day, an air meet was nearing its end at Dominguez Field outside Los Angeles, where the U.S. exhibition business had begun twelve months before. The weather was cold and stormy with gusty winds. Arch Hoxsey and Walter Brookins were among the fliers who had waited all morning for the weather to improve. Finally, at 1 P.M., Hoxsey took off after announcing he would try for a new world altitude record. He was aiming for 12,000 feet. After about an hour, his barograph recorded 7,132 feet. He could go no higher. A few minutes later he was spied coming down out of the clouds in one of the Wright team's famous spiral glides. When he was a few hundred feet above the field, a gust of wind flipped him over, and his Model B somersaulted into the ground.

When the dust cleared, a sprocket wheel from the propeller transmission was seen to lie across Hoxsey's face. The motor lay on the right side of his twisted body, which was impaled on the jagged point of an iron bar, probably a part of the transmission assembly. Hoxsey's mechanic, who had witnessed the ghoulish attack on Johnstone's body at Denver, grabbed a splintered strut from the wreck and fended off souvenir hunters. Brookins broke down and cried like a child.

Even more lives would be lost in aircraft accidents in the coming year than in 1910. The air above the racecourses and fairgrounds where air shows were held had become as heavy with the presentiment of death and disaster as with blue exhaust and the aroma of the castor oil used to lubricate the hot, heavy motors of those fragile aircraft of cloth, wood, and wire. By October 14, 1911, the number of flying-machine fatalities throughout the world reached an even hundred when a pilot named R. Level was killed in a crash at Reims.

In November 1911, one year and six months after the Wright exhibition team made its debut at the Indianapolis Speedway, the Wright company withdrew from the exhibition business. Of the three most famous Wright pilots—Walter Brookins, Ralph Johnstone, Arch Hoxsey—Brookins was the only one to die in bed. Hoxsey was not the last fatality, however. Clifford Turpin, who had flown with the Wright team in 1911, continued to fly on his own. On May 30, 1912, he flew his plane into a grandstand during an exhibition at Seattle. Two days later, Phil Parmalee died when the biplane he was flying at the North Yakima fairgrounds in Washington was overturned in midair by a sudden gust and crashed. Arthur Welsh, one of Orville's first pupils at Montgomery in 1910, stayed on with the Wright Company as an instructor after the exhibition team was disbanded. In June 1912 he was sent to College Park, Maryland, to conduct tests of a new Wright Model C purchased by the U.S. Army. On June 11, as he was flying with a passenger, the Model C went out of control and nosedived from seventy-five feet, killing both Welsh and his passenger.

Although the Wright brothers were no more responsible for the deaths brought about by the machine they had invented than Count Zeppelin was responsible for the *Hindenburg* disaster of 1937, they were glad when the exhibition business was behind them. What they wanted most of all was to be completely free of the business their invention had created. Wilbur expressed himself on the subject in a letter he wrote in December 1910:

> Orville and I have been wasting our time in business affairs and have had practically no time for experimental work or original investigations. But the world does not pay a cent for labor of the latter kinds or for inventions unless a man works himself to death in a business way also. We intend however to shake off business and get back to the other kind of work before a year is out.

The year whose end Wilbur anticipated so eagerly was out in December 1911, but the Wright brothers were as deeply involved in business as ever.

# 42

## *Who Invented Wingwarping?*

INFRINGEMENT OF THE Wrights' wingwarping claim had been the decisive factor in Judge Hazel's January 1910 decision in *Wright* v. *Curtiss.* Knowing that the simultaneous use of ailerons and vertical rudder would be an equally important issue in the court battles ahead, Glenn Curtiss made flights at the Los Angeles air meet that month with his vertical rudder fixed in a neutral position. Witnesses of these demonstrations testified that they could detect no turning effects when ailerons were used without the rudder. The Wrights maintained that the witnesses were not sufficiently trained to note what was really occurring in such flights. "We state positively," they declared in court, "that machines with fixed vertical tails are death traps and of no practical value as flying machines." Curtiss went to even greater lengths to circumvent the Wrights' wingwarping claim. He tried every possible variation of ailerons—ailerons on the trailing edges of rigid wings, ailerons between the wings, ailerons operated one at a time rather than simultaneously. He even considered the use of sliding panels to increase the span of one wing while decreasing the span of the other. In every case, the courts decided that these mechanisms were variations of the wingwarping principle of the Wright patent.

There was one other way to get around the wingwarping claim, and that was to show that the Wright brothers had not been the first to warp their wings. Wilbur and Orville were understandably bitter about such attempts. In a letter to Henry Peartree, Flint and Company's attorney in Paris, they wrote: "It must be remembered that today, when everyone knows the Wright invention, and the world has assigned certain words to describe it, these words now produce a mental picture which they did not and could not produce when men knew nothing of this method of control." And in a letter to Albert Zahm, written a few weeks after Judge Hazel's January 1910 decision in *Wright* v. *Curtiss,* Wilbur wrote: "The objections to our legal claims are technical, being based on old publications which did not lead to any result, and which are now of use only as a means of depriving us of legal rights in an invention which we independently conceived, worked into shape, and presented to the world at a time when effort in that line was considered a foolish waste of time and money. At present there seems to be a general tendency to concede our moral right to the invention, but to deny that we have any right to expect any monetary pay."

In the mad scramble to prove that the Wrights had not invented wingwarping, it was generally overlooked that their patent covered warping as a means of lateral control and that their predecessors had all but ignored lateral control. Two of their contemporaries, however, claimed that they had not only invented wingwarping but had used it for lateral control several years before the Wrights. The first to do so, as might be expected, was Augustus Herring. Before *Wright* v. *Curtiss* went to trial in December 1909, Herring filed an affidavit for the defendants in which he asserted that he had anticipated both major claims of the Wright patent by incorporating in his Lilienthal-type glider of 1894 a "method for controlling lateral balance by setting surfaces to different angles of incidence on the right and left sides of the machine and correcting the difference in their resistances by means of an adjustable vertical tail." Carl Dienstbach made a last-minute effort to publicize Herring's suddenly recollected discovery in a short-lived aeronautical journal, but the court refused to accept this nebulously documented claim as an anticipation of the Wright patent. The other experimenter who claimed to have used wingwarping for lateral control before the Wrights was John Joseph Montgomery of California.

The earthquake that leveled San Francisco in 1906 put an end to the experiments Montgomery had been conducting with tandem-wing gliders. He would be a mere footnote in aeronautical history today had not Victor Lougheed seen fit to reinflate the hot-air balloon of Montgomery's collapsing reputation just as the patent wars of 1909–17 were heating up. Lougheed was an automotive engineer living in Chicago—he was the author of *The Motor Car Handbook* and *How to Drive an Automobile*—but he kept one eye cocked on developments in aviation. After reading in a Chicago paper of Daniel Maloney's balloon-drop flights in the Santa Clara glider in March and April 1905, he initiated a correspondence with John Montgomery and in 1907 traveled to California to discuss the feasibility of putting a motor and propeller on one of Montgomery's gliders.

Whether Lougheed was genuinely impressed by Montgomery's experiments and his naïve theories of flight or whether he merely planned to use Montgomery and his theories to his own advantage can never be known. That the theories expounded in Montgomery's *Aeroplane* pamphlet of 1905 were taken seriously can only be explained by the fact that aerodynamic forces were neither well defined nor clearly identified at the time. In October 1907, Montgomery was invited to present a paper, "Principles Involved in the Formation of Winged Surfaces and the Phenomena Involved in Soaring," to an international aeronautical conference in New York. In the wake of the furor created by Wilbur's flights at Le Mans the following year, the journal *Aeronautics* published Montgomery's conference paper in its entirety in four monthly installments from October 1908 to January 1909.

Of greater interest to subscribers of *Aeronautics* than these abstruse conjectures about the forces that keep a bird or an airplane in the air was the article that accompanied the final installment of the four-part "Principles" ("Some Early Gliding Experiments in America"), in which Montgomery makes some astonishing statements regarding the balloon-drop flights made by Daniel Maloney and David Wilkie in 1905 and 1906. Glider exhibitions, he says, were given in Santa Cruz and Sacramento, California, in addition to those known to have taken place in Santa Clara, San Jose, and Oakland, and that five or six gliders were used in these performances. However, until some ardent Montgomery supporter produces photographic or other evidence, these vague references to flights made in Santa Cruz and Sacramento with a half dozen gliders can be attributed only to Montgomery's imagination. The article is illustrated with two photographs of Maloney being towed into the air in a tandem-wing glider by a balloon at the San Jose racetrack on May 21, 1905—photos that have been reproduced many times since then, always without reference to the fact that the two flights attempted that day were aborted.

Of even more interest to aeronautical historians is the brief introduction to Montgomery's *Aeronautics* article, which refers to his gliding experiments of the 1880s. Whereas Chanute's *Progress in Flying Machines* of 1894 gives Montgomery credit for one glide of 100 feet, in *Aeronautics* it is stated that the greatest distance covered was between 100 and 200 yards, which implies that there were at least two other glides of less than 100 yards. A small matter, but that statement would become the nucleus of a snowball of information about Montgomery's early gliding experiments that would result thirty years later in an accretion of allegations so conflicting and confusing as to make it seem doubtful that any glide was made at all.

"Some Early Gliding Experiments in America" appeared in January 1909, but Montgomery's reputation as an aeronautical pioneer did not burst brightly into bloom until Victor Lougheed's *Vehicles of the Air* was published that November. Lougheed's book is aeronautical history reflected in an amusement-park mirror. Eight of the twenty-eight pages describing the accomplishments of Chanute, Langley, Lilienthal, the Wrights, and other pioneers are devoted to Montgomery and his "wonderful machine," just as if the Santa Clara glider of 1905 were making routine flights in 1909, competing with propeller-driven aircraft for speed, distance, and altitude records. The Wrights receive fewer than four pages. Their two greatest contributions to flying are identified as their catapult-assisted method of launching and their use of sledlike runners for alighting, both of which had been abandoned by the time the second edition of *Vehicles of the Air* appeared in 1910.

The summit of fatuity is reached when Lougheed drops the dreadful hint that it was not until after Montgomery's patent was issued that the Wrights commenced to be conspicuously successful by employing parabolically curved wings like those in the Santa Clara glider and by using a system of wingwarping closely resembling that of the Montgomery patent. Lougheed temporarily forgets that Montgomery's patent was issued four months after the Wright patent of May 1906 and intimates that it covered wingwarping. What it covered was a means of lowering the trailing edges of the wings on a glider, one at a time, or together if the operator wished to descend.

On April 21, 1910, the day the Aero Club of America announced that it had agreed to sanction air meets only after prior arrangements had been made with the Wright brothers, the Aeronautic Society of New York, a renegade Aero Club organization, invited John Montgomery to lecture on the timely topic of wingwarping. The New York society had recently joined seven other eastern and midwestern Aero Club organizations to form the American Aeronautic Association, with Victor Lougheed as secretary, in order to loosen what its members deplored as the Wrights' deathlike grip on flying in the United States. In his lecture, "The Origin of 'Warping,' " Montgomery revealed for the first time that he had invented wingwarping a decade and a half before Wilbur twisted that empty inner-tube box in the bicycle shop on West Third Street.

The lecture began with a description of Montgomery's early gliding experiments. In the article in the January 1909 *Aeronautics,* they were said to have taken place in 1884. Montgomery now states that they "commenced about 1883 and were continued until 1886." There were other slight differences from previous versions of that famous first glide. In the Chanute account in *Progress in Flying Machines,* young Montgomery "gave a jump into the air without previous running" to launch his glider. In his 1910 wingwarping speech, Montgomery recollected after a lapse of twenty-seven years that "there was a little run and a jump," and the distance of the glide, upped from "about 100 feet" in 1894 to "between 100 and 200 yards" in 1909, was now a more assured "about 600 feet."

"When I found the machine would follow my movements in the seat for balancing," Montgomery told the Aeronautic Society, "I felt I was self buoyant. This experience led to what is now a very important question, one that is agitating the whole country, the question of wing-warping. Wingwarping was born at this moment." If so, it was a long moment, for it transpired that Montgomery applied wingwarping not to his first glider, the only one that he claimed had flown, but to a second glider built in 1885 with perfectly flat wings. A triangular section at the rear of each wing, he said, was held in position by springs that could yield to undue pressure on either side. This was a far cry from wingwarping as practiced by the Wrights or aileron control as practiced by anybody.

Montgomery's talk to the Aeronautic Society was recorded by a short-hand reporter from *Aeronautics*. That monthly journal may have had qualms about publicizing Montgomery's wild claim, for the talk was published, by permission, in the British journal of the same name in May 1910, and it was not until November 1911 that the New York journal printed "The Origin of 'Warping,' " and then only after deleting the final paragraph, in which Montgomery told of his meeting with Octave Chanute in 1893 during the Chicago World's Fair: "Then for the first time I made known to him the device by which I controlled the lateral equilibrium, the warping."

Having been ranked by Lougheed with the world's greatest physicists and mathematicians and having established himself as the originator of wingwarping, fifty-two-year-old Montgomery took a new lease on life. On June 30, 1910, he married Regina Cleary, sister of a former college classmate. In October 1910 he attended the International Aviation Tournament at Belmont Park, Long Island, where he met the Wright brothers and treated them to a colorful account of the glider flights made by Maloney and Wilkie in 1905 and 1906. Orville reported their conversation in a letter he wrote to Thomas Baldwin a year later: "Montgomery told us in perfect seriousness that the control of his machine was so great that the 'boys,' as he called them, were looping the loop time after time; in fact, were doing it so much that he was compelled to make the controls so that they could be operated but a slight extent in order to prevent their doing this kind of flying all the time!"

Before the year was over, Victor Lougheed found a backer for the project he had suggested during his trip to California in 1907—applying a motor and propeller to a Montgomery glider. On the last day of 1910, Lougheed, Montgomery, and James Plew, a wealthy Chicago sportsman, met in Plew's library in Chicago and signed a contract. By its terms, Montgomery agreed to build two gliders. One would remain in California for testing. The other would be sent to Chicago, where it would be fitted out with a motor and propeller by Lougheed. Plew would supply the funds.

Sometime during the spring of 1911 Montgomery produced two gliders of a new design. One he shipped to Chicago in a shallow box twenty-five feet long and five feet wide. Lougheed defaulted on his contract—probably after he opened the box and considered the problem, if he ever intended to consider it at all, of installing a motor and propeller weighing three or more times as much as the frail craft itself, a project tantamount to packing a 200-pound power plant into a baby carriage.

The baby-carriage analogy is not too farfetched. Montgomery's new glider was designed to be launched on a hillside by running it down a pair of wooden rails on four fourteen-inch baby-carriage wheels. It was a monoplane with a large dartlike tail. The tandem-wing arrangement of his previous gliders had been consigned to the wastebaskets of history, but Montgomery had not abandoned his belief that a flexible, sinuous wing of deep camber was the best of all possible wings, and in some photographs of the new glider, his head is all but obscured by the umbrellalike droop of the wing. The glider's fuselage consisted of four bamboo poles and two metal uprights, between which the pilot sat in something called a rocker seat, which may have controlled the upward or downward movement of the tail. There was no side-to-side movement of the tail, but the trailing edges of the wings could be lowered by a yoke-wheel control devised by Montgomery's mechanic Cornelius Reinhardt. It was Reinhardt's job to construct and assemble the new glider and to photograph it in flight as Montgomery and Joseph Vierra, a second assistant, took turns gliding down a hillside on the Ramonda Ranch in Evergreen Valley southeast of San Jose, California.

It is not easy to fathom what Montgomery was trying to accomplish in the gliding experiments that began on October 17, 1911. In the San Francisco *Call* of January 3, 1911, he was quoted as saying that he had solved the problem of equilibrium in 1905 and was now about to solve the problem of motive power for aircraft. By 1911, it was clear to everyone but Montgomery that the problem of motive power had been solved as long ago as 1903, and he had not come any closer than Octave Chanute or Augustus Herring to solving the problem of equilibrium (for equilibrium, read automatic stability).

The Wright brothers had deliberately eschewed the will-o'-the-wisp of automatic stability until they had perfected their flying machine. Then sometime after 1905 they began secretly to develop a mechanism to relieve pilots of the routine job of adjusting rudder, elevator, and ailerons—or their equivalent—for every irregularity of air movement in straightway flight. They applied for a patent on this device in February 1908. The public flights later that year and the next and the subsequent Wright Company business interrupted the work, but by the fall of 1911 Orville had developed the automatic stabilizer to the point where it was ready for testing. Instead of testing it in a fast-moving aircraft he decided to try it out first in a glider at the old campgrounds at Kill Devil Hills in North Carolina in the fall of

1911 and, by an odd coincidence, at the very time that Montgomery was gliding down a grassy hill in Evergreen Valley on the other side of the continent.

The 170-pound Wright glider built for the automatic-stabilizer tests was half again as heavy as the 1902 glider. The elevator was in the tail with the vertical rudder. The pilot operated the control levers sitting upright, rather than in a prone position, and the only protuberance in front of the wings was a large fixed vertical fin, cannibalized from the vertical rudder of the 1905 Flyer, wrecked in May 1908 and left behind in the old camp building. On October 10, Orville arrived at the camp with his brother Lorin, Lorin's ten-year-old son Horace, and Alexander Ogilvie. Ogilvie had come over from England to fill in for Wilbur, who was too tied up with work on the infringement suits to help with the experiments. Orville had hoped to conduct the tests in relative secrecy, but four newsmen appeared on the scene before the glider was even assembled. When two more reporters arrived after the experiments began, Orville and Ogilvie altered their plans and resigned themselves to the pleasurable task of gliding for sport. The secret stabilizer would not be tested in the air until after the patent had been published in 1913 and secrecy was no longer a factor.

During the last two weeks of October, almost a hundred glides were made down the sides of the three Kill Devil Hills. There were several spectacular accidents, in one of which Orville was caught in a whirlwind that turned the glider around and ran it into the sand hill, where it turned over. On October 24, Orville and Ogilvie made a score of glides longer than one minute in duration. In one 5 1/2-minute glide, the machine rose fifty feet above the top of the hill. Two glides lasted 7 1/2 minutes each, and in the best glide of the day Orville soared for 9 minutes 45 seconds—a world record that would stand until 1921, when the Germans, prohibited by the Treaty of Versailles from building power machines, took up gliding in earnest and the modern era of gliding flights over long distances began.

When Victor Lougheed read the news of Orville's long glides, he hurried to Kill Devil Hills. After returning to Dayton, Orville reported the visit in a letter to Thomas Baldwin:

> A rather amusing incident happened when we were at Kitty Hawk last month. It seems that Montgomery was doing some gliding in California at the same time that we were experimenting at Kitty Hawk. Evidently he was not doing anything that had the least appearance of soaring, for, when the report went forth that I had remained in the air for nearly ten minutes without the use of artificial power, one of Montgomery's staunch supporters, Victor Loughead [sic], went all the way down to our

camp in order that he could "set us right before the world." When he learned at first-hand from a half dozen different persons who had been eyewitnesses of the flights that the reports were really true, he skipped out without ever even seeing the machine! On his first appearance he told reporters that he knew we must have been misrepresented in the reports, since it would be utterly impossible to remain aloft five minutes without the use of artificial power.

Montgomery was not bothered by reporters. The only observers of the glides being made on the other side of the United States were Montgomery's wife, his two assistants Reinhardt and Vierra, and five boys who were asked to leave after a few days because they were in the way. Most of the information about the performance of Montgomery's monoplane glider comes from Reinhardt, who told Montgomery's biographer many years later that the fifty-five flights made between October 17 and 31, 1911, featured "rising, maneuvering, and then circling in the breeze back to the hilltop" with only occasional landings in the grassy bottomland for practice. Since photographs of Montgomery taken at the time show him to have been a chunky little man, it would have taken a highly maneuverable glider with wings of efficient camber to keep the fifty-three-year-old novice pilot afloat on the way down the hill and a wind of cyclonic proportions to carry him back uphill to the starting point.

On October 31, the glider rolled down the hillside for the last time with Montgomery in the rocker seat. The baby-carriage wheels had just left the starting rails when a sudden gust lifted the monoplane with its huge tail about twenty feet above the hillside. Montgomery lost control. The glider sideslipped to the ground and flipped over on its back.

According to Montgomery's biographer, who apparently based his account on details provided by Reinhardt, Mrs. Montgomery ran down the hillside toward the wreck, but Reinhardt got there first. He had been worried for some time about the stove bolts used in the bamboo fuselage and when he reached the wreckage he discovered that one of the long bolts had pierced Montgomery's head behind the right ear. Blood and what he took to be part of Montgomery's brain were oozing from the wound made by the bolt. Reinhardt considerately pinched off the bit of bloody gray matter before Montgomery's wife reached the scene. In the meantime Vierra ran to the ranch house and phoned for a doctor. The Ramonda Ranch was not an easy place to find. The doctor made a wrong turn. When he arrived at the ranch two hours later, Montgomery was dead.

And there, for the second time, the story of John Montgomery might have ended if Victor Lougheed had not published another book on aeronautics the following year that was even more lavish in its praise of the California inventor than *Vehicles of the Air* and in time would inspire Montgomery's heirs—his wife, mother, brothers, and sisters—to initiate a suit against the holders of the Wright patent that would rival *Wright* v. *Curtiss* in duration.

# 43
## *Vin Fiz*

EXHIBITION FLYING WAS not the only type of flying to harvest headlines in those early years. Cross-country flying had become both practical and, for a few lucky aviators, profitable. After Louis Paulhan returned to Europe from his aborted American tour in April 1910, he won the £10,000 London *Daily Mail* prize for a cross-country flight from London to Manchester. On May 29, Glenn Curtiss won the $10,000 offered by the New York *World* for a New York-to-Albany flight. He made the flight in the reverse direction, down the Hudson, in 2 hours 51 minutes, with two stops for gas and oil. On September 29, Walter Brookins set a new U.S. record when he flew 192 miles from Chicago to the fairgrounds at Springfield, Illinois, with two stops on the way (Wilbur followed in a special car attached to an Illinois Central train). On November 10, Phil Parmalee made the first aerial freight delivery when he flew from Dayton to Columbus, Ohio, with several bolts of silk strapped to the passenger seat of his Model B. The Morehouse-Martens department store of Columbus paid the Wright Company $5,000 for the delivery and within two days realized a profit of $1,000 by selling pieces of the silk as souvenirs of the flight.

The first record-breaking U.S. cross-country flight of 1911 was made by Harry Atwood, who flew 1,300 miles from St. Louis to New York in August in a Wright Model B in twelve days. Atwood had his sights set on the $50,000 prize offered by newspaper publisher William Randolph Hearst for the first coast-to-coast flight made in thirty days or less. He was unable to secure backing for the flight before the offer expired on October 10, 1911, but two other Wright-trained pilots managed to compete. Robert Fowler left San Francisco on September 11 in a Model B but was unable to clear the Donner Pass and started all over again from Los Angeles. He reached Jacksonville, Florida, on February 8, 1912, 112 days after leaving the West

Coast and eighteen weeks after the Hearst offer expired. The only other pilot to make it all the way from coast to coast was Cal Rodgers. With ample backing from the Armour Meat-Packing Company of Chicago, Rodgers' progress as he lurched across the continent from the Atlantic to the Pacific in a battered Wright biplane called the *Vin Fiz* completely overshadowed Fowler's grueling flight from west to east.

Like Atwood, Rodgers had learned to fly at the Wright Company flying school at Simms Station, Dayton. Students were required to spend several hours practicing on a primitive flight trainer at the Wright factory. The trainer was a retired biplane without engine or tail, supported on a wooden trestle and attached to a motor-driven mechanism that tipped the wings to one side or the other. Only when the student learned to manipulate the wingwarping control so as to respond automatically to an imbalance was he allowed to solo.

In May 1911 the Army sent two young lieutenants to Simms Station for training by Orville Wright—Thomas Milling and Henry (Hap) Arnold. Both would serve as generals in the Army Air Forces in World War II. Lieutenant John Rodgers of the U.S. Navy was sent to Simms for training at the same time. While he was learning to fly, his cousin Cal Rodgers dropped by for a visit and stayed on in Dayton to take a few lessons himself. Cal (for Calbraith) Rodgers was fond of automobile and motorboat racing and was something of a playboy, but he was not a typical pilot. When he learned to fly, he was thirty-two years old, six feet four inches tall, close to two hundred pounds in weight, and a heavy cigar smoker. A star pupil, he soloed after an hour and a half of instruction and in August went on to fly as an independent pilot at the international air meet in Chicago, where he won the prize for duration flying by spending a total of twenty-seven hours in the air during the nine-day meet. A month later he set off on the coast-to-coast flight that became the premier aviation event of 1911 in the United States.

The machine Rodgers purchased from the Wright Company for his transcontinental flight was a modified version of the EX, a single-seater biplane developed for use by the Wright exhibition team in 1911. Its thirty-two-foot wingspan was midway between that of the standard Model B and the tiny Baby Grand flown at Belmont Park in 1910. Its top speed was 55 miles per hour. The Armour Company had not guaranteed to pay Rodgers five dollars for every mile flown out of the goodness of its heart. A subsidiary of the company was in the midst of a campaign to launch a new carbonated soft drink—Vin Fiz—made of grapes from the Armour vineyards. "VIN FIZ" was painted in large letters on the undersides of the airplane's lower wing and the elevator in the tail, where it would be seen by the thousands of persons who could be counted on to crane their necks for a sight of cigar-puffing Cal Rodgers and his EX as they made their way across the country. Rodgers would have to pay for his own fuel, spare parts, and repairs, but the company arranged for a special three-car train to follow him on his trip. It consisted of a luxurious private Pullman car for living and eating quarters, a day coach for reporters and minor Armour Company officials, and a converted baggage car equipped with a first-aid center, repair shop, spare plane parts, and an automobile. "VIN FIZ (5¢ Sold Everywhere)" was painted in bold letters on either side of the sliding baggage-car door amid clusters of purple painted grapes.

Before setting off on his transcontinental odyssey, Rodgers announced that he hoped to be in Chicago four days after taking off from Sheepshead Bay, Long Island. He also announced that he had secured the services of Charlie Taylor, whom he described as the greatest airplane mechanic in the country, to follow him in the hangar car of the special train. Both statements were premature. It took Rodgers twenty-one days to reach Chicago, rather than four, and Charlie Taylor had not yet left the Wright Company when the *Vin Fiz,* after being formally christened with a bottle of that bubbly soft drink, lifted off from the racetrack at Sheepshead Bay. Leaflets advertising the new drink were soon fluttering from the sky onto the boardwalk at Coney Island as Rodgers passed over. He headed north over Brooklyn, crossed the East River, and flew up Broadway over the heads of the New Yorkers who had congregated in droves to cheer him on. At 6:16 P.M. he landed at Middletown, New York. Confident that Chicago was only a few days away, he took off early the next morning. As he passed under some telegraph wires a few seconds later, his rudder caught on a tree and the *Vin Fiz* slammed into a chicken coop in the backyard of a nearby house. Rodgers climbed out of the wreckage with a bleeding scalp, the cigar still clamped between his teeth. The next day Charlie Taylor arrived in Middletown to superintend the reconstruction of the *Vin Fiz.*

Wilbur was in New York at the time. The first he knew of Taylor's having been lured away from his twenty-five-dollar-a-week job at the Wright Company was when he read it in the papers. Early in September, when Cal Rodgers had come to Simms Station to test his EX airplane, he had taken Charlie Taylor aside and offered him ten dollars a day and expenses to follow him across the country in the hangar car of the Vin Fiz special train. The offer was tempting: Mrs. Taylor had been in poor health since the birth of her third child in August, and the increase in pay would come in handy. Furthermore, Charlie did not feel that his position in the Wright Company was secure. For some time the Wrights had been dissatisfied with factory manager Frank Russell, under whom Taylor worked as foreman of the engine shop. Russell had been asked to resign, but had stayed on instead and sowed dissension among the men in the factory—in Taylor's case by hinting that he was being carried on the payroll as "a sort of charity patient."

The Wright brothers reacted to Charlie's leaving each in his own way. Wilbur, in a letter to Mrs. Taylor, who had taken her baby daughter and two older children to California after Charlie left Dayton, attributed her husband's defection to the dissension created by factory manager Russell. He denied vehemently that either he or Orville had ever referred to Charlie as a charity patient. While he didn't blame Taylor for feeling as he did, Wilbur wrote: "I do blame him for letting anyone tell him stories about us without asking us about it, and finding out whether they were true." Orville seems to have been closer to Charlie Taylor than Wilbur had been during their ten-year association. He told Charlie to look on his trip to the coast as a leave of absence and to be sure and come back.

In Middletown, New York, Charlie Taylor reconstructed the wrecked *Vin Fiz* in two days. The process was repeated twice before Rodgers arrived in Chicago, three weeks after leaving Long Island. "Whether I get fifty thousand dollars or fifty cents," Cal Rodgers told reporters, "I am going to be the first to cross the country in an aeroplane." On October 10, the day the Hearst offer expired, he had got only as far as Springfield, Illinois, but he kept on. By the time he reached Kansas City, Armour's Vin Fiz subsidiary was counting pennies, and Rodgers's fee was reduced from five dollars to four dollars per mile. In Kansas City, Charlie Taylor received a telegram from his wife, who was seriously ill in a Los Angeles hospital, but the *Vin Fiz* needed his attention as desperately as his wife and children, and he stayed with the hangar car for another two weeks. At Sanderson, Texas, he bade a tearful goodbye to Rodgers's entourage and boarded the train for Los Angeles.

On November 3, Rodgers crossed into California, having covered almost 4,000 miles in approximately eighty hours' flying time. Halfway across the state, a connecting rod in his motor broke through the crankcase, and he spent two hours in a doctor's office having bits of metal removed from his right arm. Then, on November 5, exactly seven weeks after leaving Long Island, he landed at Tournament Park in Pasadena. A wild mob rushed the plane, pelted it with flowers, and wrapped the pilot in an American flag, giving the impression his odyssey was over, although his goal, Long Beach, was twenty-seven miles away. A week was spent in Pasadena, overhauling the engine and reconditioning the *Vin Fiz*. There had been eleven major accidents along the way, four of which had required an almost complete reconstruction of the aircraft. Not much of the original *Vin Fiz* was left. Charlie Taylor came from neighboring Los Angeles to supervise the job.

On November 12, Rodgers took off on the last leg of his journey. While banking to avoid some high-tension wires, he lost altitude, and the *Vin Fiz* plunged into marshy ground a dozen miles from Long Beach. Rodgers wound up semiconscious in the hospital in Pasadena with two sprained ankles, a twisted back, and a slight concussion. The cure was three weeks' convalescence in a wheelchair in a Pasadena hotel under the care of his wife and his mother, followed by a week on crutches. Cal Rodgers was as much in need of rest and rebuilding as the *Vin Fiz*. In the meantime, Charlie Taylor put together an almost completely new EX with parts ordered from the Wright factory at an estimated cost of $4,000. At last, on December 10, 1911, twelve weeks after leaving Long Island, Rodgers flew the final twenty-seven miles to Long Beach and landed on the ocean sands to the hysterical cheers of a huge crowd that surged forward with such enthusiasm that the *Vin Fiz* was pushed back into the surf.

To capitalize on his momentary fame, Cal Rodgers considered forming an aeronautical company back East. But the urge to fly was too strong, and after a few months he returned to Long Beach with the Model B he had flown at the air meet in Chicago the previous August. He went into business in a small way, taking up passengers at two dollars each for short flights over the ocean and along the boardwalk. On April 3, he went up for a flight by himself to test his engine, which had been giving him trouble. To watchers on one Long Beach amusement pier, he seemed to be flying lower than usual when he encountered a flock of sea gulls and banked to get away from the birds. At the same time he tried to climb over another pier, but he had banked too sharply, and instead of climbing, his Model B plunged into the surf not far from the spot where he had landed in triumph five months before. The engine fell on Cal Rodgers and broke his neck. He is said to have died instantly, although some observers thought that he died more slowly —from drowning—as hundreds of souvenir hunters waded into the shallow waters and fought for souvenirs.

# 44

## *Wilbur*

IN 1911 IT WAS Wilbur's turn to attend to affairs in Europe. In Paris on March 24, he testified in a trial involving suits against twelve French aviators and manufacturers accused of infringing the Wright patents. The suit against Santos-Dumont was dismissed on the grounds that he built aircraft for his own use rather than for profit, but the eleven other cases were decided in favor of the Wrights. Blériot, the largest manufacturer involved, wanted to settle, but the other ten defendants insisted on appealing the decision. Two years later the court of appeals sustained the 1911 decision but permitted the defendants to set up a board of experts to resurvey the case. This would have entailed further delays. Since the French patent expired in 1917, the case was abandoned. (In 1920 Orville would dispose of the brothers' 5,000 shares in the French Wright company for $1,800.)

The outlook for the suit against infringers of the German Wright patent was equally discouraging. The matter would not be decided until February 22, 1912, when the court ruled that descriptions of the Wright control system in Wilbur's 1901 Chicago address and in Chanute's talk to the French Aéro-Club in April 1903 constituted prior disclosure. French and German patent laws required that the wording of the disclosure must render the material covered by the patent usable. Wilbur did not consider that either his description or Chanute's was sufficiently detailed to enable anyone to build and use the control system described. The German court thought otherwise. The decision went against the Wrights, who promptly appealed. While Wilbur was in Berlin in June 1911 he looked into the German Wright business and found it to be in almost as poor shape as the French. Orville had been ready to give up the foreign business altogether after his trip abroad the year before. Wilbur was inclined to agree. "I do not feel that we are in debt to either the French or German companies," he wrote Orville from Berlin. "All the money we ever get from either of these countries will be fully paid for by future work and worries."

Wilbur returned from Europe in August 1911 and once more became involved in the suits against U.S. infringers. He had a knack for presenting difficult aeronautical concepts clearly and concisely in the courtroom at a time when most of the phenomena encountered in flight required defining and redefining at almost every stage of a trial. Defendants were hard put to find experts whose testimony would sound authentic to judges who were straining every faculty to understand the issues involved. One expert with the requisite background was Albert Zahm, friend of the Wright brothers and erstwhile professor of mathematics and physics, who had danced attendance on Orville during his stay in Washington in 1908. A few weeks after Judge Hazel's decision of January 3, 1910, in *Wright* v. *Curtiss,* Zahm wrote the Wrights a letter in which he intimated that his services as an expert witness would be made available to the highest bidder: "You will probably regard me as a renegade friend, if the defense in the approaching litigation succeed in securing my professional services against you; but I hope you will remember that I have never declined, or hesitated to serve you when an opportunity presented itself."

"Naturally we regret that you will be lined up against us even in a professional capacity as confidential adviser in the legal struggle," Wilbur replied, "but we do not think that such service carried out in a spirit of fairness need interrupt the friendship which has always existed between us."

"Apparently you are not very much concerned about my position in the patent litigation, seeing that you made no effort to secure my professional services," was Zahm's petulant reply. "However, the only thing I have done thus far is to sign a deposition covering statements which I had previously made in print or prepared for publication. I have not yet accepted a retainer or bound myself to future services."

The Wright brothers did not rise to the bait. They had no need of Zahm's services, but Glenn Curtiss did, and Albert Zahm became a witness for the defense in *Wright* v. *Curtiss.* By September 1911, when Zahm's history of aviation was published—*Aërial Navigation: A Popular Treatise on the Growth of Air Craft and on Aëronautical Meteorology*—his friendship with the Wright brothers had dissolved into enmity. In *Aërial Navigation,* he denigrates the work of the Wrights by innuendo. After praising Lilienthal for not withholding or concealing the results of his experiments, Zahm writes: "Such is the *espirit de corps* which has ever prevailed among truly scientific men, as distinguished from the mercenary and commercial." He approves of the impetuous Santos-Dumont, who "could not realize the necessity for spending months, or years, cautiously coasting downhill to acquire the adroitness requisite to speed a flying chariot over the plain." He summarizes the work of the Wrights through 1905, then reminds the reader that Chanute's biplane glider "was estimated to have ample efficiency for successful flights with existent motors." Any intelligent artisan could power a Chanute glider and soar aloft, he writes, and concludes: "The aeroplane would thus appear to be the sudden outgrowth of fertile and mature conditions, rather than the product of uncommon originality."

Zahm supplies ammunition to the defendants in the Wright infringement suits by inserting references in *Aërial Navigation* to the prevalence of wing-warping and ailerons prior to the publication of the Wright patent, as well as to their use in conjunction with the vertical rudder. He himself, he writes, had proposed the three-torque system of airplane control covered by the Wright patent in a paper delivered at the 1893 International Conference on Aerial Navigation in Chicago, thus proving that "the combination of the torsional wings and a double rudder, either fixed or movable, has been public property since that date." (Zahm's proposal was considered by Judge Learned Hand in one Wright infringement suit but was rejected as "at most only a speculative suggestion never reduced to practical form.") Any inventor, Zahm contended, could have patented such a system. As a matter of fact, he wrote, "it has been patented in one form or another by many practical aviators, some endeavoring to claim the whole broad contrivance, others claiming more restricted devices." No doubt it was these maddening, offhand references in *Aërial Navigation* to the antedating of the Wright patent claims that inspired the following comments in a letter Wilbur wrote in April 1912:

> It is rather amusing, after having been called fools and fakers for six or eight years, to find now that people knew exactly how to fly all the time. People who had not the least idea of flying until within the last year or two now attempt to write books stating what the situation of the flying problem was in 1900 and 1901, when we made our first experiments at Kitty Hawk. In view of our experiences in 1901 it is amusing to hear them tell that the science of aerodynamics had been reduced to a very exact basis, so that anyone could calculate without difficulty the lift and drift of aeroplane surfaces. After the real truth had been discovered, old experiments seemed to have an importance in value sometimes which they did not have at the time.

In 1912 Wilbur wrote three articles for the Aero Club of America's *Bulletin* to set the record straight in regard to three aeronautical pioneers —Clément Ader, Louis Mouillard, and Otto Lilienthal—two of whom, Ader and Mouillard, had been grossly overpraised in Zahm's book. Ader had become an issue in *Wright Company* v. *Louis Paulhan* early in 1910. An affidavit had been filed on behalf of Paulhan stating that the Wright patent was not entitled to the liberal interpretation that had been placed upon it by Judge Hazel, for the reason that Ader had flown almost 1,000 feet in 1897, several years before the Wrights had left the ground in a flying machine. Later in 1910, the secret report of the French commission that had observed Ader's experiments in 1897 was at last made public. It proved that Ader had made no such flight. The report had not been translated into English, however, and in his zeal to discredit the Wrights, Albert Zahm felt free to ignore its existence.

In France, it was no longer possible to claim that Ader had flown, but when Wilbur testified in Paris in the trial against French infringers in March 1911, the defendants tried a new tack. Ader, they said, had controlled the lateral balance of his machine by a means similar to wingwarping. The court was required to consider this claim and adjourned to inspect Ader's *Avion* in the Musée des Arts et Métiers, where it was then on display. Both Ader and Wilbur were present. When Ader was asked to describe his equivalent of wingwarping, he explained that running one of the propellers at greater speed than the other had the same effect as wingwarping. It was clear to the court as well as to Wilbur that this would affect the steering rather than the lateral balance, and the claim was dismissed. A few days later Wilbur returned to the museum and borrowed a ladder from the curator so that he could examine the *Avion* at his leisure. There was a mechanism for throwing the wings forward or backward, he discovered, but it was operated by a worm winch requiring twenty or thirty turns of a nut working on a screw. Moreover, the wings were not fitted with enough ribs to give any constant curvature. "The whole machine," he stated in a letter to Orville, "is most ridiculous."

In his article "What Ader Did" in the May 1912 Aero Club *Bulletin,* Wilbur included a complete translation of the official report of the trial of the *Avion,* which revealed, for the first time in English, that the rear wheel of the *Avion*'s tricycle landing gear was the only wheel to leave the ground before the machine was overturned by a gust of wind as it waddled around its circular track on the military ground at Satory near Paris on October 14, 1897.

In "What Mouillard Did," the first of Wilbur's three articles to appear, he pointed an accusing finger at the Ligue Aérienne, a chauvinistic society whose members "made it their purpose to convince themselves and the world that France was the birthplace of human flight." When it was proved that the Wrights had flown before Santos-Dumont, the Ligue fell back on Ader. When Ader was shown not to have flown, they fell back on poor Louis Mouillard, not as a maker of powerplane flights but simply as the "father of aviation." The Ligue accused Octave Chanute of stealing the secret of wingwarping from Mouillard and transmitting it to the Wright brothers. Wilbur defended Chanute, saying Chanute not only had given Mouillard considerable sums of money when he was an invalid but had furnished him with funds to secure a U.S. patent on his glider. The patent, Wilbur wrote, included a substitute for a vertical rudder, which Mouillard's glider lacked —that is, the rear edges of the wings could be pulled down on one side or the other to effect a turn. Wilbur made it clear that he and Orville considered Mouillard's book on ornithology, *L'Empire de l'Air,* one of the most remarkable pieces of aeronautical literature ever published, but while they had the highest regard for Mouillard as a missionary of flight, his gliders, they admitted, were mediocre and his efforts at gliding feeble.

The last of Wilbur's three articles, "Otto Lilienthal," was a sincere tribute to the German experimenter qualified with a few caveats. Lilienthal's tables of pressures and resistances of arched surfaces were not accurate enough to enable anyone to construct a glider with full assurance that it would fly, and the rate of Lilienthal's progress made it doubtful that he would have solved the problem of flight, even if his life had been spared. Nevertheless, Wilbur conceded, Lilienthal's efforts were the greatest contribution to the final solution of the flight problem made by any nineteenth-century experimenter.

Wilbur's article on Lilienthal, which did not appear until September, was written in the spring of 1912, a crucial time in the suit against Curtiss. Early in May a Wright Company lawyer suggested postponing hearings on the case until the following autumn. Wilbur became disturbed. "Unnecessary delays by stipulation of counsel have already destroyed fully three fourths of the value of our patent," he wrote the lawyer. "The opportunities of the last two years will never return again. At the present moment almost innumerable competitors are entering the field, and for the first time are producing machines which will really fly." Wilbur spent almost three weeks in February and March preparing a lengthy deposition for the use of Wright Company lawyers. His deposition was a virtual history of the evolution of the airplane, a chronological account of what the Wright brothers and to a certain extent others had accomplished. Wilbur was described as coming home white after these sessions with the lawyers. This did not escape the notice of his father. "The amount of his intellectuality, in describing their invention, was marvelous," Bishop Wright wrote in his diary on February 14. "It must have greatly wearied him." In April, Wilbur left for New York to negotiate a contract with the Aero Club of America for the Wright Company. At the end of the month he was in Boston, probably to consult with Frederick Fish, one of the lawyers retained as counsel in the suit against Curtiss. While in Boston, Wilbur suffered an indisposition, which he attributed to fish eaten in his hotel. When he returned home, his strength was still at a low ebb, but he went with Orville, Katharine, and Bishop Wright to look over the site of a new home.

Until 1908 the house on Hawthorn Street had fitted the family as comfortably as an old shoe. But fame had brought an increase in worldly possessions that threatened to outgrow the modest seven-room dwelling on Dayton's West Side, and the brothers decided to build a larger house on a seventeen-acre plot in Oakwood, two miles southeast of Dayton's business district. An architect had been hired to design the new house. Orville, however, had planned many of its features himself while Wilbur was in Europe in the spring of 1911. "I see that most of the rooms are smaller than in the original plans, and only the price has been enlarged," Wilbur wrote after looking over the designs that Orville had forwarded to Paris. "You are wasting entirely too much space on halls &c." He proposed a new plan for the south bedrooms, one of which was to be his. "In any event," he admonished Orville in big-brother tones, "I am going to have a bath room of my own, so please make me one."

On Thursday, May 2, the four Wrights tramped over the small hill on which the new house was to be built, then returned to Hawthorn Street. Later that day, Wilbur went with Orville to Simms Station to look over the Model C airplane ordered by the U.S. Army. Orville took the machine up for a short flight with Arthur Welsh as passenger. Welsh was to accompany the machine to College Park, Maryland, and instruct Army personnel in its use.

On Friday, Wilbur went back to Simms Station with Orville. He was quieter than usual, and when they went home to dinner he had a slight fever. It was Carrie Grumbach's day off and Katharine, who had prepared the meal herself, noticed that Wilbur hardly touched his food. On Saturday he went to the office over the bicycle shop and wrote a letter to Boston lawyer Frederick Fish. Then he went home for lunch and lay down after eating. When he got up, he decided to go to Simms Station, but Katharine refused to let him go and called Dr. Conklin, the family doctor. Conklin diagnosed Wilbur's condition as a touch of malaria and sent him to bed. After four days in bed, Wilbur was a little better, but it was obvious he was not suffering from malaria. "There seems to be a sort of typhoidal fever prevailing," Bishop Wright wrote in his diary that night. "It usually lasts about a week."

Whatever Wilbur's father may have meant by "typhoidal fever," typhoid fever itself was not a disease with a duration of one week. A common source of the disease in those days was shellfish contaminated by sewage. Wilbur had become ill after eating fish, or perhaps shellfish, in a Boston hotel at the end of April. He had become feverish on Friday, May 3, and had been put to bed the next day. On Friday, May 10, he still had a high fever. Having witnessed the mentally debilitating effects of typhoid in its advanced stages in Orville in 1896, Wilbur sent for Ezra Kuhns, a Dayton lawyer, and dictated his will—a grim acknowledgment that at forty-five he might not have the stamina to withstand the onslaught of the disease Orville had survived at the age of twenty-five.

The methodical Bishop Wright kept a daily record of Wilbur's progress or lack of it. Other matters sometimes got mixed up in the record. There was a presidential election coming that November, and ex-President Theodore Roosevelt was running on the Bull Moose ticket.

*Wednesday, May 15.* Wilbur has not as high fever as some days. Roosevelt spoke in Dayton tonight, and Orville went to hear him, but was crowded out, and heard a suffragette.

*Thursday, May 16.* Wilbur's fever is unchanged. Orville left for Washington City, at 9:00, to deliver a machine to the Government.

Wilbur was entering the third week of his ordeal, the week in which symptoms of deterioration could be expected to appear—convulsions, wasting away, and delirium. The doctor had assured Orville that it would be all right for him to go to Washington to deliver the Model C airplane ordered by the Army, but when Wilbur learned on Friday that Orville had left Dayton, he became excited and was given a sedative by injection.

*Saturday, May 18.* Wilbur is no better. He has an attack mentally, for the worse. It was a bad spell. He is put under opiates. He is unconscious mostly.

*Sunday, May 19.* Wilbur ceases to take opiates, but is mostly quiet and unconscious. His sickness is very serious.

Lorin was at Wilbur's bedside each day. Reuchlin was advised to come from Kansas. Orville hurried back from Washington and arrived home on Monday, May 20. On Tuesday a still deeper shadow was cast over the deathwatch on Hawthorn Street by news of the first fatal accident at Simms Station. Frank Southard, a would-be pilot, had purchased a plane from the Wrights and had had a few flying lessons but had shown so little ability as a pilot that Orville forbade him to fly until he had taken a few more lessons. Early Tuesday morning, May 21, the impulsive Southard broke the lock on the hangar door at Simms Station, trundled out his late-model Wright, and took off. When he was about fifty feet in the air, the plane rolled over and Southard was dashed to his death.

*Wednesday, May 22.* The doctors had Dr. Bushheimer of Cincinnati come in to consult in Wilbur's case. The doctors think him better.

Wilbur was now entering the fourth week of the siege, the week in which, if a patient was to recover, there was a gradual reduction of fever and a change for the better.

*Friday, May 24.* Wilbur seems, in nearly every respect, better. The doctors have a long examination before noon. Spitler and then Conklin's father. Reuchlin came from Kansas today.

This encouraging state of affairs lasted through Saturday. Wilbur seemed so much better Sunday that Katharine left the house for the first time in two weeks and went out for a walk. When she came back, Wilbur was worse.

*Monday, May 27.* Both Conklin and Spitler came at 7:00 morn. They think the case very bad. His fever was higher and he has difficulty with the bladder, and his digestion is inadequate. Agnes Beck called. Reuchlin saw him in the afternoon. I slept with my clothes on. We thought him near death. He lived through till morning.

*Tuesday, May 28.* Wilbur is sinking. The doctors have no hope of his recovery.

Word spread throughout the neighborhood that Wilbur was dying. Children were sent to other streets to play. Grown-ups tiptoed gravely past the house. Except for the occasional tinkling of a telephone, Hawthorn Street was silent.

*Wednesday, May 29.* Wilbur seemed no worse, though he had a chill. The fever was down but rose high. He remained the same till 3:15 in the morning, when, eating his allowance 15 minutes before his death, he expired without a struggle.
  His life was one of toil.
  His brain ceased not its activity till weeks of his last sickness had expired. Then it ceased.

All day Thursday and Friday telegrams of condolence and flowers poured into the house on Hawthorn Street. One of the telegrams was from Glenn Curtiss. Enough flowers were sent from New York by the Wright Company to fill a baggage car.

*Saturday, June 1.* The undertakers put Wilbur in the burial casket. Took him to the church at nearly ten. Many relatives come; many friends.

The family would have preferred a private funeral, but that was no longer possible, and there was a public viewing of Wilbur's wasted remains in the First Presbyterian Church of Dayton, with which no member of the family had ever been affiliated. An estimated 25,000 people filed by the casket. At three o'clock there was a half-hour ceremony in a church crowded to suffocation. The Presbyterian minister read an account of Wilbur's life prepared by Reuchlin, and a representative of the Church of the United Brethren read, rather than sang, Luther's hymn "A Mighty Fortress Is Our Lord." There was no music. Only the family and eight pallbearers were present when the casket was lowered into the soil of the family plot in Woodland Cemetery, but at three-thirty all business and industry in Dayton came to a standstill for three minutes. Streetcars and automobiles stopped. Phone service was discontinued. Men and women stood on the sidewalks in silence.

*Monday, June 3.* Wilbur is dead and buried! We are all stricken. It does not seem possible that he is gone. Probably Orville and Katharine felt his loss most. They say little. Many letters. Ezra Kuhns comes, reads Wilbur's will, and leaves copies.

It was not a complicated will. Wilbur left $50,000 each to his brothers Reuchlin and Lorin and to Katharine. He knew his father would be well taken care of as long as any of his four other children were alive, so to Bishop Milton Wright he left "my earnest thanks for his example of a courageous, upright life, and for his earnest sympathy with everything tending to my true welfare; and, in addition, I give and bequeath to him the sum of One Thousand Dollars ($1,000.00) which I desire him to use for little unusual expenditures as might add to his comfort and pleasures." (Wilbur also knew how difficult it was for his father to slough off lifelong habits of thrift. "I hope you have got poor old daddy's fan going for him all night," he had written Katharine from Berlin during his last trip to Europe, after reading in the paper that the temperature back home was between 105 and 110 degrees. "Don't let him shut off the fan during the nights to save money.") The remainder of Wilbur's estate, estimated at $126,000, was left to Orville, "who," the will read, "has been associated with me in all hopes and labors both of childhood and manhood, and who, I am sure, will use the property in very much the same manner as we would use it together in case we would both survive until old age."

Bishop Wright continued to make daily entries in his diary, his florid, gnarled syntax eloquently expressive of the family and the nation's grief. Among the "Notes for 1912" jotted down on the blank pages at the end of his leatherbound diary for the year were these comments on his third and most famous son:

> In memory and intellect, there was none like him. He systemized every-thing. His wit was quick and keen. He could say or write anything he wanted to. He was not very talkative. His temper could hardly be stirred. He wrote much. He could deliver a fine speech, but was modest.

# 45

## *Company President*

I N February 1913, Orville and Katharine sailed for Europe. They were met in London by their English friends Alexander Ogilvie and Griffith Brewer. For several years there had been talk of establishing a Wright company in England. The proposals were too much in the nature of stock-promotion schemes to satisfy the brothers, but the picture had changed. On February 21, 1913, the British Wright Company Ltd. was organized with Orville as chairman of the board. A year and a half later, an amicable arrangement was worked out by which the British government paid the Wright Company £15,000 for all unauthorized uses of the Wright patent before the establishment of the company.

From London, Orville and Katharine went to Germany. They were in Leipzig on February 26 when the German Supreme Court rendered its decision in the infringement suit that had gone against the Wrights in 1912 on the grounds of prior disclosure and had been appealed. The court's decision was strangely ambivalent. The claim for the combined use of wingwarping and rudder was honored; the wingwarping claim was not. After a week in Paris, Orville and Katharine sailed for home and were back in Dayton in time for Easter—and in time for the most devastating flood in Dayton's sixty-five-year history.

Easter came early that year. It was celebrated on March 23 under dripping skies and in ominous winds. The day after Easter, some small towns north of Dayton were already under water. Floods were not uncommon in the city itself, most of which was built on low ground about the curving Miami River. The low-lying West Side, bounded on the east and south by a bend of the Miami and on the north by Wolf Creek, was particularly vulnerable. On Monday night the downpour continued. On Tuesday morning the levees gave way and waves of brown, debris-laden water poured into the streets on either side of the swollen Miami.

Water first appeared on Hawthorn Street at 8 A.M. Bishop Wright was taken away in a canoe brought to fetch Mrs. Wagner, the Wrights' next-door neighbor. Orville and Katharine, who had been moving books and small pieces of furniture to the second floor, were offered a ride in a moving van while it was still possible for teams and wagons to navigate the rising waters, and were taken to the house of friends on Summit Street, five blocks west of Hawthorn. Having no idea where their father was, they posted notices asking that anyone knowing the whereabouts of Bishop Milton Wright communicate with them at the home of E. L. Lorenz on Summit Street. The next day, a Mr. Siler read one of the notices and informed them that their father was safe in a house on Williams Street.

Tuesday night the rain continued. Fires broke out all over town, adding to the horrors of the flood and lighting up the otherwise totally dark city. Orville worried not only about his father but about the bicycle shop on West Third Street, where the water was twelve feet deep. Although he did not know it at the time, the water did not quite reach the second-floor office where all his aeronautical data were stored, and whereas several other buildings in the block caught fire and burned in spite of the rain, the bicycle shop was spared. The shed at the rear of the shop, where the remains of the world's first flying machine, the 1903 Flyer, were stored, was protected from the flames by several feet of water and a layer of mud, but nobody in Dayton that night was worrying about the fate of that expendable artifact.

It was three days before the waters receded and the damage could be assessed. Three hundred and seventy-one lives had been lost, and the loss in buildings and real estate amounted to $100 million, none of it insurable. Asphalt pavement had been rolled up like carpets by the racing floodwaters. Dead horses and streetcars lying on their sides littered the streets. So many pianos of all sizes and descriptions had floated off and been stranded by the receding waters that they had to be hauled away like so many dead horses and burned in a huge pyre on the bank of the Miami. The player piano that had found its way into the Wright household in 1909 as an advertising ploy was among the missing. The family's personal losses, estimated at $3,000 to $5,000, were slight compared to those of the hundreds of families and merchants who had lost everything. Most of the downstairs furniture was ruined. More irreplaceable than the furniture were the glass-plate negatives in the shed that served as a darkroom behind the house. The negatives had been under water for several days. Many of these pictorial records of early Wright gliders and flying machines suffered from peeling emulsion, but the damage to the priceless image of the first flight of December 17, 1903, was limited to a small triangular area in the lower left-hand corner of the glass plate and an inconsequential smudge at the bottom.

The fashionable Oakwood area, where the new Wright house was under construction, had been untouched by the floodwaters. The Wright Company factory, just off West Third Street about two miles west of the bicycle shop, was also on high ground. It had not been harmed by the flood and reopened two weeks after the water began to recede. Orville had succeeded Wilbur as president of the company, but he went about things as he always had. When a small item such as a metal fitting was needed for a new type of aircraft he would go into the shop with Charlie Taylor, who was back with the company after a year in California, and design it with Charlie's help while matters of greater moment waited for his attention and letters piled up unanswered on his desk. He attended as few conferences and technical meetings in New York as possible. Rather than travel to the factory every day he found it more comfortable to transact most business from his office in the bicycle shop, where he was abetted in his habit of putting off the making of important decisions by Mabel Beck, the sharp-tongued secretary he had inherited from Wilbur.

Orville, like Wilbur, had been at odds with factory manager Frank Russell since the founding of the firm and was looking for a competent engineer to replace him. While he was in New York in July 1913, he interviewed Grover Loening, the young man who had turned up on Governors Island with a letter of introduction to Wilbur during the Hudson-Fulton Celebration of 1909. Loening had graduated from Columbia University in 1910 with the first master of arts in aeronautics in the United States. During the interview in Orville's hotel room, Loening hestitantly disagreed with one or two things Orville said. A week later, he replaced Russell as manager of the Wright factory in Dayton and became the same sort of partner in argument to Orville that Wilbur had been. Loening also found himself in the less enviable position of buffer between Orville and the New York office. Wilbur had always gotten along well with the wealthy directors of the Wright Company. Orville had not, although he had one good friend on the board of directors—Robert Collier, owner of *Collier's Weekly.* He particularly disliked Wright Company secretary-treasurer Alpheus Barnes, a genial, cigar-smoking Easterner with a fund of funny stories. Orville had been known to resort to forced coughing in Barnes's presence to indicate that cigar smoke was not to his liking, and Barnes had been heard to refer to Orville's Dayton businessmen friends, more than once, as Ohio hicks.

By 1913 the standard Wright airplane, the Model C of 1912, was being rapidly outclassed, and Barnes made frequent trips to Dayton to see what could be done about prodding Orville into redesigning and modernizing the airplanes being turned out by the Wright factory. Hydroplanes were a case in point. The pontoons used by the Wright hydroplanes caused trouble, but Orville would not think of copying Curtiss's more successful designs and would never have approved the Wright Aeroboat of 1913–14 if its stubby hull had not been so different in appearance from the Curtiss flying boats that were at least two years ahead of the Wright models. He was just as reluctant to convert to tractor propellers—propellers in front of the wings rather than behind—arguing that tractor propellers interfered with a pilot's ability to see for scouting. To Orville, the development of new Wright airplanes was secondary to his work on an automatic stabilizer.

Grover Loening once described flying in a Wright aircraft as "like sitting on the top of an inverted pendulum ready to fall off on either side at any moment." The Wright brothers had applied for a patent on a stabilizer to correct this condition as early as 1908. Orville had been unable to test this device at Kill Devil Hills in 1911, but he had been working on it, off and on, ever since. He was not alone in the search for a mechanism that would automatically stabilize an airplane. In 1912 Lawrence Sperry adapted a balancing mechanism invented by his father, Elmer Sperry, for counteracting the rolling and pitching of ships and installed it on a Curtiss hydroplane. The Sperry device used two gyroscopes as frames of reference. The Wright automatic stabilizer used a pendulum and a vane. The pendulum was connected to a battery so that whenever it swung out of the vertical, the wingwarping control was activated to restore balance. Fore-and-aft stability was obtained by a horizontal vane, whose displacement from the horizontal activated the elevator control. In the original device, the source of power was compressed air. In the final version, a small windmill set in motion by the slipstream activated the controls. Since the pilot could set the vane at any angle desired, the device could be used for climbing or descending. The apparatus weighed less than thirty pounds and could be switched on or off by the operator at will.

In the fall of 1913 Orville installed the stabilizer in a special one-place Wright Model E with a single pusher propeller and made several short test flights. Details of the stabilizer were kept secret, even from the Wright Company, although the patent had been granted in October. Orville had entered it in competition for the Collier trophy awarded annually by the Aero Club of America for the most significant contribution to aeronautics made during the year. The silver trophy, donated by Robert Collier, had been awarded in 1911 to Glenn Curtiss for his first successful hydroplane. In 1912 it had gone to Curtiss again for his development of the flying boat. Orville was determined to win the award in 1913, but with his usual penchant for testing and retesting everything over and over again, he put off his official try for the trophy until the last day of the year.

December 31, 1913, was a damp, snowy day. Grover Loening kept the press at bay while Orville checked and rechecked his plane, his motor, his propeller, and the pendulum and vane on the stabilizer. Finally he turned up the collar of his coat, fastened bicycle clips around the bottoms of his trousers, donned a pair of goggles, and took off. He made seventeen flights in all before the Aero Club judges. The most spectacular flight comprised seven circuits of the field, during which he flew with both hands off the control levers. The stabilizer maintained practically the same angle of bank and an almost constant altitude. Alexander Ogilvie and Griffith Brewer, Orville's English friends, had both been privy to the tests of the automatic stabilizer that autumn, for which reason, perhaps, Orville's winning of the Collier trophy was first reported in the London *Daily Mail.* "The news that Orville Wright has made a new contribution to the art of flying only second in importance to his invention of the first practical aeroplane will thrill the world," declared the London paper. "When Orville Wright makes the claim that his stabilizer renders flying 'as nearly foolproof as anything can be,' the world will believe him, for it knows he is no talker and boaster." In the American journal *Aeronautics* Orville made a prediction: Because of his automatic stabilizer, within ten years people would think no more of entering an airplane than of stepping into an automobile.

Alas! poor Orville. His automatic stabilizer never came into general use. Within a year, most aircraft were being constructed with cockpits. Cockpits required fuselages, and the fuselage surface provided the stability whose lack was so noticeable in machines in which the pilot sat in the open air between the wings, and when airplanes were developed to the point where automatic piloting became desirable in long flights, it was Sperry's gyroscopic device that swept the field rather than Orville's stabilizer with its pendulum and vane.

Another aeronautical instrument developed by Orville in 1913 was the incidence indicator. Relatively inexpensive and never patented, it was placed on the market that July and installed on the airplanes being turned out by the Dayton factory in the hope that it would put an end to accidents due to nosedives, most of which had occurred in Wright machines. The first of these accidents—the one in which Wright Company pilot Arthur Welsh and his passenger Lieutenant Leighton Hazelhurst had been killed at College Park, Maryland—had taken place on June 10, 1912, in a Wright Model C. The C, successor to the Model B of 1911, resembled the B except that the triangular blinkers attached to the front of the vestigial skids in the Model B had been replaced by a pair of vertical vanes, and the C had a more powerful motor. Three months later, Lieutenant Lewis Rockwell, flying a Model B with Corporal Frank Scott as passenger at the same airfield, came in for a landing at a steep angle. Instead of straightening out, his aircraft plowed into the ground, killing both men instantly.

In 1913 the Army shipped one Model B and two Model Cs to the Army flying school in the Philippines near Manila. They were equipped with pontoons for flights during the rainy season. The Model B and one Model C were soon destroyed, fortunately without loss of life. On July 8, Lieutenant Loren Call was flying a Model B at the Army training school at Fort Sam Houston in Texas when his aircraft tilted suddenly downward and he fell to his death. He was the seventh U.S. Army officer to be killed in a flying accident.

Orville suspected that most of these accidents were caused by stalls and that the stalls occurred when the pilot misjudged the angle of incidence of the wings of his aircraft (in modern terminology, their angle of attack). The incidence indicator had been designed to alert the pilot to the imminence of a stall. It consisted of a small horizontal vane mounted on the airplane close to the pilot. The vane rode edgewise to the wind when the wings were at the normal angle of incidence for straightway flight. A pointer attached to the vane indicated deviations from that angle, including deviations too small for the pilot himself to feel. The surplus of power available in a Wright airplane, Orville warned, was for use in climbing only. If the full power of the motor was used in straightway flight, the angle of incidence would become critical, just as if the aircraft were descending rapidly at too sharp an angle. In straightway flight, the angle of incidence should be kept between 5 and 10 degrees; otherwise the center of pressure on the wing would be critically displaced. If pilots paid careful attention to the position of the pointer on the indicator, Orville predicted, 90 percent of the accidents caused by stalling would be eliminated.

When the Army's lease on the field at College Park, Maryland, ran out in June 1913, three of its six Model Cs were sent to the Army flying school on North Island in San Diego Bay, California. On September 4, Lieutenant Moss Love met his death there when his Model C turned over on its back and crashed. On November 24, student pilot Lieutenant Hugh Kelly and chief instructor Eric Ellington—who had complained to Grover Loening that the Model C was tail-heavy and did not answer controls properly—were killed in the crash of the second of the three Model Cs sent to North Island. Only ten days before, Lieutenant C. Perry Rich, a student at the flying school in the Philippines, was gliding down for a landing in a Model C equipped with pontoons when it nosedived into the water, and he too was killed.

On December 5, in answer to a letter from the head of the North Island flying school about the growing number of accidents, Orville wrote that he found the accidents distressing—"more distressing because they can be avoided." He stubbornly insisted that the Model C was the best machine and the safest ever built by the Wright Company. The trouble was that its surplus of power and ease of maneuvering tended to make aviators careless. He reiterated his belief that stalling was the cause. "Proper care in observing the angles on incidence indicators, such as placed by our department on its machines, will positively eliminate it."

The incidence indicator was not the solution to the Army's problem that Orville hoped it would be. On February 9, 1914, Lieutenant Henry Post set a new altitude record above San Diego Bay in the Army's last Model C and after reaching 12,140 feet came down at a very steep angle. It was thought he tried to pull out when he was 600 feet above the water, but his aircraft nosed down and smashed into the bay. His death brought the number of Army officers killed in aircraft accidents to a round dozen. Six of them had been killed in Wright Model Cs. The Army board investigating the crashes concluded that the plane's elevator was too weak and condemned the Model C as "dynamically unsuited for flying."

The situation on North Island had become desperate. Oscar Brindley, who managed the Wright flying school at Simms Station with Walter Brookins, traveled to California to evaluate the Army's pilot training program. Brindley was shocked at what he found. Aircraft maintenance at North Island was a shambles. What was needed was a competent engineer to oversee the entire program. The ideal man for the job was Grover Loening. On July 14, 1914, after one year and four days with the Wright Company, Loening resigned and was appointed Aeronautical Engineer, U.S. Army Signal Corps. One of his first actions was to condemn the use of all pusher planes, Curtiss machines as well as Wright. They stalled too easily, and when they crashed, the motor too often fell on the pilot. After Glenn Martin of California sold the Army its first tractor trainer that July, Army pilots spent three to four times as many hours in the air as before. Of the twenty-nine men trained in tractor aircraft during the next six months, there was only one fatality—a pilot who lost his life when he was blown out to sea in a storm.

Grover Loening wrote Orville several times during the year he was with the Signal Corps, but Orville seldom answered his letters. Loening felt that Orville never forgave him for outlawing planes with pusher propellers. Tractor propellers would not appear on a Wright Company aircraft until the Model K, a seaplane produced for the U.S. Navy at the end of 1915, when Orville was no longer president of the company. The Model K was not only the first Wright machine to be equipped with such propellers but the first in which the outmoded wingwarping mechanism was replaced by ailerons on the trailing edges of the wings, the method of lateral control then in almost universal use.

# 46

## *The Aerodrome Affair*

IN BUFFALO, New York, on February 27, 1913, Judge John R. Hazel handed down his second decision in *Wright* v. *Curtiss,* confirming his opinion of January 3, 1910, that the Wright patent was entitled to a broad interpretation, and granting the Wright Company's petition for an order restraining Glenn Curtiss from manufacturing and selling machines that infringed the Wright patent. Curtiss appealed. The Court of Appeals decision, handed down on January 13, 1914, was a clear-cut victory for the Wright Company; it concurred with previous decisions in the four-year-old case "that the patentees may fairly be considered pioneers in the practical art of flying with heavier-than-air machines, and that the claims should have a liberal interpretation."

Orville had refrained for many years from making public his feelings about Glenn Curtiss. It would be a month before the Court of Appeals decree would be formally issued, but when it was, Orville let himself go and submitted to an interview that appeared on page one of the *New York Times* on February 27, 1914. The way was now clear, he announced, for the Wright Company to collect royalties of about 20 percent on the sale of all aircraft manufactured in the United States. A lenient policy would be adopted toward most manufacturers who had infringed the Wright patent in the past —but not toward Curtiss. He went to some lengths to justify his position by relating how Curtiss had stolen the airplane from the Wright brothers over a period of years, beginning with the 1906 visit to Dayton of Curtiss and Thomas Baldwin. ("We told them all there was to tell.") He went so far as to accuse Curtiss of contributing indirectly to Wilbur's death. It was the long infringement suit against Curtiss, he said, that had "worried Wilbur, first into a state of chronic nervousness, and then into physical fatigue, which made him an easy prey for the attack of typhoid which caused his death."

Glenn Curtiss responded with a press release in which he labeled Orville's charges that he had copied the Wrights' work as absurd and malicious. He appended to his release an editorial from the Boston *Transcript* that attributed Orville's attack to personal animosity and predicted that the January decree of the Court of Appeals would "numb what little life remains in aviation in America."

Henry Ford believed that the Wright patent was having the same stifling effect on the development of aircraft that the Selden patent had had on the development of automobiles. He convinced Curtiss that he should carry on the legal battle and let himself be represented by W. Benton Crisp, the attorney who had done so much to break the stranglehold of the Selden patent on the automobile industry. Crisp was accordingly appointed chief counsel of the Curtiss Aeroplane Company. His advice was for Curtiss to consider some action that would force the Wright Company to reopen the case and give the defendants an opportunity to introduce additional evidence. Since the court prohibited Curtiss from manufacturing airplanes in which the right and left ailerons were operated simultaneously, it was decided that all airplanes he manufactured in the future would be equipped with ailerons that could be operated independently. This had the desired effect of luring the Wright Company into filing a new complaint against Curtiss. This was not done until November 1914, which gave Curtiss and Crisp plenty of time to look into every possibility that would serve to undermine the primacy of the Wrights as aviation pioneers.

Early in 1914 a meeting took place to discuss such possibilities. It was attended by Curtiss, Crisp, and Albert Zahm, who had served as Curtiss's expert witness in the past and would serve in that capacity in the new trial. It was at this meeting that the Smithsonian Institution became involved in *Wright* v. *Curtiss*. In 1913 Zahm had been appointed director of the reactivated Langley Aerodynamical Laboratory in the Smithsonian and in that capacity was custodian of the remains of Langley's Aerodrome, the man-carrying flying machine that had twice plunged into the Potomac in 1903 with Charles Manly in the pilot's car. Zahm now suggested that it would be interesting to rebuild and retest the Aerodrome to determine if certain features of its design, such as the tandem-wing arrangement, were viable. Crisp thought the suggestion excellent. If it could be shown that Langley's Aerodrome was capable of flight and—if it had not been prevented by a faulty launching mechanism—could have flown before the Wrights first flew, this would go a long way toward convincing the court in the new trial that the brothers were not entitled to the broad interpretation placed upon their patent.

Albert Zahm's suggestion to rebuild and fly the Langley Aerodrome was not the first such proposal. In 1907, Charles Manly had written that he intended to reequip and try to fly the old machine as soon as he could find the time. There had been a further flurry of interest in the wrecked Aerodrome in 1908 when the trial of the Wright Army Flyer at Fort Myer was announced, and General James Allen of the Signal Corps was bullied by the press into acknowledging that if the Wright brothers failed to deliver a satisfactory aircraft, the Langley machine might be given another trial, but the success of the second Wright Army Flyer the next year made it hard to justify putting together Langley's old machine just to see if it could fly if it was properly launched.

What was needed was a motive, and in 1914 a motive was at hand. As a matter of fact, there were several motives. The project smacked of collusion from the beginning. In January, Lincoln Beachey, the most successful of all Curtiss-trained exhibition pilots and a stockholder in the Curtiss Aeroplane Company, sent a telegram to the secretary of the Smithsonian asking permission to restore the old machine and fly it with a modern motor. Beachey's motive, as he expressed it publicly, if inelegantly, was to show that "you can fly a kitchen table if your motor is strong enough." His proposal drew this comment from the *New York Times:* "People with minds naturally suspicious are likely to look for a connection between certain patent litigation and the announcement by Lincoln Beachey, the aviator, that he is going to prove that if Prof. Langley had been able to put a modern motor in his aeroplane it would have sailed the air as well as those since made."

The Smithsonian Institution's motives for permitting the retesting of the Aerodrome in 1914 were set forth in the Institution's *Annual Report* for that year by Albert Zahm, who stated that the Aerodrome had been reconstructed, first, to find out if the machine as originally designed was capable of sustained free flight and, second, to determine after certain modifications had been made the advantages, if any, of the tandem-wing configuration. Charles D. Walcott, Samuel Langley's successor as secretary of the Smithsonian, went even further in a phone conversation with Alexander Graham Bell—who as a member of the Institution's Board of Regents would have to endorse such a project—by pointing out that he and Albert Zahm hoped that the tandem-wing principle would provide a solution to the tragic accidents caused by the nosedives of airplanes with superposed wings.

These official motives gave the project an aura of respectability and served to mask the underlying motive, which was stated bluntly by Glenn Curtiss in a letter he wrote to Lincoln Beachey shortly before Beachey dropped out of the project and left for Europe: "I think I can get permission to rebuild the machine, which would go a long way toward showing that the Wrights did not invent the flying machine as a whole but only a balancing device, and we would get a better decision next time." On March 30, Secretary Walcott met with Curtiss and Alexander Graham Bell at Bell's home in Washington, D.C., and agreed to pay Curtiss $2,000 to reconstruct and test the Langley flying machine.

The frame, fittings, and other surviving parts of the Aerodrome were shipped to the airplane plant in Hammondsport, and the reconstruction was carried out in April 1914 with the help of Albert Zahm and Charles Manly. Manly's task was overhauling the 52-horsepower radial motor, which he had played such a large part in developing. After a decade of rust accumulation, the best the repaired motor could produce in 1914 was 40 horsepower and that only after an automobile-type carburetor had been substituted for the original fuel-feed system. A new intake manifold was also installed. A modern honeycomb-type radiator replaced the radiating-fin cooling system of the original, and the old dry-battery ignition system was replaced by magneto ignition with a hotter jump spark. Because the engine would not run to full speed with the canvas-covered propellers in their original condition, a triangular section was cut from the leading corner of each blade to increase rotation.

Since it would have been impractical to duplicate Langley's houseboat launching platform, the Aerodrome was equipped with pontoons for taking off from the surface of Lake Keuka. The 350 pounds of additional weight and the corresponding amount of drag were considered such serious handicaps that it was assumed at the time that if the machine could fly for even a few seconds with this added weight, it would have been capable of a much longer flight in 1903 if it had been properly launched. This would have been a reasonable, if unprovable, assumption if the wings had been restored to their original condition, but in that case it would not have been possible to equip the machine with pontoons. In the original machine, the trussing wires had been attached to a single guy post above each pair of wings and to a single guy post below. In the 1914 machine, the post above was replaced with an inverted V, and below the forward pair of wings the single post was replaced with four much heavier wooden struts to accommodate the pontoons. The struts not only provided additional bracing points for the guy wires but were located thirty inches farther to the rear than the guy posts in the 1903 machine and so coincided more nearly with the center of pressure on the wings in flight. This eliminated the backward pull that, in Orville's opinion, had caused the collapse of the wings in both tests in 1903 rather than any failure of the launching apparatus. The wings themselves were further strengthened by reinforcing the center spar with an extra wooden member extending under each wing for about two-thirds of its length, and the cotton wingcoverings were varnished, as they had not been in the original.

Three other changes in the wings improved their aerodynamic efficiency. These were changes in camber, shape of leading edge, and aspect ratio (ratio of span to chord). When Langley began work on his Aerodrome he gave his wings a camber of 1:18. About 1900 he decided to "quicken" the curve by adding 23.8-centimeter extensions to the ribs in front of the forward spar. The resulting hooked-nose ribs, as Albert Zahm called them, had a camber of 1:12 and gave the wings a sharply arched look. The leading edge of each wing was then no thicker than the one-sixteenth-inch wire strung from rib to rib. When the machine was reconstructed in 1914, the extensions to the ribs were eliminated, so that the front, cylindrical spar, one and a half inches in diameter, tapering to one inch at the wingtips, supplied a more desirable, rounded leading edge. The omission of the rib extensions reduced the camber to a more efficient 1:18 and increased the aspect ratio by about 5 percent. Thus, although the loss of power in the original engine and the added weight and drag of the pontoons were offset to an undetermined extent by the improvement in the aerodynamic efficiency of the wings and by the way they were strengthened, the Aerodrome could by no means be said to be in its original condition except for the addition of pontoons, as Glenn Curtiss and Albert Zahm claimed at the time and would continue to claim over the years.

The testing of the remodeled Aerodrome at Hammondsport on May 28, 1914, was a gala event. Reporters and photographers stationed on the shore of Lake Keuka were treated to a virtual air show with as many as six aircraft buzzing over the lake at one time. Albert Zahm had been appointed official observer for the Smithsonian, but Secretary Walcott was also present when the Aerodrome was launched into Lake Keuka with Glenn Curtiss in the low-slung pilot's car. It went skimming over the surface of the lake on its pontoons until it was too far from shore for clear photographs to be taken; then, in the words of Zahm's official report, it "rose in level poise, soared gracefully for 150 feet, and landed softly on the water." What the observers had witnessed, they were given to understand, was a preliminary test only. More extensive tests would soon be made. Government observers would be invited.

The papers the next day were full of the news that "Langley's Folly," so mercilessly vilified for its failure in 1903, had all along been capable of flight. As to the extent of the success achieved, the *New York Times* noted a few weeks later, when questions were raised about what had actually taken place, "accounts differ widely, some leaving, as evidently was intended, the impression of a real and prolonged movement through the air, while observers who watched the proceedings from the shore failed to see that the machine rose at all from the water." The legal implications of what had taken place were brought to public attention by the same paper three days after the flight, by an editorial writer who pointed out that the Wright brothers' case against Curtiss had been "won upon the fact that no other aeroplane had ever maintained itself in air with human freight, and inferentially, could not. What effect Mr. Curtiss's demonstration with the Langley Aerodrome will have in modifying the recent decision of the Circuit Court in favor of the Wrights' contention no one can now tell."

On June 2, the Aerodrome was tested for the second time or, as the Smithsonian *Annual Report* for 1915 put it, "subsequent short flights were made in order to secure photographs of the craft in the air." Two photographs were obtained on June 2 of the machine with its pontoons just above the surface of Lake Keuka. No estimates of time or distance were given for either flight, which implies that they were both shorter than the flight of May 28, alleged by Zahm to have been 150 feet, and no Langley or Curtiss supporter has ever claimed that they were not. After the pictures were taken, Curtiss told reporters that no official demonstration would be made until "motor and machine are tuned up to concert pitch." No official demonstration of the Aerodrome "in its original condition" before disinterested observers was ever made, however, and when Secretary Walcott left Hammondsport for Washington, he authorized the installation of an 80-horsepower Curtiss motor on the machine for the second-phase experiments to determine the value of the tandem-wing arrangement.

It happened that Griffith Brewer was visiting Orville in Dayton that June. He had recently signed a contract for a book on the conquest of the air. The book never did get written, but it was discussed with Orville. Discussing books, particularly unwritten ones, was never a popular pastime with Orville and he told Brewer he would do better to go to Hammondsport and find out what Glenn Curtiss was doing to falsify the history of aviation. Brewer made the trip. He hired a rowboat and in the company of a reporter from a British newspaper managed to get close enough to the Aerodrome on the shores of Lake Keuka to note some of the changes being made while it was being refitted with a powerful Curtiss motor and a single wooden tractor propeller. He then wrote a letter to the *New York Times,* giving several reasons why the Aerodrome had not flown in 1903—the inference being that if it had been restored to its original condition it could not have flown in 1914. He asked several questions that cast doubt on the motives behind the experiment. The most pertinent was: "Why, if such a demonstration were decided on, was not some impartial, unprejudiced person chosen to make the tests, instead of the person who had been found guilty of infringement of the Wright patent?"

The reactions to Brewer's letter when it was printed on June 22 were mixed. The *Times* urged its readers to remember that "between a brief rise into the air and flight, properly so called, there is a vast difference." The *Scientific American,* on the other hand, commented that Glenn Curtiss had nothing to gain from the experiments since wingwarping was not involved and concluded its remarks with a burst of organ music: "His is an act of piety which deserves commendation."

Further tests were made of the Aerodrome in the fall of 1914 by Elwood Doherty, a graduate of the flying school at Hammondsport, using the high-powered Curtiss motor. The pilot's position had been moved to the top of the machine, and changes had been made in the control surfaces and their manipulation. On September 17, three 450-foot hops were made; on September 19, two flights of about 1,000 feet and another of 3,000 feet. On October 1, five flights were timed, ranging from 20 to 65 seconds in duration. Photographs were obtained of the Aerodrome off the water on all three days.

That November the Wright Company filed its new complaint against the Curtiss Aeroplane Company and *Wright* v. *Curtiss* resumed its slow way through the courts. Hoping that the Aerodrome tests would help to prolong the litigation, attorney Crisp urged Curtiss to continue the experiments into the new year. In April 1915 sled runners were attached to the Aerodrome for a few experiments on the ice of Lake Keuka. With the coming of warm weather, the runners were replaced by pontoons and the testing resumed. To discover what was going on, Orville sent another emissary to Hammondsport—his brother Lorin, who would be as difficult for the Curtiss people to recognize as Griffith Brewer.

Lorin roamed about the hangars of the Curtiss flying school on the shore of Lake Keuka all Friday afternoon, June 4, waiting for chief instructor Walter Johnson to take the Aerodrome out on the water. From a student pilot he learned that Johnson had recently made a quarter-mile flight about five feet above the lake and in the next trial would attempt a turn. The purpose of Lorin's visit was not suspected and he was allowed to take whatever photographs he wished. When he was sure that no flight would be made that afternoon because of the wind, he left for the town of Bath, eight miles away, and registered for a hotel room under the name of W. L. Oren.

On Saturday morning he returned to the flying school with his camera and a pair of binoculars. Stationing himself a few hundred yards from the Aerodrome, he watched the preparations being made for a flight without being observed. At about 10 A.M. Walter Johnson climbed into the pilot's seat, the motor was started, and the Aerodrome sped off into the lake on its pontoons. Then a remarkable thing happened—remarkable, that is, in that a Wright brother was on hand to witness it. "The machine gradually acquired speed," Lorin wrote in a memorandum later that day, "and after running as near as I could judge about 1,000 ft. the rear wings broke about midway the length of the spars and folded upwards. They also broke or pulled from sockets at points where they joined to frame. When the machine stopped the outer edges dropped and dragged in the water."

While the Aerodrome was being towed ashore and dragged up the runway, Lorin left his hiding place and took several photographs before he was detected by a workman. The scene that ensued was reminiscent of Wilbur's scuffles with photographers at Les Hunaudières racetrack in 1908 and at Fort Myer in 1909. Walter Johnson demanded that Lorin turn over the exposed film. When Lorin refused, he was surrounded by loyal Curtiss workmen and told he could not leave until he surrendered the film. When he asked why, he was told that no photographs could be taken of the machine in its present condition because of "legal complications." He finally turned over the film, and a boy was sent uptown on a bicycle to purchase a fresh film pack. Lorin sat down on the edge of the wooden runway used to launch the Aerodrome and watched the dismantling of the broken wing until the boy returned. When Lorin refused to accept the fresh film, the impasse was broken by placing the film pack on his knee, whereupon he got up, put the pack of unexposed film on the runway, and left.

There was no mention of the collapse of the Aerodrome's wings in the reports of the Aerodrome experiments in the Smithsonian *Annual Reports* for 1914 and 1915. The 1914 report by Albert Zahm, "The First Man-Carrying Aeroplane Capable of Sustained Free Flight—Langley's Success as a Pioneer in Aviation," was illustrated with several photographs, including two of the machine rising from the water on June 2, 1914, and five showing it several feet above the water in September and October during its flights with the more powerful Curtiss motor. If the word "Pioneer" had been included in the title to impress the court in the new suit against Curtiss, it was a failure, for the experiments did not result in a reversal of the opinion that the Wright patent claims were entitled to a broad interpretation because of the brothers' status as aeronautical pioneers.

From a psychological standpoint, however, the Aerodrome experiments were a success. "Up to the year 1914," Orville wrote many years later, "there was no room for question in history or in the public mind as to which was the first aeroplane capable of sustained free flight, or as to whose research furnished the foundation of modern aviation." That was all changed when Albert Zahm wrote of the rebuilt Aerodrome in the 1914 *Annual Report* of the Smithsonian: "It has demonstrated that with its original structure and power, it is capable of flying with a pilot and several hundred pounds of useful load. It is the first aeroplane in the history of the world of which this can truthfully be said."

Annual reports were not popular reading matter in those days, any more than now, and Langley's elevation to a position in the aeronautical hierarchy above that of the Wright brothers was not brought graphically to the attention of the general public until 1918, when the long-suffering, battered old Aerodrome was restored to its original, 1903 condition and placed on display in the U.S. National Museum with a label that read:

> The first man-carrying aeroplane in the history of the world capable of sustained free flight. Invented, built, and tested over the Potomac River by Samuel Pierpont Langley in 1903. Successfully flown at Hammondsport, N.Y., June 2, 1914.

The date "June 2" represented a subtle manipulation of the facts, since the only flight of any length ever claimed for the Aerodrome with the Manly motor was the 150-foot hop of May 28. But two photographs had been obtained on June 2, showing that the Aerodrome had been airborne, for at least a second or two, whereas there was no proof at all that it had been in the air on May 28. Not so subtle was the claim that the Aerodrome had been capable of sustained free flight. By no stretch of the imagination could the alleged flight of May 28, 1914, or the two unmeasured, untimed hops of June 2 be considered sustained. Nor was this a mere matter of semantics, depending on how one defined "sustained free flight." It was a lie pure and simple, but it bore the imprimatur of the venerable Smithsonian and over the years would find its way into magazines, history books, and encyclopedias, much to the annoyance of those familiar with the facts. To Orville Wright it was more than an annoyance. It was the culmination of Curtiss's campaign to demean and devalue all that the Wright brothers had accomplished.

Before 1914, a good case could be made for the integrity of Glenn Curtiss. As a respected and competent airplane designer, he seems sincerely to have believed that ailerons did not infringe the Wright patent. The Aerodrome experiments of 1914–15, however, did much to legitimatize the bitter feelings of Wilbur, Orville, and their family toward Curtiss. Wright exhibition pilot Frank Coffyn once told how the exhibition team had it drummed into them when Wilbur was still alive that the Curtiss crowd was no good at all, although he was later surprised to find out that they were a "pretty nice bunch." Grover Loening, during his year with the Wright Company, thought that Orville and Katharine's hatred of Glenn Curtiss was getting the better of them, and Wright family friend James Cox, governor of Ohio, reported that he once heard the ladylike Katharine say of the Aerodrome tests of 1914, "That Langley fake of last summer was so raw that it seems incredible that it could have succeeded."

The Aerodrome affair would not be forgiven or forgotten. When Langley's man-carrying flying machine was restored to its original condition and placed on display in the Smithsonian beside its misbegotten label, a first-class scandal emerged from the dusty pages of the Institution's *Annual Reports* into the limelight. The resulting controversy, which has been called the *cause célèbre* of American aviation, would take a quarter of a century to resolve.

# 47

# End of the Patent Wars

IN THE SPRING OF 1914, Orville, Katharine, and Bishop Wright moved into their new home on Harmon Avenue in Oakwood, south of Dayton—the neoclassical mansion that had been planned while Wilbur was still alive. It was named Hawthorn Hill, not in memory of the small white clapboard house on Hawthorn Street in which Orville and Katharine had been born but because of the many hawthorns on the seventeen-acre site. A winding drive led over a steeply sloping lawn, shaded with elms and maples, to the porticoed entranceway. The building of light brick was ornamented in front and in back with four white, fluted two-story columns and flanked on either side by wide covered porches with tiled floors.

Carrie Kayler Grumbach and her husband, Charlie, were an integral part of the new household. They were treated like friends rather than domestics, but to Carrie, who had been with the family since 1900, Orville would always be "Mister Orv." Carrie had lost none of her skill in cooking. Charlie acted as caretaker and served table. On Thanksgiving and other festive occasions there would be an elegantly set table with candles. On Christmas Eve there would be two silver platters of homemade chocolate ice cream in watermelon molds, garnished with red and green maraschino cherries, and beside the place of each young grandniece and grandnephew an envelope with money in it—a far cry from the single orange and inexpensive present that the Wright children would find next to their plates on Christmas morning at 7 Hawthorn Street in the old days.

The bicycle shop had been within walking distance of the old house. It was more than three miles from the new house, but that was no problem, for Orville loved to drive. He had bought himself a Franklin roadster with a big air-cooled engine and had the car equipped with special springs and upholstery to lessen the pains that bumps and jolts caused to his injured leg and hip. While he had been recovering from his Fort Myer accident in 1908, he had contributed an article on flying to the magazine *Country Life in America* in which he made the astonishing statement: "It is the spice of uncertainty, of a possible accident, which makes swift automobiling so great a pleasure, and it will be the same way with the aeroplane." In 1913 Orville was threatened with an arrest for speeding, but the local police were unwilling to arrest such a prominent citizen and they learned to look the other way as Orville sped through the streets of Dayton on his way to the Wright Company factory or to his office above the old bicycle shop, where he preferred to do business.

The board of directors of the Wright Company in New York had looked upon the January 1914 decision of the Court of Appeals in *Wright* v. *Curtiss* as a signal for the company to exercise a monopoly as enriching as Bell's monopoly of the telephone, but they found Orville strangely uncooperative. He was apparently willing to sit back and collect royalties from other manufacturers without expanding the business. When Curtiss claimed that the airplanes he manufactured circumvented the Wright patent because their ailerons were not operated simultaneously, the Wright Company directors were impatient to institute a new legal action, but Orville's occasional flare-ups with secretary-treasurer Alpheus Barnes and his failure to answer letters or pursue the matter on grounds that he was too busy with research held up the filing of the complaint against the Curtiss Aeroplane Company until November 1914.

Orville's delaying tactics were deliberate. They were a part of his plan to get out of business altogether. As early as the spring of 1914 he had begun to buy up stock from the company directors, one at a time, by guaranteeing that each stockholder would receive a 100 percent profit on his investment, including dividends. To accomplish this, he had to borrow money for the first time in his life. The risk paid off. When he had bought out all the stockholders except for his good friend Robert Collier, Orville dismissed the odious Alpheus Barnes and put the company up for sale. On October 15, 1915, it was purchased by a group of eastern capitalists headed by mining tycoon William Boyce Thompson—a group more concerned with patent licensing and manufacturing than with creating a monopoly. The price was never disclosed but was rumored to be in the neighborhood of $1.5 million, a larger sum, after Orville had paid back the loan, than all that the brothers had ever received for their invention during Wilbur's lifetime.

Orville was retained by the company as consulting engineer at an annual salary of $25,000. He was now able to devote himself to research, which he loved, rather than to business, which he detested. What he needed was a laboratory larger and better equipped than the workroom behind the old bicycle shop. It happened that brother Lorin had had a hand in planning and constructing a store and apartment building on the corner of West Third Street and North Broadway, half a block from the bicycle shop. There was space behind the new building for the laboratory Orville wanted. Work was started in June 1916 and the building was ready for occupancy that December.

The airplane business was in a state of flux. Ten months after Orville sold his company, it was merged with Glenn Martin's California manufacturing enterprise and in August 1916 became the Wright-Martin Aircraft Corporation with a capitalization of $10 million. The company lost several millions in the first few months of operation but was later awarded a contract for 450 Hispano-Suiza airplane motors—the first big European wartime contract awarded to an American company—and moved its manufacturing operations to New Jersey.

In 1916 the Curtiss Aeroplane Company was the largest aircraft manufacturer in the United States. The Hammondsport plant was so swamped with orders that the company was reorganized as the Curtiss Aeroplane and Motor Corporation and moved to Buffalo, New York. Curtiss had profited from two flying-boat patents and a patent for an air-intake heater. Like the Wright brothers in 1910, he now found it necessary to notify other manufacturers that they must obtain licenses if they wished to continue manufacturing.

There were over a hundred American aeronautical patents on the books by then. Many were of no value, but those that were applicable were creating a manufacturing bottleneck. At the very time that the U.S. Army and Navy were attempting to expand their air arms, the payment of royalties or threat of infringement suits was making the operation of small aeronautic firms all but unprofitable. Early in 1917 the government called a meeting of leading aircraft manufacturers to see if a way could be found out of the patent muddle. Meetings were still underway when the United States entered the war in April 1917 and a settlement of the patent situation became mandatory. The outcome was a cross-licensing agreement drawn up by Curtiss's chief counsel, W. Benton Crisp. The agreement was to be administered by an organization called the Manufacturers Aircraft Association. The association would charge a flat fee for the use of any and all aeronautical patents in its patent pool. Holders of patents who surrendered their holdings to the association would be reimbursed according to the relative values of their patents. The principal beneficiaries of the agreement were the Wright-Martin Corporation, which had acquired the Wright patents in December 1916, and the Curtiss Aeroplane and Motor Corporation. Each firm received $2 million in exchange for all its patent rights.

When the Manufacturers Aircraft Association agreement went into effect on August 17, 1917, the death knell was sounded for *Wright* v. *Curtiss*.

Orville's days in court were not over, however. During the next eighteen years he was required to make depositions in three infringement suits, the most important and time-consuming of which involved the patent granted John Montgomery in 1906 for his tandem-wing glider.

The story of that eccentric inventor did not end with his death in a glider accident in California in 1911. New impetus was given to the Montgomery myth when Victor Lougheed's *Aeroplane Designing for Amateurs* was published the year after Montgomery died. This smallish handbook had few purchasers, but it had a far-reaching effect on the reputation of the professor from Santa Clara. It was dedicated to "the pioneer to whose rare vision and splendid genius it was given more than to any other, to wrest from the inscrutable mysteries of force and matter the greatest marvel of engineering perfection and practical significance, which ever has loomed upon the horizon of human endeavor . . ." Half of Lougheed's thirteen-page preface is devoted to the three gliders Montgomery was said to have built during the 1880s. The second half concerns the glides made by Maloney and Wilkie in 1905 and 1906 in Montgomery's tandem-wing gliders. "Similar performances," Lougheed states blandly, "were repeated some fifty or sixty times in the course of exhibitions that Montgomery gave around California to secure funds for the continuance of his experiments." Actually, there were only half a dozen nonaborted flights, in one of which Maloney met his death. Lougheed takes an even wilder flight of fancy when he writes that when the 1906 earthquake put an end to Montgomery's experiments, "he was just at the point of making a gliding flight across the Santa Clara Valley from a station on the side of Mt. Hamilton near the Lick Observatory, over four thousand feet above sea level." The image of the pudgy Santa Clara professor sailing off into the sunset on the sinuous wings of a forty-two-pound glider four thousand feet above the city of San Jose is complemented by an image of the sedentary theoretician and man of science as, elsewhere in his book, Lougheed reproduces a truncated version of Montgomery's aeronautical "Principles" in all their grisly unsophistication.

Several years later, Orville would write of Victor Lougheed (whose last name he insisted on spelling Loughead): "Whether it was from ignorance, from personal interests, or from a combination of the two, that he started and so zealously pushed the case of Montgomery, I am unable to say. But I am convinced that it was he who led the Montgomery family, apparently a group of sincere and loyal members, into believing there had been a great and profound thinker in their family, and that his contributions to aviation had been unappreciated and ignored by mankind. They had been deceived by the praise heaped upon Montgomery by Loughead. I have felt sorry for them."

Two suits were filed by Montgomery's widow, his aging mother, and his surviving sisters and brothers in 1917. The defendant in the first suit was the Wright-Martin Aircraft Corporation, holder of the Wright patents. The defendant in the second suit was the United States government—accused of purchasing planes constructed under the agreement administered by the Manufacturers Aircraft Association. Those aircraft, the plaintiffs argued, infringed Montgomery's glider patent of 1906. The suit against Wright-Martin was dropped in 1921, but the suit against the government dragged on for eleven years. Many of the affidavits filed were solicited to prove that Montgomery had flown in the 1880s, years before the Wright brothers had taken to the air. The testimony produced by the plaintiffs ran to hundreds of pages. Some of it was serious, some of it farcical, some of it pathetic. Orville made a lengthy deposition in January 1920 in answer to the question from counsel for the defense: "When and under what circumstances did you and Wilbur Wright first become interested in the problem of flight?" Like Wilbur's 1912 answer to a similar question in *Wright* v. *Curtiss,* Orville's deposition constitutes a more or less complete history of the early Wright experiments and has been quoted from or reprinted in part many times in books and articles on the brothers.

What Montgomery's heirs were trying to prove was that the Wrights had constructed airplanes with curved wings like those described in Montgomery's patent, whereas the Wright patent specified "normally flat" wings only. (Actually, the phrase "normally flat" had been inserted in the patent by the Wrights' patent attorney and the patent examiner.) With unintentional irony the court chose to interpret Montgomery's 1906 patent literally. Since it referred to wings with a parabolic curvature and since a parabolic curvature was aerodynamically inefficient, the claim was disallowed. As to another claim made by the plaintiffs, that Montgomery had invented wing-warping, the court declared: "It seems to us idle to contend that Montgomery was a pioneer in this particular field." As to the claim that he had made gliding flights years before the Wrights: "He preserved no data, kept no record of measurement and left no reliable information from which a court or one skilled in the art might profit from what he did, or ascertain the means he employed to do it."

The tragic waste of time and money came to an end on May 28, 1928, when *Montgomery* v. *The United States* was decided in favor of the defendants. But the belief that Montgomery had made successful glides in the 1880s, more than a decade and a half before the Wright brothers, refused to die. In the October 1930 issue of *Popular Science Monthly,* the recollections of Montgomery's brother James were the basis of an article with the title "American Unknown to Fame: First Man on Record to Leave the Earth on Wings." James claimed he had been present when his brother made the world's first successful glide at Otay Mesa near San Diego on March 17, 1884

—the first time a date had been assigned to that event. This attempt to pump new life into the Montgomery myth attracted little attention. It was not until ten years later that the apotheosis of John Joseph Montgomery began in earnest with the publication in *Harper's Magazine* in June 1940 of "He Flew in 1883," by Winsor Josselyn.

Once again the story of Montgomery's legendary first flight is drawn by an enterprising journalist from brother James, with an assist from other surviving members of the family. Now, fifty-seven years later, James remembers that it was not on March 17, 1884, that the first glide took place, as he had believed in 1930, but on an August morning in 1883. He now recalls that forty feet of rope was tied to a crossbeam on the glider and that he ran ahead with the rope and towed John into the air. In the account of the single 100-foot glide that Montgomery himself described to Octave Chanute at the time of the Chicago World's Fair, the glider was caught by the wind immediately afterward and smashed beyond repair. In James's version, the first glide was merely one of many.

Whatever else it was, the article in *Harper's* was seminal. It spawned a number of similar stories in magazines and newspapers during the next three decades with titles such as "California's First Flier," "Father of Flight," "The First Birdman," "He Gave Us Wings," and, more to the point, "The American Who Flew Before the Wright Brothers." James had failed to mention the distance of Montgomery's longest glide in the *Harper's* article. In September 1946, when he was eighty-nine, James remedied that omission in *Flying* magazine, where it was revealed that the length of that first, great glide at Otay Mesa was 603 feet, "determined by pacing it off after landing." That same year the works and martyrdom of John Montgomery entered California folklore in a more potent, if ephemeral form with the release by Columbia Studios of the movie *Gallant Journey*.

A more solid memorial to Montgomery's memory was erected in 1946 on the campus of Santa Clara University: a granite shaft marking the site of Daniel Maloney's flight in the Santa Clara glider of April 29, 1905. The inscriptions that cover the small obelisk must puzzle the less gullible undergraduates who are exposed daily to this four-sided feast of misinformation. Not to be outdone, Southern California dedicated a few memorials of its own. On May 20, 1950, the airfield at San Diego was officially christened Montgomery Field, and a plaque was unveiled in memory of the man "who made the first winged flights in the world at Otay, San Diego County, in August 1883." A more majestic monument was dedicated the next day at the Otay Mesa site—a ninety-foot stainless-steel airplane wing, marking the spot where Montgomery "made man's first controlled winged flights." At its base is the inscription:

HE OPENED FOR ALL MANKIND THE "GREAT HIGHWAY OF THE SKY"

One site was unmarked until 1961, when Santa Clara County erected a historical marker not far from the spot in Evergreen Valley where Montgomery met his death. As if further certification were needed, Walt Disney Studios began its television history of aviation, *Man in Flight,* released that year, with an animated-cartoon portrayal of that now famous flight at Otay Mesa. But the most reverent memorial of all was a full-length biography, *John Joseph Montgomery: Father of Basic Flying,* by Father Arthur Spearman, S.J., archivist of Santa Clara University, published by the university in 1967—an act of canonization as naïve as it is sincere.

The year Father Spearman's book was published, the state of California got into the act by the simple expedient of replacing the county historical marker in Evergreen Valley with an official state marker that included this sentence: "Here the basic principles of aerodynamics discovered by Montgomery were combined by his engineering skill and technology to produce a heavier-than-air flying machine which had complete control: the cambered wing, rear stabilizer, flexible wingtips, and the wing-warping aileron."

The unadorned truth, however, is that Montgomery discovered no previously undiscovered principles of aerodynamics; his 1911 monoplane glider did not have complete control; its wings had too deep a camber for efficient flight; its vertical stabilizer lacked the movable rear edge needed for a smooth bank and turn; and its wingwarping, so called, was not the equivalent of modern aileron action or even of the Wrights' wingwarping mechanism, since there was no reciprocal movement of the opposing wing.

In a letter to Thomas Baldwin, written a few weeks after Montgomery had been killed, Orville Wright said the kindest thing that could be said about Montgomery without distorting the truth. That was the letter in which he referred to the boasts made by Montgomery when they met for the first and only time at the Belmont Park air meet in 1910: that the control of Montgomery's tandem-wing gliders was so effective that Maloney and Wilkie looped the loop time after time until he was compelled to limit the amount of control. "It was hard to tell whether his statement was a result of an illusion," Orville wrote, "or whether it was simply a plain falsehood. But the poor man is dead now, and we will try to think it was the former."

# 48

## War Comes to Dayton

BEFORE THE Wright-Martin airplane plant closed in March 1917, Edward A. Deeds, vice-president, later president, of Dayton's National Cash Register Company, recruited some of the Wright-Martin department heads for an airplane company he planned to establish with three of his friends— Charles F. Kettering, Harold E. Talbott, Sr., and Harold E. Talbott, Jr. Kettering was co-founder with Deeds of the Dayton Engineer Laboratories, known as Delco, a company set up to exploit the self-starter and other automotive systems invented by Kettering. The two Talbotts were owners of a local construction firm. In 1915 the same four men had founded the Dayton Metal Products Company, which specialized in refrigeration accessories but soon turned to the more profitable manufacture of fuses and other war materials. All four men were friends of Orville Wright. Orville had had his fill of New York businessmen, but he had nothing but warm feelings for his businessmen friends in Dayton and was willing to lend his name to the airplane company they wanted to establish—a name that would do a good deal to bring wartime aviation business to Dayton if and when the United States became involved in the war that had been going on in Europe since 1914.

The United States declared war on Germany on April 6, 1917. Five days later the Dayton-Wright Airplane Company was incorporated. (During World War I, the spelling "aeroplane" was replaced by "airplane," a spelling accepted almost universally except by Orville Wright and Great Britain.) Orville was not a stockholder in the new company but he served as a director and consulting engineer. The Dayton plant of the Wright-Martin Aircraft Corporation had been sold to an automotive concern, so a new aircraft factory was built at Moraine City, just south of Dayton, on property belonging to Deeds.

Two weeks after the Dayton-Wright Company was established, Orville was commissioned a major in the Signal Corps reserve on the same day his friend Thomas Baldwin was commissioned a captain. For most of his life, Baldwin had been called Captain Baldwin, a rank that county-fair balloonists and airship operators bestowed upon themselves. When war came the country had need of Baldwin's services. As a bona fide captain he served as Chief U.S. Balloon Inspector throughout the war. Promoted to major, he was not discharged until October 1919, when he was well into his sixties. Unlike Baldwin, Orville never wore a uniform. He did little work directly for the government, and most of his work for the Dayton-Wright Airplane Company was done in his laboratory on North Broadway.

None of the founders of the Dayton-Wright Company had any experience in aircraft manufacture. Their interests and those of their two other Dayton companies, Delco and Dayton Metal Products, were aligned with those of the automobile industry. Edward Deeds, the leader of the group, did not have a very high opinion of airplane manufacturers, with the exception of Glenn Curtiss, but Curtiss's Buffalo plant was concentrating on the JN-4 trainer plane, known affectionately as the Jenny, and posed no threat to Dayton-Wright. The automotive industry had had its eye on the wartime aviation market long before the United States got into the war. Howard Coffin, president of the Hudson Motor Car Company, had close ties to the Administration and was a personal friend of Chief Signal Officer George Squier at a time when Army aviation was still under the control of the Signal Corps. When the United States entered the war, the Secretary of War appointed Coffin chairman of a hastily assembled Aircraft Production Board. The civilian members of the board, of which Edward Deeds was one, all had close ties with the automotive industry. Deeds was in charge of aircraft procurement. In August 1917 he was commissioned a colonel and made chief of the Equipment Division of the Signal Corps under General Squier. After divesting himself of his Dayton-Wright holdings, he was in a position to divert a sizable amount of business to the companies run by his friends in Dayton.

U.S. aircraft production had fallen far behind that of Europe. In 1916, only 411 aircraft had been manufactured in the United States. In 1917, the demands made on the United States for warplanes were staggering. For training American pilots alone, 2,500 trainers would be needed, and the Allies were asking for ten times that number of combat aircraft. The only possible way to meet the latter demand was to install American motors in American-built copies of European aircraft that had already proved themselves in the war. The Dayton-Wright Airplane Company was awarded two aircraft contracts. The more lucrative contract was for 4,000 De Havilland 4s—or DH-4s—the versatile British two-seater fighter-bomber designed by

Geoffrey de Havilland; the other was for 400 J-1 training planes.

In May 1917, Aircraft Production Board chairman Howard Coffin predicted that 3,500 American-built aircraft would be in the air by the end of the year—and within two years as many as 100,000. The board had complete confidence in the ability of American industry to make those predictions come true. So did Orville Wright. On July 1, 1917, *The New York Times Magazine* went to press with his picture on the cover under the headline "Orville Wright Says 10,000 Aeroplanes Would Win the War Within Ten Weeks: An Interview with Earl Findley." In Orville's opinion, the word of the businessmen on the Aircraft Production Board was as good as their bond. "The men of the Board," he was reported to have said in the interview, "have made a habit of success; each man on it has a record of definite accomplishments in whatever he has undertaken. And these men are working day and night, without salary, and to the financial detriment, of course, of the concerns of which they are the moving spirits. They are actuated by no motives other than that there shall be assembled the greatest number of airplanes of the best sort in the least time." When the true story of that interview was told many years later, it was revealed that Orville had refused to talk for publication. Instead, Earl Findley had interviewed Edward Deeds, who had dropped into Hawthorn Hill to say goodbye to Orville before leaving for Washington. When Findley showed Orville the interview, Orville admitted that he agreed with every word Deeds had said—including the praise heaped on the patriotic members of the Air Production Board, who were "working night and day, without salary," or to be more explicit, for a dollar a year—and he permitted Deeds's words to be attributed to him.

The Aircraft Production Board's rosy predictions not only failed to come true but inspired the German *Amerikaprogramm,* which doubled air defenses on the Western Front in preparation for the anticipated onslaught by U.S. aircraft. The 400 trainer planes that the Dayton-Wright Company promised to deliver by December 1917 were not delivered until March 1918 and then were found to suffer from excessive vibration and danger of fire from their rigid motor mountings. The production of DH-4s was an even greater disaster. The first sample airframe arrived from England on August 17, 1917, but the drawings that accompanied it had to be redone to conform to American standards and the first American-produced DH-4 was not flown until the end of October. Further changes were required and subcontracts had to be let for components from compasses to spruce for airframes. Deliveries were held up by shortages and strikes, so that the first Dayton-Wright DH-4 did not reach France until May 1918, and the first flight of an American DH-4 over the front lines did not take place until August 9, 1918, three months before the end of the war.

The one product that the U.S. automobile industry was equipped to produce in quantity was the airplane motor, but American motors with their interchangeable parts could not produce the power put out by handcrafted European airplane motors. To solve this problem, Edward Deeds rounded up a few of the most competent automotive engineers and draftsmen in the business and locked them up in a suite in the Willard Hotel in Washington, D.C. They emerged five days later in a fine flurry of publicity with designs for an eight-cylinder aircraft engine, but when the prototype was tested by the Bureau of Standards in July 1917, its ignition and lubrication systems were found wanting. Redesigned, with less publicity and more success, as a twelve-cylinder, 440-horsepower engine, the Liberty Engine, as it was called, proved to be a significant contribution to the winning of the war. There were the usual bottlenecks. Eleven thousand Liberty Engines were promised for February 1918. By the end of May only 1,100 had been delivered, but production soon picked up. Eight thousand were delivered between July and September, and when the war ended in November, they were coming off the production lines at the rate of 150 a day.

If airframes could have been manufactured with the mass-production techniques that made the Liberty Engine possible, the Aircraft Production Board might have been forgiven for turning over to the automotive industry the lion's share of the $640 million appropriated by Congress for wartime aviation. As it was, resentment on the part of the struggling airplane industry had built up a powder keg of ill will. It was not an airplane manufacturer who lit the fuse, however, but the patriotic sculptor Gutzon Borglum, remembered today for his four gigantic heads of U.S. Presidents carved on the side of Mount Rushmore in South Dakota. Borglum, who suffered from a form of intellectual gigantism, considered himself an authority on airplanes as well as sculpture. As early as 1904 he had expressed the opinion that the airplane should be modeled not on the bird but on the fish, whose winglike fins should be used to steady its flight—not, apparently, to provide lift. In September 1917 he offered to supply the Aircraft Production Board with a fleet of eighty aircraft capable of one thousand hours of continuous flying. When the board rejected his fantastic offer, he went to the White House and charged the board with mismanagement and profiteering. He was told to put his charges in writing. This he did in December 1917, recommending that President Woodrow Wilson appoint a three-man commission to investigate the aircraft procurement situation with himself as its head. "There are no principles related to flying heavier-than-air machines that I am not thoroughly familiar with," he wrote the President. "I feel as Da Vinci did when seeking a commission." The President's equivocal reply was interpreted by Borglum as authorization to conduct an investigation of the aircraft procurement program on his own. He did this with relish, but when he submitted his report it was ignored by the President, who was only too aware of the sculptor's appetite for controversy. Borglum then took his case to the New York *World,* which published his charges in two installments in March 1918, and the Aircraft Scandal was out in the open.

Colonel Deeds was the principal target of the investigation. Borglum had harbored a grudge against Deeds since 1912, when a group of Dayton citizens headed by Deeds had advanced him money to design a bronze memorial to the Wright brothers to be erected at the site of the former Huffman Prairie. The Dayton flood of 1913 intervened, and Borglum blamed Deeds for the cancellation of the project. The rabidly patriotic sculptor now claimed that Deeds's real name was Dietz, a name with a suspiciously German ring, and that Deeds's overpowering Teutonic personality had hypnotized the other members of the Aircraft Production Board. With the air full of the more serious charges of profiteering and favoritism in the letting of contracts, President Wilson was compelled to act. He appointed Charles E. Hughes, his Republican opponent in the 1916 election, to head a full-scale investigation of the Aircraft Production Board. In the meantime, a subcommittee of the U.S. Senate conducted an investigation and released a report, which the *Scientific American* called "extravagantly hostile and critical," but which confirmed many of Borglum's charges and affirmed that Deeds had assigned profitable contracts to his associates in Dayton, who were woefully ignorant of the problems they would encounter in aircraft production.

The more thorough Hughes investigation began in May 1918 and ended five months later after gathering thousands of pages of testimony from more than 250 witnesses, including Orville Wright. The inquiry stopped short of leveling charges of fraud against Deeds, but criticized him for awarding contracts to companies in which his friends had an interest and for acting as confidential adviser to his former business associates while he was in uniform. The findings were turned over to the Secretary of War with the suggestion that Deeds be tried by court-martial to determine if there had been any violation of military regulations. The Army's Judge Advocate Board of Review added 10,000 words to the record, but decided that a court-martial was not in order, much to the delight of Deeds's friends and supporters, one of whom accused Hughes of gunning for an elephant and coming home with a squirrel.

Reforms had already been made before the Hughes investigation began. In February 1918, Deeds had been replaced as chief of the Signal Corps's Equipment Division by William C. Potter, a banker with connections to the mining rather than the automotive industry. In May military aeronautics was taken out of the Signal Corps and placed under a new department, with copper magnate John D. Ryan as head of its Bureau of Aircraft Production. Conditions improved, but it was a case of too little and too late. By the end of the war more than 1,000 DH-4s had arrived in France, but fewer than 200 saw action at the front, and those that did quickly acquired a reputation as deathtraps because the gas tank between the pilot and the gunner had been known to explode when hit by incendiary bullets. After the war, Ivonette Wright, Lorin Wright's daughter, brought her fiancé, Lieutenant Harold Miller, to Hawthorn Hill to be introduced to her famous uncle. At dinner Orville asked Miller, who had just returned from France, what he thought of the DH-4s. Miller was not aware that Orville had had anything to do with the American-built De Havillands and answered frankly that the American pilots were afraid of them and called them "flaming coffins." Orville's response was a dead silence. The subject was never mentioned again, even after Harold Miller married Orville's niece and became a member of the family. "Flaming coffins" was a bit unfair, since DH-4s were no more vulnerable than other World War I aircraft with nonself-sealing fuel tanks, but Lieutenant Miller was quite correct. Americans did call them that, and the name had stuck.

At this late date, it is hard to get at the truth of the aircraft procurement scandal of 1917–18. The line between what was strictly legal and what was inherently unethical was as fuzzy in those days as in these. Orville was never a target of the investigations, but it is doubtful whether the four Dayton businessmen who organized the Dayton-Wright Company without any previous experience in airplane manufacture would have been able to secure those valuable wartime contracts if he had not allowed them to use the name of Wright as window dressing for their company. According to the testimony Orville gave when he was interrogated during the Hughes investigation, his role as consultant to the company was a minor one. After the sample British DH-4 was received from England in August 1917, he was in almost daily consultation with engineers at the Dayton-Wright plant in regard to changes made in redesigning the machine. His part in that, he said, was limited to preventing any more changes being made than were absolutely necessary. After the first American-built DH-4 was tested in October 1917, he had nothing more to do with the De Havillands turned out by the company—until May 13, 1918, when he donned a leather flying jacket and helmet and flew an ancient Wright 1911 biplane alongside an American-built DH-4 to demonstrate the changes that had taken place in aircraft design in a short seven years.

That was the last flight Orville ever made as a pilot. He spent the last year of the war working on an aerial torpedo, the brainchild of Charles Kettering. Lawrence Sperry had been experimenting with a flying bomb for the Navy, using a gyroscopic method of control, and Kettering had convinced General Squier that the Dayton-Wright Company could deliver a better and cheaper aerial torpedo for the Signal Corps. Working with two company engineers, Orville designed a bomb-carrying pilotless biplane with a fifteen-foot wingspan, an airframe of steel tubing, and wingcoverings of muslin and heavy, treated brown paper. The control surfaces were pasteboard, and the engine was a four-cylinder motor costing forty dollars. The guidance system was developed independently by the Dayton Metal Products Company.

The best the aerial torpedo could do in its first test in September 1918 was a 100-yard flight a few feet above the ground. On October 4, when it was tested for the third time, the instrument board came loose, and the unarmed flying bomb set off on a wild flight, chased by more than a hundred men in automobiles. It came down, out of gas, twenty-one miles from Dayton. When Kettering drove up after dark, several farmers, who had discovered the unmanned aircraft, were searching everywhere with lanterns for the missing pilot. Kettering refused to give up until October 1919, when the project came to a humiliating end as the aerial torpedo went into a steep dive during its final test in Florida and came apart in the air.

Because of Orville's status as senior statesman of aeronautics, a role left vacant for several years by the death of Octave Chanute in 1910, his pronouncements on the role of the airplane in war were always eagerly sought. In October 1917, when the United States had been at war for only half a year, his faith in the airplane as an instrument of peace because of its scouting capabilities was unshaken. "The nation with the most eyes will win the war and put an end to war," he told a reporter. "That is what we planned and that is what will happen." In November 1918, four days before peace was declared, he admitted that the airplane had become an angel of destruction as well as of peace: "The aeroplane has made war so terrible that I do not believe any country will again care to start a war." He held to this view throughout the 1920s. In 1923 he stated in a radio address (which he refused to deliver himself): "The possibilities of the aeroplane for destruction by bomb and poison gas have been so increased since the last war that the mind is staggered in attempting to picture the horrors of the next one. The aeroplane, in forcing upon governments a realization of the possibilities for destruction, has actually become a powerful instrument for peace."

World War II changed all that. In August 1945, when the war had been over for only two weeks, Orville commented sadly to a friend who had just congratulated him on reaching his seventy-fourth birthday, "I once thought the aeroplane would end wars. I now wonder whether the aeroplane and the atomic bomb can do it."

# 49

## *Orville Alone*

ON April 2, 1917, four days before the United States entered World War I, Bishop Milton Wright made the last entry in his diary and went to bed in his room on the second floor of Hawthorn Hill. When he failed to appear at breakfast the next morning, Orville went upstairs and found that his father had died in his sleep. The bishop was buried beside his wife in Woodland Cemetery in the same plot as Wilbur, who lay buried at their feet.

A few weeks before his father died, Orville brought home a St. Bernard puppy. He named it Scipio. Over the months and years, Scipio's weight increased from sixteen pounds to one hundred sixty, but like many large dogs, he suffered from rheumatism and his life was a short one as dogs' lives go. Orville did not take many photographs in his later years, but in the collection of photos made from the Wright brothers' glass-plate negatives in the Library of Congress there are no fewer than ten pictures of Scipio, one of which Orville carried in his wallet until the day he died. He had a soft heart for the big, rheumatic dog, having suffered from sciatic pains himself ever since his accident at Fort Myer in 1908. In December 1915 he experienced such intense back pain while driving that he was brought home in an ambulance. He was bedridden for eight weeks, but by the following summer was well enough to vacation on Waubec Island in Georgian Bay on Lake Huron. He fell in love with this Canadian vacation spot—and with its blueberries, which Carrie, who made the trip with other members of the family, turned into memorable pies. Before returning to Dayton, Orville explored nearby Lambert Island. There was a fine view of the bay and the Canadian mainland from its windswept hill. In September he bought the twenty-six-acre island and its three cottages as a summer retreat.

In 1917 Orville was too tied up with war work to take a vacation, but in 1918 as many family members—including Scipio—as could be rounded up began the cycle of summer visits to Lambert Island that was to last until World War II. The first trips were made by train. In 1929 Orville bought a seven-passenger Pierce-Arrow with special air-oil shock absorbers that provided an almost bumpless ride all the way to Penetanguishene on Georgian Bay. After parking the car in town, he would herd family and visitors onto a launch powered by an old airplane motor—later replaced by an elegant boat with a cabin and mahogany trim—and head for his island out in the bay. The main cottage, a hundred feet above the waterline, was surmounted with an observation room, equipped with a telescope. The two-bedroom cottage nearby was Orville's. A third cottage, with three bedrooms, was for visitors. There was a workhouse, an icehouse, a pump house, and a boathouse next to a small sandy beach. There were also mosquitoes, poison ivy, and no indoor bathrooms until 1933, but there were always blueberries for pies, and life on the island was made easier by devices built or invented by Orville, such as the funicular operated by a cable wound on a revolving drum. Powered by a one-cylinder outboard motor, it was capable of transporting 300 pounds of equipment, luggage, lumber, or cakes of ice from the boathouse up to the cottage on top of the hill.

Katharine Wright spent her summers on Lambert Island until 1926. She had a guest that year, Henry J. Haskell, associate editor of the Kansas City Star. Haskell had been a classmate of Katharine's at Oberlin College in the 1890s and a friend of the family ever since. What Orville didn't know that summer was that his fifty-two-year-old sister had been engaged to Haskell for a year. Because Orville had become almost too dependent on her presence at Hawthorn Hill, Katharine had put off telling him about her engagement until he was in a receptive mood. Orville's mood, when he found out about the engagement, has been described as alternately furious and inconsolable. On November 20, 1926, the wedding was held in Oberlin, Ohio, at the home of an Oberlin College professor, rather than at Hawthorn Hill.

On March 3, 1929, shortly after her husband had become editor and part owner of the Kansas City Star, Katharine caught pneumonia and died at her home in Kansas City. Orville had all but read her out of the family by then, but at the last moment he relented and was at her bedside when she died. She was brought back to Dayton for funeral services at Hawthorn Hill and buried beside Wilbur in Woodland Cemetery.

Reuchlin, the oldest Wright brother, had died in 1920. Lorin, born in 1862, the year after Reuchlin, lived until 1939. His loss by death was almost as grievous a loss to Orville as the loss of Katharine by marriage. By serving Wilbur and Orville well in the early days of their flying-machine business and by his help to Orville after Wilbur died, Lorin had earned the right to be known as the unsung third Wright brother. He had failed Orville only once. That was in December 1916 during the move from the bicycle shop on West Third Street to Orville's new laboratory around the corner, where the carpenters were still at work. The contents of the old shop had been stowed into a moving van for the short run to 15 North Broadway—except for the two balances that Wilbur and Orville had used in their wind-tunnel experiments of 1901. As the first such instruments to yield measurements of use in constructing a practical flying machine, they had historical as well as sentimental value. Rather than entrust them to the movers, Orville put them in a metal container and gave them to Lorin to carry to the new laboratory. When the move was over and everything was in its place, the balances could not be found. Orville accused Lorin of stopping somewhere on the way and leaving the precious balances behind. Lorin indignantly denied this, but the balances seemed lost forever. Then in December 1946, seven years after Lorin had died, Orville hired some workmen to help him clear out the attic above his laboratory. One of the items handed down to him by the workmen was a dusty, apparently empty, metal case for a long-defunct Smith Premier typewriter. Before adding it to the pile of accumulated trash, Orville gave it a precautionary shake and heard a rattling within. The rattling was caused by the two balances that had been carried from the old bicycle shop to the new laboratory exactly thirty years and three days before. Lorin was posthumously pardoned.

Unlike the mansion in Oakwood with its fluted columns where Orville lived alone with Carrie and Charlie Grumbach after Katharine moved to Kansas City, the laboratory on North Broadway presented a plain, somewhat enigmatic front to the world. Behind the austerely symmetrical one-story brick front was Orville's office, a square unadorned room with a rolltop desk, a few chairs, some books on the history of flying, a drawing table, and a worn carpet. The laboratory at the rear of the building was well equipped. Orville had designed a wind tunnel three by three feet in cross section with an air current of up to 50 miles per hour, provided by a 10-horsepower General Electric motor. Charlie Taylor left his job in the airplane factory to work for Orville when the laboratory was new. He helped with experiments and kept Orville's car in running order, but he missed the excitement of life in the workroom behind the old bicycle shop. After the war he took a job with the Dayton-Wright Company and left Orville alone in the brick laboratory building with his faithful secretary, Mabel Beck. Orville's brothers, their wives, his nieces, and his nephews all cherished Carrie Grumbach, who kept house for Orville at Hawthorn Hill, but they did not have much use for the formidable Mabel, who typed Orville's letters, maintained his files, and warded off unwanted visitors. What went on inside the laboratory was something of a mystery to Daytonians. One day two boys climbed a tree next to one of the windows and peered in while Orville was at work. One boy must have asked the other what he was doing, for Orville heard the other boy reply, "He's inventing."

Inventing the airplane was a hard act to follow. The only significant aeronautical invention to emerge from the laboratory after the war was the split-flap airfoil, or slotted wing—not to be confused with the split trailing-edge flap used on some modern aircraft. While experimenting with hydroplanes in the Miami River in 1914, Orville had discovered that a cambered strip of steel placed above the forward edge of a hydrofoil prevented the water from separating from the hydrofoil's upper side and thus reducing its lift. In his wind tunnel in the laboratory he found that a similar arrangement produced a small increase in the lift of of a model airfoil. He developed the idea further with James Jacobs of the Dayton-Wright Company, and they applied for a patent in 1921. The patent was issued three years later, but, like Orville's automatic stabilizer of 1913, the split-flap airfoil was brought to a state of usefulness by another inventor—in this case Frederick Handley Page, who developed and patented a slotted wing independently in England. Although the invention is sometimes attributed to Orville, he himself admitted that the split-flap airfoil patented by himself and Jacobs did not secure a lift at all comparable to Handley Page's slotted wing.

Oddly enough, the only invention patented by Orville after the war that earned a profit was a patent for a toy. At the annual Christmas Eve dinner at Hawthorn Hill in 1923, he entertained his assembled grandnieces and grandnephews with a toy he had made, modeled on one he had seen many years before. It featured two wooden clowns at either end of an eighteen-inch base. When a springboard at one end was released, it sent one clown flying through the air to a double trapeze at the other end, to which the other clown was attached. The flying clown caught the upper trapeze with the hooks on its arms and sent it spinning around, while both clowns hung grimly on. The toy was patented in 1925, and a Dayton factory began manufacturing it under the name Flips and Flops. When more orders flowed in than the company could finance, Lorin Wright bought his way into the company and wound up as its president. When the demand for Flips and Flops was satiated, a toy airplane that could be used for advertising was produced by the company. It was called, not unexpectedly, the Wright Flyer.

Retiring by nature, Orville Wright had no choice but to accept the honors heaped upon him in his old age. These included a Distinguished Flying Cross, awarded by Congress in 1928, ten years after he had made his last flight, three honorary doctorates in science, two in law, and one in engineering (after which it was Dr. Wright this and Dr. Wright that on formal occasions), and a miserly master of arts from Yale. It was customary for notables visiting Dayton to pay their respects to the co-inventor of the airplane. In June 1927, when young Charles Lindbergh landed at Wright Field on his triumphal return trip to St. Louis after his flight across the Atlantic, he was met by Orville and the commander of Wright Field and taken to Hawthorn Hill for dinner. Lindbergh hated welcoming committees as much as Orville did. To avoid the impromptu celebration staged in downtown Dayton, they found their way to Oakwood by a roundabout route, assuming they had been undetected, but when they sat down to dinner, the porch next to the dining room rapidly filled with people. Soon the lawns about the stately mansion were full. More hordes appeared on the hill behind the house. Shrubbery was trampled. Trees were climbed. To save house and grounds from further depredation, Lindbergh and Orville made a brief appearance on the small balcony above the entranceway, and the mob dispersed.

Orville lived long enough to become a legend in his own time, but he was a strangely colorless one. In 1930, *The New Yorker* sent a reporter to Dayton to interview Orville in his laboratory for one of that magazine's "Profiles." The reporter described the man who had made the world's first airplane flight as "a gray man now, dressed in gray clothes. Not only have his hair and his mustache taken on that tone, but his curiously flat face. . . . a timid man whose misery at meeting you is obviously so keen that, in common decency, you leave as soon as you can."

But the protective coloration that enabled Orville to disappear into the background in public did not extend to his private life. He was anything but shy with relatives and friends, willing at the drop of a hat to express an opinion on issues of the day that interested him—with the exception of Prohibition, which he approved of but which most of his friends did not. He was vehement on the evils of advertising and scoffed at the flying-saucer fad. He did not believe in insurance for car, home, or life, and carried none himself. Having had a sweet tooth since childhood, he was against his dentist's antisugar campaign, insisting that he had fewer cavities when he ate a lot of candy. He had little use for avant-garde art or literature. "I wonder is it modern art or is it indigestion," he wrote a grandnephew who was studying painting. He had little patience with Picasso or with Gertrude Stein, about whom he made the odd observation that "Gertrude had a sensitive nose for discovering things stinkingly vulgar." It is not likely that he had read more than a few words of Stein, but it is possible he peeked into her book of biographical sketches, *Four in America,* published in 1947, the year before he died. One of Gertrude Stein's *Four* was "Wilbur Wright" ("It is not a sad story not at all a sad story the story of Wilbur Wright. Listen to me while I tell it to you right"), but the thirty-six pages devoted to Wilbur must have puzzled Orville, since Wilbur was portrayed as a painter like

Picasso, rather than as an inventor ("Anyway it is not necessary not at all necessary to say, to say what he did because everybody knows that").

Among family and friends, Orville had a reputation as a tease and a practical joker. His skill in this line was demonstrated during one of the many visits Griffith Brewer made to Hawthorn Hill. Brewer was president of the Aeronautical Society of Great Britain at the time. While discussing inventions with Orville, and how simple some inventions seemed in hindsight, he quoted a remembered fragment of blank verse by a poet whom he had been trying for years to identify:

> . . . *so easy it seemed*
> *Once found, which yet unfound most would have thought*
> *Impossible . . .*

The two men looked through standard books of quotations in Orville's library, but could find no trace of this passage. The next morning, Orville received a letter from a man in Spokane, asking for his autograph. By sheer coincidence, the autograph-seeker quoted those very lines of verse, undoubtedly in regard to the invention of the airplane, and gave the source of the lines—Book VI of *Paradise Lost*. Without telling Brewer, Orville located the passage in his own copy of Milton. Then he put the book back on the shelf and pulled the book on the shelf directly above it out a fraction of an inch. After dinner, Orville announced that he would use psychic power to identify the author of Brewer's quotation. Brewer was skeptical, but his skepticism was tempered by a story Orville told him of how his psychic abilities had once saved both himself and Wilbur from asphyxiation. That had happened back in the days before the house on Hawthorn Street had been wired for electricity. Wilbur had come home late from the bicycle shop one night, and Orville, who was already in bed but not yet asleep, had suddenly thought for no apparent reason that when Wilbur went to bed he would blow out the gaslight in his room without turning off the gas. Afraid to go to sleep, Orville stayed awake until all the lights were out. Then he went into Wilbur's room and found that Wilbur had indeed blown out the light without turning off the gas.

Brewer was sufficiently impressed by this story to give Orville another chance to test his psychic abilities. Following instructions, he blindfolded Orville and led him to the bookcase, where Orville groped his way along the shelves until he felt the protruding book. Dropping his hand, he pulled out the copy of Milton on the shelf below. Brewer removed Orville's blindfold, but he was still skeptical. The words didn't sound like Milton's to him. Orville riffled through the pages of Book VI until he came to the proper page; then he ran his finger down the page until he came to lines 499 through 501.

Fred Kelly was at Hawthorn Hill that night. When he retold the story of the finding of the quotation in *Miracle at Kitty Hawk,* he wrote that Griffith Brewer went to his grave convinced that Orville had genuine psychic ability. And Fred Kelly went to his believing the story about the blowing out of the gas. It may even have been true.

# 50

## A Feud and a Celebration

DURING THE 1920s, Orville's feud with the Smithsonian Institution became almost as much of an obsession as his preoccupation during the previous decade with *Wright* v. *Curtiss*. His antagonistic feelings toward the Smithsonian were not due solely to the 1914 tests of the Langley Aerodrome and its subsequent enshrinement in the National Museum. They also involved the stand taken by that institution in regard to another historic aircraft—the Wright Flyer of 1903. In 1910, Smithsonian secretary Charles Walcott had asked the Wright brothers to contribute one of their machines to the national aeronautical collections. Since parts of the 1903 Flyer were still in existence, Wilbur suggested reconstructing it for the museum. The Smithsonian, however, expressed a preference for a quarter-size model of Orville's 1908 Army Flyer, or a reconstruction of that machine itself. In either case, the Wright machine would be exhibited alongside Langley's steam-driven models of 1896 to demonstrate what Walcott called "two very important steps in the history of the aeronautical art." The Wrights took that to mean that the Smithsonian was simply not interested in displaying the first successful man-carrying airplane and decided not to contribute any machine at all.

The remains of the damaged 1903 Flyer, which had been under water for several days during the Dayton flood of 1913, remained in storage until 1916, when Orville was induced to reconstruct the machine for exhibit at the dedication of some new buildings at the Massachusetts Institute of Technology in Cambridge. Alexander Graham Bell was a guest of honor at the dedication exercises. He had not been aware that the 1903 Flyer was still in existence and expressed amazement that the Smithsonian had not acquired it for the National Museum. He made it his business to see that Secretary Walcott approached Orville on the subject. Six months later, Orville met with Walcott in Washington to discuss the matter, but he left the meeting convinced that the secretary did not share Bell's enthusiasm for the acquisition of the world's first man-carrying airplane by the Smithsonian.

During the next five years the 1903 machine was put together, displayed, and taken apart four times, twice in New York—at the Pan American Exhibition in the Grand Central Palace in February 1917 and at the New York Aeronautical Show in March 1919—and twice in Dayton—at a meeting of the Society of Automotive Engineers in June 1918 and again in January 1921 for the purpose of obtaining testimony in the suits brought by John Montgomery's heirs against the former Wright-Martin Company and the United States.

In the meantime, Langley's Aerodrome, rebuilt in its original condition after the Hammondsport tests of 1914, remained on display in the Smithsonian's National Museum, described as the first flying machine in the history of the world capable of flight with a man. When Griffith Brewer made his annual pilgrimage to Hawthorn Hill in the spring of 1921, he and Orville took steps to bring the Aerodrome controversy back into the limelight. They spent two months compiling a list of changes that had been made in the Langley machine when it had been reconstructed for testing in Hammondsport in 1914. Brewer incorporated this information in a paper, "Aviation's Greatest Controversy," which he planned to deliver to the Aeronautical Society of Great Britain in October after his return to England. Copies of the paper were sent in advance to the four men associated with the Aerodrome affair—Smithsonian secretary Charles Walcott; Albert Zahm, who had acted as official observer for the Smithsonian; Charles Manly, who had reconditioned the Aerodrome motor; and Glenn Curtiss, who had supervised the reconstruction. Each was given an opportunity to respond to Brewer's charges, with the understanding that their responses would be printed along with the paper in the journal of the Aeronautical Society in December. Before that, however, "Aviation's Greatest Controversy" was published in the United States in the October 1921 issue of *U.S. Air Service,* together with the replies of Walcott and Zahm. The next two monthly issues of the magazine contained the replies of Manly and Curtiss and Brewer's responses to the replies of all four.

As Orville had hoped, the series of charges and countercharges once more brought the Aerodrome controversy out into the open. Zahm called Brewer's list of changes made in the Aerodrome during its reconstruction "multitudinous, minute, inconsequential, they read like a laundry list . . . the objection of a bookkeeper, rather than an engineer." Challenged to prove his statement that the Langley machine in its original condition was capable of sustained free flight, Zahm wrote: "The principle of the proof is this: From the short flights of an overloaded and less efficient plane one may infer the feasibility of a longer flight with a lighter and more efficient plane of the same type." In case this was beyond the comprehension of a layman like Brewer, he simplified his proof further: "If an eagle with some wing feathers gone makes a short flight with a child in its talons, a scientist infers the possibility of a longer flight with unimpaired feathers and without the child." To which Brewer replied that Zahm's "simile of the eagle and the baby is inapplicable to the Langley machine, because the eagle had flown before losing its feathers. The bird he must choose to correct the simile is an ostrich."

Before Orville read Secretary Walcott's reply to Brewer's charges, he had assumed that the Smithsonian secretary had been an innocent dupe of Glenn Curtiss and that the radical alterations made in the Aerodrome before it was tested in 1914 had been made without his knowledge. The realization that Walcott had been as culpable as Curtiss and Albert Zahm intensified the bitterness of Orville's feelings toward the Smithsonian at the very time he was looking for a permanent home for the 1903 Flyer. He was beginning to worry about the condition of that fragile artifact. It had survived the Dayton flood, but fire was an ever-present danger. In October 1924, it was reassembled and exhibited at the International Air Races in Dayton. When it was dismantled—for the sixth time in nine years—the wingcovering had deteriorated to the point where it had to be discarded. Griffith Brewer had already suggested that the Flyer would find a more receptive home in the Science Museum in South Kensington, London, and offered to work out the details of such an arrangement. Orville raised no objection but reserved the right to withdraw the Flyer at any time after it had been in England for five years. On April 30, 1925, he announced in two Dayton newspapers that a home had been found for the original Wright Flyer in a British museum.

The purpose of the announcement seems to have been to give the Smithsonian Institution another chance to acquire the Flyer, for it was in no condition at the time to be shipped abroad. On May 2 Orville prodded Secretary Walcott into action by issuing another statement to the press in which he accused the Smithsonian of incorrectly describing the Langley Aerodrome as capable of flight. Two days later Secretary Walcott issued a statement: The wording on the label describing the Langley machine had been reviewed. There was no mistake. The Aerodrome was capable of flight. Orville's next move was to appeal to Chief Justice William Howard Taft, former President of the United States. On May 14, 1925, he wrote a letter urging Taft, in his official capacity as chancellor of the Smithsonian, to make an impartial investigation of the Aerodrome affair. "When proofs on both sides concerning these changes are shown," Orville wrote, "I do not think it will take you five minutes to make up your mind whether the changes were made and whether they were of importance." Taft replied that his duties as Chief Justice of the Supreme Court left him no time to decide questions that should be decided by the secretary of the Smithsonian, not the chancellor. On May 29, Orville made his final offer to the Smithsonian through an intermediary. He would keep the 1903 Flyer in the United States if the Smithsonian would publish both sides of the controversy in its next *Annual Report* and display the Flyer in the National Museum with a label describing it as the world's first man-carrying airplane.

Secretary Walcott's response was to ask two members of the National Advisory Committee for Aeronautics, of which Orville was also a member, to look into the matter of the 1914 Aerodrome tests and to settle, once and for all, the question of which aircraft was the world's first man-carrying airplane. The two men, Joseph S. Ames of Johns Hopkins University and Rear Admiral David W. Taylor, submitted their report in June. They admitted that some wrong had been done the Wright brothers. To rectify the situation they suggested that the label on the Langley machine should be changed to read: "In the opinion of many competent to judge, this was the first heavier-than-air craft in the history of the world capable of sustained free flight under its own power, carrying a man." This was done in October 1925. An addition to the label stated that the Aerodrome "slightly antedated" the 1903 Wright machine.

These palliatives only strengthened Orville's conviction that the Smithsonian was not the proper home for the Flyer. On the other hand, he was in no hurry to send it abroad. It was not until December 1926 that the deteriorating 1903 machine was reconditioned with the help of James Jacobs. Wooden members that were in disrepair were either repaired or replaced, and a new muslin covering was made for the wings. Mabel Beck helped with the sewing.

In February 1927, Charles Walcott died, and by the time a new Smithsonian secretary was appointed in January 1928, the repaired Flyer was on its way to the Science Museum in London. Nevertheless, the new secretary, Charles G. Abbot, wanted to put the Aerodrome affair behind him and proposed a conference with Orville. The conference did not take place until April, a month after Orville had published an article, "Why the 1903 Wright Aeroplane Is Sent to a British Museum," in the March 1928 issue of *U.S. Air Services* (that journal had added an *s* to its name in 1924). In his article, Orville accused the Smithsonian of initiating a subtle campaign after Langley's death to take from the Wright brothers much of the credit for inventing the airplane and bestowing it on the former secretary. Since the Smithsonian had refused his requests to appoint a disinterested scientific body to investigate the 1914 Aerodrome tests, he felt justified in sending the 1903 Flyer to England.

Orville's April meeting with Secretary Abbot took place at a luncheon in Washington. He presented the new Smithsonian secretary with a list of six ways in which he felt the Smithsonian had dealt unjustly with the Wright brothers, then he returned to Dayton and waited for a reply. Abbot's reply took the form of a pamphlet published in September: *The Relations Between the Smithsonian Institution and the Wright Brothers,* in which the secretary conceded: that the Smithsonian had made inaccurate statements regarding the Wrights; that its report of the 1910 awarding of the Langley medal to the Wrights had given the impression that the brothers' success was not due entirely to their own research; and that the 1914 Aerodrome experiments should have been conducted and described in a way that would have given no offense to Orville Wright and his friends. Although it was a matter of opinion whether or not the Aerodrome was capable of flight, Abbot wrote, the label beside the machine in the National Museum would be changed to read simply: "The Original Samuel Pierpont Langley Flying Machine of 1903. Restored." In a letter to a friend, Orville described the Smithsonian pamphlet as "mostly a hollow gesture" that "scarcely made a start toward clearing up the serious matters in the controversy."

Secretary Abbot meant well, but his effort at reconciliation was academic. By the time *The Relations Between the Smithsonian Institution and the Wright Brothers* was published, the 1903 Flyer had been on display in the Science Museum in London for more than six months. That it should be on display somewhere that year was obligatory. December 17, 1928, would be the twenty-fifth anniversary of the first four flights. Plans for an elaborate celebration and the erection of a memorial at Kill Devil Hills had been underway for more than a year. Congress had appropriated $25,000 for the start of the project, but neither Congress nor the Fine Arts Commission could agree on what kind of memorial to erect. Senator Hiram Bingham, who as president of the National Aeronautic Association had some say in the matter, envisioned the memorial as a sort of Greek temple (the granite to be quarried from his home state of Connecticut), but as the anniversary drew near, all that Washington could agree on was a cornerstone-laying ceremony on top of Big Kill Devil Hill. Three months before the anniversary, Army engineers began erection of a speaker's platform and anchored a derrick in the sand for the laying of the cornerstone, although no one was sure what it would be the cornerstone of.

A second memorial was to be dedicated at the same time—a boulder marking the spot where Orville took off on the world's first airplane flight. Cutting a block of granite to look like a boulder was no problem. The problem was where to put it. Pinpointing the location of the takeoff site in the shifting sands of the Outer Banks after a quarter of a century was like trying to locate the North Pole with a Boy Scout compass, but three surviving witnesses of the first flight were willing to try. On November 4, 1928, Will Dough and Adam Etheridge of the old Kill Devil lifesaving station and Johnny Moore—who as a boy from Nags Head had just happened to wander by on the windy morning of December 17, 1903—looked over the area at the behest of the National Aeronautic Association. After taking into consideration various landmarks, the three men documented their findings in an affidavit: "We proceeded to agree upon the spot, and We individually and collectively state without the least mental reservation, that the spot We located is as near correct as it is humanly possible to be without the data in hand to work from after a lapse of twenty five years." Today a six-foot boulder marks the spot with granitic certainty. Meanwhile a third memorial had been erected and dedicated with almost no fuss at all in Bill Tate's front yard at Kitty Hawk—a simple obelisk on which an image of the 1900 glider was carved in bas-relief above an inscription proclaiming the site to be the spot where Wilbur began the assembling of the Wright brothers' first glider in 1900.

An International Civil Aeronautics Conference had been planned that year so that the two hundred delegates, meeting in Washington, could be transported to the dedication ceremonies at Kill Devil Hills. They were to travel from Washington with Orville, other members of the Wright family, several of their neighbors, and a number of government officials. The road to Kitty Hawk was as beset with natural and man-made perils in 1928 as in the early years of the century. The steamer on which the party was to make the first stage of its journey was scheduled to leave Washington at 10 P.M. on Saturday, December 15, but was held up by fog until 2 A.M. and had to pick its way down the Potomac through heavy mists and more patches of fog. The travelers spent Sunday night aboard the ship at Norfolk, Virginia. On Monday morning they piled into buses for the seventy-five-mile trek to the Outer Banks. North Carolina was building a road down the Currituck County peninsula to Point Harbor at its bottom, but the road was unfinished. When the buses could go no farther, the passengers were transferred to a fleet of seventy automobiles, and the cavalcade moved slowly south over temporary corduroy and mud roads, making occasional detours through private farmlands and across front lawns. At Point Harbor a ferry was waiting to take the pilgrims across the sound to Kitty Hawk. On the way, an aircraft beacon specialist from Wichita by the name of Woody Hockaday fell overboard in his heavy overcoat and would have gone under if a quick-thinking sailor had not slipped a boat hook under his coat collar and hauled him back on board. At Kitty Hawk a second fleet of cars took the travelers over a road recently cut through the woods and swamps by the farmers of

Dare County to a pavilion where the ladies of the county had prepared a barbecue and turkey lunch. After lunch, the cars plowed through the sand to Kill Devil Hills.

Big Kill Devil Hill had not changed much since Orville's last visit in 1911, when he had set a world record for gliding. Shrubs and stub grass had been planted about its base, but the only way to get to the top was on foot. During the dedication speeches, high winds whipped the words from the mouths of Senator Bingham and Secretary of War Dwight Davis. Orville was observed to be scanning the horizon as if he were thinking of other things. After the cornerstone laying, the Norfolk Naval Station band played "The Star-Spangled Banner," and the celebrants trudged down the side of the hill to the site of the takeoff of the first flight. The six-foot boulder was sheathed in a parachute of white silk. Amelia Earhart, all but unrecognizable in a cloche hat, stood beside Orville during another round of speeches. When the parachute silk was withdrawn from the boulder, a sailor from the Norfolk Naval Station released a flock of fifteen carrier pigeons. As the band played the national anthem for the second time, the pigeons spiraled upward and disappeared in the direction of Norfolk.

Few details of the return to Washington from Kill Devil Hills have survived, but it was compared in one account to Napoleon's retreat from Moscow. Some of the local drivers of the automobiles had gone home to get warm, and a party of delegates who missed the ferry had to be taken across Currituck Sound in a leaking rumrunner patrol boat. The pilot became lost and had to inquire the way from local boatmen. On the ferry itself, Allen R. Heuth, one of the three men who had donated land for the Kill Devil Hill memorial, dropped to the deck while he was talking to the Secretary of War, and died.

In February 1931, the foundations of the $275,000 Wright Memorial were sunk thirty-five feet into Big Kill Devil Hill. It was estimated that the hill had moved four hundred feet from its position in 1903, but it had been tamed in the two years since the cornerstone laying by encircling it with a band of wood mold three hundred feet wide and anchoring it down with a covering of heavy vetch and Bermuda grass. On November 19, 1932, there was another pilgrimage by steamer and car for the dedication of the completed memorial. The trip was made easier this time by a new road and by the recently opened Wright Memorial Bridge, spanning Currituck Sound and making the Outer Banks accessible to motorists for the first time without resorting to ferryboats. The weather, however, was even more inhospitable than in 1928. A heavy downpour that had started at dawn continued all through the ceremony. During the speeches, a sudden wind squall tore the canvas covering from over the platform, drenching orators and spectators alike. A letter from President Hoover was read aloud and then handed to

Orville, who said, "Thank you," and tucked the rain-splotched letter in his pocket. At last, aviatrix Ruth Nichols pulled the cord that officially consummated the dedication of the memorial—a 61-foot-high triangular pylon of Mount Airy granite. The cord released an American flag that concealed the word GENIUS in the inscription about the base of the memorial:

IN COMMEMORATION OF THE CONQUEST OF THE AIR

BY THE BROTHERS WILBUR AND ORVILLE WRIGHT CONCEIVED BY

GENIUS

ACHIEVED BY DAUNTLESS RESOLUTION AND UNCONQUERABLE FAITH

Wilbur and Orville's names were inscribed in large letters on the side of the memorial facing Collington Island in the sound. On each of the other two sides, which tapered toward the sea, was a huge folded-back wing in relief.

A warmer, more personal memorial to the Wright brothers was dedicated six years later at Henry Ford's Greenfield Village in Dearborn, Michigan, just outside Detroit, where whole houses and factories had been moved from their original sites and reconstructed to satisfy Ford's desire to preserve for posterity a three-dimensional portrait of life and industry in pre–World War I America. Notwithstanding his belief that the Wright patent had had an adverse effect on the development of aviation, Ford had nothing but respect for Orville's inventive genius. In 1936 he purchased the old Wright bicycle shop on West Third Street in Dayton and the former Wright home on Hawthorn Street, which had been rented to Lottie Jones, the family laundress, when Katharine and Orville moved to Hawthorn Hill in 1914, and sold to Lottie after Katharine's death. Both structures were carefully dismantled and painstakingly reconstructed, side by side, on a grassy plot in Greenfield Village.

Charlie Taylor had been as much a part of the old bicycle shop as the one-cylinder natural-gas engine that drove the lathe and operated the fan in the Wright brothers' original wind tunnel, but Orville had lost track of his old mechanic when he moved back to California in 1928. Taylor had taken a job in a machine shop in Los Angeles. Then the Depression came along, Mrs. Taylor died, and Charlie was laid off. After losing his life's savings in a real estate venture, he returned to Los Angeles and got a job with North American Aviation when he was down to his last nickel. He was making thirty-seven and a half cents an hour when Henry Ford tracked him down and brought him back East to Greenfield Village.

For almost four years, Charlie was a virtual fixture in the workroom behind the bicycle shop. In 1941 he grew restless again and returned to California to take a wartime job, working sixty hours a week beside men half his age. In 1945 he suffered a heart attack and was forced to quit working. Every December 17, on the anniversary of the first flight, Charlie would receive a letter from Orville. The last letter he received concluded: "I hope you are well and enjoying life, but that's hard to imagine when you haven't much work to do. —Orv."

Charlie Taylor outlived Orville by eight years. His only income at the time of his death in 1956, aside from Social Security, was an $800 annuity from a fund left by Orville.

# 51

## *End of the Feud*

ONE OF ORVILLE'S principal concerns after Wilbur died was that the story of the brothers' experiments should be told in such a way as to ensure them their proper place in the history of the airplane. When Orville put pen to paper, the result was always readable, but he hated to write and as early as 1915 was looking for a writer he could trust to do the job for him. The most acceptable candidate at that time was Earl Findley, a newspaper reporter who had interviewed Orville that March and published his opinions regarding the use of the airplane in war, in the New York *Tribune.* Findley agreed to write a series of biographical articles about the Wrights with the understanding that they might later be expanded into a book, but he was not sure he could do the job alone and sought the research assistance of a forty-year-old journalist friend, John R. McMahon. Findley and McMahon spent part of the summer of 1915 at Hawthorn Hill, where they were given access to the diaries of both brothers, to the files of their letters, and to the fund of family anecdotes stored up over the years by Bishop Wright, Katharine, and Orville himself.

Findley made the mistake of submitting what he had written for Orville's approval at an ill-chosen time—apparently in December 1915, after Orville had been brought home in an ambulance and confined to bed for several weeks with severe sciatic pains. Never one to mince words, the bedridden Orville glanced through Findley's manuscript and told his secretary, Mabel Beck, to inform the aspiring young author, "I'd rather have the sciatica." Findley had been counting on the sale of the articles and their subsequent publication as a book to rescue him from the straitened circumstances in which he found himself after working for half a year on the manuscript. He was deeply hurt, but swallowed his pride and in time became one of Orville's most trusted friends.

The episode convinced Orville that if a credible book about the Wright brothers was ever to be written, he would have to write it himself. Two years later, the secretary of the McGraw-Hill Book Company heard that Orville was at work on a book of technical memoirs and wrote him a letter of inquiry. "I have been prevented by one thing and another from even getting started on the work," Orville responded. "However, when I do get ready for publication, I will be glad to take up the matter with you." Almost five years later, he wrote George Spratt: "I am about to begin the writing of a history of the development of our first aeroplane," and asked for photostats of letters that he and Wilbur had written to Spratt in the early years of their friendship, but that friendship had soured and the photostats were not forthcoming. A few months later, Orville received a letter from the editor of the magazine *World's Work* suggesting that he write his book in collaboration with Burton J. Hendrick, a competent journalist and biographer, with whose work Orville was already familiar. "I have discussed your letter with Katharine," he replied. "She is rather impatient to see some account of the work of my brother and myself published, and is afraid that I will never get down to actual writing. But I think she agrees with me that such an account, though not so well written, coming first-hand will be more convincing than one coming second-hand from a much better writer."

In 1930 Orville was beaten to the draw with the publication of *The Wright Brothers: Fathers of Flight,* promoted as "the first adult book in any language dealing exclusively with the Wrights and the airplane." The book was by John R. McMahon, based on information he had obtained during his visit to Hawthorn Hill with Earl Findley in 1915. Orville deplored its inaccuracies and winced at its many imaginary conversations, but what must really have set his teeth on edge was McMahon's depiction of penury in the Wright household at a time when the brothers were privileged to draw on Flint and Company for whatever funds they needed. By 1907, according to McMahon, their invention "had swallowed all their savings and later had put them in debt to their sister, who had mortgaged the Hawthorn Street home, then owned by her, in order to aid them." Nor did it help matters for Orville to read that, when he was lying in the hospital at Fort Myer, Katharine had burst into the room with a hearty "Hello! Orv, the children want to know when you are coming home to help them make candy." After describing the luxuries of Hawthorn Hill, McMahon has Katharine say (with moist eyes): "We were happier down in Hawthorn Street"—a remark that Orville must have resented because it may actually have been made.

McMahon's retelling of the Smithsonian controversy and the Wright infringement suits could not have displeased Orville, for they were fair and accurate, but there was still a crying need for Orville himself to tell the true story of the invention of the airplane. The case of Lawrence Hargrave,

Australian inventor of the box kite, was a case in point. Over the years Orville received five different inquiries from Australia requesting information on the brothers' debt to Hargrave, most of the letter writers having heard from supposedly reliable sources that the design of the world's first successful airplane had been based on the results of Hargrave's kite experiments, which had been made known to the Wrights through their correspondence with Octave Chanute.

The campaign to discredit the brothers had not ended with the termination of the suit against Curtiss in 1917. The anti-Wright propaganda had never ceased to proliferate, and its source in Orville's opinion was Albert Zahm. Zahm had left the Smithsonian's Aerodynamical Laboratory in 1915 to become chief research engineer of the Curtiss Aeroplane Company. Two years later he left Curtiss to become director of the U.S. Navy Aerodynamics Laboratory. In 1925 he was awarded the Laetare Medal by his alma mater, Notre Dame University, as the outstanding Catholic layman of the year for his work as scientist and pioneer in the field of aerial navigation. When the Guggenheim Chair of Aeronautics was established in the Library of Congress in 1929, Albert Zahm became the chair's first incumbent. Since his primary task as chief of the library's Aeronautics Division was to acquire aeronautical material for the library's collections, he was in an ideal position to carry out his campaign of belittlement. The claim of any person to have flown before the Wright brothers was carefully considered. Zahm's most successful effort in this line was the creation of a revival of interest in the discredited German-American Gustave Weisskopf—or Whitehead—who claimed to have made at least two flights before the Wright brothers first flew in 1903. In 1897, Whitehead had been hired to build a glider for the Boston Aeronautical Society. Society member Samuel Cabot's first impression of the man was that he was "a pure romancer with a supreme mastery of the gentle art of lying." Whitehead's glider never flew. In 1900 he moved to Bridgeport, Connecticut, where he claimed to have made a flight of half a mile on August 14, 1901, in his twenty-first flying machine. The story of the flight was carried in a Bridgeport paper—four days later. Before the flight, the reporter asserted, Whitehead sent the machine up loaded with 230 pounds of sand but without a pilot, which may have accounted for the drawings of four witches on brooms with which the newspaper story was embellished. Then on January 17, 1902, Whitehead announced that he had made a seven-mile flight over Long Island Sound in a new machine that had taken fourteen men to construct.

Stanley Beach, son of the publisher of the *Scientific American,* induced his father to advance Whitehead close to $10,000 over a period of several years with which to build a flying machine. The result was the Beach-Whitehead biplane exhibited at the New York Aeronautic Society show of

November 1908 at Morris Park. It never flew, but its motor caused one visitor to comment that "the machinery, pulleys, belts, and brackets to carry all this appeared more suitable for a steam roller than an aeroplane." The Beaches eventually dropped Whitehead. Whitehead eventually dropped aviation, took up religion, and died a penniless fanatic in 1927. His preposterous claims were happily forgotten until January 1935, when an article in *Popular Aviation* by Stella Randolph and Harvey Phillips retold the story of Whitehead's 1901 and 1902 flights as fact rather than fiction. The Harvard University Committee on Research in the Social Sciences became interested and funded an investigation into the matter. The results were published in December 1936 in the *National Aeronautic Magazine.* One of the two witnesses that Whitehead said had been present at the half-mile flight of 1901 was located. He was of the opinion that the story had grown out of comments Whitehead had made while discussing what he hoped to do, rather than out of what he actually did. He had never heard of the other witness. As to the seven-mile flight over Long Island in 1902, Whitehead's wife and children, interviewed in the course of the investigation, could not remember that Whitehead had ever mentioned making such a flight.

That would have been the end of the Gustave Whitehead story, except for the publication in 1937 of *The Lost Flights of Gustave Whitehead,* by Stella Randolph. Orville Wright called it "too incredible and ridiculous to require serious refutation." He had heard from several sources that Albert Zahm was behind its publication. Stella Randolph, who worked in a doctor's office in Washington, D.C., and had no particular interest in aviation, had been induced by Harvey Phillips to collaborate on the *Popular Aviation* article about Whitehead, and Zahm had apparently encouraged her to expand the article into a book. In May 1935, a few months after the appearance of the *Popular Aviation* article, Zahm had written a letter to Emerson Newell, one of the attorneys who had represented Glenn Curtiss in the Wright Company suit, asking Newell to forward to the Library of Congress any authentic accounts of flights by Whitehead that remained in the files of *Wright v. Curtiss.* "In his frenzy of malicious spite," Orville wrote a friend several years later, "poor old Zahm was not able to get the support even of the law firm with which he had been associated in opposing the Wrights." Unknown to Zahm, Emerson Newell had died in 1931, and Zahm's letter was forwarded to Orville by a member of Newell's old law firm with a friendly warning: "It appears that someone is trying to throw a cloud on your position as the first successful flyer."

Zahm's thirty-five-year campaign to malign the Wrights, begun in 1911 with the publication of *Aërial Navigation,* culminated in 1945 with the publication by the University of Notre Dame of a forty-page booklet, *Early Powerplane Fathers.* Gustave Whitehead was merely the most successful of

Zahm's four powerplane fathers (men who had either invented the airplane or flown before the Wrights). Orville had heard for some time that Zahm was working on a book which would constitute an attack on the Wright brothers without mentioning them by name. "I presume this is that book," he wrote the editor of *Aviation News,* who had received a copy of *Early Powerplane Fathers* for review and had forwarded the book to Orville. "I do not think those at Notre Dame who let Zahm use them for his fell purpose knew what they were doing," his letter concludes, "but I feel sure in time they will be ashamed of it."

Albert Zahm retired from the Library of Congress in 1945, the year *Early Powerplane Fathers* was published. Early that year there had been a resurgence of interest in the all-but-forgotten Gustave Whitehead. It began with a national network radio broadcast that presented Charles Whitehead to listeners as the son of Gustave Whitehead, the first man to fly. This was followed with an article on the broadcaster ("The Man Who Knows Everything First") in the popular weekly *Liberty,* in the course of which it was stated that no one had ever been able to disprove "that Gustave Whitehead, a little be-mustached Bavarian, made the first motor-controlled flight in the world, sped farther, faster, and better than the Wrights." In July 1945, Whitehead's fame was multiplied exponentially when the *Liberty* article was condensed and trumpeted to the world in the pages of *Reader's Digest.* It took a canard of this dimension for Orville to overcome his aversion to writing. "The Mythical Whitehead Flight," by Orville Wright, appeared in the August 1945 issue of *U.S. Air Services.* The readership of that esoteric journal was infinitesimal, however, compared to that of the *Digest,* whose millions of readers were in the habit of accepting predigested revelations as holy writ, and the Whitehead myth died hard, if it can be said to have died at all.

Orville's paper on Whitehead was the first piece of writing he had done for publication in more than twenty-five years. It was also his last. That he would never get around to writing his own account of the invention of the airplane had been clear for some time. "It is a tragedy," Charles Lindbergh wrote after talking the matter over with Orville at a meeting of the National Advisory Committee for Aeronautics in October 1939, "for Wright is getting well on in years, and no one else is able to tell the story as he can." It occurred to Lindbergh that the best way to goad Orville into some kind of action would be to find him a competent collaborator. During a trip to Washington in September 1940, he broached the subject to his friend Earl Findley, then editor of *U.S. Air Services,* thinking Findley would be an ideal author for the book that Orville would never write himself. To his astonishment, he learned that Findley had already written such a book back in 1915 and that the manuscript of that misbegotten venture was still in existence.

Findley was reluctant to let Lindbergh discuss the book with Orville, but Lindbergh was persistent and he tackled Findley again at a luncheon in Washington a few months later. At that time the manuscript, presumably the same one Orville had likened to an attack of sciatica, was in a box beside Findley's bed in his Washington apartment. In spite of its availability, he was unwilling to reopen old wounds and perhaps risk a rupture in his long friendship with Orville by a second attempt at collaboration. "The subject is so sensitive to him," Lindbergh wrote in his diary that night, "that I think I shall not try to press it farther." Earlier the previous year, on April 18, 1940, at a luncheon celebrating the twenty-fifth anniversary of the National Advisory Committee for Aeronautics, Lindbergh had prodded Orville on the subject of selecting a suitable collaborator for the book and had found Orville "pleasant and courteous, as usual, but not at all encouraging."

In fact, Lindbergh may not have been a very close friend of Orville's. Politically, they were poles apart. Lindbergh was the darling of the America First movement, which was doing its best to keep the United States out of the war against Hitler. He was against interfering with what his wife had defined as the Wave of the Future—that is, Hitler's reorganization of society along lines that the Lindberghs considered inevitable but that most of the rest of the world considered unendurable. A lifelong Republican, Orville was nevertheless wholeheartedly with the Roosevelt administration in its aid to Britain and opposition to Hitler. Another indication of a cooled friendship, which may never have been very warm anyway, is that on the two occasions when Lindbergh mentioned the matter of Orville's finding a writer with whom to cooperate on his book, Orville had not considered it worthwhile to inform Lindbergh that he had already found an acceptable collaborator.

The first time Lindbergh mentioned the subject to Orville, in October 1939, a twelve-page article had just appeared in *Harper's Magazine*, "How the Wright Brothers Began," which was the result of just such a collaboration as Lindbergh had suggested. It was by Fred C. Kelly, who as a young reporter had written an article in *Collier's* in 1915 based on an interview with Orville. Kelly's survey of the Wrights' early years in *Harper's* seems to have been a trial balloon, sent up to determine if such a collaboration would work. It did, and shortly thereafter Kelly set to work on a biography of the Wright brothers with the understanding that Orville would have the right to go over every page of the manuscript in detail before it was published. All went well until the book was half finished and Orville grew tired of the project. He offered to pay Kelly to forget the whole thing. It was then that Kelly adopted a strategy that saved the day. With Orville's permission, he initiated a correspondence with Smithsonian secretary Charles Abbot in an attempt to end the controversy over Langley's Aerodrome once and for all. The time was ripe. For several years, Abbot had been trying to come to terms with Orville, but all his efforts had been rejected out of hand. "It is a difficult situation," Lindbergh wrote in his diary in April 1939, after trying to intervene. "I believe the fault lies primarily with the Smithsonian people, but Orville Wright is not an easy man to deal with in the matter." As if to demonstrate the truth of that statement, Orville found a new reason for distrusting the Smithsonian in January 1942, the very month that Kelly began his attempt to bring the feud to an end.

The trouble this time was that the National Advisory Committee for Aeronautics was considering naming its Cleveland engine laboratory after Charles Manly, who had designed the motor for Langley's 1903 Aerodrome. That motor had been attributed solely to Manly until 1931, when the *New York Times* had revealed that Stephen Balzer of New York had been responsible for the original design. Actually, Manly's 52-horsepower radial motor bore little resemblance to the unsuccessful 8-horsepower rotary motor that Balzer had contracted to build for Langley, but to Orville the Balzer-Manly question was just another example of Smithsonian perfidy. He was against naming the engine laboratory after Manly and wrote a long letter expressing his feelings to the secretary of the National Advisory Committee for Aeronautics. The gist of the letter was that it was time that the committee "disregard the constant importunities of the Smithsonian to use the committee as a cat's-paw in its controversies." To avoid further controversy, the committee voted not to name the Cleveland engine laboratory after Manly.

Determined to write finis to the Aerodrome affair before the year was out, Secretary Abbot composed and submitted to Orville in October 1942 a paper in which he incorporated the list of changes made in the Aerodrome before it was tested in 1914 and conceded that Curtiss's contract to reconstruct the Langley machine had been ill considered and open to criticism. More importantly, he admitted that the 1914 Aerodrome tests "did not warrant the statements published by the Smithsonian Institution that these tests proved that the large Langley machine of 1903 was capable of sustained flight carrying a man."

Abbot's paper was published both as a pamphlet and in the Smithsonian *Annual Report* for 1942. His apologia was also reprinted in Fred Kelly's *The Wright Brothers: A Biography Authorized by Orville Wright,* which appeared the following year and represented a double victory for Orville—the completion of a book he had never been able to write himself and a personal triumph over the Smithsonian Institution that had taken him almost thirty years to achieve. He wrote a conciliatory letter to Abbot when it was all over: "I can well understand the difficult position you found yourself in when you took over the administration of the Institution at a time when it had on its hands an embarrassing controversy for which you were not responsible, so I appreciate the more your effort to correct the record of the tests at Hammondsport in 1914 which brought on that controversy."

That the 1903 Flyer would be brought back to the United States was now a foregone conclusion, but the machine had been placed in underground storage for the duration of the war to protect it from the bombs being rained on London by the Luftwaffe. Since there was no possibility of bringing it home until after the war, it was decided to withhold the official announcement of its eventual return until December 17, 1943, the fortieth anniversary of the first flights. There was to be a gala dinner in Washington that night, at which President Franklin Roosevelt would announce the return of the Flyer. The Collier trophy for 1943 was to be awarded to the U.S. Army Air Forces at the same time and accepted on their behalf by General Hap Arnold, who had learned to fly at the Wright flying school at Simms Station back in 1911.

Orville disliked formal dinners, but accepted the invitation because the President himself was to make the announcement about the return of the Flyer. The President, however, had recently returned from conferences at Teheran and in North Africa and was unable to attend the dinner. Orville became upset when he learned that Secretary of Commerce Jesse Jones, who was standing in for the President, had arranged for Orville to present the Collier trophy to General Arnold while newsreel cameras recorded the event and the ceremony was broadcast on a national radio network. Before the dinner, Orville reminded Jones that he had agreed to attend only on condition that he would not be required to take an active part in the program, but after Jones had made the announcement about the return of the 1903 Flyer and the awarding of the Collier trophy, he read aloud the concluding words of the President's message: "In closing I can think of only one additional tribute to General Arnold. Will you please ask Orville Wright, the greater teacher, to act for me in handing the Collier trophy to General Arnold, the great pupil."

Confronted with a microphone, Orville remained adamantly tight-lipped. There was absolute silence on the air until the radio announcer filled in by saying that Orville was now presenting the trophy to General Arnold. Arnold rose to the occasion gracefully. There was no one, he said, from whose hands he would rather receive the trophy than Orville Wright.

Orville vowed he would never attend another official dinner in Washington. He had written the directors of the Science Museum that the Flyer could be exhibited in London for six months after the war in order to give the museum time to make a copy of the aircraft. In July 1945, two months after the war ended in Europe, the Flyer was removed from storage, but it was not sent back to the United States at the end of six months. It remained on exhibit in the Science Museum all through 1946 and 1947. It was not returned to the United States and installed in a place of honor in the Smithsonian National Museum until December 1948, eleven months after Orville Wright had died.

# 52

## *Orville's Shoes*

ORVILLE HATED TO be late. On October 10, 1947, he was late for a luncheon appointment with his friend Edward Deeds, president of the National Cash Register Company. As he hurried up the steps of that company's Dayton offices, he suffered a heart attack and was rushed to the Miami Valley Hospital. After a brief spell in an oxygen tent, he recovered and early in November was back at work in his laboratory. Most of his time now was spent in answering letters or in putting his files of correspondence and other papers in order with the help of Mabel Beck. Those files included the letters from Octave Chanute and the wind-tunnel tables and propeller formulas that Wilbur once claimed could be used to make the design "of flyers of other sizes and speeds a science as exact as those of marine engineering"— documents, Orville believed, that would one day tell the story of the invention of the airplane in a way that would give the Wright brothers full credit for their scientific approach to the problem, something that Fred Kelly's brief but readable biography did not.

Orville no longer did any laboratory work. The wind tunnel at the back of the building had not been used in some time. Its motor was the subject of a letter he wrote to the General Electric Company on January 24, 1948:

> I have a 10-H.P. General Electric motor that I would like to sell. This motor was purchased in 1917 for use in my laboratory on a wind tunnel. I would estimate it had about 200 hours of running. I am quoting from the invoice of the General Electric Company of Schenectady of February 10, 1917: 1 KT-322-10-10-720/685-220 V 60 cyc "B" motor 1186788 DRL-1891926 amps 28.
>
> Would you be interested in purchasing it or do you know of an interested purchaser?

The carbon of this letter was the last to be found in Orville's files and is the last document to appear in the two-volume *Papers of Wilbur and Orville Wright,* published in 1953. Marvin McFarland, the editor of those volumes, commented in a footnote that the letter "shows a mind as busy and as thorough as ever." Thorough it certainly is, but one can only imagine the amazement with which the letter was received by that giant corporate entity known as General Electric and passed from hand to hand. It is not every day that a millionaire tries to sell a used motor back to the company from which it was purchased thirty years before.

On Tuesday, January 27, three days after writing that letter, Orville spent part of the morning at home trying to fix the front doorbell. It was a cold morning with snow on the ground. He was in and out of the house several times and made several trips up and down the basement steps before leaving for the laboratory. Later that morning the telephone rang at Hawthorn Hill. It was Mabel Beck. Orville had collapsed at his office. Carrie was to come at once.

Carrie arrived at 15 North Broadway at the same time as the ambulance that took Orville to the hospital. A few years later, after Hawthorn Hill had been purchased by the National Cash Register Company as a guest house for distinguished visitors, and Carrie and Charlie Grumbach had retired to a small house of their own, Marvin McFarland was in Dayton. He talked with gray, grandmotherly Carrie and when he returned to Washington wrote down what Carrie told him of an incident that took place at the Miami Valley Hospital the day of Orville's second heart attack:

> While Carrie was visiting him that afternoon, the nurse came in and suggested he might like something to eat or drink. Yes, he would have a bit of scraped apple and a few sips of ginger ale. After the nurse had begun to prepare the food, Orville Wright, full of solicitude for Carrie, who had cared for him and for Wilbur and Katharine and his father for so long, said gently: "You had best let Carrie do that, Miss—she knows all my cranky little ways."

On Wednesday, Orville's condition was reported as serious. On Thursday, it was announced that his heart attack was complicated by congestion in his right lung. On Friday, January 30, the family was called to the hospital. At ten-thirty that night Orville died. His death was a quiet death compared to the long-drawn-out wasting away of Wilbur in his prime. It came as a surprise to many in the world outside Dayton who assumed that Orville had been dead for almost as long as Wilbur, but Daytonians knew better. Orville's passing was attended with all the pomp and ceremony due the city's most distinguished citizen. On February 2, the day of his funeral, flags were flown at half-staff, schools were let out at noon, and city and municipal offices were closed. There was a minute of silence at 2:30 P.M. throughout Dayton.

Orville had not been a churchgoer since his youth, but funerals of the famous require a house of God, and Orville's took place in the First Baptist Church of Dayton because its minister, the Reverend Charles Seasholes, was one of the only two clergymen in Dayton of whom Orville approved. As the funeral procession wound through the streets to Woodland Cemetery, four jet fighters from Wright Field roared overhead in a five-plane formation. The fifth plane, missing from its slot in the formation, was the equivalent of the riderless horse in a full-dress military funeral. When the procession reached the cemetery, the jets made a pass over the four graves—Susan Wright's, Milton Wright's, Wilbur's, and Katharine's—and the rectangular void that was to receive the last member of that once happy household.

Orville left an estate of more than a million dollars. The largest bequest, approximately $300,000, went to Katharine's alma mater, Oberlin College. Smaller bequests went to Reuchlin's widow, Orville's boyhood friend Ed Sines, Carrie Grumbach, Charlie Taylor, Mabel Beck, and Charlotte Jones, the Wright family laundress. The bulk of the fortune went to Orville's nephews and nieces and their children. As to the disposition of the 1903 Flyer, which was still in the Science Museum, London, Orville's will, which dated from 1937, simply stated that the Flyer should be returned to the United States if a letter authorizing its return had been written by him. That such a document existed, no one doubted, but when Harold Miller, who was known to be co-executor of the estate, attempted to obtain the letter shortly after Orville's death, Mabel Beck refused to turn over any files until the executors of the estate had been officially appointed. It took a confrontation with Edward Deeds in the office of the president of the National Cash Register Company and a long-distance phone call from Washington by Earl Findley, one of Orville's oldest friends, to dislodge the document. A final flare-up ensued when Mabel Beck refused to work for the family at the same salary for which she had worked for Orville and asked for a raise. The family put its foot down, and Mabel was fired at the end of February.

Why Orville had been so dilatory in arranging for the return of the Flyer has never been explained. The letter addressed to the director of the Science Museum authorizing the return of the 1903 Flyer—also called the Kitty Hawk—was dated December 8, 1943. It stated merely: "I have decided to have the Kitty Hawk plane returned to America when transportation is less hazardous than at present," but the war in Europe had been over for almost three years when Orville died, and it was not until October 18, 1948, that the Flyer was taken apart and packed in three crates for shipment to the United States on the *Mauretania*.

While the *Mauretania* was still at sea, the captain learned of a dock strike in New York and took the ship to Halifax, Nova Scotia. There, the three crates were transferred to the U.S. escort carrier *Palau,* which had been recalled from South American maneuvers for the purpose, and brought to Bayonne, New Jersey. At Bayonne a Navy truck was waiting to haul the crates to Washington. Lettered on the sides of the truck above the legend OPERATION HOMECOMING were the words: "The original Wright Brothers Aeroplane 1903 The 'KITTY HAWK' enroute from London England to Washington DC for permanent exhibition in the U.S. National Museum." The Navy truck traveled from Bayonne to Washington, via Philadelphia, in a two-day triumphal procession. After some unavoidable legal maneuvering, the Flyer was sold to the U.S. government by Orville's heirs for one dollar. Suspended from the ceiling of the Arts and Industries Building, which housed the Smithsonian's aeronautical collections at the time, it became a permanent exhibit of the national museum in an elaborate ceremony on December 17, 1948.

Since 1903, this aging museum piece has been assembled, dismantled, and reassembled more than a dozen times, a process more debilitating and destructive than the buffeting it received from the sand-laden winds at Kill Devil Hills in 1903, but thanks to judicious replacement of its ailing members it has survived. In 1976 it was taken from the Arts and Industries Building and suspended in the entrance hall of the Smithsonian's new National Air and Space Museum. In 1985 it was taken down one more time, completely dismantled, and refurbished piece by piece. The yellowing wingcovering was replaced with gleaming white muslin, so that what one sees today is not a dusty, decaying original but a sturdy re-creation of the big white biplane that struggled into the air on the memorable morning of December 17, 1903. In this respect, the original Wright Flyer is like the long-suffering Scarecrow of Oz, whose mangled and dismembered body was repaired and restored time after time without any appreciable change in appearance or loss of identity. The body was merely the outward manifestation of the deathless spirit within.

Admittedly, the scarecrowlike dummy lying prone on the lower wing of the Flyer in the entrance hall of the museum adds a slightly macabre note to the exhibit, but without a waxwork pilot to indicate the direction of flight, anyone unfamiliar with early airplanes might assume that the front rudder was the tail and that the Flyer was headed out the south door of the museum, rather than north in the direction of Washington's Mall. That supine waxen figure represents Orville as he was on the day he made the first airplane flight in history—although there will always be some question about which of the four flights made that day deserves to be called the first in history. There is no question that the Flyer did all that was claimed for it on Orville's first

flight ("raised itself by its own power . . . sailed forward without reduction
of speed, and . . . landed at a point as high as that from which it started"),
but that brief, untimed, unmeasured flight could hardly be called sustained.
It was not until Wilbur's accurately timed and measured 59-second, 852-foot
flight, the fourth of the day, that the Wright Flyer proved itself capable of
sustained free flight with a man. A picture is worth a thousand words,
however, and because of a picture it is Orville up there on the Flyer in the
museum rather than Wilbur. Orville had set up the camera on its tripod
before the first trial of the day, John Daniels of the Kill Devil lifesaving
station tripped the shutter just after the machine left the starting rail, and
the resulting photograph swept away all doubt about which brother made
the first flight.

Yet even then Orville was destined to play second fiddle to Wilbur.
When John Daniels squeezed the rubber bulb that tripped the shutter,
Wilbur had just let go of the Flyer after steadying it down the track. Wilbur's
figure, arms akimbo, left leg bent, jacket and pant legs flapping, adds as
much to the forward movement of the big white Flyer as its whirling
propellers. Cover his figure and the Flyer hangs as motionless above its
shadow on the sand as if it were already suspended by wires from the ceiling
of a museum. It is the image of Wilbur, silhouetted against sand and sky,
that imprints itself on the memory. His younger brother, flat on his stomach
on the lower wing, is doing all the work, of course, fighting to control the
unruly Flyer in a wind of more than 20 miles an hour—yet the clearest
impression we retain of Orville in those first few golden seconds of the air
age is not an image of the man himself but the sharply focused image of his
shoes.

# Notes

Abbreviations are used for the names of authors whose works are cited most often:

| | |
|---|---|
| AR | Arthur G. Renstrom |
| FK | Fred C. Kelly |
| G-S | Charles H. Gibbs-Smith |
| McM | John R. McMahon |
| OC | Octave Chanute |
| OW | Orville Wright |
| WW | Wilbur Wright |

Abbreviations are also used for the two works cited most frequently:

| | |
|---|---|
| MK | *Miracle at Kitty Hawk* |
| PW | *The Papers of Wilbur and Orville Wright* |

Both books will be found in the Bibliography under Wright, Wilbur and Orville.

## 1. THE HOUSE ON HAWTHORN STREET

The primary source for this chapter is Fred C. Kelly's *The Wright Brothers.* Additional sources are cited below.

| | | |
|---|---|---|
| 3 | *fining library users* Conover, 23. | |
| 4 | *the toy helicopter* OW, *Century.* | |
| 5 | *Yale divinity school* Miller, 170. | |
| 6 | *Orville in the printing business* | Charnley, 24–30. |
| | *the house in 1885* McM, 20. | |
| | *an occasional spanking* McM, 27, 31. | |
| 7 | *Santa Claus was outlawed* McM, 42. | |
| | *Sunday school* Coles. | |

*family nicknames* PW, 32 n., 40 n., 881 n.; McM, 18, 20–21.
*family sayings* PW, 31, 825, 922, 1023; McM, 22, 40; Charnley, 16.
*"and then the boiler bust"* "When the Wright Brothers Were Boys," *American Magazine,* June 1909.
*Lorin's letter* Tom Crouch, *The Bishop's Boys.* Norton, 1989, 72.
*Lorin's job as bookkeeper* Johnson, 32.

8   *the printing business* Ibid., 36–37, 45.
*Paul Laurence Dunbar* PW, 695–96 n.; Goulder, 21–22.

9   *the first two bicycle shops* Johnson, 39–40.

10   *humming the same tune* McM, 66; Sullivan, 588.
*Orville and tobacco* McM, 64.
*Orville as prankster* PW, 1107.
*Fourth of July picnic* Coles.
*house improvements* PW, vol. 1, xxxix.

11   *photographs and darkroom* PW, p. 6, 255 n.
*the Wrights and the church* McM, 50.
*"I have been thinking"* MK, 9.
*"Yes, I will help you"* MK, 10.

12   *a third location* Johnson, 34–35. In 1895–96, for about one year, the Wrights maintained a shop at 23 West Second Street in downtown Dayton. Almost nothing is known about this shop except its location and the fact that it faced competition from more than a dozen shops in the downtown area. (Johnson, 21.)
*bicycle manufacturing in the 1890s* The Engineer (New York), May 9, 1896, 112.
*left half of a remodeled building* Johnson, 41–43. The right half of the first floor was occupied by Fetters and Shank, Undertakers. Their operations in those cramped quarters remain something of a mystery.
*work in the bicycle shop* Charnley, 43.
*sold for $100* McM, 60.

13   *Lorin had married* Johnson, 33.
*"newspapers of that day"* WW, 115.

14   *Orville's illness* According to Bishop Wright's diary, Orville sat up in bed for the first time in six weeks on Oct. 8 (Young and Fitzgerald, 16). This indicates that, until at least Aug. 27, he was well enough to sit up and discuss such matters as Lilienthal's death.

## 2. THE FLYING MEN

15   *first read of Lilienthal* PW, 3.
*thought it had been in 1895* FK, 45.
*Gibbs-Smith's opinion* G-S, *Aviation,* 94 n.
*Otto Lilienthal* OC, *Progress,* 276–90; " 'The Flying Man': Otto Lilienthal's Flying Machine," by "Vernon," *McClure's Magazine,* Sept. 1894.

16   *the two encyclopedias* FK, 27.

17   *Langley and his models* Vaeth, 28–48.

18   *tied red tape* OC, "Experiments in Flying."

*pointed out the fallacies* OW, "Possibilities."

*not sufficiently quantitative* OC correspondence, OC to Means, Mar. 20, 1910.

19     *a series of swirling waves* OC, "Experiments in Flying."

*Butusov soared for miles* OC correspondence, OC to Means, Jan. 28, 1897.

*Augustus Herring* See entry in *Dictionary of American Biography.*

*Herring's thesis* Ibid.; Martin; Inglis; Crouch, *Dream,* 146.

20     *Herring at the Smithsonian* OC correspondence, OC-Herring letters, Nov.–Dec. 1895.

*"the known . . . should be tested"* OC, "Gliding Experiments."


## 3. IN THE DUNES OF INDIANA

The primary source for this chapter is Octave Chanute's diary (PW, 641–54), supplemented by Means, 30–75, and OC, "Gliding Experiments" and "Experiments in Flying."

23     *a steamy letter* PW, 651 n.

25     *two separate articles* OC, "Recent Experiments in Gliding Flight"; Herring, "Recent Advances Toward a Solution of the Problem of the Century" (Means, 31–53, 54–74).

26     *Herring's gold-dredging machine* OC correspondence, OC to Means, June 20, 1897.

*Herring's 1897 glides* Crouch, *Dream,* 210–13. The Chicago *Times-Herald* (Sept. 29) reported that on Herring's second day of experimenting (Sept. 3), he was making 300-foot glides in a 40-mile-an-hour wind and that 600-foot glides the next day were not uncommon—feats so improbable that their publication can only be attributed to the reporter's gratitude for having been allowed to make a glide himself. Apparently, no reporters were present until Sept. 6.

*No formal records were kept* OC correspondence, OC to Herring, Nov. 21, 1897.

*Oct. 1896 flights in a triplane glider* The only sources for these glides are Herring's article (Means, 70–74) and his remarks appended to Chanute's 1897 talk to the Western Society of Engineers (OC, "Gliding Experiments"). The only indication that such a glider ever existed is a photograph of a three-wing glider at the end of Herring's article, captioned "Gliding Machine in Flight." It may be a photograph of Chanute's new glider taken on Saturday, Aug. 29, the day on which the glider was tested for the first and only time in its original three-wing form. Another possibility is that the photograph of the triplane was originally a photo of the double-decker, made from one of the two negatives Herring helped himself to before leaving camp on Sept. 13, and that a third wing was added by a photo retoucher. Like many of the photographs reproduced in the 1897 *Aeronautical Annual,* it appears to have been heavily retouched.

*never mentioned such a glide* Herring's alleged glides in a triplane glider seem never to have been mentioned in any aeronautical history until Crouch's *Dream of Wings* was published in 1981, but Crouch's only source (p. 323, n. 6) is Herring's article in the 1897 *Aeronautical Annual.* The present writer is aware of only one other reference to those glides—an indirect one in McMahon. In paraphrasing a letter Wilbur wrote to his father reporting his 43-second glide of Oct. 3, 1903, McMahon wrote: "He did not deign to mention that an American Munchausen of his acquaintance had claimed forty-eight seconds" (McM, 132).

27    *specialist in lightweight motors* On December 18, 1898, the Chicago *Tribune* reported that Herring had invented a ten-pound motor that produced 8 horse-power and ran so smoothly it could be operated on top of a cardboard box.

*alleged flights of Oct. 1898* OC correspondence, Herring to OC, Mar. 17, 1901; Crouch, *Dream,* 215–20. The Niles, Michigan, *Mirror* story of Oct. 28, 1898, did not appear until six days after the event (quoted in Crouch, 220). The information it contains, presented as if the reporter were actually present, may have been supplied by Herring himself. Roseberry (p. 134), after describing an alleged flight by Herring in 1908, writes: "As in the case of his purported 1898 flight, he later sought out a newsman and volunteered an account with no one to substantiate it."

*attempted to verify the story* Zahm, 222.

*a few wild claims* OC, "Experiments in Flying."

28    *Wilbur's article on Mouillard* "What Mouillard Did," *Aero Club of America Bulletin,* Apr. 1912; reprinted in *Aeronautical Journal,* July–Sept. 1916, 107–10. In his article, Wilbur refers to *L'Empire de l'Air* as a book, but there is no indication that he ever read more than the extracts translated by the Smithsonian.

## 4. THE TWISTED BOX

30    *bandy-legged desk* PW, pl. 6; MK, 21.
31    *Hiram Maxim* Maxim, 291–94.
    *Maxim told reporters* OC, *Progress,* 246.
32    *Clément Ader* G-S, *Aviation,* 59–61.
    *Percy Pilcher* Ibid., 86–87.
    *the kite model* PW, 9–11.
33    *had been shellacked* PW, 22 n.
    *birds' method of lateral control* WW, 118.
    *Orville on birds* PW, 1168–69.
    *Orville made a sketch* FK, 49.
34    *inner-tube-box story* PW, 9 n. 4; FK, 49–50; McM, 75–76.
    *letter to Sullivan's assistant* PW, 1143.
35    *test of the kite model* PW, 11.
    *Weather Bureau letter and reply* PW, 12.
36    *Sunday afternoons* Miller, 2, 3, 72–73, 156.
    *mandolin lessons* Ibid., 4.
    *photo of Katharine* MK, photo insert.
    *Carrie Kayler* MK, 17–19.
    *turkey stuffing* MK, 119.

### 5. A Perilous Passage

38    *Wilbur to Chanute* PW, 15.
39    *Chanute to Wilbur* PW, 19.
40    *Wilbur to Kitty Hawk Weather Bureau station* MK, 25 n.
      *Dosher to Wilbur* Omega G. East, *Wright Brothers National Memorial*
      (Washington, D.C.: National Park Service, 1961), 13.
      *Tate to Wilbur* MK, 25.
      *total cost of materials* FK, 57.
      *Wilbur wrote his father* MK, 27.
41    *"The trip will do him good"* PW, 23.
      *trip to Kitty Hawk* PW, 23–25, 25 n. 9; MK, 28–30; FK, 58–59.
42    *an "African"* PW, 39.
      *a movie script* When *Miracle at Kitty Hawk* was published in 1951, Jack
      Warner optioned the movie rights, and part of a script was submitted to Fred
      Kelly for review. It was circulated (with much merriment) in the Aeronautics
      Division of the Library of Congress in 1952, where the Wright papers were
      being edited.
      *noticeably nervous* Taylor.
      *name of Perry's boat* Albertson, 13.
43    *"those 'bars' up North River"* PW, 33.

### 6. The Outer Banks

44    *Kitty Hawk* PW, 25, 28, 37.
      *"mosquito (or "skeeter") hawk"* Albertson, 25.
      *Nags Head* Outlaw, 28–30, 34, 35, 45, 46.
      *descendant of a Scottish sailor* Tate, "I Was Host."
45    *lifesaving stations* Wechter, 60–61.
      *the Tate house* PW, 25–26.
      *a strange gentleman* Tate, "With the Wrights."
46    *breakfast and room and board* Albertson, 14–15.
      *Mrs. Tate's sewing machine* PW, 28 n. 5.
      *believed in a good God* Tate, "With the Wrights."
      *Wilbur to his father* MK, 30.
47    *makes no mention of Orville* With two exceptions, there is not a whisper in
      the letters and documents of this period to indicate that Orville was involved
      in Wilbur's work on the flying problem. The exceptions are Wilbur's Nov. 27,
      1899, letter to the U.S. Weather Bureau and his acknowledgment of the receipt
      of information on Dec. 9 (WP, 12). In both letters he uses "we" throughout.
      His letter to the Smithsonian begins: "I have been interested in the problem
      of mechanical and human flight ever since as a boy I constructed a number
      of bats of various sizes." This refers to the attempt to build imitations of the
      toy helicopter of 1878, which Orville, in his 1908 *Century Magazine* article,
      describes as a joint effort. Wilbur's letter of Sept. 3, 1900, to Bishop Wright,
      who had evidently been away from Dayton for some time, uses the first person
      singular exclusively ("It is my belief that flight is possible. . . . I am taking

up the investigation for pleasure rather than profit"). There is the same chorus of "I's" in the letter Wilbur wrote his father from Elizabeth City on Sunday, Sept. 9 ("I supposed you knew that I was studying up the flying question. . . . I chose Kitty Hawk. . . . I have no intention of risking injury").

The omission of Orville's name from this correspondence would not be so significant if the literature that has grown up around these early years did not, almost invariably, take it for granted that the brothers collaborated closely in their experiments from the very beginning. John E. Walsh, in *One Day at Kitty Hawk*, dissents. He suggests that Kelly's biography, prepared with Orville's help, represents a bid by Orville to usurp for himself an equal if not greater role in the invention of the airplane. Orville's 1920 deposition *(How We Invented the Airplane)* gives the impression that he was as involved as Wilbur from the beginning.

*the old trunk* PW, 27.

*"Tell Harry to sell"* MK, 32.

48      *"At any time we look out"* PW, 31.

*the gasoline stove* OW, *How We Invented,* 25 n.

*offered to buy their stove* Albertson, 16.

*food at Kitty Hawk* PW, 33–34.

49      *Orville's long Sunday letter* PW, 33.

*the 1900 glider* PW, 18, 41–42, 1184.

*warping was achieved* There is no contemporary description of how the wing-warping mechanism was operated in the 1900 glider. The only reference to the method used is in Kelly, who states that in the 1900 and 1901 gliders "the wing-warping mechanism had been worked by movement of the operator's feet" (FK, 79).

*raised or lowered by hand* Again, the exact means used has never been described and cannot be determined from photographs of the 1900 glider. The only reference to the mechanism used seems to be by Griffith Brewer: ". . . the operator lying face downward on the machine and grasping a bar capable of receiving a twisting motion, which enabled the man, by twisting his outstretched hands, to guide the machine up or down when elevating or depressing the forward elevator" (Brewer, "Wilbur Wright," 73).

*would reduce the head resistance* PW, 47–48.

50      *gliding experiments* PW, 29–44, 105–7; OW, *How We Invented,* 31–32; FK, 63–66.

*Tom Tate* PW, 36, 39.

51      *"tried it with tail in front"* PW, 38.

*Orville's last letter home* PW, 37–40.

52      *road down the side of the bay* Outlaw, 52.

*maintain balance by shifting his weight* PW, 336 and n. 7.

*one month to twenty years later* PW, 40–44, 63, 106–7; WW, 119 (1912 deposition); OW, *How We Invented,* 32 (1920 deposition).

53      *could salvage the materials* Tate, "With the Wrights."

*Wilbur's summary* PW, 106–7.

## 7. A Two-Man Association

54     *Chanute's speech at Cornell* MK, 21.
55     *The long silence was broken* PW, 40.
       *"This is a magnificent showing"* PW, 47.
       *he drafted two articles* PW, 58–63.
56     *"Can you give us any advice"* PW, 53.
       *correspondence on anemometers* PW, 53–54.
       *Charles Taylor* Taylor.
57     *lunch was served* PW, 52 n. 8.
       *a letter from Chuckey City* PW, 57.
58     *glad to have the assistance* PW, 63.
       *first Sunday letter home* PW, 71–76.
59     *first day in camp* PW, 73–75.
       *mosquito menace reached a peak* Outlaw, 13, 41.

## 8. The Camp at Big Hill

61     *Huffaker at the Smithsonian* Adler, 251.
       *Huffaker at the Wright camp* PW, 118, 139.
62     *Spratt's medical background* Shortly after graduating from medical college in 1894, Spratt gave up medical practice as too strenuous for his heart and took up instead the more strenuous occupation of farming on the family farm four miles north of Coatesville. He lived for another four decades. (Trimble, 46; *New York Times,* Nov. 28, 1934, 15.)
       *the mosquitoes persisted* PW, 73–75.
       *the new glider* PW, 1184–85.
       *could be raised or lowered* OW, *How We Invented,* 30.
       *wingwarping mechanism was activated* FK, 79.
63     *glides of July 27* PW, 7, 75, 108–9, 158.
       *kite tests of July 29* PW, 76.
       *tested the pull of the machine* PW, 78.
64     *itemized the good points* PW, 77–78.
       *constructed two small model wings* PW, 112.
       *Wilbur in the dry-goods store* McM, 91.
       *difficulty due to a sudden reversal* PW, 76, 78.
       *"The balancing of a gliding . . . machine"* PW, 101.
65     *Huffaker detected this reversal* Crouch, *Dream,* 239–40.
       *Spratt had also investigated* PW, 108.
       *both men had pointed out* PW, 110.
       *center-of-pressure experiment* PW, 80–81, 109–11.
66     *experiments during Chanute's visit* PW, 81, 158.
       *Chanute-Huffaker glider* PW, 118–19.
       *Chanute's letter of advice* PW, 83.
67     *problem in making turns* PW, 82, 84; OW, *How We Invented,* 36–38; FK, 70.
       *"He looked rather sheepish"* PW, 118.

"*When we looked at the time and money*" WW, 120.
*one of the few after-dinner speeches* PW, 934.
*Orville's recounting of the story* FK, 72.

## 9. TRADE SECRETS

68   *Two years later* "The Outlook for the Flying Machine," *The Independent,*
     Oct. 22, 1903.
     *H. G. Wells as prophet*      *The Nineties* (New York: American Heritage,
     1967), 143.
69   *Chanute's invitation* PW, 91.
     *made a show of nagging* PW, 92.
     "*don't hear anything but flying machine*" Ibid.
     *homemade motor* Tom Crouch, *The Bishop's Boys.* Norton, 1989, 112–13.
     "*Pathetic,*" *he replied* PW, 95.
     *ladies' night* PW, 93.
     *Wilbur's trip to Chicago* PW, 99 n. 2.
     *Wilbur's clothing* MK, 47.
70   *Wilbur's address to the society* PW, 99–118.
71   *reprint of Wilbur's address* AR, *Bibliography,* 2.
     *entertained its readers* Freudenthal, 48.
72   "*Do not be afraid*" PW, 119.
     *aerodynamic experiments, Sept.–Dec. 1901* PW, 120–82, 475–93, pls. 114–27.
     *included some disparaging remarks* FK, 73–74.
73   *Lilienthal's table* PW, 127.
74   *Langley described an experiment* Langley, *Experiments,* 22, 23.
76   "*It is perfectly marvelous*" PW, 156.
     "*I am amused*" PW, 168.
     "*I get lost*" PW, 184–85.
     "*I do also*" PW, 171.
     *he offered to help finance* PW, 139.
     "*Practically all of the expense*" PW, 142.
     "*I happen to know Carnegie*" PW, 183.
     "*Andrew is too hardheaded*" PW, 187.
     "*You will need to publish*" PW, 183.
     *Wilbur's long Sunday letter* PW, 192–205.
77   *a new wind tunnel* PW, 283.
     "*As soon as our condition is such*" OW, *Century,* 650.

## 10. WELL-DIGGING

78   *flying machines being constructed* PW, 212–13.
     *the mercenary idea* PW, 205.
     *Charles Lamson* PW, 223; Crouch, *Dream,* 111–13.
     *Chanute wrote Wilbur; Wilbur's reply* PW, 223, 226–27.
79   "*I will not experiment any more*" PW, 233.

*Herring's ups and downs* OC correspondence, Herring to OC, Sept. 30 and
Oct. 28, 1900, Feb. 10, 1901; ibid., OC to Langley, Dec. 6, 1898.

80     *the* Britannica *article* PW, 651–52 n.

*"a first class show"* OC correspondence, Herring to OC, Jan. 5, 1902.

*Maxim-Chanute exchange* Ibid., May 13 and May 25, 1902.

*"to beat Mr. Wright"* Ibid., OC to Langley, Oct. 21, 1902.

*"will be all right with us"* PW, 234.

81     *attempted to decline the unwanted gifts* PW, 235–36.

*William Avery* PW, 237, 244, 249.

*Wilbur reminded Chanute* PW, 237–38.

*committed his misgivings to paper* PW, 247–48.

82     *"Will spins the sewing machine"* PW, 244.

*"that church business"* PW, 233, 238 and n. 9, 493 and n. 5; MK, 65–66.

*"really ought to get away"* PW, 243–44.

*trip to Kitty Hawk* PW, 244–45; MK, 70.

83     *remodeling the camp building* PW, 245–49.

*best water in all Kitty Hawk* MK, 71–72.

*the living room* MK, 72.

*eggs in numbered sequence* McM, 93.

*descendants of the hogs* Outlaw, 41.

84     *assembling and testing the glider* PW, 249–60, 321–22, 1185.

*increased pressure on the side* FK, 81–82.

85     *"Almost instantly it reared up"* PW, 321.

*making the tips lower* PW, 258, 322.

86     *Orville made his first free glides* It is not easy to determine what the Wrights
meant by "free glides." In tests of the Lamson-Chanute glider, Orville reported: "These flights were only partly free" (PW, 274). This may mean that
the men who helped launch the machine ran alongside and helped to keep the
wings level, as the Wrights had done in their flights of 1900 and 1901, when
they flew with the wingwarping control tied down. Walsh takes it for granted
that Orville had not made a glide of any kind until Sept. 23, 1902. The accounts
by both brothers of the dozen glides made in 1900 are vague as to who did
the gliding. In Renstrom's *Chronology* all the attributed glides of 1901 are
Wilbur's, so Walsh may be right. However, Orville's diary for Sept. 23, 1902,
states that he made a number of short glides "to learn the new method of
working the front rudder," which seems to indicate that he had been on the
machine when the movement of the rudder bar had been opposite to what it
was in 1902. In that case, Orville's "I here took my first free flight" refers to
his first free flight of 1902. (PW, 258, 259.)

*"a heap of flying machine"* PW, 260.

*when the slope was 15 to 20 degrees* PW, 253–54.

*the buzzards they observed* PW, 252.

87     *recorded the incident* PW, 262.

*events of Sept. 27–Oct. 3* PW, 264–69.

*Reuchlin Wright* Miller, 147; Johnson, 74.

88     *Orville's version, as told to Kelly* FK, 81–82. The story of Orville's sleepless
night and the discovery of the cause of well-digging appears first in McMahon
(p. 117), but there is no mention there of the explanation of well-digging being
made known to Wilbur at breakfast. In Kelly's biography, the story is told

as it is given here, except that Orville does not involve Lorin by winking at him before launching into his explanation. That detail was added by Kelly, three years after Orville's death, in *Miracle at Kitty Hawk* (p. 81), where the incident is told in approximately the same words as in the biography. Combs, in *Kill Devil Hill* (p. 169), attributes the entire breakfast-table story, including the wink, to Lorin. Walsh, who consistently champions Wilbur at Orville's expense, gives Wilbur sole credit for "piecing the puzzle together."

89      *Wilbur's version* WW, 121–22.
         *Orville's diary entry* PW, 269.

## 11. MOVABLE WINGS

90      *events of Oct. 4–14* PW, 270–75.
         *the new rudder* PW, 1185.
91      *rock about a transverse axis* PW, 1014.
         *a curious passage in McMahon* McM, 113.
92      *Chanute himself was later to admit* PW, 276.
         *events of Oct. 15–24* PW, 276–80.
         *"a fine fellow to be with"* PW, 279–80.
         *"Regarding the ten dollars"* PW, 284.
93      *he spent the night in Kitty Hawk* PW, 283 n. 10.
         *strong winds made it easier* PW, 325.
         *may have been the* Ocracoke PW, 356.
         *trip to Elizabeth City* PW, 284.
94      *he wrote Wilbur* PW, 276.
         *letter to Moedebeck* OC correspondence, Oct. 21, 1902.
         *"more are to be carried out"* PW, 664.
         *proposals to exhibit Chanute gliders* PW, 426, 429, 538, 753–54, 756, 757.
         *would have taken six to eight weeks* PW, 538.
         *Wilbur wrote Chanute* PW, 757.
         *ripped off in a violent storm* PW, 862.

## 12. TWO TALKS

95      *side trip to Washington* PW, 282 n. 9.
         *wrote Chanute the next day* OC correspondence, Oct. 17, 1902.
         *an indirect application for employment* Ibid., Langley to OC, Oct. 23, 1902.
         *Chanute's reply* Ibid., Oct. 21, 1902.
96      *sent a wire to Wilbur* McM, 121.
         *Wilbur's answer* PW, 283.
         *neither he nor Orville* PW, 290.
         *Chanute next wrote* PW, 291.
         *Wilbur apologized* PW, 291–92.
         *Chanute's European trip* PW, 293, 299–301, 303–5.
97      *"the American inventor"* PW, 655.

*Chanute's Aéro-Club talk* PW, 654–59; G-S, *Rebirth,* 59–63.

*stated more explicitly in L'Aérophile* "This is how Mr. Chanute entered into relations with the Wright brothers, his present devoted collaborators. In 1900, the Wright brothers, bicycle manufacturers, at Dayton, Ohio, wrote to Mr. Chanute to ask him for some details about his experiments. They desired to renew them but with sport only as an object. Mr. Chanute very willingly furnished them the information they wanted, and Messrs. Wright brothers then had constructed, on his data, machines similar to those of Mr. Chanute, with which they thereupon experimented with real success." (PW, 924 n.)

*the Wrights and the Patent Office* Worrel.

98  *article in the Aug. 1903 L'Aérophile* PW, 659–73.

99  *found everywhere an impression* PW, 984.

*dispute over computations of glides* PW, 325, 337–45.

100  *sent a copy of his article* PW, 340.

*"this is news to me"* PW, 342.

*"advise me as soon as possible"* Ibid.

*cited three additional errors* PW, 345.

*informed Chanute the next day* PW, 346.

*"I was puzzled"* PW, 348.

101  *Wilbur's conciliatory letter* PW, 349.

*planning to visit Dayton* PW, 308.

*letters written the following day* PW, 315; OC correspondence, OC to Langley, June 7, 1903.

*Wilbur and the Redpath Lyceum Bureau* MK, 87.

*Wilbur's June 24 lecture* PW, 318–35.

102  *"When I speak of soaring"* PW, 319–20.

## 13. THE FIRST FLYER

104  *urged them to apply a motor* PW, 1014.

*system called end control* PW, 280.

*the 1903 Flyer* PW, 312, 1187–89; Taylor; OW, "How We Made."

105  *wind-tunnel tests of Jan. 1903* PW, 297, 314.

*Chanute questioned the accuracy* PW, 314.

*the Flyer's ribs* PW, 312.

*Milton Wright in the bicycle shop* Miller, 68.

*blocked the passage* Taylor.

106  *the Flyer's motor* Ibid.; Hobbs; PW, 1210–12; OW, *How We Invented,* 52.

*keeping a diary since he was twenty-eight* Miller, 201.

*"broke their little gas motor"* PW, 298.

107  *"Very generally speaking"* Langley, *Experiments,* 88.

*the Wright propellers* PW, 594–636; Taylor; McM, 130; OW, *How We Invented,* 53.

*"What at first seemed a simple problem"* OW, *Century,* 648.

108  *arguments over propeller theory* MK, 19–20; Taylor.

109  *Orville's letter to Spratt* PW, 313.

*"back at your old trick"* PW, 305.

*"You make a great mistake"* PW, 306.

110     "*not my intention*" PW, 307 n.
        *flimsy imitation of the 1901 glider* G-S, *Rebirth*, fig. 11.
        *italics by Archdeacon* PW, 658.
        *Chanute received a letter* PW, 355 n.
        *Chanute informed Ferber.* Ibid.
        "*Not hearing from you*" PW, 335.
111     *Ferber's experiments* G-S, *Rebirth*, 70, fig. 14.
        "*has still time to beat me*" PW, 348 n.
        *Chanute translated Ferber's letter* PW, 348.
        "*If we had facilities*" PW, 349.
        "*a little nest of dishes*" PW, 354.
112     *gave his sons a dollar* Charnley, 162; McM, 146.


### 14. A RACE WITH THE WEATHER


113     *1903 trip to Kill Devil Hills* PW, 355 n., 356–57.
        *the new building* PW, 359.
114     *Monday's glides* PW, 358.
        *the four-day storm* PW, 362–63, 365–67.
115     *something of a weather prophet* PW, 388.
        *the Flyer's wing* PW, 363–64.
        *Orville's postcard* PW, 369–70.
        *anemometer tests* PW, 369, 384–85.
116     *glides of Oct. 21* PW, 370–71.
        *Dan Tate's opinion* OW, *Century*, 647.
        *glides of the following week* PW, 373.
        *carbide-can stove; Dan's strike* PW, 374–75 n. 1; MK, 105–6.
117     *Spratt pitched in* PW, 376.
        *twisted propeller shaft* PW, 376–77; OW, "How We Made."
        *Chanute's stay in the camp* PW, 377–79.
118     *the Wright launching system* PW, 379, 381, 385 n.; FK, 96.
        *proposed purchase of the Ader machine* PW, 381.
        "*thinks we could do it!*" Ibid.
119     *testing the starting rail* Ibid.
        *testing the framework* PW, 382.
        *the friction test* PW, 387; FK, 92–93.
        *Orville's letter to Taylor* PW, 386.
120     *he wrote in his diary* PW, 380.
        *a letter to his sister* MK, 108.
        *studying languages* PW, 382.
        *Chanute had written from Europe* PW, 300.
        *Nov. 17 and ensuing cold spell* PW, 382–83.
121     *tightening the sprocket wheels* PW, 385–86.
        *bought a batch of writing paper* MK, 103.
        *determining thrust* PW, 384, 386.
        *anemometer testing* PW, 384–85.
        *loaded the truck with sand* PW, 385.

testing the hip cradle Ibid.

122    gas consumption; broken bicycle hubs Ibid.
Thanksgiving Day through Nov. 28 PW, 388.
flight-data recording instrument MK, 350–53.

123    Wilbur filled in the time PW, 388–89.
estimate of the Flyer's cost MK, 112.


### 15. AN EXPERIMENT IN AERODYNAMICS


124    *"scant regard for etymology"* G-S, *Aviation,* 63.
whirling-table experiments Vaeth, 32–33.
*"vitiating the results"* Langley, *Experiments,* 24; PW, 20.

125    Langley's Law Ibid., 3, 106, 108, 113.
having *"brought to a close"* Smithsonian Institution, *Annual Report* 1906, 327.
seeking help from Octave Chanute OC correspondence, Langley to OC, June 8 and Dec. 1, 1897.
reference to aeronautical surveillance Vaeth, 66.
not until the drawings were approved Crouch, *Dream,* 132.

126    entrusted to an experienced carpenter Ibid., 264.
on the verge of bankruptcy Vaeth, 74.
framework of tubular steel Adler, 250.
trouble with propeller shafts Meyer, *Aero Engine,* 122.
the floating workshop Langley, *Memoir,* 156.

127    quarter-size model Ibid., 226–33.
news had been leaked to the press Meyer, *Aero Engine,* v.
the reporters' camp Vaeth, 75–76.
*Langley's ark* Meyer, *Model Engine,* 83.
flight of the model Ibid., 78; Langley, *Memoir,* 261.
entirely successful, he said New York Times, Aug. 9, 1903, 11.

128    a zealous workman Langley, *Memoir,* 258.
the Aerodrome's control system Ibid., 207, 215–16.
*"Referring to the general plans"* Ibid., 215.
a flight of a few miles Ibid., 217.

129    preferred a ground-level launching Vaeth, 78.
the Aerodrome's funding Crouch, *Dream,* 277.
events of Sept. 3 Vaeth, 81.
flight of Oct. 7 Ibid., 81–83; Langley, *Memoir,* 261 ff.
*"like a handful of mortar"* Washington *Post,* Oct. 8, 1903.

130    The *Post* gleefully reported Sullivan, 563.
The *Times* editorialized Oct. 8, 1903, 6.
on the vaudeville stage Sullivan, 568.
the houseboat during November Vaeth, 86–87.
the small lug was removed Langley, *Memoir,* 270.
trial of Dec. 8 Ibid., 270 ff; Vaeth, 87–89.
Its progress was plainly visible Sullivan, 583.

131    he was on the tug New York Times, Dec. 9, 1903, 1.

"*voluble series of blasphemies*" Adler, 256.
*a halfhearted attempt was made* Sullivan, 567.
*it is generally conceded* Crouch, *Dream,* 288, 290–91.
132      "*stuffers of birds and rabbits*" Sullivan, 563.
*the War Department report* G-S, *Aviation,* 67.
*embezzlement scandal* Vaeth, 99.
*Adler's tribute* Smithsonian Institution, *Annual Report* 1906, 529–30.

## 16. THE FIRST FOUR FLIGHTS

133      *events of Dec. 12–13* PW, 391, 402.
*flight of Dec. 14* PW, 391–92, 402; OW, "How We Made"; FK, 95–96.
*a blanket invitation* OW, *Century,* 649.
134      *the rope fastening the machine* PW, 392. Ten years later, Orville referred to
the rope as a "*restraining wire*" (OW, "How We Made").
*events of Dec. 15–16* PW, 394.
135      *unidentified stranger* OW, "How We Made."
*events of Dec. 17* PW, 394–97, 401–3; OW, *Century,* 649; OW, *How We
Invented,* 55–57.
*John Daniels* Daniels was interviewed by W. O. Saunders for Saunders's
article in *Collier's,* Sept. 17, 1927. His account is the only eyewitness account
of the events of Dec. 17 to find its way into print—aside from those of Wilbur
and Orville. Daniels supplies several colorful but highly suspect details. He
describes the flights as taking place on the beach and remembers carrying the
Flyer "back up the hill." Some details of Daniels' account, which must have
made Orville wince when he read them, have been used in writings about the
Wrights since Orville's death. Both Crouch and Combs have the brothers
shaking hands before the flight, hanging on to each other "sort o' like they
hated to let go," and both seem to believe that Wilbur urged the men "not to
look sad, but to laugh and hollo and clap our hands and try to cheer Orville
up." Combs adds a colorful, if unlikely, detail from an unnamed source,
noting that before the first flight, Orville "doffed his usual bowler and put on
a cap, taking the extra precaution of fastening it with a safety pin" (Combs,
213).
*sociable, hospitable places* Outlaw, 49.
*the possibility of salvaging lumber* FK, "How the Wright Brothers Began,"
*Harper's Magazine,* Oct. 1939, 481.
137      *Johnny Moore's age* Sixteen (McM, 308); eighteen (Albertson, 11).
*Mrs. Moore and the cow* Outlaw, 49.
*Johnny Moore and the chicken* OW, "How We Made."
139      *first three flights largely estimated* The most reliable contemporary record is
Orville's diary (PW, 395–96). *1st flight:* "about 100 feet from the end of the
tracks," but the machine lifted two-thirds of the way down the sixty-foot
track, making the distance about 120 feet. Wilbur forgot to stop his stopwatch,
and the stopwatch on the Flyer was set back to zero by the jolt of the landing,
so the 12-second duration is an estimate only. *2nd flight:* "about the same in
time. Dist. not measured but about 175 ft." Orville attributed the extra length
to a slackening of the wind speed, but since the wind was not measured, it

could just as well have been due to an overestimation in the duration of the first flight. *3rd flight:* "about the same distance" as the second flight; no time given. (Orville in his 1913 article in *Flying* says this flight was 15 seconds and a little over 200 feet.) *4th flight:* measured 852 feet, 59 seconds. In all four flights the shock of the landings set back the stopwatch on the machine, so the last flight must have been timed by the stopwatch in Orville's hand.

*shaken about like a rattle in a box* OW, *Century,* 649.

*sending the wire from Kitty Hawk* FK, 102–3.

*through a spyglass* MK, 153.

140 *"If we should succeed"* MK, 108.


## 17. FICTION AND FACT

141 *receipt of the telegram* MK, 118–19.

142 *press reaction to the telegram* FK, 106–7; MK, 430.

Virginian-Pilot *story of the flights* FK, 104–9; MK, 431; Sullivan, 593–94.

144 *besieged by the press* PW, 399–400.

*telegrams received at Kill Devil Hills* PW, 398–99.

*telegram that interested them most* Wilbur wrote two letters to the editor of the *Century Magazine* (Jan. 7 and Feb. 20, 1904; both letters are in the Archives and Library, Henry Ford Museum and Greenfield Village, Dearborn, Mich.). The first indicated that the magazine's telegram had been answered from Kitty Hawk. In the second, Wilbur said he would send an article when he had one ready. The article was finally written—by Orville—and sent to the magazine four and a half years later, on June 22, 1908.

145 *Orville's wire from Huntington* PW, 400.

*encounter with the reporters* Ibid.

*dairying the milk* MK, 120.

*Christmas oranges at breakfast* McM, 42.

*Orville's gift to Katharine* McM, 149.

*Chanute's letter to Wilbur* PW, 401.

*Wilbur's telegram to Chanute* Ibid.

*letter written the same day* Ibid.

146 *Chanute's letter to Katharine* PW, 398 n.

*Chanute's address to the AAAS* PW, 406.

*Wrights' release to the AP* PW, 409–11.

*omitted the paragraph* PW, 411 n.

*852 feet up in the air* Arthur W. Page, "How the Wrights Discovered Flight," *World's Work,* Aug. 1910, 13317.

*sneering references* FK, 110–11.

147 *they were stored in a shed* AR, *Chronology,* 14.

*Charlie Taylor remembered* Taylor.


## 18. THE YEAR OF THE FAIR

148 *described their situation* PW, 538.

*$4,900 tucked away* PW, 409.

*320-acre farm* FK, 113; McM, 153.

*Rather than abandon the business* FK, 120–21.

149   *Huffman Prairie* FK, 122–23; PW, 426 n. 8, 441; photoreproduction in the Wright State University archives of a map drawn by Orville Wright, May 7, 1935.

*Amos Stauffer and David Beard* FK, 123.

*the Wright patent* PW, 409, 415, 417; Worrell.

150   *"Experiences of a Flying Man"* PW, 422, 428, 430.

*the editor's apologies* The Independent, Feb. 25, 1904, 455; Mar. 10, 1904, 374.

151   *Herring's letter* Dec. 26, 1903; copy in OC correspondence, Herring volume; MK, 128; PW, 413.

*wrote Chanute another letter* OC correspondence, May 13, 1903.

152   *Chanute offered his services; Wilbur's reply* PW, 414–15.

*Herring's British patent* OC correspondence, OC and Thomas Moy, 1898–1901; OC to Herring, Mar. 1, 1898, Mar. 24 and May 19, 1901.

*went to St. Louis* PW, 421.

153   *Wilbur pointed out* PW, 421 n.

*notified the rules committee* PW, 439.

*that old "church business"* PW, 433.

*they sent a letter* FK, 123.

*events of May 23–May 26* The four-day sequence presented here is based on Milton Wright's diary and Wilbur's May 27, 1904, letter to Chanute (PW, 436–48). Orville's 1908 *Century* article describes Monday's and Thursday's events as if they occurred on two consecutive days. In Kelly, the two aborted flights occur on Monday and Tuesday (FK, 123–25). In Walsh, they occur on Wednesday and Thursday (Walsh, 161–62).

154   *gave the distance as 60 feet* OW, *Century,* 649.

*Chanute's letter to Wilbur* PW, 437.

*was able to write Chanute* PW, 439.

155   *an ingenious deception* Walsh, 160–62, 275–76. If they had really planned to abort the flight of May 26, Orville would merely have had to turn the front rudder down and come to a skidding stop without creating the damage that it took the brothers a week to repair—a week that they could not afford to lose if they were to try out their Flyer before entering the St. Louis competition. Combs (pp. 238–40) makes a valiant effort to disprove Walsh's theory by showing graphically that the air density at Huffman Prairie was such that it prevented the Wrights from making any substantial flights until they used their catapult launcher in September. The fact is that the brothers made thirteen flights of over 600 feet that summer without any significant modifications in machine or motor before using the catapult launcher. Two of these flights covered one-quarter of a mile and lasted for 36 seconds each. It took four days of flying and nine flights with the launcher before they were able to better their pre-catapult record.

*"an attempt . . . to spy upon us"* MK, 165.

*they fooled the newspapers* FK, 140–41.

*"We certainly have been 'Jonahed' "* PW, 440.

*"In a light wind"* PW, 441.

*Santos-Dumont arrived* Wykeham, 197.

156
*wring a few concessions* PW, 445.
*"It is true that the tortoise"* PW, 442.
*The tortoise was having troubles* Wykeham, 194–95; Horgan.
*inability to control its undulations* PW, 446.
*They solved the problem* PW, 467; FK, 121.

157
*flights of Aug. 1904* PW, 447–52.
*Orville's accident* PW, 1065.
*his back might have been broken* FK, 127.
*sore all over* PW, 452.
*German and English contributions* Walker, vol. 2, 11.
*the French airship* Horgan.
*the American balloon* Walker, vol. 2, 13.

158
*Chanute's launching apparatus* *Aeronautics,* May 1910, 12.
*Avery's demonstrations* PW, 450, 458–59; Horgan.
*"He is getting over it"* PW, 455.
*Knabenshue and the* California Arrow Horgan.

159
*funds were impounded* Roseberry, 42.


19. THE FINISHED FLYER


160
*launching device* FK, 128.
161
*first flights with the launching device* PW, 453–56, 460.
*Amos Root* FK, 117–19, 142–43; Hallion, 110–15.
162
*may not have been a coincidence* Walsh, 167.
*sent a copy* FK, 143.
*Chanute had been invited* PW, 433.
*On Oct. 5 Wilbur wrote* PW, 459–60.
*flights of Oct. 26–Dec. 9* PW, 462–67.
*they broke both skids* PW, 462; FK, 129.
163
*the wings had been burned* PW, 1190.
*paid a call on his congressman* PW, 494–95.
*letter to Nevin* FK, 149–50.
164
*Nevin was ill* PW, 495.
*the Board's letter to Nevin* FK, 150.
*"Imagine the Secretary of Defense"* Walsh, 278.
165
*a flat turndown* PW, 495.
*sent a letter to England* FK, 148.
*Alexander's visit* PW, 291 n.
*a large part of his fortune* Walker, vol. 1, 99.
*invited to their camp* PW, 413 n. 3.
*Capper in America* Walker, vol. 2, 13, 18, 44.
166
*correspondence with the British* Ibid., 24–34; FK, 151–52.
*a separate handle* PW, 520.
*blinkers* OW, *How We Invented,* 61.
167
*the old and new motors* PW, 1215.
*officials of the interurban railway* PW, 463; FK, 135–36.

168

169

*asked Chanute for advice* PW, 481, 483, 485.
*that old "church business"* PW, 493 and n. 5; AR, *Chronology*, 16.
*flights through July 14* PW, 492–501.
*an exhausting task* PW, 517.
*"If an older woman"* Taylor.
*Huffman Prairie was under water* PW, 506.
*a new front rudder* FK, 134.
*twice forced to land* PW, 507.
*the larger vertical rudder* FK, 134.
*flights of Sept. 7 and 8* PW, 509.
*rewiring the wings* PW, 411.
*"little jokers"* PW, 510 and n.
*changes made a few weeks later* PW, 514.

## 20. A BOLD PERFORMANCE IN CALIFORNIA

171

172

173

174

176

*"I enclose an account"* PW, 483.
*an unsuccessful inventor* Connick, 35, 51, n. 12.
*clan had become worried* Spearman, 18, 31.
*Montgomery's gliding experiments* OC, *Progress*, 248–49.
*sought Chanute's help* OC correspondence, Oct. 5, 1893–Oct. 30, 1895.
*Montgomery at Santa Clara* Spearman, 36.
*Thomas Baldwin* Roseberry, 36–37; Crouch, *Eagle*, 506–9, 515–18.
*That November he wrote Montgomery* Smithsonian Archives, Montgomery file.
*he visited Montgomery* Ibid., Montgomery to his mother, Dec. 15, 1903.
*signed an agreement* Ibid., Court of Claims No. 33852, May 28, 1928, 5.
*was writing his brother* Ibid., May 15, 1904.
*Curtiss's motor and Baldwin's flight* Roseberry, 35–41.
*idea for his new propeller* OC correspondence, Montgomery to OC, Apr. 11, 1905.
*the equivalent of an education* San Jose *Mercury*, Dec. 17, 1904, 7.
*inflated in flight* OC correspondence, Montgomery to OC, Apr. 20, 1905.
*dirigible-parachute* Spearman, 169.
*1904 tests of the glider* *Aeronautics*, Nov. 1911, 153.
*proposal for balloon-glider flights* Spearman, 45, 49.
*March flights at the Leonard ranch* Spearman, 49–57.
*Maloney told a reporter* Ibid., 55.
*he wrote Montgomery* OC correspondence, Apr. 4, 1905.
*"Baldwin entered into a contract"* Ibid., Apr. 11, 1905.
*sent Montgomery's letter to the Wrights* PW, 488.
*wrote his mother* Smithsonian Archives, Montgomery file, Mar. 21, 1905.
*flight of Apr. 29* Spearman, 58–75; San Jose *Mercury*, Apr. 30, 1905, 5, 9.
*report seen by the Wrights* PW, 490.
*his next letter to Chanute* OC correspondence, Apr. 30, 1905.
*sent one of his two copies* PW, 494.
*Wilbur wrote back* PW, 496.
*"Much of it is bosh"* PW, 497.

*most wonderful exhibition of daring* PW, 493.

*had tried to obtain data* OC correspondence, Apr. 16, 1905.

*advised Montgomery to borrow* Ibid., May 23, 1905.

*exhibition at San Jose* Ibid., Montgomery to OC, June 17, 1905; Spearman, 78–83; Connick, 41.

177     *two legal actions* Connick, 38, 52 n. 24.

*identified as Captain Baldwin* Spearman, 252.

*countersuit for libel* PW, 484 n.

*had undermined his confidence* OC correspondence, June 15, 1905.

*events of July 18* San Jose *Mercury,* July 19, 1905, 1, and July 20, 7; Spearman, 84–88; OC correspondence, Montgomery to OC, Nov. 12, 1905.

*Wilbur's letter to Chanute* PW, 504–5.

178     *Chanute wrote Wilbur* PW, 508.

*Wilbur warned* PW, 511.

*motion-picture projectionist* Spearman, 117.

*so-called cowboys*    *Aeronautics,* Nov. 1911, 153.

*Wilkie's training* OC correspondence, Montgomery to OC, Dec. 29, 1905.

*The second and last exhibition* The impression persists that there was a whole series of such exhibitions (see notes to Chapter 47). After describing Maloney's flight of Apr. 29, 1905, Victor Lougheed wrote (in *Airplane Designing for Amateurs,* 24): "Similar performances were repeated some fifty or sixty times in the course of exhibitions that Montgomery gave around California, in an effort to secure funds for the continuation of his experiments." If that was so, Maloney must have given four to five exhibitions each week before being killed eighty days later. There are no records of such exhibitions, and the only known Montgomery glider flights are those cited in this chapter and described in greater detail in Spearman's definitive biography.

*Wilkie's flight of Feb. 22* Spearman, 115–17; OC correspondence, Montgomery to OC, May 27, 1906.

*wrote a long, complaining letter* Ibid.

*Chanute forwarded the letter* PW, 715.

180     *a promotion campaign* See Chapter 42.

*"opened for all mankind"* Inscription at the base of the ninety-foot stainless-steel airplane wing erected to Montgomery's memory at Otay Mesa near San Diego.


## 21. THE THORN TREE


181     *spent every day that week* PW, 512–13.

*Wilbur stalled the machine* PW, 510.

*unable to level the wings* PW, 511.

*flight of Sept. 28* PW, 512–13, 520–21; OW, *Century,* 649; FK, 131–32.

182     *solution to their last major control problem* One of those disturbing circles of confusion throws the Wright story slightly out of focus at this climactic moment. A letter Wilbur wrote to George Spratt eleven days earlier, on Sept. 17, 1905, indicates that the principle involved in the solution to their control problem was already known: "When turning a very small circle with the outside wing much elevated it is hard to bring the inside wing up again, or

stop turning, unless the machine is high enough in the air to allow the whole machine to be turned downward for a short time. As we have heretofore been flying at heights of not over thirty feet, and usually only ten to twenty feet, we frequently touch the lower wing to the ground before we can bring it up to the level." (MK, 147.) The Wrights, however, may not yet have had an opportunity to test this maneuver at a high enough altitude until Orville's thorn-tree flight of Sept. 28, made at an altitude of about fifty feet.

*"When we had discovered"* PW, 521.

183 *oil had been added* G-S, *Rebirth,* 178.

*flights of Oct. 3–5* PW, 513–14.

*"the back of my neck would break"* FK, 214.

*three newspapermen had descended* PW, 511.

*Luther Beard* FK, 139–41.

184 *did not know the difference* PW, 684.

*badgered by interurban trolley passengers* FK, 134–35.

*the* Daily News *story* PW, 517, 684.

*keeping the news from going out* PW, 684.

*men and women with cameras* Weaver.

*a wire from Dayton* PW, 519.

*"Went to Dayton to see"* PW, 519 n. 7.

185 *turned over to Torrence Huffman* MK, 193–94.

## 22. ONE MILLION FRANCS

186 *the French glides* PW, 432–33.

*blamed the poor performance* PW, 433–34.

*the half dozen gliders* FK, 168.

*surfaces called élevons* G-S, *Rebirth,* 154–55.

187 *Deutsch-Archdeacon prize* Ibid., 137.

*Archdeacon wrote the Wright brothers* Ibid., 149–50.

*The Wrights replied evasively* PW, 488.

*a letter from Captain Ferber* PW, 506.

*Chanute asked the brothers outright* PW, 493.

*"The American Government has apparently"* Ibid.

*"We still do"* PW, 495.

188 *decided to renew their proposal* PW, 514–15.

*the Board's reply* McM, 173–74.

*The Wright brothers replied* McM, 174–75.

*another offer to intercede* PW, 531.

*the Wrights were not interested* PW, 532.

*Chanute volunteered his help* PW, 500.

*"not anticipating an immediate visit"* PW, 516.

189 *second round of negotiations* PW, 528–29 and n.; Walker, vol. 2, 35–42.

*Alexander's reading of the Wrights' letter* PW, 698.

190 *a personal attack on the Wright brothers* PW, 697.

*two letters to Ferber* PW, 524 n. 2; FK, 170–71; *L'Aérophile,* Dec. 1905, 267–68.

191 *some inconclusive experiments* G-S, *Rebirth,* 161–62.
*"the German Emperor in a truculent mood"* PW, 703.
*"seeking a fuss"* PW, 702.

191 *widely disbelieved in Germany* For example, by the editor of the *Mitteilungen,* Major Hermann Moedebeck, whose vehemence made up for a lack of fluency in English. "I do not believe what pretend the Wright brothers!" he wrote Chanute. "You have not seen them flying all round and witnesses the names of them they have now given are not competent people for me. . . . Such a machine has after my private opinion no value for warfare. That was a dream! I wish to the Wright brothers that very much nations might purchase their flying machine except the German nation." (OC correspondence, Apr. 8, 1906.)
*the initial French reaction* G-S, *Rebirth,* 179.
*Archdeacon's challenge* Ibid., 191.
*"burst into such laughter"* PW, 536.
*Lahm and the cable to Weaver Jr.* PW, 530; FK, 175–79.

192 *Weaver Sr.'s trip to Dayton* Weaver.

193 *Coquelle's visit to Dayton* FK, 179; G-S, *Rebirth,* 192.
*Aviation Committee meeting, Dec. 23* Ibid., 180.

194 *meeting of Dec. 29* Frank S. Lahm, "The Frenchmen Changed Mind in Regard to Wright Aeroplane," Mansfield, Ohio, *News,* Oct. 24, 1908.
*was treated like a visionary* G-S, *Rebirth,* 171.
*suggested that a commission be appointed* FK, 172.
*Ferber's letter and cable* FK, 182–83.

195 *Lahm's cable* PW, 536.
*identity of Ferber's friend* PW, 536–37, 540.
*indefatigable diarist since 1857* Wright State University archives.
*Dec. 28 and 30 diary entries* PW, 540.

## 23. FAME, BUT NOT WEALTH

196 Scientific American *asked its readers* Jan. 13, 1906, 40.
*"As you profess"* PW, 694.
*"It flies"* PW, 1164.
*wrote the Wrights a letter* PW, 698 n. 4.

197 *offered to exchange information* PW, 236.
Scientific American *recanted* Apr. 7, 1906, 291–92.
*French negotiations* PW, 677–79, 705–8, 718–19, 727–28; 807–8; MK, 459–60; McM, 176–81; AR, *Chronology,* 20–21.

198 *the Moroccan question* Douglas Porch, *The Conquest of Morocco* (New York: Knopf, 1983), 144–46.

200 *British negotiations* PW, 713–14, 720–21; Walker, vol. 2, 51–61.
*Samuel Franklin Cody* G-S, *Aviation,* 129.
*John W. Dunne* Walker, vol. 2, 59, 204; Gollin, 196, 230, 233, 270, 272.

201 *U.S. negotiations* PW, 716–17; FK, 157–59; MK, 176. Unknown to Chanute or the Cabots, the Wrights made a move of their own to reopen negotiations on May 21, 1906. They wrote William Loeb, Jr., President Theodore Roosevelt's

secretary, that they were contemplating a trip East and requested an interview with the President. When Loeb sent word from the White House that they could pay their respects to the President any day at noon except Tuesday and Friday but could not expect an extended interview, they canceled plans for the trip. (PW, 714–15.)

*each had made offers* PW, 353, 355, 531–32.

*Chanute had been in Boston* PW, 723.

*Samuel Cabot's letter* OC correspondence, Sept. 11, 1906.

202    *forwarded Cabot's letter* PW, 728.

*"do not exactly understand"* PW, 729–30.

*"I cheerfully acknowledge"* PW, 730.

*Wilbur's next letter* PW, 731.

*a quick solution was not possible* PW, 737.

*"I do not understand"* PW, 738.

*"It is the complexity"* Ibid.

*"did not believe that there was a secret"* PW, 740.

203    *"I still differ with you"* Ibid.

*six propeller-driven flying machines* G-S, *Rebirth,* 232.

*Santos' prediction    My Airships* (New York: Dover, 1973), 8.

*Santos' biplane* Wykeham, 205, 269.

*trials of the 14-bis* Ibid., 206–18.

*Santos' balloon* Ibid., 210–11; Crouch, *Eagle,* 543.

204    *Chanute crowed to Wilbur* PW, 733.

*wrote Chanute the next day* PW, 734–35.

*"Santos is not now as far along"* PW, 738.

*horizontal surfaces between the wings* G-S, *Rebirth,* 225.

205    *"first real indication of progress"* PW, 740.

*"There is much in the papers"* Ibid.

*Eddy's visit* FK, 194–95.

*Flint and Company    New York Times,* Feb. 14, 1932, 22 (obituary).

*Father of Trusts* Sullivan, 315, 318.

*wrote Chanute the next day* PW, 741.

*had already planned a trip to New York* Ibid., 741.

*Aero Club show, Jan. 1906    Fly,* Nov. 1908, 10.

*asked to send their 1903 motor* PW, 1214.

206    *a surviving photograph* Crouch, *Dream,* 170.

*display of Herring's propellers    Scientific American,* Jan. 29, 1906, 93.

*Augustus Herring in 1906* Roseberry, 467–68.

*Patrick Alexander* PW, 741, 746, 749, 906; FK, 191.

*offices of Flint and Company* FK, 195.

207    *side trip to Coatesville* PW, 742 n., 743.

*"I am sorry to find you"* PW, 390.

*"We have not wished to deprive you"* PW, 967–68.

*wrote Spratt asking for copies* Ibid., 1134.

208    *letter to another Pennsylvanian* PW, 1135 n. George Spratt's unhappy life ended in Nov. 1934, a month after he finally managed to get into the air in an odd biplane of his own design (*New York Times,* Oct. 14, 1934, pt. 9, 7, and Nov. 26, 15). At the time there was still a forlorn hope that someone might produce an aircraft that would do for flying what Henry Ford's Model T had

done for automobiling, and newsreel cameramen were on hand in Coatesville to record the flight of Spratt's candidate for "Flivver of the air." The film is preserved in a collection of old newsreel clips called *Aeronautical Oddities,* screened from time to time in the movie theater at the U.S. Air Force Museum near Dayton for the entertainment of visitors to the museum. The ancient newsreels show men leaping from bridges in unflyable gliders, attempting to get into the air on flapping wings, or displaying their incompetence in other ways guaranteed to draw guffaws from the audience. Some of the film clips are hilarious, some merely titillating, some sad. Saddest of all is the sight of George Spratt, one month before he died, suspended like the weight on a pendulum several feet below the wings of the frail biplane that was said to incorporate all the theories about aircraft stability and control that he had devoted the better part of his life to discovering (Trimble, 34). Spratt's aeronautical theories, which Octave Chanute had found incomprehensible and unscientific, were published in three issues of *Fly* magazine (Aug., Sept., Oct. 1912).

## 24. BELL'S BOYS

209     *moved his airship operation* Roseberry, 49.
        *Bishop Wright's diary entry* PW, 726.
        *discussions in the bicycle shop* MK, 435.
210     *Baldwin's letter* PW, 749 n.
        *Curtiss's letter* Roseberry, 53.
        *a sinister significance* PW, 749 n.; MK, 435.
        *motor ordered by Bell* PW, 725.
        *Bell's Canadian home* Bruce, 300–3.
        *"Alec is simply gone"* Ibid., 359.
        *Bell's box kite* Ibid., 365, 431.
211     *considered the Wright Flyer dangerous* Parkin, 6.
        *most fantastic hope of all* Bruce, 430–31.
        *adequately documented and photographed* Parkin, 16, 43.
        *the* Frost King  Ibid., 15, fig. 13.
212     *Curtiss arrived with a motor* Ibid., 43.
        *Bell's young recruits* Ibid., 33–34; Roseberry, 71.
        *motorcycle races at Providence* Ibid., 76.
        *"little mother of us all"* Ibid., 120; Parkin, 40.
        *addiction to note-taking* Bruce, 356.
        *inclined to be impulsive and impatient* Ibid., 366.
213     *each member would be given a chance* Parkin, 45; Roseberry, 74–75.
        *tests of the* Cygnet Ibid., 84–85; Parkin, 47–48; Bruce, 447–48.
214     *bowed to a majority decision* Roseberry, 85.
        *letters of Curtiss and Wilbur* Ibid., 81–82.

## 25. THE BROTHERS ABROAD

215    *Negotiating a contract* PW, 743–45.
       *Flint and Lady Jane* Flint, 246–47.
       *offered the Wrights $50,000* PW, 750.

216    *plan to fly to Jamestown* PW, 753 n., 1137–38; FK, 160–61; AR, *Chronology,*
       23.
       *fourth attempt to sell a Flyer* PW, 754–55; FK, 162–65; AR, *Chronology,* 23.

217    *booked passage for Wilbur* FK, 196.
       *Hart Berg        New York Times,* Dec. 10, 1941, 22 (obituary).
       *wrote to the New York office* MK, 205–7.
       *talking business* PW, 764–65.
       *forming a company in France* PW, 772–74; FK, 197–200.

218    *"a rambunctious mood"* PW, 772.
       *Henri Letellier* Letellier *fils* would acquire a degree of fame and notoriety as
       the original of the boulevardier and bon vivant Pierre Revel, played by
       Adolphe Menjou, in Charlie Chaplin's 1923 film *A Woman of Paris* (David
       Robinson, *Chaplin: His Life and Art* [New York: McGraw-Hill, 1985], 289,
       309).

219    *Charles Humbert* PW, 809–10 n.; Gollin, 258–59; *New York Times,* Feb. 29,
       1918, 3.
       *dealings with Humbert* FK, 201; PW, 781–83.

220    *"have Orville send me"* MK, 217.
       *"I would give three cents"* PW, 772.
       *exchange of cables* PW, 765–98.
       *appeared to be an indirect refusal* PW, 789.

221    *meeting with Major Targe* PW, 791–92.
       *"You and Charlie come"* PW, 795.
       *drafted a contract* PW, 806, 808.
       *letter complaining of Flint's* PW, 793–94.
       *he wrote his father* PW, 803–5.

222    *he wrote Katharine* MK, 223–24.
       *nine weeks in Paris* MK, 210–12, 217, 232.

223    *Ferber's meeting with Wilbur* PW, 780–81 n.
       *Wilbur's balloon ride* PW, 798; AR, *Chronology,* 24.
       *"Flying as a Sport" Scientific American,* Feb. 29, 1908, 139.

224    *La Patrie* PW, 790–91, 807; Zahm, 118.
       *Zeppelin's fourth dirigible* Toland, 43.

225    *"Comparison of Airships with Flyers"* PW, 799–802.
       *fate of* La Patrie        Zahm, 465–66.
       *Orville in Paris* PW, 809–18.
       *"We have been real good"* MK, 232.

226    *"I did not anticipate"* MK, 234.
       *Charlie Taylor in Paris* PW, 816.
       *Wilbur in Berlin* MK, 231.
       *final French proposal* PW, 818–19.
       *the Stewart business* PW, 822–24.

227    *letter to Barnum and Bailey* MK, 196.

*found a letter from Wilbur* MK, 236–38.
*received a cable* PW, 824.
*Wilbur and Orville in Berlin* FK, 204–5.
*"The Gebrüder Wright"* PW, 825.

228 *sailed for the United States* AR, *Chronology,* 26.
*Orville stayed in Paris* PW, 853.

## 26. A LETTER OF INFORMATION

229 *Aeronautical Division established* Tillman, 13.
*assignment of Selfridge and Lahm* Ibid., 209–10.
*made a trip to Dayton* PW, 745.
*a letter to the Paris* Herald FK, 192–93.
*international balloon race* Crouch, *Eagle,* 543–44; Chandler and Lahm, 59–60.
*Lahm's convalescence and meeting with the Wrights* PW, 779, 810; FK, 207.

230 *Lahm wrote a letter* Tillman, 14–15.
*the Board's long-delayed response* FK, 165.
*Orville wrote the Board* PW, 825–26.
*Wilbur stopped off* PW, 834.
*a formal meeting with the Board* PW, 850.
*an emergency fund* Chandler and Lahm, 149.
*advertisement for bids* Hallion, 116.
*to forestall criticism* PW, 855.

231 *"not a known flying-machine"* FK, 209–11.
*"I believe that Minerva"* OC correspondence, Means to OC, Jan. 20, 1908.
*bids received* Chandler and Lahm, 146–47.
*Scott's bid* Ibid., 150.
*maker of unobserved flights* At a Jan. 1908 meeting of the Aero Club of America, it was reported that Herring had "made several long flights in past years and has built a number of very successful aeroplanes" (*New York Times,* Jan. 14, 1908, 3).
*just such a proposition* FK, 212; MK, 407–8.
*his warm personal friend* PW, 696.
*a New York City musician* FK, 169.

232 *"Herring's Work"* American Aeronaut, May 1908, 154–55.
*a contract with the French* PW, 859.
*Delagrange in 1907* G-S, *Rebirth,* 249.

233 *Issy-les-Moulineaux* Zahm, 261.
*Blériot in 1907* G-S, *Rebirth,* 235–36.
*would one day write of Blériot* Smithsonian Institution, *Annual Report* 1910, 153.
*Farman in 1907* G-S, *Rebirth,* 345–46.
*Wilbur's letter to Chanute* PW, 847.
*attempt to reopen the debate* PW, 841.
*Farman and Delagrange in 1908* Peyrey, 291, 303; *New York Times,* Mar. 22, Apr. 12, May 31, June 25, and July 7, 1908.

234					*Farman at Brighton Beach* Ibid., Aug. 2–15, 1908.
					*AEA gliding experiments* Parkin, 49–50; Casey, 6–7; Roseberry, 85–86.
					*Selfridge's letter; Wrights' reply* MK, 248–49; McM, 195–96.
235					*made a study of the patent* Roseberry, 86.
					*ribs of the AEA machines* Casey, 11.
					*the* Red Wing			Parkin, 54–58; Casey, 8–11; Roseberry, 90–95.
236					*the* White Wing			Parkin, 54–58; Casey, 12–15; Roseberry, 96–101.
					*the* June Bug			Parkin, 58–69, table IV; Casey, 16–21; Roseberry, 102–18.
					*did his best to lure the brothers* PW, 904 n.
237					*"The builders will duplicate this machine"* Roseberry, 101.
					*"are using our patents"* MK, 279.
					*advised Orville to inform Curtiss* MK, 284.
					*Orville wrote Curtiss* PW, 907.
					*Curtiss replied* McM, 198–99.
					*Curtiss's $10,000 offer* Parkin, 156.
					*flying into a storm cloud* Parkin, 53.
238					*had released priceless data* Loening, *Takeoff*, 32.


27. RETURN TO KITTY HAWK


Unless otherwise noted, the source for this chapter is Wilbur's diary, Apr. 6–May 20, 1908 (PW, 860–82).


239					*the Mighty Midgetts* Wechter, xi, 2–3.
240					*"expect you to arrive with relief "* MK, 258.
					*Charles Furnas* MK, 259–60; Combs, 359.
242					*a ten-mile flight over the ocean* FK, 216–17.
					*D. Bruce Salley* FK, 218–19.
					*Salley's report of Wednesday's flight* Sullivan, 603.
243					*noted in his diary* PW, 875.
					*Newton was on his way* Sullivan, 607.
					*lanky, loose-jointed Salley* Ruhl, 19.
					*reporters' trek to their hiding place* Sullivan (pp. 607–13) condensed and para-
					phrased Newton's reminiscences, originally printed in the New York *World*,
					Dec. 16, 1923, and added comments by Ruhl, Orville, and Hoster in the
					footnotes. The various accounts do not agree on dates and are confusing in
					several other respects.
244					*afraid of compromising his fellow reporters* FK, 223.
					*the family from Collington Island* MK, 261–62.
245					*flights of May 14* Based on Wilbur's diary for the day and the map made by
					Orville (PW, 889), on which he charted his long morning flight and Wilbur's
					aborted afternoon flight. After Wilbur left Kill Devil Hills, Orville went over
					the ground with Charles Furnas and charted the flight paths on the basis of
					distances from the camp building of several checkpoints, using turns of the
					wheel to measure the distances in feet (PW, 888–90).
					*a hot engine bearing* The heating was in the rear-cylinder crank bearing and
					was caused by the machine being tilted forward on the starting track, so that
					oil escaped through an overflow momentarily, leaving little or no lubrication
					in that section of the engine. "The heating occurs during these first minutes,"

Wilbur wrote in his diary. "After the machine is in flight for a longer period this section fills up and the lubrication is all right." (PW, 878.) There was something else the matter with the motor, as Orville found out when he checked it over a month later in Dayton. The motor had run a few horsepower short at Kill Devil Hills. Orville was sure the difficulty was due to the new splash system of oiling, which had been responsible for the heated bearings. He was considering reverting to the former system when he and Charlie Taylor, suspecting that something might be lodged in a bend in the gas feed line, blew backward through the tube with compressed air. Something—they were never sure exactly what—flew out, after which Orville was sure they would have no trouble in making at least 40 miles per hour in the Army tests. (PW, 894.)

*Wright engines had no mufflers* It was not until 1913, when the Wright Company produced a six-cylinder motor with water-cooled cylinder heads that it was possible to use mufflers. An extra charge was made to purchasers who wanted this refinement. (PW, 1217.)

*"One did not hear much"* Harper, 112.

246    *almost crazed with grief* Charnley, 247.

*"I do wish though"* PW, 881, 883.

247    *the only course to follow* PW, 895.


## 28. Wilbur Has the Jimjams


248    *finest thing he had ever read* PW, 890.

*severing his connection with the* Herald   FK, 222.

*as Orville put it* PW, 890.

*the* Herald's *revelations* PW, 890–91; Charnley, 252.

*information from the Wright French patent* Actually there were three French patents. The first patent, similar to the basic U.S. Wright patent, had been granted Sept. 1, 1904. Two patents supplementing the basic patent—that is, containing improvements that it was hoped would strengthen the original claims—were applied for Feb. 17, 1907, and granted Mar. 30, 1908. (PW, 1230.) The *Herald* was able to draw on all three patents in describing the Wright brothers' "secrets."

249    *described the situation to Orville* PW, 886.

*"Our position is improving"* Ibid.

*Bollée's weight* MK, 322.

250    *Au Petit Bonheur* AR, *Chronology,* 29.

*hotel in Le Mans* MK, 277.

*Wilbur's soup* Ibid.

*a scathing letter* PW, 900.

*the French had opened the crates* MK, 270.

*responded by blaming the damage* PW, 901 n.

*In his old age he would chuckle* MK, 274–75.

*troubles in getting work done* PW, 890.

251    *negotiations with the British* Walker, vol. 2, 68–75.

*an indignant Bishop Wright* MK, 306.

252 *stories of two short flights* PW, 882.
*he admonished Orville* PW, 882–83.
*$500 for an illustrated account* PW, 890.
*a letter from Le Mans* PW, 903–4.
*still at it a week later* PW, 906, n. 5.
*"glad to make such adjustment"* OW to Robert Johnson, July 6, 1908 (letter in the Archives and Library, Henry Ford Museum and Greenfield Village, Dearborn, Mich.).

253 *grumbled in a letter to Orville* MK, 275.
*"fixing at things"* PW, 902.
*Wilbur's scalds* PW, 905–6, n. 4.
*insisted on walking the mile* New York Times, July 5, 1908, pt. 2, 5.
*humorous letter home* MK, 281–82.

254 *"I would really save time"* MK, 283.
*move to Les Hunaudières* FK, 212 (photo); MK, 291.
*a dirt floor* PW, 901.
*the privy* PW, pl. 150.
*in any photograph ever taken of the camp* In the Wright State University archives, there is a photograph of the camp in which a privy is clearly visible, but it was taken in 1911 during Orville's last gliding experiments.
*René Pellier* MK, 293–94.
*restaurant, farmhouse, boy linguist* MK, 289.
*the midweek weather* New York Times, Aug. 7, 1908, 2.
*"As the day was the finest"* MK, 291.

## 29. "*NOUS SOMMES BATTUS*"

256 *Everyone lounging on the steps* Photos reproduced in Peyrey, 143, and *L'Aéro-phile*, Aug. 15, 325. Combs (p. 281) states that only twenty-six spectators were present on Aug. 8. The photograph in Peyrey, however, shows that about sixty people were present in one section of the grandstand alone, which suggests that there were between two and three hundred spectators.
*Ernest and Paul Zens* Peyrey, 314–15.
*René Gasnier* Ibid., 308.
*Blériot's monoplane* Ibid., 386.
*launching derrick and track* Ibid., 144.

257 *Archdeacon pointed out* FK, 237.
*Berg's chauffeur* Ibid.
*flight of Aug. 8* PW, 911 n.; Peyrey, 146–48; FK, 237–38; G-S, *Rebirth*, 279–80.
*Many Frenchmen seriously believed* Peyrey, 206.
*ten mistakes during the flight* FK, 259.

258 *paled with emotion* Peyrey, 148.
*flushed with pleasure* McM, 213.
*kissed Wilbur* PW, 920.
*Paul Zens's comments* G-S, *Rebirth*, 287.
*René Gasnier's comments* Ibid.
*Louis Blériot's comments* Ibid., 286.
*reaction of* Le Figaro Quoted in *New York Times*, Aug. 10, 1908, 2.

259     *François Peyrey* Peyrey was aeronautical editor of *L'Auto*. A revised edition
        of his book, expanded from 78 to 154 pages so as to include Wilbur's flights
        made later at Auvours and Orville's flights at Fort Myer, would be published
        in January 1909 (AR, *Bibliography*, 22, *Chronology*, 36). The revised edition,
        with additional material, would be incorporated in *Les Oiseaux Artificiel*,
        published later in 1909—the work cited as "Peyrey" through the present
        volume.
        *flights of Aug. 10* PW, 912.
        *between 300 and 500 feet* Ibid.; MK, 300.
        *confronted the Frenchman* New York Times, Aug. 11, 1908, 1.
        *Delagrange's comments* G-S, *Rebirth*, 288–89.
        *flight of Aug. 11* New York Times, Aug. 12, 1908, 3.
260     *flight of Aug. 12* Ibid., Aug. 13, 1908, 3; L'Aérophile, Aug. 15, 1908, 327.
        *flights of Aug. 13* PW, 912, 919–20; L'Aérophile, Sept. 1, 1908, 338.
        *Henry Kapferer's remarks* PW, 912.
        *Edouard Surcouf's comments* G-S, *Rebirth*, 287.
        *letter he wrote to Orville* PW, 912.
261     *Archdeacon insisted* G-S, *Rebirth*, 286.
        *Blériot amended his comments* Ibid., 289–90.

## 30. FORT MYER

262     *an air carnival in St. Louis* Roseberry, 88.
        *Selfridge designed the propeller* Ibid., 104.
        *Signal Corps Dirigible No. 1* Tillman, 27; *Fly*, Feb. 1909, 8–9. Future airship
        development was relegated to the U.S. Navy.
263     *fourteen Army men* Tillman, 33.
        *the balloon building* Chandler and Lahm, 81.
        *Orville had written Wilbur* PW, 839.
        *the Cosmos Club* In 1908, the club occupied the Dolley Madison House at the
        southeast corner of Madison Place and H Street NW.
        *the following response from Wilbur* MK, 286.
264     *admitted to his sister* MK, 301.
        *"the most remarkable rivalry"* American Aeronaut, May 1908, 154.
        *"more or less shrouded in mystery"* George H. Guy, "Real Navigation of the
        Air," American Review of Reviews, Sept. 1908, 316.
        *thinking of flying it to Washington* PW, 915.
        *approached the inventor in his shop* Charnley, 249.
        *Glenn Curtiss suspected* Roseberry, 121.
        *"a little thing"* PW, 899.
        *hurt a finger* Roseberry, 121.
        *extended his delivery date* Chandler and Lahm, 168.
        *announced to the press* New York Times, Sept. 12, 1908, 1.
        *tests of the Flyer's motor* PW, 916–17. The Wrights had been working on
        improvements to their motor ever since 1905. Wilbur remodeled the engine
        that had powered their 1905 Flyer, while Orville worked on designing an
        entirely new engine with the four cylinders in a vertical position. Orville's
        motor was so promising that Wilbur abandoned work on the motor that had
        served them so well since 1903. Tests made in the summer of 1906 showed that

the new motor developed eight more horsepower than the 1905 motor and weighed fifteen pounds less. (PW, 732.) With Taylor's help, they continued to tinker. By April 1907, the new motor was producing 30 horsepower and weighed only 160 pounds, fifty pounds less than the motor of 1903.

In the 1903–5 motors, the speed could not be varied once the Flyer was in the air. In the new Flyers, a pedal on the footrest crossbar was connected to the magneto by a wire, so that the motor could be slowed down or speeded up by advancing or retarding the spark. An exhaust-valve-opening device permitted the propellers to rotate in a glide. That is, the valves remained open when the pilot shut off the power by pulling a wire connected to a lever at the front of the crankcase. This permitted the propellers to continue rotating. If the pilot wanted to resume power flight, he had only to manipulate the lever that reactivated the valve springs, and the windmilling propellers automatically started the engine. The usual method of starting the engine on the ground was for someone to hold a piece of waste saturated with gasoline over the air inlet. Fumes would be sucked into the engine as the propellers were turned over by hand. (PW, 1216; Chandler and Lahm, 301.)

One of the new motors with vertical cylinders was sent to France with the new two-seater machine in 1907. In Nov. 1907, after Wilbur and Charlie Taylor left for home, Orville stayed behind in Paris for the purpose of having the motor that had been in storage in the customs shed at Le Havre duplicated by the firm of Bariquand and Marre. This gave rise to newspaper reports early in 1908 that the Wright motors were of French design and manufacture. ("Our Aeroplane Tests at Kitty Hawk," *Scientific American,* June 3, 1908.)

265     *portability test* PW, 917, pls. 154–57.

*a day of jinxes* PW, 917.

*a friend of Tom Selfridge*    *New York Times,* Sept. 18, 2.

*flight of Sept. 3* PW, 917–18; FK, 227–28; Tillman, 1, 3, 37; Washington *Evening Star,* Sept. 4, 3.

266     *what it called the "vessel"* FK, 288.

*Friday's flight* PW, 918.

*letters and telegrams had gone unanswered* PW, 798.

*"a lot of embarrassing reports"* MK, 305.

*Curtiss's letter to Bell* Roseberry, 125; Parkin, 71.

267     *had taken Albert Zahm's word* Casey, 11.

*wind-tunnel experiments had demonstrated* PW, 297–98.

*"not been able to make the motor . . . run"* PW, 918 n.

*"I like Foulois"* MK, 303.

*"the others . . . are very friendly"* By "others" Orville meant Lt. Lahm and other Signal Corps personnel, as well as Thomas Baldwin, who was to remain a good friend of the Wrights in spite of his close connections with Curtiss and other AEA members. Orville wrote a letter to Fred Kelly in 1940 in which he referred to something Baldwin told him at Fort Myer in 1908: "In speaking to me of the experiments in aviation being carried on by Curtiss and the younger members of the Aerial Experiment Association at Hammondsport, he said, 'They are a gang of pirates. I hear them talking. They intend to steal everything you have.' " (MK, 436.) If Baldwin actually spoke those words in 1908, he either was walking a high wire between the Wright and Curtiss camps

or was wildly unsure about whose side he was on. He seems intent on being a friend to all men, an enemy to none.

*Delagrange's flight* Peyrey, 291.

*Orville's flights of Sept. 7 and 8* PW, 920–21.

268    *flights of Sept. 9* PW, 921; *New York Times,* Sept. 10, 1908, 1; Augustus Post, "The Man-Bird and His Wings," *Cosmopolitan,* May 1910, 633; AR, *Chronology,* 165–66.

*flights of Sept. 10–12.* PW, 922; *New York Times,* Sept. 11–13, 1908.

269    *first two flights at Camp d'Auvours* AR, *Chronology,* 155.

*shed at Camp d'Auvours* Brewer, "Wilbur Wright," 129.

*early flights at Auvours* AR, *Chronology,* 155–56.

*Sunday letter to Orville* MK, 311.

270    *"If at any time Orville"* PW, 881.

*advice began to flow* MK, 293, 297, 300.

*"advise you most earnestly"* MK, 297.

*"next flight of the aeroplane"* Washington *Evening Star,* Sept. 16, 1908, 3.

271    *ordered to follow Foulois to Missouri* Roseberry, 125. ("After that," Alexander Graham Bell wrote Curtiss, "he will probably fly the Wrights' machine.")

*Delagrange's flights* Peyrey, 291.

*Walther Nernst* PW, 926–27.

*a cablegram had arrived* PW, 925; Peyrey, 195–96; FK, 245; Washington *Post,* Sept. 19, 1908, 2.

272    *Gleichen's account* Edward Gleichen, *A Guardsman's Memories* (Edinburgh: Blackwood, 1932), 303, quoted in Gollin, 300.

*Peyrey's account* Peyrey, 195–96.

## 31. A Tragedy and a Comic Interlude

273    *accident of Sept. 17, 1908* PW, 936–37; Tillman, 43–49; Washington *Post,* Sept. 18, 1908, 1; Washington *Evening Star,* Sept. 18, 1908, 1; *New York Times,* Sept. 18, 1908, 1. Forty years later, when Taylor was interviewed by *Collier's,* he added a footnote to the happenings of that eventful afternoon that is not unlike stories of frustrated steamship passengers who were unable to use their tickets for the *Titanic* because they either were stricken with illness at the last moment or arrived at the dock after the ship had sailed. Taylor claimed that Orville had offered to take him up for his first airplane ride that day. "I was in the passenger's seat and we were preparing to take off when a high-ranking officer asked Orville if he would mind taking an Army observer instead. Naturally I got out and Lieutenant Thomas E. Selfridge took my place." (Taylor, 68.) Orville had been in his grave for almost a year when that whopper appeared in print.

275    *Bishop Wright was in Greens Fork* Washington *Evening Star,* Sept. 19, 1908, 1.

*entry in his diary* PW, 925.

*Katharine in Washington* AR, *Chronology,* 32; Washington *Evening Star,* Sept. 19, 1908, 1.

276      *Orville's bad day* Ibid.

         *the two Charlies* MK, 333.

         *the cause of the accident* PW, 936–38, 953–54; Washington *Post,* Sept. 18, 1908, 1.

         *Wilbur had the final say* PW, 954.

277      *a letter he wrote to Katharine* PW, 925–26.

         *"In so far as the responsibility"* PW, 954.

         *testing and redesign of the propellers* Ibid.

         *an extension of time* PW, 928.

         *a firsthand report* PW, 929–30.

278      *became involved in an incident* Ibid.; Roseberry, 130–31; Washington *Evening Star,* Sept. 22, 1908, 9.

279      *"I shall keep my contract"* Ibid.

         *Herring once intimated* New York Times, Sept. 9, 1908, 2.

         *so-called technical delivery* Chandler and Lahm, 168; Inglis; Roseberry, 133–35.

280      *The first and only trial* Aeronautics, Nov. 1908, 7; Roseberry, 134.

         *A fourth and final extension* New York Times, May 29, 1909, 8.

         *Orville's convalescence* PW, 934, 936–39, 941.

         *put the injured leg in a cast* Miller, 9.

281      *previous scrapes with death* PW, 260, 452, 501, 512–13.

         *X rays made a dozen years later* FK, 231.

## 32. CAMP D'AUVOURS

282      *"This will cheer Orville"* McM, 210.

         *"Orville sera content"* Peyrey, 172.

         *the dog Flyer* PW, vol. 2, xxi.

         *soldiers were called on* New York Times, Aug. 21, 1908, 4.

         *bored a peephole* Ibid., Aug. 22, 1908, 5.

283      *couldn't even take a bath* MK, 294.

         *"feel like quitting the whole thing"* MK, 310–11.

         *"The distance overcome"* MK, 320.

         *Almost every evening* MK, 310.

         *Princes and millionaires, he wrote* MK, 323.

         *worked the same hours* McM, 212.

         *took up a collection* MK, 294.

         *French for "old oilcan"* Combs, 284.

         *the song "Il Vole"* MK, 295.

         *nicknamed his artist friend* Robert Hughes in *The New Yorker,* Jan. 26, 1981, 26.

         *a fleet of taxicabs* FK, 243.

         *"Vreecht caps"* MK, 310.

         *Wilbur's birdlike features* "There was something strange about the tall, gaunt figure. The face was remarkable, the head suggested that of a bird, and the features, dominated by a long prominent nose that heightened the birdlike effect, were long and bony." (London *Daily Mail,* Aug. 17, 1908, quoted in Gollin, 364.)

*a postcard caricature* MK, photo insert.

284     *"Dear me! How thin"* PW, 930.

*barraged with bouquets* MK, 294.

*very little of the wine* "All the wine I have tasted since leaving home would not fill a single wine glass," Wilbur wrote his father during his first trip to Europe—which indicates that he at least went through the motions of taking a sip now and then when dining with others (MK, 232).

*feted half a dozen times* AR, *Chronology,* 30–35.

*Peace Society medals* Ibid., 30; MK, 297.

*quoted and misquoted so often* FK, 245; PW, 933 n. 5. Some of the other versions:

> Well, if I talked a lot, I should be like the parrot, which is the bird that speaks most and flies least (Buist, 129).
>
> Among the feathered tribe the best talker and the worst flyer is the parrot (Flint, 245).
>
> The bird that talks most is the parrot, but it does not happen to be a bird of very high flight (Harper, 114).
>
> The only birds who talk are parrots, and they are not birds of high flight (Hodgins, 30).
>
> Parrots talk . . . don't fly (Loening, *Takeoff,* 51; the ellipses are Loening's; Wilbur was not quite that saving of words).

There are other discrepancies. Kelly (p. 244) gives the date of the dinner as Sept. 12. So does Peyrey (p. 199), but according to *L'Aérophile* (Oct. 1, 1908, 383), which contains no mention of the parrot remark, the dinner in honor of Wilbur's flight of Sept. 21 was given on Sept. 24. It is generally assumed that Wilbur's speech consisted of that single sentence. Peyrey gives the seven-sentence speech in a footnote, but does not say whether the parrot remark preceded or followed the rest of the speech. Buist claims that the remark was made by Wilbur to Mrs. Griffith Brewer. Flint in his memoirs, which are rich in error regarding other matters, writes that the remark was made by another person altogether at the dinner given for Wilbur in Paris on Nov. 5, 1908. About all this proves is that the remark was made by someone at a dinner given for Wilbur sometime between Sept. 12 and Nov. 5, 1908.

*120 flights* AR, *Chronology,* 155–64. In his preface, Renstrom states that since the Wright brothers kept no systematic records of their flights after the May 1908 trials at Kill Devil Hills, the primary sources of all subsequent flights recorded in the flight-log section of his *Chronology* are the 'brothers' scrapbooks and contemporary accounts in American and European newspapers and in aviation and technical journals. . . . Consequently, it is exceedingly difficult to record all flights for these periods, and no claim is made for completeness."

*created greater astonishment* PW, 931, n. 3.

*the hobble skirt* FK, 247.

*purchased 100,000 shares* PW, 912.

285     *Painlevé's flight* PW, 931; FK, 247–48.

*his first letter to Octave Chanute* PW, 935.
*blue-misted mornings and early twilights* Peyrey, 180.
*began to put on weight* Ibid., 180 n.
*made a trip to Paris* PW, 934–35; MK, 327–28; AR, *Chronology,* 34.
*Aeronautical Society's gold medals* Ibid.
*"about the size of a small can"* McM, 215.

286    *"The dangerous feature"* MK, 295.
*Farman's ailerons* G-S, *Rebirth,* 134.
*Farman's cross-country flight* Peyrey, 303.
*Blériot's movable wingtips* G-S, *Rebirth,* 128–29.
*Blériot's wingwarping system* Ibid., 315.
*"The Wright machine is astonishing"* Bonney, 96–103 (quoting from Frederick Lanchester, "The Wright and Voisin Types of Flying Machines," *Aeronautical Journal,* Jan. 1909).
*Clément Ader* Peyrey, 353 n.
*the* Avion *and its power plant* Ibid., 356, 361.
*the* Avion's *propellers* G-S, *Clément Ader: His Flight-Claims and His Place in History* (London: Her Majesty's Stationery Office, 1968), 35, 62, 109. The semi-flexible blades were supposed to take on a finer pitch during takeoff.

287    *the* Avion *at the Paris Exposition* Peyrey, 353; Zahm, 226.
*indignantly refuted that claim* G-S, *Aviation,* 61.
*knew that Ader was lying* MK, 459–60.
*Oct. 14, 1897, test of the* Avion This was its first and only test before the full commission. Two days before, on Oct. 12, 1897, in the presence of General Mensier, who headed the commission, the *Avion* made a trial run around the 1.5-kilometer track prepared for it, but the full commission was not convened until October 14. Ader also claimed that he had made a flight in his first machine in 1890. During Samuel Langley's annual jaunt to the Continent in the summer of 1892, the Smithsonian secretary wrote Octave Chanute that he had heard that Ader was "a clever, i.e. 'sharp' man, who tried to get money out of Rorier the banker by some scheme for aerial flights. He never flew at all, or anything like it." (OC correspondence, Aug. 2, 1892.)
*Le Matin published a letter* G-S, *Rebirth,* 290–91.
*the* Avion *in the Grand Palais* Zahm, 222; *Fly,* Apr. 1909, 9 (photo).
*twenty-five-meter altitude prize* There is confusion about who actually won this prize. Kelly (pp. 248–49) states that Wilbur won it on Nov. 18, 1908. Peyrey (p. 303) states that Henri Farman won the prize on Oct. 31.

288    *privately offered an extra $5,000* PW, 932.
*"If I felt sure of decent weather"* MK, 327.
*"I do not like the idea"* PW, 938.
*Wilbur thought of withdrawing* PW, 932.
*two flights of more than 40 minutes* Peyrey, 303.
*Wilbur's fears of being overtaken* PW, 948.
*flights of Dec. 18* Peyrey, 172–74.

289    *flight of Dec. 30* AR, *Chronology,* 163.
*flights of Dec. 31* PW, 947; Peyrey, 178.
*Barthou and the Legion of Honor* PW, 947; Peyrey, 178.
*four brief flights* AR, *Chronology,* 164.

*Orville and Katharine in Paris* Ibid., 35; McM, 217–18.
*Carrie had recently been married* Miller, 9.

290     *collided with a slow local train* Peyrey, 197; FK, 250.

## 33. THE HOMECOMING

291     *a preference for Biarritz* McM, 218.
*flying field at Pont-Long* Peyrey, 212–13; Buist.
*a French chef* FK, 251; McM, 218.
*flights at Pont-Long* AR, *Chronology*, 167–71.

292     *Wilbur's training system* G-S, *Rebirth*, 203. Wright pilots were designated either right-hand or left-hand pilots. Pilots trained by the Wright brothers themselves sat on the right and learned to manipulate the wingwarping-rudder lever, which was between the two seats, with their left hand. These were the left-hand pilots. When a left-hand pilot trained another pilot, the student sat in the seat at the left and learned to manipulate the lever with his right hand and was therefore known as a right-hand pilot. Orville once attempted to fly a Wright machine as a left-hand pilot, that is, sitting in the seat at the right and manipulating the wingwarping-rudder stick with his left hand. "That was the wildest flight of my life," he admitted. "I never again attempted to pilot using the left-hand controls." (PW, 1159.)
*solo flights* PW, 948 n.
*the canard* G-S, *Rebirth,* 301.
*family of vaudeville acrobats* McM, 251.
*visit of King Alfonso* FK, 252.
*preceded by a careful search* McM, 220.
*King Edward's visit* McM, 225.
*Wilbur's hawklike features* Reporters were not the only ones to describe Wilbur as birdlike. Frank Coffyn, Wright exhibition pilot, remembered Wilbur as "a tall raw-boned man with keen eyes dominating sharply chiseled features aptly suggesting the brooding alertness of the eagle." (Coffyn, "Flying as It Was")
*Wilbur's trousers* Buist.
*According to the same journalist* Ibid.

293     *named corespondent in a divorce suit* AR, *Chronology*, 36; *Fly,* Feb. 1909, 6.
*Peyrey's comments on the Wrights* Peyrey, 196 n.
*an offer of $10,000* PW, 947.
*offered by Weiller to the Musée* Peyrey, 218.
*was sent on to Rome* AR, *Chronology,* 38.
*a Sunday letter to Orville* PW, 949–50.

294     *Orville and Katharine in Rome* McM, 226.
*Wilbur lived in a cottage* Ibid.
*Lt. Calderara* PW, 951.
*Calderara's accident*     *New York Times,* May 8, 1909, 4.
*without benefit of falling weights* PW, 951 n. A photograph of the Italian Flyer in the Wright State University collection is labeled: "Towerless launch, track going downslope."

*a bronze statuette* McM, 230.

295 *gained a dozen pounds* PW, 950.

*discarded his cane* Ibid.

*Aero Club luncheon*      *Fly,* June 1909, 9.

*"suppress the 'spontaneous' uprising"* MK, 308.

*arrival in Dayton* Arthur Page, "How the Wrights Discovered Flight," *World's Work,* Aug. 1910, 13317; *New York Times,* May 14, 1909, 7.

*elms and poplars on Hawthorn Street* Young and Fitzgerald, 128.

*seldom left alone* PW, 953.

296 *extended their deadline* New York Times, June 11, 1909, 2.

*delivered in eight boxes* Ibid., June 17, 1909, 16.

*the official homecoming celebration* PW, 956; FK, 258–59; Miller, 10; Chandler and Lahm, 155; Conover, 297–98; *New York Times,* June 18–19, 1909; *Harper's Weekly,* July 3, 1909, 7; Charles J. Bauer, "Ed Sines, Pal of the Wrights," *Popular Aviation,* June 1938, 40, 78.

297 *"the excuse for an elaborate carnival"* PW, 953.

*the player piano* McM, 234.


## 34. CROSS-COUNTRY

299 *Albert Zahm in 1909* PW, 1093–95 n.

*temperature was in the nineties* Washington *Post,* June 21–28, 1909.

*misspelling of Foulois's name* Peterson, 35, 43, 45.

*a pest with his questions* Foulois, 62.

300 *the split-handle lever* G-S, *Wright Brothers,* 14–15. Gibbs-Smith writes that the split-handle control was not used until Orville flew in Germany, later in 1909, but Chandler and Lahm (pp. 299–301) state that it was used in the 1909 Army Flyer. (Lahm was at Fort Myer in 1909.)

*a piece of cotton twine* Foulois, 60–61; Chandler and Lahm, 301.

*events of June 28*      New York Times, June 29, 1909, 1; *Harper's Weekly,* July 10, 1909, 7.

*a page-one headline*      New York Times, June 29, 1909.

301 *flights of June 29–July 1* Ibid., July 1, 1909, 6; PW, 957–58.

*accident of July 2* PW, 953; *New York Times,* July 3, 1909, 1.

*Orville returned to Dayton* PW, 958 n.

302 *events of July 12–16* PW, 959; *New York Times,* July 17, 1909, 7.

*flights of July 17–24* Ibid., July 18, 1909, 1; PW, 959–60.

*the ex-President's daughter*      New York Times, July 10, 1909, 3.

*young Charlie Taft* Peterson, 13.

*two-and-a-half-minute flight* PW, 960; *New York Times,* July 27, 1909, 1.

*flight of July 27* Ibid., July 28, 1909, 1; Peterson, 35.

303 *did a gleeful little dance* Ibid.

*Farman's cross-country flights* Peyrey, 301; *New York Times,* July 4, 1909, 1, and July 24, 1909, 1.

*After going over the grounds* PW, 914.

*Foulois's height and weight* Brewer, "Wilbur Wright," 132; *New York Times Magazine,* Sept. 27, 1929, 9.

304 *events of July 28*      New York Times, July 29, 1909, 14.

*events of July 29* Ibid., July 30, 1909, 1.

*speed test of July 30* PW, 961 n. 1; Foulois, 63–65; Tillman, 61–69; Chandler and Lahm, 157–59; FK, 260; Frank P. Lahm, "The Wright Brothers as I Knew Them," *Air Force,* Mar. 15, 1939; R. and M. Comley, "I Saw It Fly," *Army,* Dec. 1928; *New York Times,* July 31, 1909, 1, 2.

306     *The telegram Bishop Wright received* PW, 961.

*true speed would be an average* When the Wright brothers submitted their bid in Jan. 1908 (PW, 856–57), they objected to item 5 of the Signal Corps specification: "The speed accomplished during the trial flight will be determined by taking an average of the time[s] over a measured course of more than five miles, against and with the wind." To show that this would not give the true speed of a flying machine, the Wrights cited the example of a machine capable of making 40 mph in still air that makes a 20-mile flight against a wind of 10 mph and a 20-mile return trip with the same wind at its back. It would take the machine 40 minutes to fly the 20 miles against the wind (at a ground speed of 30 mph) and 24 minutes to make the return trip (ground speed 50 mph). If the average of the two *times* were used to calculate the speed (40 + 24 = 64 ÷ 2 = 32 minutes), the speed (40 miles in 32 minutes) would be given as 37.5 mph. The *true* speed, the Wrights argued, could be determined only by averaging the two *speeds* (speed against the wind and speed with the wind), or in this case 30 mph against the wind and 50 mph with the wind (30 + 50 = 80 ÷ 2 = 40 mph). The Signal Corps conceded that its specification was in error and determined the official speed of the Army Flyer by averaging its speed to Alexandria and its speed on the return flight, each speed being itself an average of the stopwatch figures recorded by all the judges. The true speed was therefore 37.735 mph (to Alexandria) + 47.431 mph (return trip) = 85.166; 85.166 ÷ 2 = 42.583 mph. (Data from AR, *Chronology,* 42.)

*$30,000 for the Flyer* A $20,000 check was given to Wilbur by Lt. Foulois on Oct. 19, 1909. The balance was paid Nov. 4, two days after Wilbur completed training the Army pilots at College Park, Maryland. (AR, *Chronology,* 45; Chandler and Lahm, 167.)

### 35. HERRING AND CURTISS

307     *Blériot's cross-country flight* Zahm, 287. This was a 26-mile flight from Etampes to within eight miles of Orléans, with one stop en route, made ten days before Farman flew his 40-mile cross-country to Reims.

*the Channel flight* Lieberg, 70–74; Zahm, 287–91.

308     *AEA meeting in Bell's home* Roseberry, 131.

the *Silver Dart* Parkin, 70; Casey, 35.

*he wired Curtiss to come* Roseberry, 147.

*American Aerodrome Company* Ibid., 150–52; Parkin, 160–61.

*wooed by telegram from New York* Roseberry, 152.

309     *a member of the Aero Club delegation* Ibid., 94–95.

*turned up again at Hammondsport* Scharff and Taylor, 74–75.

*Eighteen years of litigation* Bruce, 271.

*a somewhat similar business proposition* Herring's letter to the Wrights, Dec. 26, 1903 (see Chapter 18).

310    *experiments with* Cygnet II *and the* Silver Dart    Roseberry, 153–55.

*Something of a snake-oil salesman* Peterson, 76–77, reproduction of pp. 374–75 of *Current Literature,* 1909, which refers in turn to a recent article by Baldwin in *The World's Work.* Baldwin wrote that a friend of his had been completely cured of consumption by flying a balloon from St. Louis to the Atlantic coast. Another friend, whose lungs had been badly injured by the inhalation of iron and copper dust, required more than one balloon trip. Baldwin claimed that he himself had overcome a severe attack of rheumatics during an airship flight, every drop of blood in his body turning from black to bright red within a few hours.

*no difficulty in persuading Baldwin* Roseberry, 153.

*Cortlandt Field Bishop* Berle, 2, 3, 6; *Fly,* Apr. 1909, 7.

*Herring now hinted to Bishop* Roseberry, 156–57.

*had been championing Herring* PW, 842 n. 8.

311    *greeted him in the railroad station* Roseberry, 157.

*press conference at the Aero Club* Ibid.; *New York Times,* Mar. 4, 1909, 9.

*the Herring-Curtiss Company was incorporated* Roseberry, 159–60.

*an adulatory article*    *Fly,* Apr. 1909, 5.

312    *the only other investors*    Roseberry, 157, 238.

*David Bishop* Berle, 11, 12.

*he wired Curtiss* Roseberry, 158–59.

*Marian Bell Fairchild at Hammondsport* Scharff and Taylor, 82.

*in fast company* Ibid.

*evening of Mar. 31, 1909* Roseberry, 161–62.

*failure of* Cygnet II *and the* Silver Dart    Parkin, 84–86, table IV.

313    *Cygnet III* Ibid., 331–32; Bruce, 454. *Aeronautics* (Apr. 1912, 140) printed a picture of *Cygnet III,* under which the magazine stated, "McCurdy made a number of straightway flights with it over the ice of Lake Bras d'Or in Nova Scotia on March 1st to 17th." Neither Bruce nor Parkin mentions any such flights.

*Bell's hydrodromes* Bruce, 474–75.

*"an old man's toy"* Dorothy H. Eber, *Genius at Work* (New York: Viking, 1982), 135–36.

## 36. THE RACES AT REIMS

314    *had never approved of the tapered wings* Parkin, 247; Roseberry, 167.

*"This taper stuff"* Studer, 161.

*Aeronautic Society of New York* The name would be changed to Aeronautical Society in 1910 (Casey, 55).

*the agreement was kept secret* Ibid., 41.

*the* Golden Flier    Ibid., 43; Roseberry, 167–68.

*the* Gold Bug    Roseberry, 488–89.

*wingspans* Casey, 29, 39.

315    *Curtiss had suspected* Roseberry, 158–59.

*a triangular fixed fin* Casey, 44.

*also reduced maneuverability* Hatch, 146.

*the first circling flight* Roseberry, 139, 172.
*rules for the competition* PW, 905 n. 2.
*Curtiss at Hempstead Plains* Roseberry, 173; *New York Times,* July 18, 1909, 1.
*Herring and the Reims races* Ibid., Apr. 16, 1909, 18.

316     *his foreign patents would be forfeit* Ibid., May 29, 1909, 8.
*General Allen's letter to Herring* Ibid., July 1, 1909, 6.
*managed to make himself unpopular* Roseberry, 179.
*manufacture of toy airplanes* Ibid., 238.
*site of the air races* Ibid., 188; Hatch, 163; Lieberg, 34.

317     *opening day* Peterson, 70.
*Cockburn's race with the train* Lieberg, 97.
*prizes won by de Lambert and others* Ibid., 217–18.
*Lefebvre at Reims* Ibid., 30.
*One Parisian paper speculated* Peterson, 74.
*Wilbur on the French Wrights* Peterson, 62 (Los Angeles *Times,* Aug. 28, 1909).
*a falling out with the Voisin brothers* Lieberg, 122.
*winning of the Grand Prix* Peterson, 59 (Los Angeles *Examiner,* Aug. 27, 1909).
*race for the Gordon Bennett trophy* Lieberg, 127–32; Scharff and Taylor, 106–7.

318     *more than doubled its investment* Peterson, 70.
*crashed into haystacks* Lieberg, 80.
*skimmed the ground so closely* Ibid., 49.
*Blériot's close calls* Ibid., 99, 147; Peterson, 58.
*Lefebvre was killed* Peterson, 100.
*had competed at Reims* Lieberg, 27.
*Ferber was crushed* G-S, *Rebirth,* 257.

## 37. The Last Public Flights

319     *Count Zeppelin's fourth dirigible* Toland, 43–47.
*Lokal-Anzeiger contract* AR, *Chronology,* 37.
*German Wright company* Ibid., 40.
*the Hotel Esplanade's finest suite* MK, 343; McM, 238.

320     *the zeppelin in Berlin* Zahm, 163–64; Peterson, 74–75.
*Orville's flights at Tempelhof* AR, *Chronology,* 179–80.
*zeppelin flight to Mannheim* FK, 262–63.
*touring Europe by automobile*     *New York Times,* Sept. 1, 1909, 4.

321     *longest flight Orville was ever to make* The flight was notable for another reason. The air above the Tempelhof parade ground was full of whirlwinds and rolling gusts. One of these sudden gusts lifted Orville eight to ten inches from his seat. He avoided sailing out of the Flyer altogether only by pushing his back tightly against the back of the seat and riding in this position for several seconds. In describing the incident to Wilbur, Orville announced that he would anchor himself more firmly to the Flyer in the future. "I am going to tie myself to the seat with string" are the words he used (MK, 346). It is

hoped he had something stronger than string in mind. Strange as it seems, seat belts were not considered necessary in 1909. Harris (p. 216) gives a possible reason for this: Most pilots thought it was better to be thrown clear of an aircraft in a crash rather than to be trapped inside the wreckage by a belt. Apparently the first seat belt on record was one devised by Lt. Benjamin Foulois in 1910 when he lashed himself to the Wright Army Flyer with a homemade safety belt made from a four-foot trunk strap (Tillman, 90).

*Orville's flights at Potsdam* AR, *Chronology,* 182–83.

*presented Orville with the stickpin* FK, 264.

*reached 155 meters at Reims* Lieberg, 49.

*observed from a steamer* Peterson, 109.

322     *offered Wilbur $15,000* Wilbur was paid $2,500 in advance. Another $10,000 was received in October. "It is doubtful whether I ever get any more," he wrote his father on Oct. 31, "as the treasury is about empty" (MK, 352–53). Eventually he agreed to accept $1,000 in lieu of the $2,500 balance, but the Aeronautical Committee was able to scrape up an additional $500, so that he received, all told, $14,000 (*U.S. Air Services,* Dec. 1934, 33).

*Curtiss's contract* Roseberry, 208.

*Loening at Governors Island* Loening, *Our Wings,* 9–12.

*breach between Wilbur and Curtiss* Ibid., 11.

*meetings with Curtiss and Marconi*     *New York Times,* Sept. 23, 1909, 3.

323     *Curtiss's reception in Hammondsport* Roseberry, 212–14.

*accepted $5,000 from Wanamaker's* Ibid., 200, 211.

*the flight Curtiss made Wednesday* Ibid., 217.

*Wilbur's flights of Sept. 29* AR, *Chronology,* 181; Peterson, 105, 106.

324     *airship flights* Peterson, 105, 106; Roseberry, 216–17.

*an attempt to redeem himself* Ibid., 218; *New York Times,* Oct. 4, 1909, 1.

*Herring, acting as his agent* Studer, 195.

*Wilbur's Hudson River flight*     *New York Times,* Oct. 5, 1909, 1, 2; Peterson, 109, 110; "Wilbur Wright Pays Grant's Tomb a Flying Visit," Earl Findley's Oct. 5, 1909, report in the New York *Tribune,* reprinted in *U.S. Air Services,* Oct. 1931, 11.

325     *accident to the motor*     *New York Times,* Oct. 5, 1909, 2.

*his last public flight* Peterson, 110.

326     *the field at College Park* Chandler and Lahm, 162–63.

*Foulois was assigned* Tillman, 71.

*training flights* AR, *Chronology,* 184–86.

*Lahm grazed a wing* Tillman, 77–78.

*ordered Humphreys back* Ibid., 80.

*"taken a woman into the air"* Arnold, 25.

*completed his training by correspondence* Ibid., 79.

*Only $150 was allotted*     *New York Times Magazine,* Sept. 27, 1925, 9.

*the 1909 Army Flyer restored* Tillman, 123–24; Chandler and Lahm, 187.


### 38. THE PATENT WARS BEGIN


327     *their basic patent* Filed Mar. 23, 1903, the patent went through numerous changes before being granted May 22, 1906. Two additional "flying-machine"

patents, filed Feb. 17, 1908, were granted Oct. 14, 1913, and Dec. 29, 1914 (PW, 1228). Wilbur described these patents to Octave Chanute: "They cover broadly the idea of using horizontal surfaces adjustable about a transverse axis so as to face forward at different angles on right & left sides, in combination with means of correcting the resulting disturbance of balance about the vertical axis by the use of rudders, vanes, or resistances in front, behind, or on the wing tips. They also cover detail features, such as imparting helicoidal warp to the aeroplanes; and in addition the particular means of doing it in [a] double-deck machine" (PW, 858). Applications for two other aeronautical patents were filed in 1908, one for an automatic stabilizer, which would not be perfected and patented until 1913, and a mechanism for flexing the horizontal front rudder, granted Jan. 5, 1909, and described by Wilbur as a "flexible rudder capable of being curved simultaneously with its adjustment to different angles above or below the horizontal."

*movement to purchase U.S. patent rights* McM, 184–85.

*"If the subscription"* MK, 319.

*Bishop's meeting with the Wrights* Roseberry, 170–71.

328     *"They told me certain things"* Ibid.

*a bill of complaint was filed* AR, *Chronology,* 43. The next day a suit was filed against the Aeronautic Society of New York to prevent further exhibition of the society's Curtiss-built *Golden Flier.* Wilbur explained the situation in a letter to Orville, Aug. 21, 1909. "As Hammondsport is in a different district from New York it was necessary to bring two suits, one against the Aeronautic Society and one against Curtiss and Herring-Curtiss Co." (PW, 962 n. 4). There is no further reference to this suit in the literature. It may have been either dropped or incorporated into the suit against Curtiss.

*Wheeler issued a statement* Scharff and Taylor, 116–17.

*their basic patent was duplicated* PW, 1229–32.

329     *Bishop confidently told reporters* Peterson, 151.

*Each had assumed that the other* Roseberry, 190.

*they met Wilbur in New York* AR, *Chronology,* 46.

*$40,000 from Germany* MK, 344.

*British and Italian contracts* PW, 951.

*Clinton Peterkin* FK, 269–70.

330     *formation of the Wright Company* FK, 271–72; MK, 352.

*only a subsidiary issue* Hayward, 507.

*Thomas Hill* "Status of the Wrights' Suits," *Aeronautics,* Oct. 1909, 122. Hill was retained as defense counsel in the Wrights' suit against the Aeronautic Society of New York (Roseberry, 218; see note to *a bill of complaint was filed,* above).

331     *"airplane chauffeurs"* PW, 972.

*Hazel's federal judgeship* Roseberry, 336.

*Hazel and the Selden patent* Ibid., 343–45.

332     *opinion handed down Jan. 3, 1910* Hayward, 507–8. Judge Hazel also handed down opinions on two minor issues. The defendants contended that the Wright patent claims applied only to aircraft with "substantially flat surfaces," as wings were defined in the patent. A slight arching of the wings, Judge Hazel wrote, did not constitute a material departure from the patent, which, he insisted, "does not belong to the class of patents which requires narrowing the details of construction." He also agreed with the Wrights that

the defendants had had access to information obtained from the brothers before constructing aircraft of their own. They had obtained detailed information on wind pressures on wings through the Wrights' Jan. 1908 letter to AEA secretary Selfridge and on the Wrights' method of lateral control through Herring's presence in the camp at Kill Devil Hills in 1902. But as Roseberry (p. 335) points out: "The judge's knowledge of the work of the A.E.A. was manifestly skimpy; and he was far off base in presuming that Herring had anything whatever to do with the design of the Curtiss plane."

*Hazel's injunction was vacated* Roseberry, 336.

*Ford's challenge of the Selden patent* Ibid., 345.

*praising the author's chapter* Hayward, xv.

*Hayward on the Wright and Bell patents* Ibid., 506–7.

333      *"Are the Wrights Justified?"*       *Aeronautics,* Apr. 1910, 141.


### 39. END OF A FRIENDSHIP


335      *the joint product* PW, 1146.

      *his brief acceptance speech* PW, 998.

336      *the presentation ceremony account* Smithsonian Institution, *Annual Report* 1910, 22–23. The complete text of all three speeches was printed on pp. 104–10 of the "Proceedings" section of the report.

      *a letter to Octave Chanute* PW, 737.

      *had quoted Wilbur's words* PW, 739 n.

      *Rathbun had recommended* PW, 5 n. 7.

337      *both misleading and inaccurate* See Chapter 9, "Trade Secrets." It was Wilbur, incidentally, who later that year saved the Smithsonian from making an embarrassing error. A tablet was to be placed in the entrance hall of the Smithsonian building commemorating Langley's work in aeronautics, and Secretary Charles Walcott had written the Wrights, asking their opinion of the inscription to be placed on the tablet. The inscription contained a reference to Langley's Law, considered to be the former secretary's chief contribution to aeronautics. Wilbur in his reply cited the computations in *Experiments in Aerodynamics* that had led Langley to enunciate the law, then added: "A careful reading shows that he never actually tried the experiments of which he professed to give the result" (PW, 1009). When the tablet was finally unveiled in May 1913, a year after Wilbur's death, the reference to Langley's Law had been omitted, but the inscription now gave Langley credit for discovering "the relations of speed and angle of inclination to the lifting power of surfaces moving in the air." Orville commented on this part of the inscription in a letter to the editor of *Collier's Weekly*: "He tried to do this, as did Duchemin, Lilienthal and others before, but failed" (MK, 416–17).

      *a press release* PW, 409–11.

      *Chanute had taken exception* PW, 414.

      *Wilbur's diplomatic response* PW, 415.

      *had a hand in constructing* PW, 424 n. 4.

      *Renard to Chanute* OC correspondence, Oct. [Nov. ?] 8, 1908. "As a matter of fact," Renard wrote, "the Wright brothers have been your pupils and through their contact with you they obtained the first idea of aviation and took their first lessons to take up the 'trade as birdmen' which they practice perfectly today."

*Chanute replied modestly* PW, 940–41.

338 *Chanute's reply was even shorter* PW, 951–52.

339 *he wrote the editor* PW, 962.

*spent two evenings with Chanute* Roseberry, 222.

*In an interview* Scharff and Taylor, 129–30.

*he dashed off a letter* PW, 972.

340 *New York* World *headline* Freudenthal, 224.

*Chanute was quoted* PW, 980 n. 8.

*a short, sharp letter to Chanute* PW, 979–80.

*Chanute's reply* PW, 980–82.

341 *three examples of "warping"* Two of the examples were from *Progress in Flying Machines* (pp. 96–97, 106). In 1864, the French Count d'Esterno patented a birdlike glider, the rear of whose wings could be raised or lowered. The wings themselves were meant to be flapped and could be twisted, but what the twisting was for was not stated. It was certainly not for lateral control, since equilibrium was to be maintained by shifting the weight. The second example was a glider whose wings were modeled on those of the albatross, built by a French mariner, Jean Marie Le Bris, in 1867. The glider had *rotules,* which Chanute translated as "knee pans." They "imparted a rotary motion to the front edge of the wings, and also permitted of their adjustment to various angles of incidence with the wing." The third example was the Mouillard patent, which Chanute had applied for in his own name as well as Mouillard's (PW, 19 n. 4). The patent, granted in the United States a few months before Mouillard died in 1897, but never applied for in Europe, was for a glider, the rear corners of whose wings were double so that one or the other could be turned down to steer to right or left. When pulled downward together, the movable sections were supposed to act as a brake. The patent was examined by Judge Learned Hand in *Wright* v. *Paulhan.* In his opinion of Feb. 24, 1910, Judge Hand stated: "In no one of the 19 claims is there anything which in any way foreshadows the patent in [the Wright] suit" (PW, 963 n.).

*Wilbur's long letter* PW, 982–86.

343 *The enclosure was a clipping* PW, 986 n.

*brought suit against the brothers* PW, 993; AR, *Chronology,* 110.

*wrote his friend George Spratt* PW, 987 n.

*broke the silence of three months* PW, 991–92.

344 *"I am in bad health"* PW, 993–95.

*wrote a letter to Chanute's son* PW, 1008. Wilbur was also thinking of the importance of those letters to contemporary aeronautical practice. In his letter to Charles Chanute, Wilbur wrote: "I am writing to request that you do not permit any person *interested in flying as a business* to have access to these letters and talks at this time." The italics were Wilbur's. He feared that the correspondence might be of use to defendants in the infringement suits then in the courts, a fear that turned out to be well founded when it was discovered, many years later, that the brothers' erstwhile friend Albert Zahm had gone through the first two years of the correspondence at a time when he was employed as a witness for the defendants in *Wright* v. *Curtiss* (PW, 1008 n.).

345      *the many misconceptions* The most persistent misconception is that Chanute
provided the Wrights with much useful advice and data during 1900, the first
year of their correspondence. The truth is as follows:

*May 13, 1900.* Wilbur asks two questions in his first letter: Where can he
find a suitable locality for gliding? How can he obtain an account of Percy
Pilcher's experiments?

*May 15.* Chanute recommends as gliding sites one in California and one
in Florida, both deficient in sand hills, but suggests the coasts of Georgia and
South Carolina as alternatives. (The Wrights instead chose the North Carolina coast on the basis of information supplied by the U.S. Weather Bureau.)
Chanute did supply a source for information on Pilcher's experiments and
additional sources for information on other experimenters.

*June 1.* Wilbur writes he would "be pleased to have the benefits of your
advice when my plans are more fully matured."

*Aug. 10.* Wilbur's plans are now mature. He makes two inquiries of Chanute: What Chicago firm can supply spruce for spars? What is a suitable
varnish for wingcoverings?

*Aug. 14.* Chanute provides the address of a Chicago lumber dealer but
recommends Cincinnati as a source of spruce closer to Dayton. (The
Wrights use white pine instead of spruce for spars.) Chanute sends a recipe
for wing varnish. (The Wrights decide not to varnish the wings of their
gliders.)

*Nov. 16–Dec. 3.* After returning from Kitty Hawk, Wilbur writes Chanute
four letters containing information on the 1900 gliding experiments. Chanute
responds with three letters, in the second of which he calculates the diminish-
ment of head resistance for a glider operator in a prone, rather than upright,
position. In replying, Wilbur points out an error in Chanute's calculations and
shows how his own computations result in less than half the air resistance of
Chanute's. In these last letters of 1900, Wilbur does not ask for advice, nor
does Chanute proffer advice of any sort.

The Wrights never made a secret of the fact that they had adopted the
biplane configuration and the Pratt system of trussing used by Chanute in his
double-decker glider of 1896. But Chanute did not claim to have originated
the biplane, and the Wrights' trussing system was a decided improvement over
Chanute's. The biplane had been used earlier by British experimenters George
Cayley and John Stringfellow, and Chanute's successful double-decker was a
biplane only by default. It originally had three wings, but the bottom wing was
removed after it was found to drag along the ground—"as a matter of pru-
dence," as Chanute explained in a letter to James Means on Nov. 14, 1896, and
he added: "When I make sure there are no hidden defects I will restore the
third surface." He never did.

While Chanute was the first to apply the Pratt system of trussing to glider
wings, he cautioned in his writings that wire stays should be employed as
sparingly as possible. "Not only do they vibrate when the machine is underway and so increase the resistance, but they get loose and allow the apparatus
to become distorted" (Means, 52). The Wrights overcame the latter difficulty
quite simply by crossing the wires in the manner shown in the diagram in
Wilbur's letter to Chanute of Nov. 16, 1900 (PW, 41), so that by using turnbuckles and "by tightening a single wire every other wire is tightened." In the

margin of Wilbur's letter, opposite the sketch, Chanute made the notation "Remarkably good construction" (PW, 41 n.).

### 40. EXIT HERRING

346    *the infringement suits* FK, 287; AR, *Bibliography,* 105–13.
       *"bring suit against importers"* MK, 347.
       *Paulhan was served* Peterson, 144; Roseberry, 230–31.
       *a strong response abroad* *Aeronautics,* Apr. 1910, 141.

347    *Los Angeles air meet* Peterson, 173; Roseberry, 231–33; Harris, 166–67.
       *a preliminary injunction* AR, *Bibliography,* 110; *Chronology,* 48.
       *made a round $100,000* Freudenthal, 235.
       *suit against Grahame-White* AR, *Chronology,* 57, 58.
       *Curtiss at the Los Angeles meet* Roseberry, 231–33.
       *Herring and the Herring-Curtiss Company* Ibid., 238–39, 243; Scharff and Taylor, 118–19; Studer, 88.

348    *patent applied for jointly* OC correspondence, OC to Herring, Mar. 24 and May 19, 1901; Herring to OC, Jan. 5, 1902.
       *bankruptcy; Curtiss's new company* Roseberry, 254, 257–59.

349    *who had sided with Herring* Scharff and Taylor, 120.
       *Herring and Burgess* Ibid., 120–21; Bonney, 145; Roseberry, 179–80; Bart Gould, "Burgess, Herring-Burgess," *WWI Aero, The Journal of the Early Aeroplane,* Sept. 1986, 18–29. Burgess later went into the aviation business with a new partner, Greely H. Curtis (with one *s*). In Jan. 1911, Burgess learned to fly at the Wright flying school in Atlanta and changed the name of his company to Burgess-Wright—the first company in the United States outside of Dayton licensed to manufacture Wright aircraft. (PW, 1208; AR, *Chronology,* 54.) The license expired Dec. 31, 1912. All Burgess-Curtis machines manufactured after that date were considered infringements of the Wright patent. (PW, 1075–76.)
       *Herring filed suit against Curtiss* Roseberry, 433–34.

350    *a lengthy biographical sketch* *The Libertarian,* Oct. 1924, 589–608.
       *a minor-league Herring* Loening, *Our Wings,* 22–23, 159–60. Loening identifies Martin as one of a number of promoters, cranks, and self-styled inventors hired in 1911 by the wealthy playboy owner of the Queen Aeroplane Company of New York. In 1925 Martin testified before the House Committee of Inquiry into the Air Services, which also heard testimony from General Billy Mitchell and Grover Loening. Martin complained to the committee that he was being discriminated against by a pernicious aircraft trust. Martin's story is told in some detail in Boyne (pp. 100–5), who writes: "Martin was a competent, daring pilot with some very advanced ideas; he was also something of a charlatan, who lived as much by the press as by his inventions."
       *had worked for Herring in 1909* Freudenthal, 194. Freudenthal swallowed the *Libertarian* article whole. She gives Herring credit for "undoubted brilliance" and a "keen, inventive mind" and refers to Martin's "serious, well-documented claims on Herring's behalf."
       *Herring's obituary* *New York Times,* July 19, 1926, 12.
       *the suit was carried on* Roseberry, 435.

351     *Curtiss's death* Ibid., 453–55.
        *settlement with Herring's heirs* Ibid., 479. A letter to the author from Eugene
        Husting, received while this volume was in press, states that Herring's daugh-
        ter once assured Husting that the amount of the settlement was indeed half
        a million dollars but that only $30,000 filtered down to the heirs. This would
        seem to indicate that the remaining $470,000 went for court costs and legal
        fees, in the manner of *Jarndyce and Jarndyce* in Dickens' *Bleak House*.


                    41. THE EXHIBITION BUSINESS


352     *had licensed Short Brothers* PW, 951.
        *French and German business* PW, 1001–2.
        *wrote Wilbur from Berlin* PW, 1004.
        *American Wright Company* FK, 272; MK, 375.
353     *agreement with the Aero Club*     *Aeronautics,* Apr. 1910, 141; AR, *Chronol-
        ogy,* 50.
        *The usual fee* PW, 1024. According to Frank Coffyn, the Wright pilots were
        among the most poorly paid in the business. They received $20 per week, plus
        $50 for every day they flew. The maximum weekly pay was thus $320 for a
        six-day week, since they were not allowed to fly on Sunday. Members of the
        Wright team were offered two-year contracts at the Indianapolis meet in June
        1910, the first in which they participated. Brookins was spokesman for the fliers
        who were dissatisfied with the terms, but it was a case of signing or not flying.
        When Brookins won the $5,000 altitude prize at Atlantic City in July, for
        instance, he was paid only $50 for the day's flying, in addition to his weekly
        salary of $20. The prize money went to the company. Many years later, Coffyn
        wrote that he himself had been happy to fly as a member of the Wright team,
        regardless of the pay. (Coffyn, "Flying with the Wrights"; Harris, 220.)
        *Roy Knabenshue* FK, 273.
        *leaving Wilbur free* McM, 243.
        *a temporary flying school* AR, *Chronology,* 187–90.
        *Walter Brookins* Harris, 155; Peterson, 192.
        *Spencer Crane* Harris, 159.
        *J. W. Davis* Coffyn, "Flying as It Was."
        *Arch Hoxsey* Peterson, 216; Dwiggins, 18.
354     *fliers trained at Simms Station and flights made there* AR, *Chronology,* 191–98.
        *Duval La Chapelle* Coffyn, "Flying as It Was."
        *a trick bicyclist* Coffyn, "Flying with the Wrights."
        *close to 250 flights* One day, while he was flying alone at Simms, Orville
        encountered a puzzling phenomenon. After climbing to almost half a mile, he
        spiraled down until he was about 1,500 feet above the ground and discovered
        that even though the machine was pointed steeply downward and his motor
        was at full throttle, he was no longer descending. He circled for a full five
        minutes without making any appreciable descent, a sensation he described as
        like running in a dream without making any headway. He later deduced that
        he had flown into a whirlpool of air that was rising as fast as his machine could
        descend, and whose diameter was greater than his spiral of descent. Had he
        stopped circling and flown a straight course he would have reached nonrising

air in a few seconds. At the time, however, he was so astonished he could think of no reason for the phenomenon and continued his dreamlike circling until the rising whirlpool of air passed and he could complete his descent. (PW, 1126–27.)

*It was the last flight* Wilbur made at least one more flight as pilot, in Germany. On June 28, 1911, he wrote Orville from Berlin: "The poor Captain [probably Paul Engelhard, whom Orville had taught to fly] . . . would not believe that I could carry two men with 375 turns of the propellers till I took him up and did it" (MK, 383). Wilbur may also have done some flying in England during his stay with Alexander Ogilvie on the Isle of Sheppey in June, before he left for Berlin.

*"Higher, Orville"* PW, 996 n. 5.

*Aviation Day* FK, 280.

*"Orville comes on his flyer"* PW, 999.

*Indianapolis air show* Peterson, 192, 193, 195.

355     *Montreal two weeks later* Ibid., 195.

*exhibition at Atlantic City* Ibid., 200, 201.

*first Flyers with wheels* PW, 998; AR, *Chronology,* 197.

*Brookins's accident* Peterson, 212, 213; "When the Wrights Joined the Flying Shows," *U.S. Air Service,* Dec. 1923, 22.

*were slightly injured* Including a boy whose arm was broken. All recovered, but the Wright Company was sued for $25,000 on behalf of the boy. This was the first case of its kind to come to trial in the United States. Two years later, it was thrown out of court when it was shown that the accident was not due to negligence on the part of the pilot. (*Aeronautics,* July 1912, 37.)

*Asbury Park meet* Peterson, 216; Harris, 186.

*Star Dust Twins* Ibid., 215.

*the Wright Model B* PW, 1197; AR, *Chronology,* 52.

356     *meet at Squantum Meadows* Peterson, 222.

*Hoxsey's accident* Ibid., 22. Five women and three men were said to have been seriously injured. Newspapers tended to exaggerate reports of such accidents, but the Wright Company was sued eight months later for $5,000 for injuries alleged to have occurred when Hoxsey "swooped down on" Miss Sadie I. Fuller of Oshkosh, Wisconsin. (AR, *Chronology,* 55.) The outcome of the suit is not reported.

*Johnstone's accident* Peterson, 228.

*"I am very much in earnest"* PW, 998.

357     *deaths from flying-machine accidents* Peterson, 202, 215; Villard, 242, 243; *New York Times,* Jan. 3, 1912, 6; Zahm, 318–19.

*Curtiss's candidate* Roseberry, 292.

*Grahame-White's powerful Blériot* Liebling, 153.

*Wright Roadster* PW, 1199.

*the Baby Grand* Ibid.

358     *the only eight-cylinder motor* PW, 1216–17.

*left arm wrapped about an upright* PW, 1119, pl. 210.

*arrived at Belmont Park* AR, *Chronology,* 52.

*set a new U.S. altitude record* Peterson, 235.

*Tuesday's flights* Ibid., 236; PW, 999 n.; Harris, 202, 204.

*Wednesday's and Thursday's flights* Peterson, 238–39.

*Brookins made a trial flight* Ibid., 239.

*Bennett trophy race* Ibid.

359     *Sunday's and Monday's flights* Ibid., 240, 241.

*$20,000 paid to the Wright Company* A few weeks later the Wright Company sued the managers of the meet for an additional $15,000, which it claimed was due the Wright team for participating. The chairman of the arrangements committee called the demand outrageous. Wilbur didn't think so. "The Belmont swindlers are still trying to unload the results of their own incompetence on us," he wrote Orville, who was then in Europe. "I intend to have the money collected." In Jan. 1912, the suit was dismissed on the grounds of insufficient cause for action. (PW, 1007; AR, *Chronology,* 53; Roseberry, 294.)

*Baltimore air show* Peterson, 242–44.

*Denver air show* Ibid., 245–47; Harris, 215–16; Dwiggins, 21–22.

*an almost perpendicular dive* It was impossible to determine the exact cause of the disaster, but after comparing the various versions of what happened, Wilbur thought that the trouble began with Johnstone falling off the seat after turning the machine up on its side at the beginning of the spiral glide and that he involuntarily pushed the elevator lever to its limit in trying to force himself back onto the seat (PW, 1007).

360     *Moisant's air circus and death* Villard, 114; *New York Times,* Jan. 1, 1911, pt. 2, 1, 2.

*Los Angeles air meet* Ibid.; Harris, 216–18.

*fended off souvenir hunters* Dwiggins, 31; Harris, 217 (photo).

*castor oil* Villard, 126.

*reached an even hundred*     *Aeronautics,* Nov. 1911, 154.

*withdrew from the exhibition business* Johnson, 27.

*the only one to die in bed* Brookins died in 1953. There were twelve candidates for the Wright exhibition team, according to Renstrom's *Chronology,* but three dropped out for various reasons: J. W. Davis, Spencer Crane, and Duval La Chapelle (Coffyn, "Flying as It Was"; Harris, 159). Three of the remaining nine trained at Montgomery, Alabama, in the spring of 1910: Walter Brookins, Arthur Welsh, and Arch Hoxsey (AR, *Chronology,* 187). Four trained later that year at Simms Station: Frank Coffyn, Phil Parmalee, Ralph Johnstone, and Clifford Turpin (Ibid., 191). Two others, Leonard Bonney and Howard Gill, joined the team later and flew at Chicago in August 1911 (Ibid., 56). Six of the nine team members died in aircraft accidents: Johnstone, Hoxsey, Parmalee, Welsh, Gill, and Bonney. Bonney would be killed in 1928 while testing a gull-wing aircraft of his own design (Vecsey and Dade, 179).

*Turpin's accident and Parmalee's death*   *New York Times,* May 31, 1912, 1; June 2, 1912, pt. 2, 1.

361     *death of Arthur Welsh* Tillman, 156–58.

*a letter he wrote in December* MK, 377–78.

## 42. WHO INVENTED WINGWARPING?

362     *wingwarping had been the decisive factor* Hayward, 507.

*with his vertical rudder fixed* Roseberry, 233–34.

*they declared in court* Ibid., 340.

*tried every possible variation* Loening, *Takeoff,* 82; Studer, 212.

*a letter to Henry Peartree* PW, 1019.

*a letter to Albert Zahm* PW, 987.

363    *Herring filed an affidavit* PW, 971.

*last-minute effort to publicize* The *American Aeronaut* (Oct. 1909, 110), a monthly journal co-published and co-edited by Dienstbach in New York, reprinted a two-page article from the *American Engineer* of Jan. 1894 describing three Lilienthal-type gliders built by Herring. An introduction, "The Wrights' Legal Action," preceding the reprinted article stated that the "supplementary surfaces" mentioned in the 1894 article were used for lateral control and that this action was combined by Herring with movement of the horizontal and vertical rudders. But in the reprinted article itself, the movable auxiliary surfaces were said to have been used "to maintain an approximate constant angle of advance," which indicates that they were intended for either fore-and-aft control or for yaw control, and in the illustration of the third and final version of Herring's glider (it weighed only nineteen pounds), there is no vertical surface at all.

*would be a mere footnote* "What fame attends the name of John J. Montgomery in aviation history is due almost altogether to the propaganda put out by Victor Loughead," Orville Wright wrote three decades later. "It is astonishing to what lengths propaganda will be used when financial interests are involved!" (MK, 448). Lougheed spelled his last name with two *e*'s, although his family—and Orville Wright—spelled it Loughead. If the name has a familiar ring, it is because Victor's half-brothers Allan and Malcolm founded the Loughead Aircraft Corporation in 1916, changed the name to Lockheed in 1928 to avoid problems in pronunciation, and later sold the few remaining assets of the failing company to the present Lockheed Corporation (Vecsey and Dade, 236).

*Lougheed and Montgomery* Spearman, 122; Connick, 45.

364    *neither well defined nor clearly identified* It would be hard otherwise to explain the publication of "New Principles in Aerial Flight," by John Montgomery, in the Nov. 22, 1905, Supplement to the *Scientific American* (pp. 24991–93), even though the editor added a disclaimer that Montgomery's "principles" did not comply with any known physical laws.

*"Some Early Gliding Experiments"*     *Aeronautics,* Jan. 1909, 151–54.

365    *their two greatest contributions* Lougheed, 152.

*the dreadful hint* Ibid., 151.

*the day the Aero Club* AR, *Chronology,* 50.

*American Aeronautic Association*     *Aeronautics,* June 1910, 78.

*Montgomery's lecture—Aeronautics* (London), May 1910, 63–64; *Aeronautics* (New York), Nov. 1911, 51–54. The New York journal stated that it was publishing the lecture "for the first time." The editors forgot that they had given permission to their sister journal to publish the talk in England in 1910. A note on page 63 of the London *Aeronautics* for May 1910 reads: "In publishing this report we are indebted to the courtesy of the editor of *Aeronautics* (New York)."

366    *ranked with the world's greatest physicists* Lougheed (pp. 173–203) reprints Montgomery's "principles" in their entirety, with no elucidation or comment except for a brief aside in a footnote: "The time is certain to come when the clear logic and brilliance of these remarkable investigations and

conclusions . . . will rank their author not merely with present-day aviators but with the world's greatest physicists and mathematicians" (Lougheed, 181 n.).

*he met the Wright brothers* PW, 1028.

*James Plew* Plew purchased the second airplane turned out by the Herring-Curtiss Company (Roseberry, 228). He controlled the operation to the extent that when Curtiss tried (unsuccessfully) to form an organization to license the manufacture of aircraft under non-Wright patents, he wrote to Plew regarding the availability of the Montgomery patent, rather than to Montgomery or Lougheed (Spearman, 119).

*in a shallow box* Ibid., 77 n. 10.

*Lougheed defaulted* Connick, 45. The only experiment ever carried out with a motorized Montgomery machine is described in *Popular Science Monthly,* Jan. 1931, pp. 40–42, in the article "My Forty Years with Flying" by Thomas Baldwin's nephew Horace Wild. Wild writes: "Several of us in Chicago built a Montgomery-type tandem plane in 1910 and fitted it with a small Bates air-cooled engine." Wild claimed that speeds of up to 60 miles per hour were achieved, although each flight ended with smashed wheels and struts. This sounds like an impressive experiment, but a close examination of the two photographs illustrating the motorized aircraft reveals no pilot, no pilot's seat, no means of control. The alleged powerplane is merely a model of indeterminate size, yet in Spearman's biography, Wild's article is cited to show that Montgomery's machines not only were capable of propeller-driven flight but achieved speeds greater than the 1910 Wright and Curtiss machines.

367 *Montgomery's new glider* Spearman, 123–31.

*in the San Francisco* Call     Connick, 45.

*They applied for a patent* AR, *Bibliography,* 100.

368 *1911 Wright glider and gliding experiments* PW, 1024–28; AR, *Chronology,* 199–202; Miller, 193.

*two more reporters arrived* The reporters weren't sure they weren't being hoodwinked. During the second week of experiments, a small bag containing eight pounds of sand, later increased to twelve, was attached to the end of a pole and suspended several feet in front of the wings. Reporters suspected this was the automatic stabilizer. When Orville was questioned about this, he assured them it was "a special stability device." This was literally true, although the sole function of the bag of sand was to bring the glider's center of gravity slightly forward. (Miller, 193.)

*a letter to Thomas Baldwin* PW, 1030.

369 *Montgomery's gliding experiments* Spearman, 123–31.

*Montgomery's death* Spearman, 129. In keeping with other important events in the Montgomery story, there are a number of conflicting versions of what actually happened. The magazine *Fly,* purporting to give Mrs. Montgomery's own version, stated that Montgomery suffered compound fractures of the skull and internal injuries. A doctor summoned from Santa Clara—by telegraph—drove Montgomery back to his home in Santa Clara, where he died in his wife's arms one and a half hours later, conscious to the end. According to *Aeronautics* (Nov. 1911, 5), Montgomery landed on his right hip and head. Not believing himself seriously hurt, he talked for a while with his wife in the tent where the glider was kept but later complained of pains in his back. The pains grew worse until he died. The San Jose *Mercury* and San Francisco *Examiner* reported that Montgomery suffered a blow on the head and that although he remained conscious for three hours, the blow proved fatal.

### 43. VIN FIZ

371     *Curtiss won the $10,000* Roseberry, 272–79.
    *Brookins set a new U.S. record* AR, *Chronology*, 52; FK, 279. Kelly ignores Curtiss's 150-mile trek down the Hudson and calls Brookins's flight "the first long cross-country flight." This sounds less like an oversight than a reflection of Orville's anti-Curtiss bias.
    *first aerial freight delivery* FK, 280; Johnson, 50.
    *Harry Atwood* Harris, 258; G-S, *Aviation,* 159.
    *Robert Fowler* Harris, 259, 268.

372     *Wright Company flying school* The company operated three schools in 1911. A school was opened in January at Augusta, Georgia, under the supervision of Frank Coffyn. In June, Arthur Welsh was placed in charge of a school at Belmont Park, Long Island, scene of the 1910 air races.
    *a primitive flight trainer* Arnold, 17–19; Stein, 29.
    *Milling, Arnold, and John Rodgers* AR, *Chronology,* 55.
    *Cal Rodgers* Stein, 141, 269–70.
    *Rodgers's coast-to-coast flight* The primary source is Stein. Villard 136–37; *New York Times,* Sept. 10–Dec. 11, 1911.
    *a modified version of the EX* PW, 1137, 1199; AR, *Chronology,* 203.

373     *Wilbur's letter to Mrs. Taylor* Oct. 9, 1911 (original in the Archives and Library, Henry Ford Museum and Greenfield Village, Dearborn, Mich.).
    *his trip as a leave of absence* Taylor. In his 1948 interview in *Collier's,* Taylor said, "Some of the personal feeling of the old days when there were just the three of us, was gone."
    *Not much of the original* Vin Fiz Harris, 256. Harris writes that the *Vin Fiz* was rebuilt so many times that the only original parts left when Rodgers reached California were the rudder, engine drip pan, and a strut or two. The *Vin Fiz* that landed at Long Beach was flown at exhibitions in 1912 and 1913 by Charles Wiggins, one of Rodgers' mechanics, who later married Rodgers' widow. In 1914 Rodgers' mother sent the *Vin Fiz* to Dayton for restoration so that it could be donated to the Carnegie Museum in Pittsburgh. She was unable to pay for the work, and the aircraft was destroyed in 1916. (Stein, 346–47.) According to Stein: "When in 1927 the Carnegie Institute decided to resurrect the machine, odds and ends were stitched together . . ." (ibid., 347–48). The odds and ends were parts of a Wright Model E if the following excerpt from a letter written on May 29, 1925, by Orville Wright to Congressman James M. Magee is to be believed:

> The Carnegie Institute at Pittsburgh . . . has no exhibit of historical nature in aviation. The Rodgers machine, which it now has, is not the one with which Cal made the transcontinental flight, but is the one on which Cal took part of his training in flying here at Dayton. The plane used in the transcontinental flight was almost totally destroyed in an accident in

California. The few remaining parts were shipped by Mrs. H. S. Sweitzer (Cal Rodgers' mother) to the Wright Company at Dayton in 1914, for the purpose of having it restored for presentation to the Carnegie Institute. But when Mrs. Sweitzer learned the cost of such restoration she gave up the idea of having that machine restored. The parts were still at the factory when I sold my interests in the company, and were later in 1916 destroyed. (PW, 1136–37.)

After being exhibited at the 1933 Century of Progress Exhibition in Chicago, the Carnegie Institute's "resurrected" *Vin Fiz* was sent to the Smithsonian Institution, where it underwent a final restoration and emerged as the *Vin Fiz* now on display in the National Air and Space Museum.

375     *hundreds of souvenir hunters*    *New York Times,* Apr. 4, 1912, 1.

## 44. WILBUR

376     *French infringement suits* McM, 258, 276; *New York Times*, Apr. 30, 1911, pt. 3, 1.

*the Wright patents* The French version of the basic patent had been granted Sept. 1, 1904. Two other patents, covering improvements that would strengthen claims for the basic control system, were applied for in 1907 and approved in 1908, although the equivalent U.S. patents would not be approved until 1911 and 1914. (PW, 1230.)

*5,000 shares* AR, *Chronology,* 27.

*the German Wright patent* The basic Wright patent, issued in Germany in July 1906, was the only one involved in the suit at the time Wilbur was in Berlin. The two supplementary patents were not issued until Oct. and Nov. 1911, after Wilbur had returned to the United States. (PW, 1230.)

*the German infringement suit* PW, 1040–41.

*the German Wright business* MK, 384–85.

377     *Zahm wrote the Wrights* PW, 1094 n.

*"Naturally we regret"* PW, 987.

*"Apparently you are not"* PW, 1094 n.

*dissolved into enmity* Orville suspected that one of the reasons for Zahm's virulent attacks on the Wrights was that shortly after being rebuffed in his offer to serve as a witness for them, he had been made to appear ridiculous in court. On Mar. 16, 1910, in one of his first appearances as witness for Curtiss, Zahm testified under oath that it was not necessary to use the vertical rudder to maintain lateral balance. Aileron movement, his testimony implied, did not produce torque about a vertical axis in a Curtiss machine or any other machine. The Wrights revealed in court that Zahm himself had applied for a patent on a device that would overcome the torque produced by the difference in drag of two ailerons adjusted at opposing angles—which "often happens," Zahm had stated in his patent application. "There was much mirth in the court room over Zahm's embarrassment when he tried to explain why he did not want to produce the document [his patent application]." (MK, 457–58.)

*Zahm on Lilienthal, Santos-Dumont, and Chanute's glider* Zahm, 216, 256, 250.

378     *"The aeroplane would thus appear"* Ibid., 250.
*three-torque system of control* Ibid., 230.
*Judge Hand on Zahm's proposal* McM, 246.
*Any inventor, Zahm contended* Zahm, 231–32.
*"It is rather amusing"* PW, 1041–42.
*An affidavit had been filed* PW, 992.

379     *felt free to ignore* Zahm, 222–26.
*Ader's* Avion *at the Musée* McM, 257.
*Wilbur returned to the museum* PW, 1022.
*a worm winch* Peyrey, 370.
*article on Ader*     *Aero Club of America Bulletin,* May 1912; reprinted in
*Aeronautical Journal,* July–Sept. 1916.
*article on Mouillard*     *Aero Club of America Bulletin,* Apr. 1912; reprinted
in *Aeronautical Journal,* July–Sept. 1916.

380     *article on Lilienthal*     *Aero Club of America Bulletin,* Sept. 1912; extracted
in MK, 389–90. In Apr. 1911, when Wilbur was in Germany, he ascertained
that Lilienthal's family was in need. In December the Wright brothers sent
Frau Lilienthal a check for $1,000 as a token of their appreciation of her
husband's contribution to aeronautics. (MK, 381; AR, *Chronology,* 57.)
*Wilbur to the Wright Company lawyer* PW, 1042.
*a lengthy deposition* WW, 115–24.
*described as coming home white* McM, 266.
*Bishop Wright wrote in his diary* PW, 1037.
*Wilbur in New York and Boston* AR, *Chronology,* 59.
*Frederick Fish* McM, 242.
*suffered an indisposition*     *New York Times,* May 31, 1912, 4.

381     *"most of the rooms are smaller"* MK, 382.
*tramped over the small hill* McM, 268.
*Orville took the machine up* AR, *Chronology,* 205.
*Wilbur on Friday and Saturday* McM, 268.
*letter to Fish* PW, 1042–43.
*"a sort of typhoidal fever"* PW, 1043.
*A common source of the disease* This and other references to the disease and
its course are from the (contemporary) article on typhoid fever in the 11th
edition of the *Encyclopaedia Britannica,* 1911.

382     *dictated his will* PW, 1043 n.
*kept a daily record* PW, 1044–46.
*death of Frank Southard* PW, 1044; Harris, 161–62.

383     *sent to other streets to play* Young and Fitzgerald, 128.
*telegram from Curtiss* Ibid., 131.

384     *Wilbur's funeral*     *New York Times,* June 2, 1912, 1; McM, 274.
*Wilbur's will* PW, 1043 n.
*"poor old daddy's fan"* MK, 385.

385     *"In memory and intellect"* PW, 1046 n.

45. COMPANY PRESIDENT

386    *sailed for Europe* AR, *Chronology*, 61.
*stock-promotion schemes* FK, 284.
*British Wright Company* Brewer, "Wilbur Wright," 80.
*paid the Wright Company* Ibid.; AR, *Chronology*, 65.
*German infringement suits* Ibid., 58, 61, 62; McM 275–76. It is not clear who profited by the decision. Griffith Brewer said that what the decision meant was that flying machines that used only warping were free to use the Wright patent, but those that used warping and rudder action were not. (*Flight*, Mar. 15, 1913, 300.)

387    *the Dayton flood* PW, 1060–61; Miller, 15–16; Conover, 112, 267–68, 275–76, 295; Marcosson, 140–42; Young and Fitzgerald, 134–35; Cox, 165–69.

388    *Orville as Wright Company president* Loening, *Our Wings*, 43, *Takeoff*, 55–56.
*sharp-tongued secretary* Miller, 118.
*hiring of Loening* Miller, 79–80.
*first master of arts* Loening, *Our Wings*, 15.
*Alpheus Barnes* Loening, *Takeoff*, 54–61.
*hydroplanes a case in point* Ibid.

389    *Loening once described flying* Loening, *Our Wings*, 7.
*had applied for a patent* PW, 771–72. According to McMahon, the stabilizer was largely the work of Orville, Wilbur's contribution being limited to the idea of the horizontal vane to control fore-and-aft balance (McM, 291).
*the Sperry device* Roseberry, 327–28.
*Wright automatic stabilizer New York Times*, Jan. 6, 1914, 1.
*the Wright Model E* PW, 1203, 1205.
*stabilizer tests* AR, *Chronology*, 206.
*Curtiss and the Collier trophy* Roseberry, 321, 330.

390    *Orville's winning of the trophy New York Times*, Jan. 6, 1914, 1 (in which the London *Daily Mail* was quoted); AR, *Chronology*, 206; Miller, 84.
*made a prediction Aeronautics*, Jan. 1914, 4.
*never came into general use* Charnley, 235.
*placed on the market that July* AR, *Chronology*, 62.
*first of these accidents* Tillman, 156–57.
*the Wright Model C* PW, 1200–1.
*Model B accident* Tillman, 162–64.

391    *two accidents in the Philippines* Ibid., 154.
*death of Lt. Call New York Times*, July 9, 1913, 7.
*Orville suspected* PW, 1085. The ideas behind the incidence indicator were later incorporated into a paper, "Stability of Aeroplanes," delivered at the Franklin Institute, Philadelphia, May 20, 1914, and published in the institute's journal in Sept. 1914 (reprinted in PW, 1078–87, and in the Smithsonian Institution *Annual Report* 1914, 209–16). In his paper, Orville contended that most of the accidents that had been occurring resulted from a stall when the aviator glided down from a height and then tried to check the downward plunge by pulling back on the elevator. This not only decreased the speed but increased the drag until the machine began to stall and dived downward in spite of every

effort of the pilot to stop the descent. If the operator were able to "feel" exactly the angle at which his wings met the air, he would be able to avoid the danger. Since most pilots were not able to do this, the incidence indicator had been designed to do it for them.

*deaths of Ellington and Kelly* PW, 1067 n.
*death of Lt. Rich* Tillman, 154.
*found the accidents distressing* PW, 1068.

392      *death of Lt. Post* Tillman, 185.
*the plane's elevator was too weak* Ibid.
*"dynamically unsuited for flying"* Ibid., 155.
*Oscar Brindley at North Island* Loening, *Our Wings,* 48.
*Loening and the Signal Corps* Ibid., 50–51.
*Glenn Martin* Tillman, 187.
*felt that Orville never forgave him* Loening, *Takeoff,* 69.
*the Wright Model K* PW, 1208.

## 46. THE AERODROME AFFAIR

393      *Hazel's second decision* AR, *Chronology,* 61.
*Court of Appeals decision* Ibid., 63–64.
*"patentees may fairly be considered"* McM, 280.
*It would be a month* PW, 1074.
*Orville's interview* Thomas Baldwin was questioned about Orville's statements to the press and in the next day's *New York Times* (Feb. 28, 1914, 6) was quoted as saying, "Since Orville Wright took the whole country into his confidence, it is high time for all the rest of us to step up and admit that not a one of us would have known what it was to get off the ground in flight if the Wrights had not unlocked the secret for us." Kelly quotes Baldwin as saying in the same interview that he had warned Curtiss in 1906 "that he was asking too many questions, but he kept right on" (FK, 289). Roseberry (p. 353) also quotes passages from Baldwin's interview that refer to Baldwin and Curtiss's visit to Dayton in 1906, but neither the Kelly nor the Roseberry quotes are in the microfilm edition of the *New York Times.*

394      *Curtiss's press release* New York Times, Mar. 9, 1914, 7.
*Ford, Crisp, and independently operated ailerons* Scharff and Taylor, 218–19; Roseberry, 357–58.
*a meeting took place* Scharff and Taylor, 220.
*thought the suggestion excellent* Ibid.

395      *Manly had written* Aero Club of America, 190.
*a further flurry of interest* Roseberry, 123.
*Lincoln Beachey* FK, 308; Roseberry, 382–83; *New York Times,* Jan. 27, 1914, 8.
*the Smithsonian's motives* Smithsonian Institution, *Annual Report* 1914, 218.
*a phone conversation with Alexander Graham Bell* Roseberry, 385.
*he wrote to Lincoln Beachey* Ibid., 384.

396      *agreed to pay Curtiss $2,000* Griffith Brewer wrote that Walcott told Orville in Apr. 1921 that the Smithsonian had paid only for transporting the Aero-

drome from Washington to Hammondsport (*U.S. Air Service,* Dec. 1921, 26). Walcott himself insisted that the Smithsonian paid Curtiss $2,000 and that the Institution had Curtiss's receipt on file (ibid., Oct. 1921, 19). Loening (*Takeoff,* 85) reproduces a Smithsonian voucher for $2,000 made out to Curtiss and signed by him, but the voucher has no date of any kind. McMahon says that, according to some newspaper reports, Curtiss was paid three years later (McM, 202). Roseberry writes that there was no such disbursement in the 1914 and 1915 report of the Board of Regents' Executive Committee and suggests that it is "barely possible" that Walcott and Bell shared the cost, as they had privately talked of doing.

*roles of Zahm and Manly in the reconstruction* Although neither man was affiliated with the Curtiss Aeroplane Company at the time, Zahm would become chief research engineer of the company in 1915 (*New York Times,* July 24, 1954, 13), and Manly would serve Curtiss's company as consulting aviation engineer, 1915–19, and as assistant general manager, 1919–20 (Dictionary of American Biography).

*changes in the motor* FK, 331; Roseberry, 387.

*changes made in the Aerodrome during reconstruction* FK, 327–32. The changes were originally itemized by Orville in an affidavit filed Apr. 24, 1915, in the second suit against Curtiss (AR, *Chronology,* 66). According to Griffith Brewer (*U.S. Air Service,* Oct. 1921, 10), they were based on a comparison of drawings and photographs of the original Aerodrome in the *Langley Memoir* of 1911 with photographs taken in 1914, supplemented by data from an affidavit filed by Zahm in the same suit.

Roseberry (p. 436) complains that Orville failed to differentiate between the changes made in rebuilding the Aerodrome and those made when the more powerful motor was added after the tests of May 28 and June 2. The latter changes, however, were mostly improvements in methods of control, repositioning of the pilot's car, and modifications made to accommodate the new motor and propeller. Changes in wing camber, leading edge, aspect ratio, and bracing were made before the experiments began. This is apparent in the photographs taken May 28. Both Zahm and Manly (*U.S. Air Service,* Oct. 1921, 23; Nov. 1921, 26) state that the 23.8-cm rib extensions used in the 1903 machine were omitted in 1914. This gave the wings a more efficient camber, leading edge, and aspect ratio. The so-called extensions are described and illustrated in the *Langley Memoir* (p. 205 and pl. 66). They are not visible in any of the photographs of the machine made at Hammondsport, but are clearly visible in photographs of the Aerodrome in the Smithsonian after it was restored to its original condition.

Brewer is partly responsible for giving the impression that the camber was changed after the tests of May 28 and June 2. In *Fifty Years of Flying* (p. 108), he writes that when he visited Hammondsport in June 1914, "I watched them changing the camber on the shores of the lake." (How does anyone watch a camber being changed from a rowboat?) He also writes that his letter to the *New York Times* enumerated the changes made in the Aerodrome. His letter does no such thing, however. Roseberry quotes both statements as if they were facts rather than an old man's imperfect recollections of thirty-two-year-old events.

*thirty inches farther to the rear* FK, 312.

397  tests of May 28, 1914 New York Times, May 29, 1914, 1, 2.
     "rose in level poise" Smithsonian Institution, Annual Report 1914, 219.
     noted a few weeks later New York Times, June 23, 1914, 8.
     The legal implications Ibid., May 31, 1914, pt. 3, 4.
398  "subsequent short flights were made" Smithsonian Institution, Annual Report
     1915, 121.
     two photographs were obtained Ibid. 1914, 217–22, pl. 2.
     Brewer made the trip Brewer, Fifty Years, 108.
     wrote a letter to the Times June 22, 1914, 10.
     The Times urged its readers       Ibid., June 23, 1914, 8.
399  "an act of piety" Roseberry, 391.
     Further tests were made Smithsonian Institution, Annual Report 1914, 220.
     urged Curtiss to continue the experiments Loening, Takeoff, 86.
     experiments with sled runners Roseberry, 392.
     Lorin's visit to Hammondsport PW, 1087–92.
400  The 1914 report by Zahm Smithsonian Institution, Annual Report 1914, 217–22.
     it was a failure PW, 1088 n.
     "there was no room for question" PW, 1151.
     "It has demonstrated" Smithsonian Institution, Annual Report 1914, 221.
401  a label that read Abbot, 10.
     the integrity of Glenn Curtiss   Roseberry (pp. 338–39) quotes Glenn Curtiss
     on the reconstructed Aerodrome: "It is true that it was flown without a single
     change that could have improved its flying qualities. The only changes were
     the replacements of the broken parts and the addition of the floats." The italics
     are Curtiss's. As an airplane manufacturer, he must have known that changes
     in camber, aspect ratio, and leading edge would seriously affect the flying
     qualities of any but the most crudely designed aircraft. Curtiss also ignores
     the changes in trussing and repositioning of the guy posts, which kept the
     wings from collapsing—until June 5, 1915. The chances are that no one today
     would know that the Aerodrome's wings had collapsed in 1915 if Lorin Wright
     had not been present to witness the collapse.
     had it drummed into them Harris, 220.
     Orville and Katharine's hatred of Curtiss Loening, Takeoff, 56.
     "That Langley fake of last summer" Cox, 89.


### 47. END OF THE PATENT WARS


403  Hawthorn Hill McM, 285–86.
     the many hawthorns Johnson, 71.
     "Mister Orv" PW, 57, n. 8.
     homemade chocolate ice cream Johnson, x.
     the single orange McM, 42.
     a Franklin roadster Miller, 80.
404  an article on flying "The Future of the Aeroplane," Country Life in America,
     Jan. 1909.
     threatened with an arrest Miller, 160
     Orville strangely uncooperative Loening, Our Wings, 46, Takeoff, 62–63.

*Orville's delaying tactics* FK, 285; MK, 403.
*dismissed the odious Alpheus Barnes* Loening, *Takeoff,* 63.
*more concerned with patent licensing* Ibid., 89.
*in the neighborhood of $1.5 million*     *New York Times,* Oct. 14, 1915, 8.
*a larger sum* OW, *How We Invented,* 73.
*as consulting engineer* AR, *Chronology,* 67.

405     *a store and apartment building* Miller, 15.
*the laboratory Orville wanted* AR, *Chronology,* 67.
*Wright-Martin Aircraft Corporation* Ibid., 68; PW, 1102; Loening, *Takeoff,* 89–90. After World War I, the company changed its name to the Wright Aeronautical Corporation and in 1929 merged with the Curtiss Aeroplane and Motor Corporation to become the Curtiss-Wright Corporation. Curtiss was reported to be pleasantly titillated by a report that Orville had waxed indignant at the idea that Curtiss's name should precede that of Wright, although neither man was party to the manipulations that preceded the merger. (Roseberry, 448–49.)
*Curtiss's business and patents* Ibid., 360, 401.
*more than a hundred American aeronautical patents* Mingos, 26.
*a cross-licensing agreement* Roseberry, 361.
*had acquired the Wright patents* AR, *Chronology,* 68.
*Each firm received $2 million* Roseberry, 361.

406     *three infringement suits* AR, *Bibliography,* 112–13. The two suits other than the Montgomery suit involved the 1917 flying-machine patent of George Francis Myers, which Myers claimed was based on a patent applied for in 1897. Orville made four depositions in these two suits between 1925 and 1935.
*Lougheed's book* The complete title is *Aeroplane Designing for Amateurs: A Plain Treatment of the Basic Principles of Flight Engineering—Including Heretofore Unpublished Facts Concerning Bird Flight and Aerodynamic Phenomena* (Chicago: Reilly & Britton, 1912).
*It was dedicated* Lougheed managed to get Montgomery's middle name wrong. He dedicated his book to "Professor John James Montgomery."
*"repeated some fifty or sixty times"* Lougheed's preface, 24. Father Arthur Spearman, Montgomery's biographer, who had access to all of Montgomery's records and so knew better, could not resist quoting Lougheed's false statement in his biography, but he kept his skirts clean by laundering Lougheed with a tidy ellipsis so that the quotation comes out: "Similar performances were repeated . . . in the course of exhibitions that Montgomery gave," etc. (Spearman, 91).
*half a dozen nonaborted flights* All of which are described in Chapter 20.
*"a gliding flight across the Santa Clara Valley"* Lougheed's preface, 24.
*Orville would write of Lougheed* MK, 450.

407     *some of it was farcical* Typical of the affidavits produced by the plaintiffs was one by a resident of San Diego who swore that as a boy of twelve he helped Montgomery construct and fly several propeller-driven airplanes. On one occasion, he said, Montgomery had tried to operate a propeller by hand but found the control of the wings and tail required his entire attention. (Spearman, 23.)
*some of it pathetic* Montgomery's mother, then in her nineties, testified to her

son's obsession with flight. Even as a small boy, she said, he would lie on the floor with a pillow under his stomach and pretend to fly (Spearman, 9).

*Orville's 1920 deposition* The most significant portions have been printed in OW, *How We Invented the Airplane.*

*chose to interpret Montgomery's patent literally* Court of Claims of U.S. No. 33852, Decisions May 28, 1928, 29. Copy in Smithsonian Archives, Montgomery file.

*"It seems to us idle"* Ibid., 23.

*"He preserved no data"* Ibid., 15.

*"American Unknown to Fame"* Robert Martin, *Popular Science Monthly,* Oct. 1930.

408     *the* Harper's *article* June 1940, 28–31.

*the first glide was merely one* Only Orville Wright seems to have taken the trouble to determine the feasibility of Montgomery's having made even a single glide in a machine like the one described in Chanute's *Progress in Flying Machines.* "Today," Orville wrote in 1944, "all aeronautical engineers know that a machine having only 90 ft. wing area, with camber as used by Montgomery, can not lift more than 20 pounds at a speed of 8 miles per hour, and not more than 45 pounds at 12 miles per hour—one-eighth to one-fourth of the weight of Montgomery and his machine" (MK, 449).

*a number of similar stories* Spearman, 227–33.

*James remedied the omission* "Forgotten Pioneer," *Flying,* Sept. 1946, 52.

*movie* Gallant Journey—Replicas of the Montgomery machines used in the movie were airworthy in ways the originals were not. The wings of the 1905 Santa Clara glider replica were rigid without the original's droop and deep camber. They were equipped with ailerons operated by a control stick strapped to the pilot's back out of sight of the camera. (*Flying,* Sept. 1946, 52–53.)

*four-sided feast of misinformation* The primary inscription on the obelisk states that Montgomery "from this point sent aloft on April 29, 1905, the first heavier than air glider in controlled flight and maintained equilibrium." The second side quotes Victor Lougheed: "Eye witnesses of the California flights as a rule seemed to imagine that something akin to a parachute jump was in progress, few realizing that the one great problem of aerial navigation from the beginning had been that of controlled flight and maintained equilibrium, which, for the first time in history, it was their privilege to witness." Both these inscriptions, chiseled in granite, assume that the Wright brothers never made a controlled flight or maintained equilibrium until after Apr. 29, 1905. The other two sides of the monument contain quotations from Octave Chanute ("One of the most daring feats ever attempted," which is true, at least from the viewpoint of Daniel Maloney, whose name and death are not mentioned) and Alexander Graham Bell ("All subsequent attempts in aviation must begin with the Montgomery machine," which is patently untrue). Both quotes are from page 139 of Lougheed's *Vehicles of the Air,* where no source is given for either quotation. Chanute wrote Montgomery on Apr. 16, 1905, regarding the March flights of Maloney (not the Apr. 29 flight): "I congratulate you most heartily on the boldest feat ever attempted in gliding flight." Lougheed may merely have altered this quote in his book and omitted the qualifying phrase

"in gliding flight." It would be interesting to have the context of Bell's comment. It is impossible to believe that either he or Octave Chanute would have sanctioned the use of their words and names on such a monument.
*ninety-foot stainless-steel airplane wing* Spearman, 149.

409      *as naïve as it is sincere* As when Spearman discovers a parallel between Montgomery's forty-two-pound tandem-wing glider and a modern bomber: "Montgomery recognized the value of flexibility in the structural design of his wing. The same quality of flexibility exists in the wings of the great modern aircraft of today. The B-52 bomber is said to have had 22 feet of 'give' up and down." (Spearman, 161.)
*Evergreen Valley memorial* Ibid., 150.
*a letter to Thomas Baldwin* PW, 1209.


### 48. WAR COMES TO DAYTON


410      *Dayton Metal Products Company* Leslie, 77.
*Dayton-Wright Airplane Company* AR, *Chronology,* 69. Actually two companies were incorporated. The other was the Wright Field Company, organized for the training of civilian pilots. Orville was a director and consulting engineer of both companies. In 1916 Deeds and Kettering purchased between 100 and 200 acres of land about a mile north of downtown Dayton, where, with Orville's cooperation, they hoped to establish a flying field for training civilian pilots. It was to be called Wright Field. (It was also referred to as North Field, to distinguish it from South Field, the airfield on Deeds's Moraine Farm estate used for testing aircraft produced by the Dayton-Wright Company.) The field had been only partially cleared when the United States entered the war. After Deeds was commissioned a colonel, he sold his interest in the property to Kettering, who leased it to the government through his Dayton Metal Products Company. Renamed McCook Field, it was activated in Dec. 1917 to centralize the government's aviation research and testing activities. (PW, 1115; Johnson, 94–97; Marcosson, 271.)

411      *Orville's commission* AR, *Chronology,* 69.
*Thomas Baldwin in the war* Crouch, *Eagle,* 562.
*did not have a very high opinion* Loening, *Takeoff,* 99.
*Howard Coffin* Ibid., 100–1.
*only 411 aircraft* Roger E. Bilstein, *Flight in America 1900–1983* (Baltimore: Johns Hopkins, 1984), 35.
*2,500 trainers* Mingos, 27.
*Dayton-Wright contracts* PW, 1116; Johnson, 63.

412      *Howard Coffin predicted New York Times,* May 21, 1917, 1.
*the true story of that interview* McFarland.
*the* Amerikaprogramm  Arnold, 58.
*400 trainer planes* Loening, *Takeoff,* 109.
*the sample airframe* Boyne, 157.
*American DH-4s in France* Loening, *Takeoff,* 110.

413      *the Liberty Engine* Ibid., 109; Loening, *Our Wings,* 81–82; Marcosson, 240–41.
*Gutzon Borglum and his investigation* Ibid., 255–62; Rex Alan Smith, *The Carving of Mount Rushmore* (New York: Abbeville, 1985), 56–59; Robert J.

Casey and Mary Borglum, *Give the Man Room: The Story of Gutzon Borglum* (Indianapolis: Bobbs-Merrill, 1952), 142, 245.

414  *the Senate investigation* Marcosson, 271.

*the Hughes investigation* Ibid., 272–82; Loening, *Takeoff,* 112; PW, 1111–21.

*Reforms had already been made* Loening, *Takeoff,* 110–12.

*American-built DH-4s in France* Ibid., 113.

415  *Harold Miller* Miller, 20.

*"Flaming coffins" was a bit unfair* Boyne (p. 162) writes that of the total of 289 aircraft lost by U.S. pilots, only 33 were D-H4s, and of those, only 8 went down in flames; 25 were lost from other causes. Loening (*Takeoff,* 113) claimed that the American-built DII-4s flew as well as if not better than their British counterparts. Boyne (p. 155) claims that the gas tank was not well fastened to the fuselage and in a crash usually came loose and either crushed the pilot against the hot engine or exploded.

*it is hard to get at the truth* Marcosson, in his biography of Deeds, and Leslie, in his book on Kettering, try hard to justify their subjects' actions. Loening, in his two books, reviews the scandal from the standpoint of aircraft designers who were cold-shouldered by the Aircraft Production Board. Mingos defends the automobile industry. Borglum, according to all accounts, was contentious and inclined to exaggerate. Orville had nothing but praise for Deeds, Kettering, and the two Talbotts, at least before the disastrous failures in production. In May 1917, when these four men were considering building trainer planes for the government, Orville wrote Glenn Martin: "I do not know of anyone who could undertake a job of that kind and put it through more successfully than those men could" (PW, 1101). Deeds remained a close friend for the rest of Orville's life.

The founders of the Dayton-Wright Airplane Company had hoped to make Dayton the airplane manufacturing center of the United States. That hope foundered in 1923 when the company, which had been acquired by General Motors in 1919, discontinued aeronautical work, but Dayton was to profit in another way from the wartime activities of Edward Deeds and his friends. Deeds was instrumental in leasing to the government 2,000 acres of Miami Conservancy District land, on which Wilbur Wright Field, eight miles east of McCook Field, was established as a military aviation training center in May 1917. (The new field included the former Simms Station airfield, which had been closed in 1916.) In June 1917, the Fairfield Aviation General Supply Depot was established on an adjoining forty acres near the town of Fairfield, now Fairborn.

After the war, McCook Field was enlarged to 254 acres and used for both military and civil aviation research, but it was small and close to the populous Dayton downtown area. In the early 1920s, when the government threatened to move its aviation research activities elsewhere, a group of citizens calling themselves the Dayton Air Service Committee raised more than $400,000 for the purchase of 5,000 acres adjoining Wilbur Wright Field and presented the land to the government. A new airfield, named Wright Field after both Wright brothers, was dedicated in 1927. It assumed the functions of McCook Field, which was closed the same year. In 1931 the former Wilbur Wright Field, which was then a part of Wright Field, was combined with the Fairfield Depot and established as Patterson Field, named after Lt. Frank Patterson, who had been killed in a DH-4 accident at Wilbur Wright Field in 1917. In 1948 the two military airfields were merged and became the flourishing U.S. government aeronautical technical center known today as Wright-Patterson Air Force Base. (Johnson, 87–90, 97.)

*the testimony Orville gave* PW, 1111–21.

*Orville's last flight as a pilot* PW, pl. 224; AR, *Chronology,* 71, 208. The DH-4 flown by Howard Rinehart on that occasion was the first DH-4 produced by the Dayton-Wright Company in 1917. It is now in the National Air and Space Museum, Washington, D.C. In 1944, when Orville was seventy-two, he took over the controls of an Army four-engine Lockheed Constellation for a brief period while flying over Dayton (AR, *Chronology,* 106).

*Kettering's aerial torpedo project* Leslie, 80–86; Arnold, 74–76.

416     *a humiliating end* Leslie (p. 85) describes the final test, before U.S. and British Army and Navy personnel, as "a humiliating display of technical failures."

*"The nation with the most eyes"* Aerial Age, Oct. 15, 1917, 579.

*"The aeroplane has made war so terrible"* PW, 1121.

*"The possibilities of the aeroplane"* Young and Fitzgerald, 151.

*"I once thought the aeroplane"* PW, 1176.


## 49. ORVILLE ALONE


417     *death of Milton Wright* PW, 1077 n. 8; Young and Fitzgerald, 147.

*the dog Scipio* Miller, 19, 61.

*brought home in an ambulance* AR, *Chronology,* 67.

*vacations at Waubec and Lambert islands* Miller, 98–109, 139, 141, 152; Johnson, 74.

418     *Orville's Pierce-Arrow* Miller, 106, 143.

*Katharine's marriage and death* Goulder, 117–18, 122–23; McM, 298–99. There is no mention of either her marriage or her death in Kelly. After Katharine's 1913 visit to Europe with Orville, she simply disappears from the biography authorized by Orville.

*alternately furious and inconsolable* Goulder, 117.

*all but read her out of the family* From a 1972 conversation between the writer and the late Marvin McFarland. McFarland learned of Orville's attitude toward his sister from Charles Gibbs-Smith, who had recently been shown Katharine's correspondence with the Griffith Brewers, in whom she confided.

*deaths of Reuchlin and Lorin* AR, *Chronology,* 73, 102.

419     *missing wind-tunnel balances* Ibid., 108; Miller, 38; U.S. Air Services, 1949, 17; New York Times, Dec. 18, 1948, 32.

*Orville's laboratory* Hodgins; Aerial Age, Oct. 15, 1917, 579 (photo); New York Times Magazine, Sept. 1927, 23–25.

*General Electric motor* PW, 1179.

*Taylor in the laboratory* Taylor.

*feelings about Mabel Beck* Miller, 28–29, 43.

*two boys climbed a tree* Ibid., 195.

420     *the split-flap airfoil* PW, 1144, 1148–49; MK, 462; AR, *Chronology,* 100.

*Handley Page's slotted wing* In 1928, Orville wrote: "We did not secure a lift at all comparable to that secured by Handley Page. . . . It is Handley Page who has brought the slotted wing to a state of usefulness, and I do not think that anything we previously may have done along that line ought to affect the validity of his patent" (PW, 1149).

*Orville's patented toy* Miller, 24–25; AR, *Bibliography,* 101; Johnson, 74.

*a Distinguished Flying Cross* AR, *Chronology,* 89.

*honorary degrees* Ibid., 66, 72, 91, 92, 96, 106, 109. These degrees were in addition to the degrees awarded both brothers during Wilbur's lifetime: bachelor of science degrees from Earlham College, June 1909; doctor of laws degrees, Oberlin, June 1910 (ibid., 41, 51).

421     *Lindbergh's visit* PW, 1141 n.

*"a gray man now"* Hodgins.

*Orville on Prohibition* Cox, 84.

*Orville on advertising and flying saucers* Miller, 119, 151.

*Orville on insurance* Young and Fitzgerald, 162, 164.

*Orville's sweet tooth* Johnson, x; Miller, 120.

*"I wonder is it modern art"* Ibid., 164.

*"Gertrude had a sensitive nose"* Ibid., 167.

*Gertrude Stein's "Wilbur Wright"*     *Four in America* (New Haven: Yale, 1947), 83–117 (quotations are from pp. 109, 107).

422     *Orville's practical joke* MK, 463–64; FK, "A Psychic Mystery of Aviation," *Michigan Alumnus Quarterly Review,* Aug. 9, 1958, 352–53.

*a story Orville told* MK, 20.

### 50. A FEUD AND A CELEBRATION

424     *Walcott had asked* FK, 303–7.

*Bell and the MIT dedication* FK, 307–8. The machine had been reconstructed with the help of James Jacobs, who later worked with Orville on the split-flap airfoil. A new crankcase was cast for the motor. The crankshaft and flywheel of the original motor, which had been loaned to the Aero Club of America for exhibit in Jan. 1906, could not be found, so the flywheel and crankshaft of the 1904 motor were used, after being modified to make them fit the 1903 chain-guide bearing. Charlie Taylor made new parts for the motor. (PW, 1214; Taylor.)

425     *displayed and taken apart four times* PW, 1189; AR, *Chronology,* 69, 71, 72, 74.

*spent two months compiling a list* Brewer, *Fifty Years,* 111.

*published in the United States*     *U.S. Air Service,* Oct. 1921, 9–19 (Griffith Brewer, "Aviation's Greatest Controversy"), 19–20 (Charles D. Walcott, "Smithsonian's Answer to Griffith Brewer"), 21–24 (Albert Zahm, "Review of Experiments with Rehabilitated Langley Airplane in 1914"); Nov. 1921, 21–26 (Charles Manly, "The Langley Machine at Hammondsport: Being a Reply to Griffith Brewer"); Dec. 1921, 26–29 (Griffith Brewer, "Langley Machine and Hammondsport Trials: Replies to Walcott, Zahm, Manly, and Curtiss"), 29 (Glenn Curtiss, "The Langley Machine at Hammondsport"). The papers were also published in the British *Aeronautical Journal,* Dec. 1921, 620–64, with illustrations that were not included in *U.S. Air Service.*

426        *had been an innocent dupe* FK, 316.
           *beginning to worry about the condition* MK, 408.
           *exhibited at the International Air Races* AR, *Chronology,* 78.
           *the wingcovering had deteriorated* Beck, 10.
           *Brewer had already suggested* MK, 408–9.
           *announced in two Dayton newspapers* AR, *Chronology,* 79.
           *another statement to the press* Ibid.
           *Walcott issued a statement* Ibid.
           *appeal to Chief Justice Taft* FK, 316–17.

427        *made his final offer* AR, *Chronology,* 80. The intermediary was Grover Loen-
           ing.
           *report of Ames and Taylor* Abbot, 11–25.
           *the label changed to read* Ibid., 13, 34.
           *reconditioned 1903 Flyer and its shipment to England* Beck, 10; AR, *Chronol-
           ogy,* 82, 85.
           *Orville's article*        *U.S. Air Services,* Mar. 1928, 30–31, reprinted in PW,
           1145–48.

428        *meeting with Secretary Abbot* FK, 319; Abbot, 1.
           *"mostly a hollow gesture"* PW, 1151.
           *Congress had appropriated $25,000* AR, *Chronology,* 85.
           *Senator Bingham* Hodgins.
           *erection of a speaker's platform* Ibid.
           *cutting a block of granite* New York Times, Dec. 18, 1928, 18.

429        *"We proceeded to agree"* Aeronautic Review, Dec. 1928, 190. Even if any trace
           of the 1903 camp buildings had remained, it would have been difficult to locate
           the takeoff point. The starting rail had wandered over the years. Orville's
           diary, Dec. 17, 1903, does not mention its location. Wilbur's letter to Chanute,
           written twenty-five days after the event, places the starting rail two hundred
           feet west of the camp buildings (PW, 402). In 1913, when Orville wrote up the
           story of that day in greater detail for *Flying* magazine, it had moved to "about
           one hundred feet north of the new building" (OW, "How We Made," 35). In
           his 1920 deposition in *Montgomery's Heirs* v. *Wright-Martin,* he located it
           about a hundred feet *west* of the building. That is where it remained when
           Kelly excerpted the 1913 *Flying* article in his biography (FK, 98). In 1933,
           Orville, through his secretary, Mabel Beck, supplied some information about
           the first flights to a James Smith, in which the track was located sixty to
           seventy-five feet "away" from the camp buildings (PW, 1161 n.). In 1928, the
           takeoff point could have been located almost as accurately with a dowsing rod,
           but they had to put the boulder somewhere.
           *a third memorial* AR, *Chronology,* 86. It was dedicated May 2, 1928.
           *a conference had been planned* New York Times, Dec. 17, 1928, 20.
           *trip to Kill Devil Hills and cornerstone ceremonies* Ibid., Dec. 17, 1928, 20,
           Dec. 18, 18; *Aeronautic Review,* Jan. 1929, 4–7; Hodgins.

430        *Napoleon's retreat from Moscow* Hodgins.
           *death of Allen Heuth* New York Times, Dec. 18, 1928, 18.
           *taming of Big Kill Devil Hill*        U.S. Air Services, Nov. 1932, 25.
           *dedication of the completed memorial* Ibid., Dec. 1932, 21–22; *New York
           Times,* Nov. 20, 1932, 2; AR, *Chronology,* 92; Miller, 28.

431        *Greenfield Village* AR, *Chronology,* 97–99.
           *the Wright family laundress* Johnson, 34; Young and Fitzgerald, 165–66. The

house had been given to Katharine by her father when the bishop disposed of his farm in Iowa in 1902 and divided the money among his four sons.

*reconstructed, side by side* A 1971 television production about the Wrights, filmed partly in Greenfield Village, showed the brothers scurrying back and forth between home and bicycle shop over a well-kept lawn, a convenience denied them in the days when the bicycle shop was on West Third Street and the house on Hawthorn Street.

*Charlie Taylor* Taylor; Combs, 360; Stein, 346.

## 51. END OF THE FEUD

433     *had interviewed Orville* AR, *Chronology,* 66.

*Findley and McMahon at Hawthorn Hill* Ibid.; McM, 13; McFarland.

*Orville's rejection of Findley's manuscript* Walsh, 4, 5, 250; McFarland. McFarland's 1956 version of the rejection differs in particulars from that of Walsh, who apparently based his version on a letter he received from McFarland almost two decades later. Walsh's version is used here. In the McFarland version, it is Katharine who breaks the news to Findley. "I am sorry, Earl," she says. "He said he would rather have the sciatica than read your manuscript."

*Findley's reaction to Orville's rejection* Lindbergh, 383.

434     *Orville and the McGraw-Hill Book Company* PW, 1110. The company had proposed the publication of a book by the brothers as early as 1909. In 1953, on the fiftieth anniversary of the first four flights, McGraw-Hill published *The Papers of Wilbur and Orville Wright.*

*"I am about to begin the writing"* PW, 1134–35.

*"I have discussed your letter"* Ibid., 1135–36.

*"the first adult book in any language"* From the jacket of McMahon's book. Other, shorter books in French and German on the Wright brothers had been published in 1908 and 1909.

*penury in the Wright household* McM, 192, 200.

*"Hello! Orv"* McM, 209.

*"happier down in Hawthorn Street"* McM, 286.

*Lawrence Hargrave* PW, 1176–77; MK, 454.

435     *chief research engineer*     *New York Times,* July 24, 1954, 13 (obituary).

*to acquire aeronautical material* One of Zahm's most important acquisitions was that of the letters and other papers of Octave Chanute, deposited in the library in 1932 by Chanute's two daughters, including the more than five hundred letters exchanged by Chanute and the Wright brothers. It is possible that Zahm did some manipulating of the Chanute papers. He and Chanute had corresponded frequently, but in the Chanute correspondence in the Library of Congress, no more than half a dozen letters from Zahm are included in the collection, which suggests the possibility that he may have removed any of his letters to Chanute that might have proved embarrassing in any way. (PW, 532–33 n. 4.)

*hired to build a glider* Crouch, *Dream,* 118, 317.

*Cabot's first impression* OC correspondence, Cabot to OC, May 7, 1897.

*Whitehead's flights of 1901 and 1902* Crouch, *Dream,* 120–22.

*close to $10,000* PW, 710 n.

*the Beach-Whitehead biplane* Arch Whitehouse, *The Early Birds* (Garden City, N.Y.: Doubleday, 1965), 136–37.

436     *died a penniless fanatic* Crouch, *Dream,* 308.

*an article by Randolph and Phillips* "Did Whitehead Precede the Wrights in World's First Power Flight?" *Popular Aviation,* Jan. 1935, 22–24, 55–57. Three decades after the Wrights had made the name Kitty Hawk world-famous, Randolph and Phillips were spelling it Kittihawk! Their article states that although the airplane in which Whitehead claimed to have made his first flight in 1901 was called No. 21, it was actually No. 56. He had evidently not bothered to number the first 35.

*an investigation into the matter* John B. Crane, "Did Whitehead Actually Fly?" *National Aeronautic Magazine,* Dec. 1936, 11–14. In 1949, Crane contributed to the Whitehead myth by completely reversing his position in an article, "Early Airplane Flights Before the Wrights," in the Winter 1949 issue of *Air Affairs.* "By suppressing all reference to his former article and not once questioning the sources he had held up to ridicule eleven [actually thirteen] years before, Dr. Crane succeeds in performing one of the most spectacular journalistic flip-flops in aeronautical history" (PW, 1167, n. 8).

Lost Flights of Gustave Whitehead    PW, 1164–65, 1165 n. Stella Randolph's book contained fourteen affidavits by people claiming to have seen Whitehead fly. Some of these verged on sheer silliness, like the statement of the man who swore he had been "firing the boiler" in the back of a plane flown by Whitehead in Pittsburgh in 1899 when it hit a three-story building. Others were aimed more squarely at the Wrights, like the affidavit stating that Wilbur and Orville had visited Whitehead in Bridgeport during the early 1900s. "After they had gone away," the signer of the affidavit stated, "Mr. Whitehead turned to me and said, 'Now since I have given them the secrets of my invention they will probably never do anything in the way of financing me.' " The Wright brothers were never in Bridgeport, although they passed through the city once, on a train.

*"too incredible and ridiculous"* MK, 458.

*"In his frenzy of spite"* Orville to Alexander McSurely, Feb. 5, 1946, in the Wright papers in the Library of Congress; reprinted, but only in part, in MK, 455–60.

437     *"I presume this is that book"* Ibid. The other three "powerplane fathers" were the Englishman William Henson, who envisioned but never constructed a passenger-carrying monoplane in 1842; M. A. Goupil, a Frenchman who designed a machine with the body as well as the wings of a bird, but never got around to building a motor to fly it; and Clément Ader.

*retired from the Library of Congress* Zahm died in 1954 at the age of ninety-two. His obituary in the *New York Times* (July 24, 1954, 13) states that "among his inventions [is] the three-torque control of airplanes." It was the Wright brothers' three-torque control system, of course, described in their patent of 1906, that taught the world to fly.

*"The Man Who Knows Everything First"* Mort Weisinger, *Liberty,* Apr. 28, 1945. The "man" was Joseph Nathan Kane.

*the Whitehead myth died hard* In 1966, Stella Randolph shuffled her affidavits and retold the Whitehead story in a book for children, *Before the Wrights Flew: The Story of Gustave Whitehead* (New York: Putnam, 1966). In 1982, William J. O'Dwyer, a retired Air Force officer of Stratford, Connecticut, restirred the pot by calling in the Associated Press and accusing the Smithsonian Institution of refusing to release a 1901 photograph of Whitehead in flight, because if it did, he said, it would lose "display rights" to the Wright 1903 Flyer (Washington *Post,* Aug. 23, 1982, C 10). The following year an obscure press in Baton Rouge, Louisiana, published a book co-authored by the same retired Air Force officer with the titillating title *History by Contract: The First Motorized Flight in History* (Baton Rouge: Zeppelin, 1983). Whose flight that was can be deduced from the identity of the airman's co-author— the apparently ageless Stella Randolph. For more recent revivals of the Whitehead myth, see *New York Times,* Feb. 20, 1986, pt. 2, 1; Washington *Post,* Mar. 9, 1986, G 1; and *Christian Science Monitor,* Dec. 9, 1986, 33, 36.

*"It is a tragedy"* Lindbergh, 276–77.
*he broached the subject* Ibid., 383–84.

438     *he tackled Findley again* Ibid., 446–47.
*prodded Orville on the subject* Ibid., 336.
*wholeheartedly with the Roosevelt administration* PW, 1167. "We should give every possible aid to Britain. I feel this way, not on financial grounds, nor for political reasons, but I look upon it solely as a *moral* question" (Orville's italics; quoted in *U.S. Air Services,* May 1941, 9).
*"How the Wright Brothers Began"*    *Harper's Magazine,* Oct. 1939, 473–84.
*an article in* Collier's "Flying Machines and the War: An Interview with Orville Wright," July 31, 1915.
*initiated a correspondence* Miller, 32.

439     *trying to come to terms with Orville* FK, 323.
*"a difficult situation"* Lindbergh, 188.
*the Cleveland engine laboratory* PW, 1169–72.
*Abbot's paper* "The 1914 Tests of the Langley 'Aerodrome,' " reprinted in FK, 324–33.
*"I can well understand"* MK, 440.

440     *had been placed in underground storage* "They have it in a reinforced concrete air raid shelter where I guess it will be perfectly safe" (Orville to Chalmers Roberts, June 12, 1941, quoted in the Washington *Post,* Dec. 17, 1983).
*a gala dinner in Washington* PW, 1174, 1174–75 n. 5; *New York Times,* Dec. 18, 1948, 10; Miller, 34–35.

441     *the 1903 Flyer in England, 1945–48* AR, *Chronology,* 106, 111.


### 52. ORVILLE'S SHOES


442     *heart attack of Oct. 10, 1947* PW, 1177 n. 8; Miller, 38–39.
*"flyers of other sizes and speeds"* PW, 721.
*wrote to the General Electric Company* PW, 1179.

443     *"shows a mind as busy and as thorough"* PW, 1179 n.
*second heart attack* Ibid.; Miller, 39.
*Hawthorn Hill had been purchased* AR, *Chronology,* 111.

*"While Carrie was visiting him"* PW, 1179 n.

*complicated by congestion* New York Times, Jan. 30, 1948, 35.

444    *Orville's funeral* Ibid., Feb. 3, 1948, 25; Miller, 40; Young and Fitzgerald, 178.

*one of the only two clergymen* Johnson, 22. The other was "a colored minister" on the West Side.

*Orville's estate* Ibid., 180; *New York Times,* Mar. 19, 1948, 25.

*Mabel Beck refused* Miller, 41–43.

*letter authorizing the Flyer's return*    *U.S. Air Services,* Feb. 1948, 15.

445    *return of the Flyer* Hallion, 53–54.

*the sides of the Navy truck* Young and Fitzgerald, 179 (photo).

*the Flyer was sold* Miller, 45.

*the scarecrowlike dummy* When Paul Garber, curator of the National Air Museum in 1948, dressed the original dummy, he had trouble finding any of the high stiff collars worn by the Wright brothers. He finally unearthed a lode of these all-but-extinct items in a haberdashery in the Willard Hotel in Washington. The haberdasher stocked the collars for sale to Herbert Hoover during the ex-President's frequent trips to the capital. (Young and Fitzgerald, 181.)

# Bibliography

Abbot, Charles G. *The Relations Between the Smithsonian Institution and the Wright Brothers.* Washington: Smithsonian Institution, Sept. 29, 1928.

Adler, Cyrus. *I Have Considered the Days.* Philadelphia: Jewish Publication Society of America, 1941.

Aero Club of America. *Navigating the Air.* New York: Doubleday, Page, 1907.

Albertson, Catherine. *Wings over Kill Devil Hill and Legends of the Dunes.* Elizabeth City, N.C., 1928. "Wings over Kill Devil Hill," by William Tate (pp. 7–18), is reprinted from a privately printed edition of 25 copies.

Arnold, Henry H. *Global Mission.* New York: Harper, 1949.

Beck, Mabel. "The First Airplane After 1903." *U.S. Air Services,* Dec. 1954, 9–10.

Berle, Beatrice Bishop. *A Life in Two Worlds.* New York: Walker, 1983.

Bonney, Walter T. *The Heritage of Kitty Hawk.* New York: Norton, 1962.

Boyne, Walter J. *The Aircraft Treasures of Silver Hill: The Behind-the-Scenes Workshop of the National Air and Space Museum.* New York: Rawson, 1982.

Brewer, Griffith. "The Life and Work of Wilbur Wright" and "Wilbur Wright." *Aeronautical Journal,* July–Sept. 1916, 68–84, 128–35.

———. *Fifty Years of Flying.* London: Air League of the British Empire, 1946.

Bruce, Robert V. *Alexander Graham Bell and the Conquest of Solitude.* Boston: Little, Brown, 1973.

Buist, H. Massac. "The Human Side of Flying: Being an Attempt to Introduce the Reader to Messrs. Orville and Wilbur Wright at Pau." *Flight,* Mar. 6, 1909, 128–29; Mar. 13, 141–43.

Casey, Louis S. *Curtiss: The Hammondsport Era, 1907–1915.* New York: Crown, 1981.

Chandler, Charles de Forest, and Frank P. Lahm. *How Our Army Grew Wings: Airmen and Aircraft Before 1914.* New York: Ronald, 1943.

Chanute, Octave. *Progress in Flying Machines.* New York: Forney, 1894.

———. "Gliding Experiments: An Address by Octave Chanute . . . Delivered 20th of October, 1897." *Western Society of Engineers Journal,* Nov. 1897, 593–628.

———. "Experiments in Flying: An Account of the Author's Own Inventions and Adventures." *McClure's Magazine,* June 1900, 127–33.

———. Correspondence. Typewritten copies, National Air and Space Museum Library.

Charnley, Mitchell V. *The Boys' Life of the Wright Brothers.* New York: Harper, 1928.

Coffyn, Frank T. "Flying with the Wrights." *World's Work,* Dec. 1929, 80–86.

———. "Flying, as It Was—Early Days in the Wrights' School." *Sportsman Pilot,* May 15, 1939, 14–15, 30, 32.

Coles, Thomas R. "The 'Wright Boys' as a Schoolmate Knew Them." *Out West,* Jan. 1910, 36–38.

Combs, Harry, with Martin Caidin. *Kill Devil Hill: Discovering the Secret of the Wright Brothers.* Boston: Houghton Mifflin, 1979.

Connick, George P. "John Joseph Montgomery: His Life in Brief," in *Santa Clara County Pioneer Papers.* San Jose: Smith & McKay, 1973.

Conover, Charlotte Reeve. *Dayton, Ohio: An Intimate History.* New York: Lewis Historical Publishing Co., 1932.

Cox, James M. *Journey Through My Years.* New York, Simon & Schuster, 1946.

Crouch, Tom. *A Dream of Wings: Americans and the Airplane, 1875–1905.* New York: Norton, 1981.

———. *The Eagle Aloft: Two Centuries of the Balloon in America.* Washington, D.C.: Smithsonian Institution Press, 1983.

Dwiggins, Don. *Famous Flyers and the Ships They Flew.* New York: Grosset, 1969.

Flint, Charles R. *Memories of an Active Life: Men and Ships, and Sealing Wax.* New York: Putnam, 1923.

Foulois, Benjamin D. *From The Wright Brothers to the Astronauts.* New York: McGraw-Hill, 1968.

Freudenthal, Elsbeth E. *Flight into History: The Wright Brothers and the Air Age.* Norman: University of Oklahoma, 1949.

Gibbs-Smith, Charles H. *The Aeroplane: An Historical Survey.* London: Her Majesty's Stationery Office, 1960.

———. *The Wright Brothers: A Brief Account of Their Work, 1899–1911.* London: Her Majesty's Stationery Office, 1963.

———. *Aviation: An Historical Survey from Its Origins to the End of World War II.* London: Her Majesty's Stationery Office, 1970.

———. *The Rebirth of European Aviation, 1902–1908: A Study of the Wright Brothers' Influence.* London: Her Majesty's Stationery Office, 1974.

Gollin, Alfred. *No Longer an Island: Britain and the Wright Brothers, 1902–1909.* Stanford, Calif.: Stanford University Press, 1984.

Goulder, Grace. *Ohio Scenes and Citizens.* Cleveland: World, 1964.

Hallion, Richard P., ed. *The Wright Brothers: Heirs of Prometheus.* Washington, D.C.: Smithsonian Institution Press, 1978.

Harper, Harry. *My Fifty Years in Flying.* London: Associated Newspapers Ltd., 1956.

Harris, Sherwood. *The First to Fly: Aviation's Pioneer Days.* New York: Simon & Schuster, 1970.

Hatch, Alden. *Glenn Curtiss: Pioneer of Naval Aviation.* New York: Messner, 1942.

Hayward, Charles B. *Practical Aeronautics.* Chicago: American School of Correspondence, 1912.

Hobbs, Leonard S. *The Wright Brothers' Engines and Their Design.* Washington, D.C.: Smithsonian Institution Press, 1971.

Hodgins, Eric. "Heavier Than Air." *The New Yorker,* Dec. 13, 1930, 29–32.

Horgan, James J. "Aeronautics at the World's Fair of 1904." *Missouri Historical Society Bulletin,* Apr. 1968, 214–40.

Inglis, William. "The Problem of Flight Solved." *Harper's Weekly,* Oct. 24, 1908, 2–8, 27.

Johnson, Mary Ann. *A Field Guide to Flight: On the Aviation Trail in Dayton, Ohio.* Dayton: Landfall Press, 1986.

Kelly, Fred C. *The Wright Brothers: A Biography Authorized by Orville Wright.* New York: Harcourt, 1943.

Langley, Samuel Pierpont. *Experiments in Aerodynamics.* Washington, D.C.: Smithsonian Institution, 1891.

———. *The Internal Work of the Wind.* Washington: Smithsonian Institution, 1893.

———. *Langley Memoir on Mechanical Flight.* Washington: Smithsonian Institution, 1911. Completed by Charles M. Manly.

Leslie, Stuart W. *Boss Kettering.* New York: Columbia University, 1983.

Licberg, Owen S. *The First Air Race: The International Competition at Reims, 1909.* Garden City, N.Y.: Doubleday, 1974.

Lindbergh, Charles A. *The Wartime Journals.* New York: Harcourt, 1970.

Loening, Grover. *Our Wings Grow Faster.* New York: Doubleday, 1935.

———. *Takeoff into Greatness: How American Aviation Grew So Big So Fast.* New York: Putnam, 1968.

Lougheed, Victor. *Vehicles of the Air: A Popular Exposition of Modern Aeronautics.* Chicago: Reilly & Britton, 1909.

Marcosson, Isaac F. *Colonel Deeds: Industrial Builder.* New York: Dodd, Mead, 1974.

Martin, James V. "When Will Merit Count in Aviation? The Life Story of Augustus M. Herring, Inventor of the Aeroplane." *The Libertarian* (Greenville, S.C.), Oct. 1924, 589–608.

Maxim, Hiram S. *My Life.* London: Methuen, 1915.

McFarland, Marvin W. "Orville Wright and Friend." *U.S. Air Services,* Aug. 1956, 5–7.

McMahon, John R. *The Wright Brothers: Fathers of Flight.* Boston: Little, Brown, 1930.

Means, James, ed. *Aeronautical Annual 1897.* Boston: Clarke Co., 1897.

Meyer, Robert B., Jr. *Langley's Aero Engine of 1903.* Washington, D.C.: Smithsonian Institution Press, 1971.

———. *Langley's Model Aero Engine.* Washington, D.C.: Airplanes and Engines, 1976.

Miller, Ivonette Wright, compiler. *Wright Reminiscences.* Dayton, privately printed, 1978.

Mingos, Howard. "The Birth of an Industry." In G. E. Simonson, ed., *The History of the American Aircraft Industry: An Anthology.* Cambridge: MIT, 1968, 10–95.

Outlaw, Edward R., Jr. *Old Nag's Head: Some Personal Recollections...* Norfolk: Liskey Lithograph Corp., 1956.

Parkin, J. H. *Bell and Baldwin: Their Development of Aerodromes and Hydrodromes at Baddeck, Nova Scotia.* Toronto: University of Toronto, 1964.

Peterson, Houston. *See Them Flying: Houston Peterson's Air-Age Scrapbook, 1909–1910.* New York: Richard W. Baron, 1969.

Peyrey, François. *Les Oiseaux Artificiel.* Paris: Dunod et Pinat, 1909. (Incorporating and updating, through April 1909, *Les Premiers Hommes-oiseaux: Wilbur et Orville Wright.* Paris: Guiton, 1908.)

Prendergast, Curtis. *The First Aviators.* Alexandria: Time-Life Books, 1980.

Renstrom, Arthur G. *Wilbur & Orville Wright: A Bibliography.* Washington, D.C.: Library of Congress, 1968.

———. *Wilbur & Orville Wright: A Chronology.* Washington, D.C.: Library of Congress, 1975. ("Flight Log, 1900–1918," pp. 123–208.)

Roseberry, C. R. *Glenn Curtiss: Pioneer of Flight.* Garden City, N.Y.: Doubleday, 1972.

Ruhl, Arthur. "History at Kill Devil Hill." *Collier's Weekly,* May 30, 1908, 18–19, 26.

Scharff, Robert, and Walter S. Taylor. *Over Land and Sea: A Biography of Glenn Hammond Curtiss.* New York: McKay, 1968.

Spearman, Arthur Dunning. *John Joseph Montgomery, 1858–1911: Father of Basic Flying.* Santa Clara: University of Santa Clara, 1967.

Stein, E. P. *Flight of the Vin Fiz.* New York: Arbor House, 1985.

Studer, Clara. *Sky Storming Yankee: The Life of Glenn Curtiss.* New York: Stackpole, 1937.

Sullivan, Mark. *Our Times: The United States, 1900–1925.* Vol. 2: *America Finding Herself.* New York: Scribner's, 1927.

Tate, William J. "With the Wrights at Kitty Hawk." *Aeronautic Review,* Dec. 1928, 188–92.

———. "I Was Host to Wright Brothers at Kitty Hawk." *U.S. Air Services,* Dec. 1943, 29–30.

Taylor, Charles E. "My Story of the Wright Brothers, as told to Robert S. Ball." *Collier's Weekly,* Dec. 25, 1948, 27, 68, 70.

Tillman, Stephen F. *Man Unafraid.* Washington, D.C.: Army Times, 1958.

Toland, John. *The Great Dirigibles: Their Triumphs and Disasters.* New York: Dover, 1972.

Trimble, William F. *A History of Aeronautics in Pennsylvania.* Pittsburgh: University of Pittsburgh, 1982.

Vaeth, J. Gordon. *Langley: Man of Science and Flight.* New York: Ronald, 1966.

Vecsey, George, and George C. Dade. *The Pioneers of Aviation Speak for Themselves.* New York: Dutton, 1979.

Villard, Henry S. *Contact! The Story of the Early Birds.* New York: Crowell, 1968.

Walker, Percy B. *Early Aviation at Farnborough.* Vol. 1: *Balloons, Kites and Airships.* Vol. 2: *The First Aeroplanes.* London: Macdonald, 1974.

Walsh, John Evangelist. *One Day at Kitty Hawk: The Untold Story of the Wright Brothers and the Airplane.* New York: Crowell, 1975.

Weaver, Henry M. "Letter read by Mr. Frank Lahm before the Aviation Committee of the Aéro-Club de France, December 29, 1905." *Aeronautical Journal,* July–Sept. 1916, 97–99.

Wechter, Nell Wise. *The Mighty Midgetts of Chicamacomico.* Manteo, N.C.: Times Printing Co., 1974.

Worrel, Rodney K. "The Wright Brothers' Pioneer Patent." *American Bar Association Journal,* Oct. 1979, 1512–18.

Wright, Orville. "The Wright Brothers' Aeroplane, by Orville and Wilbur Wright" (actually by Orville only). *Century Magazine,* Sept. 1908, 641–50.

———. "How We Made the First Flight." *Flying,* Dec. 1913, 10–12, 35, 36.

———. "Possibilities of Soaring Flight." *U.S. Air Service,* Dec. 1922, 7–9.

———. *How We Invented the Airplane,* edited and with commentary by Fred C. Kelly. New York: McKay, 1953.

Wright, Wilbur. Deposition of February 15, 1912. Excerpted in *Aeronautical Journal,* July–Sept. 1916, 115–24.

Wright, Wilbur and Orville. *Miracle at Kitty Hawk: The Letters of Wilbur and Orville Wright,* Fred C. Kelly, ed. New York: Farrar, Straus and Young, 1951.

———. *The Papers of Wilbur and Orville Wright: Including the Chanute-Wright Letters and Other Papers of Octave Chanute,* Marvin W. McFarland, ed. New York: McGraw-Hill, 1953.

Wykeham, Peter. *Santos-Dumont: A Study in Obsession.* London: Putnam, 1962.

Young, Rosamond, and Catharine Fitzgerald. *Twelve Seconds to the Moon: A Story of the Wright Brothers.* 2nd ed.; Dayton: U.S. Air Force Museum Foundation, 1983.

Zahm, Albert Francis. *Aërial Navigation: A Popular Treatise on the Growth of Air Craft and on Aëronautical Meteorology.* New York: Appleton, 1911.

# Index

# ABOUT THE AUTHOR

Fred Howard served as a bombardier-navigator with the U.S. Army Air Force from 1942 to 1945. After the war he became an aeronautics librarian at the Library of Congress, where he handled the scientific and technical aspects of the editing of *The Papers of Wilbur and Orville Wright*. Since 1958 he has worked as editor on a number of scientific publications and for several publishing houses. He is the author of a novel, *Charlie Flowers and the Melody Gardens*, and coauthor, with his wife Janet, of *Whistle While You Wait*, a book of wartime letters.

A CATALOG OF SELECTED
**DOVER BOOKS**
IN ALL FIELDS OF INTEREST

# A CATALOG OF SELECTED DOVER
# BOOKS IN ALL FIELDS OF INTEREST

CONCERNING THE SPIRITUAL IN ART, Wassily Kandinsky. Pioneering work by father of abstract art. Thoughts on color theory, nature of art. Analysis of earlier masters. 12 illustrations. 80pp. of text. 5⅜ x 8½.                23411-8 Pa. $3.95

ANIMALS: 1,419 Copyright-Free Illustrations of Mammals, Birds, Fish, Insects, etc., Jim Harter (ed.). Clear wood engravings present, in extremely lifelike poses, over 1,000 species of animals. One of the most extensive pictorial sourcebooks of its kind. Captions. Index. 284pp. 9 x 12.                23766-4 Pa. $12.95

CELTIC ART: The Methods of Construction, George Bain. Simple geometric techniques for making Celtic interlacements, spirals, Kells-type initials, animals, humans, etc. Over 500 illustrations. 160pp. 9 x 12. (USO)                22923-8 Pa. $9.95

AN ATLAS OF ANATOMY FOR ARTISTS, Fritz Schider. Most thorough reference work on art anatomy in the world. Hundreds of illustrations, including selections from works by Vesalius, Leonardo, Goya, Ingres, Michelangelo, others. 593 illustrations. 192pp. 7⅛ x 10¼.                20241-0 Pa. $9.95

CELTIC HAND STROKE-BY-STROKE (Irish Half-Uncial from "The Book of Kells"): An Arthur Baker Calligraphy Manual, Arthur Baker. Complete guide to creating each letter of the alphabet in distinctive Celtic manner. Covers hand position, strokes, pens, inks, paper, more. Illustrated. 48pp. 8¼ x 11.                24336-2 Pa. $3.95

EASY ORIGAMI, John Montroll. Charming collection of 32 projects (hat, cup, pelican, piano, swan, many more) specially designed for the novice origami hobbyist. Clearly illustrated easy-to-follow instructions insure that even beginning papercrafters will achieve successful results. 48pp. 8¼ x 11.                27298-2 Pa. $3.50

THE COMPLETE BOOK OF BIRDHOUSE CONSTRUCTION FOR WOOD-WORKERS, Scott D. Campbell. Detailed instructions, illustrations, tables. Also data on bird habitat and instinct patterns. Bibliography. 3 tables. 63 illustrations in 15 figures. 48pp. 5¼ x 8½.                24407-5 Pa. $2.50

BLOOMINGDALE'S ILLUSTRATED 1886 CATALOG: Fashions, Dry Goods and Housewares, Bloomingdale Brothers. Famed merchants' extremely rare catalog depicting about 1,700 products: clothing, housewares, firearms, dry goods, jewelry, more. Invaluable for dating, identifying vintage items. Also, copyright-free graphics for artists, designers. Co-published with Henry Ford Museum & Greenfield Village. 160pp. 8¼ x 11.                25780-0 Pa. $10.95

HISTORIC COSTUME IN PICTURES, Braun & Schneider. Over 1,450 costumed figures in clearly detailed engravings–from dawn of civilization to end of 19th century. Captions. Many folk costumes. 256pp. 8⅜ x 11¾.                23150-X Pa. $12.95

STICKLEY CRAFTSMAN FURNITURE CATALOGS, Gustav Stickley and L. & J. G. Stickley. Beautiful, functional furniture in two authentic catalogs from 1910. 594 illustrations, including 277 photos, show settles, rockers, armchairs, reclining chairs, bookcases, desks, tables. 183pp. 6½ x 9¼. 23838-5 Pa. $9.95

AMERICAN LOCOMOTIVES IN HISTORIC PHOTOGRAPHS: 1858 to 1949, Ron Ziel (ed.). A rare collection of 126 meticulously detailed official photographs, called "builder portraits," of American locomotives that majestically chronicle the rise of steam locomotive power in America. Introduction. Detailed captions. xi + 129pp. 9 x 12. 27393-8 Pa. $12.95

AMERICA'S LIGHTHOUSES: An Illustrated History, Francis Ross Holland, Jr. Delightfully written, profusely illustrated fact-filled survey of over 200 American lighthouses since 1716. History, anecdotes, technological advances, more. 240pp. 8 x 10¾. 25576-X Pa. $12.95

TOWARDS A NEW ARCHITECTURE, Le Corbusier. Pioneering manifesto by founder of "International School." Technical and aesthetic theories, views of industry, economics, relation of form to function, "mass-production split" and much more. Profusely illustrated. 320pp. 6⅛ x 9¼. (USO) 25023-7 Pa. $9.95

HOW THE OTHER HALF LIVES, Jacob Riis. Famous journalistic record, exposing poverty and degradation of New York slums around 1900, by major social reformer. 100 striking and influential photographs. 233pp. 10 x 7⅞. 22012-5 Pa. $10.95

FRUIT KEY AND TWIG KEY TO TREES AND SHRUBS, William M. Harlow. One of the handiest and most widely used identification aids. Fruit key covers 120 deciduous and evergreen species; twig key 160 deciduous species. Easily used. Over 300 photographs. 126pp. 5⅜ x 8½. 20511-8 Pa. $3.95

COMMON BIRD SONGS, Dr. Donald J. Borror. Songs of 60 most common U.S. birds: robins, sparrows, cardinals, bluejays, finches, more–arranged in order of increasing complexity. Up to 9 variations of songs of each species. Cassette and manual 99911-4 $8.95

ORCHIDS AS HOUSE PLANTS, Rebecca Tyson Northen. Grow cattleyas and many other kinds of orchids–in a window, in a case, or under artificial light. 63 illustrations. 148pp. 5⅜ x 8½. 23261-1 Pa. $4.95

MONSTER MAZES, Dave Phillips. Masterful mazes at four levels of difficulty. Avoid deadly perils and evil creatures to find magical treasures. Solutions for all 32 exciting illustrated puzzles. 48pp. 8¼ x 11. 26005-4 Pa. $2.95

MOZART'S DON GIOVANNI (DOVER OPERA LIBRETTO SERIES), Wolfgang Amadeus Mozart. Introduced and translated by Ellen H. Bleiler. Standard Italian libretto, with complete English translation. Convenient and thoroughly portable–an ideal companion for reading along with a recording or the performance itself. Introduction. List of characters. Plot summary. 121pp. 5¼ x 8½. 24944-1 Pa. $2.95

TECHNICAL MANUAL AND DICTIONARY OF CLASSICAL BALLET, Gail Grant. Defines, explains, comments on steps, movements, poses and concepts. 15-page pictorial section. Basic book for student, viewer. 127pp. 5⅜ x 8½. 21843-0 Pa. $4.95

BRASS INSTRUMENTS: Their History and Development, Anthony Baines. Authoritative, updated survey of the evolution of trumpets, trombones, bugles, cornets, French horns, tubas and other brass wind instruments. Over 140 illustrations and 48 music examples. Corrected and updated by author. New preface. Bibliography. 320pp. 5⅜ x 8½. 27574-4 Pa. $9.95

HOLLYWOOD GLAMOR PORTRAITS, John Kobal (ed.). 145 photos from 1926-49. Harlow, Gable, Bogart, Bacall; 94 stars in all. Full background on photographers, technical aspects. 160pp. 8⅜ x 11¼. 23352-9 Pa. $12.95

MAX AND MORITZ, Wilhelm Busch. Great humor classic in both German and English. Also 10 other works: "Cat and Mouse," "Plisch and Plumm," etc. 216pp. 5⅜ x 8½. 20181-3 Pa. $6.95

THE RAVEN AND OTHER FAVORITE POEMS, Edgar Allan Poe. Over 40 of the author's most memorable poems: "The Bells," "Ulalume," "Israfel," "To Helen," "The Conqueror Worm," "Eldorado," "Annabel Lee," many more. Alphabetic lists of titles and first lines. 64pp. 5³⁄₁₆ x 8¼. 26685-0 Pa. $1.00

PERSONAL MEMOIRS OF U. S. GRANT, Ulysses Simpson Grant. Intelligent, deeply moving firsthand account of Civil War campaigns, considered by many the finest military memoirs ever written. Includes letters, historic photographs, maps and more. 528pp. 6⅛ x 9¼. 28587-1 Pa. $11.95

AMULETS AND SUPERSTITIONS, E. A. Wallis Budge. Comprehensive discourse on origin, powers of amulets in many ancient cultures: Arab, Persian Babylonian, Assyrian, Egyptian, Gnostic, Hebrew, Phoenician, Syriac, etc. Covers cross, swastika, crucifix, seals, rings, stones, etc. 584pp. 5⅜ x 8½. 23573-4 Pa. $12.95

RUSSIAN STORIES/PYCCKNE PACCKA3bl: A Dual-Language Book, edited by Gleb Struve. Twelve tales by such masters as Chekhov, Tolstoy, Dostoevsky, Pushkin, others. Excellent word-for-word English translations on facing pages, plus teaching and study aids, Russian/English vocabulary, biographical/critical introductions, more. 416pp. 5⅜ x 8½. 26244-8 Pa. $8.95

PHILADELPHIA THEN AND NOW: 60 Sites Photographed in the Past and Present, Kenneth Finkel and Susan Oyama. Rare photographs of City Hall, Logan Square, Independence Hall, Betsy Ross House, other landmarks juxtaposed with contemporary views. Captures changing face of historic city. Introduction. Captions. 128pp. 8¼ x 11. 25790-8 Pa. $9.95

AIA ARCHITECTURAL GUIDE TO NASSAU AND SUFFOLK COUNTIES, LONG ISLAND, The American Institute of Architects, Long Island Chapter, and the Society for the Preservation of Long Island Antiquities. Comprehensive, well-researched and generously illustrated volume brings to life over three centuries of Long Island's great architectural heritage. More than 240 photographs with authoritative, extensively detailed captions. 176pp. 8¼ x 11. 26946-9 Pa. $14.95

NORTH AMERICAN INDIAN LIFE: Customs and Traditions of 23 Tribes, Elsie Clews Parsons (ed.). 27 fictionalized essays by noted anthropologists examine religion, customs, government, additional facets of life among the Winnebago, Crow, Zuni, Eskimo, other tribes. 480pp. 6⅛ x 9¼. 27377-6 Pa. $10.95

FRANK LLOYD WRIGHT'S HOLLYHOCK HOUSE, Donald Hoffmann. Lavishly illustrated, carefully documented study of one of Wright's most controversial residential designs. Over 120 photographs, floor plans, elevations, etc. Detailed perceptive text by noted Wright scholar. Index. 128pp. 9¼ x 10¾. 27133-1 Pa. $11.95

THE MALE AND FEMALE FIGURE IN MOTION: 60 Classic Photographic Sequences, Eadweard Muybridge. 60 true-action photographs of men and women walking, running, climbing, bending, turning, etc., reproduced from rare 19th-century masterpiece. vi + 121pp. 9 x 12. 24745-7 Pa. $10.95

1001 QUESTIONS ANSWERED ABOUT THE SEASHORE, N. J. Berrill and Jacquelyn Berrill. Queries answered about dolphins, sea snails, sponges, starfish, fishes, shore birds, many others. Covers appearance, breeding, growth, feeding, much more. 305pp. 5¼ x 8¼. 23366-9 Pa. $8.95

GUIDE TO OWL WATCHING IN NORTH AMERICA, Donald S. Heintzelman. Superb guide offers complete data and descriptions of 19 species: barn owl, screech owl, snowy owl, many more. Expert coverage of owl-watching equipment, conservation, migrations and invasions, etc. Guide to observing sites. 84 illustrations. xiii + 193pp. 5⅜ x 8½. 27344-X Pa. $8.95

MEDICINAL AND OTHER USES OF NORTH AMERICAN PLANTS: A Historical Survey with Special Reference to the Eastern Indian Tribes, Charlotte Erichsen-Brown. Chronological historical citations document 500 years of usage of plants, trees, shrubs native to eastern Canada, northeastern U.S. Also complete identifying information. 343 illustrations. 544pp. 6½ x 9¼. 25951-X Pa. $12.95

STORYBOOK MAZES, Dave Phillips. 23 stories and mazes on two-page spreads: Wizard of Oz, Treasure Island, Robin Hood, etc. Solutions. 64pp. 8¼ x 11. 23628-5 Pa. $2.95

NEGRO FOLK MUSIC, U.S.A., Harold Courlander. Noted folklorist's scholarly yet readable analysis of rich and varied musical tradition. Includes authentic versions of over 40 folk songs. Valuable bibliography and discography. xi + 324pp. 5⅜ x 8½. 27350-4 Pa. $9.95

MOVIE-STAR PORTRAITS OF THE FORTIES, John Kobal (ed.). 163 glamor, studio photos of 106 stars of the 1940s: Rita Hayworth, Ava Gardner, Marlon Brando, Clark Gable, many more. 176pp. 8⅜ x 11¼. 23546-7 Pa. $12.95

BENCHLEY LOST AND FOUND, Robert Benchley. Finest humor from early 30s, about pet peeves, child psychologists, post office and others. Mostly unavailable elsewhere. 73 illustrations by Peter Arno and others. 183pp. 5⅜ x 8½. 22410-4 Pa. $6.95

YEKL and THE IMPORTED BRIDEGROOM AND OTHER STORIES OF YIDDISH NEW YORK, Abraham Cahan. Film Hester Street based on Yekl (1896). Novel, other stories among first about Jewish immigrants on N.Y.'s East Side. 240pp. 5⅜ x 8½. 22427-9 Pa. $6.95

SELECTED POEMS, Walt Whitman. Generous sampling from *Leaves of Grass*. Twenty-four poems include "I Hear America Singing," "Song of the Open Road," "I Sing the Body Electric," "When Lilacs Last in the Dooryard Bloom'd," "O Captain! My Captain!"—all reprinted from an authoritative edition. Lists of titles and first lines. 128pp. 5³⁄₁₆ x 8¼. 26878-0 Pa. $1.00

THE BEST TALES OF HOFFMANN, E. T. A. Hoffmann. 10 of Hoffmann's most important stories: "Nutcracker and the King of Mice," "The Golden Flowerpot," etc. 458pp. 5⅜ x 8½. 21793-0 Pa. $9.95

FROM FETISH TO GOD IN ANCIENT EGYPT, E. A. Wallis Budge. Rich detailed survey of Egyptian conception of "God" and gods, magic, cult of animals, Osiris, more. Also, superb English translations of hymns and legends. 240 illustrations. 545pp. 5⅜ x 8½. 25803-3 Pa. $13.95

FRENCH STORIES/CONTES FRANÇAIS: A Dual-Language Book, Wallace Fowlie. Ten stories by French masters, Voltaire to Camus: "Micromegas" by Voltaire; "The Atheist's Mass" by Balzac; "Minuet" by de Maupassant; "The Guest" by Camus, six more. Excellent English translations on facing pages. Also French-English vocabulary list, exercises, more. 352pp. 5⅜ x 8½. 26443-2 Pa. $8.95

CHICAGO AT THE TURN OF THE CENTURY IN PHOTOGRAPHS: 122 Historic Views from the Collections of the Chicago Historical Society, Larry A. Viskochil. Rare large-format prints offer detailed views of City Hall, State Street, the Loop, Hull House, Union Station, many other landmarks, circa 1904-1913. Introduction. Captions. Maps. 144pp. 9⅜ x 12¼. 24656-6 Pa. $12.95

OLD BROOKLYN IN EARLY PHOTOGRAPHS, 1865-1929, William Lee Younger. Luna Park, Gravesend race track, construction of Grand Army Plaza, moving of Hotel Brighton, etc. 157 previously unpublished photographs. 165pp. 8⅞ x 11¾. 23587-4 Pa. $13.95

THE MYTHS OF THE NORTH AMERICAN INDIANS, Lewis Spence. Rich anthology of the myths and legends of the Algonquins, Iroquois, Pawnees and Sioux, prefaced by an extensive historical and ethnological commentary. 36 illustrations. 480pp. 5⅜ x 8½. 25967-6 Pa. $8.95

AN ENCYCLOPEDIA OF BATTLES: Accounts of Over 1,560 Battles from 1479 B.C. to the Present, David Eggenberger. Essential details of every major battle in recorded history from the first battle of Megiddo in 1479 B.C. to Grenada in 1984. List of Battle Maps. New Appendix covering the years 1967-1984. Index. 99 illustrations. 544pp. 6½ x 9¼. 24913-1 Pa. $14.95

SAILING ALONE AROUND THE WORLD, Captain Joshua Slocum. First man to sail around the world, alone, in small boat. One of great feats of seamanship told in delightful manner. 67 illustrations. 294pp. 5⅜ x 8½. 20326-3 Pa. $5.95

ANARCHISM AND OTHER ESSAYS, Emma Goldman. Powerful, penetrating, prophetic essays on direct action, role of minorities, prison reform, puritan hypocrisy, violence, etc. 271pp. 5⅜ x 8½. 22484-8 Pa. $6.95

MYTHS OF THE HINDUS AND BUDDHISTS, Ananda K. Coomaraswamy and Sister Nivedita. Great stories of the epics; deeds of Krishna, Shiva, taken from puranas, Vedas, folk tales; etc. 32 illustrations. 400pp. 5⅜ x 8½. 21759-0 Pa. $10.95

BEYOND PSYCHOLOGY, Otto Rank. Fear of death, desire of immortality, nature of sexuality, social organization, creativity, according to Rankian system. 291pp. 5⅜ x 8½. 20485-5 Pa. $8.95

A THEOLOGICO-POLITICAL TREATISE, Benedict Spinoza. Also contains unfinished Political Treatise. Great classic on religious liberty, theory of government on common consent. R. Elwes translation. Total of 421pp. 5⅜ x 8½. 20249-6 Pa. $9.95

MY BONDAGE AND MY FREEDOM, Frederick Douglass. Born a slave, Douglass became outspoken force in antislavery movement. The best of Douglass' autobiographies. Graphic description of slave life. 464pp. 5⅜ x 8½. 22457-0 Pa. $8.95

FOLLOWING THE EQUATOR: A Journey Around the World, Mark Twain. Fascinating humorous account of 1897 voyage to Hawaii, Australia, India, New Zealand, etc. Ironic, bemused reports on peoples, customs, climate, flora and fauna, politics, much more. 197 illustrations. 720pp. 5⅜ x 8½. 26113-1 Pa. $15.95

THE PEOPLE CALLED SHAKERS, Edward D. Andrews. Definitive study of Shakers: origins, beliefs, practices, dances, social organization, furniture and crafts, etc. 33 illustrations. 351pp. 5⅜ x 8½. 21081-2 Pa. $8.95

THE MYTHS OF GREECE AND ROME, H. A. Guerber. A classic of mythology, generously illustrated, long prized for its simple, graphic, accurate retelling of the principal myths of Greece and Rome, and for its commentary on their origins and significance. With 64 illustrations by Michelangelo, Raphael, Titian, Rubens, Canova, Bernini and others. 480pp. 5⅜ x 8½. 27584-1 Pa. $9.95

PSYCHOLOGY OF MUSIC, Carl E. Seashore. Classic work discusses music as a medium from psychological viewpoint. Clear treatment of physical acoustics, auditory apparatus, sound perception, development of musical skills, nature of musical feeling, host of other topics. 88 figures. 408pp. 5⅜ x 8½. 21851-1 Pa. $10.95

THE PHILOSOPHY OF HISTORY, Georg W. Hegel. Great classic of Western thought develops concept that history is not chance but rational process, the evolution of freedom. 457pp. 5⅜ x 8½. 20112-0 Pa. $9.95

THE BOOK OF TEA, Kakuzo Okakura. Minor classic of the Orient: entertaining, charming explanation, interpretation of traditional Japanese culture in terms of tea ceremony. 94pp. 5⅜ x 8½. 20070-1 Pa. $3.95

LIFE IN ANCIENT EGYPT, Adolf Erman. Fullest, most thorough, detailed older account with much not in more recent books, domestic life, religion, magic, medicine, commerce, much more. Many illustrations reproduce tomb paintings, carvings, hieroglyphs, etc. 597pp. 5⅜ x 8½. 22632-8 Pa. $11.95

SUNDIALS, Their Theory and Construction, Albert Waugh. Far and away the best, most thorough coverage of ideas, mathematics concerned, types, construction, adjusting anywhere. Simple, nontechnical treatment allows even children to build several of these dials. Over 100 illustrations. 230pp. 5⅜ x 8½. 22947-5 Pa. $7.95

DYNAMICS OF FLUIDS IN POROUS MEDIA, Jacob Bear. For advanced students of ground water hydrology, soil mechanics and physics, drainage and irrigation engineering, and more. 335 illustrations. Exercises, with answers. 784pp. 6⅛ x 9¼. 65675-6 Pa. $19.95

SONGS OF EXPERIENCE: Facsimile Reproduction with 26 Plates in Full Color, William Blake. 26 full-color plates from a rare 1826 edition. Includes "TheTyger," "London," "Holy Thursday," and other poems. Printed text of poems. 48pp. 5¼ x 7. 24636-1 Pa. $4.95

OLD-TIME VIGNETTES IN FULL COLOR, Carol Belanger Grafton (ed.). Over 390 charming, often sentimental illustrations, selected from archives of Victorian graphics—pretty women posing, children playing, food, flowers, kittens and puppies, smiling cherubs, birds and butterflies, much more. All copyright-free. 48pp. 9¼ x 12¼. 27269-9 Pa. $7.95

PIANO TUNING, J. Cree Fischer. Clearest, best book for beginner, amateur. Simple repairs, raising dropped notes, tuning by easy method of flattened fifths. No previous skills needed. 4 illustrations. 201pp. 5⅜ x 8½. 23267-0 Pa. $6.95

A SOURCE BOOK IN THEATRICAL HISTORY, A. M. Nagler. Contemporary observers on acting, directing, make-up, costuming, stage props, machinery, scene design, from Ancient Greece to Chekhov. 611pp. 5⅜ x 8½. 20515-0 Pa. $12.95

THE COMPLETE NONSENSE OF EDWARD LEAR, Edward Lear. All nonsense limericks, zany alphabets, Owl and Pussycat, songs, nonsense botany, etc., illustrated by Lear. Total of 320pp. 5⅜ x 8½. (USO) 20167-8 Pa. $6.95

VICTORIAN PARLOUR POETRY: An Annotated Anthology, Michael R. Turner. 117 gems by Longfellow, Tennyson, Browning, many lesser-known poets. "The Village Blacksmith," "Curfew Must Not Ring Tonight," "Only a Baby Small," dozens more, often difficult to find elsewhere. Index of poets, titles, first lines. xxiii + 325pp. 5⅜ x 8¼. 27044-0 Pa. $8.95

DUBLINERS, James Joyce. Fifteen stories offer vivid, tightly focused observations of the lives of Dublin's poorer classes. At least one, "The Dead," is considered a masterpiece. Reprinted complete and unabridged from standard edition. 160pp. 5³⁄₁₆ x 8¼. 26870-5 Pa. $1.00

THE HAUNTED MONASTERY and THE CHINESE MAZE MURDERS, Robert van Gulik. Two full novels by van Gulik, set in 7th-century China, continue adventures of Judge Dee and his companions. An evil Taoist monastery, seemingly supernatural events; overgrown topiary maze hides strange crimes. 27 illustrations. 328pp. 5⅜ x 8½. 23502-5 Pa. $8.95

THE BOOK OF THE SACRED MAGIC OF ABRAMELIN THE MAGE, translated by S. MacGregor Mathers. Medieval manuscript of ceremonial magic. Basic document in Aleister Crowley, Golden Dawn groups. 268pp. 5⅜ x 8½. 23211-5 Pa. $8.95

NEW RUSSIAN-ENGLISH AND ENGLISH-RUSSIAN DICTIONARY, M. A. O'Brien. This is a remarkably handy Russian dictionary, containing a surprising amount of information, including over 70,000 entries. 366pp. 4½ x 6⅛. 20208-9 Pa. $9.95

HISTORIC HOMES OF THE AMERICAN PRESIDENTS, Second, Revised Edition, Irvin Haas. A traveler's guide to American Presidential homes, most open to the public, depicting and describing homes occupied by every American President from George Washington to George Bush. With visiting hours, admission charges, travel routes. 175 photographs. Index. 160pp. 8¼ x 11. 26751-2 Pa. $11.95

NEW YORK IN THE FORTIES, Andreas Feininger. 162 brilliant photographs by the well-known photographer, formerly with *Life* magazine. Commuters, shoppers, Times Square at night, much else from city at its peak. Captions by John von Hartz. 181pp. 9¼ x 10¾. 23585-8 Pa. $12.95

INDIAN SIGN LANGUAGE, William Tomkins. Over 525 signs developed by Sioux and other tribes. Written instructions and diagrams. Also 290 pictographs. 111pp. 6⅛ x 9¼. 22029-X Pa. $3.95

ANATOMY: A Complete Guide for Artists, Joseph Sheppard. A master of figure drawing shows artists how to render human anatomy convincingly. Over 460 illustrations. 224pp. 8⅜ x 11¼. 27279-6 Pa. $10.95

MEDIEVAL CALLIGRAPHY: Its History and Technique, Marc Drogin. Spirited history, comprehensive instruction manual covers 13 styles (ca. 4th century thru 15th). Excellent photographs; directions for duplicating medieval techniques with modern tools. 224pp. 8⅜ x 11¼. 26142-5 Pa. $12.95

DRIED FLOWERS: How to Prepare Them, Sarah Whitlock and Martha Rankin. Complete instructions on how to use silica gel, meal and borax, perlite aggregate, sand and borax, glycerine and water to create attractive permanent flower arrangements. 12 illustrations. 32pp. 5⅜ x 8½. 21802-3 Pa. $1.00

EASY-TO-MAKE BIRD FEEDERS FOR WOODWORKERS, Scott D. Campbell. Detailed, simple-to-use guide for designing, constructing, caring for and using feeders. Text, illustrations for 12 classic and contemporary designs. 96pp. 5⅜ x 8½. 25847-5 Pa. $2.95

SCOTTISH WONDER TALES FROM MYTH AND LEGEND, Donald A. Mackenzie. 16 lively tales tell of giants rumbling down mountainsides, of a magic wand that turns stone pillars into warriors, of gods and goddesses, evil hags, powerful forces and more. 240pp. 5⅜ x 8½. 29677-6 Pa. $6.95

THE HISTORY OF UNDERCLOTHES, C. Willett Cunnington and Phyllis Cunnington. Fascinating, well-documented survey covering six centuries of English undergarments, enhanced with over 100 illustrations: 12th-century laced-up bodice, footed long drawers (1795), 19th-century bustles, 19th-century corsets for men, Victorian "bust improvers," much more. 272pp. 5⅝ x 8¼. 27124-2 Pa. $9.95

ARTS AND CRAFTS FURNITURE: The Complete Brooks Catalog of 1912, Brooks Manufacturing Co. Photos and detailed descriptions of more than 150 now very collectible furniture designs from the Arts and Crafts movement depict davenports, settees, buffets, desks, tables, chairs, bedsteads, dressers and more, all built of solid, quarter-sawed oak. Invaluable for students and enthusiasts of antiques, Americana and the decorative arts. 80pp. 6½ x 9¼. 27471-3 Pa. $8.95

HOW WE INVENTED THE AIRPLANE: An Illustrated History, Orville Wright. Fascinating firsthand account covers early experiments, construction of planes and motors, first flights, much more. Introduction and commentary by Fred C. Kelly. 76 photographs. 96pp. 8¼ x 11. 25662-6 Pa. $8.95

THE ARTS OF THE SAILOR: Knotting, Splicing and Ropework, Hervey Garrett Smith. Indispensable shipboard reference covers tools, basic knots and useful hitches; handsewing and canvas work, more. Over 100 illustrations. Delightful reading for sea lovers. 256pp. 5⅜ x 8½. 26440-8 Pa. $7.95

FRANK LLOYD WRIGHT'S FALLINGWATER: The House and Its History, Second, Revised Edition, Donald Hoffmann. A total revision–both in text and illustrations–of the standard document on Fallingwater, the boldest, most personal architectural statement of Wright's mature years, updated with valuable new material from the recently opened Frank Lloyd Wright Archives. "Fascinating"–*The New York Times.* 116 illustrations. 128pp. 9¼ x 10¾. 27430-6 Pa. $11.95

PHOTOGRAPHIC SKETCHBOOK OF THE CIVIL WAR, Alexander Gardner. 100 photos taken on field during the Civil War. Famous shots of Manassas Harper's Ferry, Lincoln, Richmond, slave pens, etc. 244pp. 10⅝ x 8¼. 22731-6 Pa. $9.95

FIVE ACRES AND INDEPENDENCE, Maurice G. Kains. Great back-to-the-land classic explains basics of self-sufficient farming. The one book to get. 95 illustrations. 397pp. 5⅜ x 8½. 20974-1 Pa. $7.95

SONGS OF EASTERN BIRDS, Dr. Donald J. Borror. Songs and calls of 60 species most common to eastern U.S.: warblers, woodpeckers, flycatchers, thrushes, larks, many more in high-quality recording. Cassette and manual 99912-2 $9.95

A MODERN HERBAL, Margaret Grieve. Much the fullest, most exact, most useful compilation of herbal material. Gigantic alphabetical encyclopedia, from aconite to zedoary, gives botanical information, medical properties, folklore, economic uses, much else. Indispensable to serious reader. 161 illustrations. 888pp. 6½ x 9¼. 2-vol. set. (USO) Vol. I: 22798-7 Pa. $9.95
Vol. II: 22799-5 Pa. $9.95

HIDDEN TREASURE MAZE BOOK, Dave Phillips. Solve 34 challenging mazes accompanied by heroic tales of adventure. Evil dragons, people-eating plants, blood-thirsty giants, many more dangerous adversaries lurk at every twist and turn. 34 mazes, stories, solutions. 48pp. 8¼ x 11. 24566-7 Pa. $2.95

LETTERS OF W. A. MOZART, Wolfgang A. Mozart. Remarkable letters show bawdy wit, humor, imagination, musical insights, contemporary musical world; includes some letters from Leopold Mozart. 276pp. 5⅜ x 8½. 22859-2 Pa. $7.95

BASIC PRINCIPLES OF CLASSICAL BALLET, Agrippina Vaganova. Great Russian theoretician, teacher explains methods for teaching classical ballet. 118 illustrations. 175pp. 5⅜ x 8½. 22036-2 Pa. $5.95

THE JUMPING FROG, Mark Twain. Revenge edition. The original story of The Celebrated Jumping Frog of Calaveras County, a hapless French translation, and Twain's hilarious "retranslation" from the French. 12 illustrations. 66pp. 5⅜ x 8½. 22686-7 Pa. $3.95

BEST REMEMBERED POEMS, Martin Gardner (ed.). The 126 poems in this superb collection of 19th- and 20th-century British and American verse range from Shelley's "To a Skylark" to the impassioned "Renascence" of Edna St. Vincent Millay and to Edward Lear's whimsical "The Owl and the Pussycat." 224pp. 5⅜ x 8½. 27165-X Pa. $4.95

COMPLETE SONNETS, William Shakespeare. Over 150 exquisite poems deal with love, friendship, the tyranny of time, beauty's evanescence, death and other themes in language of remarkable power, precision and beauty. Glossary of archaic terms. 80pp. 5³⁄₁₆ x 8¼. 26686-9 Pa. $1.00

BODIES IN A BOOKSHOP, R. T. Campbell. Challenging mystery of blackmail and murder with ingenious plot and superbly drawn characters. In the best tradition of British suspense fiction. 192pp. 5⅜ x 8½. 24720-1 Pa. $6.95

THE WIT AND HUMOR OF OSCAR WILDE, Alvin Redman (ed.). More than 1,000 ripostes, paradoxes, wisecracks: Work is the curse of the drinking classes; I can resist everything except temptation; etc. 258pp. 5⅜ x 8½.     20602-5 Pa. $5.95

SHAKESPEARE LEXICON AND QUOTATION DICTIONARY,. Alexander Schmidt. Full definitions, locations, shades of meaning in every word in plays and poems. More than 50,000 exact quotations. 1,485pp. 6½ x 9¼. 2-vol. set.
Vol. 1: 22726-X Pa. $16.95
Vol. 2: 22727-8 Pa. $16.95

SELECTED POEMS, Emily Dickinson. Over 100 best-known, best-loved poems by one of America's foremost poets, reprinted from authoritative early editions. No comparable edition at this price. Index of first lines. 64pp. 5³⁄₁₆ x 8¼.
26466-1 Pa. $1.00

CELEBRATED CASES OF JUDGE DEE (DEE GOONG AN), translated by Robert van Gulik. Authentic 18th-century Chinese detective novel; Dee and associates solve three interlocked cases. Led to van Gulik's own stories with same characters. Extensive introduction. 9 illustrations. 237pp. 5⅜ x 8½.     23337-5 Pa. $6.95

THE MALLEUS MALEFICARUM OF KRAMER AND SPRENGER, translated by Montague Summers. Full text of most important witchhunter's "bible," used by both Catholics and Protestants. 278pp. 6⅝ x 10.     22802-9 Pa. $12.95

SPANISH STORIES/CUENTOS ESPAÑOLES: A Dual-Language Book, Angel Flores (ed.). Unique format offers 13 great stories in Spanish by Cervantes, Borges, others. Faithful English translations on facing pages. 352pp. 5⅜ x 8½.
25399-6 Pa. $8.95

THE CHICAGO WORLD'S FAIR OF 1893: A Photographic Record, Stanley Appelbaum (ed.). 128 rare photos show 200 buildings, Beaux-Arts architecture, Midway, original Ferris Wheel, Edison's kinetoscope, more. Architectural emphasis; full text. 116pp. 8¼ x 11.     23990-X Pa. $9.95

OLD QUEENS, N.Y., IN EARLY PHOTOGRAPHS, Vincent F. Seyfried and William Asadorian. Over 160 rare photographs of Maspeth, Jamaica, Jackson Heights, and other areas. Vintage views of DeWitt Clinton mansion, 1939 World's Fair and more. Captions. 192pp. 8⅞ x 11.     26358-4 Pa. $12.95

CAPTURED BY THE INDIANS: 15 Firsthand Accounts, 1750-1870, Frederick Drimmer. Astounding true historical accounts of grisly torture, bloody conflicts, relentless pursuits, miraculous escapes and more, by people who lived to tell the tale. 384pp. 5⅜ x 8½.     24901-8 Pa. $8.95

THE WORLD'S GREAT SPEECHES, Lewis Copeland and Lawrence W. Lamm (eds.). Vast collection of 278 speeches of Greeks to 1970. Powerful and effective models; unique look at history. 842pp. 5⅜ x 8½.     20468-5 Pa. $14.95

THE BOOK OF THE SWORD, Sir Richard F. Burton. Great Victorian scholar/adventurer's eloquent, erudite history of the "queen of weapons"–from prehistory to early Roman Empire. Evolution and development of early swords, variations (sabre, broadsword, cutlass, scimitar, etc.), much more. 336pp. 6⅛ x 9¼.
25434-8 Pa. $9.95

AUTOBIOGRAPHY: The Story of My Experiments with Truth, Mohandas K. Gandhi. Boyhood, legal studies, purification, the growth of the Satyagraha (nonviolent protest) movement. Critical, inspiring work of the man responsible for the freedom of India. 480pp. 5⅜ x 8½. (USO) 24593-4 Pa. $8.95

CELTIC MYTHS AND LEGENDS, T. W. Rolleston. Masterful retelling of Irish and Welsh stories and tales. Cuchulain, King Arthur, Deirdre, the Grail, many more. First paperback edition. 58 full-page illustrations. 512pp. 5⅜ x 8½. 26507-2 Pa. $9.95

THE PRINCIPLES OF PSYCHOLOGY, William James. Famous long course complete, unabridged. Stream of thought, time perception, memory, experimental methods; great work decades ahead of its time. 94 figures. 1,391pp. 5⅜ x 8½. 2-vol. set.
Vol. I: 20381-6 Pa. $12.95
Vol. II: 20382-4 Pa. $12.95

THE WORLD AS WILL AND REPRESENTATION, Arthur Schopenhauer. Definitive English translation of Schopenhauer's life work, correcting more than 1,000 errors, omissions in earlier translations. Translated by E. F. J. Payne. Total of 1,269pp. 5⅜ x 8½. 2-vol. set.
Vol. 1: 21761-2 Pa. $11.95
Vol. 2: 21762-0 Pa. $12.95

MAGIC AND MYSTERY IN TIBET, Madame Alexandra David-Neel. Experiences among lamas, magicians, sages, sorcerers, Bonpa wizards. A true psychic discovery. 32 illustrations. 321pp. 5⅜ x 8½. (USO) 22682-4 Pa. $8.95

THE EGYPTIAN BOOK OF THE DEAD, E. A. Wallis Budge. Complete reproduction of Ani's papyrus, finest ever found. Full hieroglyphic text, interlinear transliteration, word-for-word translation, smooth translation. 533pp. 6½ x 9¼.
21866-X Pa. $10.95

MATHEMATICS FOR THE NONMATHEMATICIAN, Morris Kline. Detailed, college-level treatment of mathematics in cultural and historical context, with numerous exercises. Recommended Reading Lists. Tables. Numerous figures. 641pp. 5⅜ x 8½.
24823-2 Pa. $11.95

THEORY OF WING SECTIONS: Including a Summary of Airfoil Data, Ira H. Abbott and A. E. von Doenhoff. Concise compilation of subsonic aerodynamic characteristics of NACA wing sections, plus description of theory. 350pp. of tables. 693pp. 5⅜ x 8½. 60586-8 Pa. $14.95

THE RIME OF THE ANCIENT MARINER, Gustave Doré, S. T. Coleridge. Doré's finest work; 34 plates capture moods, subtleties of poem. Flawless full-size reproductions printed on facing pages with authoritative text of poem. "Beautiful. Simply beautiful."—*Publisher's Weekly.* 77pp. 9¼ x 12. 22305-1 Pa. $6.95

NORTH AMERICAN INDIAN DESIGNS FOR ARTISTS AND CRAFTSPEOPLE, Eva Wilson. Over 360 authentic copyright-free designs adapted from Navajo blankets, Hopi pottery, Sioux buffalo hides, more. Geometrics, symbolic figures, plant and animal motifs, etc. 128pp. 8⅜ x 11. (EUK) 25341-4 Pa. $8.95

SCULPTURE: Principles and Practice, Louis Slobodkin. Step-by-step approach to clay, plaster, metals, stone; classical and modern. 253 drawings, photos. 255pp. 8⅛ x 11.
22960-2 Pa. $11.95

THE INFLUENCE OF SEA POWER UPON HISTORY, 1660–1783, A. T. Mahan. Influential classic of naval history and tactics still used as text in war colleges. First paperback edition. 4 maps. 24 battle plans. 640pp. 5⅜ x 8½. 25509-3 Pa. $12.95

THE STORY OF THE TITANIC AS TOLD BY ITS SURVIVORS, Jack Winocour (ed.). What it was really like. Panic, despair, shocking inefficiency, and a little heroism. More thrilling than any fictional account. 26 illustrations. 320pp. 5⅜ x 8½. 20610-6 Pa. $8.95

FAIRY AND FOLK TALES OF THE IRISH PEASANTRY, William Butler Yeats (ed.). Treasury of 64 tales from the twilight world of Celtic myth and legend: "The Soul Cages," "The Kildare Pooka," "King O'Toole and his Goose," many more. Introduction and Notes by W. B. Yeats. 352pp. 5⅜ x 8½. 26941-8 Pa. $8.95

BUDDHIST MAHAYANA TEXTS, E. B. Cowell and Others (eds.). Superb, accurate translations of basic documents in Mahayana Buddhism, highly important in history of religions. The Buddha-karita of Asvaghosha, Larger Sukhavativyuha, more. 448pp. 5⅜ x 8½. 25552-2 Pa. $12.95

ONE TWO THREE . . . INFINITY: Facts and Speculations of Science, George Gamow. Great physicist's fascinating, readable overview of contemporary science: number theory, relativity, fourth dimension, entropy, genes, atomic structure, much more. 128 illustrations. Index. 352pp. 5⅜ x 8½. 25664-2 Pa. $8.95

ENGINEERING IN HISTORY, Richard Shelton Kirby, et al. Broad, nontechnical survey of history's major technological advances: birth of Greek science, industrial revolution, electricity and applied science, 20th-century automation, much more. 181 illustrations. ". . . excellent . . ."–Isis. Bibliography. vii + 530pp. 5⅜ x 8¼. 26412-2 Pa. $14.95

DALÍ ON MODERN ART: The Cuckolds of Antiquated Modern Art, Salvador Dalí. Influential painter skewers modern art and its practitioners. Outrageous evaluations of Picasso, Cézanne, Turner, more. 15 renderings of paintings discussed. 44 calligraphic decorations by Dalí. 96pp. 5⅜ x 8½. (USO) 29220-7 Pa. $4.95

ANTIQUE PLAYING CARDS: A Pictorial History, Henry René D'Allemagne. Over 900 elaborate, decorative images from rare playing cards (14th–20th centuries): Bacchus, death, dancing dogs, hunting scenes, royal coats of arms, players cheating, much more. 96pp. 9¼ x 12¼. 29265-7 Pa. $11.95

MAKING FURNITURE MASTERPIECES: 30 Projects with Measured Drawings, Franklin H. Gottshall. Step-by-step instructions, illustrations for constructing handsome, useful pieces, among them a Sheraton desk, Chippendale chair, Spanish desk, Queen Anne table and a William and Mary dressing mirror. 224pp. 8⅛ x 11¼. 29338-6 Pa. $13.95

THE FOSSIL BOOK: A Record of Prehistoric Life, Patricia V. Rich et al. Profusely illustrated definitive guide covers everything from single-celled organisms and dinosaurs to birds and mammals and the interplay between climate and man. Over 1,500 illustrations. 760pp. 7½ x 10⅛. 29371-8 Pa. $29.95

*Prices subject to change without notice.*

Available at your book dealer or write for free catalog to Dept. GI, Dover Publications, Inc., 31 East 2nd St., Mineola, N.Y. 11501. Dover publishes more than 500 books each year on science, elementary and advanced mathematics, biology, music, art, literary history, social sciences and other areas.